CARNEGIE

CARNEGIE

Peter Krass

John Wiley & Sons, Inc.

Published by John Wiley & Sons, Inc., Hoboken, New Jersey
Published simultaneously in Canada

For general information about our other products and services, please contact our Customer Care Department within the United States at (800) 762-2974, outside the United States at (317) 572-3993 or fax (317) 572-4002.

Wiley also publishes its books in a variety of electronic formats. Some content that appears in print may not be available in electronic books.

Library of Congress Cataloging-in-Publication Data:

Krass, Peter.
    Carnegie / Peter Krass.
      p. cm.
    Includes bibliographical references and index.
    ISBN 0-471-38630-8
    1. Carnegie, Andrew, 1835–1919. 2. Industrialists—United States—Biography.
    3. Philanthropists—United States—Biography. 4. Steel industry and trade—
    United States—History. I. Title.

CT275.C3 K73 2002
338.7′672′092—dc21

2002010162

Printed in the United States of America

10 9 8 7 6 5 4 3 2 1

For Diana

Contents

Preface

Like many men working in the hellish Carnegie mills, my great-grandfather William Danziger imbibed quantities of beer and liquor to soothe his pains and to make him feel alive again. He didn't reach sixty years of age, while Carnegie lived to the ripe age of eighty-four. In the summer of 2001, I visited my great-grandfather's gravesite in a cemetery not far from his old frame house in Carnegie, Pennsylvania, a suburb of Pittsburgh. I found a congested cemetery bordered by busy streets. There was no peace there. I also visited Andrew Carnegie's grave in the bucolic Sleepy Hollow Cemetery, near Tarrytown, New York. Carnegie has a spacious corner lot, nestled among evergreens and fern. It appears he has found a measure of peace. The contrast of the two gravesites raises one of the poignant themes to be explored in reconstructing the complicated life of a titan who came to power in America's Gilded Age: the unequal distribution of wealth that marked that era in our history.

To gain perspective on that theme, we should join Carnegie on his commute from his home to the iron and steel mills. At one time in the mid-1860s, Carnegie lived in the elite Homewood suburb of Pittsburgh with its grand Federal-style and Victorian homes. He and his affluent neighbors had toilets, hot-and-cold running water, forced-hot-air furnaces, gas lighting, and iceboxes, which were not only status symbols, but means to healthy living and relative longevity. Upper-class areas like Homewood also had sewers, paved roads, and garbage incineration. The paved roads were courtesy of the city council, which funded them with bonds, a debt that was paid by poor and rich alike, although the poor districts received not one paved road, and wouldn't for at least another decade. On the streets of Homewood, Carnegie encountered fashionably dressed men—or dandies, as they were called—smelling wonderful thanks to a discreet sachet. Style demanded creaseless trousers, coats buttoned high on the chest, bowlers or stovepipe hats, pomaded hair, thick mustaches, and Dundreary whiskers rippling to their chests. If not too early in the day, he passed a lady or two in polonaise and bonnet and holding a fringed parasol overhead.

As Carnegie approached the mills and the adjacent tenement buildings, he left the paved roads for those of dirt—roads where horse droppings and human refuse became putrefied in the hot summers. There were few water lines accessible to flush the stinking excrement and garbage, because in a bout of perfect logic, the Pittsburgh City Council's Water Commission had decided that the size of the water pipe being laid on a given street would be determined by the amount of potential revenue it would bring; in other words, big pipes were laid in the rich neighborhoods, while the poor tenement districts in desperate need of water were granted smaller pipes that fed communal outlets. Keeping a clean house and washing the men's grimy clothes were impossible chores under such conditions.

The Pittsburgh Board of Health declared the tenement homes "the filthiest and most disagreeable locality within the limits of the city," where people were renting "the merest apologies for houses," the structures characterized as "tumble down houses in rows."[1] Most were dilapidated brick or frame buildings that provided no ventilation in the hot summers and were cold and damp in the winters. The neighborhoods around the mills were populated with churches, taverns, and brothels; every imaginable spirit was available in a number of forms. Carnegie would have had to notice the churches' cemeteries were cluttered with tombstones. One-fifth of all Pittsburgh men, most in the prime of their life, died due to accidents—a large majority were in the iron, steel, railroad, and construction industries—and the rate was probably even higher as many accidents went unreported.[2] Thousands of men also fell to typhoid over the years, when, to quench their thirst after a hot day in the mills, they drank directly from Pittsburgh's polluted Monongahela and Allegheny Rivers.

To ease their pain, the workers did have a good number of taverns and brothels to select from, and after work many of the men slipped into the tavern, sidled up to the bar, and, with a foot on the rail, ordered a shot of whiskey and a beer. Whiskey was considered medicinal by the workers looking to clear the dust from their throats and to soothe their aching muscles and bruised bones. The working men might have a round or two, then play some cards, or head home, or perhaps visit a brothel. Some brothels served the well-to-do; however, after hours, Carnegie was more likely to find his wealthy peers in one of the city's chophouses or oyster grills. Other favorite evening pastimes of the rich included dancing—the polka, the valse, and the mazurka—or playing charades, twenty questions, and backgammon. Surprise parties were the rage.

As Carnegie approached the mills, hundreds of smoking furnaces, poking and bleeding the sky black, rose above him; showers of soot swept down; and ammoniacal air wafting from the stables mingled with acrid fumes from the mills. The mill buildings themselves, warehouselike with as many as ten smokestacks each, offered no aesthetic pleasure. Once inside he encountered ambivalent men in patched cotton trousers and sweat-stained shirts open at the collar. Dark lines of soot marked the creases in the skin around their mouth and eyes as they gazed at him with vague, desperate looks.[3] All the men in the mill had reason to be ornery characters, because, in addition to contending with the heat and the physical strain, the incessant roaring furnaces added immeasurable stress. There was no time for rest and relaxation. They worked seven-day weeks, and the only holidays granted by the mill owners were Christmas and the Fourth of July. Meanwhile, Carnegie took months to gallivant across Europe.

Adding to the mill workers' sour temperament was the constant worry about money. While Carnegie made well in excess of $100,000 a year (in 1870 dollars), his rollers earned $1,200 to $2,000 a year, puddlers and other skilled workers $600 to $1,000, and unskilled workers $300 to $550.[4] On payday, Friday, regardless of the amount, they would take out a portion for tobacco and the taverns, and the remainder was handed over to their wives. The wife was in charge of the budget and did her food shopping on Saturdays, before the money disappeared. While the laborers struggled to meet daily needs, Carnegie amassed a fortune of over $300 million (in 1900 dollars).

Was Carnegie just another robber baron who squeezed every penny he could from his men before they dropped dead, like my great-grandfather? Or was there more to this man who considered himself a lord of creation, a trustee of civilization, who gave away his fortune? It is too easy to execrate Carnegie as a robber baron or to extol him as the hero of the exemplary Horatio Alger rags-to-riches story. In taking on this biography—not the first, nor the last, to be written on Carnegie—I needed to better understand what inspired this man, how he justified his great wealth while his men starved, and whether it was possible to reconcile the differences between capital and labor. He left behind thousands of letters for those with questions about his life, and, as I sifted through them, a man who wore many masks emerged from the pages. Before me arose a titan I both disdain and respect. Carnegie's sanctimoniousness is repulsive at times, but his extreme loyalty to family and boyhood friends is highly admirable. He is full of internal conflict and contradiction. I came to think of him as a flawed Shakespearean protagonist—a Macbeth, a King Lear, a Prospero.

Not until I traveled to Scotland and watched my children play in Carnegie-funded parks and traveled to Pittsburgh and watched my children soak in the displays of the Carnegie Museum of Natural History did I begin to fully appreciate what Carnegie achieved. Both purposefully and unwittingly he planted seeds for civilization. While trampling asunder thousands of workingmen, he ultimately uplifted millions of people in the future. With this hindsight, I can begin to justify Carnegie's fantastic fortune, as well as those amassed by Rockefeller, Morgan, and America's other gilded titans. I don't think my great-grandfather or his wife, Bertha Danziger, would have entertained such forgiving thoughts; but perhaps, if they had understood the great internal conflicts Carnegie the man suffered, they would have mustered a degree of empathy.

CHAPTER 1

Flesh and Blood

On a bleak twenty-fifth day of November in 1835, a quixotic clan gathered in the one-room ground floor of a weaver's cottage in Dunfermline, Scotland, to await the arrival of its newest member. That day, Andrew Carnegie—or Andra as his relatives would call him—was born into a large family of political activists, radicals, and eccentrics. These blood relations, with all their passions and idiosyncrasies, would inspire and haunt Andra; they would infuse him with proletarian social and political convictions that would create merciless internal conflict as he came to embody the quintessential American rags-to-riches story.

The first in the family tree on record to protest the British monarchy and the oppressive living conditions suffered by the working class was James Carnegie, Andra's great-grandfather, who was of Celtic blood.[1] A shadowy figure in family lore, James had settled in Pattiemuir, just north of Edinburgh, where he leased land for farming and took up weaving. The village encompassed about a dozen cottages with red-tiled or thatched roofs nestled among softly rolling pastureland. During the Meal Riots of 1770, which followed a bad harvest, he was arrested for sedition against the local gentry who controlled the land and bore the blame for the food shortages. While he was in prison, a mysterious lady visited him and gave him a jewel-encrusted snuffbox, which prompted rumors that the Carnegie lineage was of a more exulted rank than mere peasant weaver. The earls of Northesk and of Southesk both bore the name Carnegie, but the family proudly denied any connection. Although James escaped conviction and quietly returned to his family, the name Carnegie, a Gaelic compound word meaning "fort at the gap," would be forever associated with the radical element.

James's oldest son and Andra's grandfather, Andrew Carnegie, was more of an eccentric than a radical. Also a natural leader, he was more blithe than his father and lived by the Scottish proverb "Be happy while you're living, for you're a long time dead"—a trait he bequeathed to Andra, who later reflected,

1

"I think my optimistic nature, my ability to shed trouble and to laugh through life, making 'all my ducks swans,' as friends say I do, must have been inherited from this delightful old masquerading grandfather whose name I am proud to bear."[2] Grandfather Carnegie relished consorting with the hamlet's men either at the smithy or the Black Bull Inn. In order to instigate political and social debate, he founded Pattiemuir College, which was no more than a single-room cottage in the village center were the men gathered weekly to argue over the important issues of the day.[3] Grandfather Carnegie was dubbed the Professor, as were most of his cohorts, and considering that the so-called professors far outnumbered the students, whispers in town that rumored the college to be "a drinking place" were not unfounded.[4]

To initiate the meetings, Grandfather Carnegie would climb upon his throne and, lifting his dram of malt whiskey, toast the common man's king of poets, Robert "Rabbie" Burns, or some other Scottish icon. Although the temperance movement was actively attempting to put an end to public and private drinking, the ability to imbibe, otherwise known as "quaffing the goblet" or "chasing the rosy hours," said a good deal about a man, and these men had much to say. After a benedictory toast, he would instigate heated debate by reading the news from either the London *Times* or the *Edinburgh Scotsman*. Topics ranged from theological matters to corruption in Parliament to factory reform. Regardless of the issue, whether national or foreign, Professor Andrew proved to be the expert. He was celebrated for his power of persuasion, his passion for debate, his skilled storytelling, his devotion to democratic ideals, and his righteous indignation (particularly true after a few drams at the college)—all traits that later manifested themselves in Andra, who would become renowned for his grandiloquence and derive exceptional pleasure from startling people with his wild stories and radical ideals.[5]

As a second-generation weaver, Grandpa Carnegie accompanied his father, James, to cities such as Dunfermline and Edinburgh to sell their linens. During one such excursion to the nearby coastal town of Limekilns, he became smitten with Elizabeth Thom, the daughter of a customer. Their courtship began in earnest, but there was a major obstacle: Elizabeth's wealthy father, a sea captain and shipowner, wanted his precious daughter to have nothing to do with a village weaver who offered no sign of being "specially successful in the acquisition of worldly gear."[6] (Here the characters of Grandpa Carnegie and his namesake Andra diverged completely; Andra would prove himself a prodigal capitalist.) Despite the wizened captain withdrawing Elizabeth's dowry, she and Andrew married for love, eventually producing ten children.

Andrew and Elizabeth's seventh child was William, born on June 19, 1804, the future father of the world's most rapacious steel master. The flaxen-haired boy with blue eyes bright against his milk-pale skin became a third-generation weaver and eventually specialized in damask, a craft involving the use of a lustrous fabric such as cotton, linen, or silk to create flat patterns in a satin weave. The patterns were intricate and beautiful, and William produced spectacular tablecloths as his feet worked the treadles and his hands deftly moved the shuttle from side to side. At that time, Dunfermline, two miles north, was the center for the damask trade. William, realizing an independent life in Pattiemuir would put few shillings in his pocket, journeyed there circa 1830, his father to follow.[7] It was a brave act moving from a mere hamlet to a burgh of more than ten thousand people, but William was young and ambitious.

Nicknamed "Auld Grey Toun" because all the buildings were constructed of gray sandstone, the seemingly dour Dunfermline nevertheless had a certain romantic lure that pervaded the inhabitants' spirits, including that of Andra. It stood on high ground overlooking the Firth of Forth, a long, narrow bay backed by the silhouette of the Pentland Hills beyond, and had once been the capital of Scotland. Rich with tradition and treasure, at the start of the fourteenth century Dunfermline's "Abbey and Monastery buildings stood unrivalled in Scotland for their extent and 'noble adornments,'" according to town historian Ebenezer Henderson.[8] On his death in 1329, King Robert the Bruce was buried in the center of the abbey, surrounded by past kings and queens, including Queen Margaret, the patron saint of Scotland. But in the mid-1400s, the capital was relocated to Edinburgh, a far more powerful military seat, with its imposing fortress and ability to protect the royal family. When William Carnegie made his way to Dunfermline, the majestic monastery and royal palace were but ruins, though the air of nobility and pride remained, the noble ghosts of William Wallace and the Robert the Bruce alive in the streets.

William rented half of a cottage duplex on the corner of Moodie Street and Priory Lane, paying between $15 and $20 a year. He set up his loom on the main floor, the room's dimensions a mere eight paces by six, and his living quarters in the cramped attic above. He shared the stairs with the other renters, along with the privy out back. While Captain Thom had thumbed his nose at William's father, in Dunfermline the damask handloom weaver was considered aristocracy, the nobility of the working class and relatively prosperous, in stark contrast to the suffering tenant farmers, coal miners, and factory workers who were paid starvation wages.[9]

Recognized as a sober and skilled weaver, William Carnegie quickly made friends, including the Morrison family, who lived up the street. He became smitten with Margaret Morrison, who was born on June 19, 1810, the third of six children. Her father, Thomas, was a political activist, reminding William of his own radical heritage. Like all Morrison women, Margaret had a stout body and strong, dark facial features, her square chin and high cheekbones prominent in what was otherwise a plain face. As a polite Scotsman would say, she was a "wiselik" girl, or "She's better than she's bonny." In other words, she was a woman with character. Considering her mother died when Margaret was just four, she had little choice but to become strong-willed, and it was her penetrating eyes with heavy, almost seductive lids that first captivated

The Dunfermline, Scotland, cottage in which Andrew Carnegie was born in 1835. The Carnegie family shared "the duplex" with another family. (Courtesy of the Carnegie Library of Pittsburgh)

William. No fool, he recognized an efficient woman of good stock, and in December 1834 he took her hand in marriage. Although Andra was named after his paternal grandfather and had his father's blond hair and blue eyes, he would inherit his mother's resoluteness and tenacity, as well as the fiercely independent fighting spirit of his maternal ancestors.

The bellicose Morrison spirit was due to their Norse blood, their Viking ancestors having invaded northern Scotland and conquered the people there in the ninth and tenth centuries. They then migrated south. Some seven hundred years later found Thomas Morrison's father, John, to be a prosperous leather merchant in Edinburgh. Thomas married Ann Hodge, the daughter of a wealthy Edinburgh merchant, and was running the family's leather business when, according to family legend, he made some speculative investments and lost both the business and his wife's inheritance.[10] He moved the family to Dunfermline to begin anew, to rebuild his life. There he became a respectable cobbler, a trade he had learned as a boy.

Although a widower since 1814, Thomas found the time to pursue political activities, and derived great satisfaction in haranguing audiences about his favorite topic, land reform. It was time for the monarchy, the lords, and the privileged few to relinquish the land they had controlled since the beginning of the feudal system. In one torrid lecture, "Rights of Land," he delivered his core doctrine: "Our rule is *Each shall possess; all shall enjoy;* Our principle, *universal and equal right;* and our 'law of the land' shall be *Every man a lord; every woman a lady;* and *every child an heir.*"[11] His brooding black eyes would stare out at the crowd, and his wild outcropping of sable hair would shake as he gestured wildly with each point he shouted, his strong jaw jutting outward. His extravagant use of body language—a thrown-out chest, rollicking lips, violent hand motions—were so identically reproduced in Andra that it unnerved his relatives. As for Thomas Morrison's politics, they were embraced by the entire clan, including Andra, who came to despise inherited privilege and aristocratic tendencies in any form.

To further his political agenda, Morrison organized a Dunfermline political union of fellow radicals in the 1820s, which had the adopted battle cry "Agitation is the order of the day—the night of monastic ignorance is passed."[12] He also founded *The Precursor,* a newspaper "devoted to the interests of the Tradesmen and Mechanics in particular," but it was considered so provocative that only a radical printer in Edinburgh would set it in type.[13] Whether it was a readership too timid to buy the paper or the cost of sending each manuscript the sixteen miles to Edinburgh via horse-drawn carriage, the newspaper was declared defunct after just three issues. Enthusiasm unabated, Morrison took up his pen against the district's representative to Parliament, the Tory nobleman Lord Dalmeny, and in an audacious stream of correspondence he advised and criticized Dalmeny on everything from his support of the monarchy to his grammar. A land reform evangelist until the end, Thomas Morrison died on the road in 1837, haranguing the public and collecting money to continue his mission.

There was good cause for Morrison's land reform agitation, as well as the general desire for revolution that pervaded Britain's working class: the country's deteriorating economic and living conditions had become unbearable. While Andra was yet too young to comprehend his immediate world, he was a creature of his environment, and these threads of history would be woven into the fabric of his soul. Social conditions, now and in the future, would shape his moral convictions.

No longer ignorant, voiceless peasants taking swipes at the monarchy by poaching deer on the nobility's properties, the members of the disenfranchised working class were becoming more vocal, organizing themselves into trade unions, demanding reduced work hours and reasonable wages, and their leaders were inserting themselves into the political fray. Several issues in particular stirred the public's ire, but, foremost, the middle and lower classes demanded the seemingly basic rights to vote, which would give them representation in Parliament, and to own property. Another thorn was the Corn Laws, which artificially supported the price of corn and wheat to benefit the farmers. The majority of the working class, however, lived in factory and mining towns where they couldn't grow their own food and were forced to pay the artificially inflated prices or face starvation. It became difficult to earn a living wage and conditions continued to deteriorate, a situation described so depressingly well by Charles Dickens in such classics as *Oliver Twist* (1838). These problems were not just political; they were also the side effects of the Industrial Revolution, a revolution that was beyond the control of politicians.

Great Britain had taken an early lead in the Industrial Revolution. The isles, with rich coalfields to provide fuel for steam engines, many natural waterways for cheap transportation, and a booming international trade with its colonies, was ideally suited for a transformation from an agricultural-based economy to a manufacturing-based economy, from a handicraft system to a factory system. As country folk, in search of steady jobs, migrated to the cities in increasing numbers, the transition proved painful because already poor living conditions in urban centers were exacerbated by a population explosion. Contributing to this unprecedented growth were the Irish, who, seeking work, arrived in waves. Thus, employers had such a large labor pool to select from that they were able to dictate low wages and long hours, further suppressing the working poor.[14] Disillusioned and embittered, the working class formed both trade and political unions to exert pressure, and activism increased dramatically.

Nationalistic-minded Scotland raised a collective cry of protest as industrial towns such as Dunfermline, Glasgow, and the mining towns that sprang up around the expansive central coalfields suffered more than most. The police superintendent of Glasgow, reporting on his own city streets, observed, "There is concentrated everything that is wretched, dissolute, loathsome, and pestilential. These places are filled by a population of many thousands of miserable creatures. The houses in which they live are unfit even for sties . . . dunghills lie in the vicinity of the dwellings; and from the extremely defective sewerages, filth of every kind constantly accumulates."[15] Thirty-nine miles to the northeast of Glasgow, Dunfermline was certainly not immune to the pestilential conditions. In the coalfields that ringed the town, visitors discovered the squalid conditions of Glasgow, with women and girls working alongside men and boys in the pits. Sanitary conditions were deplorable. Not only was clean water scarce, but miners were creatures of superstition and preferred not to bathe, perhaps hoping their filth would keep death at a distance.

On the more immediate outskirts of Dunfermline, tenant farmers were equally destitute. A prominent radical activist and friend of the Morrison family, William Cobbett, described the living conditions of the farmer he encountered on his way visit to the Morrison household: "I found the 'bothie' to be a shed, with a fire-place in it to burn coals in, with one doorway, and one little window. The floor was the ground. There were three wooden bedsteads nailed together like the berths in a barrack-room, with boards for the bottom of them. The bedding seemed to be very coarse sheeting with coarse woolen things at the top; and all seemed to be such as similar things must be when there is nobody but men to look after them. . . . There was no back-door to the place, and no privy."[16] A wry observation made more than once was that the cows were housed as well as the men and the pigs ate better. The factories in Dunfermline proper also offered horrific scenes; even government commissions found them filthy and ill ventilated.[17] As in the coal mines, here, too, children labored. One commission inspector reported on eleven-year-old Margaret Methven, whose "feet and legs often swell and give her pain" from the long hours, her workday beginning at a quarter before 6 A.M. and lasting until 8 P.M., with half an hour for dinner.[18]

Cholera and typhus were a constant threat in the overpopulated town of Dunfermline, with its narrow streets and inadequate housing. When a cholera epidemic swept across Europe in 1832, the townspeople fearfully tracked its progress in the newspapers. The disease found its way to northeastern England in February of that year, and on September 2 it struck its first Dunfermline victim.[19] Not long after, the dead cart rumbling through the streets became a familiar sight, but behind it trailed no mourners for fear of being infected. Such were the conditions of the new industrial society, characterized by glorious advances in technology and mass production, overcrowding, squalor, and an acute sense of mortality—for the working class, a bleak, Dickensian place that held out little hope to their children. This was the world, country, and town into which Andrew Carnegie was born.

The boy was the offspring of Celtic and Norse blood, and from both the Carnegie and the Morrison sides little Andra would take a piece for himself. From his mother and father, his aunts and uncles he would learn of family traditions and legends, some more embellished than others. Fate would play a prominent role in his own legend, too, for that cold, foggy November day of his birth was a day for Shakespeare's witches to rule on the heath, stirring their cauldron and prophesying the future as they did for the ambitious Scotsman Macbeth. "All hail, Macbeth," they cried, "that shalt be king hereafter!"[20] The seed was planted for Macbeth to kill his king, and a battle between determinism and freewill ensued. Carnegie would face the same battle for control, reckoning with forces that began with his birthplace. "No bright child of Dunfermline can escape the influence of the Abbey, Palace, and Glen," he reflected. "These touch him and set fire to the latent spark within, making him something different and beyond what, less happily born, he would have become."[21] He believed in fate, and fate would indeed light that "latent spark within." The stage was set.

At the pulpit in the austere church in Dunfermline, the minister spoke of sin. His stern voice lost in its profundity, he preached the standard Calvinistic doctrine that mankind is spiritually incapacitated by sin, having been born into the original sin of Adam and Eve. He used these thorny words: *infant damnation*. Will Carnegie could take no more of this Presbyterian diatribe— how could his slaphappy baby, his wee Andra, be living in sin?—and he admonished the minister, declaring, "If that be your religion and that your God, I seek a better religion and a nobler God." That was the family story of Will's break with the church, a story Andra cherished his entire life.[22] It would also lead to young Andra growing up in a house divided on religious matters. As a result, he would become devoutly agnostic, preferring to seek immortality in his temporal life than concerning himself with theological thereafters.

Will's rejection of the Presbyterian Church of Scotland, which was based on John Calvin's doctrines, was not unusual; most radicals of that time considered the church to be part of the Tory-Anglican establishment that had opposed voter reform in 1832. Another factor influencing Will was that Calvin's God was not a benevolent God, nor a particularly judicious one in light of the fact that Calvinism denies the will of the individual, as well as blesses and condemns people indiscriminately. Will did not want his child growing up handicapped by such deterministic principles. No doubt, Margaret was pleased by her husband's choice because her family had forsaken the church years ago, and she herself was taken with the impassioned William Ellery Channing, the American minister who wrote a biography of Henry David Thoreau and advocated Unitarianism. (This Protestant sect believes that God is one person, not part of a Trinity, and trusts in the moral abilities of the individual.) Although Unitarianism had existed in Transylvania since the 1560s, it was Channing who did much to popularize the church's beliefs in the early 1800s. Not only did Channing preach that the Calvinist God was corrupt, which was welcomed by the radical Morrisons, but he greatly elevated mankind's state from depravity. He believed that man and woman followed a divine pattern in their own spiritual evolution, and the greatest good was that mankind could "hold intellectual and moral affinity with the Supreme Being."[23] Margaret took delight in this viewpoint, and she imagined such greatness for her Andra; he would not submit to the Calvinist's wanton deity, but walk with God. Still, she did not attend any Unitarian church services, not with housework and cooking to be done; as a Scottish woman, she could never shirk her Calvin-based puritan streak.

Not convinced Unitarianism was the answer, Will elected to join the Swedenborgian church, a very small congregation attended by other members of the Carnegie and Morrison families. The church was based on the teachings of Emanuel Swedenborg, a Swedish scientist, theosophist, and mystic, who, after a tranquil career of studying mathematics and the natural sciences, experienced a mystic illumination in 1745. Based on his vision, he constructed three realms of existence: the divine mind, the spiritual world, and the natural world, corresponding to love, wisdom, and use, respectively. And each could be found in both God and humankind. Life was a shared experience with God, according to Swedenborg, who believed divinity equated to eternal love. This was the benevolent God Will sought, regardless of whether Swedenborg was a theosophist quack with delusions of being a prophet. Truth be known, Will was a bit of a dreamer, too, who was liable to forsake the loom for religious meditation. Neighbors referred to him as a "thawless chiel" on occasion, suggesting he was dreamy and impractical.[24]

Although both churches believed humankind was not born in a depraved state, nor were individuals predestined for salvation or damnation, Will and

Margaret didn't share the other's enthusiasm for their respective religions. Impressed upon Andra were beliefs from each religious practice, which would manifest themselves later in life; and while the Carnegie family denied the Presbyterian Church a place in their lives, Calvinism was so strong in Scotland that its spirit pervaded the family's soul, a spirit that included moral austerity and family piety, thrift, industry, and sobriety. Andra recalled that "the stern doctrines of Calvinism lay as a terrible nightmare upon me," but the nightmare later faded.[25] Faded, but not forgotten, especially when Andra achieved wealth and fame, for he came to believe he was one of Calvin's blessed, a sanctified trustee for all of civilization.

Now a confident master weaver, Will decided to take on apprentices and add looms; with the small, half cottage on Moodie Street no longer adequate, he moved the family to larger quarters on Edgar Street, overlooking a park and lush green. On the bottom floor of the Edgar Street home Will installed four looms; the family still lived above the workshop, but this time in a spacious apartment, not a cramped attic. Far more driven than her husband by material gain, a temporarily satisfied Margaret looked forward to the time when they would reach the social status of others in the Morrison clan, especially her older sister Seaton, who had married George Lauder, a well-to-do merchant with a shop on High Street. At Edgar Street, Andra found new entertainment for himself besides flinging porridge about: he discovered money. When allowed, he would take all the pennies his mother had diligently saved in her cash box and stack them up, only to swat them down. A neighborhood lad, John Kirk, who used to baby-sit occasionally for Margaret, later recalled the game: "The ploy he seemed to like best was tae get haud o' as mony pennies as he could, build them up on the tap o' each ither, an' then knock them o'er wi' his haund."[26]

Life was grand for a year, and then pennies were no longer playthings. Due to a business downturn in 1837, the growth of the damask trade quickly reversed, exacerbated by the fact that not only was there less work, but the number of looms in Dunfermline had reached a saturation point, almost doubling in the previous twenty years.[27] Weavers employed in shops were paid off and let go; hundreds were without work, with the unemployment rate among weavers nearing 30 percent, making it necessary to start a relief fund. Compounding the distress, influenza and typhus fever struck Dunfermline, and there was also a poor harvest.[28] All William could do was go to his closet to pray, which was his habit, but the damask trade would never be the same.

Now more desperate to wield political power, the working class created formidable political unions that encompassed all workers in all geographic locations. Two organizations came to the forefront in early 1838: the London Working Men's Association (LWMA) and the Birmingham Political Union. The LWMA, with little fanfare, published its manifesto, *The People's Charter*, which was aimed at suffrage reform, beginning with "a vote for everyman twenty-one years of age, of sound mind, and not undergoing punishment for crime."[29] It was the old story of fair representation for all.

In May, the Birmingham Political Union, with its power base in the industrial town of Birmingham, sent its most eloquent and electrifying speakers on tour—Dunfermline was on the itinerary—in support of the charter. The speakers also presented the union's National Reform Petition, which, like the charter, demanded voter and parliamentary reforms, and called for everyone to sign. By early June, the petition was adopted in Dundee, Dunfermline, Edinburgh, Glasgow, and Perth, among other towns, and as the movement picked up momentum the supporters became known as Chartists. The Chartists were to be the unifying power that was supposed to bring about the downfall of the British government.

Both William Carnegie and his brother-in-law Thomas Morrison Jr. enthusiastically took up the Chartists' mantle, which would impact Andra. Margaret's eldest brother, Thomas, a member of the town council since 1833 and nicknamed "the Bailie," was the carrier of the family's radical torch and quickly took a leadership role in Dunfermline's chapter of the London Working Men's Association. Like his father, he was an impressive sight when haranguing the public, a forceful and sometimes supernatural-appearing specter. A tremendous walking stick—"as big as a post"—thumping down city roads always announced his arrival. A lean, upright man, Morrison added to his imposing figure by always donning a long frock coat and a lum hat, a chimney-shaped headpiece. Public speakers opposing Morrison feared the sight of his piercing eyes and his bushy beard in the crowd because he was renowned as "a determined and clever heckler," showing contempt with a cuckoo singsong of "hear, hear, hear!" The *Dunfermline Journal,* a conservative newspaper, described his heckling as "most disgusting" and deplored how he could "laugh at the most sacred emotions of the human heart."[30] From Thomas, Andra would inherit a mocking, biting humor and a willingness to startle, stun, and otherwise disrupt his enemies.

When not humiliating the enemy or being chastised by the press, Thomas hosted other prominent British radicals and Chartists. Among them were those who espoused violence to achieve the charter; they were the physical force men who thirsted for armed revolution. Thomas, while a fiery character, did not advocate the use of physical force; instead he was a moral suasionist, believing that peaceful, logical discussion would effect change. Already a tenuous coalition as different tradesmen envisioned different goals, the Chartist movement would fracture over the point of violence versus pacifism. Decades later, Andra would also be faced with this basic choice between using physical force or peaceful persuasion in dealing with labor strikes like that at his Homestead steel mill in 1892; he would find himself and his lieutenants so divided on the issue that indecision would lead to tragedy. While strikes would be anathema to Andra, his uncle Thomas was not averse to calling for disruptive strikes, and helped establish a Cessation-from-Labour committee. Their purpose was "to go on strike and 'not to resume the production of wealth until the People's Charter becomes law.' "[31] To not produce wealth was a prospect that did indeed intimidate the authorities, landowners, and sundry lords. Troops and cavalry were sent from Edinburgh to patrol Dunfermline and prevent seditious meetings, so the town's defiant Chartists held a meeting in nearby Torryburn—with Tom Morrison and his club at the podium.[32]

Often at his brother-in-law's side at many of the gatherings, Will developed into a forceful speaker, too, and little Andra, when attending the political rallies, would push through the thick human brush of legs and coats to see his father. Will also took up his pen for the cause, writing a bold letter to the editor of the *Edinburgh Monthly Democrat*, a newly founded Chartist newspaper, that was printed in the July 7, 1838, inaugural issue. He extolled Dunfermline's Chartist movement, noted that 6,106 citizens had signed the Chartist petition, and concluded, "The work goes on gloriously here."[33] Despite Will's optimism, the next spring the proposals in the Chartist petition were soundly rejected by the House of Commons, 235 votes to 46. Radical activity would thereafter become more desperate.

Andrew Carnegie was not yet three years old when the Chartist movement began in 1838, and he could hardly understand the social and economic dynamics behind it; however, the excitement it generated in his parents worried the boy. Childhood in the Carnegie home offered little enjoyment with Father at the loom ten to twelve hours a day, Mother laboring through chores, and the Carnegie-Morrison clan dedicating hours to planning the reform campaign. A voracious reader who cofounded a small library for weaver families, Will spent any other precious free minutes reading the papers and *Bentley's Miscellany*'s monthly installments of the latest Charles Dickens novel, such as *Oliver Twist* or *Nicholas Nickleby*.

The one sanctuary Andra could escape to for attention and boyhood pleasures was his uncle George Lauder's grocery store on High Street. By instinct, he gravitated toward this surrogate father, who, after his wife Seaton's premature death, turned his attention to his son, George Jr., and Andra, hoping to forget his grief in their young enthusiasm. Andra spent many hours of the day with his uncle and his cousin George, and the boys, close in age, became like brothers. Unable to say each other's names as toddlers, George called his cousin by a piece of his last name, Naig, and Andrew, using a piece of no one knows what, called him Dod; the names stuck for their entire lives. When there were no customers, Uncle Lauder, as the family called him, would pull up a couple of crates and, in a hushed tone, recount stories of Scotland's history, including the boys' favorite—the heroic exploits of William Wallace. Wallace emerged from obscurity to lead Scottish forces against the ruthless English King Edward I, whose army was defeated on September 11, 1297. Anointed guardian of Scotland, Wallace later resigned and was eventually captured. For his crimes he was hanged, decapitated, his head mounted on London Bridge, his internal organs burned, and his body cut into four parts to be displayed in Scotland as a gentle reminder to not question the king's authority. No doubt, Uncle Lauder edited the story a bit to soften the blow. The message imparted was that a commoner had risen up to become the guardian of Scotland, comparable to being king, and so, too, could the boys elevate themselves to greatness. Wallace upset the natural order, the hierarchy of the social class, and for Andra, "everything heroic centered in him."[34]

The exploits of King Robert the Bruce, who won Scotland's independence on the heels of Wallace's heroics, were also favorites of the boys: how his three brothers were captured and executed; how his wife was held prisoner for eight years; how he risked his wealth and estates for all-out war against the English; how he single-handedly slew three would-be ambushers; how he made and broke alliances to secure victory; and how he mingled with all his soldiers to win loyalty. These stories were dramatic lessons for Dod and Naig to be applied later in life, and to ensure the boys remembered their history, Uncle Lauder offered pennies as rewards for memorizing facts. It worked. A neighbor recalled that Andra developed a spongelike memory; for one of the girls he played with he would commit to memory favorite songs and poetry, then stand on the kitchen chair and recite them back.[35] His power of memorization and fine public performing would serve him well, and he later wrote that his uncle's "influence over me cannot be overestimated."[36] At this early age, Andra also associated the monetary rewards with success, the only measurement he would know how to use as an adult.

Outside of Uncle Lauder's shop, the ruins of the Meal Mill on Monastery Street became the boys' castle for imaginary sieges and battles, the dam of an old barley mill made for a moat and drawbridge—until the stagnant water became dangerously polluted—and the hilly, cobbled streets lined with single-story cottages with red-tiled roofs were also the playground.[37] The preferred games were marbles, or "plounkie," and grounders. Athletic competition, such as high jumping and racing base, was popular, too, for the blue-collar boys who couldn't afford more luxurious sporting events such as foxhunting or dressage or cricket. The absolute favorite, however, was cavalry fighting, in which Andra would perch on the shoulders of a stronger lad and try to knock off a similarly mounted antagonist. Blood and broken bones were not unknown, and the games instilled in the young men a will to win.[38] Competition, violence, bloodshed, and even death, it seems, could not be ignored; they were everywhere in Andra's life, from Scottish history to the coal mines ringing Dunfermline to the streets on which he walked.

There was one place, an oasislike paradise in Dunfermline, where Andra was banned from playing—the Pittencrieff estate and its parklike grounds. Owned by the Hunt family, Pittencrieff was the largest estate in town, the property encompassing the historically important ruins of the mythical monastery and palace, along with more than sixty acres of grand lawns, high hills, deep woods, and beautiful views of the firth. Although the Hunts were an inhospitable bunch, protecting their estate with formidable stone walls and iron gates, every May, in an annual display of generosity, the family would open the grounds to the public, except to those descended from Thomas Morrison Sr. The radical had publicly fought with James Hunt over greater access to Dunfermline's heritage—the ruins—and a spiteful Hunt barred all Morrisons and descendants from ever stepping on the property. With Uncle Thomas still riling the Hunt family, the feud continued a generation later, and Andra could only daydream of magic among the ruins. One day he would exact revenge and procure the estate.

As Andra grew older and prepared to become a fourth-generation weaver, work became part of his daily routine. For hours, he'd watch his father weave, fascinated by the rhythmic movement and clatter of the handheld driver stick and the batten; and when needed, he fetched supplies, such as spools of yarn and buckets of water. Water was a scarce commodity in Dunfermline, so every morning queues formed at public wells to pump the day's first supply, a chore Andra enjoyed only because he could antagonize the old ladies. "The supply was scanty and irregular," he recalled. "Sometimes it was not allowed to run until late in the morning and a score of old wives were sitting around, the turn of each having been previously secured through the night by placing a worthless can in the line. This, as might be expected, led to numerous contentions in which I would not be put down even by these venerable old dames. I earned the reputation of being 'an awfu' laddie.' In this way I probably developed the strain of argumentativeness, or perhaps combativeness, which has always remained with me."[39] Never intimidated by the ladies' clucking reproaches, brash Andra, with flaxen hair and sturdy, stumpy legs, always ignored their cans and scurried to the front of the queue.

Occasional emergencies at Uncle Lauder's shop required Andra's help. Once, when Dod and Naig were about nine or ten years of age, Lauder bought one hundred pints of exceptionally ripe gooseberries that had to be peddled immediately. "Well Naig," Uncle Lauder said, "will you and Dod go to Crossgates with John Vock and his Cuddy Cart and sell these grosets for me?" It was a big job, but Andra was already displaying an aptitude for selling and performed admirably, according to Uncle Lauder, who in a letter to Andra, reflected, "This was a lesson in self reliance—and nobly did the lads acquit themselves."[40]

Self-reliance and independence: These were traits bred in young Andra's bone and because he was small in physical stature, reaching only five feet three inches in adulthood (five feet seven inches was the American adult male average), he had no choice but to rely on a quick wit to solve problems. As a boy, he showed this acumen when he started keeping rabbits. His father was good enough to build a rabbit hutch, but when it came to feeding the rabbits (who multiplied unmercifully, as rabbits are apt to do) Andra was on his own. To manage the task, the boy gathered his chums and made his first business deal: if they gathered dandelions and clover to feed the frisky rabbits, he would name a rabbit after each of them. Playing upon vanity, the manipulative Andra learned at a young age, was a clever means to motivate others and to profit. It was a technique he used time and again to secure his desires.

As for a formal education, which was then voluntary, doting Will and Margaret promised their only child they would not ship him off to school until he was quite ready. By the time he reached age seven and was still showing no inclination to attend school, Will and Margaret were regretting their promise. Finally, they approached Robert Martin, head of the nearby Rolland School, and asked him to take Andra on a little outing to discuss the merits of schooling. To his parents' relief, the eight-year-old boy took to Mr. Martin and was enrolled in the school at a cost of a few pennies a week. Between 150 and 180 students attended the Rolland School, the entire flock in a single room. The master taught the lessons to the older students, who in turn helped the younger with studies that included spelling, memorizing, doing sums in arithmetic, and writing in copybooks. The students would form a semicircle around the teacher to "say their lessons," a duty the demonstrative Andra excelled at—and a good thing, too, because "Snuffy" Martin, as the headmaster was secretly called, was a taskmaster. If one of his cretinous charges misbehaved, he threw a leather strap at the perpetrator. The child then brought the strap to Snuffy and took a smart whack on the open palm.

Far from being a hooligan, Andra was a boy who tried too hard in the eyes of his peers and was nicknamed "Martin's Pet," a name snarled at him in passing. Although he despised the moniker, Andra couldn't help but be a diligent student. In his teacher, as he had in Uncle Lauder and as he would throughout his life, he astutely recognized another worthy mentor. Andra had the canny ability to latch on to both men and women from whom he could absorb wisdom and information and who could further his career. From Mr. Martin's perspective, he claimed that Andrew Carnegie was "one of the smartest lads who had ever passed through his school."[41] Besides the nickname Martin's Pet, the only other souring experience at school was having to recite a daily dose of two double verses of the Psalms. Due to his father and mother's rejection of traditional church, religion was not Andra's forte, immediately demonstrated on the first day of school when he was asked to recite a proverb. Proudly, he responded, "Take care of your pence, the pound will take care of themselves."[42] That particular proverb's source was Andra's mother, not the Good Book, and his classmates had a hearty laugh at his expense. It was only fitting that Margaret Carnegie held more power over her son than any god: she was the single greatest motivational force behind his success.

CHAPTER 2

Odyssey to America

I t didn't matter that the economy improved in 1840. It didn't matter that Margaret gave birth to a girl and named her Ann, after her sister. It didn't matter that George Lauder and Tom Morrison considered their plans ill-advised and traitorous. Margaret's younger sister Annie and her husband, Andrew Aitken, were finished with Dunfermline, and in 1840 they emigrated to Allegheny City, a suburb of Pittsburgh. They arrived in Philadelphia on July 2 and searched for Annie's sister Kitty, who had emigrated there earlier with her husband, Thomas Hogan. The Aitkens and Hogans, including Thomas Hogan's brother Andrew, then pushed on to Allegheny, otherwise known as Slabtown—a nickname less appealing and, perhaps, less inviting than Auld Grey Toun.

One of the first letters home suggested they had indeed made a mistake. In October 1840, Annie wrote, "My dear Margaret things being in such an unsettled condition in this country at present, it would be the height of folly to advise you . . . to venture out at this season at any rate, as it is very difficult for one to get employment of any kind, and more particularly weaving which is scarcely carried on here at all."[1] As evidence of their growing frustration with Scotland's political and economic situation, Will and Margaret were obviously entertaining the idea of emigrating as well if Annie's reports offered hope. But the United States was mired in a depression precipitated by crop failures, restricted bank credit, and a financial panic three years earlier. So what would they be escaping to? A town where the weaving trade was nonexistent and unemployment rampant? Abandon their beloved "toun" for that?

Then again, Andra's baby sister, Ann, was born into a Dunfermline that was not the town of her parents' youth. Smokestacks now pierced the skyline in a series of thrusts, and each year the soot hung heavier in the air. Filth slithered through window cracks and across doorsills. Disease, like a tireless parasite, sought more victims, including families living on Edgar Street. Death, which had so far been avoided by the Carnegie family, took its first victim in 1841—baby Ann—and the Carnegie-Morrison clan descended into depression, broken by innocent death, defections to America, and a dispirited Chartist movement following the defeat of the petition.[2]

The Carnegie-Morrison clan found renewed purpose in the economic downturn of 1842, during which more than eight hundred Dunfermline looms sat idle and some sixteen hundred weavers and other laborers, as well as their families, were in a state of destitution.[3] The downturn reinvigorated the Chartist movement as a new call for reforms filled the air, especially when, in August 1842, the large, controlling linen manufacturers threatened to cut wages again. The average weaver had already witnessed a 50 percent drop in wages from 1810 to 1840, and they could take no more. Violence erupted. Men and boys and even women, faces blackened, clubs in hand, took to the streets, and they attacked the loom shops, warehouses, and homes of the reviled manufacturers—hurling stones, setting fires, and looting. Thomas Morrison threw himself into the seething mob, the moral-suasionist Chartist imploring the people to end their rampage. To no avail. Enniskillen Dragoons were ordered in to suppress the uprising, and the sheriff now had his excuse for making several highly visible arrests.

One night, not long after the rioting, there was a tap at the back window of the Carnegie house. There were hushed whispers. Six-year-old Andra awoke to discover the sheriff had arrested Uncle Thomas for holding an illegal Chartist meeting, and he was now being held in jail, located above the town council chamber. The situation quickly became explosive as sympathizers marched on Town Hall and threatened to forcibly free their leader, which prompted the panicked provost to petition Tom to ask his supporters to go home. A riot was averted.[4] After several days, he was released. Formal charges were never brought against Thomas—one of the more lucid decisions by the authorities, according to the Carnegie-Morrison clan. The incident was burned into Andra's memory, however; his world, it seemed, was on fire. Years later, he framed a handbill describing the charges levied against his uncle, which he displayed proudly in his study and called his "title to nobility."[5]

Carnegie would question whether his parents realized the impact those events had on him: "Along with the most advanced ideas which were being agitated in the political world—the death of privilege, the equality of the citizen, Republicanism—I heard many disputations upon theological subjects which the impressionable child drank in to an extent quite unthought of by his elders."[6] Peace and love were not the words whispered across his parents' lips; Andra was anything but a cuddly, kilt-clad Scotsman. "It is not to be wondered at that, nursed amid such surroundings," he reflected, "I developed into a violent young Republican whose motto was 'death to privilege.'"[7] This disciple of Wallace believed that he "could have slain king, duke, or lord, and considered their deaths a service to the state and hence an heroic act."[8]

For all the brave talk and agitation, conditions in Dunfermline continued to deteriorate. For the first time, in 1843, the Auld Grey Toun had its own poorhouse—or "porridge house," as it was unaffectionately known—and by December there were twelve pawnbrokers welcoming the destitute to part with their family heirlooms. Two years later, a new prison would be finished, with room for 262, and a police force of 12 would be established for night duty.[9] The proliferating poverty and crime had to be eradicated from the streets. Will Carnegie struggled to find work as the great wave of the Industrial Revolution broke over him, his skills replaced by sophisticated looms in the steam-powered factories. Although Will's income was shrinking, the size of the Carnegie family increased with the birth of a son, Thomas, in 1843. Not long after, Will was forced to dismiss an apprentice and sell one of his looms, and the next year the weaving trade was again depressed with five hundred unemployed.[10] But there were also small victories for the reformers in the coming years: the 1844 Factory Act, which reduced hours for children and women, and provided for stricter factory sanitation; the hated Corn Laws were repealed on June 26, 1846, inspiring a grand jubilee in Dunfermline that transformed the town into a "fairy land"; and then Parliament passed the 1847 Factory Act, which ultimately limited the hours of weekly labor to fifty-eight—a real concession to the working class.[11] Such acts, however, did nothing to alleviate the situation of the independent artisan like Will.

Finally, from America, there came a bit of good news. Annie, writing for the first time in over a year, reported: "Business here is much better now, as most individuals can find employment although some are out of a job yet, & wages are considerably reduced. . . . This country's far better for the working man than the old one, & there is room enough & to spare, notwithstanding the thousands that flock into her borders."[12] Margaret was both pleased and jealous—jealous because the better life she had dreamed of was slipping away. Will was forced to sell off his other two extra looms and dismiss the apprentices, and now degraded, the family moved back to a small cottage on Moodie Street. With more than ten years gone since Will and Margaret married, they were no better off—and their future prospects looked grim.

As the weavers soon realized, neither petitions nor violence were going to reinstitute higher wages because there were plenty of workers taking jobs for a pittance—namely, the Irish. When the potato famine struck Ireland in 1846, more than 346,000 left the country over the next two years, many traveling the short distance to England and Scotland. These people were escaping abject poverty and starvation, so a poor-paying job in the Dunfermline mills was a step up and readily accepted. However convenient it was to lay blame on the Irish, who became the easily targeted scapegoat, for handloom weavers there was a far greater force at work—the Industrial Revolution. With perfect retrospection, Andrew Carnegie wrote, "My father did not recognize the impending revolution, and was struggling under the old system."[13] James Watt had patented an improved steam engine in 1769; the power loom had been introduced in 1783; and the Jacquard loom had made its debut in 1825. Programmed by large punch cards, the Jacquard loom was able to make as intricate designs as the handloom weavers, so fewer men could now produce equitable products. Whatever work was left for handloom weavers, men like

Will were last on the list to hire because they had alienated themselves by becoming radicals and by leaving the church. Essentially, Will the Chartist was campaigning against the very men he depended on to buy his webs.

After the move back to Moodie Street, Andra became aware of the family's impending doom: "I remember that shortly after this I began to learn what poverty meant. Dreadful days came when my father took the last of his webs to the great manufacturer, and I saw my mother anxiously awaiting his return to know whether a new web was to be obtained or that a period of idleness was upon us."[14] Andra's mother came to the rescue; her thin upper lip stiffened, she opened a small shop in their cottage, displaying cabbages, leeks, carrots, and sweets for the children in the front window.[15] Come evening, she bound shoes for her brother Tom; and now, instead of assisting his father at the loom, Andra helped his mother by threading her needles. Years ago, Margaret's father had written an essay on the importance of learning a craft to achieve self-reliance. "How is it that I enjoy health, competence, serenity, independence and even respectability," he wrote, "in the best sense of that term? All these, and other enjoyments, I owe to handication. Blessed be God, I learned in my youth to make and mend shoes: the awls were my resource and they have not failed me."[16] Morrison belittled what was called "heddekashun"—education of the head, an education in the humanities, an education that created imbeciles, according to him. As Margaret and Andra bound shoes, she recalled the essay, emphasizing the importance of practical training and self-reliance. He would not forget the lesson.

During this period, Margaret, who was imbued with a more tenacious constitution than her husband, displaced Will as Andra's hero, and he elevated her to a demigod status, a position she would forever retain. "I feel her to be sacred to myself and not for others to know," he wrote in his autobiography.[17] The idolatry knew no bounds, and Carnegie admitted that "I cannot trust myself to speak at length" of her. He strived to please her, to repay her, and to honor her.

Unemployment was widespread by the end of 1847 and deepened in early 1848, sparking food riots in Edinburgh, Glasgow, and several other towns. The Carnegie dinner table witnessed less cod, haddock, and kippers bought from the fishwife, and more oatcakes, porridge, and potatoes—oats and potatoes were easily grown in the northern climate and became their food staples. In the Hungry Forties, as this period became known, a pot full of potatoes was a feast, many a bowl of meal was sent to destitute neighbors, ever more children went to bed without supper, and even the street lamps were lit late and extinguished early to save a few pennies. Typhus became rampant, and the *Dunfermline Journal* warned its readers of the importance of clean living: "TEMPERANCE, CLEANLINESS, *and* BREATHING PURE AIR, *are three of the surest means of securing health, and preventing attacks of typhus fever, or any other diseases.*" The article concluded with an harangue concerning whiskey:

Andrew Carnegie's mother,
Margaret Morrison Carnegie,
saved the family from destitution.
(Courtesy of the Carnegie Library
of Pittsburgh)

"NO DRINKER EVER RISES ABOVE THE LOWEST POVERTY. Mark this, too, TYPHUS
FEVER FINDS OUT THE DRUNKARD, AND FASTENS ON HIM."[18] To be sure,
Andrew Carnegie never overindulged in whiskey or any other alcohol, any
desire purged by what he witnessed as a boy.

Finally, the day came when Will trudged home and haltingly admitted to
his boy, "Andra, I can get nae mair work."[19] Once considered the aristocrat of
the working class, the handloom weaver was now obsolete. There had been
approximately 84,560 handloom weavers in Scotland in 1840; there would be
only 25,000 in 1850.[20] Ten years had passed since Will wrote that buoyant letter to the *Edinburgh Monthly Democrat* in 1838, declaring a Chartist victory
was at hand, but all that idealism and promise had gotten him nowhere—he
had failed his boy Andra. Will's fall had been slow and painful, and it ate at
the family's dignity like termites eating at their home's foundation.

The family weighed its options: Will could apply at one of the factories to
be a power-loom operator; or Will could break rocks for relief pay; or Will
could drive stakes on the Dunfermline-Stirling railroad that was under construction. The handloom weavers, however, were a proud group and not readily willing to subject themselves to such manual labor. As they debated their
dire situation, a line from Annie's 1844 letter—"This country's far better for
the working man than the old one, & there is room enough & to spare,

notwithstanding the thousands that flock into her borders"—was a refrain for every thought and consideration. There was only one option: to flee. To flee to America, where the citizens already had the charter and life would be better—if not for Margaret and Will, then most definitely for the boys. They would join Aunt Annie in Allegheny City, across the river from Pittsburgh, then known as "the Gateway West." Having the funds for the *flitting*—Scottish for "moving house"—was another matter.

The Carnegies decided to auction off all of their household items and furniture to raise money for their flitting. As Will made preparations, he sang:

> To the West, to the West, to the land of the free,
> Where the mighty Missouri rolls down to the sea;
> Where a man is a man even though he must toil
> And the poorest may gather the fruits of the soil.[21]

Hundreds of miles to the south, in London, future U.S. labor leader Samuel Gompers would learn the same song. "It was typical of the feeling among English wage earners of my boyhood days," he recalled, "that the two most popular songs were 'The Slave Ship' and 'To the West.' I learned both and sang them with such fervor in which all my feeling quivered and throbbed."[22] Gompers and Carnegie would be buried in adjoining lots in Sleepy Hollow Cemetery in Tarrytown, New York, some eight decades later—an ironic twist of fate.

The proceeds from selling their furniture and Will's last loom were severely disappointing and left the family £20 short of what was needed. Fortunately, Margaret's best friend, Ailie Henderson, who had helped deliver Andra, offered the difference.

The Carnegie family, accompanied by Andra's uncles Tom and Lauder and his cousin Dod, boarded the horse-drawn omnibus that would take them the five miles to Charleston, a seaport on the Firth of Forth. Dreamy Will was forty-three and defeated; proud Margaret was thirty-seven and humiliated; effervescent Andra was twelve and fearful; innocent Tom, with white hair and beautiful black eyes, was five and mercifully oblivious. As the omnibus pulled out of town, the last sight was the magnificent abbey tower with all the glory it invoked; and then it, too, disappeared.

In Charleston the family took a rowboat out to a steamer sailing for Edinburgh. When they pulled along the steamer, Andra clung to Uncle Lauder, who urged him to go and pressed a sovereign into his hand. "I cannot leave you! I cannot leave you!" Andra cried. For so long a child observer, he was now an innocent victim, forced to leave his extended family: Uncle Lauder, his surrogate father, Dod, his cousin/brother, Mr. Martin, his beloved mentor; and Dunfermline, with its rich heritage. His parents had rejected the traditional church, refused to adapt to the changing economy, brought indignities upon the family, and now it seemed they were rejecting Scotland, a country Andra had been taught to be so very proud of. There was only one person—his father—to blame for their flight from Scotland with nothing but some clothes, a few household essentials, and assorted mementos. Their destination: a town where the weaving trade was nonexistent. Their lives would have to be reinvented.

Andy, the name he now assumed to facilitate his assimilation into American culture, was but one of 188,233 British emigrants who journeyed to the United States in 1848, a year that witnessed a surge in emigration due to Ireland's Great Potato Famine, as well as tumultuous political events and depressed economic conditions in Europe.[23] For the confidence men and the corrupt emigration agents waiting on the shores of America, it proved to be a windfall year. The first concern for the Carnegie family, however, was simply making it to the United States alive. The voyage across the Atlantic was slow, unpredictable, and extremely hazardous.

On the first leg of what would become a four-thousand-mile odyssey by water, the Edinburgh steamer cut almost directly across Scotland to Glasgow, the journey permitted by a canal linking the two coasts. It took the day, the landscape changing from farmfield to the dismal Glasgow slums to the city's bleak harbor, the Broomielaw on the Clyde, where the Carnegie family was immediately transferred to the ship *Wiscasset*, to depart the next morning for America. Ten years earlier, a transatlantic competition was held between the steamers *Sirius* and *Great Western*, the latter recording a blistering time of fifteen days and five hours from Bristol, England, to New York City.[24] The event ushered in the era of the deluxe ocean liner. There was no such luxury for Andy and his family, however. Accommodations consisted of thin mattresses strewn across the cargo holds, with each family assigned their space—steerage was the only option. And the *Wiscasset* was a large, three-masted, square-rigged schooner that was *not* built for speed; it was a whaling ship built in Wiscasset, Maine, designed to spend years at sea.[25] Joining the Carnegies were other weavers and their families, but the majority were farmers and laborers hailing from all parts of Scotland. They would live together for the next fifty days.

On May 17, the ship hoisted anchor and rode the tide out of the firth and into the Atlantic, where the expansive skies and waters were a welcome sight for those suffering through the oppressive Hungry Forties; many danced on the decks and sang in high spirits. Of course, what was welcomed now would become hated over the coming weeks as the monotony of the horizon took its toll. Agitated seas that rolled the ship with violence and the accompanying sickness also became anathema; and on days when the winds were not favorable, there was the nerve-racking threat of an extended voyage resulting in food and water shortages. In addition to nature's hazards, the passengers had to be ever-vigilant of petty thieves in their midst; old men and women, in particular, were robbed to their last shilling. The passengers brought their own food for the trip, so that, too, was guarded. Disease was another menace, for there was no place to escape a sudden outbreak of cholera. Not all survived the voyage. As for the corpses, the heads and shoulders were sewn up in an old jacket, a bag of coal was tied to the feet, the captain read the burial service, and the crew committed the body to sea. The passengers would quickly forget the whole affair—they had to.[26]

While a prison to his parents, the *Wiscasset* was a pirate schooner, a Spanish galleon, and a man-of-war to Andy and brother Tom. The brothers saw the trip as a grand adventure, and precocious Andy wasted no time in making himself known to the sailors. "During the seven weeks of the voyage," Carnegie reflected, "I came to know the sailors quite well, learned the names of the ropes, and was able to direct the passengers to answer the call of the boatswain, for the ship being undermanned, the aid of the passengers was urgently required."[27] A square-rigged ship could be handled by just a captain, a mate, a cook, and four hands—a bare-bones crew that maximized the shipping company's profits—but with a hold full of passengers, help was indeed required. On a regular schedule, the mattresses were brought up to air and the ship scrubbed, more often after rough seas and bouts of sickness. Eager and bright-eyed, Andy directed dumbstruck Scots, some quadruple his age, to assist with the chores; as a reward for his help, he was treated to plum pudding in the sailors' mess on Sundays.

Just after the Fourth of July, the ship made its way into New York City's harbor. As the ship approached the lower tip of Manhattan, Bedloe's Island, the future home of the Statue of Liberty, came into view. But it was Fort Columbus on Governor's Island, with its round bastion patrolled by smartly uniformed soldiers and defended with rows of cannons, that caught Andy's fancy. As the boy's eyes followed the cannons pointing across the harbor to Manhattan, he encountered hundreds of masts stabbing the sky, the ships draped like a primitive necklace of splintered wood around the lower portion of the island. Beyond them, the gothic spire of Trinity Church rose like a beacon. The *Wiscasset* dropped anchor off the Castle Garden, a premier theater that was circular, two-tiered, and sitting in the water, tethered to the Battery by a wooden bridge.[28] The city commissioners reported that 189,176 immigrants landed in 1848—many of them ravaged by the odyssey.[29]

One contemporary, Isabella Bird, observed a group of seven hundred English immigrants just deposited dockside and noted: "They looked tearful, pallid, dirty and squalid. . . . Many were deplorably emaciated, others looked vacant and stupefied."[30] Andy admitted to being bewildered and overwhelmed by the city's great hive of human activity, for as the boy crossed the threshold between old country and new, every sense was attacked.[31] The stench of fish and excrement burnt his nostrils; the clatter of hooves and wooden wheels against cobblestone rung in his ears; newsboys shouted the day's headlines and peddlers hawked their wares; foul beggars from Five Corners Slums pleaded for mercy; slinking among the wooden boxes and crates and trunks piled precariously high, runners hissed promises of shelter and directions. Runners, a notorious bunch identified by their bright green neckties, lured the green arrivals to boardinghouses on Greenwich Street or to ticket agents who booked them passage on steamers and canal boats traveling north, south, and west at prices that amounted to robbery. The charter was not going to be freely handed over in the land of the free.

William Carnegie ignored the runners and sought advice for traveling to Pittsburgh from emigration agents. Railroads were not yet an option, so the family would have to travel on packet boats and steamers via canals, rivers, and Lake Erie. After haggling with the agents over ticket costs, the Carnegies retired to the more tranquil promenade along Bowling Green at Castle Garden, where women with fashionable bonnets and parasols and men with top hats and canes strolled along with great dignity. There, one of the *Wiscasset's* sailors, "decked out in regular Jackashore fashion, with blue jacket and white trousers," caught Andy up in his arms, he recalled, and took him over to a refreshment stand.[32] He bought the boy a glass of sarsaparilla, a sweetened, carbonated drink flavored with sassafras; for a brief moment, Andy drank in the beauty of America. So very briefly.

When the Carnegies landed, the city was still abuzz over the July Fourth celebrations, with the *New York Herald* reporting two days later on the front page: "The celebration on Tuesday was splendid—nay magnificent. . . . From daylight to midnight the city was enveloped in the smoke of gunpowder and crowded with people from all parts of the surrounding country."[33] Home to Edgar Allen Poe, Herman Melville, and Walt Whitman in 1848, New York was a worthy place to come celebrate and a top tourist attraction. In addition to the popular Castle Garden and Trinity Church, visitors flocked to the Customs House, with its Grecian Revival columns, and Wall Street, already recognized in the United States and Europe as a powerful financial center. But the number one attraction was Barnum's American Museum, the building looming over Broadway just south of Ann Street, the facade adorned with a colorful snake mural. No time for tourism, the Carnegies boarded the 6 P.M. overnight steamer to Albany—again, this was no luxury liner and safe passage was not guaranteed. Even in 1848, steamers' boilers tended to overheat and occasionally set a ship on fire or simply exploded. Invariably, there were enough casualties for enterprising undertakers from New York to send up loads of coffins on speculation.

The rising sun introduced yet another boat, a packet boat that would take the family through the Erie Canal, which, running through farmland and forest, village and city, offered a dramatic, surreal juxtaposition of modern technology and brute labor, of sprawling countryside and urban centers, of the organic and the artificial. Not only did it symbolize technological progress, but Manifest Destiny, the slogan for America's righteous march westward to civilize the land and the native heathens.[34] The cigar-shaped packet boats, able to transport forty passengers at night and triple that during the day, were no more than 78 feet long and 14½ wide, and had a single-level cabin that extended almost its entire length, so the cabin roof served as observation deck. At night, the cabin was divided into ladies' and gentlemen's quarters by a curtain. Tiered berths were pulled out of cabin walls and additional cots were strung from the ceiling. The passengers were packed together like pigs in a pork warehouse. Although the boats were a marvel in their efficient use of space, passengers had to contend with bunks ripping out of walls and falling on those below, incessant snoring, babies crying, and mosquitoes feasting.

Delays were numerous. Canal gridlock often ensued when aqueduct walls crumbled, canal banks collapsed, and locks malfunctioned. At many of the locks, Margaret had to shield her boys from the brawls that erupted over various problems. A tough crowd, the canallers relished swearing, drinking, gambling, and whoring; even the children who comprised about one-quarter of the workforce were a profane bunch. The vulgarities washed over Andy. "Nothing comes amiss to youth," he reflected, "and I look back upon my three weeks as a passenger upon the canal-boat with unalloyed pleasure."[35] Andy's optimism was irrepressible, whether he was on a hazardous five-week ocean crossing or a tedious three-week canal tour, prime examples of the ability to make "all my ducks swans" inherited from Grandpa Andrew. But what better way to mask fear than with effusive optimism? Andy varnished his youth to soothe the pain.

The plodding pace of the packet boat and the oppressive July heat took their toll. The family was disturbed by being separated each night; moreover, body sores developed from the hard bunks, as did rashes from the heat, and they became lethargic from confinement and revolted by the monotonous diet. Finally, ten days later, the Carnegies arrived in Buffalo, where they boarded the steamer to Cleveland and then another packet boat down the Ohio & Erie Canal to Akron, Ohio. From there it was to Beaver, Pennsylvania, located at the confluence of the Ohio and Beaver Rivers. They arrived late in the day and were forced to spend the night on a wharf boat sitting in backwater. Throughout the dark hours, mosquitoes had a feast at the family's expense, and the next morning Margaret's face was so swollen she could hardly see. It was the last indignity—of the journey, anyway.

A paddle wheeler took the family up the Ohio to Pittsburgh, where Margaret's anxious sisters awaited their arrival. Smoke in the sky, not the Dunfermline Abbey tower, now became the family's beacon for home, and the closer the dark blanket, the more excited they became. Uprooted and detached from any semblance of a stable home for so long, the Carnegies rejoiced at the sight of fellow clan members on the Wood Street wharf. There to meet them were the Hogans, Annie Aitken, and Margaret's older brother William, who had emigrated to a farm in East Liverpool, Ohio, forty miles distant via the Ohio River. They clung to one another as though they had been brought back from the dead.

As the Carnegies stood on the wharf, gazing at the many raised arms of smoke that entwined into a great body overhead, and then at the hustle and bustle of man, beast, and cart in the streets, they were in awe. As one businessman passing through Pittsburgh on his way to Wisconsin observed, "This is one of the most active, business-like places I have ever seen, with every appearance of present prosperity and future greatness; manufactures of iron, glass, and machinery are carried on extensively, and under great advantages; iron abounds in every valley, and bituminous coal of the best quality comes cantering down from surrounding mountains. . . . A place so situated must rise to greatness."[36]

Just days after their arrival, the Carnegies were shocked to hear the news that an army of ax-wielding females had taken control of Allegheny's Penn Cotton factory and routed the sheriff. Apparently their adopted home was as riotous as the one they left, and the reasons for why the town's cotton mill workers were striking the same as those of the textile workers in Dunfermline: better wages, better hours, and better conditions. Had nothing changed for the desperate emigrants in search of opportunity?

Not until mid-August did the cotton mill workers return to their bobbin wheels, only to strike again in September. Over the next months the owners of Blackstock Cotton Mill, Gray's Allegheny Cotton Factory, and the Penn factory were met in Slabtown's streets with curses, rotten eggs, tomatoes, and rocks. The 1848 Cotton Mill Riots initiated a tradition of labor violence in the greater Pittsburgh area, but then Pittsburgh already had a tradition for violence and bloodletting dating back to 1749, when the French sent an expedition to assert their claims over Ohio country and to incite the Indians against the English settlers there.

After increasingly violent skirmishes, in 1758, the English, in force under General John Forbes (who happened to own the Pittencrieff estate in Dunfermline for a period) marched on Fort Duquesne to permanently vanquish the French. Hopelessly outnumbered, the French retreated posthaste and burned the fort—black smoke rising over the area for the first time. On arrival, General Forbes rechristened the smoldering ruins Pittsburgh, in honor of the English prime minister William Pitt. To ensure complete domination of the Ohio lands, the English built Fort Pitt, and the Forks never again fell to Frenchman or Indian. Many of the Scottish Highlanders and Irish who served under Forbes and subsequent commandants of the fort chose to settle in Pittsburgh. Their town motto became "A compound of worship on Sunday and whiskey on Monday, thus blending the spirits." The mountains to the east of Pittsburgh obstructed access to the seaboard, so the town quickly became economically and socially independent.

While the town was just a fur-trading post at first, the hardworking settlers soon began to tap the area's rich natural resources that would transform Pittsburgh into a powerful industrial center. Saline wells were discovered along the Allegheny and saltworks lined its banks, timber rafts 350 feet long and 40 feet wide were floated down the Ohio to lumber mills, rich deposits of coal and iron were discovered seemingly everywhere. The first iron furnace was built in 1793, and a Pittsburgh foundry supplied cannons, howitzers, shells, and balls to America's fleet on Lake Erie during the War of 1812. Four years later, the city was incorporated, the population now six thousand, and complaints about the smoke had begun. "Pittsburgh is by no means a pleasant city for a stranger," *Darby's Emigrant's Guide for 1818* stated. "The constant volume of smoke preserve the atmosphere in a continued cloud of coal dust."[37] Regardless, in a sign of Pittsburgh's growing respectability as an important manufacturing center, renowned New York governor DeWitt Clinton visited in 1825, as did William Carnegie's favorite author, Charles Dickens, in 1842.

Eying continued expansion, business prospectors surveyed the land across the Allegheny River from Pittsburgh, the north side, and built a second industrial center. All eight square miles of Allegheny City was incorporated in 1840. The population was then ten thousand, and the ethnic groups were well segregated, with the Germans ensconced in the town's eastern end, nicknamed Deutchtown, and the Irish and Scotch-Irish in the western end.[38] There were ironworks, slaughterhouses, food-processing plants, cotton mills, and tanneries. Allegheny City was a premier leather tanning center, making harness leather, sole leather, belt leather, and lighter leather for shoes and clothing. While the pride of the modest city, the tanneries were the chief perpetrators in polluting water supplies with rotting flesh and stinking tree bark. Typhus was rampant.

Will and Margaret Carnegie envisioned Allegheny City as the American version of Dunfermline. In contrast to Pittsburgh and its heavy industry, Allegheny City was "a hive of family workshops" that attracted artisans like Will, although by the time the family arrived the population had exploded to twenty thousand, substantially larger than Dunfermline's thirteen thousand citizens.[39] At least Slabtown was rich with Scottish traditions, for many of the area's most successful families were Scottish and Scotch-Irish, as well as of New England descent.[40] It was infused with a spirit of independence, self-reliance, and the puritan work ethic—all qualities admired by the Carnegies.

Preparations had been made for the Carnegies' arrival. Kitty Hogan, her husband, Thomas, Andrew Hogan, and Annie Aitken lived together in a black, two-story frame house tucked among other bleak homes and squalid hovels on Rebecca Street, said to be more rundown and muddy than any other street. (Annie's husband, Andrew, had died several years earlier.) At the rear of the house facing the muddy back alley, Thomas and Andrew had built a loom shop with two rooms on a second floor, which were now converted into living quarters for the Carnegies. The rickety house was no Dunfermline cottage with a view of the Firth of Forth, but it was rent free until they were settled. The Hogans and Annie Aitken could afford the generosity, as they were making an honest go of it: Thomas worked as a clerk in a crockery shop, and Aunt Annie worked as a nurse and later was the proprietor of a grocery store.

Will immediately encountered three major obstacles in finding work: riots, depressed trade, and soldiers. At first brush, a job at a cotton mill seemed ideal for the onetime damask weaver, but the riots put an immediate end to fourteen hundred jobs and that possibility. While there were other industries to explore, the particularly low river levels that summer and the completion of the Cincinnati & Sandusky Railroad to Lake Erie diverted trade from Pittsburgh, forcing unemployment on the area. Not only was the job market tight, but the unemployed ranks swelled with both immigrants and returning soldiers—the Treaty of Guadalupe Hidalgo had been signed earlier in 1848, formally ending the Mexican War. It was just as well; Will preferred to work the loom, so he commandeered the Hogans'. Unlike in Dunfermline, where the merchants supplied the materials and then sold the finished webs, Will had to buy his own supplies and then hawk his tablecloths and other wares door-to-door. He soon discovered there was little market for his fine linens; they were far too expensive compared to the factory-made versions. A ball of fear, familiar from the last months in Dunfermline, hit Andy's gut hard when the boy recognized that for his dad's work "the returns were meager in the extreme."[41] Had the voyage been for naught? There was no turning back. How would they eat?

CHAPTER 3

$1.20 a Week

Mother Margaret again came to the rescue; as Andy recalled, "There was no keeping her down."[1] Two doors away lived Henry Phipps, an Englishman with two sons, John and Henry Jr., who were close in age to Andy and Tom, and the boys immediately became playmates and fast friends. Henry Sr. also happened to be a shoemaker, a trade Margaret knew well, and, with plenty of work, he paid her $4.00 a week to sew shoes for him. As his mother's heroic proportions increased in Andy's esteem for her, his father's continued to fall. All the family needed to feed their four hungry mouths was a mere $7.50 a week, but they couldn't manage it; so eyes now turned to Andy, who was thirteen years old. Schooling was a luxury that could no longer be afforded, but what could the undersized boy do to earn money? Any heavy labor was out of the question. One evening, Uncle Tom Hogan weighed in: he suggested that a basket be fitted for Andy to wear and then filled with knickknacks to peddle around the wharves. A considerable sum could be made!

Margaret sprung to her feet and shook outstretched hands in Tom's face. "What! My son a peddler and go among rough men upon the wharves! I would rather throw him into the Allegheny River. Leave me!" She pointed at the door. Her boys would never linger among vagrants—death was better. It was not only love, but ambition that drove her decision; she wanted her boys to be among a better class of people, at any cost. Immediately regretting the outburst, Margaret broke into sobs and gathered her sons into her arms and told them not to mind her foolishness. Yet the strain of survival was becoming too much. Survival was consuming her spirit. For Andy, "the prospect of want had become to me a frightful nightmare."[2]

The heated cotton mill strike finally broke in January, and Will Carnegie found work at a bobbin wheel at the Blackstock Cotton Mill on Robinson Street, which ran parallel to Rebecca Street three blocks to the south. Once on the job, Will discovered that the mill employed many boys to handle menial tasks, so he approached the owner, Mr. Blackstock, about finding a position for Andy. While the mill owner was a good capitalist, he was also a Scotsman and not without compassion for his fellow countryman. He offered Andy a position as a bobbin boy at $1.20 a week for twelve-hour days every day but Sundays. "It was a hard life," Andy recalled, his usual enthusiasm suppressed. But he understood that "what I could get to do, not what I desired, was the question."[3] Bobbin boys scurried about the factory floor with supplies of bobbins to be loaded on the spindles; and then once the yarn was wound onto the bobbins, the boys removed them. While not physically stressful, the work was monotonous and the days long. The first winter was the worst: "In winter father and I had to rise and breakfast in the darkness, reach the factory before it was daylight, and, with a short interval for lunch, work till after dark."[4] No longer sheltered by a doting mother, Andy had joined the ranks of the children he had seen back in Dunfermline who were forced to work as colliers or in the textile mills. His childhood had been taken from him; life was now about being a man, a real man. He had no choice but to work; he had no freedom but to take a job. Slavery was more apt of a description, and Andy admitted as much.[5] The silver lining, he said, was being a breadwinner and contributing to the family coffers. And if Will could keep his job, however distasteful to his artisan spirit, the family would be able to eat reasonably well.

Not long after, another Scotsman and a manufacturer of bobbins, John Hay, offered Andy a job at $2 a week. His factory was on Lacock Street, just one block south of Rebecca. Lured by the money, Andy found himself in his own inferno in the dark cellar of the bobbin factory, firing the boiler of a small steam engine that powered the machinery on the floor—the blocking saws, the boring machines, the roughing and finishing lathes. Woodchip refuse, not coal, was used in the fire, so the actual firing of the boiler wasn't so bad; shoveling the woodchips was clean work, it was a warm burrow for the winter, and only carelessness resulted in flesh being seared. The monitoring of the boiler's temperature and pressure struck terror into Andy, however. Blood-chilling nightmares denied him sleep and peace of mind: "It was too much for me. I found myself night after night, sitting up in bed trying the steam gauges, fearing at one time that the steam was too low and that the workers above would complain that they had not power enough, and at another time that the steam was too high and that the boiler might burst."[6] Although himself ready to explode, Andy never told his parents, keeping his troubles hidden and masking his emotions. Instead, he relied on the inspiring stories of William Wallace and Robert the Bruce to give him strength. And every single day, Andy looked for a way out.

The chance came when Mr. Hay, a poor penman and without a clerk, was struggling to write out some bills and decided to give Andy a test. Snuffy Martin's schooling paid off, and Andy was given a reprieve from the factory bowels to handle the bills. The office work consumed little time, however, so now Andy was also charged with bathing the newly made bobbins in vats of oil. Confined to a small room, the stench of the oil overwhelmed him; it stuck to his fingers and clung to his clothing. Nausea often got the better of him, so that he regurgitated breakfast and lunch into a convenient pail, but the ever-ebullient Andy merely observed that he had all the more appetite for supper. All the hours in solitary confinement—first in the fiery, satanic dungeon and then in the oil-laced cell—hardened the young man. The thirteen-year-old had passion, but began to lose compassion; the boy had a conscious, but began to lose a conscience. He was consumed with driving away the wolf of poverty.

For the rest of the year, Andy trudged to Lacock Street and back—alone. His father never adapted to factory work and quit Blackstock's soon after Andy moved on. But at least on Sundays, Andy could meet new friends. He eventually became part of a group that called itself the Original Six; its members were like blood brothers to each other and developed lifelong loyalties. It included Andy, John Phipps, William Cowley, Thomas Miller, James R. Wilson, and James Smith. The Original Six took themselves quite seriously, with part of every Sunday reserved for debating the day's issues—just as Grandfather Andrew had at Pattiemuir College, only without the whiskey. First glimpses of Andy's idealistic, radical temperament flashed, echoes of his ancestors. Based on his experiences in the factory, where he realized that without labor there would be no material progress, Andy penned an essay that he read to the boys. He glorified the industrious and declared, "A workingman is a more useful citizen and ought to be more respected than an idle prince."[7] The respect he demanded for laborers would dissipate with time, however; and once he became the capitalist, his workers would be nothing but drones with an associated cost in the ledger books.

Together, the Original Six kicked through the ruins of Allegheny's first great fire in July 1849, which striking firemen let burn. Together they loitered around the White Horse Tavern, which served as a meeting place for the borough council, and where the wide porch offered a produce stand for the surrounding farmers and the lawn a stockyard for cattle and horses. Together they explored the surrounding woods and the waterfront. Together they stood at the bridge spanning the Allegheny River to the great smoky city beyond, where they lost themselves in the billowing, black clouds, their minds conjuring up images of dragons and fire, knights and swords, power and riches. Yes, hidden behind the dark veil was treasure to be had. Feeding off one another's enthusiasms, in the winter of 1849–1850, Andy, Tom Miller, and William Cowley decided to go to a Pittsburgh night school to learn double-entry bookkeeping. Considering Mr. Hay used the single-entry method, Andy hoped that he could permanently escape the oil vat room by acquiring more sophisticated clerical skills. Despite the inherent dangers posed by the smoky city, Margaret encouraged him. Always ready with a Scottish proverb, she knew gentility will never boil the pot. Her boy would have to cook up some attention for himself.

Every member of the Original Six gang was determined to rise above his humble beginnings. Sitting are Will Cowley, John Phipps, and Andrew Carnegie. Standing are Thomas Miller and James R. Wilson. Missing is James Smith. (Courtesy of the Carnegie Library of Pittsburgh)

Boys would not be boys without a few scraps in the street. The Original Six exchanged slurs and scrapped with the native Alleghenians—"the bottom hoosiers," as they were called. The bottom hoosiers didn't take kindly to Andy and his thick Scottish burr, hooting, "Scotchie! Scotchie! Scotchie!" Unfazed, Andy shouted back, "Aye, I am Scotchie, and I'm prood o' the name!"[8] There was little else he could boast of. With Andy's father unable to keep the factory job, the family was now struggling to make the needed $7.50 a week, and life in America remained tenuous. During these first years, there were no letters of braggadocio written to Dunfermline—a true sign of the family's desperate situation.

A shrewd and determined Yankee, David Brooks always enjoyed a keen game of checkers with his friend Thomas Hogan. One evening, Brooks, who was manager of a Pittsburgh telegraph office, casually mentioned to Hogan that the telegraph business was exceedingly good. Another telegram delivery boy was needed, he said, and did he know where a good boy might be found? Hogan thought of his fourteen-year-old nephew Andy, struggling to and from the Hay bobbin factory, living the life of an impoverished mole. The boy deserved better, but he was a wee laddie—would he measure up? Yes, Hogan answered, he knew a good boy, his nephew. Send him round tomorrow, Brooks said, for the position had to be filled immediately, no delay.

Later that night, a family council was held. Uncle Hogan explained that Andy would have to walk to Pittsburgh, to the corner of Fourth and Wood Streets, that the job involved delivering incoming telegraph messages to area businesses and residences, and that there'd be some night work, but that it paid $2.50 a week, amounting to a 25 percent raise. Andy hooted with joy; here was a chance to escape his dungeon! For Margaret, her brother-in-law had redeemed himself from the day he suggested Andy peddle wares down at the wharf, and she supported the move. But Will did not, thinking it was too much for his son. At $2.50 a week, he figured a larger and older boy was expected. And what of the night work? Pittsburgh was a den of exotic dangers. There were unlawful cockfights, dogfights, bare-knuckle prizefights, bowling and billiards, and horse racing through the streets that resulted in more than one oblivious citizen being trampled to death. Also, there were gamblers, thieves, killers, and disease. The city was coming to the end of a cholera epidemic, during which fumigating coal fires or pitch pots burned on many a street to beat back the disease. Another of Will's concerns was ongoing labor violence. Just recently, Pittsburgh proper had been rocked with disorder when over twelve hundred ironworkers went on strike over wage cuts and then rioted when strikebreakers were imported from the east.

After considering the spectrum of dangers, Will concluded, "Ye better let weel enough alone."[9] He was outvoted, however, his authority long undermined. Hardly able to contain himself, the next day Andy dressed in his Sunday best—a white linen shirt, a jacket, and navy blue pants—and his father and he marched double time the two miles to the Atlantic and Ohio Telegraph Company office managed by Brooks. Determined to get the job himself, Andy asked his father to wait outside the two-story office. Secretly, the boy also feared his father's broad Scotch accent would do more harm than good— Andy had purged his own burr to assimilate. Fate at hand, the boy walked up the seemingly endless flight of stairs to the operating floor where Mr. Brooks awaited, and then the bobbin factory worker made his case. "I took care to explain that I did not know Pittsburgh," Andy recalled, "that perhaps I would not do, would not be strong enough; but all I wanted was a trial."[10] The opportunity the burgeoning telegraph industry offered could not be overstated.

The Atlantic and Ohio Telegraph Company, owned by Henry O'Reilly, had generated much excitement in 1846 when it opened for business. "Mr. Brooks was the object of special wonder as he patiently explained the mechanism, and the meaning of the sounds," wrote James Reid, then a telegraph superintendent in Philadelphia. "A long-legged hoosier, who had gazed at the 'crittur' for some time, at last determined to turn his chance to practical account. So stepping over the barrier he walked rapidly up to the register, and placing his mouth very near the instrument, said in a kind of confidential and yet anxious tone, 'I say, mister, can you tell me the price o' corn?'"[11] The telegraph evoked both wonder and fear—in 1849 it was even blamed for the spread of cholera.

As Andy's interview drew to a close, Brooks said, "When can you go to work?"

"Right now!"[12] Quick to pounce on every opportunity, Andy was certainly not going to leave the office for fear of another boy coming along who might be more suitable.

Brooks summoned his one other messenger, George McClain, who immediately set about showing Andy the ropes; meanwhile, poor Dad stood on the corner and wondered, until Andy finally remembered his father and dashed down to tell him the good news. It was a turning point in his life, made possible by an innocent game of draughts. "Upon such trifles do the most momentous consequences hang," he reflected. "A word, a look, an accent, may affect the destiny not only of individuals, but of nations. . . . The young should remember that upon trifles the best gifts of the gods often hang."[13] A sense of destiny, the notion that perhaps the gods favored him, now took hold in Andrew Carnegie—and that sense of Calvinistic predestination would strengthen.

The quality of Andy's life changed dramatically: "I was lifted into paradise, yes, heaven, as it seemed to me, with newspapers, pens, and sunshine about me. There was scarcely a minute in which I could not learn something or find out how much there was to learn and how little I knew. I felt that my foot was upon the ladder and that I was bound to climb." It was indeed the first rung in a ladder as high as Jack's beanstalk.

Watching the telegraph operators, Andy was immediately mesmerized by "the tick of those mysterious brass instruments on the desk annihilating space and standing with throbbing spirits ready to convey the intelligence of the world."[14] As the steel pen embossed the dots and dashes of the Morse alphabet on a narrow strip of paper—an electric current moving the pen—the boy learned of international, national, and local happenings. Most important, at age fourteen, Andy was riding the wave of a new technology and privy to much business correspondence passing through the office. He learned which businesses were buying, which were selling, which were growing, and which were failing. He learned of deals for land, for resources, and for companies— all inside information that he eventually used to his benefit.

First, he had to keep the job: "My only dread was that I should some day be dismissed because I did not know the city; for it is necessary that a messenger boy should know all the firms and addresses of men who are in the habit of receiving telegrams. But I was a stranger in Pittsburgh."[15] At night, instead of dreaming of the satanic boiler, he closed his eyes and worked on memorizing the various firms in the order they lined the streets, and then he worked on knowing the businessmen and city leaders. Pittsburgh then was classified as a "walking city," one in which people walked both to work and to conduct business, so it was not uncommon to meet the telegram addressee in the street. In that environment, Andy's ability to greet respectfully the addressee by name often resulted in a small tip and definitely a good impression. B. F. Jones Jr., whose father was a wealthy iron mill owner, recalled that Andy "was fond of telling me whenever we met that his especial reason for liking the job of delivering messages to my father was because he always received a tip of a quarter of a dollar for doing so. He was a sharp and keen youngster and had an eye for business even then, as a result of which he was on the lookout for messages directed to Jones & Laughlins and was usually the first at the desk to obtain them and run out to deliver them."[16]

The telegraph business continued to boom and soon there were four couriers, two boys handling messages coming in from the east and two assigned to the west. Andy made lifelong friends that first year, including David McCargo, later superintendent of the Allegheny Valley Railway; Henry Oliver, later an iron and ore tycoon; and Robert Pitcairn, later the Pittsburgh superintendent of the Pennsylvania Railroad. Always on their toes for fear of dismissal, the boys were driven to a higher level of tremulous excitement by Superintendent James Reid's inspections. Reid later recalled that Andy "was prompt, intelligent and industrious . . . and performed his duties well and cheerfully."[17]

As Andy ventured into Pittsburgh, he discovered a city still rebuilding from its great fire of 1845, in which twelve hundred buildings burned to the ground. The streets and sidewalks were clogged by merchants hawking their wares, by draymen and stablemen with parked horses and wagons, and by loafers. In addition to the thriving business community, Andy also encountered culture at the Pittsburgh Theater. The owner, a Mr. Foster, was provided with complimentary telegraph correspondence; in return, the operators were given free admission. Because this barter did not explicitly extend to the messengers, the more clever boys would hold onto Foster's telegrams until evening, and then present them at the door in hopes of being invited in for the show. The rose- colored boxes, the crimson seats edged with velvet and brass nails, the crystal chandeliers, and the gold-embroidered draperies gave Andy a taste of society life. When the theatre presented Shakespeare's *Macbeth*, the play captured his imagination: "Never before had I realized what magic lay in words. The rhythm and the melody all seemed to find a resting-place in me, to melt into a solid mass which lay ready to come to call. It was a new language and its appreciation I certainly owe to dramatic representation, for, until I saw 'Macbeth' played, my interest in Shakespeare was not aroused."[18]

The boys appreciated their exalted rank of messenger; it sure beat the bobbin factory or some other hellish job. Granted, blistered feet and being on duty until 11 P.M. every other day were causes for complaint; and sometimes the boys had to shin up a telegraph pole to help adjust the wire, a job Andy tried to avoid because he was an admittedly "poor climber."[19] There was one bone of contention among the boys—dime messages. Because these telegrams took the boys to the outskirts of Pittsburgh, they were rewarded with an extra dime, but quarrels arose over boys taking dime messages out of turn, a serious infraction. Displaying the astute capitalist's tendency to create cooperative pools to eliminate destructive competition, Andy proposed they pool the dimes and "divide the cash equally at the end of each week." Naturally, he was appointed treasurer. He later said of his "first essay in financial organization" that "peace and good-humor reigned ever afterwards."[20] It would prove to be the first and last of his pools in which peace and good humor reigned; once in the iron and steel industry, Carnegie's cooperative relationships with competitors would be exceptionally stormy.

Up against a violent city in which death took victims indiscriminately, Andy, now making $11.25 a month, continued to fight that wolf of poverty, saving every one of those additional dimes. Meanwhile, the other boys spent their bonuses at the neighboring confectioner's shop, even establishing running accounts that drew on future dimes. Unable to ignore his comrades' spendthrift ways, Andy attempted to police their habits by notifying the confectioner that he would not be responsible for any debts contracted by his greedy comrades. One of Andy's friends from that period said to him years later, "The whole trend of your mind seemed to be towards big things. Indeed, I recall that your efforts to do the pranks of the average boy struck me at the time as being almost grotesque. You would not follow the fashion in dress, because, I supposed, you believed it to be the evidence of a little mind."[21] The boys disparaged Andy for his formal dress suits and for his extreme frugality because they didn't appreciate how much every penny counted in the Carnegie home. Not only were they trying to build a new life, but spare half-dollars were hidden in one of Margaret's stockings to eventually repay the £20 loaned by Ailie Henderson for the flitting.

Andy also received additional heckling for assisting Mr. Glass, the office manager. John P. Glass's job entailed receiving the messages from the public to be forwarded to the operators, distributing incoming telegrams to the messengers, and handling the finances. On occasion, when he stepped away, he asked Andy to watch the office for him and direct the messages—a reprieve from scurrying through the streets and another rung up the ladder. But then, on one of the monthly paydays, Andy thought that the worst had occurred, that he had made a fatal error and was to be dismissed: "We stood in a row before the counter, and Mr. Glass paid each one in turn. I was at the head and reached out my hand for the first eleven and a quarter dollars as they were pushed out by Mr. Glass. To my surprise he pushed them past me and paid the next boy. . . . My heart began to sink within me. Disgrace seemed coming. What had I done or not done? I was about to be told that there was no more work for me." After paying the other boys, Mr. Glass took Andy aside and said to him that he was worth more than the other boys; he was giving Andy a raise to $13.50 a month.[22] He alone was now earning almost a half of the $30 required monthly for their family to live with reasonable comfort.

The moment the last fifty cents hit his hand, Andy bounded out the door and ran the entire two miles home. He gave his mother the usual $11.25, but he divulged nothing of the raise—and he wouldn't until the next morning, with great dramatics. That night in bed he confided in Tom, telling him about the extra money and about some bigger plans he had in mind: "It was then, for the first time, I sketched to him how we would go into business together; that the firm of 'Carnegie Brothers' would be a great one, and that father and mother should ride in their carriage."[23] The dreams were vague, perhaps, but they were big, the sense of a glorified destiny beginning to formulate.

Every morning Andy arrived early to sweep out the office, one of the other required chores. The operators had yet to arrive, so he was able to practice with the technological wizardry. For more than a year, Andy picked up pieces here and there on Morse code, sending and receiving practice messages to other aspiring messengers down the lines. Then one day he turned to his friend Tom David and, with eyes sparkling, said, "Tom, I can read nearly every word of that."[24] Regardless of their proficiency with Morse code, the boys never dared to interfere when the lines opened for business; that is, until Andy could contain himself no longer. One morning, he was sweeping the floors as usual when a death message came clicking over the line from Philadelphia. Death messages were obviously quite important to those concerned, and the operator sending this one seemed particularly excited. With no operators present, Andy, who was supremely confident at a young age, brazenly answered that he would take the message. It was risky; a mistake would cause others serious distress and cost him his job. Later that day, Andy explained his daring initiative to David Brooks, who complimented the action but warned him to be careful. From such experiences came one of Andy's lifelong mantras: "The rising man must do something exceptional, and beyond the range of his special department. HE MUST ATTRACT ATTENTION."[25] Or, as his mother would say, he must light the fire to boil the water.

Not long after, Carnegie started relieving the operators who desired a break, just as he had sat in for Mr. Glass; and when the company's operator in Greensburg, thirty miles away, took a two-week vacation in June 1851, Brooks assigned Andy as his replacement.[26] While in Greensburg, he was so determined to win a permanent position that he manned his post during a lightning storm, which was rather ill-advised. Sure enough, a blast of electricity threw him from his stool, but he survived the lesson. His stint was a complete success, of course; and as soon as there was an opening, Andy was promoted to full-time operator and given a raise to $4 a week. At age sixteen, he was the family's unchallenged breadwinner.

Finally there was good reason for him to write to Dunfermline. On Sunday, June 22, 1851, a hot summer day with the thermometer reaching ninety-two, Andy found shelter under a tree and composed a letter to his cousin Dod, the first of many they would exchange in their lifetimes. He divulged his new job as telegraph operator and proclaimed that someday he would return to Dunfermline, "for I can easily manage to save as much money if I behave well."[27] Prospects were indeed good that Andy would save enough money for a visit; but he would wait until he could arrive in grand fashion, or not at all.

The family finances had improved considerably, and every so often they were able to buy a piece of furniture or some knickknack. Will had sporadic requests for webs and was now working in a vineyard belonging to the Allegheny City chapter of the Swedenborgian Society. Andy, Tom, and Aunt Annie accompanied Will to the Swedenborgian services. Andy joined the choir, but he couldn't sing on key, incurring the wrath of the conductor, who occasionally rapped him on the knuckles with his baton. Although somewhat tone-deaf, music was the only aspect of church Andy found inspiring.

Margaret still sewed shoes and was now helping out at her sister Annie's grocery store. After three years, she was finally realizing the fruits of the emigration and her cultivation of Andy, for it was she who instilled in him the puritan work ethic, infused him with pride, confidence, and the conviction that he would rise gloriously above all the rest. Almost every day for over a year, even if he didn't return home from work until midnight, she washed and pressed her boy's clothes so he would be smartly dressed the next day. She also pushed her small son physically to give him strength. "When the other boys of the neighborhood weren't allowed to skate on the pond on the 'Sabath,'" a neighbor recalled, "she urged 'Andra' to go as exercise and the fresh air was more important to them than community criticism." Now was not the time to ease off, so right after his promotion to operator she encouraged Andy "to wean himself from his boyhood playmates, and make new and more dignified ties in keeping with his future."[28] Sentimental friendships could not be an impediment to his success, but Andy wanted to be sentimental and yearned to duplicate the strong emotional bond he had had with his cousin Dod. As a result, his mother's urging to sever ties with certain friends confused and troubled him.

Late in 1851, a friend asked Andy and Tom to pose together for a photo. As they did, the elder brother draped his arm awkwardly and coldly around the other's shoulders. Tom's hands rested comfortably in his lap, his lips and eyes shaped into the whimsical, genial smirk of an untroubled boy. In sharp contrast, Andy's eyes were wide, serious, and melancholy, and he wore a natural frown set in place for years. Although he considered himself an incurable optimist, he was equally dour and gloomy.

At age sixteen, Carnegie, who both protected and bullied his younger brother, Tom, was a telegraph operator and the family's breadwinner. (Courtesy of the Carnegie Library of Pittsburgh)

*   *   *

Not long after Andy's promotion, one of the other operators in the office, a Mr. Maclean, started taking messages by ear, transcribing the clicking sound directly to words. He challenged Andy to do the same, which the young man excelled at in no time. Reputed to be one of only three in the country who could do it, Andy became a local celebrity, with folks stopping in to see him at work. Although the celebrity was soon earning $25 a month for his skills, it was not enough, and for $1 a week he agreed to make five copies of the incoming news for a newspaper pool reporter who would then distribute the copies to the local papers. Andy pushed everything to the next level and did anything to get ahead.

Now the Carnegies were financially prepared to emerge from their two small rooms over the loom shop, as they once had in Dunfermline, moving from the cramped Moodie Street cottage to the spacious Edgar Street home. Coincidently, the Hogans decided to move to East Liverpool, Ohio, and put the house on the market; but an untimely Allegheny River flood in the early spring of 1852 damaged the home, so instead of listing it for the $700 they had originally hoped for, the Hogans settled on $550.[29] Able to afford this price, the Carnegies bought it, taking a loan to be paid back in two years. At long last they were landowners, a prospect denied them in Scotland. An extremely buoyant Andy immediately sent a lithograph of their home to Uncle

Lauder, along with a letter in which he described the flood: "Every season when the snow melts on the mountains the Rivers raise very high but they have not been so high for 20 years before. It rained for 3 weeks almost constantly and both rivers rose at once. It was up to the ceiling in our house and for 2 days we had to live upstairs and sail about in rafts and skiffs. It was a great time." Every disheartening setback continued to be glossed over by Andy as he disguised his inner feelings.

His social and political consciousness emerged in this letter as Andy reported on the upcoming presidential election: "The politicians here are all in great excitement about the presidency. Every candidate (and there are about twenty) is trying everything he can think of to gain popularity. They write letters to different associations flattering them, make speeches on popular questions taking every occasion to flatter the Enlightened Citizens of the Great Republic & c & c. You would laugh to see how low they have to bow to their sovereigns *the People*. . . . I take great interest in politics here and think when I am a man I would like to dabble a little in them. I would be a Democrat, or rather a free soil Democrat—free soilers get that name from their hatred of slavery and slave labor. Slavery I hope will soon be abolished in this country." The year Franklin Pierce was elected president, Andy recognized the tradition of American politicians to pander to special interest groups, a political weakness he would be sure to take advantage of. He would not become a Democrat, however; laissez-faire Republicans would be more to his capitalist taste. As for himself, Andy wrote, "I am sure it is far better for me that I came here. If I had been in Dunfermline working at the Loom its very likely I would have been a poor weaver all my days, but here, I can surely do something better than that if I don't it will be my own fault, for any one can get along in this country, I intend going to night school this fall to learn something more and after that I will try to teach my self some other branches."[30] His drive was evident, and he alone took responsibility for bettering himself—a perspective on success he would never abandon.

Not surprisingly, Andy's responsibilities increased at the telegraph office. When the flood that damaged the Hogans' home also knocked out the telegraph line between Steubenville and Wheeling, Andy was sent to Steubenville to set up a temporary office for receiving incoming messages. He then shipped the telegrams the twenty-five miles to Wheeling, where they were forwarded to Pittsburgh. While in Steubenville, he learned his father would be passing by on his way to Cincinnati to sell a tablecloth, and they made plans to meet. He recalled what was a sad exchange between father and son:

I remember how deeply affected I was on finding that instead of taking a cabin passage, he had resolved not to pay the price, but to go down the river as a deck passenger. I was indignant that one of so fine a nature should be compelled to travel thus. But there was comfort in saying:

"Well, father, it will not be long before mother and you shall ride in your carriage."

My father was usually shy, reserved, and keenly sensitive, very saving of praise (a Scotch trait) lest his sons might be too greatly uplifted; but when touched he lost his self-control. He was so upon this occasion, and grasped my hand with a look which I often see and can never forget. He murmured slowly:

"Andra, I am proud of you."[31]

Will fully recognized that Andy was now a man, the man of the house; the handshake was the passing of responsibility and a blessing.

CHAPTER 4

The Scotch Devil

Visitors to the Atlantic and Ohio Telegraph Company couldn't help but notice the buoyant, hustling, white-haired Andy. They included Thomas A. Scott, general superintendent of the Pennsylvania Railroad and a regular customer, who took a paternalistic liking to the young man. Those at the telegraph office couldn't help but notice Scott. All the railroad officials were pandered to, but Scott's classic good looks—a strong chin, high cheekbones— and personable demeanor made him particularly attractive. Now, with the railroad having strung its own telegraph lines, he decided to hire a personal clerk who would double as his telegraph operator. Andy was his first choice. The lad hesitated in accepting, however.

His mentor, Mr. Glass, was now running the entire office, and Andy rightly envisioned himself in Mr. Glass's position someday. Life was comfortable, and Glass did offer to increase Andy's salary to $400 a year if he elected to stay, so why make a change? But Glass knew the railroad would offer a chance at real advancement, so even though he hated to lose an experienced operator, he encouraged the change, explaining that the most Andy could make at the telegraph office was $700 or $800 a year, while the railroad held unlimited prospects. Andy's friend and fellow telegrapher, the reliable Tom David, recalled how difficult the decision was in a letter to his friend: "It took some persuasion on the part of John P. Glass to convince you that it offered better opportunities. I saw you and Mr. Glass having an earnest talk and to my question, 'What is wrong with Andy?' he intimated that you did not like to make a change."[1] Only after consulting with his mother, which Andy did for every important decision, and only after she concurred with Mr. Glass, did he agree to join Scott.[2]

Andy revised the story later in life, claiming he was eager to join the Pennsylvania Railroad, which he promulgated in interviews and in his autobiography:

> One day I was surprised by one of his [Scott's] assistants, with whom I was acquainted, telling me that Mr. Scott had asked him whether he thought

that I could be obtained as his clerk and telegraph operator, to which this young man told me he had replied:

"That is impossible. He is now an operator."

But when I heard this I said at once:

"Not so fast. He can have me. I want to get out of a mere office life. Please go and tell him so."[3]

The purpose of the revision was to place himself in a more proactive role when it came to what was a significant turning point in his career. Rather than the scenario of Scott plucking him from the office and Andy reluctantly accepting the change, he wanted it to be him who aggressively pursued the opportunity. While seemingly a trivial revision, it was not, because it was part of a more duplicitous pattern of revisionism that emerged once Andy began to attain prestige. He felt it necessary to refine, aggrandize, and sanitize much of his life, some of it to prove painful to others.

When Andy joined the Pennsylvania Railroad on February 1, 1853, at $35 a month, he came under the tutelage of a strong-willed man in Scott, a debonair man who considered himself a dashing speculator willing to exploit most anyone to make a dollar. Andy's new workplace was an office at the Outer Depot, a twenty-acre property on the outskirts of Pittsburgh. That first morning, as he approached the depot, he encountered a breathtaking sight: an intense hive of activity within a maze of railroad track and colossal structures. There was a vast locomotive and car-repair shop, 240 feet by 220 feet; blacksmith's, tinner's, painter's, carpenter's, and trimming shops; storehouses and offices; a freight house, 300 feet by 70 feet; iron and lumber yards; and one of America's largest circular engine houses, 900 feet in circumference and containing stalls for forty-four locomotive engines and tenders.[4] Since the locomotives burned wood, tremendous rows of cordwood were stored on the grounds—not until the 1860s did coal become the dominant fuel. The shrieking steam whistles, clanging bells, and hammering of iron, the heavy smoke and flying cinders, steam fouled with iron, and the deep driving chug of the locomotives all jarred Andy's senses.

Even more so than the equipment and the brick structures, he was impressed by the men:

> I was now plunged at once into the company of coarse men, for the office was temporarily only a portion of the shops and the headquarters for the freight conductors, brakemen, and firemen. All of them had access to the same room with Superintendent Scott and myself, and they availed themselves of it. This was a different world, indeed, from that to which I had been accustomed. I was not happy about it. I ate, necessarily, of the fruit of the tree of good and evil for the first time. . . . I passed through this phase of my life detesting what was foreign to my nature and my early education. The experience with coarse men was probably beneficial because it gave me a "scunner," to use a Scotism, at chewing or smoking tobacco, also at swearing or the use of improper language, which fortunately remained with me through life.[5]

Andy's righteous indignation concerning the coarse men was the same indignation his mother had displayed when Uncle Thomas suggested Andy work at the waterfront. Margaret and her son placed themselves in a higher class than British society would ever have given them, and, although the family had preached the charter, they remained imbued with a class consciousness that caused them to snub the crude and feckless.

Just as the canal had been on the rough-and-tumble frontier of American commerce, the railroad was now, and it attracted the same vulgar characters who had migrated to the canals twenty-five years earlier. The laborers, stinking of sweat and smoke, clomping about in heavy boots and ratty jackets, were mostly Irishmen who took on the backbreaking work of building the lines. Trapped in their daily drudgery, they were oblivious to the impact of the railroads, which were making for a transient United States. People were leaving their hometowns never to return, were migrating from the countryside to the cities, from city to city, searching for opportunity; pleasure seekers were able to expand their horizons, and workers were able to commute much longer distances; new industries were realized, and commerce was maximized. The railroad perpetuated the exchange of ideas and cultures. It also brought conflict. Many people feared the railroad, the way it created and destroyed towns, depending on where the main and feeder lines were built. Many felt railroad companies took advantage of the public and the local governments, from demanding land to charging discriminatory rates. Most condemning, the railroad, for all its promise to unite the country economically and socially, did not prevent the Civil War.

Any romance the railroad offered was quickly dispelled at Andy's new job because most of his tasks—and Mr. Scott's, for that matter—were mundane, such as routing trains, clearing tracks, and policing the behavior of employees. Regulations were strict. Twice a week old material and brush had to be cleared away and stacked neatly in designated areas; station houses and yards had to be kept clean. Conductors were drilled to be most considerate of travelers and to quickly eject any passengers using profanity or acting disorderly or drunk. The relatively frequent crashes did provide excitement. Stray animals were often the culprit; the trains could handle a sheep, but a cow or a horse moseying along the tracks was another matter.

A month after being hired, Andy penned a letter to Uncle Lauder, explaining his new job with Mr. Scott, of whom Andy wrote, "I have met with very few men that I like so well in this country—and I am sure we will agree very well." The job was equally agreeable; instead of working until eleven o'clock at night, he was finished at six, which left him "not so much confined."[6] The free evenings were not for pleasure, however, not as far as Andrew Carnegie was concerned; they were for self-improvement.

Andy was a voracious reader, like his father, and the one place in Allegheny City he could satisfy his appetite was Colonel Anderson's library on

Federal Street. James Anderson, who fought in the War of 1812 and made his fortune as an iron manufacturer, donated fifteen hundred volumes of religious, scientific, and historical books to the town. His purpose was to provide a building of knowledge, free of charge, for apprentices for whom school was not an option. Voluntary subscriptions of $2 a year were requested from other patrons to support the library. Andy's friend Thomas Miller, who lived near the colonel, introduced Andy to the local hero; and before long, the Original Six were frequenting the library. As working boys, they were permitted entry at no charge. "Colonel Anderson opened to me the intellectual wealth of the world," Carnegie reflected. "I became fond of reading. I reveled week after week in the books. My toil was light, for I got up at six o'clock in the morning, contented to work until six in the evening if there was then a book for me to read."[7] He always sought environments conducive to his evolutionary progress, whether it was Uncle Lauder's shop, Colonel Anderson's library, or debates with the Original Six. He would never forget what that small library meant to him, how the books fed his imagination and knowledge. As a result, library giving would become the mantelpiece for his philanthropy.

In 1853, Anderson's library, called The Mechanics' and Apprentices' Library, was moved to 611 West Diamond Street, and the new administrators began to charge all patrons $2 except true apprentices, defined strictly as those bound to another. Andy was aghast that he was now forced to pay; after all, he reasoned, he was a working boy (although seventeen years old) with no chance to continue schooling. His radical spirit came to the fore. He argued with the librarian, but it proved futile, so he took his dispute to an open forum— the newspapers. On May 13, 1853, a letter to the editor of the *Pittsburgh Dispatch* appeared:

MR. EDITOR:

   Believing that you take a deep interest in whatever tends to elevate, instruct and improve the youth of this country, I am induced to call your attention to the following. You will remember that some time ago Mr. Anderson (a gentleman of this city) bequested a large sum of money to establish and support a Library for working boys and apprentices residing here. It has been in successful operation for over a year, scattering precious seeds among us, and although fallen "by the wayside and in stony places," not a few have found good ground. Every working boy has been freely admitted only requiring his parents or guardian to become surety. But its means of doing good have recently been greatly circumscribed by new directors who refuse to allow any boy *who is not learning a trade* and *bound* for a stated time to become a member. I rather think that the new directors have misunderstood the generous donor's *intentions*. It can hardly be thought that he meant to exclude boys employed in stores merely because they are not bound.

   A Working Boy though not bound.

In the spirit of his father and Uncle Thomas Morrison, Andy opened his letter with a moral-suasionist argument: the library should remain free to working boys because it improves youth. He then left the moral ground and attempted to refute the logic of the new directors' decision through sheer speculation serving his own agenda. The tone became presumptuous and combative.

Oblivious to the radical forces behind Andy's personality, an anonymous librarian responded with a letter on May 16, in which he corrected Andy's facts about the exact nature of Anderson's gift, but he didn't bother justifying the changes, except to allude to reasons. The letter was a slap on the hand — petty, as far as Andy was concerned. The very next day he retorted, "The question is, was the donation intended for use of apprentices only in strict meaning of the word, viz. persons learning a trade and *bound*, or whether it was designed for working boys whether bound or not? If the former be correct then the managers have certainly misunderstood the generous donor's intentions."[8] The trivial mistakes pointed out by the librarian were excusable to Andy, especially since they were his own. There was no moral argument now; only the main thrust of his point mattered — namely, that he should be admitted for free. Others clamored to support Andy's cause, so the anonymous librarian called for a summit, at which the matter was settled to Andy's satisfaction. The Original Six anointed him their undisputed king for restoring their privileges.

Andy had clung instinctively to these boyhood friends — the Original Six, as well as his telegraph messenger comrades — even though his mother had advised otherwise. He needed those friends. He needed to compete against them in work and play and to measure himself against them in salary and social standing. His friends gave him value. At Andy's urging, two friends from the telegraph office, David McCargo and Robert Pitcairn, joined the Pennsylvania Railroad. The Original Six gang would continue to remain tight, as well, keeping up with their Sunday debates, joining the Webster Literary Society, which met weekly to discuss classic literature, and forming a club that subscribed to Horace Greeley's *New York Weekly Tribune*.

Now very cognizant of the power of the pen in a public forum, Andy was briefly inspired to become a news reporter and an editor like Horace Greeley, his latest hero. But instead, using the resources made available to him at Colonel Anderson's library, Andy now brought his pen to bear upon his cousin Dod, who had challenged him to debate the political systems of the United States and the United Kingdom, respectively. "It will no doubt be beneficial to both of us to examine into the systems of Government by which we are ruled and it will prompt us to read and reflect on what perhaps we would never have done without the stimulant," he wrote Uncle Lauder. "I have therefore accepted Dod's challenge, and am now reading the Early

History of our Republic and I find that the obstacles which our revolutionary fathers had to surmount and the dangers they had to encounter were far greater than I had imagined and worthy to take a place among the deeds of Scotland's heroes."[9] His loyalties were shifting.

In an early salvo, Naig sent Dod a copy of the U.S. Constitution along with a condescending and ridiculing letter in which he demanded to see the (nonexistent) British Constitution.[10] George Bancroft's *History of the United States*, which Andy was reading, came in most handy for the debate; even in Bancroft's introduction he discovered an arsenal of ideological weapons to use and expand upon. Bancroft touted the Constitution's "capacity for improvement; adopting whatever changes time and the public will may require, and safe from decay, so long as that will retains its energy."[11] Echoing the historian, Andy wrote Dod, "Our Con. was made by the People and can be altered amended or done away with by them whenever they see fit." He also directly borrowed from Bancroft in discussing America's policies for managing the treasury and the armed forces.[12] Andy was absorbing Bancroft's words and ideas, as well as those of other prominent writers and thinkers such as Greeley, taking bits and pieces and making them his own as he reinvented himself in his adopted country. The letters to Dod helped him build a new sense of identity, of belonging to America.

Greeley, in particular, would have a lasting impact on Andy's evolving personality and his philosophy for both life and business. Picturing America as a harmonious whole, Greeley promoted a grand economic vision in which the country tapped its tremendous natural resources to become self-sufficient. He believed the federal government should encourage and protect capitalism through high tariffs and other measures. Andy adopted both the vision and the position on tariffs. Not all of Greeley's ideas meshed with Andy's, however, as the proletarian newspaperman supported the laborer and was a voice for the poor. Too much was expected of the poverty-stricken and uneducated, Greeley argued, and circumstances in the new industrial order were such that the poor could not be expected to help themselves. Andy was diametrically opposed on this point. In a country that had the charter, Andy devoutly believed, every man had an equal chance to make something of himself. He was becoming a Republican capitalist, not a radical Chartist. As these two forces—capitalism and radicalism—continued to pull him in opposite directions, he developed a fragmented personality that would manifest itself in hypocritical behavior.

In his ebullient enthusiasm, Andy was blinded by the dazzling idealism imbedded in a democracy and worshiped his adopted country like it was a living, breathing hero. In an August 18, 1853, letter to Dod, the budding Republican displayed all the glory of the Republic, pronouncing that "our government is founded upon justice and our creed is that the will of the People is the source and their happiness the end of all legitimate Government." Greeley's voice was strong in this letter. Just three months prior, the newspaperman had written an editorial that included this passage: "In a Monarchy, the Government rules and the People obey—the rulers and the ruled being distinct and often antagonist; but in a Republic, based on Popular Education and Universal Suffrage, rulers and ruled are essentially the same."[13]

In his letter, Andy proceeded to introduce his evidence as to why the U.S. political system is superior to Britain's in every aspect, from the limited armed forces to the political equality: "An Irishman becomes a useful and patriotic citizen with us; he feels that he is on an equality with his neighbors, with no drawbacks upon his industry, no merciless landlord to crush him." There was no mention of the cotton and iron riots in which the police forces were routed, not a word of slavery, Indian relocation, or women's suffrage in discussing equality of voice. Andy had a selective memory; he preferred to ignore America's underside, as he would when making his millions in steel while his exploited workers died by the dozens. Displaying no empathy for his relatives or sentiment for Scotland, Andy took a callous stab at the charter: "We now possess what the working classes of Your country look forward to as constituting their political millennium. We have the charter which you have been fighting for for years as the Panacea for all Britain's woes, the bulwark of the liberties of the people." He clearly and ruthlessly drew the we/you line. Hard eco-demographic evidence of America's superiority was introduced in the remainder of the letter, a glossy picture of material progress during the Industrial Revolution. "Everything around us is in motion," he concluded, "mind is freed from superstitious reverence for old customs, unawed by gourgeous and unmeaning show and form. This 'doing of a thing' because our grandfathers did it I can assure you is not an 'American Institution.'"[14] As the last lines suggest, traditions and his father's way of doing things had no place in Andy's world; any sentiment had burned away in Mr. Hay's boiler room.

Intoxicated by the Republic's vast resources and industrial power, Andy measured America's success in terms of prosperity and material progress, and that was how he learned to measure his own success. Another insight offered by the cousins' debate: Andy sought historical and economic information not to better himself in a moral or spiritual sense, but to beat Dod in competition. The other endeavors for self-improvement—learning double-entry bookkeeping, using Colonel Anderson's library, joining a debate society—were all means to achieve similar goals: material gain, winning a competition, or simply dominating other people.

The Crimean War provided Dod with a weapon for a counterattack. Czarist Russia was seeking to expand its power in the Balkans and, in 1853, Russian forces occupied Turkish dependencies that were part of the Ottoman Empire. Dod questioned why Andy's freedom-loving United States was not speaking out for the rights of an unjustly occupied nation—Turkey. The ongoing debates had become very personal to Andy, and he ruthlessly assaulted both the message and the messenger. He took the generally accepted American viewpoint that Britain, which came to Turkey's defense, was only concerned for its economic interests, not Turkey's. After the stinging rebuke, Andy answered why the United States should not become involved: "I want to give you the American doctrine in regard to our interference in European affairs, which is, in the language of Washington, 'Friendship with all, entangling alliances with none.'"[15] Unfortunately, Andy was quoting a misquote; the words were spoken by Thomas Jefferson at his first inaugural speech. But it was a mistake he could forgive; it was the message that counted. The phrase "Friendship with all, entangling alliances with none" would reappear almost fifty years later as his primary business dictum, a testament to how tenaciously he clung to ideas he was exposed to in his youth and how intertwined his personality was with the United States. What was good for the country was good for him, and vice versa.

As their dueling correspondence continued unabated over the next several years, each chiseling at the other's ideology, Dod found another weak chink in his cousin's armor: slavery. "The burden of your letter as usual is upon the slavery question. 'Still harping on my Daughter' as Polonius says," Andy replied to one attack, and then attempted to place the blame on Britain for introducing slavery to the colonies. It sickened Andy to think of "one man trafficking in flesh of another," of "women & children lashed like cattle."[16] But there was little else Andy could use in defense except to say he was, like Greeley, an "ultra abolitionist."[17] He concluded so nobly with "I hope I shall never be found upholding palliating oppression in any shape or form"; yet, once he was a capitalist, a capricious Andy would oppress his workers in a variety of forms.

Dod also attacked the Maine Liquor Laws and the prohibition of the manufacture and sale of liquor in certain states. How, he wondered, could this happen in the land of the free? Andy retorted, "There is no liberty in serving the Devil." His diatribe on abstinence went on for pages, and he beseeched Dod to never indulge in liquor. While there was a moral tone to the letter, Andy's support for the Maine Liquor Laws focused on economics— in particular, Maine's decreased pauperism, which took a burden off the state and its residents.[18] For Andy, his arguments always returned to the material progress and growth of the nation, not the inner spiritual development of the individual. Yet again his sentiments echoed Greeley, who believed liquor contributed to pauperism and who wrote that the prohibition measure was "a necessary result of the progress of the age."[19]

By age eighteen, Andy had a strong, although jaded, grasp of the country's complex political and economic machinations; the young man felt the substance of the United States, and it made him substantial.

Work for the railroad also strengthened Andy's sense of being, righteous character, and destiny. Even mishaps contributed to his confidence. A particularly memorable one occurred after the Pennsylvania Railroad breached the Allegheny Mountains, directly connecting Pittsburgh with the eastern seaboard. As of February 15, 1854, the Philadelphia-Pittsburgh journey could be made in fifteen hours or less, prompting the *Pittsburgh Gazette* to crow that such speed "ought to satisfy the fastest of this fast generation."[20] It was now a smaller Pennsylvania and a smaller country. With the line complete, one of the mundane tasks Scott gave to Andy was to fetch the monthly payroll and checks from Altoona, the railroad's operational headquarters in Pennsylvania; but even the mundane could turn adventurous. Andy always enjoyed the overnight adventure, which gave him a chance to meet powerful men within the railroad—that is, until one return trip took a dreadful turn.

Just as he had many times before, Andy tucked the payroll package with checks into his waistcoat and climbed onto the locomotive. The roar of the engine, the flying cinders and sparks, and the rough track distracted him, until he reflexively felt for the package and was horrified to find it missing. "There was no use in disguising the fact that such a failure would ruin me. To have been sent for the pay-rolls and checks and to lose the package, which I should have 'grasped as my honor,' was a dreadful showing. I called the engineer and told him it must have been shaken out within the last few miles. Would he reverse his engine and run back for it? Kind soul, he did so."[21] The engineer surely wanted his check, too. As the train moved slowly backward, a fretful Andy watched for the package and soon spotted it a few feet from standing water. Still, with the engineer and conductor as witnesses to his neglect, he feared there would be reprisals; but not wanting to ruin the boy, they promised to keep it a secret. Based on the experience, Andy decided to never be too hard on a young man who made a mistake or two; and he also realized fate had blessed him. That day the lost payroll package "seemed to be calling: 'All right, my boy! the good gods were with you, but don't do it again!'"[22] More than ever, he was certain he had a destiny to fulfill.

Under Tom Scott, Andy asserted himself with the same audacity he had displayed at the telegraph office when he took the death message. One morning, he arrived at the depot to discover a serious accident had tied up traffic along the entire line, not an uncommon event considering there were almost 150 train wrecks in 1853 alone. At the moment, an eastbound passenger train was crawling along with a flagman scouting each curve, the westbound passenger train was delayed, and the freight trains had sat on the sidings all night, afraid to move. Only carefully orchestrated orders from Scott could get the trains rolling again, but he was nowhere to be found. Andy mulled over the situation. He had given similar orders many times before at Scott's direction, but never on his own, and if he alone did attempt to unravel the snarl and failed, it could result in his dismissal or worse—the death of others. After a brief hesitation, the eminently confident lad hunkered down at the telegraph and tapped out orders for the various trains, signing each with his boss's initials. When Scott finally arrived at the office, he tentatively explained his actions, justifying each. Days later, the depot's freight agent told Andy what Scott said to him after the incident:

> "Do you know what that little white-haired Scotch devil of mine did?"
> "No."
> "I'm blamed if he didn't run every train on the division in my name without the slightest authority."
> "And did he do it all right?"
> "Oh, yes, all right."[23]

Andy continued to adhere to his modus operandi, which was to make opportunities by drawing attention to himself, and the story of the Scotch Devil quickly made its way through the ranks to Scott's immediate superior, Herman Lombaert, and to the railroad's president, J. Edgar Thomson.

A brilliant understudy, Andy had proven his worth. Subsequently, Scott gave him more responsibilities, such as routing the trains, as well as an unsolicited raise to $40 a month. Moreover, when Scott was away for two weeks, Andy was put in charge of the division. But his first stint as a manager ended in failure. At the time, if there was a crash due to negligence or a trainman was caught drinking, among other infractions, reprisals were always swift and harsh, with the railroad holding what they termed a court-martial for alleged offenders. When, under Andy's watch, an accident occurred due to the negligence of a ballast train crew, he was faced with having to dole out punishment or waiting until Scott's return. Determined to make his mark, he held a court-martial and summarily dismissed the chief offender and suspended two others. To the older, contemptuous railroad men, he appeared as a young, baby-faced Napoléon striding before the court, too eager to wield authority. Even Scott suspected Andy had behaved impetuously, but didn't want to erode the young man's authority, so the decision remained. Had Andy already forgotten his pledge the day he lost the payroll—to forgive a mistake or two— or did the older men deserve their punishments? For certain, he suffered himself, but never other fools.

When the esteemed President Thomson paid a visit to the Pittsburgh depot, he made time to meet the audacious clerk, whom he greeted as "Scott's Andy." Lombaert also began calling him Scott's Andy. The moniker, a respectable step above Martin's Pet from the Dunfermline days, didn't bother him; Scott was the perfectly paternal boss and he was proud to be attached to him. "Mr. Scott was one of the most delightful superiors that anybody could have," Andy said, "and I soon became warmly attached to him. He was my great man and all the hero worship that is inherent in youth I showered upon him."[24] Like Snuffy Martin and Uncle Lauder, Scott joined the ranks of surrogate fathers and heroes. He was surrogate because Andy's own father was a failure, but the younger man's relationship with Scott would become more complicated than that of a father and son, especially after the death of Will Carnegie.

Will had filed for U.S. citizenship in November 1854, but never had the chance to take the oath. On October 2, 1855, his long slide finally came to an end.[25] As Andy had written insightfully to his Uncle Lauder several years before, his father had not changed and was never going to adapt to the American way and the new economy. He had become a burden to the family, and a long illness leading up to his death put a financial strain on them. In his autobiography, the usually ornate writer offered a spartan eulogy: "Fortunately for the three remaining members life's duties were pressing. Sorrow and duty contended and we had to work."[26] To the family, Will had died long ago; his physical death was a mere formality.

Tree of Knowledge

U nder the tutelage of Tom Scott, a powerful man in a company that would soon be the largest in America, Andy learned the management skills, the financial dealings, and the political maneuvers to build an empire. To understand the relationship that developed between Scott and Andy was to understand the relationship between Scott and his boss, J. Edgar Thomson. A surveyor by training, Thomson, who was born in 1808, worked through the ranks of Pennsylvania's state-owned railroad in the 1820s and then of the Georgia Railroad, where he was made chief engineer. When he joined the Pennsylvania Railroad in 1847, he was an imposing figure. At five-foot-nine and with a tendency toward portliness, always dressed in a dark suit with a waistcoat, with a thick gold watch chain draped from his pocket, he had the reserved manner of a clergyman as opposed to a railroad pioneer. Mutton-chop whiskers that went to the collar framed his serious face. Dark eyebrows protruded above gray eyes, which had heavy bags below, and thinning black hair was combed across his scalp. Years on the road, along with twelve-hour workdays, made relationships with women all but impossible, so, not married until age forty-six, Thomson took a paternalistic approach to his railroad; he even bequeathed the bulk of his estate to a fund that was then distributed to female orphans of railway men. Filling the family void included surrounding himself with a bright young management team and forging a father-son relationship with Scott, who was fifteen years his junior.

Scott's street smarts, work ethic, and charm brought him to Thomson's attention, and the president quickly recognized a kindred spirit—both rarely took vacations, could juggle numerous complex projects, and had an eye for speculation. He took Scott, whose father died in 1835, under his wing and was soon teaching him to make savvy investments. While at the Georgia Railroad, Thomson first learned to speculate in advance of the railroad and made tremendous profits. Knowing where the Georgia and other railroads were building, he bought into local real estate and commodities and also invested in companies that would thrive from railroad construction. It was a technique he taught Scott, who would in turn teach Andy. By the mid-1850s, Thomson and Scott were investing in advance of the Pennsylvania Railroad, taking stakes in coal, lumber, freight, and telegraph companies, as well as real estate. When a coal company approached them in need of a rail line to access a newly discovered deposit, they bought into the company. When they found out where another railroad was planning to bridge a river, they bought the land on the river's banks. And so on. This insider investment technique was 100 percent guaranteed, and there were no laws preventing it.

When Scott encountered Andy, he, too, found a kindred spirit in the brash, hardworking boy; he found a surrogate son for himself and cultivated their relationship just as Thomson had with him. Only Scott was a more dangerous speculator than Thomson; he was unafraid to push into a gray zone of what was potentially criminal. To a degree, he was Dickens's Fagin, while Andy played Oliver. Having lived through the Hungry Forties, the boy was an easy target, especially considering he was so quick to lionize.

After two and a half years with Scott, in May 1856, Andy was invited in on his first investment deal—the opportunity to buy $500 worth of stock in a package delivery company that relied on the Pennsylvania Railroad. A $110 premium was also required. Thrilled to be included, Andy regrettably had to admit he didn't have much savings. Scott immediately offered to loan him the money, and on May 17, 1856, Andy wrote an IOU for $610, payable in six months.[1] Now the proud owner of ten shares of Adams Express stock, Andy was a capitalist at last—a leveraged capitalist, anyway. When the six-month date rapidly approached, Andy didn't have close to the $610 and was forced to borrow $400 at 8 percent interest per annum from a George Smith, the stock certificates handed over as collateral.[2] Shortly thereafter he borrowed another $100 from Smith to invest in the Insurance Company–Monongahela Company of Pittsburgh. Good dividends were expected, but the 8 percent interest paid to Smith ate into the family's income, so Andy and his mother decided to mortgage their house, which had been paid off, at a lower rate than Smith offered and then pay him.[3]

It was a series of crude transactions, but it worked. More significant, Andy was demonstrating a willingness to assume great risk—in this instance, the loss of their house—and the first inkling of complicated transactions to follow. In fact, he would make his early fortune in stocks and bonds, and that nest egg would finance his triumphant rise in the steel industry. Any current anxiety over taking risks was dispelled when the dividend checks started arriving. "It gave me the first penny of revenue from capital—something that I had not worked for with the sweat of my brow," he recalled. "'Eureka!' I cried. 'Here's the goose that lays the golden eggs.'"[4]

From the advantageous position of being Scott's clerk and telegrapher, Andy was privy to other investments and sophisticated business decisions made by his boss and Thomson that would affect his philosophy. In particular, the concept of setting up an allegedly independent company that would have the Pennsylvania Railroad as an immediate and reliable customer or client was very enticing. Scott and Thomson did the very thing in 1856 when they established their own construction company, the Western Transportation Company, to build the Pittsburgh & Steubenville Railroad, which was to be owned and controlled by the Pennsylvania Railroad—a nifty interlocking of companies bound to augment their bank accounts. This new company required a Virginia charter and to obtain it they hired the well-connected Simon Cameron, a U.S. senator from Pennsylvania who would prove a profitable partner, especially when he became secretary of war in the Lincoln administration. While Andy did not have the capital to join them in these other ventures, he continued to absorb their methods of both speculating in advance of the railroad and creating parasitic entities to feed off existing railroad operations.

Andy was also exposed to the political astuteness of Scott and Thomson. Although the railway business boomed, the one thorn in Thomson's side was the freight tonnage tax levied against the Pennsylvania by the state legislature. Its original purpose was to protect the state-owned canal business, but it eventually resulted in raising the transportation costs to such a degree that it hurt local industries. The cost of domestic coal was pushed to a point where it was cheaper to buy imported English coal in Philadelphia than Pennsylvania or West Virginia coal mined not more than a few hundred miles away. In addition, there was the state-controlled and strategically located Philadelphia & Columbia Railroad, which charged the Pennsylvania Railroad high tolls for through traffic. To win lower taxes and tolls, Thomson took his argument to the state legislature, using personal appeals and lobbyists, as well as giving free train passes to the right people and placing newspaper advertisements to arouse public pressure. Meanwhile, Scott convinced newspaper editors to take their side by pledging heavy advertising; he also promised prominent business leaders preferred rates if they used their influence with state politicians to eliminate the tonnage tax. As a result of his aggressive campaign, charges of bribery were leveled against Scott, who tended to push his tactics to the edge of impropriety. Regardless, not only was the tonnage tax repealed, but the Pennsylvania became the new owner of the Philadelphia & Columbia Railroad.[5]

As the Pennsylvania Railroad expanded, competition with other railroads, canals, river steamboats, and Great Lakes steamers became fierce. To prevent crippling rate wars, Thomson and Scott joined price-fixing schemes—yet another opportunity for the prodigal capitalist Andy to learn from his masters. Because the executives feared not knowing what their competition was up to, officers from the Pennsylvania Railroad, the Baltimore & Ohio, and the Ohio & Mississippi, among others, started meeting annually at New York City's St. Nicholas Hotel to fix rates. The key was to charge high-enough prices to enjoy healthy profits, but keep them low enough to encourage capacity traffic. The newspapers quickly got wind of the meetings but reported on them without prejudice; it was assumed both big business and the people would benefit.[6] Everyone knew free competition was harmful, and it was quite natural for Andy to join similar schemes in the iron and steel industry, even after price-fixing was made illegal by the Sherman Antitrust Act in 1890.

Invariably, price wars broke out, alliances were shattered, and the railroad officers were forced to start from scratch frantically in a business world not ready to wholly pursue the doctrine of survival of the fittest. (Charles Darwin's *On the Origin of Species* was published in 1859 and would have a profound impact on both evolutionary and social thinking.) Such fickle maneuvering was not foreign to Andy's Scottish blood; his hero the Robert the Bruce, as well as many a clan throughout the centuries, had formed and broken alliances to further their own agendas.

Changes at the Pennsylvania Railroad were afoot in late 1857, prompted by a stock sell-off on Wall Street and a financial crisis in autumn. Railroads had issued vast amounts of watered stock during a period of rapid expansion, Europeans had sought safe haven in U.S. investments during the Crimean War, and easy money had encouraged stock manipulation. But now, with the war over, the European bankers withdrew their prodigious funds, crippling an already stalled U.S. economy and contributing to a spike in unemployment. Wall Street's gambling pirates were blamed for the financial panic as bread riots erupted in New York and other cities. To survive, Thomson desperately needed greater efficiencies, especially a new organizational structure that would both remove him from the daily operations and provide him with more accurate cost information for setting rates and determining profits. His thoughts turned to what the Erie Railroad had done two years prior, which was to decentralize, segmenting the company's line into operating divisions. Thomson decided to reorganize the company into staff and line departments, with each line department responsible for a segment of the Pennsylvania Railroad and with the corporate staffs coordinating efforts between the segments. Lower-level employees were empowered to make decisions, authority and accountability were clearly defined, forms were standardized, and information was directed through efficient channels. Empowering managers and knowing the costs were crucial to success in the new industrial order, and Thomson's re-organization, effective on January 1, 1858, of one of the largest companies in the United States was a major step in the evolution of business management.

Andy, who was digesting Thomson's every move, was affected as Scott was promoted to general superintendent, which required the transfer of him and his protégé to Altoona, almost a hundred miles east.[7] Having to leave family and friends behind, Andy was initially melancholy about the move. "This breaking up of associations in Pittsburgh was a sore trial," he reflected, "but nothing could be allowed to interfere for a moment with my business career. My mother was satisfied upon this point, great as the strain was upon her."[8] The Carnegie family nucleus remained tight, extending to Aunt Annie and the relatives in Ohio, where the Carnegies spent summer vacations.

        ✳   ✳   ✳

At age twenty-two, Andy rightly considered himself a man, but his most striking features were his short stature (five-foot-three), his particularly small hands
and feet, and his clean-shaven baby face. He took his diminutive traits in
stride, even recounting more than once a story about how he bet a young lady
friend he could fit in her shoes and won, exclaiming, "My foot wabbles in it."
To project a more rugged image, the once-dapper Andy now preferred wearing heavy boots and an overcoat, as opposed to the shined shoes and the
pressed suits from his telegraph days. Any limitations in physical stature were
made up for by a personality that filled the room with its animation. He was
cocksure and opinionated, charming and inquisitive, both at work and in
social settings. To some acquaintances, his extreme confidence bordered on
arrogance; however, one of the more poignant observations concerning Andy
discerned that it was his "absorbing self-reliance" that "made him appear
arrogant and disregardful of the opinions of others."[9] After the depravities his
family had suffered, no less than a puritanical self-reliance should have been
expected.

The first months in Altoona did indeed require self-reliance on the part
of Andy and Scott. They shared a hotel room, were without family, and had
few friends; and to make matters worse, the trainmen were threatening to
strike for better wages. Thomson, who considered the laborers as just another
resource to be had at the lowest cost, demanded wage cuts ranging from 10
to 25 percent, depending on the job. The cuts went into effect on November
1, 1857, and by early 1858 Scott faced a spreading rebellion as the trainmen
and shop workers organized work stoppages. Unexpectedly, Andy found himself in the position of playing spy. One night, walking home, he realized he
was being followed. Turning to confront his shadow, he recognized a blacksmith for whom he had found work. Feeling obliged to Andy, the blacksmith
explained in a hushed tone that "a paper was being rapidly signed by the
shopmen, pledging themselves to strike Monday next."

"There was no time to be lost," Andy recalled. "I told Mr. Scott in the
morning and he at once had printed notices posted in the shops that all men
who had signed the paper, pledging themselves to strike, were dismissed and
they should call at the office to be paid."[10] The aggressive tactic to preempt
the strike succeeded. And Grandpa Thomas Morrison rolled over in his grave.
Had Andy forgotten the weavers' strikes back in Dunfermline and the desperate fight for a decent life, for something more than a starving wage? Had he
turned his back on his radical heritage because it no longer served him? Or
was he taking Greeley's view that although the workingman must be supported, strikes were disharmonizing and a waste of time? Beyond such speculation, there were two key business lessons here: depressed markets justified
harsh wage cuts, and strikers had to be dealt with in a unilateral manner.

Margaret and Tom eventually joined Andy in Altoona. They set up home
in a rented house with an added luxury; able to realize his dream of relieving
his mother of toilsome housework, Andy hired a servant. It was time for her

"to play the lady."[11] Horses were another luxury he could now afford, and with the help of the railroad's chief mechanic, Colonel John L. Piper, Andy bought a spirited horse named Dash. Hard riding in the surrounding hills became a favorite pastime. After a day on horseback together, Tom Miller determined his friend to be "reckless."[12] It was also time for the spirited young man to learn how to play the gentleman.

Scott, whose wife died the same year Andy's father did, had settled into a new home with his two daughters and niece, Rebecca, who served as governess. Andy took a liking to Rebecca, but not in a romantic way—at least he didn't admit as much. A smoking locomotive was his best girl for now, according to lifelong friend Miller, who, in a series of letters, recorded incidents from those days. In illuminating Andy's dedication to the railroad, he recalled how his friend had "to go to 26th Street, 2 miles or more and no street cars and snow quite deep and falling—but there was a wreck at Derry, and you buttoned your great coat on, and were off in a burst of glory, as if going to see your best girl—!"[13] As for Rebecca, Andy wrote in his autobiography, "she played the part of the elder sister to me to perfection, especially when Mr. Scott was called to Philadelphia or elsewhere. We were much together, often driving in the afternoons through the woods."[14] When with Rebecca, Andy had to soften the rough edges he had acquired around the trainmen, and she taught him etiquette and how to socialize. Once, when Tom Miller came to visit, Rebecca had them over for a formal dinner. Years later, Tom reminded his friend of "the awe you felt—or was it exultation?—when I took dinner with you at Scott's and 'Beck' Stewart was our hostess? She went out for some service, and you hastily took up a cream pitcher and said 'Real Silver, Tom!'"[15] By the way he reacted to the silver, one would think Andy was still playing the ragamuffin boy from a Dickens novel—or, more likely, in another measure of personal success, he was touting his rich friends to Tom.

His relationship with Rebecca became more complicated when Scott asked them to hold two stocks in their name for him. He made inside investments in the Phoenix Lumber Company and the Y. H. & Y. Coal Company; but to avoid attracting the attention of the companies' respective board members, he preferred to hold his shares anonymously. Andy and Rebecca were eventually to pay him the cost and interest on his investment, and then later they would be allowed to assume ownership of the stocks.[16] While this discreet practice was not uncommon, Scott was slowly pulling Andy into suspect territory. On the other hand, the most important investment in Andy's life fell into his lap while living in Altoona, courtesy of Scott.

T. T. Woodruff, the celebrated inventor of the sleeping car, had started his business career as an apprentice to a wagon maker and progressed from there until he became a master railroad car builder for the Terre Haute, Alton & St. Louis Railroad. Legend has it that Woodruff was riding atop a freight car when he was knocked off by a low bridge, after which, while recovering, he sketched out plans for his sleeper. In December 1856, the Terre Haute, Alton & St. Louis Railroad's chief engineer Orville W. Childs helped Woodruff obtain two patents necessary for his sleeping car—one for a seat and another for a couch that converted into beds.[17] After securing financial backing, Woodruff organized T. T. Woodruff & Company, later to be renamed the Central Transportation Company, and built the first demonstrator car; orders from several railroads soon followed. When he pursued a contract with the Pennsylvania Railroad, he found the perfect customer in Thomson.

The Pennsylvania's president was forward-thinking when it came to plant and equipment (another trait Andy would adopt), always demanding first-class conditions and seeking new developments to incorporate into his railroad. Under Thomson, the Pennsylvania introduced iron bridges, gas lighting, and stoves to heat the cars, and was one of the first railroads to experiment with and then to widely use coal-burning fireboxes. He immediately recognized the value of Woodruff's sleepers, but just to be certain, he requested Scott's opinion. Once Scott concurred, an order for four sleeping cars was placed. There remained just one issue: Woodruff needed capital to meet the burgeoning orders. Because it was another interlocking investment that couldn't fail, as far as Scott and Thomson were concerned, they stepped in with money and took shares in Woodruff's company. "One of the conditions of the said agreement was that a certain specified interest therein should be held for another person," Woodruff later wrote, "and represented (as the talk ran) by a boy then in the superintendent's office at Altoona. . . . When we came to consummate the agreement in a written form, I learned that the boy alluded to was 'Andie Carnegie.'"[18] He was given a one-eighth interest in the firm.

Although Andy was considered a deserving son, there can also be no doubt Scott recognized the prodigal capitalist in Andy. From the day the Scotch Devil had the guts and vision to get the trains running in the name of his boss, Scott perceived Andy's ability to see patterns, to understand cause and effect, and to organize with efficiency. In the near future, Scott knew, the young man would be a very valuable partner, a vigilant protector of their investments, so he fronted the money for the Woodruff investment. To repay this latest IOU, Andy borrowed $217.50 from a local bank and then used dividends.[19] How could Andy fail? The trio was invested in a company of which they were a large customer. There can be no mistake concerning the importance of the one-eighth interest Andy was given in the Woodruff concern; by 1863, it was generating a superlative $5,050.00 in annual dividends and providing the funds for other lucrative investments.[20] Carnegie later conceded that "the first considerable sum I ever made was from this source. . . . Blessed be the man who invented sleep."[21]

The vice president of the railroad, William B. Foster, died unexpectedly in late 1859, and it was rumored Scott would take his place in Philadelphia, where there was no supporting role for Andy. He dreaded a catastrophe, as such a move would leave him with either a new boss or in the cold. He recalled, "To part with Mr. Scott was hard enough; to serve a new official in his place I did not believe possible. The sun rose and set upon his head so far as I was concerned. The thought of my promotion, except through him, never entered my mind."[22] After a ceremonial interview with Thomson in Philadelphia, Scott was indeed given the job and returned to Altoona to discuss Andy's fate. He explained that Enoch Lewis, a division superintendent, was to be promoted to general superintendent, which would make him Andy's new boss.

"Well," Scott continued, "Mr. Potts [superintendent of the Pittsburgh Division] is to be promoted to the transportation department in Philadelphia and I recommended you to the president as his successor. He agreed to give you a trial. What salary do you think you should have?"[23] Surprised by the sudden turn of events, Andy blurted out that the money didn't matter, just the job. To be in charge of a division, now called the Western Division, to be signing the initials A. C. instead of T. A. S. to every order, was glory enough for Andy. Money did matter, of course, and Scott promptly offered him $1,500 a year, a substantial raise over the $780 he was then making. On December 1, 1859, Andy took charge, his march up the corporate ladder astoundingly quick. He was only twenty-four years old and already had his first taste of real power.

The Carnegie family moved into a downtown house on Hancock Street, later renamed Eighth Street, and here they experienced smoky Pittsburgh in all its industrial might with soot permeating every corner of their home. "If you placed your hand on the balustrade of the stair," Carnegie recalled, "it came away black; if you washed face and hands they were as dirty as ever in an hour. The soot gathered in the hair and irritated the skin, and for a time after our return from the mountain atmosphere of Altoona, life was more or less miserable."[24] The city had continued to expand; it was the sixteenth largest in the United States now, and home to one hundred different industries. Iron and metalworking was the most important sector, with twenty-six rolling mills, followed by glassmaking, with twenty-three glassworks.[25] Paddle steamers lined the wharves like magnificent horses at a trough. Irish and German immigrants shouted for friends and family as they clamored down gangplanks by the thousands, eager to make their fortune. The city was soon to be a metropolitan polyglot. And the Carnegies wanted out.

David A. Stewart, Scott's nephew and the division's freight agent, suggested a move to Homewood, where he lived. Located about ten miles east of Pittsburgh, Homewood—or Point Breeze, as it was also known—was described as a "romantic place, highly cultivated," and was served by two railroad stations. The family immediately took his advice and, to their delight, discovered one of their neighbors was the Honorable Judge William Wilkins, who had served under President Andrew Jackson as minister to Russia and under President John Tyler as secretary of war.[26] The Wilkins home, a redbrick mansion with a Greek portico entrance and a marble roof supported by fluted Ionic pillars set on 650 acres, was the epicenter of the Homewood social and political scene. It took only a few social gatherings for Andy to realize that for all of his self-improvement, he was unrefined compared to the aristocratic social set he now found himself among. But he was not totally unprepared.

While living on Hancock Street, Andy had met Leila Addison, who, picking up where Rebecca left off, made it her duty to infuse him with culture. She had a European education, was fluent in French, Italian, and Spanish, and knew her grammar. In a moment of humility, Andy admitted, "It was through intercourse with this family that I first realized the indescribable yet immeasurable gulf that separates the educated from people like myself."[27] He meant to cross that gulf, cross it and excel past those on the other side. In response to Leila's criticisms, he strived to improve his writing skills, from punctuation to vocabulary; he studied the English classics and French; and he focused on refining his social skills and table manners. *L'amour* had yet to enter his vocabulary, however, so Leila served only as another matriarchal figure. Andy never forgot Leila, and later in life he made lucrative investments on her behalf.

Soon a regular at the Wilkins home, he was reasonably confident he would not make a fool of himself. He relished these social gatherings because they were yet another opportunity to better himself, to add another dimension: "Musical parties, charades, and theatricals, in which Miss Wilkins took the leading parts furnished me with another means of self improvement." He worked on his ice skating, hiking, fishing, and riding, all popular outdoor activities. Also, Andy became as enamored with the judge's name-dropping as he had with the Scott's silver tea service: "I shall never forget the impression it made upon me when in the course of conversation, wishing to illustrate a remark, he said: 'President Jackson once said to me,' or, 'I told the Duke of Wellington so and so.'"[28] Through these gatherings, the Carnegies and David Stewart's family became good friends, and Andy met a man who would be a lifelong chum in John "Vandy" Vandevort, a dashing figure who played a howling violin.

While his mother settled into the life of a country lady among the gardens of their modest, tawny, two-story frame house, Andy asserted himself at the railroad. He appointed Davey McCargo superintendent of the telegraph department and boyhood friend George Alexander a conductor; he hired his cousin Maria Hogan to be a freight station telegraph operator and his brother, Tom, who had finished school and learned the telegraph, to be his secretary. While the appointment of Maria raised some eyebrows, a progressive-minded Andy was certain that women would prove more reliable as operators. Once the Civil War broke out, his foresight would pay dividends as the war siphoned the men away from the railroad, as well as all industries, and women stepped into their places. To strengthen his position, Andy was surrounding himself with people he could trust, and the appointments also demonstrated how loyal he was to family and boyhood friends.

Andy may have hired family and friends, but they received no preferential treatment. George Alexander could attest to that the day Andy, Mrs.

Carnegie, and he visited the Forrester family, friends who lived several miles outside of the city. "We had a delightful time until about 10 o'clock when there came up a terrible wind and rainstorm," George recalled. "It simply poured. I was a passenger conductor at that time and my train left the depot at two o'clock A.M. I knew there was no train for me to get to Pittsburgh on, and I did not fancy much the idea of having to get there for that train, so I approached the Supt. (A.C.) and asked him how about my getting to town to take out my train. He replied, 'Well, George, you know that train goes out at two o'clock and it can't go very well without a conductor.' That is all the satisfaction I got and there was nothing left me but to foot it through the storm and I arrived at the depot just in time to get on the train, soaked to the skin."[29] The men had to be pushed to maintain President Thomson's high standards, but Andy never pushed George and the others any harder than he pushed himself—full throttle every minute.

Regardless of Thomson's demand for quality, track conditions were deplorable. "The line was poorly constructed," observed Andy, who had some 225 miles of track under his care, "the equipment was inefficient and totally inadequate for the business that was crowding upon it. The rails were laid upon huge blocks of stone, cast-iron chairs for holding the rails were used, and I have known as many as forty-seven of these to break in one night. No wonder the wrecks were frequent. The superintendent of a division in those days was expected to run trains by telegraph at night, to go out and remove all wrecks, and indeed do anything. At one time for eight days I was constantly upon the line, day and night, at one wreck or obstruction after another."[30] When it came to repair work, Andy was a hands-on boss, hopping around the tracks and directing traffic. He was not one to be confined to the office; others described him as a man of action, rather than mood. So youthful looking, he was not always treated with respect by the laborers, as he discovered on one repair job when he inadvertently obstructed the path of a "bulky Irishman" moving logs. "Get out of me way, ye brat of a boy," the Irishman shouted, "you're eternally in the way of the men." The poor hulk was embarrassed when told the brat was his boss.[31] Although it was a Herculean task for the baby-faced Andy, he decided to grow a beard to age himself and fortunately managed a blond fringe along his jawline.

Andy's most arduous task with the railroad lay ahead during the Civil War. A little over a month after Republican candidate Abraham Lincoln was elected president in 1860, South Carolina voted to secede from the Union, followed by Mississippi, Florida, Alabama, Georgia, and Louisiana in that order in January, and then Texas in February. Many in the North, including Andy, considered Lincoln's election a righteous blessing, and the Pittsburgh streets were buzzing when on February 14, 1861, the president-elect visited en route to his inauguration. Cannons announced the arrival of his train in Allegheny City, and several elite military companies escorted him to the Monongahela

House in Pittsburgh. The next morning he delivered a speech from a balcony, declaring that the differences between the North and the South were artificial and could be solved if dealt with calmly.

Unfortunately for Lincoln, the Confederates in Charleston, South Carolina, were not interested in friendly conversation; they fired on Union forces in Fort Sumter on April 12. The news came over the telegraph lines that evening and hundreds of people took to Pittsburgh's streets, anxious and desperate for details. On the way into work the next morning, Andy found that the passenger train "resembled a bee-hive. Men could not sit still nor control themselves." Their language, he recalled, was unquotable.[32] On April 13, the *New York Tribune* succinctly announced: "The ball has opened. War is inaugurated. The batteries of Sullivan's Island, Morris Island and other points were opened on Fort Sumter at 4 o'clock this morning. Fort Sumter has returned the fire, and a brisk cannonading has been kept up. No information has been received from the seaboard yet."[33]

After being bombarded by some four thousand shells, the Fort Sumter garrison surrendered on April 14. Lincoln now issued a proclamation calling forth the militia of several states to suppress the rebels.[34] That same day, the people of Pittsburgh formed a Committee of Public Safety, commanded by Andy's neighbor, the eighty-two-year-old Judge Wilkins. The committee immediately began to recruit volunteers and to gather equipment. At the outer depot, Andy was overwhelmed by the onslaught of volunteers and supplies; in addition to making provisional plans to transport recruits, equipment, and munitions, he also had to ensure that no contraband meant for the rebels passed along his line. Scott also became immediately embroiled in the war when Pennsylvania governor Andrew Curtin placed him in charge of transporting all troops and war matériel throughout the state. The situation in Washington, D.C., meanwhile, had unexpectedly become critical. Confederates sabotaged the Baltimore & Ohio's lines and cut telegraph wires, isolating the city and leaving it open to attack. Confederate sympathizers in Baltimore ambushed Union troops, killing four, prompting the Maryland governor to expel all Federal troops and to order all bridges on the Northern Central and the Baltimore & Ohio railroad lines burned, to prevent more soldiers from arriving.

Those in defenseless Washington became more anxious as the hours passed. To reestablish the capital's lines of communication and access north, Simon Cameron, who had been appointed secretary of the War Department, called on his friend Scott, who was made an assistant secretary. Desperate for competent help, Scott immediately summoned Andy to the nation's capital. Andy's career now entered a more dynamic phase as he was forced to operate and to lead men in a volatile, fluid environment in which he had to improvise. He would also realize fantastic opportunities as war profiteering reached fevered levels.

CHAPTER 6

Blood Money
and Black Gold

Enemy territory and brutal work awaited. Andy was ordered to Annapolis, Maryland, but rail travel through that state was impossible after the governor's actions. He was forced to take a train to the shores of Chesapeake Bay, where he boarded a steamer, accompanied by a core group of railroad men— including engineers, mechanics, trackmen, and bridge builders—who were to rebuild the lines. Troops of the Sixth Massachusetts were also on the steamer, charged with protecting the railroad. His mother would have come if allowed. As it was, the intrepid woman made the hazardous journey shortly thereafter to ensure her son was minding himself.[1]

Once in Annapolis, Andy and his crew took possession of a deserted mansion and set up operations. Their first task was to repair the sabotaged railroad and telegraph lines between Annapolis and Washington to restore communications and to permit troop movement into the panicked capital. After three 24-hour days of grueling work, the team succeeded, and the capital was no longer in immediate danger. Astride the engine like a gallant knight, Andy road to Washington with the first trainload of soldiers, known as the First Defenders. Just before reaching the outskirts of the city, he spotted telegraph wires pinned to the ground and ordered the train stopped so he could release them. "When released, in their spring upwards, they struck me in the face, knocked me over, and cut a gash in my cheek which bled profusely," he later wrote. "In this condition I entered the city of Washington with the first troops, so that with the exception of one or two soldiers wounded a few days previously in passing through the streets of Baltimore, I can justly claim that I 'shed my blood for my country' among the first of its defenders."[2]

Proudly displaying his battle scar, Andy reported to Scott, who subsequently ordered him to organize what would become the Military Telegraph Corps. To help build a vital communications network for the Federal forces, he summoned David Homer Bates and three other Pennsylvania Railroad telegraphers.[3] His next job was to organize a ferry system across the Potomac River to Alexandria, Virginia, in place of a destroyed bridge. There he established a new base of operations for extending the railroad and telegraph lines from the center of Washington to Alexandria, where the Federals hoped to mass their troops and launch an attack on the rebels. That extension meant laying new track through the city and rebuilding the five-thousand-foot Long Bridge. Again the men worked day and night, accomplishing the job in an astoundingly quick seven days. Fortunately for Andy, he had the ability to fall asleep anywhere at any time, with a catnap fully revitalizing him.

Meanwhile, the Confederate forces under General Pierre Gustave T. Beauregard massed twenty miles from Washington, at Manassas, Virginia, to protect a strategic railroad station and to thwart any Union invasion. When on July 21 Union forces under General Irvin McDowell engaged them with a clever flanking maneuver, it appeared a swift victory for the North was secured as the rebel defense buckled. But then Southern reinforcements arrived, including Thomas "Stonewall" Jackson's brigade of dedicated Virginians, and rallied the broken Confederates. As the battle developed, Andy's friend Homer Bates, the telegraph operator stationed in Washington, recalled the tension in the cramped telegraph office, crowded with President Lincoln, War Secretary Cameron, and General in Chief Winfield Scott: "All the morning and well along into the afternoon, General McDowell's telegrams were more or less encouraging, and Lincoln and his advisers waited with eager hope, believing that Beauregard was being pushed back to Manassas Junction; but all at once the dispatches ceased coming. At first this was taken to mean that McDowell was moving farther away from the telegraph, and then, as the silence became prolonged, a strange fear seized upon the assembled watchers that perhaps all was not well. Suddenly the telegraph-instrument became alive again, and the short sentence, 'Our army is retreating,' was spelled out in Morse characters."[4]

Stationed in Alexandria, Andy was caught off guard by the reversal: "We could not believe the reports that came to us, but it soon became evident that we must rush every engine and car to the front to bring back our forces. The closest point then was Burke Station. I went out there and loaded up train after train of the poor wounded volunteers."[5] About 625 Union soldiers were killed and 950 wounded.[6] Then, through the shrieking steam whistles and clanging bells, came reports indicating that the Confederates were closing in, so Burke Station was abandoned and Andy jumped aboard the last train out.

Five days after the Battle of Bull Run, named by the North after a local river, or the Battle of First Manassas as the South later called it, Andy, putting a positive spin on the defeat, penned an optimistic letter to a friend: "Depend upon it, the recent defeat is a blessing in disguise. We shall now begin in earnest. Knowing our foes, the necessary means will be applied to ensure their overthrow. . . . What might have been half work, a mere scotching of the snake, will now be thorough and complete. . . . I am delighted with my occupation here—hard work, but how gratifying to lie down at night & think By George you are of some use in sustaining a great cause & making the path clearer for those who come hereafter as well as maintaining the position that humanity has, after laborious efforts, succeeded in reaching."[7]

Andy now joined Tom Scott in the War Building, where he took charge of the telegraph department. Lincoln visited the telegraph office daily and left a graphic impression on Andy, who found him to be "one of the most homely men I ever saw" but also very animated, charming, and deferential.[8] Overall, Andy was not impressed by what he witnessed in Washington: "The general confusion which reigned at Washington at this time had to be seen to be understood. No description can convey my initial impression of it. The first time I saw General Scott, then Commander-in-Chief, he was being helped by two men across the pavement from his office into his carriage. He was an old, decrepit man, paralyzed not only in body, but in mind; and it was upon this noble relic of the past that the organization of the forces of the Republic depended."[9] Optimism on the wane, Andy was frustrated by the lack of decision-making at the top; it took days to settle matters that required prompt action, and the strain of hard days and sleepless nights began to take its toll on him. He had already suffered through one bout of heatstroke under the Virginia sun, and there was the constant threat of disease as typhus was reaching epidemic proportions in the surrounding army camps. Although Andy put up a brave front, there was no doubt he would soon break—it was just a matter of when.

The high demand placed on the Pennsylvania Railroad to transport men and materials required Andy's return to Pittsburgh at the end of the summer of 1861, but there the pace was no less stressful. Men departed daily for the front, arriving at the depot in mule-drawn carts, accompanied by hoopskirted ladies, tearful good-byes, and goodies wrapped in handkerchiefs, and then were loaded on waiting cattle cars. The human cargo flowed both directions—more than a hundred thousand wounded men would eventually be transported to Pittsburgh to be cared for. Heavy artillery, small arms, ammunition, gun carriages, wagons, tents, blankets, clothing, cattle, and hogs also filled the outer depot. During the war, the city's Fort Pitt Foundry alone supplied the Union army with 1,193 cannon, some of the guns weighing 56 tons, and 10 million pounds of shot and shell.[10] The first year of the war marked the point when railroads became the dominant mode of transportation, carrying more freight than the canal boats. All of this, from the tearful good-byes to massive cannons, contributed to the logistical nightmare Andy faced. In the process, he came into his own as a manager and leader.

On October 4, he fired off a letter to General Superintendent Enoch Lewis, seeking the approval to purchase adjacent pastureland to expand the rail yard. The very next day, he sent Lewis a nine-page letter detailing the need for additional lines, locomotives, and cars to handle the increased tonnage. Competition was still a factor, too, and he argued that his Western Divi-

sion needed to reduce its passenger rates to certain outlying suburbs to compete with the newly opened Pittsburgh & Connellsville Railroad. To offset the
price reductions, Andy detailed how the railroad could cut costs, which included the elimination of a train crew change on the run between Pittsburgh
and Altoona, which would be accomplished by asking the trainmen to work
as much as thirteen hours a day as opposed to ten.[11] While he was not asking
them to work any harder than he did himself in these extraordinary times, he
now viewed—like top boss Edgar Thomson—the men as an expendable resource with a very definite cost, and reduced costs translated to greater profits.
"Mind the costs and the profits will take care of themselves" became Andy's
foremost business mantra, derived from his schoolboy's proverb, "Take care of
the pence and the pound will take care of themselves." This letter was evidence
of his evolving business philosophy, one built on three cornerstones: cut costs,
cut prices, and scoop the market. He had come to realize competitors had to
be aggressively run from the field before they could establish a position.

But Andy had to admit to Lewis that some Pittsburgh engineers were
already forced to work as many as thirty hours at a stretch, that morale was
low, and that many men "have not visited their families for several weeks."[12]
In addition to the labor and capacity problems, Andy had to contend with
escaped pigs, rotting produce, missing freight cars, dangerously overloaded
mail cars, church ministers complaining about freight trains running on Sundays, and shipments being late or going to the wrong station.[13] Another major
concern was accusations of war profiteering on the part of the Pennsylvania
Railroad and its officers.

Andy's mentor, Tom Scott, was accused of price gouging the government,
and Congress initiated an investigation. As Congress scrutinized the practices
of the Pennsylvania Railroad, both Scott and his friend, War Secretary Cameron, who was an owner of Northern Central railroad stock, were also accused
of allocating a disproportionate share of traffic to their railroads. Although the
Pennsylvania increased its earnings by 40 percent and the Northern Central
had doubled its earnings in 1861, the defrauding of the government was impossible to prove because of conveniently poor recordkeeping.[14] While Scott
was the point man, Andy was all too aware of the practice and guilty by association. He could not disobey his superiors, however, and turned a blind eye
to their indiscretions. Slowly, a step at a time, he continued to be lured into
ambiguous moral territory. Twenty years later he would admit to his price dis-
crimination days with the railroad, but would claim to be reformed.[15] The
truth was that discriminatory pricing was a fact of business life, and a practice
Andy would become adept at using to his advantage while protecting his
companies from it.

A welcome distraction from the war that would generate prodigious dividends
landed in Andy's lap in the fall of 1861: black gold. His speculation in oil was
the first of three significant investments he made during the Civil War, each

profiting from the conflagration and each a considerable step toward attaining independent wealth.

During the war, the demand for petroleum-based products and illuminants increased dramatically, and a region some sixty miles north of Pittsburgh would find itself in the midst of an oil rush. There, ran a modest yet mystical river called Oil Creek, where slimy oil bubbled to the surface and covered the water with a slick coat. Oil wasn't considered particularly crucial, however, until the mid-1850s, when Samuel M. Kier, a Pittsburgh merchant who was selling it as the most wonderful remedy for "the torturing pains of RHEUMATISM, GOUT, and NEURALGIA," succeeded in refining the crude oil to a point where it was clean enough to burn in lamps.[16] Once word spread of the refined oil being used as an illuminant, the craze was under way. Then, in August 1859, the first derrick struck oil. Soon it was the California gold rush incarnate. One Pittsburgh group intent on investing in the oil included William Coleman, one of Andy's Homewood neighbors. In 1859, the group leased the Storey family farm, situated right on Oil Creek, and a number of their wells proved very productive.[17] The one major drawback, besides the filth and stink, was the wildly fluctuating price of oil, which ranged from ten cents a barrel to five dollars. To stabilize their venture, Coleman and his partners decided to reorganize as a joint-stock company to raise funds for building more efficient facilities. In his search for investors, Coleman turned to Andy.

Coleman, with a full beard laced with white, gray hair, and a straight nose, was of good puritan stock. Having already made a fortune in the iron trade, he carried himself like a general. As had Tom Scott, he took a paternalistic liking to Andy and his brother, Tom, who would marry Coleman's daughter, Lucy. He also appreciated Andy's energy and resourcefulness, and figured he would be an asset to the group. Certain a brush with the fever would convince the young man to invest, in the fall of 1861 Coleman persuaded Andy to visit the oil region. The two men traveled by steamer up the Allegheny River to the mouth of Oil Creek. From there they took a five-mile rickety carriage ride north, across rutted roads and through wild scenery, both natural and the human kind in a region where raucous men seeking treasure overwhelmed the preachers.

As Andy surveyed the scene, he was amazed to discover twenty-four-hour saloons filled with brawlers and gamblers, and suspicious houses filled with self-styled ladies, servicing the drillers and other laborers who made anywhere from $2 to $5 a day. As one visitor noted, "The orgies in Petroleum Centre sometimes eclipsed Monte Carlo and the Latin Quarter combined."[18] Conditions were definitely sordid. Even though the cheaply constructed but expensive hotels offered only scratchy straw pallets, these were in short supply, forcing many drillers to share beds. The food was worse. It included half-baked water biscuits with salt pork, pallid beans drowned in molasses, and steak so leathery it required a hatchet to cut. The streets of the mushrooming towns were cluttered with shanties, precarious pyramids of barrels, and strewn garbage, and the air was thick with the stench of oil, turning Andy's stomach as it brought back memories of the days at John Hay's bobbin factory. Due to the sin and mud and oil all churned together, the inferno area became known as Sodden and Gomorrah.

Accustomed to the rough railroad men, Andy was relatively immune to the bawdy chaos, which was later extremely glossed over in his censored memoirs: "What surprised me was the good humor which prevailed everywhere. It was a vast picnic, full of amusing incidents. Everybody was in high glee; fortunes were supposedly within reach; everything was booming. On the tops of the derricks floated flags on which strange mottoes were displayed. I remember looking down toward the river and seeing two men working their treadles boring for oil upon the banks of the stream and inscribed upon their flag was 'Hell or China.' They were going down, no matter how far."[19]

Waste, chaos, and sin aside, Andy knew a good investment. The Storey farm site was a relatively orderly affair with a tough foreman who allowed no riffraff on the property, and by 1862, the farm had twelve flowing wells. On the return trip home, Andy agreed to join Coleman in the Columbia Oil Company, which was originally capitalized at $200,000 with ten thousand shares issued. He used his dividend proceeds from the Woodruff sleeping car business to buy a block of discounted $10 shares.[20] In 1863, the company paid stockholders over $300,000 in dividends, with Andy receiving a tremendous $17,868.67 for the year. To reflect the great success, the company recapitalized at $2.5 million, or $50 a share, which was $40 more than Andy had paid, or a phenomenal 400 percent increase in value. Never one to forget his loyalties, he invited Scott, Thomson, brother Tom, and friend Tom Miller to invest. Again, instead of squandering the dividends, Andy would use them to make further investments.

The sleeping car business, being neatly interlocked with the Pennsylvania Railroad, had been so easy to exploit that when a similar prospect emerged in 1862 Andy pursued it diligently. This second wartime venture would also involve a modest investment that yielded a tremendous return—the one Andy considered to "have always been my pet as being the parent of all other works."[21] It was a bridge-building concern, and this time it was the Pennsylvania Railroad's very own Altoona yard that provided the opportunity.

When Andy had been transferred to Altoona, he met Colonel John L. Piper, who was then the railroad's chief mechanic, charged with keeping the tracks and the trains in operation. A rough-mannered hulk, Piper took an immediate liking to the Scotch Devil, a delicate lad with spunk, and although side by side the two made a comical pair, they discovered they shared a love for horses. Two other members of Piper's team were Aaron Shiffler, whose specialty was maintaining the bridges, and J. H. Linville, who was chief bridge engineer. With the rampant sabotage during the Civil War, iron bridges were suddenly in high demand. This provided the impetus for Thomson and Scott to have Andy discreetly approach Piper—or Pipe, as he was known—about organizing a bridge-building company that would initially operate out of Altoona as a private company hidden within the Pennsylvania Railroad. Pipe then recruited Shiffler and Linville, who were only too happy to pocket some side profits.

The Piper and Shiffler Company was formed on February 1, 1862, and soon relocated to Pittsburgh, at Andy's suggestion, to take advantage of the many iron mills there. Thomson, Scott, Andy, Pipe, Shiffler, and Linville, who was made president, each invested $1,250 for a one-sixth interest, and once again Andy held Scott's share in his name.[22] Per the impervious Scott-Thomson modus operandi, the Pennsylvania Railroad was an instant large customer, all but guaranteeing success. Even though operations were modest in the first years, in 1863 Andy made $7,500 on his initial investment. Within ten years, the bridge-building operations would generate hundreds of thousands of dollars, clearly why Andy considered it his pet.

While Andy had built himself quite a portfolio with an income to be envied—he suddenly found himself among the wealthiest of young men in Pittsburgh—the genesis of his greatest investment during the Civil War had yet to come.

Juggling his wartime responsibilities at the railroad and his investments in oil, sleeping cars, and iron bridges was a heavy strain, and by late spring of 1862 Andy was burned out. He wasn't the only one. The stoic Thomson collapsed in April and was confined to bed for exhaustion and a pulmonary infection. A month passed before he was back in the office on a regular basis, and he would travel to Europe that summer to recuperate further.[23] Also desperate for relief and dreaming of a glorious return to Scotland, Andy applied for a leave of absence, which was granted. He received the good news while in Altoona and, with the enthusiasm of a boy going to the circus, immediately dashed off a letter to his cousin Dod: "The dream of a dozen years is at last on the very threshold of realization. *Yes I am to visit Scotland*, see and talk with you all again!—Uncles, Aunts and Cousins, my schoolfellows and companions of my childhood—all are to be greeted again. . . . Hurrah! Three cheers for this! There is nothing on earth I would ask in preference to what has just been given me. The exuberance of my joy I find is tempered by a deep feeling of thankfulness for the privilege vouchsafed—it seems so much in advance of my deserts." Andy's plans involved more than just Dunfermline; he also intended to tour the Continent and invited Dod to join him. "Whew! that's enough to make one jolly, isn't it? I confess I'm clean daft about it. I fancy I look like an ardent lover who has just obtained a flattering 'yes.' "[24] All his boyish vitality, drained by grueling work and brutal war, gushed forth in the letter. He needed not only to regain his health, but to rejuvenate his spirit and to reconnect with the past he had lost in shaping himself into an ardent Republican.

By 1862, the Civil War had taken its toll on Carnegie, who, despite his eternal optimism, could be dour and gloomy. (Courtesy of the Carnegie Library of Pittsburgh)

Andy invited his friend Thomas Miller, now the purchasing agent for the Fort Wayne & Pittsburgh Railroad, to accompany him and his mother, while Tom, now nineteen and serving as his personal secretary, remained to mind the store. Miller stood a head taller than Andy and, with a goatee and black, curly locks, had roguish good looks. He was a stormy-tempered Irishman willing to debate any topic with his Scottish friend, which made them lively traveling companions; even so, the two maintained a mutual respect. No time was to be wasted during this three-month leave of absence, so they departed for Dunfermline on June 28, three days before the leave was official, aboard a steamer far more luxurious than the *Wiscasset*, which had brought the Carnegies to America years earlier. After the ship landed in Liverpool two weeks later, the trio proceeded immediately to Scotland. As soon as they crossed the border, Andy felt like throwing himself to the sacred soil and kissing it.[25] His attitude changed, however, as they rode their carriage into town like returning heroes. The glorified image of Dunfermline he had cherished and embellished over the last fourteen years, was suddenly diminished:

> Every object we passed was recognized at once, but everything seemed so small, compared with what I had imagined it, that I was completely puzzled. Finally, reaching Uncle Lauder's and getting into the old room where he had taught Dod and myself so many things, I exclaimed:
> "You are all here; everything is just as I left it, but you are now playing with toys."

> The High Street, which I had compared with some New York estab-
> lishments, the little mounds about the town, to which we had run on Sun-
> days to play, the distances, the height of the houses, all had shrunk. Here
> was a city of the Lilliputians.[26]

From his perspective, life was on a much grander scale in the United States, and now Dunfermline wilted under the bright glory of America. Yet if Andy had demonstrated more insight, he would have realized that as a child—the last time he was in Dunfermline—everything appeared much larger than it was.

His tone was almost contemptuous in addressing his relatives and old acquaintances who were "playing with toys." When his Aunt Charlotte exulted, "Oh, you will just be coming back here some day and keep a shop in the High Street," he thought to himself, "That's her idea of triumph."[27] Once upon a time, a shop on High Street epitomized success to his mother, but that was no longer so for the Carnegie family. Still, Andy was excited to be there, and his Uncle Lauder, for one, remained of tall stature. They enjoyed long walks and talks about life in America; but to his chagrin, Andy discovered Uncle Lauder was the only one in the family supporting the Union cause.

Many in Scotland were suffering because of the Civil War. The Union's naval blockade of the South had strangled the flow of needed cotton to Scotland while at the same time U.S. orders for linen had dropped dramatically, depressing the economy in towns like Dunfermline. Uncle Thomas, among others, blamed the Union government for their privations. Such people were quite cynical in analyzing the North's true motives, convinced the North was not fighting a righteous battle to free the slaves, but to strengthen its own industrial grip on the nation. Because of their own fight for autonomy over the centuries, the Scottish radicals linked themselves romantically to the Southern rebels.

Other relatives were not so politically minded. Cousin Dod and Andy fell in together as though never separated by the Atlantic. Framed by a full brown beard flowing over his collar and accentuated by the brooding, dark Morrison eyes, Dod's stern face lighted up when the two cousins reenacted their swordplay from youth. Now an engineer, he divulged his dream of coming to America to seek his fortune. The old aunties relished telling Andy stories about his childhood, from his eating habits as a baby—he preferred to have two spoons going at once—to riding his father's shoulders as though on a mule. Between the heated political debate and Aunt Charlotte recalling his childhood days and the town itself appearing to be Lilliputian, the Dunfermline visit was a surreal experience for Andy. Sleepless nights and a head cold soon dampened the visit. He then came down with a fever, and when his condition showed no signs of improving his stern nursemaids became determined to bleed him of his ills. The ancient art of bleeding was so suc-

Andrew Carnegie, his cousin, George "Dod" Lauder, and
Thomas Miller were together in Dunfermline in 1862.
While there, Carnegie fell ill and submitted to bleeding in
hopes of regaining his health. (Courtesy of the Carnegie
Library of Pittsburgh)

cessful that it almost killed him in the process. To regain strength, Andy
escaped to the shores of picturesque Loch Leven. All told, he spent six weeks
confined to bed. Plans to visit the Continent were canceled, and once strong
enough, he sailed for home in the autumn of 1862, his ill-fated visit coming
to an abrupt end. Andy had found himself a foreigner in his native land and
estranged from his radical heritage.

Capitalism now dominated Andy's consciousness. When he wrote Dod, it was
not to debate the sociopolitical scene, but to encourage him to invest in the
fledgling oil industry, which his cousin did for a short time before deciding to
withdraw. Andy was sorry he did, but continued to push the industry on his
cousin, wanting to know if he should send him listings for oil property lots for
sale that Dod might want to market to firms in Scotland.

Once bitten by oil fever, a marked change came over Andy; while always conscious of material progress, he was suddenly far more focused on accumulating money and reveling in luxury. When Dod wrote that he was determined to "put money in his purse," Andy responded that it was a "noble resolution." In the same June 1863 letter, he continued: "Isn't it strange how little ambition most of our Scotch acquaintances have to become independent *and pthen enjoy the luxuries which wealth can (and should) procure*. For my part I am determined to expand as my means do and ultimately to own a noble place in the country, cultivate the rarest flowers, the best breeds of cattle, own a magnificent lot of horses and be distinguished for taking the deepest interest in all those about my place. . . . There, my boy! Such a picture should incite you to the extremest measures."[28] Amid the ruins of the Civil War—the bloodbaths at Chancellorsville and Gettysburg—business ruled his conscious.

CHAPTER 7

An Iron Coup

W hen Tom David stopped by that winter for a visit and asked his buddy how life was treating him, Carnegie exclaimed, "Oh, Tom, I'm rich. I'm rich!"[1] So he was. During these first years of the Civil War, Carnegie had answered a pivotal question for himself: Did he want to play the conservative company man, or did he want to assume risk, extend himself financially, and put money to work? Did he want a few chickens in the backyard, or did he want a gaggle of geese laying golden eggs? He chose the latter. He took advantage of his Homewood friends—William Coleman, Thomas Miller, David Stewart, and John Vandevort—and his Pennsylvania Railroad contacts to secure the inside track on buying stock in a variety of sure thing companies—at a discount, of course.

When preparing his personal taxes, levied by the Federal government to pay for the war, Carnegie made a statement for his 1863 income on Pennsylvania Railroad Company notepaper. It listed investments in a dozen concerns, including a few shares of Western Union, that generated over $45,000 for the year, while his railroad salary contributed a paltry $2,400. It was the railroad, however, that made it all possible. Over the next two years, he would buy into another oil field called Pit Hole; purchase stock in two insurance companies, several coal-mining companies, and a brick manufacturer, as well as increase his Western Union holdings; and acquire Homewood land.[2] He was often joined in these investments by his brother, as well as Miller, Pitcairn, Stewart, Vandevort, and John Scott, a fellow railroad executive.

Carnegie reveled in owning a piece of a company; it was like owning a piece of the glorified Republic. He bathed gleefully in his riches. Making money was noble, as he told Dod. Being rich was to be celebrated, as he demonstrated with his exclamations to Tom David. Under Scott's tutelage, he had developed a lust for money that he expressed openly, and determined to succeed on a grander scale than his father had failed, he would continue to extend himself, borrow money to invest, and assume ever-greater risk.

Money dictated his thoughts and his actions. It was pathological. It gave him respect, too.

While not quite a bon vivant, Carnegie was living the high life in ritzy Homewood, a far cry from his radical heritage. He was cultivated, refined; he attended fancy parties at the Wilkins mansion and knew how to drink tea.

Confidence brimming, Carnegie bulled his way into a web of intrigue in the fall of 1863. He was determined to help his friend Thomas Miller, who had found himself caught in a complex relationship with a local iron firm that would severely test friendships and prove to be another pivotal turning point in Carnegie's life. It eventually involved his third and final significant investment during the Civil War, a $10,000 investment in the iron firm that was the seed for the world's greatest steel empire.

Competition in the Pittsburgh iron industry was intense, including more than fifty firms, and the leading firms were determined to break the small establishments; as one ironmaster declared, "The big fish are going to swallow up the little ones."[3] Two little fish who wanted to become big fish were Anthony and Andrew Kloman, Bavarian immigrants operating a small Allegheny City forge with one trip-hammer and a steam engine. Quickly gaining a reputation for making extremely durable axles using their patented process, they couldn't keep pace with demand. Eager to expand, but without capital, Andrew Kloman approached Miller, their customer at the Fort Wayne, Pittsburgh & Ohio Railroad, and offered him one-third of the business if he anted up $1,600, the money needed to buy another trip-hammer, which would double the firm's output. Miller was intrigued. Between Kloman's expertise and his connections with various railroads—such as the Pennsylvania, where his friend Andy worked—it seemed a safe bet. There was one problem, however: Miller had a conscience. Uncomfortable with the impropriety of connecting himself with a supplier, he told Kloman he wanted to invest but would have a friend represent him.[4] It was not an unusual arrangement, and Kloman acquiesced.

The friend was Henry "Harry" Phipps, whose older brother John had been part of the Original Six until killed in a horseback riding accident at age eighteen. Still living at his father's home in Allegheny City, Harry was a bookkeeper; and with his bland features, a broad forehead, and a receding hairline, he had the countenance of a numbers man. His penny-pinching was legendary among his friends; his preferred restaurant served free bread with codfish balls. Keen to add some excitement to his dull life, he agreed to give Miller half of the $1,600 to join the scheme. This would require Phipps's father to mortgage their home, however, so Miller, having assumed the role of big brother to Harry, agreed to fund the entire $1,600 with Phipps paying off his half out of profits. The Klomans, Miller, and Phipps came to terms on November 16, 1861; the new company was called Iron City Forge, and in the articles of partnership Miller's name was left out as agreed on.

Iron City Forge flourished during the Civil War as government orders for gun carriages and axles poured in. Profits soared, but unfortunately for the other partners, Anthony Kloman became more interested in hoisting drinks in local taverns than he did iron. An overwhelmed Andrew Kloman asked Miller to buy his brother out; after a heated argument, Anthony agreed to sell his share for $20,000.[5] Trouble erupted again when Kloman, whose greed appeared to increase with profits, decided he wanted a bigger share. He aligned himself with the weaker character of his two partners, Harry Phipps, and convinced him that they should force Miller out. Kloman went so far as to place an advertisement in the newspaper stating that Miller was not a member of the firm.[6] Miller couldn't believe it: he had invited Phipps into the business; he had contributed capital when needed; and now they wanted to eject him. In the fall of 1863, he turned to Carnegie to arbitrate the matter.

"For some weeks," Carnegie recalled, "scarcely a day passed that I did not see one or more of the parties. Hearing both sides, I was fully satisfied I could not establish harmony upon the basis of a common partnership." Once it was clear to him there were irreconcilable differences between Miller and the other two, he recommended a reorganization of the company to both boost its capitalization and to redistribute the balance of power. Acknowledging Carnegie's more sophisticated business experience, the trio agreed to his suggestions, which included increasing the firm's capital to $60,000, with Kloman taking a 50 percent interest and Miller limited to only a one-sixth share. Since Phipps could not afford the remaining $20,000, Carnegie insisted his brother take half of it. He argued that Tom would bring balance and an evenhandedness to the management. Tom, with soft, dark eyes, wispy muttonchop whiskers, and a reserved manner, was exceptionally affable and was said to make friends even as he was asking for a favor. Whereas Andy tended to force his views on others and ruffle feathers, Tom was the one who smoothed the ruffled feathers. Kloman agreed to the arrangement, but he still held serious reservations about Miller. To protect against any Miller reprisals, Carnegie suggested a clause in the partnership articles allowing Kloman and Phipps to buy Miller out with 60 days' notice if his actions were deemed detrimental. It was also agreed that if Miller were expelled, one-half of his interest would go to Tom Carnegie, who now borrowed money from his older brother for his one-sixth share of the company. For the first time, Andrew Carnegie had a sizable investment, albeit a loan to his brother, in iron.

It wasn't long before squabbling broke out, and Kloman and Phipps gave Miller his notice. Miller considered Phipps's actions traitorous and disowned him, but the intrigue didn't end there. He vowed to drive Kloman and Phipps into bankruptcy. Certain his friend had been wronged, Carnegie reacted rashly and agreed to join forces with Miller to build a competing iron mill from scratch. It didn't matter that neither had any practical experience in the industry. Together they scouted property, and on July 1, 1864, they quietly leased a five-acre plot of farmland located a mere four blocks from the Kloman concern. Half-grown cabbages were cleared to make way for the foundation of a 230-foot-long by 80-foot-wide mill. On October 14, their new firm was officially registered and capitalized at $100,000, with Miller the majority owner. Also included were Carnegie, John Piper, Aaron Shiffler, John C. Mathews, who would be the manager, and Thomas Pyeatte, the company's bookkeeper. It was a savvy move bringing in Piper and Shiffler; Carnegie knew the iron firm would have a loyal customer in the bridge-building concern.

They christened the firm the ominous-sounding Cyclops Iron Company, after the one-eyed giants from Greek mythology who devoured men. In Homer's *Odyssey*, the hero was captured by a Cyclops named Polyphemus. To escape, Odysseus tricked the Cyclops into becoming drunk and then put a spear through his single eye. These monsters were also linked to the iron industry. According to myth, the Cyclopes were once companions of Hephaestus, the fire god; using great hammers, they worked molten bronze and iron drawn from Hephaestus's furnace. The question now was whether Carnegie would be blessed by the fire god or become another Polyphemus. And to those watching the construction of a new iron mill, it appeared Carnegie had turned on his brother.

Despite the distractions offered by the Kloman-Phipps-Miller squabble, "Scott's Andy," or the "Little Boss" as he was also nicknamed, continued to perform admirably for the Pennsylvania Railroad. Under the assumption that he was protected by the Conscription Act of 1863, which exempted locomotive engineers and other railroad employees vital to operations from serving, he was shocked when the federal government drafted him in the summer of 1864. At age twenty-eight and single, he was a perfect candidate, even though the Pennsylvania Railroad's ranks had thinned and the company was so desperate for competent help it was recruiting men from Europe. Still, in the eyes of the government, Andrew Carnegie was expendable. He weighed his options. Leaving cozy Homewood and joining the war was not particularly attractive. General Ulysses S. Grant, who was being denounced as a butcher, had begun his relentless drive for Richmond which, over seven weeks in May and June, had left sixty-five thousand Union soldiers dead, wounded, or missing. His other two choices, allowed under the terms of the Conscription Act of 1863, were to pay the government $300 to avoid service or to hire an alternate. Not wanting to completely dodge his patriotic duty, Carnegie hired an alternate through the services of H. M. Butler, a Pittsburgh draft agent. He paid $850, and Butler found a willing substitute in John Lindew, an Irish immigrant. Carnegie prudently signed the Certificate of Non-Liability on July 19; the deal was good for three years.[7]

With his tenure now secure at the railroad, rumors reached Carnegie toward the end of 1864 that he was to be offered the position of assistant general superintendent under Enoch Lewis. The next steps would be general superintendent and then a vice presidency, just like his mentor Scott. Thomson himself made the offer, but Carnegie hesitated in accepting. He had to weigh his loyalty to the railroad against his strong feelings of predestination for greatness. His mother certainly thought her boy Andra should answer to no man, and his radical heritage had infused him with fierce individualism. There were his personal investments to consider, too; income from them far exceeded his salary, and his portfolio demanded more attention. "I declined," Carnegie later explained with a hint of piety, "telling him that I had decided to give up the railroad service altogether, that I was determined to make a fortune and I saw no means of doing this honestly at any salary the railroad company could afford to give, and I would not do it by indirection."[8]

But then Carnegie had a crisis of conscience. It wasn't about leaving the railroad. It was about becoming a capitalist. On New Year's Day of 1865, while in a reflective and rare sentimental mood, he had a sudden urge to return to Scotland; more specifically, to take a consular position in Scotland working for the government. He wrote to Scott, hoping he could use his influence with Simon Cameron to win the appointment for him. Scott obliged, but with the war still raging and Cameron's reputation compromised, nothing could be done.[9] This brief episode, filled with doubt and questions, was Carnegie's first crisis of conscience of several, for out there, beyond the dark perimeter of material gain, he suspected there was a nobler existence.

It was a bittersweet moment on March 28, 1865, when Carnegie sat down to pen his letter of resignation. He expressed his "deep regret" at parting after twelve years of "pleasant intercourse" with the Pennsylvania Railroad and the "painful" change of breaking with intimate associates.[10] As he crafted the letter, Carnegie reflected on the first time Mr. Scott had tousled his white hair; on earning the moniker Scotch Devil; and on his first investment in the Adams Express Company. Going deeper into his personal odyssey, he had survived the Hungry Forties in Scotland and the seven-week ocean voyage as an immigrant faced with the ravages of typhus and cholera; he had worked as a bobbin boy and in the inferno of John Hay's bobbin factory for such a pittance that it amounted to slave labor; he had been lifted to the heavens all because of a checkers match and ridden the wave of a new technology that annihilated time and distance, the telegraph; and he had joined the railroad just as it was beginning to transform America socially and economically. He justifiably believed the gods were with him, the nonchurchgoer.

As the young Napoléon of business stood on his pedestal and eyed the industrial landscape, preparing for his unrelenting march to fortune, he brought with him a number of weapons given to him by Scott and Thomson. He knew intimately how to speculate in advance of the railroad, to create interlocking investments, to finance projects through bond sales, to control costs, to sink profits back into the business, to motivate lieutenants, to create

alliances with competitors and subsequently to break them, to preempt organized labor movements, and to manipulate politicians. The railroad had been
the first industry to require complex organizational hierarchies relying on
accurate information, and Carnegie had been immersed in it.

The first order of business was to deal decisively with the traitorous
Phipps and the iron business. Despite their inexperience, when Carnegie and
Miller organized Cyclops their prospects appeared to be much better than the
Kloman enterprise; after all, Cyclops had a ready-made market in the Piper
and Shiffler Company, while Kloman would lose business at war's end. But
when Cyclops manager John Mathews ordered his men to fire up the machinery in the early spring of 1865, the supporting structure proved too weak for
safe operation; it appeared to be the spear to the ogre's eye. Carnegie was
beside himself with disbelief and frustration, which he took out on Mathews,
who in turn complained it was a result of Carnegie and Miller demanding he
"build a $400,000 mill on a $100,000 capital."[11]

It was an unmitigated disaster for Carnegie. This mill was his first true
business venture, one in which he had enlisted the financial support of
friends, and it was an embarrassment. The situation had to be remedied posthaste. To some businessmen it appeared that Carnegie desperately needed
Kloman's mechanical help, while to others it was still the Kloman concern
that ultimately needed Carnegie's help to obtain customers. The truth was
they both needed each other. And so, as General Grant slowly encircled Lee
in the final phase of the Civil War, brothers Tom and Andrew opened negotiations on merging the two firms. All members of the Kloman and Cyclops
concerns were amicable to merging, except for Miller, who was still smarting.

Carnegie cajoled him with promises that he would be the largest shareholder, quipping, "You return as conqueror." Finally, Miller relented, on the
condition that he have no contact with his "former protégé" Phipps.[12] It was
agreed that for a 50 percent interest in the new firm, Carnegie and Miller
would pay the Iron City partners $50,000 cash to divvy up among themselves
and would donate the Cyclops plant and equipment. The new company was
christened Union Iron Mills to commemorate the reunion of both the country and Carnegie's friends, although Phipps was asked to step down as a director to ensure Miller would have no personal contact with him.

The Carnegie brothers, and Andrew in particular, were accused of sinister,
Machiavellian tactics in capturing control of what had once been Kloman's
iron firm. The charges were partly true. Carnegie's loan to Tom for his share
in Iron City Forge paid a handsome return of $4,250 in 1863, according to
his income tax statement; but something was wrong there. Interest on a
$10,000 loan to Tom should have amounted to no more than a few hundred
dollars that year, strongly implying the $4,250 was, in fact, a share of the Klo-
man profits.[13] Carnegie and his younger brother had struck a deal of some
kind that in a few short months yielded almost twice as much money as his

superintendent's salary. Whether this affected the eventual merger is unknown; however, Carnegie's adept skill in consummating the marriage was certain in Machiavellian terms.

He innately executed the advice offered by Machiavelli in *The Discourses* for conquering a troubled city (Iron City): "The way to do this is to try and win the confidence of the citizens that are divided amongst themselves [Kloman, Phipps, Miller], and to manage to become the arbiter between them [Carnegie], unless they should have come to arms; but having come to arms, then sparingly to favor the weaker party [Miller], so as to keep up the war and make them exhaust themselves, and not to give them occasion for the apprehension, by a display of your forces, that you intend to subjugate them and make yourself prince. And if this course be well carried out, it will generally end in your obtaining the object you aim at."[14] Carnegie played the role of arbiter to perfection.

He was able to remain loyal to both the Phipps family, who had given his mother work in their destitute days, and his bosom buddy Miller. Because his family had forsaken Scotland, maintaining such loyalties was crucial to Carnegie's sense of belonging to a community, which still needed reinforcement even though he had lived in Pittsburgh for almost twenty years. Misplaced loyalty could have dire consequences, however; two years later, Carnegie would indeed admit how foolish the Cyclops venture had been. "I knew you had previously been wronged and felt you could not forget it," he wrote Miller. "I did what I could at the time to redress the wrong and went into the most hazardous enterprise I ever expect to have any connection with again, the building of a rival mill."[15] Carnegie would have to guard himself against blind loyalties.

Carnegie's promise of making Miller the largest shareholder, his promise of money and power, had been enough to keep his friend in the firm as long as he had no contact with Phipps. When a position on the Union Iron Mills board of directors opened up in the spring of 1867, however, and Miller found Phipps in the vacated chair at the next meeting, he exclaimed, "I will not sit at the table with that man!"

"Oh come, Tom, don't act like a child," said Carnegie. "Come back, shake hands with Harry and be friends once more." An unyielding Miller stormed from the room and later resigned. "He was Irish," Carnegie observed dryly, "and the Irish blood when aroused is uncontrollable."[16] He now realized it would take more than money, so he played on two very potent emotions, vanity and guilt, a mix he would use throughout his business career to motivate and control his partners and lieutenants.

During the very period that beleaguered President Andrew Johnson and the Senate—which had failed to impeach him by one vote—were in dire need of reconciling their differences, Carnegie made a last effort to coax Miller to return and to reunite his friends. In a sharply toned letter, he played on

Miller's vanity by lavishly complimenting his abilities—abilities desperately needed by the company. He then attempted to evoke guilt by issuing reprimands laced with bursts of impatience, writing Miller that "for so large an interest as yours should receive your attention—principally upon my account, for so far from your presence being an embarrassment it would be esteemed of great value. . . . I want all parties in interest to understand that I have worked to bring matters right about as long as I intend to do so. When you know how we are placed I think instead of embarrassing us by resigning you should put your shoulder to the wheel with us. We never needed the efforts of all more urgently than now. You have of course aided us in money matters for which we are duly thankful, but your presence at the mill every morning for twenty minutes would double this obligation."[17] The scolding failed. As far as Miller was concerned, it was either him or Phipps. Carnegie had no choice but to choose Phipps because, when it came to the bottom line, Phipps contributed more than Miller. Phipps and brother Tom, Carnegie ascertained, were quite capable of managing Union Mills, while he played the role of financier and salesman at large, exploiting his railroad contacts to secure contracts. Carnegie did not spend notable time at the mills; a plush study at home provided the fertile ground for his business contemplations.

Now it became a matter of dealing with Miller's stake in the firm, because if he wasn't going to contribute, he wasn't going to share in the profits. Rather than sell it back to all the partners, who included Kloman and Phipps, Miller preferred to have Carnegie buy him out; and so the haggling between the stubborn Irishman and the tight-fisted Scotsman began. In September, Carnegie played down the company's worth, claiming that the Union Iron Mills was "going as fast as they could into bankruptcy," and said he was willing to pay only $27.40 a share, a hefty discount from the book value of $40. He employed a little more guilt, too, blaming Miller for involving him in the first place. But Miller held out for $32.75 a share. The two men came to terms in March 1868, with Carnegie buying Miller's 2,203 shares at Miller's asking price for a total of $72,148.25, giving him a controlling interest in the firm.[18]

Again, observers accused Carnegie of Machiavellian tactics, but Miller never suggested as much nor regretted what he did. Almost forty years later, in a letter to Carnegie, he confirmed his decision to sell out: "I could not stand the stink of such treachery as his [Phipps] conduct had been in 1863— indeed after 40 years, while I have forgiven him, I cannot meet him comfortably. As to yourself, what you did then was wise, you had no quarrel with Henry Phipps, you advised me well to 'let bygones be bygones'—and I loved you then Andy, as I have *ever* loved you, but Phipps had stabbed me at a critical time in my life—but why weary you with dirty linen of the past."[19]

To Carnegie, such petty, unyielding behavior when profits were to be made was incomprehensible. Hurt by Miller's defection, their friendship became strained; it would be years before they could again be called chums.

"He mellowed in old age," Carnegie reflected, "like the rose, bursting into glossy purple at last; one of the sweetest natures I have ever known; tender as a woman and true as steel."[20]

The iron business was evolving into a love-hate relationship. On the one hand, Carnegie had encountered one headache after another at the Union Mills, and the roaring furnaces reminded him of his days stoking Mr. Hay's boiler. On the other hand, iron was fast becoming the centerpiece of his portfolio; in 1867, Union Mills would yield a personal profit of $20,000. Still, Carnegie had yet to sense that his fate was tied to iron and to Pittsburgh, the forge of the universe. Instead, he continued to pursue tangential investments and scatter his capital, and in the ensuing years he would overextend himself.

CHAPTER 8

Many Hands,
Many Cookie Jars

C arnegie fancied himself an investor extraordinaire, a financier, a broker of deals. He was not a Wall Street gambler or a swindler, but he was swept up in the post–Civil War money fever, the contagion of greed unleashed after four years of horrific bloodshed. His cavalier attitude toward investing was exposed when Carnegie proposed to his friend John "Vandy" Vandevort, "If you could make three thousand dollars would you spend it in a tour through Europe with me?"[1]

"Would a duck swim or an Irishman eat potatoes?" Vandy replied. Both Carnegie and he had been reading travel writer Bayard Taylor's *Views Afoot; or, Europe Seen with Knapsack and Staff*, which inspired them to strike out for the Continent. If culture could be had, a little stock speculation was certainly excusable; and so Carnegie, like an Arabian genie, transformed a few hundred dollars of Vandy's money into a few thousand by investing in oil. Vandy was tall with a trim brown beard and seductive eyes, carried himself in an urbane manner, and relished adventure. The much shorter, plainer-looking Carnegie purposefully selected such suave, handsome friends as Miller and Vandy to offset his own physical shortcomings. Harry Phipps was also invited. Departing for a vacation to last until the next spring on the heels of the Civil War and with so many investments to monitor appeared irresponsible; however, for Carnegie, becoming a well-rounded man of culture added a dimension of power he craved. And as cousin Dod noted, "Carnegie owes a great deal to his habit of traveling. While other men were wallowing in details, he was able to take a wider view."

Upon arriving in Liverpool in late May 1865, the trio proceeded directly to Dunfermline, where Carnegie introduced his chums to the family. Contrary to the visit three years prior when he found his hometown to be of Lilliputian size, a more mature Carnegie now reveled in reconnecting with his heritage and extended family. In a letter home, he paid tribute to the Sir Walter Scott monument in Edinburgh, and no longer was his tone condescending when speaking of relatives and friends. "It was 'ondrous strange to be surrounded with old men who were our father's boon companions," he wrote Tom. "In America we are an entirely new family, and outside of Aunts Aitken and Hogan we have no relatives nor associations. Here we have a local history extending to the third generation, and many a one speaks kindly of our ancestors. You may believe this seems a very great change."[2] Never quite comfortable with his boyhood uprooting from Scotland, Carnegie relished the sense of belonging he discovered during this stay.

After a brief stay in Dunfermline, the trio returned to Liverpool, where Robert Franks, a relative of Harry Phipps, joined them. Then it was to London and the Continent, Carnegie leading the assault on France, Germany, and Italy with the same vigor he brought to business. Franks was so enamored with Carnegie that he would later become his financial secretary for life. "As to Andy's health," Franks wrote his sister, "this is so overflowing that it is extremely difficult to keep him within reasonable bounds, to restrain him within the limits of moderately orderly behavior, he is so continually mischievous and so exuberantly joyous. . . . He is full of liveliness, fun and frolic. His French is to carry us through when Vandy's German is no longer required. I had to acknowledge my obligation to him no later than yesterday when, wishing my portmanteau forwarded by rail and the German porter being so stupid as not to understand my good English, Andy kindly stepped forward to the rescue with 'Voulez vous forward the baggage to Mayence?' It is, I expect, needless to tell you that in time I found my portmanteau at its destination."[3]

Carnegie provided his own assessment: "We make up a splendid whole and go laughing and rollicking through, meeting with many laughable adventures and exciting much merriment." But rather than indulging in his companions' personalities as did Franks, he viewed each as serving a function: "Vandy is by far the most useful man of the lot. . . . He earns his grub. . . . To Harry is given the Post Office department. He mails all letters, gets them out . . . goes back after coats forgotten or guide books left at the hotel, and is par excellence the accommodating member of the quartette."[4] Each had to serve a function to be valued and included in Carnegie's circle; if not, they were cut loose like Miller. A normal, emotionally congenial friendship absent of strings was not possible with Carnegie.

Already anticipating a larger stage for himself, the ambitious Carnegie wasn't satisfied with merely writing letters home to Tom and his mother; adopting Bayard Taylor's persona, he also wrote letters to the editor of the *Pittsburgh Commercial*, in which he recounted their experiences. "This visit to Europe proved most instructive," Carnegie later reflected. "Up to this time I had known nothing of painting or sculpture, but it was not long before I could classify the works of the great painters. One may not at the time justly appreciate the advantage he is receiving from examining the great master-pieces, but upon his return to America he will find himself unconsciously rejecting what before seemed truly beautiful, and judging productions which come before him by a new standard."[5] Although Carnegie developed a degree of aesthetic appreciation for fine art, in general art remained some-thing to be classified and judged by him. Except for a growing sentimentality for Scotland, he still lacked the emotional depth to be moved in a spiritual way by an artist's inspiration—his callous spirit wouldn't allow it—and he never collected art like J. P. Morgan and other haute capitalists. He was too thrifty to spend money on priceless art and too priggish to grace his home with reclined nudes by European masters.

The various cultures Carnegie encountered were to be studied, too. "In France, all seems dead," he wrote home. "The soil is miserably farmed, and one is at a loss to account for the leading position which the Gauls have attained. I am one of those who hold that they cannot maintain it long—that they must give way to the German element which, you know is Anglo-Saxon and therefore has the right 'blend.'"[6] Again, it wasn't a spiritual experience, but a scientific one. His determination that the Anglo-Saxon had "the right 'blend'" suggested an unsavory Aryan streak in Carnegie's personality that would manifest itself more clearly as he came to view himself as a trustee of civilization and became enamored with Kaiser Wilhelm II in the early 1900s.

Political debates were unavoidable among the group. So sure was Carne-gie of his positions on various matters, Franks observed, that "on all questions grave or otherwise, Andy is ever ready 'to back his own opinions with a wager' as Byron says. . . . What with the arguments we have upon most questions, social, political, etc., Andy brimming first upon one side, then upon the other, with admirable impartiality, and possibly to keep the balance even, it must be confessed, that upon the whole we make up a tolerably lively party." Carnegie had become an admirable orator and debater, his skills honed in Mr. Phipps's leather shop on Sunday afternoons, his mind expansive and agile enough to dissect an issue from opposing viewpoints.

While the young men took in the sights of London, Paris, Antwerp, Ams-terdam, Dresden, Vienna, Naples, and Pompeii, and as they attended plays and operas and sipped lemonade at outdoor cafés, they kept an eye on busi-ness matters back home. "The boys are elated by glorious news in their letters of continued advances in prices, of stocks advancing, of their mills working double turns, of large orders pouring in, of new patents obtained and of still greater successes looming in the future," noted Franks.[7]

Reports of success didn't stop Carnegie from pushing brother Tom ever harder on all fronts as though a general commanding an army, albeit a one-man army:

> We must pull up and develop the Union Mills sure. . . . How is the Brick concern doing? . . . Am glad to see you are pushing around after trade, but my dear boy, the South is our future market. The Freedom Iron Co. made most of its profits from Southern trade. . . . I beg to urge upon you the

Harry Phipps, Andrew Carnegie, and John Vandevort
toured the European continent for five months in
1865–1866, leaving Andrew's brother, Tom, to handle
business in Pittsburgh. (Courtesy of the Carnegie
Library of Pittsburgh)

importance of sending a first class man to Nashville, Memphis, Vicksburg, etc. at once. . . . Will you please carry out these views regardless of expense of anything else? . . . The Carnegie family, my boy, are destined always to be poor, but I am poorer than I expected if $8,000 in debt. We must work like sailors to get sail taken in. . . . What about Pit Hole? My interests there requires your attention, I think.[8]

The brothers' relationship had not evolved. The twenty-nine-year-old Andy still played the bullying big brother to twenty-one-year old Tom, and with an eight-year spread in age their relationship would never be on equal ground. While emotionally insensitive to his brother's needs, Carnegie did view himself as protector of the family and their assets. As for Tom, he appeared content with being subservient; but, in fact, he was often outraged by his brother's behavior, only to internalize his feelings. To assuage his anger and sadness, he took to drink.

Thomas Carnegie would forever be smoothing over the feathers his elder brother, Andrew, ruffled. (Courtesy of the Carnegie Library of Pittsburgh)

By November 1865, Tom mustered up the courage to question his brother's prolonged absence in a letter of rebuke. Carnegie attempted a conciliatory response that came across as patronizing; he noted that the more he drank in the enjoyment of being in Europe, the more he appreciated Tom's "devoted self-denial." He continued: "It is a heavy load for a youngster to carry, but if you succeed, it will be a lasting benefit to you. Talk to Mother freely; I always found her ideas pretty near the right thing. She's a safe counselor, safer than I, probably, who have made money too easily and gained distance by carrying full sail, to be much of an adviser when storms are about, or sail should be taken in."[9] His admission of making money too easily was true, discounting his days in the cotton factory and bobbin mill, as prizes from Tom Scott had simply fallen into his lap. And while he didn't know when to take in sail, instead always pushing ahead, extending himself, it was this unwillingness to allow economic and social forces to determine his business course—a classic trait of the gambling entrepreneur—that defined Carnegie's early business career.

Even while vacationing, Carnegie sought moneymaking opportunities. During the war, Edgar Thomson had experimented with all-steel rails imported from Europe, and Carnegie had overseen their installation at Pittsburgh. The rails proved too brittle for the mainline where trains moved at higher speeds, but they did last over a year on the sidings, easily justifying the high price the

British firms exacted. The idea of steel replacing iron gnawed at Carnegie, so while he was in London in 1865, he, along with Dod, investigated iron rails capped with steel, manufactured with a new process invented by Englishman Thomas Dodds. The product was called doddized rails. If the reports proved true, these rails were stronger and cheaper than the rails with which Thomson had experimented. Carnegie realized doddized rails could be a major windfall for him, but in reporting the extremely intriguing find to his more conservative brother he promised to make no hasty investment.[10] The initial interest quickly escalated, however, and while Carnegie's friends traveled through Switzerland, he returned to London to open negotiations in earnest with Dodds to secure the exclusive American rights for the use of the Englishman's patents.

While in London, he developed an attachment to the city, writing his mother, "I wish I knew the ropes and points in business affairs in London, as well as I do in the Iron City. I would certainly try to persuade the family to come there and try it for a while at least. . . . How would you like to try a residence near Hyde Park, eh? Or if Tom *will* insist on getting married (a very proper thing to do), he might run the machines in America and I do the foreign business. Seriously, however, I am quite taken with London and would like to spend a year or two there."[11] London not only offered the first underground railway, opened in 1863, but was far more cosmopolitan than smoky Pittsburgh. The city was teeming with intellectual power, fueling debate on scientific, social, and theological issues. Stirring the kettle was Karl Marx and his comrade Friedrich Engels; philosopher John Stuart Mill, author of *On Liberty* (1859) and *Utilitarianism* (1863), who was serving his first year in Parliament; Charles Darwin, who was updating his seminal *On the Origin of Species by Means of Natural Selection*; and Herbert Spencer, a sociologist and philosopher, who believed in the preeminence of the individual over society and science over religion. Spencer took the idea of evolution and adapted it to sociological theories—comparing society to an animal organism—creating the theory known as social Darwinism. In his *Principles of Biology* (1864), he coined the phrase "survival of the fittest," a term embodying a philosophy Carnegie would later adopt with great enthusiasm.

For the moment, Carnegie was concerned with ingratiating himself with Dodds and his partners. His magnetic personality and power of persuasion were difficult to fend off, and Dodds succumbed to giving him the American rights to his patents without a shilling changing hands. "Have had to exercise every whit of my business ability to convince these gentlemen that it was far better to give our party their patents without any cash down than to get 5,000 pounds gold from others," Carnegie crowed in a letter home, "but I have succeeded, and feel repaid for the three weeks I have lost in Switzerland."[12] Aligning his own triumph with America's prosperity, Carnegie added, "I may reasonably expect to be able to 'do the States some service,' as it will be a great gain for America if we can do what I think we can. I have made a number of valuable and pleasant acquaintances in London during the time."[13] Carnegie, whose interest in manufacturing processes for iron and steel first emerged on this trip, subsequently visited ironworks in Prussia, at Ruhwort on the Rhine, and at Magdeburg.

On returning to the United States in the spring of 1866, Carnegie worked diligently to bring Dodds's steel-faced rails to his adopted country. Before the patents were even validated, he organized the American Steeled Rail Company to manufacture doddized rails. In early 1867, samples were shipped to Thomson at the Pennsylvania Railroad for testing. Thomson's report in March was anything but sanguine, as initial tests suggested the rails were unsafe for heavy loads; and in a second letter that month, he reinforced his position: "Private—a word to the wise . . . The experiments made in relation to the strength of the Doddized Rails has so much impaired my confidence in this process that I didn't feel at liberty to increase our order for these rails. . . . the process is not a success."[14] Carnegie's blind optimism and tendency to plunge into affairs got the better of him, and so, still dreaming of a windfall, he failed to heed Thomson's advice.

Carnegie continued to write enthusiastically to potential customers that "all looks favorable" and offered to send specimens that will speak for themselves.[15] Not until a number of irate customers returned the rails did he abandon the project, whereupon—quite adept at shifting culpability—he placed the blame on Dodds.[16] The failure stung, and he was so disenchanted that when Tom Scott approached him about investing in a chrome steel process, Carnegie demurred: "My advice (which don't cost anything if of no value) would be to have nothing to do with this or any other great change in the manufacture of Steel or Iron. I know at least six inventors who have the secret, all are so anxiously awaiting. . . . That there is to be a great change in the manufr. of iron & steel some of these years is probable, but exactly what form it is to take no one knows. I would advise you to steer clear of the whole thing. One will win, but many lose & you & I not being practical men would wager at very long odds. There are many enterprises where we can go in even."[17]

The one positive take-away from Dodds's experience was that Carnegie recognized his own power of persuasion, his skill as a salesman. With his storytelling skill, his ability to fall in and out of a Scottish brogue, and his earnestness, he was downright charming. As he sought to further expand his investments and garner more personal power, he would need that charisma in confronting two men who offered formidable obstacles. One was William Orton, the calculating president of Western Union; the other was George Pullman, the supremely arrogant founder of the Pullman Palace Car Company.

In 1867, Carnegie refocused on what he knew best, telegraphy and railroads, in divining treasure to be had. These were enterprises where he could "go in even," in the words he had used with Scott. In the telegraph industry, a little game was being played with telegraph bully Western Union, the game exemplifying the age's cult of opportunity, and Carnegie decided to have a go. Western Union's own greed perpetuated the game, which was modeled after the David and Goliath fable. Instead of trying to kill Goliath, the idea was to become a nuisance in Western Union's path by starting a rival concern and exacting a toll in the form of a payoff or buyout, before stepping aside. Organized in 1856 and determined to consolidate the industry, Western Union immediately began absorbing competitive firms entrenched in key cities, such as Carnegie's old firm, the Atlantic and Ohio Telegraph Company. After the Civil War, which proved how indispensable the new technology was by aiding the two armed forces, expansion accelerated. At times, the shopping spree appeared almost indiscriminate, and it was now that enterprising businessmen realized an opportunity to profit by starting rival firms that were invariably purchased by Western Union at a premium.

Carnegie, who owned Western Union stock, was well aware of how profitable the business was, so it was a logical step for him and sundry associates to join the game in 1867 by organizing the Keystone Telegraph Company. Chartered on April 9, Keystone telegraph's initial capital was set at $50,000 with one thousand shares issued. Again playing the role of venture capitalist, Carnegie, along with Thomson and Scott, invested in the company but did not take an official management position. He did, however, secure a key advantage for the company from his friends at the Pennsylvania Railroad: the right to string two wires along the railroad's poles running from Pittsburgh to Philadelphia for a nominal fee per mile. Before Keystone ever strung a wire or sank a pole, the company was approached not by Western Union, but by another large player, the Pacific and Atlantic Telegraph Company (P&A). Impressed with Carnegie's connections with the railroads and hoping that he could arrange similar deals as he had with the Pennsylvania, the Pacific and Atlantic offered a swap of six thousand of their shares, valued at $150,000, for Keystone's one thousand, tripling the value of Carnegie's company without a pole being planted.[18]

Fast becoming a wily business veteran, Carnegie aided the negotiations, consummated in September 1867, and was able to arrange for his friend David McCargo to be made the P&A's general superintendent, which gave him a strong ally in the company's upper ranks. For himself, Carnegie arranged a deal whereby he would manage the installation of the wires along the Pennsylvania's line, but he didn't want to be paid in cash. Instead, the ravenous accumulator of stock was paid $3 of stock for every $1 of construction cost.[19] Not only was he willing to sacrifice a short-term gain for a long-term windfall, but he comprehended that stock equated to power, the power to control a company and men, which thrilled him more than the jingle of money. Sacrificing short-term monetary gains for power and riches down the road was a technique he would use repeatedly.

The P&A's president, George H. Thurston, happened to be playing the game with Western Union. Determined to challenge the Goliath, he was anxious to have agreements in place for stringing lines to Chicago, St. Louis, and other major cities by the end of the year. To achieve these goals, he turned to Carnegie in hopes the energetic Scotsman could secure agreements similar to those he had with the Pennsylvania with other railroads. "Aware of the great assistance you rendered the officers of the Corporation in bringing to a successful conclusion the negotiations with the Keystone Tel. Company," Thurston wrote with lavish flattery, "I am anxious to secure your services in negotiations with other rail road Co. . . . You can open and conclude for us many advantageous negotiations, in less time and, upon perhaps more favourable terms, then the immediate officers of this corporation."[20]

Knowing he would be well compensated with additional shares in the company, Carnegie accepted the task with bravado: "The end you aim at is a great one & it will require much time and attention to accomplish it; I know if once arrived at, you will have one of the most prosperous enterprises of the day."[21]

Now was the time to provoke Western Union, a battle relished by Carnegie, who always rooted for the underdog. However, he quickly discovered not all arrangements with the railroads for stringing lines were easily negotiated. For those railroads fully or partly owned by the Pennsylvania, he merely had to write to his friend Scott, as he did concerning the placement of two wires on poles owned by the Terre Haute & Vandalia Railroad Co.[22] (The P&A awarded Carnegie 2,913 shares for his work on this negotiation.) Other railroad executives, fearing reprisals from Western Union, were not so easily convinced. Chicago & Great Eastern Railroad president W. D. Judson, for one, was hesitant, forcing Carnegie to argue his case vigorously as he demanded the same privileges offered Western Union, which was to string wires along the railroad lines for a moderate fee. "Our list of Stockholders embraces many of the prominent business men in the various cities with which we connect . . . ," Carnegie wrote with a hint of intimidation, and even alluded to possible legal action "to place us upon equal footing & let us fight it out."[23] The veiled threats worked and Judson relented; however, he unequivocally stated that his company would not be liable for any damages if Western Union were to sue the P&A. That was exactly what Carnegie hoped for—to attract Western Union's attention—and he thrived on invading the larger company's turf, setting up his bid for the big payoff. In the interim, he pocketed a good profit as the P&A paid 37.5 percent dividends in its first three years. But those high dividends didn't last because Carnegie's incursion into Western Union territory stalled.[24]

Little did Carnegie know that he was up against a tough competitor in the former commissioner of the U.S. Internal Revenue Service, Mr. William Orton. Described by Carnegie's former superior at the Atlantic and Ohio Telegraph Company, James Reid, as having "an intellect unusually alert and keen, and of an industry which was earnest almost to ferocity," the native New Yorker had risen in three years from collector of internal revenue in

New York City to the federal post.[25] While in that position, Orton befriended some very powerful businessmen; after less than a year in Washington, Orton was offered the presidency of the United States Telegraph Company. He took the job, engineered a merger with Western Union in April 1866, and then a year later was handed the presidency of the Goliath. As for the competition, gnats like Carnegie's Pacific and Atlantic were to be dealt with accordingly.

Although Carnegie had proved adept at using a mix of charm and veiled threats to convince railroad officials to allow the company to string telegraph lines along existing poles, management issues at the Pacific & Atlantic threatened the plan to force Western Union to buy the company. Growth had stalled and earnings were erratic, fluctuating wildly between $3,700 and $10,000 a month, issues Carnegie was oblivious to until his well-placed ally David McCargo sounded the warning. The two old friends began to mull over the possibility of Carnegie seizing control of the company. Convinced that Thurston, the company's president (and shyster, according to McCargo), was trying to force him out, a vulnerable McCargo appealed to Carnegie: "You must come to my rescue. Don't address me at my office as my letters might be opened through surveillance I am under by my Asst. who is ready to do any dirty work for the parties named. If they could get a catch on me. Be very careful with these figures. Don't show to anyone. I write this at my house."[26]

It was Carnegie, now a powerful shareholder in the company by taking payment in stock, who forced out Thurston in early 1873. In his place, W. G. Johnston was made president. With the change, some of the Pacific and Atlantic executives wanted to rekindle the battle against Western Union, but Carnegie understood the game was over. Supremely confident in his salesmanship, he covertly approached Orton and his representatives to gauge their interest in absorbing the Pacific and Atlantic. The two parties reached an agreement in which Pacific and Atlantic shareholders could exchange six of their shares, then trading at $12, for one of Western Union, then at $85.06, or a profit of $13.06 for every six shares.[27] For Carnegie, who had taken stock for payment of services, this was indeed a windfall, but it wasn't enough for the avaricious gamesman. Now, with McCargo's and Johnston's help, he engaged in insider trading by quietly buying Pacific and Atlantic stock before news of the profitable exchange was made public. Insider trading was not yet illegal, and during this period in history businessmen wrote the rules as they went. It was a free-wheeling time during which the clever predator enjoyed excessive successes that were never to be enjoyed again. It was a dangerous gamble on Carnegie's part, however, because an overcapitalized and overextended Western Union could renege on the deal at any moment and leave him with a pile of worthless stock certificates.

In early May, Carnegie halted his purchases, and before the month was out, the news of the exchange was made public. By the third week of May, dozens of requests from stockholders were pouring in, all wanting to capitalize on Western Union's deep pockets. Thomson, owner of 450 shares, submitted his request on May 23 and expected no delays.[28] Other close business associates and friends also demanded immediate attention. Carnegie, who had hoped for an orderly process, was spooked by the sudden avalanche, and on June 3 he wrote to Orton, alluding to trouble with Pennsylvania Railroad executives and making his own request for expedience.[29] He could only wonder if Orton detected a hint of desperation in his words; and he could only hope that invoking the powerful Pennsylvania Railroad would help. If he and McCargo were stuck with sizable amounts of stock—or other important parties, for that matter—it wouldn't just be a major embarrassment: it would be a financial disaster.

In the first few weeks of the exchange, chaos reigned, but Western Union pulled through, with Thomson for one receiving his Western Union shares and promptly selling them at a profit.[30] Then, as the days progressed, the process bogged down. Pacific and Atlantic president Johnston warned Carnegie that he'd better take care of friends first, but "others who have no claim on friendship should be informed that you cannot do anything for them."[31] Johnston and McCargo were also still pushing to buy more Pacific and Atlantic stock, as long as "we can have a speedy exchange effected."[32] As much as Carnegie would have liked to profit more from the exchange, the avalanche of requests continued through June, and he had a number of brokers riding his back who had to be satisfied first.

By September, Carnegie was forced to acknowledge to stockholders that he could no longer help them. Somewhat deceitfully as he was wont to do, he shifted the blame; this time from himself to a change of management at Western Union.[33] As for McCargo, who had first warned Carnegie of trouble in the upper ranks, he was left without a job. Loyalty never forgotten, Carnegie worked to find his old friend a job. In a letter to Pennsylvania Railroad executive George Roberts, Carnegie praised his old friend: "For integrity and devotion to his duties he is unsurpassed, and I feel quite sure if when you are in want of a man such as is here indicated, you will have cause to congratulate yourself, should you appoint Mr. McCargo."[34] What was so maddening about Carnegie was that one minute he was a deceitful trader profiting at others' expense, and the next he was demonstrating a righteous quality such as loyalty. He was imbued with qualities one despised and adored.

Another opportunity to display his deft salesmanship and to profit from insider trading arose when Carnegie clashed with George Mortimer Pullman, a Chicagoan who was intent on making his fortune in the sleeping car business. Born in 1831 and raised on a farm south of Buffalo, Pullman took over the family's building raising and relocation business when his father died in 1853. Like Carnegie, he was the family breadwinner, supporting his mother and three younger siblings. To find jobs, he started traveling as far as Chicago, which had become a major grain reception point by the mid-1850s, and he eventually moved there.

On a visit to Buffalo, he paid for a berth in the sleeping car, but he found it cramped and poorly ventilated and the bed uncomfortable, which prompted him to enter the industry. An independent soul who—again like Carnegie—hired a substitute to serve in the Civil War, Pullman didn't give a damn about patents and incorporated many of T. T. Woodruff's inventions into his own sleeping cars. Where Pullman excelled was introducing plush luxury to his car's design, which, in 1865, the *Daily Illinois State Register* declared was "superior to any that we have ever inspected."[35] Although Pullman's Palace Car Company was blocked from expanding east by the Central Transportation Company, which counted Carnegie and Pennsylvania Railroad executives among its major shareholders, Pullman solidified his position in the Midwest by selling shares of his company to railroad executives located in the Chicago area. There was one prize on the horizon he keenly eyed: the right to operate cars on the nearly completed transcontinental line, divided between the Union Pacific in the east and the Central Pacific Railroad in the west. Of course, he was not the only one interested in securing a juicy deal.

Andrew Carnegie was busy securing contracts with various railroads on behalf of the Central Transportation Company. He was also preparing his pitch for the Union Pacific officials, who had summoned to the St. Nicholas Hotel in New York all those interested in bidding for the right to operate sleeping cars on their transcontinental line. Confident that his company's size, experience, and connections through Scott and Thomson would carry the day, Carnegie was surprised to discover that George Pullman was in New York and being given equal consideration. What Carnegie didn't know was that the Union Pacific's vice president, Thomas C. Durant, had been a passenger on one of Pullman's cars and was so impressed he had made it his personal car. On finally meeting Pullman face-to-face, Carnegie quickly assessed his competitor, a strapping man with dark, piercing eyes and a bushy beard falling to his chest. "He was, indeed, a lion in the path," reflected Carnegie.[36]

He considered his options: he could go head-to-head with Pullman or, perhaps, negotiate a partnership with him. The best solution, he decided, was to create a separate and entirely new company jointly owned by Central Transportation and Pullman. One evening, after a round of meetings with the Union Pacific officials, Carnegie *just happened* to mount the broad staircase in the St. Nicholas Hotel at the same time as none other than George Pullman. "Good-evening, Mr. Pullman!" he said charmingly. "Here we are together, and are we not making a nice couple of fools of ourselves?"

Pullman played it coy. "What do you mean?"

Carnegie explained that to obtain the Union Pacific contract they were both offering sacrifices that would hurt their respective firms in the future, even if they were to win.

"Well," Pullman said, "what do you propose to do about it?"

"Unite. Make a joint proposition to the Union Pacific, your party and mine, and organize a company."

"What would you call it?" he asked.

Thinking quickly, Carnegie knew the way to Pullman's heart was to play on his vanity, just as he had with his playmates in Dunfermline when he allowed them to name rabbits after themselves. "The Pullman Palace Car Company," he said.[37] (It would be called the Pullman Pacific Car Company.) The idea of a partnership was a unilateral decision on Carnegie's part—he had not conferred with Central Transportation executives—but he was displaying that same willingness to accept risk that he had when taking the death message years ago. It was this willingness to stake it all on a single roll of the dice that would eventually yield unheralded riches.

Pullman agreed to the plan, but now Carnegie had to win approval from the Central Transportation executives, including President Otis Childs, who was not pleased. In fact, he was preparing to bring suit against Pullman for patent violations. Scrambling to save face, Carnegie proposed that the partnership agreements include compensation from Pullman for use of the patents; after all, he reasoned, a legal battle could become protracted and give Pullman time to win other rich contracts, thus providing the funds to pay any fines levied against him. Childs and company acquiesced, but then Pullman refused to consider several propositions concerning compensation. Childs was now determined to take him to court. Anxious to resolve the matter, in May 1867 Carnegie warned Pullman that the case against him was strong and insisted it was time for him offer a proposal for compensation or face the consequences. He then suggested a royalty arrangement for settling the dispute.[38] Just like the early iron adventures with Kloman, Phipps, and Miller, Carnegie had a foot in each camp, straddling a delicate situation that could turn against him with a wrong word or action, this time using his knowledge of Childs's position to help Pullman find a solution. Carnegie didn't think of himself as a Benedict Arnold aiding the enemy; instead, he viewed himself as a facilitator of peace. He believed that such conflicts were ludicrous when everyone could be profiting.

Finally, Pullman agreed to pay $20,000 for use of the patents, and the Pullman Pacific Car Company was organized that summer. To everyone's consternation, Pullman didn't pay the $20,000 and, ignoring Carnegie's offer of "sage counsel & advice," went about his business of organizing the new company as he saw fit.[39] Almost a year later, Carnegie was under increasing pressure to resolve the matter, so he wrote Pullman an imploring letter, which included a warning: "The Central Transportation patentees notify me they now wish this matter closed. Please let me hear how you propose to arrange it."[40] Pullman was too busy pouring money into construction to heed Carnegie's plea; in fact, the brazen sleeping car baron demanded money from Carnegie, who, having agreed to buy his share in the company through installments, currently owed $6,400. Along with the money, Carnegie sent a note: "It is difficult to imagine how you require so much money *all at once,* or indeed how we can judiciously put $400,000 into Cars to equip 1200 miles of line through the desert—I fear your anticipations of business upon it are not to be realized. However you know better than I. I only hope your estimates are correct."[41] For once, Carnegie feared he was in over his head. And he was, for this drama played out simultaneously with the Keystone Telegraph venture, on top of his interests in iron and bridge building.

George Pullman, who was determined to triumph over the Central Transportation gang, had never trusted Carnegie, Childs, or Woodruff; and when Childs initiated a patent infringement lawsuit against him in 1870 he knew his instincts were correct. Of course he invited the suit by not paying the $20,000 fee. At this time, Central Transportation was in a strong position—the company had recently recapitalized at $2 million, and the stockholders had realized an 18 percent return on investment in 1869—so both Pullman and Carnegie knew the infringement suit had the potential to be lengthy and costly.[42] Also, Carnegie continued to receive grief from Childs for originally agreeing to the $20,000 that was yet to be paid, so by early 1870 he wanted to wash his hands of the whole affair.

Quietly, Carnegie and Pullman opened negotiations with the former presenting two options: consolidate their sleeping car companies, or have the Pullman Pacific Car Company lease the rolling stock, franchises, equipment, and patents from Central Transportation. At the January 31, 1870, Pullman stockholders' meeting, it was agreed that the company would lease Central Transportation for $264,000 a year for ninety-nine years. In addition, the Pullman board issued a bonus of three thousand shares of stock to Richard Barclay, the alleged trustee of the Central Transportation negotiators, for distribution.[43] Barclay was the front man for Carnegie, Scott, and Thomson, so it was highly unlikely anyone but those three benefited from the stock. Also, Carnegie and Scott immediately began buying more Pullman stock, which was bound to rise once the announcement of the leasing arrangement was formally made. On signing the lease agreement, Central Transportation president Childs and the other stockholders, whom Carnegie mockingly derided as "the cautious old men in Philadelphia," were finally pleased with his performance; it certainly involved deft statesmanship. When they considered that their company realized net earnings of just over $250,000 for the fiscal year ending in August 1869, a $264,000-a-year lease was a solid victory. Carnegie had made amends for his prior failure.[44]

This triumph and the sellout to Western Union had involved quite a circus act, from juggling knives to leaping through rings of fire, but instead of moderating his investment philosophy after these treacherous episodes and enjoying the fruits of victory, Carnegie forged ahead. Building on his success, he became more brazen in speculating on businesses associated with the railroads.

CHAPTER 9

Bridges to Glory

C arnegie was certain his destiny lay among the lions of Wall Street. During negotiations with George Pullman and the Union Pacific, he had been seduced by New York City, the preeminent financial center in the United States. In late 1867, he decided to move there, to take up residence in a city ruled over by the notorious "Boss" Tweed and his Tammany Hall cronies, as well as Wall Street scoundrels like "Jubilee" Jim Fisk and Jay Gould.

"No large concern could very well get on without being represented there," he later wrote, explaining his decision, and he had grand visions of an empire, no doubt.[1] In New York, the streets were awash with money, and there was ample opportunity for him to secure more lucrative contracts for his iron and bridge-building concerns, as well as to capitalize on investment prospects not available in Pittsburgh. The move also made sense for the Carnegie family because it amounted to a divide-and-conquer maneuver, with Tom overseeing affairs in Pittsburgh. Another motivating factor in Carnegie's move was that New York, like London, was alluringly cosmopolitan, had a strong intellectual presence, and offered a plethora of music, opera, and theater, among other arts agreeable to him. Tom, who had finally married Lucy Coleman, took the Homewood house, while Andy, who got to keep Mom, took up residence on lower Broadway in the plush St. Nicholas Hotel, which had greatly impressed him when there for the Union Pacific meetings. He rented an office at 19 Broad Street and a hung a sign on the door: Investments. That said it all, except that a year after his move an episode suggested Carnegie harbored doubts about the direction his life was taking.

Precisely four years after his first crisis of conscience, when he had sought a consular position in Scotland, a second crisis attacked Carnegie. In December 1868, he penned a surprising letter to himself: it was wrought with introspection as he questioned the purpose of his existence; it was a desperate attempt to reconcile his Scottish past with his American present; and it was a violent reaction to what he discovered in Gomorrah, the underside of Gotham, his newly adopted city.

The Christmas holiday season was in full swing and the St. Nicholas Hotel shone, itself a spectacular ornament. Promoted as "the largest house of public entertainment in the world," the six-story hotel boasted six hundred rooms. Behind the white marble facade rising above Broadway were Carrara stairways and balustrades, fluted Corinthian columns, crystal gaslit chandeliers, lofty frescoed ceilings, walnut wainscoting, hot running water, central heating, steam-powered washing machines, and a telegraph in the lobby. There was even an army of private detectives to protect the clientele from prying eyes and unwanted visitors. Here Carnegie and his mother were ensconced in adjoining apartments, pampered by servants on duty in the hotel's opulent parlors and stately dining room. But as Carnegie sat at his desk on that cold December night and evaluated his various business endeavors and portfolio, the sparkling opulence faded and a certain year-end melancholy took hold.

There was little satisfaction as he scribbled down his investments, noting the number of shares, dollar holdings, and income from more than twenty concerns. His personal assets were $400,000 that year, yielding a bountiful return of over $56,000.[2] The top money winner was the Union Mills, which generated $20,000, while income from an old favorite, the Columbia Oil Company, had fallen to $2,000. Despite the material triumphs, something nagged at him. He wasn't satisfied, and after completing his financial review, he mulled over his station in life. It was, he knew, of singular dimension: money. With deliberate penmanship, reflecting Carnegie's deep reflection and forethought, he concisely expressed his thoughts:

> Dec. '68
> St. Nicholas Hotel
> N York

Thirty three and an income of 50,000$ per annum.

By this two years I can so arrange all my business as to secure at least 50,000 per annum. Beyond this never earn—make no effort to increase fortune, but spend the surplus each year for benevolent purposes. Cast aside business forever except for others.

Settle in Oxford & get a thorough education making the acquaintance of literary men—this will take three years active work—pay especial attention to speaking in public.

Settle then in London & purchase a controlling interest in some newspaper or live review & give the general management of it attention, taking a part in public matters especially those connected with education & improvement of the poorer classes.

Man must have an idol—The amassing of wealth is one of the worst species of idolitary. No idol more debasing than the worship of money. Whatever I engage in I must push inordinately therefore should I be careful to choose that life which will be the most elevating in its character. To continue much longer overwhelmed by business cares and with most of my thoughts wholly upon the way to make more money in the shortest time, must degrade me beyond hope of permanent recovery.

I will resign business at Thirty five, but during the ensuing two years, I wish to spend the afternoons in securing instruction, and in reading systematically.[3]

Shouted were these words as he reflected, dreamed, coaxed, and berated himself: "spend . . . surplus . . . for benevolent purposes"; "get a thorough education"; "education & improvement of the poorer classes"; "no idol more debasing than the worship of money"; "money . . . must degrade me beyond hope of permanent recovery"; "resign business at Thirty five."

A simple breakdown of the letter revealed both his internal turmoil and a template for living to purge his self-doubts. In the letter's opening line was a simple statement of fact: he was rich. But then Carnegie's thoughts immediately turned to philanthropy—not in the way of a charitable donation here and there, but as a continuous process, like running a business. Philanthropy as a business was a unique, bold, and gratifying concept to him, totally foreign to a world inhabited by the likes of Tom Scott. To complement the enrichment of others, he would further improve himself, too, by seeking a better education, a desire lost in his pursuit of material progress. Then, in the letter, he added the clause on public speaking. Why? So he could effectively take his message, whether it be on benevolence or improvement of the poorer classes, to the people as did his uncle Tom Morrison, a renowned public speaker. Also toward that end, like his hero Horace Greeley, Carnegie dreamed of owning a newspaper to serve as a platform for championing the lower class—only it was to be in London, a city that embodied culture and offered a stronger connection to his Scottish heritage than New York ever could. In this enlightened course of life, words and money would be his weapons.

Ah, money. Carnegie was surrounded by it at the St. Nicholas, yet in the second half of his meditative letter he spurns it, condemns it, and fears it. Not too long ago, however, he himself had worshiped money. He had gloated over his wealth to his friend Tom David. He had told Dod that his cousin's desire to win fortune was a noble resolution. He had reveled in the pleasures and comforts money brought. He had believed his accumulation of the material reflected America's grand progress. Not now. Yes, man must have an idol, he knew that, but not mammon. Carnegie's voice was pleading as he feared money would forever corrupt him, destroy any shred of his radical heritage, and he would become degraded beyond hope. Sadly, he recognized that no matter what course of life he pursued, he was condemned to always push inordinately—he must to avenge his father and to please his mother—so he had to be very careful to choose a dignified path.

Just as his flitting to New York raised so many questions, so did this letter. Why the radical change in perspective? Did Carnegie really mean what he wrote, or was he just being too hard on himself in a year-end fit of melancholy? Was it reactionary and impetuous? J. Pierpont Morgan and John D. Rockefeller were incapable of writing such a note, according to historian Joseph Frazier Wall, "nor would they have understood the man who did."[4] So where did Carnegie's contemporaries stand in 1868? Rockefeller was on a relentless march to conquer the oil-refining business, and his personal life was well grounded, too. Four years earlier, he had married Laura Celestia "Cettie" Spelman, and, with their relationship mutually supportive, he never hesitated to write her a letter about his latest triumph.[5] As for the philanderer Morgan, a refined banker's son, he was fast becoming a pillar of Wall Street; moreover, in autumn 1868 the Morgan family, which included two children, rented a house on Fourteenth Street for $5,000 a year.[6] In contrast to Carnegie, both Morgan and Rockefeller were secure in their respective industries and quite settled at home, and there was no impetus for them to question their purpose.

Perhaps, after a year in New York, Carnegie simply missed Pittsburgh and his friends there, which forced emotions to the surface. He readily admitted his defection to New York was not easy: "The change was hard enough for me, but much harder for my mother; but she was still in the prime of life and we could be happy anywhere so long as we were together. . . . For some time the Pittsburgh friends who came to New York were our chief source of happiness, and the Pittsburgh papers seemed necessary to our existence. I made frequent visits there and my mother often accompanied me, so that our connection with the old home was still maintained."[7] Spiritual emptiness was certainly a factor; after all, Tom had married and was starting his own family, while Carnegie remained a bachelor, pampered and bullied by an overbearing mother. The notion of passionately loving a woman remained alien to him, except for the complicated bond with his heroic mother. Mother and son remained inseparable, she a haunting reminder of his father's failure and the driving force in his metamorphosis from bobbin boy to capitalist. Because he could only equate love to his mother, love was a platonic thing without physical desires. In fact, carnal love was repulsive to him, for as one of his close business associates reflected years later, "Carnegie frowned on anything savoring of the flesh and the devil."[8] Not that the puritan had much spare time for wooing, anyway. Like one of his other heroes, J. Edgar Thomson, who didn't marry until late in life, Carnegie was continuously traveling and deeply immersed in the man's world of railroads and iron. Still, having a spouse was a piece of life Carnegie missed and began to explain why he desired the contrary: a semimonastic existence studying at Oxford and becoming acquainted with literary men. But there had to be even more behind the radical letter.

New York City also inspired much of Carnegie's severe backlash against money. Pittsburgh had its share of corruption and seedy politicians, and Carnegie was aware that his mentor Scott was prone to cross the line of fair business dealings; and yes, Carnegie had dabbled in speculating before the railroad and insider stock trading. But all of this was nothing close to the scale of political corruption and crooked business ventures he discovered in New York. While he was not a churchgoer, the city truly appeared to him not as Gotham, but as Gomorrah, the biblical city of sin upon which the Lord rained brimstone and fire.

With the postwar Reconstruction under way, money poured in from foreign lands as international bankers sought high returns from American industrialists thirsting for capital at any cost; money poured in to feed the steel buffaloes racing across the Great Plains; money poured in to develop the West and spur mining, lumbering, and cattle ranching; and money poured into the burgeoning brokerage houses that after the introduction of the stock ticker, patented in 1867, began to proliferate. Opportunities for spectacular get-rich-quick schemes were also plentiful, especially in railroad stocks. Dirty speculators continuously knocked on Carnegie's office door. "I was besieged with inquiries from all quarters in regard to the various railway enterprises with which I was connected," he recalled. "Offers were made to me by persons who were willing to furnish capital for investment and allow me to manage it—the supposition being that from the inside view which I was enabled to obtain I could invest for them successfully. Invitations were extended to me to join parties who intended quietly to buy up the control of certain properties. In fact the whole speculative field was laid out before me in its most seductive guise." The stock-market games played in 1867 and 1868 by Daniel Drew, Jim Fisk, and Jay Gould were particularly galling, especially their attempt to seize control of the Erie Railroad from Cornelius Vanderbilt, who was attempting to monopolize New York State railroads. It became known as the Erie War.

And then there was Boss Tweed, who made money both on stock manipulation and from bribes. He epitomized the New York government's corruption, which embarrassed the city's elite. In 1868, a prominent lawyer and diarist, George Templeton Strong, noted: "To be a citizen of New York is a disgrace. A domicile on Manhattan Island is a thing to be confessed with apologies and humiliation. The New Yorker belongs to a community worse governed by lower and baser blackguard scum than any city in Western Christendom."[9] New York had once been called the London of America, and that was what Carnegie was naively expecting. Instead, the sin of New York pricked his social conscience, which had been so calloused in Blackstock's and Hay's factories, and he was suddenly inspired to lift mankind up.

But first he was resigned to working for two more years to ensure his financial independence. Then what? Would he be able to adhere to his proclamations? Would there still be a need? After all, New York did have a pleasant upside that might entice him and compromise his resolutions. As he and his mother strolled through the streets, they encountered all the luxuries affluence could buy. A. T. Stewart's new department store at Broadway and Ninth Street was the coup de grâce for shoppers. The five-story structure, built with cast iron and painted white, boasted two thousand panes of French glass windows and Venetian-style arches, and it served customers with an army of five hundred clerks and cash boys. R. H. Macy was busily expanding his four-story shop at Fourteenth and Sixth; toys could be had at F. A. O. Schwarz; suits at Brooks Brothers; and books at Brentano's, including Horatio Alger's first rags-to-riches novel, *Ragged Dick,* published in 1867.

The American Museum of Natural History would open in 1869 and the Metropolitan Museum of Art in 1870, providing Carnegie with some of the culture he craved. A favorite pastime he could indulge in for now was horseback riding in scenic 843-acre Central Park, which, after the Civil War, had become the fashionable place to walk, ride, and drive. To reach the park, he was able to take a public omnibus from Wall Street, passing by the square, squat, fortresslike Croton Reservoir on Fifth Avenue and Forty-second Street, the future site of the magnificent public library. At the park, he was introduced to many strong-willed, independent women who relished riding and would suit Carnegie perfectly as a wife. Perhaps prior to his self-imposed exile to a monklike existence in Britain, he would find a fine woman there among the throngs.

Two years to retire. In that time Carnegie would "push inordinately" to achieve complete financial independence and he would focus his efforts on the two firms in which he held a sizable interest: the Piper and Shiffler bridge-building concern and Union Mills. His second-biggest earner in 1868, after Union Mills, was Piper and Shiffler, which brought in $15,000, and he had grand visions for the operation. From New York, he tracked proposals to build bridges across the mighty Mississippi—at St. Louis and other points—which had yet to be breeched by the railroad, and eagerly anticipated bidding on each. Much of the multimillion-dollar financing of these projects originated in New York, and Carnegie diligently sought out the men involved and ingratiated himself before the bids were requested. After all, winning the contracts to build such bridges would not only be lucrative, but would represent monuments to man's ingenuity, to the progress of America, and to the river itself, eulogized by Mark Twain in *Life on the Mississippi.*

Carnegie dreamed of the Piper and Shiffler Company building glorious structures spanning America's mighty rivers and canyons, intertwining himself with the land as well as conquering it. Beginning to fully assert himself in the everyday management of the firm, two years prior he had insisted on a reorganization to boost its capital to support expansion and proudly renamed it the Keystone Bridge Company—after Pennsylvania, the Keystone State. It was incorporated on May 16, 1865, and capitalized at $200,000. Tom Scott bought one-half of Carnegie's $80,000 allocation but kept it in his protégé's name, while Thomson held about 5 percent of the stock in his wife's name.[10] By securing relatively independent financial strength through investors like Thomson and Scott, Carnegie enjoyed a freer hand in managing his companies than men indebted to banks or Wall Street. He was free to make quick decisions and take sweeping action without answering to anyone first, which often gave him the upper hand on competitors; he could lowball a bid or make costly capital improvements without reprisals.

Carnegie's superb instinct of attaching himself to talented men—Kloman and Piper, among others—also served him well, but he knew he was the spirit that brought them together and gave them direction. It was his vision, optimism, determination, and resourcefulness that attracted these men like moths to a light, and through good-natured cajoling and ferocious demands he brought out the best in them. Carnegie's Keystone partners, however, were overwhelmed with work and were not so enthusiastic about pursuing large, complicated projects. With no patience for those unable to keep the pace, Carnegie wrote a blistering letter to President J. H. Linville, whom he thought spent too much time in Philadelphia as opposed to Pittsburgh: "The truth is Mr. Linville that you are wanted here to organize the concern, make it capable of doing an extensive business, divide the duties among competent heads & require each to attend to his own department. . . . It is proposed to have a meeting of the board Thursday week to discuss matters fully & determine upon a course of policy to be pursued.—I trust you will be present."[11]

Five days after his pointed critique, he sent a long letter to Linville and the directors, demanding investment in plant and equipment to expand their bridge-building capacity and to prevent any potential competitors from gaining a foothold. "Should we be unable to bid upon any of the several large bridges soon to be contracted for," Carnegie thundered, "we will give one of them the desired opportunity & hereafter may calculate upon a rival to cut down future profits."[12] As for upcoming bids, Carnegie had the Mississippi bridges in mind, and he concluded his letter with an exhortation in favor of expansion, pointing out that their industry was still in its infancy and that a mere $40,000 investment could double their firm's revenue to $600,000. There laid another dimension to Carnegie's genius: never taking a narrow view and pushing an idea to its full potential.

Carnegie's drive paid off less than a year later when on December 10, 1868, he signed the coveted contract with the Keokuk and Hamilton Bridge Company to supply a superstructure to span the Mississippi River, connecting Illinois with Iowa. When Carnegie later said that this was his most important project since moving to New York, he was not exaggerating; he was involved at all levels.[13]

To begin, Carnegie was compensated for his personal services in overseeing the project with sizeable chunks of stock in the Keokuk and Hamilton Bridge Company, and he would eventually become the company's president. The bridge company, of course, had signed with Keystone, which in turn subcontracted work to Union Mills, where Andrew Kloman's mechanical genius greatly aided developments in shaping beams and cutting precise pieces for bridges. But now, in yet another dimension, not only was Carnegie responsible for building the bridge, but he took on the added responsibility of managing the construction of the railroad that would cross it. He was like an octopus, wrapping each arm around a tasty morsel as each new project offered new opportunities.

Backed by Scott and Thomson, Carnegie organized the Iowa Contracting Company to build a railroad from Keokuk through southern Iowa to Nebraska City, where it would connect with a line being built from Lincoln, all of these lines partly owned by the Pennsylvania Railroad, now a gorged behemoth. Naturally, Carnegie's Iowa Contracting Company would also subcontract to Union Mills for the iron rails, stakes, and sundry needs. Completely engrossed in his industrious and industrial web, Carnegie neglected to inform brother Tom of all his actions, so when Tom received an order for iron rails from some unknown outfit called the Iowa Contracting Company, he balked at filling the order until he knew if the company's credit was good. To ascertain more on the firm, he wrote to his brother's personal secretary, Gardner McCandless. Humored by the inquiry, McCandless responded, "We consider the company good. . . . We would add that such men as Messrs. J. Edgar Thomson, Thos. A. Scott & c & c are interested in the building of the road, and the Treasurer of the Company is a reliable New York gentleman, a Mr. Andrew Carnegie with whose name you are perhaps not unfamiliar."[14]

Keystone, having just completed a 320-foot span across the Ohio River as well as winning the Keokuk contract, now enjoyed national prominence—precisely what Carnegie desired for himself.

Although the Keokuk Bridge was 2,300 feet long, it didn't require the engineering ingenuity required for the St. Louis Bridge, making the latter the prize Carnegie would continue to pursue for the next two years. A bridge across the Mississippi at St. Louis required an unparalleled engineering feat of sinking two piers in the middle of the river, which measured 1,500 feet wide at this point, with 225,000 cubic feet of water rushing by every second.[15] To finance the construction, St. Louis–area businessmen eager to encourage local trade formed the St. Louis and Illinois Bridge Company and hired Colonel James B. Eads as their chief engineer. The Civil War veteran, a slight figure but with great physical strength like a lithe jungle cat, designed a colossal bridge that was to be a 54-foot-wide two-deck roadway—a highway above and two rail lines below—with a spectacular center arch 515 feet long resting on two piers, and two additional spans of 497 feet that would connect with each shore.[16] The crucial ingredient was high-quality steel.

It took Eads time to solve the challenge of sinking the two piers in the middle of the Mississippi, but he eventually discovered the solution on a trip to Europe, where he learned about French engineers using caissons, sealed chambers of compressed air with open bottoms that rested on the water's bed, to allow the men to work underwater. In October 1869, the first caisson was floated into the Mississippi and construction on the east pier finally started. With construction successfully under way on the project's most difficult segment, the St. Louis and Illinois Bridge Company could now consider bids for the superstructure and seek capital to complete the project.

Carnegie's patient courting of Eads paid off as Keystone won the contract in February 1870. Financing the project, which was to cost more than $5 million, was now the main obstacle that the directors of the St. Louis and Illinois Bridge Company solved by deciding to sell bonds, just like the railroads did. When Carnegie read the published reports that $4 million in first-mortgage bonds were to be sold in New York and London to finance the completion of the St. Louis bridge, he pounced on the opportunity. Having proved himself the consummate salesman in peddling iron, bridges, and sleeping cars, why not bonds? With Thomson and Scott's backing, he approached the chairman of the bridge company's executive and finance committee, William Taussig, with a proposal that he sell the bonds for a commission of $50,000 in St. Louis and Illinois Bridge Company stock.[17] Again, Carnegie was willing to sacrifice a short-term gain in cash for a higher long-term bonanza, a fantastic profit considering $50,000 was as much as he had made in all of 1868. Taussig agreed. With letters of reference tucked away, Carnegie sailed for London to penetrate the hallowed halls of finance and to curry favor with the redoubtable Junius Morgan, a rising American banker operating out of London who excelled at selling U.S. investments to Europeans. This marked the beginning of a brief but wild career as a bond salesman.

Peddling bonds was initially a delight, thus setting false expectations, as Morgan graciously received Carnegie at his fashionable London office at 22 Broad Street. With skeptical, light-blue eyes set on either side of a substantial nose crowned by a prominent forehead, the six-foot-tall Morgan was softening in the middle, but the banker remained a vigilant, hardmouthed, and brooding study in reserve. As he listened to the little Scotsman, it was difficult to resist Carnegie's charm. The ebullient salesman described the monumental bridge, its significance to local trade, and the tollgate that would generate generous profits for the St. Louis and Illinois Bridge Company. Nothing before had been so glorious to Carnegie than this selling of America to Britain.

Using bonds to pay for a bridge was an entirely new concept, but Morgan was intrigued with such a "novel" project, and submitted the papers to his lawyers for review. After they scrutinized the terms, he requested a number of necessary changes before he would agree to handle the floating of the bonds.[18] "You told me that you were going up to Scotland," Morgan said. "Write your people and get the changes made and stop by here on your way back to America. If the changes are put through satisfactorily, I will buy some of your bonds." That meant a five- or six-week time period, and Carnegie, the consummate salesman, had no intention of "allowing the fish to play so long."[19] Instead, he made good use of the transatlantic cable, which had been laid in 1866, and two days later he surprised Morgan by having the approved changes in hand. Before a week passed, he was able to report home that Morgan, who appreciated the young man's resourcefulness, had agreed to take at least $1 million of the offering. This transaction was his first with European bankers, and while there would be others, none would be so straightforward. Not all men were as honest as Morgan, or as easily sold.

Fresh on the heels of his triumph with Junius Morgan, Carnegie, with the usual suspects of Thomson and Scott backing him, created yet another inter-locked business venture, modeled on the Iowa Contracting Company, that involved the construction of a railroad from Davenport, Iowa, to St. Paul, Minnesota. In 1871, the trio was the driving force in forming the Davenport and St. Paul Construction Company, with Carnegie appointed treasurer and charged with selling bonds in Europe to finance the project. There was a complication, however, that would lead to serious trouble: the company's client, the Davenport & St. Paul Railroad, wanted to survey and select the route.

Even though the road was to run through flat land parallel to the Missis-sippi, Carnegie was wary of the railroad's ability to handle the task, so to watch his flank he hired an old Allegheny City friend, William H. Holmes, as a consulting engineer to help determine the best route. Holmes and the rail-way's president, Hiram Price, immediately came into conflict. In a lengthy February 1871 letter, the handwriting a smudged scribble, Holmes warned Carnegie that an impatient Price was pushing ahead with grading a 135-mile stretch with little thought to making provisions for feeder lines. (Knowing his friend Andy expected perfection, Holmes added a postscript concerning his penmanship: "I am ashamed of the looks of this but it is written in a cold room in a printing office with smutty fingers.")[20]

As pressure was put on Price that spring to conform to Carnegie and his allies' desires concerning the railroad's route, he denounced the Pennsylvania crowd as "a pack of adventurers"—increasingly a truthful statement. By June, Carnegie and Holmes decided Price should be forced out. He did indeed resign; but Scott, while acknowledging there were lots of problems "out there," was not ready to accept the resignation. Because Price had been instrumental in handing them the project, Scott believed he deserved better treatment. Before the summer was out, Scott finally acknowledged Price had blundered in laying plans for key connections and accepted his resignation. As a some-what objective observer, Holmes was "mystified" by the manner in which Thomson, Scott, and Carnegie handled the Price affair—indecision was not the way to run a railroad—but Holmes was not attuned to the politics of money behind certain deals.

A change of management did nothing to correct the grading and line connections blunders that caused delays and cost money. By late 1872, the situation was so bad that Holmes asked Carnegie to exonerate him from any responsibility, which Carnegie did. But, for surreptitious reasons, he also warned Holmes against speaking out on the matter. Carnegie had good cause for suppressing the mismanagement: he was attempting to sell $6 million in bonds for the Davenport & St. Paul Railroad, which were guaranteed by the Pennsylvania Railroad, to finance the railroad construction, and nasty rumors would squelch any deal.

When Sulzbach Brothers, an investment-banking firm in Frankfurt am Main, Germany, expressed interest in floating the Davenport bonds, Carnegie sailed for Germany in the summer of 1872. The Sulzbachs were immediately suspicious of the interlocked venture. Many of the officers of the construction company were also the officers of the railroad, making the organization incestuous enough for the bankers to demand another guarantor of the bonds besides the Pennsylvania. The firm of Drexel, Morgan agreed to the added responsibility, with J. Pierpont Morgan taking charge.

Morgan immediately voiced impatience with the Sulzbachs' questions and delays and with Carnegie for not closing the deal promptly. He demanded of the latter, "Don't let's have any more slip ups if they can be avoided. . . . Don't leave Frankfort again till all O.K."[21] Still, in November 1872, after Carnegie had spent several months bouncing from Germany to Switzerland for relaxation, to Scotland for family visits, and then back to Germany, the negotiations continued to drag. The German firm expressed further concerns about the progress of the railroad, stating that "we should be much obliged to you by your procuring us some information about present conditions of the Davenport line, how many miles are completed and operating, when the entire line is expected to be finished and all this sort of thing; also earnings gross & net."[22] Finally, the Sulzbachs agreed to take $3 million; but as for the remaining balance of $3 million, they hesitated. In May 1873, the firm again voiced concerns over the health of the railroad, suspecting that Carnegie had not been completely forthcoming as to the facts. Also, considering 150 miles of the line had already been built, the Sulzbachs thought the sale of the first $3 million in bonds would cover the completion of the road, so when Carnegie started pressing for the balance to be sold, the bankers became even more suspicious. A note from Carnegie suggesting Sulzbach Brothers was unnecessarily concerned did little to assuage its fears, and the banking firm responded with a blistering letter: "Although you say herein that the Davenport matters should not trouble us too deeply, we must confess that they really do." The Germans, feeling insulted, demanded to know why construction had halted and why "you don't give us even any notice of it and had it not been for our inquiries we would not even know the present condition of affairs."[23]

Was Carnegie deliberately hiding trouble at the railroad to protect his own financial gain? Not if he expected to pursue future bond sales. He was quite concerned with his image and refused offers to sell bonds he considered too speculative, as he did for a mine development concern in Utah: "It would not do for me to try London on any mining scheme. I must stick to my role of first class steady-going Security man—very adverse to anything speculative, or 'too good.' Among the class I have been dealing with you frighten if anything much beyond six per cent is talked of."[24] Also, the railroad business continued to boom, and all associated with it breathed an air of invincibility. Carnegie was certain any difficulties could be overcome and the project would prove profitable. To ensure success, he spent a good deal of time in Davenport in 1871—so much so that his mother came for a visit, and the rising Napoléon of business provided his queen dowager with a tour of the area. Certainly her (omni)presence bolstered his moral conscience if it was beginning to wander, and certainly he would never allow his mother to visit a place where she might be exposed to a den of thieves.

To ease their concerns, the Sulzbachs demanded that Carnegie and his friends take $1.5 million worth of the remaining bonds to inextricably tie them to the railroad's success; in other words, if it failed, they'd all go down together. In yet another salvo, the German firm took aim at the Pennsylvania and Carnegie's reputation, ominously hinting that they would be sullied if the Davenport railroad were not completed satisfactorily: "You also have the greatest interest to see the matter arranged taking the question from the moral point & we count therefore upon your good services, reminding you of your pledge to protect & to promote our interest."[25]

After years of taking on numerous and complicated ventures, Carnegie was now stretched too thin—a ball had finally dropped—for the Davenport & St. Paul would indeed fail after the financial panic of 1873, and Carnegie would feel the wrath of the Germans. This interlocked venture would haunt Carnegie for over a dozen years.

While Carnegie found himself entangled on a number of fronts in the early 1870s, bridge construction continued at a hectic pace. Yet another opportunity emerged in the Great Plains, one that would prove more financially disastrous than the Sulzbach Brothers deal. On February 24, 1871, the Bridge Act of Congress authorized the issuance of $2.5 million in 8 percent gold bonds to finance a bridge spanning the Missouri River at Omaha. Thomson and Pierpont Morgan were made two of the three Bridge Bond trustees, and they turned to Carnegie to handle the bond sales.[26] Because the bridge would fill the last gap in the Union Pacific and Central Pacific's jointly built transcontinental railroad network, linking the western with the eastern lines, it was a noteworthy project. No longer would the railroad have to rely on ferries in the summer and temporary tracks across the ice in the winter. As with other bridge deals, the tolls would pay off the debt. What Carnegie didn't know was that a small group of Union Pacific executives were planning to use the proceeds from the bonds he sold to pay off personal debts and loans they had accrued in trying to keep the financially troubled railroad afloat. One director, Cornelius S. Bushnell, hoping to even profit from this new issue, bought a sizable block of the bonds and then made independent arrangements with

Carnegie to resell them at a profit. Independently, Bushnell also arranged for Carnegie to sell an additional $1 million to $3 million worth of other Union Pacific bonds.[27] The money was siphoned away as quickly as Carnegie sold the bonds, of course, and he discovered nothing remained to pay his commission. Greed had gotten the better of Carnegie, who should have been far more wary of dealing with the Union Pacific.

The dastardly situation in which Carnegie found himself originated when President Lincoln championed a transcontinental railroad and the necessary legislation was passed for subsidizing the construction with land grants, federal bonds, and loans. The Union Pacific Railroad was charged with building the line westward from Omaha, Nebraska, while the Central Pacific would build eastward from Sacramento, California. The Union Pacific's first board of directors included J. Edgar Thomson, Cornelius Bushnell, Brigham Young, and Thomas C. Durant, the railroad's chief, among others. Durant, however, never believed the Union Pacific would yield a cent of profit. He was, from the start, intent on making a fortune off the actual construction of the road.[28] The fact that the government was willing to subsidize the construction and guarantee loans made to the Union Pacific provided the perfect opportunity for a good, sound fleecing.

To achieve his ignoble goal, Durant organized an independent construction company to which the railroad would then subcontract the construction and called it Crédit Mobilier of America, a fancy-sounding name that hardly suggested a company whose sole mission was to drain the Union Pacific of its capital through excessive overcharging. Yes, Durant and his cronies used their construction company to steal from their own railroad. To keep the money flowing, they floated more and more Union Pacific bonds and stock, thus overcapitalizing the company while slinking out the back door with Crédit Mobilier wheelbarrows full of money. This relationship between construction company and railroad, with the interlocking directorates, was identical to what Carnegie set up in Davenport, and this fleecing scenario was precisely what the Sulzbachs feared. Both construction companies charged a premium for services—only in Carnegie's case, planning and construction blunders appeared to siphon off most of the money, not a pack of scoundrels like Durant and his associates.

Durant's scheme was so bold that as early as 1868 Congress was threatening to investigate alleged corruption. To preempt an investigation, Union Pacific officials offered key congressmen large blocks of the company's stock gratis or at severe discounts; included on the gift list were both of U. S. Grant's vice presidents, Schuyler Colfax and Henry Wilson. The well-timed bribery squelched news of the looting for the moment, but by 1869, certain Union Pacific officials were so disgusted with themselves, with the company, and, in particular, with Durant's extravagances that they forced him out. Then, in September 1870, Grant appointed a new attorney general, Amos T. Akerman, whose first initiative was to demand that all government-subsidized railroads repay accrued interest on subsidy bonds and make interest payments semiannually going forward, rather than waiting until the thirty-year bonds matured. Union Pacific executives, after reviewing the company's ledgers, realized they could not make the payments, so Bushnell, the railroad's president, Oliver Ames, and others pooled their finances and loaned the company money, with Bushnell personally arranging for and endorsing more than $600,000 in short-term loans from New York banks.[29] Wall Street was not so kind and pummeled the stock. Seeing an opportunity to extend the Pennsylvania Railroad's franchise, Thomson and Scott quickly purchased blocks of Union Pacific stock. (Pullman and Carnegie already had been given and had purchased sizable amounts due to the sleeping car connection.)

Union Pacific's financial situation became so precarious that in early 1871 Bushnell traveled to Philadelphia to seek Thomson's help in extricating the railroad from its troubles. He proposed that Thomson use Pennsylvania Railroad securities to obtain another sizable bank loan. After some negotiating, Thomson agreed. Carnegie was selected to handle the transaction, but before he approached the New York banks to facilitate the loan, Thomson invited him to his Philadelphia home, an imposing mansion designed in the Greek-revival style. Almost twenty years had passed since they had first met: now Carnegie was entering his prime, still youthful looking with his blond hair thinning only slightly at the temples; in contrast, the heavyset Thomson was showing his years, with his face baggy and pliable, his gray hair receding halfway across his skull. A crucial moment was upon these men, one still seeking glory, the other a final and fitting crown. Thomson divulged the sensitive nature of Carnegie's task: if a loan could be arranged, it would give the Pennsylvania Railroad the necessary leverage to seize control of the Union Pacific, greatly extending its franchise. There would be pecuniary benefits for him, too.

Once Carnegie secured the loan, Thomson demanded collateral from the Union Pacific, which he received in the form of thirty thousand shares of Union Pacific stock with a par value of $3 million. As an added bonus, the Union Pacific gave Thomson, Scott, Carnegie, and Pullman, who had also aided the transaction, the option of buying any or all of that stock at any time.[30] They promptly did at severely discounted prices—and those shares, along with their previous purchases, gave them de facto control of the Union Pacific. Thomson's plan had worked. On March 8, 1871, an ambushed Ames resigned. Scott was made president of the railroad, while Carnegie and Pullman joined Thomson as directors. It was a major triumph for Carnegie, who was suddenly elevated into his foremost position of power. It was about this time that he was hired to sell the Omaha Bridge bonds. He had to have been aware of Durant's fleecing and the railroad's still precarious financial situation, but he couldn't ignore the chance for another windfall.

Meanwhile, the railroad industry decried the Pennsylvania Railroad's coup and its now extensive control of transcontinental traffic. Wall Street, on the other hand, approved, and the Union Pacific stock began a steady climb higher. As it did so, the opportunity for a quick capital gain was hard to resist.

Using several different brokerage firms to mask the sizable sales, Scott and Carnegie, who personally controlled eleven thousand shares, started selling theirs and Thomson's Union Pacific shares in early spring of 1871. By late May, all but four hundred shares had been sold, leaving each participant with one hundred shares each—and a tidy $80,000 profit.[31] The other Union Pacific stockholders were hardly amused and charged the foursome with selling the loan collateral for their personal profit.

In March 1872, Carnegie, Scott, and Thomson were expelled from the board; only Pullman, who still held a sizable stake, survived. For Scott, it was particularly embarrassing and finger-pointing ensued as to who was to blame for initiating the sale. Carnegie later noted that "the transaction marked my first serious difference with a man who up to that time had the greatest influence with me, the kind and affectionate employer of my boyhood, Mr. Scott."[32] Needless to say, when it came time for Carnegie to recover his Omaha Bridge commission in the fall of 1871 and early 1872, he carried little goodwill, and his requests were summarily dismissed by Bushnell, other Union Pacific executives, and even Thomson.[33] Then, in the fall of 1872, the New York Sun broke the Crédit Mobilier scandal, exposing how the company had reaped up to $16.5 million in profits while bribing Congress by freely distributing stock. The paper estimated that James A. Garfield, a future president, and James G. Blaine, a future secretary of war and Carnegie ally, received between two thousand and three thousand shares, respectively.[34] The public was outraged; congressional hearings commenced, although it was difficult to find enough innocents to serve; and any hope of Carnegie recovering his money was now gone. "I had never been so cheated and found it out so positively and so clearly," he reflected with somewhat tainted righteousness. "I saw that I was still young and had a good deal to learn. Many men can be trusted, but a few need watching."[35]

Throughout the early 1870s, Carnegie was also engaged in a fast-paced game of speculation, personally buying and selling the very bonds he was peddling, as well as stocks. The pace became ever-more frantic as he purchased bonds and stocks on margin to bolster his profits. The high degree of risk was apparent in Carnegie's anxious tone in a letter to Thomson's personal secretary, Richard Barclay, written as he scrambled to cover a loan from Drexel, Morgan: "Mr. Scott and I have decided that you sell the Eleven hundred and thirty six shares of Pennsylvania Railroad Stock which you hold as trustee for us jointly, and remit me Seventy thousand dollars, in time to meet our note for that amount, falling due at Messrs. Drexel, Morgan & Cos., Saturday Nov. 11th. Matters of deeper interest than this loan depend upon its being paid, and under no circumstances must you fail to remit me the amount in time."[36] Not only were profits at stake, but so was Carnegie's relationship with Morgan, Scott, and Thomson. There was no margin for error.

Carnegie was frenetic to the point of being manic as he pursued, created, and promoted moneymaking deals. Thomas Miller was amazed by all of the "things" his friend was into in "those active years," and later in life, Carnegie himself was surprised and had to be reminded of them all.[37] On top of his sleeping car, oil, iron, telegraphy, and bridge enterprises, as well as his stock speculation, he participated in land deals with the McCandless family, in coal mining with Robert Pitcairn, and invested in a coal machinery patent, among other ventures. He was making investments for his immediate family, relatives, and even friends from the Slabtown days who were now counting on him. Carnegie wanted "to make Uncle Lauder comfortable in his old age from his American investments," and he was managing investments for the Hogans, as well as for the families of Original Six member James R. Wilson and Leila Addison. And, of course, there remained his mother to please, and his brother to protect.[38]

Sadly, it would be many years before he realized the dream laid out in the December 1868 letter. When the day of reckoning knocked in December 1870, the day Andrew Carnegie was to retire from active business on his own terms and pursue a more noble life, his introspective letter was tucked safely away, but no concrete plans had been laid. For now he was making over $100,000 annually, and it was no time to relent—certainly not while accepted in the world of Junius Morgan. And yet the harder Carnegie pushed into high finance, the more repulsed he was by deceitful men and deals gone bad due to any number of uncontrollable factors. In this realm, he did not have command of his own destiny. Fate was pulling him away from the likes of Morgan and pushing him toward steel.

CHAPTER 10

Epiphany of Legend

There was one other factor in Carnegie's decision not to retire, not to abandon America for Oxford, England: he was now living a privileged, cultured life in New York City. Carnegie had ingratiated himself with the Gramercy Park crowd, as dynamic a social group as could be found anywhere. Located between Third and Fourth Avenues and Twentieth and Twenty-first Streets, it was an upper-class enclave of homes built mostly in the 1850s and owned by prominent New Yorkers such as Peter Cooper, George Templeton Strong, and Cyrus Field. One resident and wealthy businessman with whom Carnegie became well acquainted was Courtland Palmer. Like Carnegie, Palmer aggressively pursued a balanced, humanistic approach to life and founded the Nineteenth Century Club, a group dedicated to discussing the social, religious, and philosophical issues of the day. Much more than the friendly Sunday debates in the Phipps cobbler shop, Palmer's Nineteenth Century Club was likened to a "religious cult" that preached positivism.[1]

This philosophy was championed by Auguste Comte, who espoused a new social order, a "sociocracy" ruled by scientists whose mission was to oversee the progress of humanity. Such words as *sociocracy* and *progress* struck a chord within Carnegie, and once admitted to the club he became a faithful member. The monthly meetings were held in the Palmers' home for many years, and then moved to the American Art Galleries. Much discussion circled around the provocative Herbert Spencer, and to bone up for the debates, Carnegie immersed himself in Spencer's *First Principles* and *Social Statics*. Many of the ideas he encountered—in addition to the survival of the fittest dictum—he would live by and apply throughout his life.

In *First Principles*, Spencer addressed evolution, which he observed to be "a change from a less coherent form to a more coherent form," which meshed well with Carnegie's obsessive demand for an ever-more efficient organization. Other poignant ideas Carnegie culled from *Social Statics* included Spencer's argument that the growth of the race depends on "partly weeding out those of lowest development, and partly by subjecting those who remain to the never-ceasing discipline of experience"; and his hypothesis that "society advances where its fittest members are allowed to assert their fitness with the least hindrance, and where the least fitted are not artificially prevented from dying out."[2] These ideas had a profound impact on how Carnegie conducted his life, manifesting themselves in how Carnegie dealt ruthlessly with his competition, his workers, and even his philanthropy. There was no room for sympathy.

Among the socialites, Carnegie met a particularly intriguing woman when in 1871 he befriended Anne C. L. Botta. An author and a critic, Anne Botta was a figure of consequence in New York's literary and art circles, making her quite an attraction. In her younger days, she had presided over soirees attended by literati that included Ralph Waldo Emerson, Margaret Fuller, Washington Irving, Bayard Taylor, and Edgar Allan Poe—the latter having recited "The Raven" in her drawing room prior to its publication. Now it was a different crowd that gathered in her home, but no less eminent, including the likes of Henry Ward Beecher, Edmund C. Stedman, Julia Ward Howe, as well as eminent newspaper and magazine editors. Carnegie was quite enamored with Madame Botta even though she was white haired and nearing sixty years of age. Just as he had taken to Tom Scott's niece Rebecca and Leila Addison as maternal tutors, so did he to Madame Botta, whom he described as a "lithe, gentle little woman."[3] She was affectionate and nurturing, qualities not readily attached to his mother. At soirees in her parlor, she found the rambunctious, seemingly contradictory radical-capitalist a curious case; and although Carnegie could be overbearing, his enthusiasm for mental stimulation won her over. They remained friends until her death twenty years later. "One of her chief characteristics was that of recognizing unknown men and women," he acknowledged, "and giving them opportunities to benefit, not only from her own stores of wisdom, but from the remarkable class she drew around her."[4]

So Carnegie, even at age thirty-five, still sought a woman other than his mother to satisfy his needs for warm nurturing. To a friend, he admitted he was eager to retire and take a wife, but he had yet to secure a woman who could fill that role.[5] Mostly it was because the bride-to-be had to measure up to his mother—an impossible standard to meet, even with her flaws. Carnegie himself, now settled into his routine of being a single man, had raised his own expectations. Impatient friends prodded him to marry, but instead of discussing candidates, he complained that the older he grew, the more particular he became. "Yes Andrew," one female companion retorted, "and the less desirable."[6]

Carnegie was not completely caught up in New York's trappings. At the same time he was penetrating the circles of the elite financiers and literati, to escape New York's sticky summer heat he purchased a summer retreat—a simple frame house christened "Braemar Cottage"—nestled in the Allegheny Mountains at Cresson, Pennsylvania. Fresh air cascaded down the hills and through the valleys, of which the cottage had a commanding view. Here, away from the clatter of hooves and carts and shouting paperboys, away from the smell of rot and burning coal, and away from the mass of people scurrying hither and thither, Carnegie rejuvenated. Many of Pittsburgh's industrialists, including B. F. Jones, had been going to Cresson for years, and the elite community was also another means for extending his business network.

There he befriended William J. Holland, who later became the director for the Carnegie Museum of Pittsburgh. They first became acquainted while taking a meal at the Mountain House, the upscale hotel where most of the cottagers dined. "We sometimes adjourned together to the assembly room and had merry discussions there," Holland recalled.

> He often called at our cottage and we called at his. He was then, as always, exceedingly fond of music, and among the guests at the hotel were Mr. Josiah Cohen (afterward Judge Cohen) and his charming wife, who was an accomplished musician. Mr. Carnegie now and then invited her to give a musical recital at his home, and, when bidden to attend these pleasant gatherings, we went. Being fond of walking, Mr. Carnegie was in the habit of taking strolls on the by-paths and roads on the mountain, and often he invited me to go with him on these rambles, or I myself extended to him an invitation to accompany me. He was greatly interested in all that we saw, and our conversations on these excursions into the woods related to the plants and animals, especially the birds, in which he took an interest. He informed me that as a boy he had at one time essayed making a collection of bird skins and had read a great deal about birds. On one occasion, I found a number of nests of the Snow-Bunting cunningly hidden under tufts of fern. I called his attention to the fact that this bird of the Canadian life zone was nesting at the top of the mountain. A day or two afterward he came to the cottage and told me that he had had the delight during a stroll of discovering a number of nests of the Junco, and was very enthusiastic in speaking to me about his discovery. "I did it myself," he said. "I did not have your help." He loved "to do things himself" if pleasant.[7]

In every endeavor, large or small, business or ornithology, Carnegie had to push inordinately.

Despite his enthusiasm to dabble in a myriad of ventures, whether business, philosophic, or scientific, by late 1872 Carnegie recognized that scattering his efforts and attempting to score quick windfalls was not the way to build an empire. He was beginning to understand what would later become one of his mantras: "Put all good eggs in one basket and then watch that basket."[8] In explanation, he wrote, "I believe the true road to preeminent success in any line is to make yourself master in that line. I have no faith in the policy of scattering one's resources, and in my experience I have rarely if ever met a man who achieved preeminence in money-making—certainly never one in manufacturing—who was interested in many concerns." Hindsight helped, of course. He now turned to steel.

But this decision was *not* an epiphany, as legend has it. Over the years, a myth evolved about how Carnegie had a sudden flash that steel would replace iron, that steel was king, and how he immersed himself full steam ahead. His entry into steel, however, was cautious and calculating. Not quite the visionary he was depicted, Carnegie had been following developments in steel ever since the mid-1860s, when J. Edgar Thomson invested in steel rails and he experienced his own doomed affair with doddized rails. He was well aware that the first steel produced in the United States using the Bessemer process had been made at a mill in Wyandotte, Michigan, in 1864, but the plant had been shut down five years later. A second company, the Albany and Rensselaer Iron and Steel Company of Troy, New York, gave it a go in 1865. Two years later, so did the Pennsylvania Steel Company, which erected its works in Steelton, Pennsylvania.

On his overseas trips to sell bonds, Carnegie made it a point to meet with British manufacturers of iron and steel. One man who fascinated him was Henry Bessemer, a renowned inventor and ironmaster. During the Crimean War, Bessemer had experimented with iron, hoping to improve it for casting cannon. As with so many great advances in science and technology, he then accidentally stumbled upon a process for making steel. One day, some molten iron was exposed to gusts of cold air purely by chance, and when he studied the effects, he realized he was onto something: the rush of air combining with the molten iron and carbon had increased the iron's temperature to such a degree that impurities were oxidized, burned off, making for a far stronger product—steel. Bessemer, who would be knighted in 1879 for his accomplishments, set about inventing a process to replicate the accident, which involved building a converter, a huge, egg-shaped container lined with fire brick into which the molten iron could be poured and then a blast of air blown in from below. He then applied for and was granted an American patent in 1856. But because making steel by this method required a high-grade, phosphorus-free iron ore, it was still a number of years before his process was perfected.

When Carnegie visited Bessemer at his Sheffield steelworks in the spring of 1872, the inventor was fifty-nine years of age. As Carnegie often did, he practically worshiped the accomplished older man. He was extremely impressed by the Bessemer process and the steel plant; it was far more successful than the struggling efforts he had witnessed in the United States. Although it was still a noisy, dirty, and hot business, the wonder of steelmaking was more alluring to him than that of iron. It involved an attraction best described by John Fitch, a social worker who, even in exploring the underside of the steel business, couldn't help but be impressed: "There is a glamor about the making of steel. The very size of things—the immensity of the tools, the scale of production—grips the mind with an overwhelming sense of power. Blast furnaces, eighty, ninety, one hundred feet tall, gaunt and insatiable, are continually gaping to admit ton after ton of ore, fuel, and stone. Bessemer converters dazzle the eye with their leaping flames. Steel ingots at white heat, weighing thousands of pounds, are carried from place to place and tossed about like toys. Electric cranes pick up steel rails of fifty-foot girders as jauntily as if their tons were ounces. These are the things that cast a spell over the visitor in these workshops of Vulcan."[9] So, while names like Morgan and Rothschild intoxicated Carnegie, the power of fire and molten iron was also alluring. Powerfully so.

As Carnegie stood before the dazzling Bessemer converter, the white ingots glowed in his eyes and the heat of the blow inflated his five-foot-three-inch frame until he was as big as President Ulysses S. Grant. He felt a surge of power, of enthusiasm, of confidence that steel would indeed replace iron, and he became determined to build a majestic steel mill. This 1872 visit with Bessemer finally convinced him of what Bessemer had comprehended the moment he had discovered steelmaking: "[W]hat a perfect revolution it threatened in every iron-making district in the world was fully grasped by the mind as I gazed motionless at that glowing ingot," Bessemer wrote, "the mere contemplation of which almost overwhelmed for the time."[10] Now that the pioneers had worked out most of the early problems associated with the Bessemer process, Carnegie, who was fond of saying, "Pioneering don't pay," knew the time was ripe to erect a steel mill, for making rails in particular; but if he were going to do it, nothing less than the largest, most advanced mill yet would satisfy him. As he was prone to exclaim when a great idea hit him, he had "got the flash."

Over the years, a debate arose as to whose idea, among the Carnegie crowd, it was to enter the steel business. Carnegie's personal secretary for a time, James Howard Bridge, credited William Coleman, Tom Carnegie's father-in-law, with hatching the idea. Once he had convinced Tom, Coleman then elicited the help of Homewood neighbors and business associates David Stewart and John Scott, while Tom attempted to interest Andrew. According to Bridge, the elder Carnegie was strongly opposed to the project until he visited the Bessemer works.[11] Taking a contrary position was William L. Abbott, who served as president of Carnegie's steelworks for several years. Even though the two parted over strained relations, Abbott claimed entering steel was entirely Carnegie's idea and that his Union Mills partners had little enthusiasm for it. Tom, for example, he said, "did not have Andrew's vast ambition. He was content with a good, prosperous, safe business and cared nothing for expansion. He disapproved of Andrew's sky-rocketing tendencies, regarded him as a plunger and as a dangerous leader. Tom wanted earnings in the shape of dividends, whereas Andrew insisted on using them for expansion. The fact was that Tom, though fraternally fond of Andrew, was temperamentally unsympathetic."[12] Considering Abbott's observations and that Carnegie took the largest financial stake in the steel mill, Andrew Carnegie was the driving force.

On his return from England in 1872, Carnegie traveled to Cresson for a quick rest and then on to Pittsburgh to propose the construction of a magnificent mill for making Bessemer steel. His enthusiasm was unrequited. Carnegie did find one ally, however. William Coleman, although now sixty-five years old, had been following developments in the Bessemer process, too, and had just completed a tour of Bessemer works in the United States, including a successful operation just fifty miles away at the Cambria Iron Works in Johnstown, Pennsylvania. It didn't appear to be such a risky affair: production problems had been resolved; the railroad boom continued; and in 1871 the protective Schenk Tariff put a costly duty on imported rails. Once the venerable Coleman voiced his support, Tom and the others joined.

Before partnership papers were even signed, Carnegie sought a name for the steelworks; after all, names were important to him. He proposed Edgar Thomson to pay homage to the great man . . . and to win his favor for when it came time to hand out profitable steel rail contracts. This playing on vanity, a recurring theme, was the same technique he had used as a child to motivate the neighborhood kids to feed his rabbits and had used in negotiating with George Pullman. All the partners agreed, so Carnegie dashed off a flattering note to Thomson requesting his permission, fawning over him by writing, "we have nothing to say except to assure you that there is not one of our party who is not delighted that an opportunity has arisen through which expression can be given, however feebly, to the regard they honestly entertain for your exalted character & career."[13]

While Carnegie waited anxiously for Thomson's reply, the Articles of Co-Partnership were drawn up, signed, and filed on November 5, 1872; the company would be called Carnegie, McCandless and Company. The partners included Andrew Carnegie, Tom Carnegie, Harry Phipps, Andrew Kloman, William Coleman, David McCandless, David Stewart, and John Scott.[14] Two new additions to Carnegie's iron and steel trade circle were McCandless, a highly respected local businessman whose name they wisely included in the company's to lend the affair more respect; and Stewart, who was president of Columbia Oil and expected to lend his management skills. Once again, Carnegie was surrounding himself with very capable, seasoned men. Capital was set at $700,000, with Carnegie contributing $250,000, much of it from his recent windfall selling bonds. Coleman anted up $100,000 and the other six partners $50,000 each, which left $50,000 to be given to the man who would manage the operation. (To ensure the capital was there to inject in the Edgar Thomson Mill, the original Kloman mill, otherwise known as the Lower Mills of Union Iron Mills, was sold to Wilson, Walker and Company, although Carnegie still held a large interest. A trusted friend, John Walker, was one of the principals.) Considering the average steelworks had capital of

$156,000 in 1869 and $267,000 in 1879, Carnegie's vision was pretty grand indeed.[15] He intended for the steel mill to catapult him into the upper echelon of the country's business elite.

Thomson soured the plans somewhat when he expressed doubts about giving his name to the mill itself because he believed U.S.-made steel rails were not up to par with the "foreign article," and he didn't want to sully his reputation. Tenacious as ever, Carnegie explained who was involved in the affair and argued that this time would be different—their rails would be up to snuff.[16] Brimming with confidence, he also suggested Thomson invest in the affair. Thomson, who knew Coleman, McCandless, and Scott well, reconsidered. On November 14, he wrote his old protégé: "As regards the Steel Works you can use the name you suggest, if the names you sent me are individually liable for its success and as I have no doubt will look after its management. I have no funds at present to invest, having been drained by the Texas & California—and Sanborne's Mexican project."[17] The "Texas & California" Thomson referred to involved a bid by Tom Scott and several other railroad chieftains to build a second transcontinental line by connecting Texas with California and Texas with the Pennsylvania Railroad's lines, and thus the East Coast. Scott had borrowed heavily and Carnegie had invested a small amount, so Thomson "having been drained" should have been a warning signal of events to come.

That fall and winter, Tom Carnegie and his father-in-law scouted property and found a strategic location for the mill about twelve miles outside of Pittsburgh at Braddock's Field, where the English general Edward Braddock had suffered a humiliating defeat at the hands of the French in 1755. Along the north edge of the 107-acre property ran the Pennsylvania Railroad, through the center the Baltimore & Ohio Railroad, and along the southern edge flowed the Monongahela. Considering the importance of cheap transportation, it was indeed strategic. As to who should design and oversee the construction of the Bessemer steel mill, Carnegie was only interested in procuring the brightest man available: the dashing and brilliant Alexander Holley. An 1853 graduate of Brown University, Holley was described as being "fairly Apollo-like in personal beauty," sporting a thick mustache curled upward at each end and wavy brown hair swept back. He had a keen mind, was cultured, and was a prolific writer—all traits that made him extremely attractive to Carnegie. While investigating armor plate and armament in Europe in 1862, Holley had visited Bessemer's works in Sheffield and had become convinced steel was the future. He procured a license from Bessemer and, along with several businessmen, organized Albany and Rensselaer Iron and Steel. As manager of the construction, Holley added a number of refinements and new ideas to Bessemer's work, prompting one observer to note, "Where Bessemer left the process which bears his name, Holley's work began."[18] After Troy, Holley went on to build a Bessemer plant for the Pennsylvania Steel Company and then for Cambria. By the time Carnegie requested his services, Holley clearly knew what was required to build the most technologically advanced Bessemer mill in the world.

Carnegie and his partners were savvy enough to give Holley free reign in the design, and he let form follow function. First he sketched in the railroad tracks and then laid out each building—the converter house with two six-ton converters, the boiler house, the gas generator house, the rail mill—ensuring highly efficient transportation of raw and finished material. After the spring thaw, excavations for the mill's foundations were started at once, during which the men uncovered numerous relics from Braddock's 1755 battle, including bayonets and swords. It was quite an exciting time for both the common laborer and Carnegie.

There was one unforeseen obstacle that threatened not only the construction, but the very survival of the steel mill: a financial panic and the country's first great depression, which would last six years. Over that time, Carnegie would demonstrate his incredible resolve to preclude external conditions from affecting his operations.

That money had become tight Carnegie knew from Thomson, as well as Scott, who both declared they had no funds to invest in the steel mill at Braddock. Pierpont Morgan also recognized credit was tightening; wary of a financial panic, he increased cash reserves and steered clear of any speculative investments. In April 1873, he informed his father, Junius, that he was only floating bonds "which can be recommended, without a shadow of a doubt, and without the least subsequent anxiety, as to payment of interest."[19] The very next month the Vienna stock market collapsed, creating a domino effect that hit Berlin, Amsterdam, Paris, and London—it was a global economy long before most realized it—and European investors dumped their American securities. As for gauging the economy's health, all one needed to know was that in 1872 the railroads had built seventy-five hundred miles of track; in 1875, the year Edgar Thomson was to open, the cash-starved railroads would only build sixteen hundred miles.

Although the economic situation deteriorated dramatically in September, Carnegie, who was still unaware as to how dire the situation would become, felt flush enough to donate $25,000 to Dunfermline for public baths, which were to be built on the site of an old slaughterhouse. It was his first major philanthropic effort, and while notable, he had yet to develop the philosophy for benefaction that would ultimately lead to him giving away more than $300 million. It did make the New York papers on September 6, publicity that didn't sit well with Carnegie's attorney, Lewis Sanders, who dashed off a note to the budding philanthropist: "I see by this morning's Tribune that Mr. Andrew Carnegie a *wealthy citizen* of *this city* has donated $25,000 as a refresher to his native town. How do you expect your lawyer to keep you off jury duty & keep your taxes down when you advertise yourself as a *resident* of

N.Y.?"[20] It appeared that while Carnegie preached American righteousness, he was not so anxious to pay his civic dues. His lawyer's scolding became the least of his problems.

Carnegie was relaxing in Cresson when disastrous news reached him, a day he vividly recalled: "The works were well advanced when the financial panic of September, 1873, came upon us. I then entered upon the most anxious period of my business life. All was going well when one morning in our summer cottage, in the Allegheny Mountains at Cresson, a telegram came announcing the failure of Jay Cooke and Co. Almost every hour after brought news of some fresh disaster. House after house failed."[21] The banking house of Jay Cooke had been trying to keep the Northern Pacific Railroad afloat with a series of short-term loans, but the railroad had finally defaulted. Subsequently, Cooke failed on September 18. Because the company was the government's leading private banker, the event shocked Wall Street. "To say that the street became excited would only give a feeble view of the expressions of feeling," a *New York Times* correspondent reported. "The brokers stood perfectly thunderstruck for a moment, and then there was a general run to notify the different houses in Wall Street of the failure."[22] The ensuing panic forced another fifty-seven investment banks to fail, the stock market crashed, and for the first time ever the New York Stock Exchange closed its doors on September 20. The post–Civil War boom, which had taken a breather or two, now came to an abrupt end.

So very vulnerable to the health of the railroads, Carnegie took two direct hits. The Davenport & St. Paul Railroad, for which he had sold bonds to the very cautious Sulzbach banking house, failed. Seeking vengeance in court, the Sulzbachs, among others, brought suit against the railroad, the construction company Carnegie created to build the road, as well as Carnegie, Scott, Thomson, and the other directors and trustees. Court proceedings would open in 1874 and entangle Carnegie for ten years. More damaging to Carnegie, however, was the tottering financial position of Scott's Texas & Pacific Railroad. The company had to be propped up immediately to pay interest on $2 million in loans or it, too, would fall into bankruptcy.[23]

Scott turned to his Andy for help, explaining that a $300,000 loan was due that Morgan and Company was willing to cover as long as Carnegie joined in the temporary financing. After all that Scott had done for the young man, he was certain Andy would pull through; but Carnegie hesitated and then, to Scott's surprise, declined. "It was one of the most trying moments of my whole life," Carnegie later explained. "Yet I was not tempted for a moment to entertain the idea of involving myself. The question of what was my duty came first and prevented that. All my capital was in manufacturing and every dollar of it was required. I was the capitalist (then a modest one, indeed) of our concern. All depended upon me. My brother with his wife and family, Mr. Phipps and his family, Mr. Kloman and his family, all rose up before me and claimed protection."[24] How self-serving his reflections were and how dependent his partners were on him was up for debate; however, he and his partners were, in fact, financially squeezed—so much so that to raise funds for the steel mill, McCandless had just sold Pittsburgh investment property owned by himself, his son Gardner, and the Carnegie brothers, among others.[25]

Scott now turned to Thomson and asked him to plead his case before Carnegie. The railroad icon was also struggling and was only too willing to approach Carnegie about endorsing the loan. Again the answer was no, that he had no money to cover such a perilous loan. Thomson, who stood to lose about $750,000, wrote Carnegie a second letter, hoping to pressure him into recruiting friends to help.[26] It was to no avail, and the Texas & Pacific went under. The failure also broke the health of both Scott and Thomson and poisoned their personal relationships with each other and Carnegie. "This marked another step in the total business separation that had to come between Mr. Scott and myself," Carnegie sadly reflected in his autobiography. "It gave me more pain than all the financial trials to which I had been subjected up to that time."[27] Carnegie had turned his back on the very men who had given him his start. Despite his claims that he had to consider his family and partners invested in the steel mill, and his contrite reflections on the pain it gave him, Carnegie had betrayed Scott, who suffered a relatively mild humiliation when the railroad went bankrupt.

There was another, murkier reason for his infidelity that can't be discounted. Scott had stolen a girl Carnegie was smitten with. When living in Homewood, Carnegie had fallen in love with a Miss Anna "Annie" Duke Riddle, the beautiful daughter of the owner of the *Pittsburgh Journal.* Intent on a more permanent relationship, Andy told his friend Tom Miller he was going to introduce Miss Riddle to Mr. Scott for his opinion of her.

"Be careful, Andy," warned Miller. "Scott is a handsome man and you are not. If he sees Annie, he'll win her away from you."

"Well, if any other man can win Annie Riddle away from me, he's welcome," rejoined Carnegie boldly. He took her to meet Scott, expecting his mentor to appraise her character and report his findings as though studying another business proposition, but Scott decided Miss Riddle required further evaluation. The two continued to meet on a regular basis. She fell for the handsome, personable railroad magnate, as Miller had warned, and they were married.[28] Although Carnegie claimed the loss of Annie Riddle was not a great one, he was deeply wounded. He always claimed he held no grudges, but that wasn't true; Carnegie could be very spiteful and never forgot what Scott had done. The friendship had been poisoned long before 1873, and old loyalties now meant nothing. Old loyalties certainly weren't going to hinder Carnegie's own success.

With the fall of Scott, Carnegie found himself the target of an inquisition by the Exchange Bank of Pittsburgh, which had loaned substantial sums to him for the construction of the Edgar Thomson Mill. During an emergency meeting with the bank's directors, the president of the Exchange Bank, a Mr. Shoenberger, decided to call in the loans before the money simply disappeared into the panic's vortex. It wasn't a surprising decision; after all, in the eyes of the older business community, this young Carnegie had a reputation as being somewhat reckless and the largest borrower in the state. Luck had been with him, but it appeared to have just run out as Shoenberger summoned him to Pittsburgh. On his arrival at the bank, an imposing Greek Revival structure built with granite, he was escorted to the director's room, where the still boyish-looking Carnegie found himself surrounded by severe, upper-crust inquisitors. The questions began. Are you connected with the Texas & Pacific? Yes. Are you a stockholder? Yes. For how much? Two hundred fifty thousand dollars. The men drew in a sharp breath of air. How much on margin? Carnegie quieted the older men with a sly grin and explained his investment was free and clear, his finances sound. He retold the story of how he had turned down Scott's request for money and for endorsing a loan, much to the bankers' relief. To Carnegie's relief, they did not call in the loans; but more money was not forthcoming from anyone, and the construction of Edgar Thomson would be halted for several months.

Although Carnegie, closing in on thirty-eight years of age, fared better than Scott and Thomson—especially Thomson, who would die on May 27, 1874, at the age of sixty-six—the financial panic took its toll on him, too. He fell terribly ill, lost weight, and was confined to bed for some time. Once-stimulating New York now offered Carnegie no solace. As he walked the streets that winter, he encountered ambitious development projects frozen in time, foreclosed properties being auctioned off, and FOR LET placards plastered across office buildings. Unemployment shot to 25 percent, forcing men, women, and children to beg in the streets. Carnegie had to circumnavigate the lines outside thirty-four soup kitchens feeding five to seven thousand daily. In 1873, five thousand families were receiving aid; the next year it was twenty-four thousand. Tramps became such a nuisance that the *New York Times* advised its readers to buy dogs that knew how to use their teeth. On January 13, 1874, a rally was held in Tompkins Square in support of the suffering poor, an event the media called communist agitation and the mayor responded to with force. Unsympathetic to the crowd of seven thousand, the police charged into the square with clubs flailing.[29]

Wall Street had threatened, the banks had threatened, even Scott had threatened, but Carnegie had survived. Now a new and far more dangerous menace arose: his partner Andrew Kloman. Kloman, imagining himself a financier à la Carnegie, had borrowed heavily and secretly created his own interlocking investment by becoming a partner in the Escanaba Furnace Company, a smelting company, and the Cascade Iron Company, a mining company. He then made certain Carnegie operations bought ore from his new investments. Escanaba and Cascade now failed, however, and the creditors came after Kloman, who could no longer hide the investment from the Carnegies and Harry Phipps, especially when the creditors threatened to seize his shares in Union Mills and Edgar Thomson. It was unthinkable to Carnegie that a third party, just days before unknown to him, might seize sizable interests in their businesses.

Subsequent meetings between Kloman and his partners were tense, the tone acidic, as they desperately sought a solution. Carnegie, who thrashed him mercilessly, recalled, "This gave us more of a shock than all that had preceded, because Mr. Kloman, being a partner, had no right to invest in another iron company, or in any other company involving personal debt, without informing his partners. There is one imperative rule for men in business—no secrets from partners. Disregard of this rule involved not only Mr. Kloman himself, but our company, in peril, coming, as it did, atop the difficulties of my Texas Pacific friends with whom I had been intimately associated."[30] There was but one choice: Carnegie insisted Kloman declare bankruptcy, have his estate assessed, and then Carnegie would buy his shares at the assessed value, which would occur in 1876. If not for Kloman's mechanical ingenuity, he would have then been thrown out of the firm, and possibly the city; however, he was permitted to keep his position.

Carnegie's outrage over Kloman typified his hypocritical streak because he found himself in the same precarious position once the Sulzbach case, among several other Davenport-related lawsuits, went to trial in 1874; as a matter of fact, Carnegie was so worried about the consequences that he kept the lawsuits hidden from brother Tom and Phipps.[31] If he were to lose, the court could very well seize his assets—and yet his own legal quandary didn't stop him from assailing Kloman. But he was not about to forfeit everything he, his mother, and his brother had worked for. Desperate measures were called for. In a covert defensive move, he and one of his codefendants living in Iowa, George French, hired an agent to lobby the Iowa congress to pass legislation that would explicitly protect members of the Davenport and St. Paul Construction Company, which had been set up to build the railroad, from personal liability. "All are agreed that the matter must be handled quietly and with as much secrecy as we can command," French wrote to Carnegie.[32] With a more devious tone, he also reported that the Davenport & St. Paul Railroad offices had burned down, conveniently destroying all records. Investigators and observers could only speculate as to who was behind the burning, if anyone.

The legal battles continued through the late 1870s. Joining Sulzbach Brothers in the suit was the First National Bank of Davenport, with the bank seeking monetary damages for a loan default and misappropriated funds; namely, it alleged that $5,000 was wrongly given to a lobbyist to influence Congress to pass an act that would give Carnegie and his cronies the right to build a bridge over the Mississippi. Tom Scott testified in the Sulzbach case, as did representatives of the Thomson estate, who placed the blame squarely on Carnegie's shoulders. Carnegie was forced to hire a top trial lawyer in New York, Colonel Ingersoll, who appreciated a wee dram of Scotch and the poet Robert Burns, and the well-connected steel master eventually emerged unscathed. In March 1879, a judge determined that the members of the Davenport and St. Paul Construction Company were not liable for the company's debts, but the decision would be appealed.[33] Suits against the Davenport and St. Paul Railroad continued to wind their way through the courts until 1884, when the U.S. Court of Appeals dismissed the case against Carnegie. Of all the men involved, only the deceased Edgar Thomson, and thus his estate, was held liable—a very convenient conclusion—for about $1 million.[34] According to the court, Thomson, a Davenport trustee, should have been more diligent.

In response to the Sulzbach lawsuit and to take advantage of a new law passed by the Pennsylvania legislature that allowed the organization of limited liability companies, crucial at this hazardous time, Carnegie, McCandless and Company was dissolved in October 1874 and reorganized as a limited partnership under the name Edgar Thomson Steel Company.[35] Carnegie's personal assets were now better protected.

One disaster followed another at the onset of the depression. On January 23, 1874, a blustery day, a fatal accident occurred at the mill construction site. Just as the men were positioning the roof frame for the converting works, a heavy squall caused it to collapse.[36] It couldn't have come at worse time, delaying construction and adding to the cost. It seemed as though the gods of fate were intent on turning against Carnegie on every front. Throughout 1874, money trickled in and work proceeded slowly until, finally, that December, Carnegie secured a loan through John Scott. He excitedly ordered his men to begin taking bids for the materials needed to finish the job and to recommence construction. Although construction had been delayed, Carnegie could take comfort in the discovery that material and men came much cheaper as the depression took hold. The cost of the plant—$1,250,000, which included $11,000 in patent fees paid to Bessemer and Holley—turned out to be three-fourths of what it might have been to build either before or after the severe years of the depression.[37] Contrary to the conservative philosophy of battening down the hatches and waiting out the storm, he realized economic downturns provided an opportunity for expansion. "Mr. Carnegie was a genius in two points," William Temple, a contemporary who became commissioner of the Steel Plate Association, said. "In the first place he exceeded any man I ever knew in his ability to pick a man from one place and put him in another with the maximum effect. . . . His other point of genius was to realize that the real time to extend your operations was when nobody else was doing it."[38] Carnegie would employ this strategy for expansion in every subsequent economic downturn and each time emerge stronger.

Success, Carnegie understood, was not contingent on financial health alone; there was also the crucial human element. Just as he had insisted on choosing Holley, the foremost expert on building a steel mill, he now demanded the best possible candidates for the general manager and superintendent positions at Edgar Thomson. He turned his eyes on the competitive ranks and they rested on Daniel Morrell, the general manager and a partner at Cambria in Johnstown, Pennsylvania, who was a no-nonsense man, antiunion, and adept at forcing down wages. He approached Morrell to become both the general manager and an investor, but while Morrell was interested in the job, money was tight and he couldn't "think of anyone that has the money to invest just now."[39] Carnegie offered him the job anyway, and he accepted. When brother Tom received a telegram with a perfunctory statement that Morrell was hired at an astounding $20,000 salary, he was flabbergasted at his brother's unilateral decision making. He quickly summoned John Scott and David McCandless for a meeting, and all agreed such a salary was unreasonable, especially considering the steelworks wouldn't earn a penny until blown in, and because Morrell was not investing. Fortunately for everyone, Morrell had second thoughts about leaving Cambria. Carnegie, realizing his impetuous behavior had chagrined his partners, didn't encourage otherwise.[40]

For general manager, Edgar Thomson partner John Scott championed William P. Shinn, who was an exceptionally competent vice president of the Allegheny Valley Railroad. Shinn was a solemn man, and to match his personality he had dour looks, with an almost fully receded hairline revealing an aesthetically displeasing bumpy skull, a gray beard pulling his long face and nose even longer, and round, determined eyes. He was a man whose only interest in life was business, and he excelled at cost management—a perfect choice. His connection with the railroad would also yield an immediate customer. By the end of January, Carnegie was won over and Shinn, who would retain his position at Allegheny, was named secretary-treasurer at a $5,000 annual salary.

As for the top candidate for superintendent, the man who would be in the trenches, he was a seasoned former Cambria employee who had been pushed out by Morrell. His name was Captain William "Bill" Jones, and he would be the initial power behind Carnegie's reputation as a steel master. A large-boned, muscular man, with red, ruddy cheeks, a half-smiling mouth, and soft blue eyes that twinkled merrily one moment and turned steely hard the next, the clean-shaven Welshman had a booming bass voice and volatile temper.

Captain Jones, born in 1839 to a Welsh nonconformist preacher and Chartist, had been in the workforce since age ten, laboring as a farmhand and then a lumberjack, afterward learning the iron business. At the outbreak of the Civil War, Jones, who was in Chattanooga, Tennessee, working on the construction of a blast furnace, subsequently fled to Pennsylvania, where he found work at Cambria. An abolitionist, Jones enlisted as a private, fighting at Fredericksburg and Chancellorsville. During one particular skirmish, Jones and his company had to wait while engineers erected a pontoon bridge across

Tom Scott introduced young Andy Carnegie to the art of financial speculation.

Captain Bill Jones greatly influenced Carnegie's ideas on management and manufacturing.

a river, but impatient to engage the enemy, he cried, "Hanged if I'll wait for the bridge," and he dove into the muddy river. It was only a few feet deep, and he split open his nose. He was also promoted to captain. After the war, Jones returned to Cambria, where he was promoted to assistant superintendent. When Cambria built its Bessemer works in 1869, he became well acquainted with Alexander Holley, who designed the mill and oversaw the construction.

Jones's boss at Cambria was Morrell, a stern Quaker with unforgiving eyes set in a large, oval-shaped face. He was not so appreciative of how Jones motivated his men, which included baseball games and going to the horse races, resulting in the occasional shutdown of the mills. When it came time to promote a new superintendent and Jones was passed over, he quit. Holley then hired him as an assistant to manage the Edgar Thomson construction. Jones drove his crews hard and always spoke his mind, which endeared him to Carnegie. After having been acquainted with Jones for well over a year, in late 1874, Carnegie and the other Edgar Thomson directors voted him superintendent. Again, he was the preeminent choice; he was highly experienced in steelmaking and had an excellent rapport with the laborers, which was immediately made evident when, as Edgar Thomson neared completion, he recruited some two hundred disenchanted Cambria men, promising better working conditions than Morrell offered. The blessed Carnegie found himself with a highly experienced crew of Bessemer steelmakers.

Despite the promises Jones made, the town of Braddock offered bleak living accommodations in these first months. One worker was quoted as saying, "We would go in some times, after having done a hard day's work, sit down to the table, a half dozen or dozen of us as it might be, look at each other and wink, taking it good-naturedly, but there was scarcely anything but bread and molasses. This did not go far after a hard day's work. Many a time we would make up our minds to quit; thoroughly discouraged and blue, the clouds hanging over us thick and black. We would go down to see Captain Jones, and after talking with him fifteen minutes, there was a ray of sunshine that pushed all the clouds away, and with a promise from him that things would be better and that he would look out for our welfare, the sky cleared, and we were made as happy as ever, and went back to work with vim and determination."[41] Jones earned his pay with charisma alone.

The first steel rail rolled off the line at Edgar Thomson on September 1, 1875, and the official opening celebration took place three days later. More integrated and larger than any steel mill in the world, the first Bessemer steel mill in the immediate Pittsburgh area was a technological marvel, a magnificent summation of all of Holley's experience and knowledge. The various dignitaries who arrived aboard a special train from Pittsburgh were greeted by a high-stepping Carnegie, who gave them a personal tour of the sprawling works, with block-long buildings and towering chimneys spewing smoke. They watched with trepidation as the workmen, some wearing colored glasses to protect their eyes, blew a blast of air through the egg-shaped converter and scintillating sparks the size of quarter dollars erupted in a pyrotechnics display. Less courageous observers took a step backward, fearing an explosion, a fear not all together unwarranted. Experienced hands knew well the dangers.

"When a charge of metal was poured into the vessel," steel master John Fritz recalled, "the blast put on, and the vessel turned up, our anxiety commenced, and as the heat increased our anxiety increased in a corresponding ratio, until both became intense. It was when the heat was greatest that accidents were most likely to happen." The molten metal might burn through the vessel's lining, hit the wet floor, and result in an explosion that sent hot metal blowing in all directions; or, if the ladle into which the steel was poured gave out, the molten metal would again spill to the floor with a good chance of causing an explosion; or highly combustible fumes might become trapped and ignite, setting off a bomb.

"When an accident occurred anywhere about the works," Fritz explained, "the first question asked would be: 'Is anyone hurt?' If not, we would go to work at once to repair with that object only in mind. If, on the contrary, some of the workmen were seriously injured, it is impossible to describe the distress of mind that the person in charge had to endure. . . . Altogether the difficulties we encountered were enough to appall the bravest hearts. My brother George once said, when at Cambria, that he did not believe there was a man who ever went onto the Bessemer business, and was responsible for the result, who did not at times wish he had never gone into it."[42] Even experienced men like Captain Jones could not avoid exposure to fatal danger, but the Captain never dithered before the great converter. "I have no patience with a wavering person," he once said, and then added prophetically, "Thank God, when I die, I will die like a man at my post of duty, or whatever helm it is."[43] Death marked pioneering efforts in American industry, whether running railroads or steel mills; the hope for men like Carnegie was that it wouldn't touch them or their valuable lieutenants.

A setback due to disaster at the mill was of the least importance as Carnegie sought to establish himself in the steel industry, which was already dominated by several well-established firms. To offset potential losses at Edgar Thomson in the first years of operation, Carnegie was counting on dividends from Union Mills, but the depression continued to have a crippling impact on the iron and steel industry. In November 1874, demands by the Pittsburgh iron manufacturers, including Carnegie, for wage reductions resulted in a lockout, which would last into 1875 as the owners, willing to sacrifice profits, tried to break the workers. The president of the Amalgamated Association of Iron and Steel Workers (AAISW), Joseph Bishop, observed sadly that the workers had little hope as time progressed: "Distress, misery, want and destitution stare them in the face and for the first time they have known what it was to want bread for themselves, their wives and little ones."[44] In Pittsburgh, the Sons of Vulcan union, which represented the ironworkers, organized relief efforts, as did the genteel rich.

Strikes and violence in the coalfields also affected the iron and steel industry by disrupting the flow of coal. In particular, it appeared the Molly Maguires were again active in the eastern Pennsylvania anthracite coal region. The Maguires, quite determined to have better working and living conditions at any cost, were a secret society that originated in north-central Ireland and was transplanted by immigrants in Pennsylvania in the late 1840s. Arriving Irish natives clashed with British miners, their employers, and authority figures in general. During the protracted coal miner's strike in 1874 and 1875, the group was accused of murdering a chief burgess, a justice of the peace, a policeman, a superintendent, two foremen, a watchman, and a miner.[45] When rumors spread the group was planning a new campaign of agitation, a prominent coal mine owner, Franklin B. Gowen, hired Allan Pinkerton. Pinkerton's agents did a superb job by posing as Irishmen to infiltrate the Molly Maguires, and a series of arrests between 1875 and 1878 resulted in twenty hangings, some justified.

The most potent threat Carnegie faced in establishing his position in the steel rail business was simply finding customers. With each passing year, railroad building declined dramatically. By 1876, half of the country's railroads would be in receivership. The average price per ton of domestic rails also fell, from $112 in 1872 to $68.75 in 1875.[46] It was going to be an extremely depressed market to enter, and Carnegie had been counting on his patron, Mr. J. Edgar Thomson, at the Pennsylvania Railroad to provide orders. The Pennsylvania Railroad had been ordering rails from the Pennsylvania Steel Company and Cambria for a number of years, but with his mill named after Thomson, Carnegie had been certain that he had an instant, gluttonous customer of steel rails. Now Thomson was dead. Come 1875, the success of the Edgar Thomson steel mill was in serious doubt as the obstacles appeared insurmountable.

CHAPTER 11

Template for Domination

Profits were for those who pursued business relentlessly," reflected Joseph Butler, one of Carnegie's peers in the steel industry.[1] Certainly, that importunate pursuit and absolute discipline in managing the steel mill were necessary to survive the first years of Edgar Thomson's (E.T.) operation, but while Carnegie garnered a reputation as a management genius, it was, in fact, his top lieutenants who greatly influenced his philosophy and efforts during this initial struggle. They were indispensable in hiring a motivated labor force, introducing progressive manufacturing processes, and managing that all-important fixation—costs.

To Carnegie's amusement and benefit, he quickly discovered that Captain Jones considered himself on equal footing with any man—Jones's salutation for Edgar Thomson's majority shareholder was not Mr. Carnegie, but simply Andy, and to Carnegie Jones was always Bill—and fearlessly expressed his opinions on the business. Shortly before E.T. opened, Jones presented his management manifesto, which set the tone:

> 1st. We must be careful of what class of men we collect. We must steer clear of the West where men are accustomed to infernal high wages. We must steer clear as far as we can of Englishmen who are great sticklers for high wages, small production and strikes. My experience has shown that Germans and Irish, Swedes and what I denominate "Buckwheats"—young American country boys, judiciously mixed, make the most effective and tractable force you can find. Scotsmen do very well, are honest and faithful. Welsh can be used in limited numbers. But mark me, Englishmen have been the worst class of men I have had anything to do with; and this is the opinion of Mr. Holley, George and John Fritz.
>
> 2nd. It should be the aim of the firm to keep the works running steadily. This is one of the secrets of Cambria low wages. The workmen, taking year in and year out, do better at Cambria than elsewhere. On steady work you can calculate low wages.

3rd. The company should endeavor to make the cost of living as low as possible. This is one bad feature at present but it can be easily remedied.

These are the salient points. The men should be made to feel that the company are interested in their welfare. Make the works a pleasant place for them. I have always found it best to treat men well, and I find that my men are anxious to retain my goodwill by working steadily and honestly, and instead of dodging are anxious to show me what a good day's work they have done. All haughty and disdainful treatment of men has a very decided and bad effect on them.[2]

Jones had a very clear vision for managing the works that at times would put him at loggerheads with Carnegie. But imbedded in this letter, this template, were ideas Carnegie would adopt and expand upon. The slighting of Englishmen put a smile on Carnegie's face, but it was the notion of keeping "the works running steadily" that appealed most to him. This dictum, which Carnegie would adapt to *run full*, was the cornerstone of his success in steel. To run full demanded that he produce rails at the lowest possible cost so that he could sell them at cutthroat prices and therefore scoop the market; that is, win orders away from the competition. In turn, it would generate the volume needed to keep the works running steadily. Carnegie savored driving his competitors from the field, just as he had wanted when he was a railroad superintendent in Pittsburgh. Achieving the necessary efficiencies to do so took time, and he relied on brother Tom, Phipps, and Shinn to institute the processes required while he played flogging taskmaster. At the moment, Carnegie focused his efforts on winning rail contracts.

Carnegie was a traveling salesman, feverishly peddling bridges, iron, and now steel rails in Philadelphia, Harrisburg, Baltimore, and other industrialized towns. He aggressively "got orders" as they said, but the prize he now desired eluded him: if E.T. could win a rail contract from the Pennsylvania Railroad, it would give the fledgling company immediate legitimacy. When Thomson had died the prior year, Tom Scott succeeded him, and the tension between him and Carnegie made it very questionable as to whether Scott would give his Andy the inside track on orders. When Carnegie heard the railroad would be ordering five thousand tons of rails in 1875, he realized it was possibly his one and only chance to convince Scott to send business his way. Without Scott's help, Carnegie knew his top two competitors, Pennsylvania Steel and Cambria, would arrange to split the order. He told Shinn, "The harder we fight for this the sooner our friends will agree to our sharing of orders" — especially if Scott demonstrated his old patronage of Andy.[3] Sharing orders with the competition, or establishing a pool, was another means for immediately gaining a foothold and thus survival.

Pools, which were the forbearers of monopolies and trusts, sought to regulate entire industries. Some of the so-called pools were no more than gentlemen's agreements that carried little weight. True pools, however, involved formal pacts for dictating prices, quotas, and geographic territories for each participating company, as well as sharing orders. Sometimes pool members even paid other companies to stay out of a particular market. The participating capitalists knew the benefits; they knew free competition wasn't good business, and in the iron industry pools were a matter of survival in a wildly gyrating market, where sustaining prices was the difference between profitability and bankruptcy. Of course, when the market was particularly strong there was a tendency to break any agreements; likewise, when the market softened, companies were quick to shatter the pool by cutting prices to keep business.

The day he had entered the iron business almost twenty years earlier, Carnegie had discovered an aristocracy made up of well-established Pittsburgh families who controlled the industry through pooling agreements. They openly resented upstarts like Carnegie, who was not welcome in their tight social circle. Because these more powerful firms attempted to dictate how business was done, he revolted. He drew a very definite us-them line and viewed himself as the underdog who would fight to the death. His contentious relationship with the Pittsburgh aristocracy explains the ruthless tactics he later employed in the steel industry.

In 1869, Carnegie entered his first pool—for iron beams—with three other firms. As with most pools, it was only a matter of time before paranoia and greed tore it apart with the venomous words and spite more suitable to lovers scorned. By late 1870, the four iron companies were sneaking about, making surreptitious deals, undercutting one another, and causing enough mischief for Carnegie to fear free enterprise at its worst—no-holds-barred competition. "The last effort at reconciliation having finally failed," he wrote fellow member Samuel Reeves at Phoenix Iron Company, "I beg to express my regret at the sad spectacle soon to be afforded to the public in general at the sole cost and expense of four unfortunate manufacturers who prefer to waste their energies and profits in an unwise attempt to injure each other. When the day of sober sense and due repentance arrives, you will always find us ready to cease the discreditable warfare."[4] Of course, Carnegie accepted no share of blame for the impending discreditable warfare. Carnegie's fickle relationship with Reeves, among other ironmasters, continued for years as a variety of pools were organized, only to be shattered. Like an adolescent couple at a town dance, these men would then come back together, awkward, unsure, but wanting each other. For Carnegie, it resembled the days of yore, he playing King Robert the Bruce, making and breaking alliances to secure ultimate victory. He was indeed able to firmly establish Union Mills, and now he was eager to join a pool for steel rails.

Here Carnegie had to contend with the aristocracy of the steel industry— the so-called patricians—including Daniel Morrell at Cambria, Samuel Felton at Pennsylvania Steel, Benjamin F. Jones at Jones and Laughlin, and Joseph Wharton at Bethlehem Steel. This elitist group, the original nucleus of America's steel industry, didn't look favorably on the upstart Carnegie, who now had a habit of publicly expressing his disdain for the aristocracy and what he considered to be their antiquated mills. Nevertheless, earlier in the summer of 1875, Morrell had invited Shinn to a meeting in Philadelphia to discuss important issues in the steel rail trade. But following that meeting, when Carnegie suggested a rail pool, an agreement among the steel rail manufacturers to establish pricing and sales quotas that would bring stability to the market, he was met with an indignant rejection.[5]

The Pennsylvania Railroad finally ordered a mere morsel of two thousand tons of rails, thanks to Scott. Unfortunately for Carnegie, the railroad's powerful board of directors played favorites in handing out contracts. Because he no longer enjoyed a favored status in the wake of the Texas & Pacific Railroad debacle, he suggested sealed bids for winning rail orders, knowing he could undercut the competition. The board rejected the idea. Desperate, Carnegie wrote an anxious note to Shinn, instructing him to enlist the help of their partners John Scott and David Stewart, who had some influence at the Pennsylvania. "Wont you please show this to Messrs. Scott & Stewart & urge them to go down. If Mr. S. went he could incidentally ascertain just where we stood—We are in grave danger—the importance of starting right is so obvious I need say nothing to impress you—now is the time to get the E.T. just right on its feet—Please telegraph me what is decided upon."[6]

That autumn, as Carnegie waited nervously for a more sizable order from the Pennsylvania, he again pushed for a rail pool; but all meetings failed to yield any agreements. Dejected, Carnegie wrote Shinn: "Of course we are in for a year of low prices. I have seen this from the day of our failure to combine, but if we meet it rightly the track will be clearer after the war is over—One year without dividend on Cambria, Penna. Steel, Joliet and North Chicago will make some amicable arrangement possible."[7]

His back against the wall, Carnegie comprehended that only aggressive tactics would win the day. Just nine days after warning Shinn that low prices were inevitable, on November 29, the irrepressible Carnegie delivered his charge:

> Two courses are open to a new concern like ours—1st Stand timidly back, afraid to "break the market" following others and coming out without orders to keep our works going—that's where we are going to land if we keep on.
>
> 2nd To make up our minds to offer certain large consumers lots at figures which will command orders—For my part I would run the works full next year even if we made but $2 per ton.[8]

Carnegie was willing to sacrifice profits in order to undercut the competition and eventually win a sizable market presence that would then yield a plentiful bounty. "Please call our people together & advise me just how low you are willing to go," he instructed Shinn. "You know my views—fill the works at a small margin of profit—get our rails upon the leading lines next year. The year after, take my word for it, you will make profit enough."[9] Shinn began by selling steel rails for $66 a ton, whereas the other firms were at $70 a ton, but that wasn't low enough for Carnegie. "I have known from the first that our hope for profit lay for sometime to come in the fact that our cost was less than others," he informed Shinn, and then added, "Don't be too greedy—'small profits & large sales' in golden letters above your desk is respectfully recommended."[10]

The patricians were extremely irritated with Carnegie for now selling rails at $61.50 a ton and immediately directed their wrath toward Shinn. Succumbing to their pressure and his own anxieties, Shinn expressed his concerns about a bloody price war as early as December: "The feeling is that we are incurring unnecessarily the opposition of the older Companies & getting down so low on our first bids as to have no room for further reduction when other large contracts are in the market. . . . The Cambria people are becoming very bitter against us for making, as they claim, unnecessary concessions in prices, so early in the season."[11]

This was war, a matter of survival, and no wavering would be tolerated by Carnegie. He had staked his entire fortune on E.T., and he viewed the steel aristocracy with the same contempt he and his ancestors viewed the British aristocracy. Here was a chance for him to win a battle over what he viewed as the privileged class, and his ruthlessness emerged. He exhorted Shinn to become "bitter too" and to take any order that offered a profit.[12] Because their performance would make or break E.T. in these first, fragile months, Carnegie kept unrelenting pressure on both Shinn and Jones.

Profits in September were $11,000, a fair accomplishment for the start-up, and October's were $18,000—the average ton of rails selling for $66.32 while costing $56.64.[13] But the prospects for success remained dim enough that Tom's father-in-law, William Coleman, who was financially overextended, elected to sell his partnership. Carnegie offered to buy him out for exactly what he put in—$100,000—with no premium to account for the firm's increased market value. "He wanted much better bargain but I could do no better," Carnegie wrote Shinn; "finally he said to write Tom what I had offered and he would talk it over. I suppose it will be arranged. Any portion of it you want you can have and I will take your obligation same as I give Coleman."[14] It was another credit to Tom that Coleman trusted him to handle the negotiations of the sale.

Tom was not quick to roll over during the ensuing negotiations, and the discussions between the two brothers extended into the spring. In April, Carnegie updated Shinn on Coleman, as well as Kloman, who was in the process of declaring personal bankruptcy: "I want to buy Mr. Coleman out & hope to do so. Kloman will have to give up his interest, these divided between Tom, Harry, you and I would make the Concern a close Corporation—Mr. Scott's loan is no doubt in some banker's hands and may also be dealt with after a little, then we are right and have only to watch the Bond conversions which will not be great as our foreign friends will want to stick to the sure thing I think."[15] The next month Coleman sold out on Carnegie's terms.[16] From his position of relative financial strength, Carnegie realized the opportunity to consolidate his personal power, another strategy to use in future financial crises. He wasn't necessarily taking advantage of his strapped partners, but he was certainly profiting from their financial troubles. Such circumstances only reinforced his belief that he was superior; in fact, it fed his ego to such a point that within the steel industry he became known as "the Great Egoist."

With the onset of 1876, Carnegie's prophecy of depressed prices was realized: in 1875 the price per ton was $68.75; in 1876, $59.25; and by 1878, it would fall to $42.25.[17] While there was enough demand to justify production, the downward-spiraling prices threatened the already slim profits, so the only hope for survival was to drastically reduce costs, a decisive strategy on which Carnegie's lieutenants focused their efforts and Carnegie monitored vigilantly. At times, he proposed such radical ideas in cutting costs that as his legend evolved, it was assumed he was the genius behind his firm's cost accounting methods. The truth was that Tom, Phipps, and Shinn played pivotal roles in developing the renowned Carnegie cost accounting system that could track the cost and use of every brick, nail, and other minute piece of material used in manufacturing.

Even in the iron industry during the boom years that immediately followed the Civil War, price was often the deciding factor in winning customers, so production costs had consumed Carnegie since the mid-1860s. From his railroad days of studying Thomson's management practices, Carnegie knew how important it was to track the financial performance by department and division. Therefore, he was all the more stunned after first becoming involved in the iron industry when he realized the lack of attention costs received: "I was greatly surprised to find that the cost of each of the various processes was unknown. Inquiries made of the leading manufacturers of Pittsburgh proved this. It was a lump business, and until stock was taken and the books balanced at the end of the year, the manufacturers were in total ignorance of results. . . . I felt as if we were moles burrowing in the dark, and this to me was intolerable."[18] Implementing a system for recording costs in detail was easier said than done. It took Tom and Harry Phipps years to perfect a system involving weighing scales and a team of clerks to track the iron and other materials used by each department. Carnegie later acknowledged, "My brother and Mr. Phipps conducted the iron business so successfully that I could leave for weeks at a time without anxiety."[19]

But that didn't stop him from writing anxious letters. Concerned about labor costs, the one variable they could control more so than others, he wrote Tom, "I HAVE EXAMINED upper mill statement sent me. The Stationary Labor, that is, all we pay by the day I know must be practically the same whether we turn out much or little, & it would require very close management to save much, if anything, out of this Department after the forces are cut down to the proper number. 28 Mechanics seems very large indeed. I wish you would look over & see what each one does, & whether the time has not come to dispense with some whose services may have been necessary while extending."[20] In the letter, Carnegie went on to review labor cost per ton of rolled and finished iron and the output of iron per puddling furnace. Believing productivity was poor, he bolstered his argument by comparing the Union Mills to one of their competitors. For Carnegie, as it was for other manufacturers, labor was a resource to be maximized, and it was his unrelenting desire to depress labor costs that would embroil him a series of conflicts. From his first days as a manager and business owner, he recognized that labor was "a problem."

Phipps also felt Carnegie's heavy hand when it came to accounting for costs; the boss wanted information recorded daily, not according to his partner's whim. "Things have come to such a pass that it is my duty to instruct you positively that the Books of the U.I. Mills must be balanced monthly," Carnegie wrote, "and kept up with the current business day by day. You will no longer consider that you have any discretion in this matter."[21] When it came to dispersing salary and dividends, Carnegie was just as vigilant, of course, and he again criticized Phipps's bookkeeping: "Can you explain why I am not credited with Salary for a long while, also why no dividends are credited. I understand you are dividing so much per month. Somehow or other we can never get a perfectly satisfactory a/c from your Dept."[22] Carnegie could hardly be blamed; his interest was significant in the Union Mills. In articles of agreement effective as of January 1, 1871, his share was 40 percent, while Tom, Kloman, and Phipps held 20 percent each.

Despite Carnegie's criticisms, Harry Phipps was recognized as a very valuable contributor in managing the books and the costs. "He was a cheese-parer in every direction," one executive commented, "making economies that would never occur to anyone else."[23] Stingy to the point of being disliked, it was he who uncovered mill foremen who were listing more men than they had on the payroll and pocketing the extra dollars come payday. He also suggested getting "rid of some very old men who are not capable of doing a days work." In November 1875, he first suggested the brilliant idea of linking the superintendents' pay to their performance in reducing costs, declaring that "tuppeny economics will not save us. We must strike for big things and when they are to be found. Tom believes something radical must be done. The plan I propose is Revolution, but is it not feasible? It upsets all the traditions of the past, which we must do, if we desire to make money."[24] It would appear that Phipps was not the timid number-crunching mouse that many of his peers depicted him as.

When Shinn came aboard, he built on the cost-tracking system Tom Carnegie and Phipps had implemented. He introduced a voucher system used at the Allegheny Railroad, which required the workmen to fill out a requisition voucher for any piece of material. Clerks then logged it in their books and management knew right down to the number of bolts what material was used where and what it cost. If costs in a particular department increased, management jumped all over the foreman. It wasn't long before every workman was conscious of material costs. The importance of Carnegie's partners could not be underestimated, although in later years, as he came to prominence, he would assume much of the acclaim.

To Carnegie's credit, he promoted such cost consciousness. Whenever a new project was undertaken, he demanded precise costs estimates, right down to the brick type. In November 1874, when the partners elected to build a blast furnace for making pig iron, he was very hands-on. "Not one dollar to be spent upon ornament—" he wrote Kloman, who was in charge of its construction, "all this is bad taste & entirely out of place & everything to be of the plainest description."[25] Five months later, Carnegie was again berating Kloman over the plans: "Will you please send me by express as soon as ready the complete drawings . . . I want everything complete remember—ground plan—foundation, hoist, everything to show to parties here—When may I expect them."[26] Such bullying was salt to Kloman's wounds, and the growing rift between the manic Scotsman and the overmatched Prussian would widen. Behind the oppressive letters was a very obsessive man.

To save on costs, Carnegie even suggested abandoning Holley's patents and redesigning the works, a proposal that horrified Shinn, who replied, "You are entirely mistaken. We could not abandon the use of Holley's patents for a cost of $100,000, as it would involve a re-construction of our converting works and then it is doubtful if we could manage economically to carry on the process."[27] Well, if not patents, why not insurance? Carnegie wrote his brother and Phipps: "We are paying double the Insurance on Buildings that we could collect in case of fire. Forty thousand dollars would replace our wooden building with iron. . . . I hope someday we shall have the entire building fire proof. If any parts of it require renewal from time to time let us put in Iron. Insurance is a deceptive thing." On another occasion, a new, more efficient converter mill at E.T. had just been built to save fifty cents a ton in costs. When the obsessive Carnegie learned that a slightly different design would yield fifty cents more in savings per ton, he ordered the mill torn down and rebuilt—no questions asked. It was no wonder that one of the more renowned quotes that circulated about Carnegie was contributed by a complaining partner: "Carnegie never wanted to know the profits. He always wanted to know the costs."[28]

Another bugaboo for Carnegie was quality. Winning a good reputation was crucial to gain the confidence of the railroads, which were biased toward English steel. That was why Carnegie was particularly galled when the New

York & New Haven Line complained of defective rails. Although he moved quickly to control any damage, he struggled for an excuse in writing his customer: "I am surprised to hear of the defects in the New Haven rails and can only account for this first and only complaint upon the hypothesis that having to divide the forces into day and night gangs to run double turn compelled us to employ ½ green men and the imperfect rails may have been shipped at night."[29] He immediately dispatched an inspector to investigate, and when the report confirmed the defects, Carnegie lashed out at Shinn: "Mr. Roysten's report on the New Haven rails is *very sad* indeed. No one can hold his head up when he looks at them. Now *this will not do* and should not be repeated. *It is ruin* to send out a bad rail especially to Eastern lines where inspection is always severe. . . . I would rather today pay out of my own pocket 5000 dollars than have had this *disgraceful failure* occur." (Emphasis added.)[30]

One customer Carnegie attempted to capture in early 1876 who was biased toward English rails was Pierpont Morgan. He had invested in several railroads and was the recently named president of the Cairo & Vincennes Railroad in Illinois. "Morgan is trying hard to buy steel rails cheap," Carnegie wrote Shinn, "& he will do it too—I could not bring him one cent above $64. . . . He has no American Steel Rails on his line but has heard of the wonderful work we have & *sixty feet lengths* (as who has not)." In dealing with Morgan, Carnegie encountered the banker's purchasing agent, General Walker, with whom he was most impressed and was determined to hire. Once again, Carnegie wanted the best of men, and Walker was to be the cornerstone of the one piece of the puzzle yet to be put in place: a highly organized sales force.

Carnegie comprehended that success of his sales organization depended on him picking the man best qualified for specific territories and compensating them well. "I have come to the conclusion that if we could get Genl Walker to take our agency South of the Ohio & West of Cina or Louisville at 50 c per ton," Carnegie apprised Shinn, "we will be the strongest seller in that region—The Genl is a West Pointer—a gentleman—much liked by Southerners—& can frequently get a preference—I consider Royston the right man for New England—With Genl Walker in the South we should want a man for the West—I could probably get Mr. Katte—not a bad selection—He has not more weight than is desirable but he is honest, well known—of good address & would try hard. Fifty cents per ton is not a high charge & you get the utmost exertion from agents in this form."[31] The fifty-cent commission per ton was indeed excellent compensation; at that rate, a man could live very comfortably for a year off a moderate five-thousand-ton order. Carnegie also advised Shinn to send one of the company's managers to visit the Short Line in Cincinnati, among other railroads, for as he explained, "Nothing like personal effort on the ground & face to face." Less than a year into E.T.'s operation, all the pieces were falling into place—

highly cost-effective production, quality, and a vigorous sales force — and Carnegie was charging ahead, ready to do battle with any rival.

The gravest danger to Carnegie's impressive start in the steel business — the final component in the template for success, as it were — was Carnegie himself. In dealing with his managers and foremen, rarely did he offer a compliment in motivating them; rather, it was biting sarcasm or a deflating What are you going to do for me next? When one lieutenant wired, "We broke all records for making steel last week," Carnegie rejoined, "Congratulations! Why not do it every week?" When a sales agent signed a big contract, Carnegie replied, "Good boy! — Next!" When his blast furnace manager reported, "No. 8 Furnace broke all records today," Carnegie responded, "What were the other ten furnaces doing?"[32] On a daily report from manager Julian Kennedy, Carnegie scribbled madly, "Why did Furnace C fall below the average today?" Dryly, Kennedy explained there could be no average unless you occasionally fell below it.[33] In dealing with his two most important men, Shinn and Jones, he was equally relentless in his oppressive management style, which threatened to undermine their desire to perform and their loyalty.

Early in their relationship, Carnegie was impressed with Shinn's work and wanted him full-time. He didn't like the idea of sharing the executive with the Allegheny Railroad; in fact, he was never a good sharer, a trait born in the empty belly of poverty. Shinn admitted that E.T. did indeed require more time than he imagined, but he stopped short of committing himself fully, so Carnegie's wooing continued: "With you at the helm, and my pulling an oar outside, we are bound to put it at the head of rail-making concerns. My preference would be for you to double your interest & manage it to the exclusion of everything else. . . . we shall not quarrel about your compensation. The only objection I think of to increasing your salary directly would be that $5,000 is considered the figure for partners. Tom, Harry, Piper, Linville, Shiffler and Kloman all get this, and it would cost me a pretty penny should they raise the standard, quoting you as precedent, but this may be arranged. You shall be satisfied one way or another if you take command."[34] For Carnegie to offer to double Shinn's interest to $100,000 was quite a testimony. Still, Shinn did not yield. Several months later, in August 1876, more cajoling from Carnegie was forthcoming: "I am naturally anxious to get *all* of you for E.T. I do not know your equal as an Ex. Officer & I always feel with you at the helm E.T. is safe but it makes all the difference whether your entire mind is bent on the concern. . . . Remember I can see no fault with your management as it is, on the contrary I assure you there are few nights in which before going to sleep I don't congratulate myself at our good fortune in having you there — Tom & Harry ditto — but we don't think we can have 'too much of a good thing' & want somehow or other to get you root and branch — compensation can be arranged — I don't care about money so much as about success."[35] Charming compliments, he knew, would eventually yield victory.

Once Shinn came to Carnegie full-time, the honeymoon was over; and once he made his first mistake, Carnegie lashed out with a vengeance. Ears hot from anger and frustration, Carnegie could not believe the note before him at his new Broadway office: the Edgar Thomson steel mill had stopped for the want of coke. Shinn was responsible, but instead of dealing with him directly, Carnegie focused his ire on John Scott, who had originally promoted Shinn for general manager, and in a shrill note he demanded an explanation.

A competent man, Scott did not take the scolding lightly and wrote a long, testy response:

> In regard to the Edgar Thomson having stopped for want of Coke, I think you are a little too fast in your remarks about that, as I think you will find on the day they were said to have stopped, they made an unexampled product, probably not excelled by any mill at any time in the world—The busy-body who made the report to you should know all the facts before he retails such nonsense. As I understand it, there was a short interruption—nearly all cars on all the roads being blockaded from a heavy fall of snow we had had.
>
> Since the mill started last as far as I can see, every person connected with it has been doing his very best . . . and I would advise you before writing those complaining letters to get all the facts, because I see your hastily written notes keep those gentlemen in a state of irritation—[36]

"I would advise you before writing those complaining letters to get all the facts, because I see your hastily written notes keep those gentlemen in a state of irritation" was a valid point because Carnegie was extremely reactionary in all matters. Some days he launched two or more letters and cables, targeting partners and managers in his continuous bombardment of criticism. But would he heed John Scott's advice, verify facts, encourage more than bully, and soften his tone?

With the reprimand in mind, Carnegie did decide to better express his appreciation for the men's efforts—at least for the workingmen in the mill. Two months later, when they were exceptionally productive and Captain Jones suggested they be recognized, Carnegie heartily agreed, offering to pay all the men in gold and silver, or to give them a gold piece, along with a note commemorating their accomplishment.[37] Shinn was not so enthusiastic and suggested "a neat circular in the form of a general order giving the product and commending them . . . would be better appreciated."[38] Well, at least Carnegie had tried. For all his bullying and maligning of men, he was always proud of E.T.'s accomplishments and touted them to industry notables, such as James Swank, secretary of the American Iron and Steel Association, and the media.[39]

The same day Carnegie offered to pay the men in gold, he wrote an effusive letter to Henry Curry, manager of an independent blast furnace company named the Lucy Furnace Company (after Tom's wife) that Carnegie had created to supply his iron and steel works with pig iron: "I desire to congratulate upon the extraordinary results of the past two weeks. I am at last satisfied that we are getting the results we had a right to expect. . . . You will soon have the 2 greatest Furnaces in the country under your charge and you are bound to make a national reputation if you continue to manage them as you are doing."[40] This lavish praise of Curry, however, opened another rift between Shinn and Carnegie.

The pig iron the Lucy Furnace Company was supplying to E.T., Shinn charged, cost more than the competition's; not only that, on several occasions the quality was suspect. Troubled by this unforeseen obstacle thrown in the road by supposed allies, in April 1877 Shinn wrote Carnegie a letter marked private and confidential. Quite reasonably, Shinn argued that if the Lucy Company was to furnish most of the pig iron, then "it is of the utmost consequence that we should have the fullest confidence in each other, and that we could feel assured at all times, that no material would be used to cheapen the metal, that would or could injure our product." In fact, he continued, cheap pig iron had recently resulted in a batch of brittle, defective rails, even though Phipps had assured everyone changes had been made to ensure quality at the furnaces. "You are most interested in our getting and keeping a reputation for making *the best rails in America*," Shinn reminded Carnegie, "and to do that we must use the *best material*. My reputation as well as my capital, is involved in the matter, and if I am to make it my life occupation, and cut loose from all RR. Associations, it can only be, as you can readily see, upon a basis of full confidence between us, and between us all as associates, in all our relations."[41] Shinn suggested that not only had Phipps been less than straightforward, but that perhaps Carnegie was guilty of unspecified surreptitious behavior, too, undermining their trust in each other. No doubt, Carnegie did not appreciate the tone of this personal letter, but the man required appeasing. Within days, he tantalized Shinn with a large partnership in a reorganized company that would consolidate all the iron and steel interests.[42]

Convinced any internal conflicts had been resolved, by the fall of 1877 Carnegie was again riding his men hard, harping on costs. Still paying the Lucy Company what he considered a premium for ore, Shinn responded bitterly, "You say that 'there is but one thing for us to do, get cost down, etc.,' We will do all we can in that respect, but when Vulcan can get metal at from a dollar to a dollar fifty below us, we have not the best show in the world for meeting them in their market."[43] Attacked repeatedly over wage reductions and other costs, Shinn's bitterness was becoming more apparent. His relationship with Carnegie began to sour, slowly at first, initiated by Carnegie's bullying, but then accelerating as Shinn's resentfulness grew over the pressures placed on him by his much younger boss. Now he secretly coveted more money and power as compensation, and he dreamed ambitious dreams that were beyond his ability to attain. It would soon become a question of whether he would heed Carnegie's advice—"Don't be too greedy"—or would take Kloman's path.

While a tempestuous Carnegie, who found it difficult to have an even-tempered relationship with anyone (except his mother) both wooed and flagellated Shinn, he pressed Jones for more productivity in a barrage of letters. In stark contrast to Shinn, who was forever on the defensive and looking for excuses, Jones took a belligerent, yet pleasantly confident, posture with Carnegie. When Carnegie specifically demanded higher production to beat an aggressive Illinois competitor, the North Chicago Rolling Mill, the superintendent rejoined with confidence and coolness: "Your last two letters have been received. In reply to last, I am free to confess what North Chicago put out is hard to beat. Yet I doubt if it would be good policy for us to attempt to beat it. . . . I feel confident that it is utterly impossible to make that amount of rails in the time specified and meet the requirements of such roads as the Pa. R. R. and its connections. I know what rail making is out west. I feel confident that at the end of the year, we will not be far behind the best. . . . We still have many difficulties to contend with, but are getting rid of them as fast as we can. Have patience and I think I can show you a thing or two."[44] Patience was one trait Carnegie was not imbued with.

At times, Jones could not hide his exasperation with his doubting, heavy-handed boss and was compelled to confront him when he didn't give credit when credit was due. On one occasion, to prove his labor cost per ton was cheaper than that of the Pennsylvania Steel Company, a prime competitor, he sent figures for both firms and demanded that his boss "be candid enough to give us credit." Captain Jones finished his letter with a flourish: "In conclusion I do think that no works in the world, can point to so successful a record as we can claim, and show, and today I am in receipt of letters making inquiries 'how we do this,' and 'how we do that?' The oldest asking the youngest for information."[45] The letter had little effect on Carnegie. The barrage of criticism, suggestions, and sundry Scottish proverbs about minding the pence continued.

The next year, when Carnegie continued to harp on labor costs, Jones, rather than whining like Shinn would, bluntly told Carnegie what was to be done: Nothing. "I must earnestly say let us leave good enough alone," he demanded. "Don't think of any further reductions. Our men are working hard and faithfully, believing that hard pan has been reached. Let them once get the notion in their heads that wages are to be further reduced and we will lose heavily. . . . Now mark what I tell you. Our labor is the cheapest in the country. Our men have 'Esprit de Corps,' and our cost of maintenance is way under that of any other works. Low wages does not always imply cheap labor. Good wages and good workmen I know to be cheapest labor. Our men are taking good care of our property and are pulling with us so heartily that I even cant dream of again attacking them."[46] Jones likened the workmen to a spirited horse difficult to rein in; they must be given their head and wages. To cultivate the esprit de corps, he encouraged his various crews on different shifts to form baseball teams and play each other, knowing the competitive spirit would carry over to steel production. He even built a baseball diamond right inside the Edgar Thomson plant.[47]

His relationship with Carnegie also became extremely competitive, each egging the other on. Supremely confident, the Captain bet Carnegie a new suit that E.T. would beat Pennsylvania Steel's production—and when E.T. did triumph, Jones wrote to collect on the bet, offering a piece of his mind, too:

> I guess you had better send that order for suit of clothes, for I fear that by the time you have compared our results with that of other works, you will feel sure that I am entitled to two suits.
>
> Now in conclusion, you let me handle this nag in this race. I think I will keep her on the track, and may keep her nose in front. I think at the end of this year, I will have her ahead, and when we stop to rub down, you will find her in excellent condition.[48]

Finally, Carnegie conceded that Jones was doing a superb job. He even asked his advice on prospects for expansion, and on consolidating the E.T. and Lucy companies. Shocked by the chance to give *solicited* advice, Jones unleashed a host of pent-up ideas. In particular, he recommended expanding their works and building more furnaces.[49] Jones, who was always eager to implement the latest technology, continued to shape Carnegie's ideas and reinforce what the Scotsman had learned from Thomson on reinvesting dividends. Reinvestment equated to greater production and greater profits in the future. As Carnegie had and would with other lieutenants and partners, he recognized Jones's brilliance and would heed his advice. But expansion would have to be paid for with money that would otherwise go toward dividends, and Carnegie, who came to believe dividends should be limited to 25 percent of the profits, would find it exceedingly difficult to convince his partners to forgo the short-term gain. Everyone's relationships would become more complicated—especially his and Shinn's—as profits complicated most everything.

Carnegie was setting the tone for the steel industry by spring of 1877 and had only scorn for the other firms sniveling over the bitter contest for rail orders. He was pushing the entire industry to a higher level of performance, forcing competitors to seek greater efficiencies and to discover new processes. By challenging the status quo, he elevated American industry. The demoralized patricians, however, decided to attempt a rail pool. Realizing it would only succeed if Carnegie were included, they reluctantly invited him to a meeting in Philadelphia.

Carnegie prepared diligently for the meeting by buying stock in each of his publicly traded competitors to receive their reports, by investigating the

By the late 1870s, Carnegie was setting the tone in the steel industry. He also remained a most eligible bachelor. (Courtesy of the Carnegie Library of Pittsburgh)

executives who would be there, and by estimating the costs each of their respective mills incurred in making rails. At the table, no faces surprised him. There was Edward Y. Townsend and Morrell from Cambria, Samuel Felton from Pennsylvania Steel, Walter Scranton from Scranton Iron and Steel, Benjamin Jones from Jones and Laughlin, and Joseph Wharton from Bethlehem Steel. Carnegie was stunned, however, to discover the group of elders had already decided each firm's share of the rail pool. Cambria was to receive 19 percent and Pennsylvania 15 percent, while E.T. was designated a paltry 9 percent.

After looking over the documents handed to him, Carnegie calmly stood, drawing himself up to his full five feet three inches, and then pounded the table. Taken aback, the haughty steel masters turned their attention to Carnegie, who declared in no uncertain terms that E.T. would have as large a piece as Cambria. The announcement was greeted with chortles of laughter. Pale and indignant, Carnegie gave them a piece of his mind. He informed them he was a stockholder in their concerns and therefore had access to their financial reports. Then, singling out each president in turn, he stated their salary and personal expenses, hoping to embarrass them. "Moreover," Carnegie declared, "Mr. Holley, the engineer who built the Edgar Thomson works has informed me that it is the most complete and perfect in the world and will turn out steel rails at cost far lower than its competition. So gentlemen, you must be interested to know that I can roll steel rails at $9 a ton. [He was bluffing.] If Edgar Thomson Co. isn't given as high a percentage of this pool as the highest, I shall withdraw from it and undersell you all in the market—and make good money doing it."[50] By the end of Carnegie's tirade, the laughter had subsided, but his demands were not met and negotiations fell apart. One of the major reasons the steel masters were not overly enthused about creating a pool was because they had already established another means for controlling the industry.

In 1866, the Pennsylvania Steel Company and several other established steel manufacturers had created the Pneumatic Steel Association, later called the Bessemer Steel Association, with the sole objective of buying and controlling the patents, such as Bessemer's, required for making steel. If the patricians wanted to limit the competition, they simply refused to license the patents or charged exorbitant fees. Pools weren't that necessary because the association effectively controlled the market. By 1877, Carnegie wielded enough power that he was granted membership in the Bessemer Steel Association, about the only friendly relationship he established with the steel aristocracy. And even then he complained bitterly about the royalty fees he had to pay.

With his men under continuous strain, Carnegie began to realize an alliance with a competitor was necessary to relieve the pressure. Although a rail pool remained elusive, a partnership with another powerful firm would bring some stability to prices and thus eliminate the incessant drive for lower costs. It would also provide Edgar Thomson with more rail orders as the respective sales forces worked in concert. In particular, he wanted to join forces with another firm to generate the critical mass necessary to attack the firms based in Chicago, now a powerful steel center, that were blocking his entry into western markets. If he could entice Cambria into a partnership, he calculated, they could crush the competition together; and then, with the others subdued, Carnegie would deal with Cambria. He struck up a relationship with E. Y. Townsend, the president of Cambria, and suggested an alliance. He wrote, "I know there is more profit for each of us in harmonious working than in fierce competition for every order that comes upon the market, and I am disposed to try any plan you think likely to make." To bolster his argument, he provided the example of two coal companies warring that eventually partnered and achieved unparalleled success:

> In like manner, if our two works obtain a lead & go forward prosperously, we shall both grow in various directions & make always a large proportion of the steel made in this country.
>   I have been charged with demoralizing the Rail Mkt. but should war between our concerns result in prices now almost undreamt of, I decline to share the responsibility.[51]

Townsend realized he could no longer ignore the threat that Carnegie posed, so he agreed to share rail orders equally, provided all sales were approved by him and all sales agents reported to him. Carnegie, more interested in the money, willingly acquiesced on this issue of control. Yet he did not entirely trust Cambria, as he apprised Shinn: "The division of orders, between Cambria and ourselves, will be made by dividing each order as far as practicable, and I will arrange the matter of division, otherwise, very carefully."[52] Now Carnegie believed he would reap a good portion of the Pennsylvania Railroad bounty that Cambria and Pennsylvania Steel had feasted upon.

In the autumn of 1877, with his Cambria relationship proving amicable enough, Carnegie pursued John Fritz, the general manager at Bethlehem Steel, as his next ally to build an even stronger regional alliance for stabilizing the local market and combating competitors. To show his interest in Bethlehem's welfare, as well as to engage in a little reconnaissance, Carnegie visited with Fritz at Bethlehem in December, then reported back to Tom and Phipps. He included information on the mixture of fuel and iron Bethlehem used to make its pig iron, along with costs for each ingredient, as well as labor.[53] Such information allowed him to evaluate where he stood and gave him the weapon needed to *kindly* induce his own managers to strive for lower costs. On the same day he relayed his findings to Pittsburgh, Carnegie wrote a glowing, complimentary note to Fritz, concluding with a cataclysmic line: "I might say that everything I saw tended to convince me that, on the Darwinian principal of survival of the fittest, you have no reason to fear the future."[54]

Even though he was seeking a harmonious relationship with Bethlehem and Cambria, after the heated battle to establish his steel mill survival of the fittest as a socioeconomic philosophy was now imbedded in Carnegie's conscious and part of his lexicon. Of course, it was Spencer who coined the social thought down to a couple of catchphrases. What mattered to Carnegie was that the survival of the fittest mentality justified any ruthless action and confirmed his elevated view of himself.

During the brutal depression, he realized life's many battles did indeed result with the victor being the one who was most fit to survive. For evidence, he only had to look as far as his own associates: Thomson was dead and Scott mired in financial chaos; Kloman had fallen prey to greed and Coleman to the panic and credit squeeze. But he, with mother Margaret at his side, he had the intellectual and moral strength to survive. He was one of Calvin's blessed. He stood alone, the fittest.

CHAPTER 12

Rekindling the Flame

C arnegie's conviction that he was the fittest, that he was superior to his peers, as was his beloved Republic to other nations, was reinforced by an eight-month voyage around the world that began in 1878. This odyssey also rekindled dormant literary aspirations and marked a new phase in his life in which Carnegie sought to vastly expand his cultural realm beyond New York and to develop intimate personal relations beyond his mother.

He had made a number of trips to Europe in the early and mid-1870s during his bond-selling junkets, but none expressly for pleasure. After wholly dedicating himself to accumulating money since his European tour with Vandy in 1865, Carnegie decided to undertake the fantastic trip, a feat accomplished by no one he knew. The dangers were inherent, what with the number of miles he would travel by rail and steamboat and the corresponding high probability of accident. There were numerous hazards in foreign lands, too, from disease to political instability to strange foods to wildlife. To accompany him, he again enlisted his faithful companion Vandy, who was now a sales agent for the Union Mills. They would go west, taking the train to San Francisco and then a steamboat to Japan, the first country on the itinerary. From there they would journey to China, India, Egypt, Italy, France, and Great Britain.

Before locking up his Broadway office, Carnegie sat at his rolltop desk and wrote a last note to Shinn: "Good bye my friend, I feel so perfectly satisfied to leave E. T. in your hands. This absolute confidence is worth everything & I daily congratulate myself that I have met you & got such a man bound in the closest manner to our party. Your fortune is secured that I do know."[1] So was Carnegie's. He had begun with $250,000 of the original $700,000 in capital. In 1878, the Edgar Thomson Steel Company's capital stock was increased to $1,250,000 with Carnegie alone adding the last $250,000 bringing his total share to $741,000, or 59 percent.[2] Now he would have the last word on everything in the partnership. At the moment there was little to criticize as 1878 profits were $401,800, an impressive 32 percent return on capital. Also, E.T. was now able to manufacture rails for less than $37 a ton and sell them for $42.50 on average, an agonizingly low price for his competitors to match.

There was one weakness Carnegie was not yet aware of. It was the highly praised Shinn, who was fast going the way of Kloman. While Carnegie was overseas and unknown to the other partners, Shinn and his brother John would form the Peerless Lime Company—the good old interlocking investment—to sell lime to E.T. at a healthy profit. Bitter over Carnegie's relentless criticisms, Shinn had decided he deserved a greater financial reward.

On October 12, 1878, Carnegie bid his office adieu. Then, with Mother and trunks in tow, he took the train to Pittsburgh, where he settled his mother in Tom's house and toured the mills, rattling off endless instructions to his brother, Phipps, and Shinn. Before her son departed, Margaret gave him a small, but handy thirteen-volume set of Shakespeare's writings, a companion to occupy his many hours at sea. Suspecting this would be a unique odyssey, he also packed notebooks for recording his experiences. Then it was to San Francisco where the SS *Belgic* awaited. When Andy and Vandy arrived dockside on October 24, they discovered they would be sailing with eight hundred downtrodden Chinamen who were returning home, an unsettling situation.

This journey was no coaching trip to Dunfermline or tour of western Europe, where Carnegie could get by with bastardized French. To find accommodations and guides, they would have to rely on connecting with American and British dignitaries stationed in the various countries, and on letters of introduction obtained in one city to be used in the next. They would encounter written languages involving ideographs and syllabic characters, Semitic and Sanskrit in origin, and spoken by people who were predominantly Buddhists, Hindus, and Muslims. How would these nations compare to the United States? For Carnegie, here was an opportunity to confirm the righteousness of the great Republic's economic and political systems. Ingrained in him was the philosophy of Herbert Spencer, which provided the lens through which to study foreign societies, governments, religions, and, of course, their commerce and industries, with the ultimate question being, How evolved were they? As Carnegie traveled from city to city, as he passed people in the street, took in art and architecture, met with dignitaries, and dined on native food, he would ask this very question over and over.

On November 15, the islands of Japan were sighted. Tokyo was stranger to Carnegie than he had ever imagined: the citizens forever bowing to the ground, the depth depending on class and rank; jinrickshaws rushing about, the men pulling them clothed in a loin rag and a hat the size of a barrel top; fishmongers and water carriers stumbling along with a basket swinging at each end of their bamboo poles; and women with painted lips, whitened necks, and those married with blackened teeth. "How women can be induced to make such disgusting frights of themselves I cannot conceive," Carnegie noted, "but Fashion—Fashion does anything."[3] Food was plentiful: beef, mutton, woodcock, snipe, hares, venison, fish, turnips, radishes, and carrots. At one market stand, Vandy measured the radishes and carrots, which were eighteen and twenty inches respectively; they concluded the soil must be rich, an important environmental factor for social evolution. Ultimately, however, Carnegie had little respect for Japanese culture, writing that, "the odor of the toyshop pervades everything, even their temples."[4]

On November 27, they sailed for the coastal city of Shanghai, China. There was a brief stopover in Nagasaki, and the two men hiked up through the terraces built on the steep coast for cultivating various crops. As they gazed down at the boxed farmland resembling a quilt, a momentary serenity enveloped Carnegie. Nagasaki was a peaceful farming community, and he could understand why the inhabitants would never want to leave such a place. As the ship made its way across the East China Sea, Carnegie eagerly anticipated China, a land that had given the world the compass, gunpowder, porcelain, and the art of printing. He even paid Confucius a compliment: "It is an old and true saying that almost any system of religion would make one good enough if it were properly obeyed; certainly that of Confucius would do so. I have been deeply impressed with his greatness and purity."[5] To highlight the point, he quoted Matthew Arnold:

> Children of men! the unseen Power, whose eye
>> For ever doth accompany mankind,
> Hath look'd on no religion scornfully
>> That men did ever find.

Carnegie habitually quoted Arnold, Burns, and Shakespeare to make his points, especially when he was attempting to develop ideas involving intellectual and emotional depth. Such quotations helped him define his thoughts and feelings as he continued to struggle with his identity, a struggle that dated back to when the Carnegie family moved to America and he found it necessary to reinvent himself.

On reaching Shanghai, Carnegie and Vandy took rooms at the Astor House in the American Settlement, part of the property the Chinese government had set aside for accommodating foreign peoples. The streets reminded Carnegie of an English town—broad, lighted with gas, and equipped with sewers—but there were no telegraph lines nor railroads yet. He was amazed to discover the obstacle to railroad building was graves; coffins were buried everywhere, many covered lightly with dirt or completely exposed, because in this region the Chinese wanted their kin to be near them in death. After nine days in Shanghai, the twosome traveled by mail steamer to Hong Kong, and then it was on to Canton. Here, as they toured the streets, they found dogs, cats, rats, and mice nicely dressed—hanging in windows, that is, for consumption. The dogs, Carnegie observed, could easily pass for a delicious young roasting pig. He found them to be of delicate flavor—yes, he bravely immersed himself in the various cultures. As for the few women he saw, they weren't as repulsive as those in Japan, but he did pity them for their lack of individual rights. They were married off into relative slavery, and were discarded if they were unable to deliver a boy. Part of the problem was evolutionary, according to Carnegie; he calculated that thousands of years of seclusion had molded the Chinese female into the same form, so men might as well marry or reject one as another.

At one point, their guide pointed out a bloodied square where criminals had just been executed, their heads put in jars and left as a reminder. Even so, Carnegie decided China placed little emphasis on warlike qualities, instead exulting triumphs in peace. "No general, no conqueror, be his victories what they may, can ever in China attain the highest rank," he wrote. "That is held only by successful scholars who have shown the possession of literary talent."[6] This was the rank that Carnegie coveted; it represented immortality for a man with no religion, a man such as himself. He would write a book on these travels, *Round the World*, to share his personal scholarship and to obtain that immortality.

Against its illustrious history, he found China an inconsistent country and determined that further development, or evolution, would require adopting more features from the Great Republic, from postage stamps to railroads. Criticisms aside, Carnegie caught the souvenir bug and managed to ship home nine boxes of curios, including a temple gong. The two men returned to Hong Kong for Christmas. There, on Christmas day, Carnegie, who was always introspective at the year's end, thought wistfully of walking to holiday services at church with the future Mrs. C.

Next on the itinerary was Saigon, where he found nothing to laud, and then to Singapore. Here, close to the equator, Carnegie appreciated the unadorned existence of the native men wearing loincloths, and nothing more. In response, the best Vandy and he could do was make a pact not to wear starched clothes on their return home. (The promise didn't last long.) While in Singapore, they did manage to reduce their dressing time to just seven minutes as vests, overcoats, and other wardrobe items were eliminated in the heat.

On January 14, they boarded an English mail steamer for Ceylon, later to be renamed Sri Lanka, where Carnegie encountered pretty women dressed in closely fitted skirts and tight jackets, all of pure white cotton or muslin, and Buddhist priests in sheets of yellow plaid silk cloth wrapped around their bodies and draped over the shoulders. It was his first encounter with Buddhism, and there was much to favor in the religion's faith in gratitude, contentment, moderation, and forgiveness, among other means for a peaceful way of life. Such a religion was a reflection of the environment, he decided, which was lush with botanical gardens and varieties of palm trees, including breadfruit, banyan, and jackfruit. The caste system was the island's only drawback, a social system Carnegie would experience to a greater degree at the next stop, India, a country ruled over by Great Britain.

A three-day journey by mail steamer brought the adventurers to Madras, India, and from there they sailed across the Bay of Bengal to Calcutta, the City of Palaces. During a jaunt to the Ganges River to watch the Hindus participate in the sacred rite of bathing, Carnegie observed sarcastically, "What a mercy that Brahma thought of elevating personal cleanliness to the rank of virtues!"[7] Cremations on the funeral pyre, the mostly naked body sitting upright in the flames, was an unsettling sight to Carnegie. He was also disturbed to discover those in charge of dressing and burning the dead were of such a low caste no one desired to associate with them. To soothe himself, he ruminated over Spencer, reflecting, "In the progress of the race such dreadful conceptions of God must apparently exist for a time."[8] He was certain the railroad and newspapers would aid the country's evolution beyond the oppressive caste system by providing the people means to trade with and to educate one another.

On February 6, Carnegie and Vandy traveled by train to the Hindu Mecca, Banaras, a mystical city where the rajah's temple was on a cliff overlooking the Ganges, then pushed on to Akbar to view the Taj Mahal. Filled with great expectations for the Taj, Carnegie claimed to be disappointed, but only slightly, when he finally toured the wonder: "Am I to be disappointed? Of course I am. I have made up my mind to that, and having just had tiffin, and drank a whole pint of bitter beer, I feel myself quite competent to criticize the Taj with the best of them, and especially well fitted just now to stand no nonsense."[9] The structure was solemn and joyous, graceful and charming, the interior adorned with exquisite mosaics of fruits and flowers, originally made from precious stones, but now colored glass that still dazzled. Shah Jahan had built the Taj Mahal, completed circa 1648, as a tomb and a memorial for his favorite wife Mumtaz Mahal. It took eleven years, twenty thousand men, and an emperor's fortune to build, but its great cost to society was justified, according to Carnegie: "Truly a costly monument, you say. No doubt, but if it has given mankind one proof that the loftiest ideal can be wrought out and realized in practice, the Taj would be cheap even if its erection had emptied the Comstock lode. . . . I would think the time and labor and money bestowed upon it well spent had it been twenty times—aye, a hundred times—as great. There is no price too dear to pay for perfection."[10] The monument intoxicated Carnegie; for him, such monuments were another form of glorious immortality.

On February 16, they arrived in Delhi, where they remained for several days before moving on to Bombay. Carnegie felt at home in that city, which he called the Rome of India and found quite modern. Here, business caught up with him when a letter from Shinn dated December 1 arrived with news that struck Carnegie to the heart: Mr. David McCandless, chairman of the

Edgar Thomson Steel Company, as well as longtime supporter and confidant, was dead.[11] Carnegie, feeling cheated, lamented he was not there to see his friend one last time. With great difficulty, he wrote to Shinn:

> It does seem too hard to bear, but we must bite the lip & go forward I suppose assuming indifference—but I am sure none of us can ever efface from our memories the images of our dear, generous, gentle & unselfish friend— To the day I die I know I shall never be able to think of him without a stinging pain at the heart—His death robs my life of one of its chief pleasures, but it must be borne, only let us take from his loss one lesson as the best tribute to his memory. Let us try to be as kind and devoted to each other as he was to us. He was a model for all of us to follow. One thing more we can do—attend to his affairs & get them right that Mrs. McCandless & Helen may be provided for—I know you will all be looking after this & you know how anxious I shall be to cooperate with you.[12]

While Carnegie's tribute was undoubtedly heartfelt, he would take advantage of his friend's untimely death to further consolidate his own power within the company. As for Shinn, he would start negotiating to replace McCandless as chairman before Carnegie even returned to the States.

While en route to Egypt, a six-day leg, Carnegie took time to reflect on India. He concluded that the country, strong in the cotton, wheat, and tea industries, had great potential; but, as he had decided about China, the quicker it adopted Western ways, including the Christian religion, he believed, the better off the people would be. So, although he had rejected the church, thinking himself evolved beyond the need for a dictatorial god, he wanted to impose Christianity on India for the country's benefit, a contradiction he didn't acknowledge. As for the British rule of India and elsewhere, he was impressed: "The more I see of the thoroughness of the English Government in the East—its attention to the minutest details, the exceptional ability of its officials as evinced in the excellence of the courts, jails, hospitals, dispensaries, schools, roads, railways, canals, etc.,—the more I am amazed."[13] Too easily seduced by genius in any form, whether in an individual or a political system, Carnegie was blind to the underside of colonialism, to the oppression and economic pillaging. For all of England's noble work, however, he did recognize it wouldn't be long before India revolted against the British Empire.

After making its way through the Suez Canal, the ship anchored off the coast of Egypt. Carnegie and Vandy then took in the sights of Cairo, a picturesque city with a commanding citadel and hundreds of mosques with slender spirals poking at the sky. There was an opera house, a circus, cafés, and the renowned museum with its haunting mummies, sarcophagi, jewelry, coins, and statues. Next came the great pyramids at Giza, where three Arabs helped Carnegie climb Cheops, one on each side and the third behind, pulling and pushing. While the pyramids held a mystical power, it was the mysterious, sad Sphinx that captured his imagination, symbolizing everything, yet nothing, he said.

As the exotic odyssey reached its end, Carnegie boiled down his foremost negative opinions of life in the East: "Life there lacks two of its most important elements—the want of intelligent and refined women as the companion of man, and a Sunday. It has been a strange experience to me to be for several months without the society of some of this class of women—sometimes many weeks without even speaking to one, and often a whole week without even seeing the face of an educated woman. And, bachelor as I am, let me confess what a miserable, dark, dreary, and insipid life this would be without their constant companionship!"[14] It was the second time he mentioned the lack of a female companion; the trip had exacerbated his emotional loneliness, his want of a woman.

On March 14, after two weeks in Egypt, they departed for Sicily, to be followed by Naples, Rome, Florence, Paris, and London. Four days later, Sicily rose from the Mediterranean. Once ashore, Carnegie inhaled the rich aromas of olive, oranges, and lemons wafting from the groves. Vandy and he ascended Mount Etna, an active volcano on the east coast, but the climb to the top was not as exhilarating to Carnegie as receiving a note from Shinn declaring E.T. had bested Cambria in steel rail production. "Pyramids & Mt Etna & Vesuvius have been our last climbs—Mt E of course we did only from the base," he replied. "Tell Capt Jones there was a proud little stout man who gave a wild hurrah when he saw E T ahead."[15]

In London, Carnegie's mother joined them, and a month was passed in England and Scotland, visiting friends and family. On June 14, the group sailed for home on a Cunard steamer. They arrived in New York ten days later, exactly eight months after Carnegie and Vandy had departed San Francisco. Carnegie went straight to Cresson to rest from his extensive vacation.

The pastoral voyage through a slice of time had come to an end, but the grand panorama remained vivid in Carnegie's mind and gave him a more expansive view of life. He was inspired to share his experience and to expose himself, or rather his thoughts and emotions during the journey that rekindled his old desire to become a writer in the vein of Horace Greeley and Bayard Taylor. Over the next several years, he organized his notes and reflections and penned a book, which he had privately printed for his family, friends, and colleagues. Although he experienced the thrill of holding the book in his hands, he was anxious over its reception: "The writer of a book designed for his friends has no reason to anticipate an unkind reception, but there is always some danger of its being damned with faint praise."[16] He was no Mark Twain or Herman Melville, but the work was regarded highly enough for Charles Scribner's Sons to purchase the rights to publish it for general readership; it would appear in 1884 under the title *Round the World*.

Having witnessed diverse cultures, many stricken with conflict, Carnegie declared himself to be growing "tolerant and liberal" and he concluded the book with a call for "the Brotherhood of Man."[17] Such a liberal and embracing view did not supersede Carnegie's combative religion of survival of the fittest. The odyssey had confirmed arguments set forth by Spencer and Darwin: "A new horizon was opened up to me by this voyage. It quite changed my intellectual outlook. Spencer and Darwin were then high in the zenith, and I had become deeply interested in their work. I began to view the various phases of human life from the standpoint of the evolutionist. . . . The result of my journey was to bring a certain mental peace. Where there had been chaos there was now order. My mind was at rest. I had a philosophy at last. . . . All our duties lie in this world and in the present, and trying impatiently to peer into that which lies beyond is as vain as fruitless."[18]

More so than ever, Carnegie found justification for his relentless pursuit of material progress: "Not only had I got rid of theology and the supernatural, but I had found the truth of evolution. 'All is well since all grows better' became my motto, my true source of comfort."[19] If his business continued to grow, then all was well. It was a faultless argument, according to Carnegie, who devoutly believed the theories of Spencer and Darwin were fact. If his friends, subordinates, and competition suffered in this battle for survival, such was evolution. There was no room for sympathy; after all, Spencer concluded that when the struggle begins "all start with equal advantages," and then those with natural ability excel. "One part of the community is industrious and prudent and accumulates property," Spencer wrote, "the other idle and improvident or in some cases perhaps, unfortunate."[20] These ideas engulfed Carnegie and became weapons in the battle for domination over competitors, partners, and labor. He would also need these weapons to block any influences of his proletarian, radical heritage as he espoused material progress.

Bachelorhood had weighed heavily on Carnegie for some time, the weight only to increase when, in November 1879, he turned forty-four years of age. After his voyage around the world, his hair had thinned, his beard was thicker with gray, and his face more weathered, reflecting his angst. Once again fully immersed in the New York social scene, he couldn't help but notice that the young ladies he had been riding with in Central Park were being married off, and those who were not failed to meet his high standards. With another New Year approaching, the feelings of loneliness, of wanting someone to share in his triumphs and battles, intensified. Carnegie needed an additional emotional pillar to complement his aging mother.

On New Year's Day in 1880, Carnegie strode out of the luxurious Windsor Hotel, at Fifth Avenue between Forty-fifth and Forty-sixth Streets, where Margaret and he had recently moved, to pay his respects to various friends, as was the custom. Dressed fashionably in a silk shirt, black waistcoat and straight trousers, patent leather button boots with suede uppers (and inserted lifts to add a good inch to his height), as well as a top hat, Carnegie cut a sharp figure. He was joined by Alexander King, a Scotsman who'd made his wealth in the thread business, and his wife Aggie. Just two blocks from the Windsor Hotel, they visited with the Kings' longtime friends, the Whitfields, a family from good Yankee stock. John W. Whitfield, having prospered as a dealer of fine dress material, had died at age forty-six in 1878, and was survived by his wife and three children. This was Carnegie's first visit since his death. Even though Carnegie, who had won the contract to supply the superstructure for the Brooklyn Bridge and was supplying beams for New York's derided elevated railway—a noisy, smoky nuisance—was known for being brash and arrogant, the Whitfield family looked forward to his ebullient company, having been introduced to him by the Kings several years earlier. When he arrived, Carnegie noticed for the first time that Louise, the eldest child, was no longer a schoolgirl, but a self-possessed twenty-two-year-old woman. She had blue eyes, brown hair, and the strong, determined jaw of Carnegie's mother. She was also a delicate woman, trained in the ways of high society, as were the many debutantes he encountered. Since her father's death, Alexander King had been inviting Louise riding in Central Park, and when he suggested a ride sometime soon, Carnegie insisted he come along. He was most impressed the society girl was willing to ride in winter.

Decked out in a short frock coat, breeches of broad corduroy, top hat and spurs, and astride his fine horse, Carnegie appeared far larger than his five-foot-three frame. His aggressive and competent riding style immediately caught Louise's eye as they toured Central Park with Alex King. Dressed in black riding habits, a tip-tilted top hat with a wisp of tulle, a snug-fitting, high-collared jacket with short tails, a long, smooth skirt, and fur-lined leather gloves, she, too, was most impressive on her beast. As they cantered through the park, their breath streams of mist in the cold winter air, Carnegie quickly recognized she was just as competent an equestrian as he, and he found himself aroused, later noting, "A woman looks her loveliest on horseback."[21] Not long after their first ride together, Carnegie asked permission to take Louise riding without King's companionship, a request Louise's mother granted.

At first it was intimidating for Louise to be out riding with a man-about-town, for he seemed to know everyone, including the other young ladies, but his worldly charm put her at ease. Her own friends immediately speculated as to Mr. Carnegie's intentions: was this a wooing in the making? It appeared the steel master had indeed found a woman who was well educated and without the airs of a spoiled society girl—a probable match. Over the course of their spring rides, Carnegie learned that the Whitfield family had lived in Gramercy Park but moved uptown to escape the congestion, as had he. He learned that she had been schooled for twelve years, had excelled in her deportment and recitations, and was fluent in French, as was he. She had toured Europe in 1873, visiting Great Britain, France, Belgium, Switzerland,

Germany, and Austria, where she had attended a Johann Strauss concert—the maestro both conducting and playing violin—and she was an avid theatergoer, having seen *Pygmalion and Galatea, The Merchant of Venice, Twelfth Night, The Pirates of Penzance,* and *The Mikado,* the latter two written by a pair of new stars, Gilbert and Sullivan. The Russian poet Pushkin, Wordsworth, and Emerson were her favorite authors. All these shards of her life were gathered by Carnegie as the horses idled between trotting and cantering and bursts into a rollicking gallop.

Carnegie was earnestly courting Miss Louise Whitfield in early 1881, but it wasn't easy. Not only was his free time very limited, but Carnegie was naive as how to best use it in expressing interest in a woman beyond casual flirtations in a social setting. So their relationship continued to revolve around horseback riding in Central Park, a common ground he found comfortable. Thrilled by the steel master's companionship, Louise wrote in her diary, "Went riding with Mr. Carnegie. Glorious time! . . . In afternoon Mr. Carnegie came and took me horseback riding. Splendid time!"[22] On one occasion, in February 1881, Carnegie sent his mother to the Whitfields to take Mrs. Whitfield and Louise's younger siblings for a carriage ride. A short time later the wily wooer followed, giving Louise and himself some time alone together before heading for the stables. Louise had a "splendid time!"[23] Just three days later, Louise, Carnegie, and his mother attended a production of *Macbeth,* and again Louise enjoyed herself.[24] Their relationship was just heating up when summer threatened to derail it.

Carnegie was planning a six-week coaching trip through Great Britain when he realized this meant leaving Louise for an extended period. After mulling over the situation, he decided to make a bold move: he would invite Louise to join him on the trip; after all, two other young, unattached ladies would be among the proposed eleven travelers, and the Kings, who could chaperon, were also planning to come. Louise was thoroughly enthralled with the idea and consulted her mother. "In afternoon went to ride," she wrote in her diary on April 6. "Had a delightful time—afraid it is my last. He told me to speak to Mama about trip and she says I cannot possibly go. So unhappy."

Apparently, Margaret Carnegie and Mrs. Whitfield had already spoken on the matter, with Margaret declaring it improper. It was a rather indiscriminate decision considering that there would be other young ladies on the trip; but then, like her son Andrew, Margaret stood for no rivals. Hopes dashed, Louise wrote, "I cannot become reconciled to my disappointment. Mr. C. has invited me to go on his drag trip but Mother says it's not proper for me to go. . . . Mr. C. came in the morning and I told him I could not go on his trip to England. Am afraid that it is the last I shall see of him. He goes to Pittsburgh tomorrow. Stayed home all afternoon and evening and Mother and I so unhappy."[25] Carnegie did not give up so easily, however. Standing up to his mother, he insisted she go to the Whitfields and encourage Mrs. Whitfield to allow Louise to join them.

When the Whitfields received Mrs. Carnegie in the drawing room, the old matriarch, now seventy years of age, was cordial but did not argue on Louise and her son's behalf. To the contrary, waiting until Louise was beyond earshot, the conniving Margaret told Mrs. Whitfield, "If she were a daughter of mine she wouldna go."[26] The next day Louise despaired, "I am so unhappy about the trip. I want to go so much and yet I see it is impossible."[27] It was for the best, reasoned Louise once the initial disappointment faded, as it seemed useless to pursue a courtship with such a busy older man. When he invited her to a concert on May 7, she declined. Two weeks later, Carnegie insisted Louise join him and his coaching party, who called themselves the Gay Charioteers, for a last dinner in New York. Not wanting to play the spoiled loser, Louise accepted with grace. "Was very sorry I went," she noted in her diary, "but did not know how to get out of it. . . . I suppose the party all got off this morning. I must learn to be satisfied with what I have and not long for more."[28]

The very day of this farewell dinner, the world bid good-bye to Carnegie's mentor Tom Scott, who died after suffering a third stroke. Not so unexpectedly, Carnegie treated his fallen hero's death with the same passing indifference as he did his own father's death, merely noting in his autobiography that the financial disaster of 1873 and subsequent humiliation "cut him [Scott] to the quick." Carnegie was far more saddened over Louise not joining the coaching party, but even here his buoyancy soon returned. Before leaving, he said to Captain Jones, "Oh Bill, when once I get on a steamer and feel myself rounding Sandy Hook, with this long vacation ahead, you don't know what a relief it is to me!"

"And you, Andy, don't know what a relief it is to all of us!"[29] Jones replied with a sardonic chuckle.

These vacations, whether odysseys around the world or a tour of Europe — which would now become an annual affair — were essential to Carnegie's personal evolution, to his contentment. If he did not delve into other cultures, did not explore other social and political landscapes, he would have completely failed the promises he made to himself in 1868. Although this junket was no 'round the world adventure, Carnegie was exceptionally thrilled to return to Britain for one reason: when the party reached Dunfermline he would participate in the groundbreaking ceremony for the construction of a public library, marking his very first donation for a public library building — to be named in his honor, of course. Giving away money for libraries, he had discovered, was not so easy. The prior year Carnegie had offered $25,000 for the building, on the condition Dunfermline invoke the Free Libraries Act, which gave it the power to levy a one-penny tax on the individual townspeople to fund operating expenses. Dickering over the costs of maintaining the library ensued, and the hometown hero's offer was initially rejected because it would cost too much to support. Relatives still living there were outraged. "How about the library (?)" his cousin Thomas Morrison wrote. "I think we have a set of muddleheads managing our municipal affairs just now. There is scarcely a man of average ability amongst them. The lukewarm manner in which they received your generous offer was disgraceful & were it not that I am certain the public think as I do, I would say withdraw it."[30] To ingratiate himself, Carnegie invited a select group of Dunfermline councilmen, their wives, and several others for a tour of the United Sates at his expense. Over the course of the ongoing discussions, he explained that he wanted to plant the seed, as it were, with the building, but then it was up to the town to also make a commitment—a philosophy for giving from which he wouldn't depart. Apparently his lobbying worked.[31]

But the furor didn't end there. Back in Pittsburgh, critics argued that Carnegie's generosity was misplaced when taking into account he had made his money from the sweat of the men in Pittsburgh area mills. Had he not already given Dunfermline $25,000 for baths? Was it not time to give back to the communities of Allegheny and Braddock, from which he had taken? Unbeknownst to his detractors, Carnegie and Jones were already planning a library for Braddock; but as Carnegie learned, it wasn't easy serving two distinct loyalties in two countries.

On June 1, the Gay Charioteers sailed for Liverpool, England, where they arrived ten days later. The American contingent included Margaret Carnegie, Jeannie Johns, Alice French, Carnegie's old friend David McCargo and his wife, Mr. and Mrs. King, Benjamin Vandevort, Harry Phipps, Gardner McCandless, and the king himself—Carnegie. He brought along two penny passbooks for notetaking in case he decided to pen another travel book, which he did, publishing *An American Four-in-Hand in Britain* in 1883, and dedicating it to "My Favorite Heroine My Mother." The *New York Herald* would receive it kindly: "Mr. Carnegie is a keen, interested, practical, and, on the whole, kindly observer; and he records his observations and experiences in quite a pleasing style."[32]

From Liverpool, it was a coach ride to London, where Carnegie mingled with the city's literati, including novelist William Black, whom he had happened to meet in Rome on his world tour and who nicknamed Carnegie the "Star-Spangled Scotchman." Black then introduced him to the poet Edwin Arnold, among others. After a five-day stay in London, the Charioteers coached south to Brighton, a coastal resort town. There, the party made final preparations for a seven-week sightseeing tour that would average thirty-two miles a day and take them north through the royal home of Windsor, Shakespeare's birthplace Stratford-upon-Avon, the industrialized Midlands, Edinburgh, Inverness on Loch Ness, and of course, Dunfermline.

The black-and-red polished coach accommodating fourteen up top, with four horses, a driver, and a footman, the men adorned in silver-and-blue uniforms, impressed Carnegie. The experience of riding behind noble steeds, according to him, was "the most exquisite pleasure in life."[33] The first notable stop was Windsor, a quaint town dominated by the royal family's Windsor Castle. While attending Windsor Church, they were surprised to see the Liberal prime minister William Gladstone and the Prince of Wales there for the services. To Carnegie, the seventy-one-year-old Gladstone, a heroic radical, appeared pale and haggard—a "sadly noble lionface"—not a vision of the majestic legend he imagined. In reflecting on the encounter, Carnegie called forth lines from Milton's poetry:

> A pillar of state: deep on his front engraven
> Deliberation sat and public care;
> And princely counsel in his face yet shone,
> Majestic though in ruin.[34]

Gladstone's unexpected physical decline troubled him, but for all of Carnegie's outward emotional and sentimental expressions—teary eyes, broad smiles, wild gesturing—he still struggled to express his feelings, to disclose to anyone his innermost thoughts and fears. Instead, he continued to use the words of others like Milton, and, by flaunting his ability to quote the great poets, he masked his own self.

At Carnegie's invitation, Sidney Gilchrist-Thomas, an inventor who greatly aided the steel industry, and his family joined the Charioteers for a Windsor dinner at which Carnegie and his mother, as they always did, made quite an impression on Thomas's sister Lillian. "His devotion to his mother, a trenchant old lady who called a spade a spade with racy Scottish wit, was delightful to see," she recalled.[35] With Louise an ocean away, Margaret did indeed take center stage. On June 19, the party celebrated her seventy-first birthday; according to Carnegie, not a dry eye prevailed at the emotional tribute dinner. Under the spotlight throughout the trip, Margaret thrived. "The Queen Dowager [Margaret] and Aggie [King] were off to paidle in the burn after luncheon," Carnegie memorialized her in his pennybook, "and as a fitting close they kilted their petticoats and danced a highland reel on the greensward, in sight of the company, but at some distance from us. They were just wee lassies again, and to be a wee lassie at seventy-one is a triumph indeed."[36] Over the course of the trip, she sang Scottish songs, including a ditty about marrying the one you love no matter what—unless you were one Andrew Carnegie.

The young and supple Louise did indeed remain on Carnegie's mind, and on June 21 he took time to pen a letter to her. He also took no pains to water down his pleasure as he described the enthusiastic party, the pretty gardens, and the sumptuous picnics. He concluded, "It is all I pictured it, and more." Louise could take some comfort when he concluded the letter by expressing desire for her company and asking her to write, care of J. S. Morgan and Company in London.[37]

As the Gay Charioteers moved north, they strolled alongside the carriage; picked handfuls of wildflowers; had roadside picnics; played lawn tennis; went fishing, rowboating, and yachting; and toured castles and cathedrals. To ward off chilly days, they nipped whiskey, sherry, or brandy, and nights were spent in country inns. In Stratford-upon-Avon, tribute was paid to Shakespeare at the bard's gravesite. "I have been there often," Carnegie wrote, "but I am always awed into silence as I approach the church; and when I stand beside the ashes of Shakespeare I cannot repress stern, gloomy thoughts, and ask why so potent a force is now but a little dust. The inexplicable waste of nature, a million born that one may live, seems nothing compared to this—the brain of a god doing its work one day and food for worms the next!"[38] Mortality forever haunted the agnostic Carnegie, who lived in an age when death was indiscriminate. Eternal life, he always recalled to comfort himself, was achieved through words: "What a man says too often outlives what he does, even when he does great things."

From Shakespeare's village, it was on to the industrial heartland of the Midlands, aptly named the Black Country. "We see the Black Country now," Carnegie wrote, "rows of little dingy houses beyond, with tall smoky chimneys vomiting smoke, mills and factories at every turn, coal pits and rolling mills and blast furnaces, the very bottomless pit itself; and such dirty careworn children, hard-driven men, and squalid women. To think of the green lanes, the larks, the Arcadia we have just left. How can people be got to live such terrible lives as they seem condemned to here?"[39] The very question social workers would ask of the Pittsburgh slums housing Carnegie laborers. When it came to living conditions surrounding his own mills, the underbelly of the American industrial town, he was either completely blind, believing so righteously in the Great Republic, or he was too fearful to confront it, or it was simply a natural condition per Spencerian philosophy to be accepted in America, where everyone had an equal chance.

Almost a week was passed in the Black Country as Carnegie toured mills and conducted business. Meanwhile, back in his adopted country, on July 2, 1881, a lone gunman shot President James A. Garfield, and the Gay Charioteers were distraught as they scoured the London *Times* for details. Apparently the assassin was a disenchanted job seeker, angered by the Garfield administration, which was scandalized by squabbles over the filling of federal jobs. Fortunately, it appeared Garfield would recover and Carnegie sent congratulations. Of the coaching party, he was the most distressed because he had dined with the president just a week before departing on the tour, a testimony to his rising success. Politicians now considered him an industrial magnate to be tapped for electoral support, financial and otherwise. At the dinner they had discussed William Black's popular *Adventures of a Phaeton*, a work Garfield had praised as Black's best. Unfortunately Carnegie's congratulations were premature; the president would die on September 19, to be succeeded by Vice President Chester Alan Arthur.

The coaching party was revitalized when, on July 16, the group entered Scotland—Dunfermline and the triumphant library dedication were only days away. By now, Carnegie's coaching trip was generating some press, too; his movements were reported daily, and wherever the handsome coach stopped crowds gathered to meet the native millionaire-hero. Carnegie embraced the publicity—the exact opposite of John D. Rockefeller, who, portrayed as rapacious dictator, became an aloof recluse. Carnegie knew he had arrived when the local police forces had to clear paths through the streets. The first night was spent in Dumfries, Robert Burns's resting place; then they moved on to Edinburgh, and finally to Dunfermline. As they neared the outskirts, a white haired, bent-over figure approached; it was Uncle Lauder, now in his sixties, determined to ride next to his surrogate son, who was to be honored for his success and benevolence.

At the entrance to the city, a triumphal arch had been built and "Welcome Carnegie" banners graced the streets. Factories and businesses were closed, sidewalks were crowded with men, women, and children in their Sunday best, faces pushed through upper-story windows, and a mile-long parade stretched through the town, following the coach, as some twenty thousand people paid tribute. "The town was ablaze with flags and mottoes and streaming ribbons," one of the Charioteers recalled,

> the American stars and stripes waving everywhere, even over the noble old abbey where the Scottish kings lie in their stone coffins. Bells were ringing, drums beating, people shouting. The Chief [Carnegie], taken by surprise, his sunburnt cheeks pale, and, as he afterward confessed, a big lump in his throat, could only bow right and left, while the crowd swarmed about the coach windows and a hundred hands were outstretched to grasp his mother's.
>
> As for the rest of us, we felt a little like members of a royal progress, and a great deal like a part of a circus.[40]

At the ceremonial laying of the first foundation stone for the library, the provost of Dunfermline handed the trowel to Carnegie, who then insisted his mother perform the rite. She spread the mortar, gave the stone three taps for good luck, and announced, "I pronounce this memorial stone duly and properly laid, and may God bless the undertaking." At the celebratory dinner, Dunfermline's provost praised Carnegie, noting that "the only flaw in Mr. Carnegie's character is that he wants a wife. I attribute that very much to the fact of his having a mother. His mother has taken good care over him, and has showed that she does not want to hand him over to the tender mercies of

Carnegie, seated next to his mother, made a triumphant return to his hometown of Dunfermline, Scotland, to dedicate his first Scottish library. (Courtesy of the Carnegie Library of Pittsburgh)

some half-cousin, or any of the half-dozen young ladies who are with him today."[41] Laughter followed, but the provost's observations cut to his heart.

So it was, on July 27, 1881, Carnegie celebrated his first major library benefaction. In the course of designing the building, the architect had asked Carnegie for his coat of arms, but he had none. Instead, he suggested a rising sun shedding its rays be carved into stone over the entrance door, along with the motto "Let there be light."[42] Libraries were his cathedrals, a holy place to worship knowledge. In these hallowed buildings, the sin of ignorance was washed away and individuals could improve their station in life. Libraries perpetuated social evolution. The founding of free public libraries was a tradition in Great Britain, which he aimed to pursue on a grand scale. He also wanted to follow in the footsteps of Ben Franklin, Colonel Anderson, and his father, who had cofounded a very modest library for weavers.

Following the tour's climax in Dunfermline, on August 13, a large crowd saw Carnegie off at Liverpool. Once back in New York, he was in a melancholy mood, his friends having gone their separate ways and Louise still at her family's summer home in the Poconos. "Two or three of the most miserable hours I ever spent were those at the St. Nicholas Hotel, where the Queen Dowager, Ben [Vandevort], and I lunched alone before starting for Cresson.

Even Ben had to take an earlier train for Pittsburgh, and I exclaimed: 'All our family gone! I feel so lonely, so deserted; not one remains.' But the Queen was equal to the emergency. 'Oh, you don't count me, then! You have still one that sticks to you.' Oh, yes, indeed, sure of that, old lady," concluded Carnegie wryly, thinking of Louise Whitfield.[43] Louise, for her part, continued to entertain other suitors and seriously questioned Carnegie's interest in her; after all, he appeared more enamored with his cultural pursuits and his business concerns. Particularly distracting in the first year of their relationship was the climax of a major conflict with Edgar Thomson's general manager, William P. Shinn, that then endangered the tenure of the invaluable Captain Jones.

CHAPTER 13

War against the
Steel Aristocracy

T he first significant fissure in Carnegie and Shinn's relationship—one that would eventually engulf Captain Jones—had appeared when Carnegie was in Rome in the spring of 1879, winding up his world tour. At that time, Shinn committed a major blunder by making a most presumptuous request. When Carnegie arrived at the Hotel du Quirinal in Rome, there awaited a lengthy letter from Shinn, who stated his case for why he should be made chairman of the Edgar Thomson Steel Company, filling the vacant seat left by McCandless. It was an audacious proposition, Carnegie thought, especially considering McCandless's untimely demise and the fact that he, the majority owner, was not yet home. (The Edgar Thomson Company would expediently purchase the McCandless estate's share in July.)[1] His reply was firm: "Your personal [letter] was a genuine surprise. It never occurred to me that you would prefer to be called chairman rather than genl. manager, on the contrary the latter was your own choice. . . . Let the matter rest until my return, & we will meet as friends, desirous of pleasing each other & I am sure our happy family will remain one. Tom cares as little for names as I do, I think, and that is simply nothing—it's the prosperity of the works we seek. That's our pride."

Carnegie considered the concern over titles, or names, rather petty. Once he had exited his fast-wheeling bond-selling days, he never did hold a formal title in any of his companies; on the other hand, the companies always had his name in their titles. Carnegie was also upset that Shinn had apparently given himself a raise from an $8,000 annual salary to $10,000, and concluded his note by saying, "Let me get a little time for breathing please—You travel fast in this direction."[2]

More so than titles and money, it worried Carnegie that Shinn was looking to expand his power while the ruler was overseas. Three days after replying to Shinn, he wrote his favorite whipping boy, John Scott, to let them know he remained vigilant:

> I think Mr. Shinn might have spared me his long letter of complaint—It has of course cut my holiday short & made me uneasy—Surely he couldn't expect me to act on such a matter until my return—What use then in annoying me—I would not have done it to him had he been away. . . . His action after what I have done for him seems to me ungracious. Then he has gone into a damned gambling operation contracting for 45,000 tons low priced rails without first covering with Pig Iron—I can't trust such speculative people as you & he appear to me to be. . . . Why can't you try to reform & make yourselves respectable manufacturers in which hope your friend Andrew will offer up today in St. Peter's a solemn prayer.
>
> Good night My Boy I am glad you are better, I like you awfully, only I must give you a piece of my mind now & then.[3]

Having been away from the business too long and now paranoid, Carnegie held Scott partly responsible for Shinn's greedy desires, and to subjugate him, he blasted Scott over the selling of rails at a low cost before procuring pig iron at a low cost, which was tantamount to gambling. (In some respects, he was a conservative businessman.) Calling him "My Boy" was particularly insulting.

Tension between Carnegie and Shinn was running high in the summer of 1879; Shinn wanted an answer on his bid to become chairman of the Edgar Thomson Steel Company, and Carnegie continued to demur. Only a trusted partner was going to sit at the head of a Carnegie company, and with Coleman and McCandless now gone, realistically it was going to be either brother Tom or Phipps. At an August meeting of the partners, Tom was the clear front-runner.

When Shinn realized he was not going to be anointed chairman, he threatened to resign as general manager and insisted on taking a vacation to the St. Lawrence River Valley for relaxation and fishing. Instead, he went to St. Louis to interview with a competitor, the Vulcan Iron Company, promising that if hired as general manager he would bring Captain Jones with him.[4] When rumors finally filtered in to Carnegie about the Peerless Lime Company, the interlocking investment Shinn had created with his brother, and about Shinn visiting Vulcan, he was livid. Determined to expel Shinn, he declared to everyone who would listen that if his general manager didn't resign, he would "make it so warm for Shinn that he would have his resignation before Christmas."[5]

On September 13, Shinn submitted his resignation, but added, "I have full confidence in the pecuniary success of the E. T. S. Co. Limited and purpose to remain your business associate; and it will be my interest, to advance its success by any and all means in my power."[6] It was a gutsy play on Shinn's part, who was hoping to retain his interest in E.T. and reap the profits, especially considering he had originally been given his share on credit, to be paid off by future dividends, and had now secured a job at Vulcan. Carnegie didn't have to sniff out the double-dealing—it was so obvious. He simply decided to cut all ties, urging Shinn that he should "go, but in that case I cannot concur with your idea that you should remain interested with us at all—surely you don't want your colleagues to do all the work & you sit down only to share ingloriously in their triumphs. No, no, if you go, go. Sell out & try another party. We want no drones in E.T. if we can help it."[7] No drones, no parasites— the message was clear.

Later that month, the Edgar Thomson board met, appointed Tom chairman, and accepted Shinn's resignation. Now there remained the issue of compensating Shinn for his shares. At the meeting's conclusion, Carnegie, Shinn, and the man who brought him into the firm, John Scott, remained in the room. Carnegie offered Shinn $105,000, the book value of his shares, only to have Shinn argue for his corresponding piece of the Kloman and McCandless interests the company had absorbed. This request, Carnegie told him, would not be considered, period. Fed up with the autocracy, Shinn spat out that working under Carnegie amounted to slavery, and the discussions came to an abrupt conclusion. Both men did agree the dispute should go to arbitration, with B. F. Jones and two other prominent Pittsburgh businessmen agreeing to arbitrate.

During the hearing, Shinn charged Carnegie with "willful and malicious mendacity," otherwise known as deceptive dealing, and Carnegie countered that Shinn was scheming to fleece Edgar Thomson.[8] That was that. Shinn withdrew from arbitration and filed suit in the Allegheny County Court. Hoping for a sympathetic judge, Carnegie petitioned that the case be removed to the U.S. Circuit Court, which was granted. Hoping to shame Carnegie into capitulating, in a clever tit for tat, Shinn secured an order for the E.T. ledger books to be submitted as evidence. The idea of exposing his company to public scrutiny was indeed anathema to Carnegie, so he quickly took a conciliatory tone and they returned to the arbitration table. With no squirming room, he handed over what Shinn demanded, close to $200,000, ending a rather ugly episode.[9]

What had gone wrong? After all, Carnegie was to become renowned for his selection of lieutenants. Inflating the ego, overpromising, and micromanagement, all of which poisoned the relationship, fell on Carnegie's liability side of the ledger. In other words, extremely resolute to succeed at Edgar Thomson, he had wooed Shinn so fervently, pushed him so hard, and promised so much that Shinn rightly expected the chairmanship. On Shinn's side, lies, double-dealing, ambition, and greed were his undoing. Too late, Carnegie had recognized what Niccolo Machiavelli had warned against more than four hundred years earlier: "When you see the minister think more of himself than of you, and in all his actions seek his own profit, such a man will never be a good minister, and you can never rely on him."[10] Prince Carnegie had no choice but to purge his minister.

*   *   *

When Shinn became chief of Vulcan, a strong enemy on the western front, it served to harden Carnegie's resolve and desire to crush any competition. The move also precipitated a conflict between Captain Jones and Carnegie, whose heavy-handedness and absentee ownership could very well be his undoing. Again, due to his prolonged absence, Carnegie wasn't aware of any problems until he sent an innocent note to his superintendent suggesting they build a library at Braddock. (With prodigious profits in his pocket, Carnegie was beginning to consider more notable beneficence.) Jones's reply started off benign enough as he fully approved of "the Library idea, but think we can wait awhile until we get all the main improvements completed about the Works." But then Jones, who was well aware of the prodigious profits, decided it was time to make a bid for a larger share for himself. He bluntly stated, "On my present salary, I can never expect to accumulate competency for myself or family. You will admit that the career of the E.T. has been unexampled in every respect to attain this, has cost me many a severe headache and many a sleepless night." He also made it clear he would prefer to remain in his current position than find work elsewhere: "Your brother, T.C. suits me exactly, and is a far more sagacious business man than the late Gen. Man [Shinn]. It is a pleasure to me to be associated with him in the management of these works and I only give utterance to my earnest convictions when I say of him, that he is the clearest brained business man I ever had connections with. You may well repose confidence in him. To you and him I appeal and with you and him I will leave this question. I can only say that I think I am worth more money than I am getting."[11]

Fearing Jones might defect to a rival concern, Carnegie immediately cabled his brother, to whom the fiery Welshman was endeared, with instructions to meet with Jones and ascertain what he was thinking.

He also wrote Jones: "I like yours of 5th much,—always be frank with us—As for you leaving your own works—that's absurd—You could never be so *proud* of any other—As for compensation we never have differed about that & wont—Tom & I appreciate you I believe more than you do yourself. All you have to do is say what you want & *don't put it low either.* . . . Tell me confidentially what would not only satisfy you—but *gratify* you as well."[12] As he had with Shinn, Carnegie offered lavish praise, yet there was the possibility that if he overindulged Jones he could set the stage for a future rift. There seemed to be no middle ground for the reactionary Carnegie; he was either extravagant with praise or brutal in his condemnation.

On the other hand, if Jones wasn't content, there was no telling what he would do, so appeasing his most important employee quickly was paramount. The Captain, after all, was known for his impulsive behavior and propensity to lather himself up into a "towering rage." Inflicted with a speech impediment, Jones's words became garbled when raging, sometimes leading to humorous castigations of subordinates—humorous to those avoiding his wrath.[13] Temper aside, the undisputed czar of Braddock was revered by the thirteen-year-old water boys and hardened mill hands alike. Most pleasant evenings would find him buying peanuts from a street vendor and then walking the town's streets as though he owned them, cracking peanut shells and greeting the men cordially.

Tom, who was forever smoothing over the feathers his brother ruffled, discovered in his talk with Jones that he had actually been to Shinn's Vulcan works for an interview and offered a substantial sum to leave E.T.—an offer still on the table. Since it was his older brother who wielded the ultimate power, Tom suggested that Jones play hardball with him because only then would he procure the money he wanted from the tightfisted Carnegie. Jones did so without delay and informed Carnegie that three different firms were vying for his services and that he was worth $15,000 a year—$5,000 *more* than Shinn had been making as chairman. Aware he couldn't afford to lose Jones, Carnegie offered him not only a salary increase, but a piece of the partnership, which he had wisely done for several managers at the Keystone Bridge Company, fully vesting them in the business's success.[14]

To Carnegie's surprise, Jones declined the partnership. Unknown to his boss, there were two reasons: Jones didn't want the men to think he was sharing in the profits of the company at their expense, and he had not forgotten how Shinn used to complain about Carnegie using the partnership to enslave him.[15] Rather than elaborate on his reasoning, Jones simply said, "No, I don't want to have my thoughts running on business. I have enough trouble looking after these works. Just give me a hell of a salary if you think I'm worth it."

"All right, Captain, the salary of the President of the United States is yours."

"That's the talk," said Jones.[16]

They ultimately settled on $25,000.

Jones was quite invigorated by the generous salary, and not long after E.T. beat Bethlehem's production. "I told you so," he crowed to the Little Boss. "Their old nag aint got the blood; wont stand a hard race."[17] Such proclamations never appeased Carnegie's appetite, however. Competition was particularly intense between E.T. and Bethlehem and Pennsylvania Steel—the latter firms headed by Carnegie's aristocratic adversaries, the patricians—and he hated to lose. Rivalry between the mills was trumpeted in the *American Manufacturer* and *Iron Age*, as daily, weekly, and monthly production records were big news, and the ironmasters and steel masters were considered the heroes of their age, literally building America.

When Cambria suddenly posted a strong production increase in November 1880, Carnegie demanded an explanation. The Captain minced no words in explaining the spike: he blamed it on Andy for allowing Cambria executives to tour E.T. "and stay with us for four days to learn how it is done," and he chastised him for being "a little too generous with the lunk heads of rival establishments." But even if the competition did glean a nugget or two of useful information, Jones was supremely confident and bet Carnegie that E.T. would beat all rival concerns in production and quality. He also warned, "Information in the future will not be so freely given."[18]

Carnegie was a victim of vanity, a deadly sin. He couldn't help but show off his steelworks, like a peacock its plumage, to Cambria executives, among others. To the arrogant Carnegie they were lunkheads, along with most of the world, for as he once told Phipps, he thought the public fools: "Where would you and I be if they weren't?"[19] Such self-promotion was anathema to brother Tom, however. "Andrew's craze for publicity was abhorrent to Tom," recalled a Carnegie lieutenant. "He used to ridicule Andrew's self-advertising tendencies."[20] Another Carnegie ally was forced to admit, "His one fault was vanity, and he was overwhelmingly vain. His pride was easily hurt, and he loved to consider himself supreme in everything."[21] If only Carnegie had studied the Bible thoroughly, in particular Ecclesiastes 1:14, he would have read, "I have seen all the works that are done under the sun; and, behold, all is vanity and vexation of spirit." Vanity in the business arena boiled down to Carnegie wanting to rub his success in the face of his competition. This form of arrogance was once again similar to his radical ancestors' brash condemnations of the British aristocracy, only Carnegie transferred it on his competitors.

For Carnegie, both business (and life in general) was about beating the privileged, well-moneyed interests. His obsession for besting them was typified when an explosion rocked one of his furnaces for making pig iron. In the fall of 1870, several Pittsburgh firms had organized an effort to build a jointly owned blast furnace to make their own pig iron from the raw iron ore, which was then used in manufacturing iron and steel. Instead of joining the consortium, the independent Carnegie gang had decided to build their own.[22] The company immediately purchased property at Fifty-first Street, conveniently located along the Allegheny River and the Allegheny Valley Railroad. It was a step toward vertical integration—a corporate structure then stumbled upon by only a few firms—giving Carnegie continuous control from the pig-iron-making stage to manufacturing beams and bridge superstructures.

The furnace was christened Lucy, after Tom's wife, for good luck; she was prolific at having children—nine over fourteen years—and the men hoped their furnace would be just as productive. Carnegie, who preferred a decentralized organization, insisted they establish a separate company, the Lucy Furnace Company, to manage the business. It took about a year to build, and when completed it was an impressive brick structure, one of the largest furnaces in the country, towering seventy-five feet high and evoking power and awe. Meanwhile, the rival group—the aristocracy—had constructed their own furnace, almost identical in size and christened Isabella, after a sister of one of the partners. When the Lucy and Isabella furnaces were put in blast in 1872, an immediate rivalry erupted as to which concern could produce the most tons. The contest was tracked by the newspapers and industry rags for all the country to see. A dozen years later, both sides had added furnaces and the competition remained fierce, so when the explosion shut down one of Carnegie's furnaces he was distraught.

His concern was not with injured or dead victims, but with beating their competitor's furnaces for production of pig iron, with beating the furnaces on the other side of the river—the Isabella furnaces. When Carnegie heard of the accident, which occurred on a Mr. Mulligan's watch, he angrily wrote his general manager of the blast furnaces, Julian Kennedy:

> My Dear Mr. Kennedy
>
> Your action, or rather lack of action, in Mr Mulligan's case, has laid the foundation for non-success of your management—
>
> Within one hour after you had heard the accident, the man who caused it, *no matter who he was*, should have been suspended that every Employee might see how determined you were to have success. You have passed it over, no moral effect has been produced upon your men—Yes, a bad moral effect has been produced—
>
> You will suffer from it now until a second opportunity occurs to show that you are a strict, exacting manager. I write to you as one who is most anxious you will succeed as *a manager*—I have resolved you shall have the fairest of trials, but I have only one gauge. Mr. Macrum & you must produce equal, or better, results than your Brother at Isabella or you must give place to others—I shall blow up the Lucy Furnace or get some man to run them successfully.
>
> We are disgraced by such accidents as the last & more disgraced by passing them over as Mr. Macrum & you have done. I am very anxious now about you and him.[23]

To suggest he would blow up the furnaces was so reactionary it called into question the forty-eight-year-old Carnegie's mental stability, but that was how intent he was on beating the Isabella furnaces.

Belatedly, the disgraced Mr. E. A. Macrum, Kennedy's right-hand man, scribbled off a note in pencil to Carnegie, reporting the accident, but he offered no further details. Carnegie's reply was even more scathing than his note to Kennedy:

> I am not satisfied to allow this serious matter to pass. The least you could have done would have been to have suspended Mr. Mulligan, so as to show the other employees that a high standard of attention was required.
>
> This whole matter shows that neither the Chairman nor the Manager of the Lucy Furnace Co insist fully on discipline; and I have lost confidence in their success.
>
> You will find that nothing but a series of accidents will result from such management as this, and *the Furnaces on the other side of the River will continue to do better than we do* [emphasis added], as long as you continue such a policy.[24]

With all the flogging, there was not one inquiry into which men were hurt; Carnegie was simply too engrossed in beating the Pittsburgh aristocracy across the river, beating them at any cost.

Even though Carnegie had a pooling agreement with Cambria in the early 1880s, he still wanted to beat them in terms of production, along with everyone else, and demanded an assessment from Jones. The superintendent reported: "I anticipate a hard struggle for the supremacy this year. Cambria has an immense advantage over us in having big 18″ ingots, powerful and well constructed blowing engines that stand right up to the works, greater superiority in steaming capacity, having more steaming capacity for their bessemer works and blooming, than we have for our entire Steel Works. Yet I know we will lather the very devil out of them. We intend to watch the points closely. Keep sober, and thereby keep our brains clear—No 'Wine & Woman in ours.' We expect you and John Scott to attend to that part of the business."[25] (Jones expected the chaste and sober Carnegie to attend to the wine and women? Apparently, Louise Whitfield had made enough of an impact on Carnegie that more than once he had mentioned her to Jones.)

To ensure he lathered the devil out of the competition, Carnegie had few options with E.T. already running efficiently, wages cut to the bone, and railroad freight rates acceptable courtesy of Tom Scott, but two possibilities included ringing more effort from his men and procuring cheaper sources for raw materials that went into making steel. In 1881, he procured both, with Jones handling the first and Carnegie the second. Jones's action, both revolutionary and unprecedented, was to reorganize the mill into three shifts of men working eight hours each, instead of two shifts working twelve. "In increasing the output of these works," he explained in a speech to steel executives, "I soon discovered it was entirely out of the question to expect human flesh and blood to labor incessantly for twelve hours, and therefore it was decided to put on three turns, reducing the hours of labor to eight. This proved to be of immense advantage to both the company and the workmen, the latter now earning more in eight hours than they formerly did in twelve hours, while the men can work harder constantly for eight hours, having sixteen hours for rest."[26] Whereas Carnegie viewed men solely as a cost on the ledger, Jones included the flesh-and-blood factor. Much has been written about Carnegie's progressive labor policy, but it was Jones who often promoted the men's needs and demanded the eight-hour day, which would prove a very fragile condition.

An excellent evaluator of men, like Carnegie, Jones was always on the lookout for a prospective star. A frequent patron of McDevitt's, a grocery and dried-goods emporium just outside E.T.'s gates, he had recently become acquainted with the store's seventeen-year-old clerk, Charlie Schwab, who was fresh from the countryside. Although Jones was only buying cigars, he couldn't help but notice the clerk's confidence and intelligence, and asked him if he had any skills that might be useful at Edgar Thomson. As it turned out, Charlie had attended St. Francis College and had received some instruction in surveying and engineering. Jones, who was currently erecting two furnaces and was sure the boy would be of some use, hired him in 1879. Charlie would remain with the firm for the next twenty-two years, eventually becoming president.[27]

Jones was a great cultivator of men, but he could be exceptionally hard-driving and spiteful, too. When a group of his men prompted their reverends and priests to call for an end to Sunday work, Jones's reaction was venomous. "I have notified our bigoted and sanctimonious cusses that in the event of their attempting to interfere with these works," he wrote Carnegie, "I will retaliate by promptly discharging any workman who belongs to their Churches and thereby get rid of the poorest and most worthless portion of our employees. If they don't want to work when I want them, I shall take good care that they don't work when they want to. We bet a dollar they will be glad to drop the agitation."[28] Clearly, the Captain was a gambling man. But then, just a few months after his lethal tirade, Jones informed Carnegie that Reverend C. DeLong, a local pastor, had approached him about procuring a Sunday school library for the church. "I listened carefully to his statements and concluded to do all I could to assist him. Rev De Long is full of faith, but minus money. I told him I knew a gentleman in New York that possesses D——d little faith, but had lots of money, and was liberal in matters of this kind."[29] Jones urged Carnegie to purchase a library of books for the congregation, while he would have E.T.'s carpenters erect the building. What a pair Carnegie and Jones made, both steeped in contradiction. Yet, in the end, Jones protected his men more than he castigated them, and he acted as a thick buffer between them and the profit-hungry Carnegie. Such a buffer was needed to maintain a reasonably congenial relationship between capital and labor, and it would be absent when needed most.

To reduce production costs during the merciless price war, Carnegie pursued cheaper raw material and was not above associating himself with the unsavory coal mining industry, including one Henry Clay Frick, the reputed king of coke and a man who would have a profound impact on Carnegie's business legacy. Coke, a strong, smokeless fuel used in iron and steel manufacturing, was derived from coal, and the best coal for coking was found in the Connellsville area of southwest Pennsylvania. Coking entailed dumping coal into beehive ovens, which were circular, dome-shaped brick structures resembling . . . beehives. Built in rows, with twelve-foot base diameters and seven-foot heights, they had openings in the top so a train could pull alongside and quickly unload the coal into the stoked ovens. For the next forty-eight hours, gases and volatile matter trapped in the coal were burned off. Front brick doors were then broken open, the coke was washed, and laborers using long-handled scrapers pulled out the coke.

Early in his iron adventure, Carnegie had discovered that determining the proper amounts of coke and the other raw materials for the concoction proved elusive and led to inconsistent quality. Advice from quack doctors was no longer welcome. Carnegie the positivist wanted facts, so the company hired a chemist—the first to do so, according to legend. (However, their competition, Cooper and Hewitt, had one on the payroll in 1867, two years prior to Carnegie, and that may have inspired him to hire one.)[30] Procuring a steady source for coke was another difficulty, so Carnegie had invested in ovens at Larimer Station, conveniently located along the Pennsylvania's line to supplement his needs. Desiring to grant his cousin Dod's wish to emigrate to America, he hired his cousin, who had gained expertise in washing coal, to manage the operation in the early 1870s. A partner for the next twenty-five years, Dod was expected to cover Naig's back, but he also provided honest appraisals: when Carnegie questioned Dod on their coke facility's production, his cousin acerbically replied, "I judge from your telegram that you must have got imbued with some strange notion of the magnitude of the works here."[31] As Carnegie often said, "Dod is the balance-wheel."[32]

In fact, not only were the works inadequate by the 1880s, it was costing Carnegie more to operate them than to buy all his coke from an independent source. It was an unacceptable situation. Desperate to unload the small but costly ventures, in late 1881 Tom Carnegie approached Frick to ascertain whether he would consider buying the properties. After studying the assets, Frick agreed, but then matters took an interesting turn. Having acquired a fair debt load, Frick was in need of a capital infusion, and figured who better to approach for financing than his anxious customer Andrew Carnegie. If Carnegie gave him money, Frick would relieve him of the coke works.

The Scotsman was very much open to investing in Frick. "The one vital lesson in iron and steel that I learned in Britain," he later wrote, "was the necessity for owning raw materials and finishing the completed article ready of its purpose."[33] An investment in Frick would be another step toward achieving that vertical integration and self-sufficient independence. Also, as early as January 1880, thrifty Harry Phipps had suggested they invest in Frick's company because it appeared quite profitable, yet no action was taken until now.[34] Learning that Frick and his wife, just married in December 1881, would be passing through New York on their way to a European honeymoon, Carnegie arranged a luncheon at the Windsor Hotel. At the table, Carnegie sized up his potential partner: Although of a medium build, slight figure, with an undistinguished trim beard, Frick possessed hard, studious eyes that made the objects of his gaze uncomfortable; these eyes displayed the genius Carnegie sought in all men. What he failed to see was the putrid bowels of the coal industry investigated by Mother Jones and the Pennsylvania secretary of internal affairs.

*   *   *

Born in 1849 to a bumbling southwestern Pennsylvania farmer, Frick never-theless had ambition. He had a rich grandfather, and during rides in his fancy carriage the young man became determined to emulate him. After spending his childhood performing chores on the family farm, at age 15 he left home to live with an uncle and attend Westmoreland College and then Otterbein University. Eventually, Frick's grandfather hired him as his chief bookkeeper, but in 1870 the old man died, at which point his elder cousin, Abraham Tintsman, invited him to become a partner in a modest coke business. On March 10, 1871, Frick signed his name to the partnership papers and put in capital for a one-fifth interest in the firm Overholt, Frick, and Company. Relying on the venerable Thomas Mellon, who had been friendly with Frick's mother since her well-to-do childhood days, Frick procured loans for expanding the operations. Two years after having entered the partnership, he gained control and renamed the firm Frick and Company. At times cold-blooded and machinelike, he was a formidable man. Under his command were two hundred ovens and four hundred acres of coal land. For all the toughness it took to succeed in the steel industry, it took that much more to survive in the brutal coal mining industry, in which labor violence and acci-dents took hundreds of lives. But Frick had the guts, motivation, and vision to triumph—as well as the callousness, for he wrung every penny he could from his men.

Many years after escaping the Connellsville coal region, Ben Shedlock, whose father and brothers worked for Frick, depicted life in the Frick realm as totalitarian. The town they lived in "was under the control of the Coal Iron Police, hired by the company. They were like the Gestapo." All purchases had to be made at the company store, which charged high prices, or the men faced losing their jobs. "They robbed the people blind in those stores," said Shedlock. "The men in the coal mines were slaves. They worked 12 hours a day. I remember my Dad coming home in winter, his clothes frozen to his body from working in the water in the mines. Of course, if you were killed in the mines, the company paid your family nothing."[35]

Conditions were so bad the Pennsylvania secretary of internal affairs opened an investigation and accused Frick of charging $9.60 for a barrel of flour when it could be bought elsewhere for just $8. The investigation also confirmed that if the Frick men didn't spend their wages in the Frick store, they were summarily fired. Over a fourteen-month period, the Frick Com-pany made $33,000 from their stores, which were supposed to *benefit* the men.[36] But men paying a premium for flour, or men dying of pneumonia, or collapsed mines burying dozens alive, or explosions killing scores more were taken in stride by such captains of war as Henry Clay Frick—or Clay, as he was known to friends. By the summer of 1881 he had earned the reputation as the cruelest employer in the industry.[37]

*   *   *

Frick's reputation as a human being didn't concern Carnegie, who was obsessively focused on beating his competition. Certainly, the taciturn Frick and buoyant Carnegie made for a seemingly incompatible combination, but before the New York luncheon was over they were partners. "Ah, Andra," his mother, who was also in attendance, whispered, "that's a verra good thing for Mr. Freek, but what do we get out of it?" A partner that would affect Andrew Carnegie's standing in history, for one. From Frick, Carnegie now had an agreement that provided for a cheaper source for coke that translated to cheaper prices for his steel rails. Effective January 1, 1882, Carnegie's company owned 11.25 percent of the H. C. Frick Coke Company, with Frick holding 11,846 shares, his prior partners, E. M. and Walton Ferguson, 23,654 shares, and Carnegie 4,500.[38] In turn, Carnegie had to buy all his coke from Frick.

The arrangement proved so profitable that unknown to Frick, Carnegie started pressing the Ferguson brothers to sell him additional shares so he could gain even more negotiating leverage over coke pricing. The steel master had little respect for them, especially after Phipps observed, "In our various negotiations have found Mr. Frick clear-headed but can not say as much for his two associates."[39] Little by little the Fergusons capitulated, and by mid-1883 Carnegie was the largest shareholder in the H. C. Frick Coke Company. To strengthen his hold on the company, over the next two years Carnegie brought in his allies, including Tom, Phipps, Stewart, Vandy, John Walker, Dod, and even Captain Jones, among others, who all became individual stockholders via shares Carnegie sold to them.[40] By August 1885, the scorecard would stand at Carnegie with 13,711 shares, H. C. Frick with 8,668, E. M. Ferguson with 8,667, Walter Ferguson with 8,665, Phipps with 3,955, and Tom with 3,780.[41]

The old fox had tricked the young one. It was a sudden reversal of fortune that didn't sit well with Frick and set a contentious tone for their relationship. Frick's displeasure with the situation was quite evident in how he reacted when Carnegie struck down a proposal to buy more operations. Assuming a snide voice, Frick wrote, "I am free to say, I do not like the tone of your letter. Outside of my desire to follow and accept your views as the largest stockholder in our Company—I have great admiration for your acknowledged abilities and your general good judgment, and would much prefer to defer to your views—in the matter of the values of the properties in question and the propriety of increasing our stock I shall have to differ from you and I think the future will bear me out."[42] Convinced of his superior knowledge when it came to coke, Frick was not going to kowtow to Carnegie or anybody else, but he came to accept the circumstances. He even dangled the prospect of more stock under Carnegie's nose when just three months after his snide letter Frick again asked for money to buy three competitors. Hoping to win approval for the deals, he encouraged Carnegie to purchase

$500,000 more of Frick stock, adding suggestively. "You will then be the owner of half of Frick Coke Co."[43] Dod warned Carnegie: "I do not see why we would wish to take these properties into the Frick Co. They are well enough as they are. . . . Let Frick worry with them is my verdict."[44] For all his vanity, Carnegie knew when to heed his lieutenants' advice and did so. By the end of the year, he and his allies controlled 50 percent of the stock, anyway, and there was nothing Frick could do about it except prove his worthiness for remaining at the helm.[45]

Carnegie was well prepared when a price war threatened his relationship with Cambria in 1882 and when, on the heels of that conflict, a debilitating war broke out with Chicago-area steel mills. The spirited competitor in Carnegie made it difficult to maintain a harmonious relationship with any of the industry's old guard, even Edward Townsend at Cambria. The trouble first surfaced when Townsend, who claimed he didn't want rail prices below $55 a ton, allegedly permitted his agents to sell some orders at $50. Carnegie's sales agents immediately reported the sudden drop in price, and he then discovered Townsend had scooped a nine-thousand-ton order. Incensed, he wrote "Dear Mr. Townsend" that "it will be impossible to overlook your recent action," and he called his actions "pernicious." Carnegie suggested they split the order and prevent future lapses: "I greatly hope that my suggestion, after you think it all over will seem to you fair & reasonable. It would be source of much personal gratification to me if you accede to it as in that case it would be unnecessary for me to report to my Brother & Mr. Stewart that a misunderstanding has arisen between us. . . . Consider it all over & try to think whether you have done to your colleagues as you would like to be done by."[46] Interestingly, Carnegie used his brother as a threat. Why? For the simple reason Tom Carnegie did indeed carry much more respect in the Pittsburgh business community than did Andrew, and a derogatory word from Tom would hurt Cambria's reputation far more than his brother's blustery tirades.

The very next day Townsend fired back: "I can furnish you evidence of many instances wherein sales have been made by your Company without any respect to the provisions of Article 4 that you quote & more 'pernicious to our agreement' that the case now under discussion."[47] Offended by the allegations, Carnegie responded not to "My Dear Mr. Townsend." Instead, he wrote:

Dear Sir,

I have received your favor of 21st instant. If you have any charge to make against us for which you have not already accepted our explanation as satisfactory and thus closed them, you have only to present them. I assure you we do not intend to reap any advantage from violations of our obligations to you or to anyone. These, however, have nothing whatever to do with our request that you shall justify your recent action before an arbiter as

required, by our contract, unless upon reflection you accede to my suggestion and place the negotiation to joint account. . . . While trying to advance
our mutual interests by holding up the prices of Rails here to figures
approved by you, I little expected to be stabbed in the back by the hand
whose duty it was to co-operate with me.[48]

Considering it was the first time Townsend had allegedly betrayed Carnegie's trust, the Scotsman's reaction was violent and demonstrated just how
strongly he felt about anyone crossing him. But as impetuous as he was, he
was equally conciliatory when it benefited him, so he quickly negotiated a
truce with Townsend. At this time, they also formulated a battle plan to capture more rail orders in booming western markets controlled by their arch
competitors in Chicago. Together they would use radical price cuts in taking
the battle to Chicago in an attempt to scoop the market.

The very next year their alliance was successfully cutting into enemy territory.
After one triumph, Carnegie's sales agent, A. L. Griffin, reported that he beat
the Chicago mills for an order of seventeen thousand tons for the St. Paul,
Minneapolis & Manitoba Railway, one of the strongest in the West: "There
was more fighting and excitement among the Chicago Mills in getting this
order than anything yet offered, and my taking it, and your taking Chicago
Burlington & Quincy has given them the worst black-eye they have yet had.
. . . Yours and Mr Townsend's idea was to hit them a square blow between the
eyes, before they had time to dodge—We did it!"[49] Nothing brought more
pleasure than hitting Orrin W. Potter, who was the reigning monarch in Chicago, and the competition between Carnegie and the Chicago firms would
remain heated as he invaded western markets that were once unassailable
due to the higher cost of transportation. The deal with Frick had negated
those added costs.

On Carnegie's home turf, a more imminent threat from Pittsburgh's iron aristocracy emerged. Andrew Kloman and several well-established ironmasters
were behind it. After parting ways in 1878, Kloman had leased an old mill in
Allegheny City to make structural steel for bridges, and when the lease
expired the following year he began construction on his own mill in Homestead, Pennsylvania, just one mile down the Monongahela River from E.T.
Several Pittsburgh businessmen offered Kloman financial backing if he joined
them in a more ambitious project, and, on October 21, 1879, he and five
partners formed the Pittsburgh Bessemer Steel Company, intent on building
a steel mill to compete with Carnegie. Along with the Homestead plant came
labor trouble that threatened to destabilize the entire Pittsburgh market.

For Kloman, who had harbored ill-feelings toward Carnegie for years, it
was a chance for revenge, and several of his partners also relished the thought

of beating the Scotsman. Although the new firm wouldn't roll its first rail until August 1881, not far into the construction Carnegie realized the planned size of the operation made Kloman a very potent threat, which contributed to his desire to gain efficiencies in the interim, like his partnering with Frick. With no intention of giving up center stage to the aristocracy, he also decided to consolidate his interests—Union Mills, E.T., and the Lucy Furnace Company—which were to be called Carnegie Brothers and Company, Limited, effective April 1, 1881, and increase capital to $5 million to immediately fund any expansion or retooling required to stay ahead of the competition.[50] The seven partners included Andrew Carnegie with a $2,737,977.95 share, Tom Carnegie with $878,096.58, Harry Phipps also with $878,096.58, David A. Stewart with $175,318.78, John Scott with $175,318.78, Gardner McCandless with $105,191.00, and John W. Vandevort with $50,000.[51] Just two months after the reorganization, the Lucy Furnace Company was spun off and sold to Wilson, Walker and Company, owned by Carnegie allies.[52] The reason for this sudden about-face was that E.T. now had two furnaces of its own, so the Lucy people were given their freedom to go after customers without worrying about E.T.'s needs. Carnegie and his partners figured an independent management would be more effective in doing so—a savvy move.

The Prussian Kloman never lived to see Carnegie squirm, however; he died in December 1880. When Jones relayed the news to Carnegie, the Welshman's only concern was that Kloman's "patent for rolling eye bars may be thrown on the market," a crucial patent Carnegie had licensed exclusively years ago.[53] (Control of such patents made a critical difference in an industry where a penny a ton gain in efficiency could translate to millions of dollars.) If there was any doubt about the mutual dislike between Carnegie and Pittsburgh's iron upper crust, one only had to read the statement issued by the Pittsburgh Bessemer Steel Company in a tribute to Kloman's character, which included this remark: "In broad charity, in great patience, *in uncomplaining endurance of wrongs,* in conscientious veracity and uprightness of integrity, in calmness and serenity of manner, we recognize the higher type of Christian manhood."[54] All swipes at Carnegie.

To Carnegie's chagrin, a man more potent than Kloman was hired to take on the general superintendent position. It was William Clark, a respected technical expert who had been awarded patents for his work in iron and steel machinery. He was also avidly antiunion, so when he discovered the Amalgamated Association of Iron and Steel Workers had infiltrated the mill by the time the furnaces were fired in February 1881, he summarily fired union sympathizers and ordered employees to sign an agreement stating they would not join the union. Another problem he faced was internal conflict between the Irish and the Welsh who dominated the works. The Irish were angry over the Welsh controlling the foreman jobs, and they complained bitterly about low wages. Clark also brought problems on himself during the first summer of operation when men at other firms were getting small advances—compensation for the hot weather—but Pittsburgh Bessemer Steel workers did not. Clark's blooming mill men struck. They won higher wages this time, but resentment between labor and capital, between mill hand and Clark, was strong at Homestead. Still, Carnegie and the rest of the industry perceived that as soon as Pittsburgh Bessemer worked out these initial problems, the company would be a force in steel.

But labor troubles continued to hamper Homestead, which suffered another strike in January 1882 when Clark demanded wage cuts. To bolster their position, the Amalgamated threatened to incite sympathy strikes at all mills owned by those men invested in Homestead. It was an alarming development never before faced by the mill owners, who considered their relationship with the workingman to be more civilized; such sympathy strikes broke the rules. For the first time, capital realized how powerful the Amalgamated had become, with agitation indeed spreading even further than expected, into mills outside of the Homestead realm.

The Amalgamated, which had been founded in 1875 when three unions representing ironworkers merged, would become Carnegie's nemesis. For now, he accepted the union as a necessary force that still negotiated reasonably, and when men working at E.T.'s furnaces also went on strike in January 1882, Carnegie and his lieutenants quickly acquiesced to their demands. The next month, Captain Jones was able to inform Carnegie, "I think our men are now getting to be satisfied, and I see signs of the old Esprit De Corps. I am going slow and carefully. I now feel sure that the Union will not get a foothold here. I will ask the Company to agree to loan such good men as I may select say from 60—$800.00 this year to assist them in building homes. This is an effective plan to keep out the Union. Every good man that wants to build, encourage. You should calculate on a reasonable investment in that direction. Give them the money on fair interest."[55] Carnegie would adopt a policy of aiding home construction that was hailed as progressive, but obviously, as Jones suggested, there was a very pragmatic goal behind it: lock out the union. Also, Carnegie falsely took and was mistakenly given much credit for yet another progressive policy, when it was Captain Jones who had championed it.

As for esprit de corps, there was no such attitude at Homestead. The ten-week-long strike was reportedly settled on March 11, but when it came to putting the new agreements in writing, Clark and the Amalgamated disagreed over what had been discussed verbally. The men struck again and Clark attempted to bring in scabs, inciting a pitched battle with the loss of life. Sickened by the mess, the Homestead owners stepped in and settled with the workers, agreeing to maintain the existing wage rates and forcing Clark to resign. Adding to the owners' woes, the mill had originally been built for manufacturing various steel shapes; but in midconstruction, changes were implemented so steel rails could also be manufactured, resulting in a poor cohesive design and no efficiency, which exacerbated financial losses when steel prices fell.

By 1883, the owners had had enough and started to look for a buyer. Although they were loathe to sell to Carnegie, there were very few prospects, so they reluctantly offered him the company at book value, not much more than the $250,000 in original capital. He didn't hesitate to buy, allowing the Homestead partners to take their proceeds in either cash or stock. Only one, William H. Singer, took $50,000 in stock—someday to be worth millions.[56] A new firm, Carnegie, Phipps and Company, was organized to manage Homestead as well as the Lucy Furnace Company, which had been under control of Wilson, Walker. Trusted business partner John Walker was named chairman of the new organization. Plans were announced to spend $4 million to revamp Homestead into what it was supposed to have been: the greatest plant in the country for manufacturing structural steel.[57] Carnegie's October 1883 purchase of Homestead marked an absolute victory over the aristocracy, but perhaps he had been too obsessive, too eager in jumping at the opportunity. Perhaps he should have more carefully considered the deep division that existed there between capital and labor.

CHAPTER 14

An Attack on Britain

Carnegie was just as feverish in attacking the British aristocracy as he was the patricians in iron and steel, and his phenomenal business success became a platform for launching into political, as well as literary, endeavors far more vigorously than ever before. Although he regretted from time to time not having pursued the course laid out in his 1868 memorandum, he now realized that with the ladles of disposable cash he possessed, he had the opportunity to seriously influence literary, political, and social movements. This tantalizing prospect first manifested itself in 1882 when he agreed to finance a proletarian newspaper chain in Britain advocating the overthrow of the privileged class. Here was a chance to carry on his father's fight for the charter.

The initial guiding force behind the newspaper chain was Thomas Graham, a Dunfermline native whom Carnegie had befriended on a train ride almost twenty years earlier. Graham was now an influential merchant in Wolverhampton who was allied with Samuel Storey, a radical member of Parliament from the industrialized Newcastle area and owner of two radical newspapers. An impressive and intimidating figure, Storey stood over six feet tall, with a bulky frame, a thick, flowing beard, and booming voice. His stature was reflected in the editorial content of his newspapers, the *Sunderland Echo* and the *Tyneside Echo*, which resounded with calls for reform. Graham wanted Carnegie to partner with him and Storey to build a radical newspaper chain targeting the industrial heartland of Great Britain.

When Carnegie had coached through Britain in 1881 (the logistics handled by Graham, not so incidentally), he spent six days with the merchant in Wolverhampton to fully understand what was involved. The industrialized Midlands were ripe for political revolution, Graham argued, and a network of newspapers located in volatile cities could incite meaningful reforms that would give more power to the people. These would be cheap papers, affordable to the workingman, with Storey and he providing the management and editorial expertise and Carnegie the financing.

While Graham talked a good game, the changing British political climate also inspired Carnegie to take an interest in a politically charged newspaper syndicate. In 1880, the atmosphere had suddenly changed when the radical Liberals overthrew Prime Minister Benjamin Disraeli, a politician Carnegie thought heartless. Leading the charge was William Gladstone, age seventy-one, who became prime minister when the Liberal Party took the Parliament by storm, winning a majority. During the campaign, he had stopped at Dunfermline, and a tremendous crowd turned out to hear the "People's William" speak. An impressive orator, the Liberal leader had stirred up the public by promising further reforms to extend the electorate and by respecting the desire for home rule in Ireland, a position Carnegie heartily agreed with. "I hear some Americans reproaching the Irish people for rioting and fighting so much," Carnegie wrote at the time, "the real trouble is they don't fight half enough."[1] The fire had not died inside him, and he predicted the destruction of the aristocracy: "Even Englishmen will soon become satisfied that no man should be born to honors, but that these should be reserved for those who merit them. But what kind of fruit could be expected from the tree of privilege? . . . The days of rank are numbered." It was time to seize the moment.

Over the next year, their plans coalesced, and Carnegie returned to England in 1882 to oversee the launch of the newspaper syndicate. The trio now owned or controlled eight modest newspapers located in industrialized cities (the number to increase to eighteen within two years) and a sizable interest in one crown jewel, the *London Echo*. Its owner, Passmore Edwards, had been railing against the Royal Family, the House of Lords, the Established Church, and anything held sacred by the conservatives in general for several years, and was making a fortune at it, too. Making money on radical politics was a perfect mix as far as Carnegie was concerned. But more significant to him, he was able to amplify his personality and further define himself through the newspapers. That first summer Carnegie appeared often in the offices of the Wolverhampton *Express* and gave rousing speeches on the burning issues of the day. His voice was heard through shrill editorial policy and content, as the newspaper syndicate supported Gladstone's initiatives, advocated universal franchise, payment of members of Parliament, curtailed power of House of Lords, and home rule.

The trio's campaign had an immediate impact as a wave of agitation swept through the laboring class, and the landed gentry feared upheaval. Not only did the conservative establishment and media not appreciate Carnegie's politics, but they found his self-aggrandizing offensive. The *St. James Gazette* counterattacked, stating that "the present agitation originated in America, and is an attempt to infuse republican sentiments into English politics. The movement, with all its paraphernalia of banners, processions, monster meetings and other factitious machinery which American politicians know so well how to handle, is entirely foreign to English sentiment, and is the result of American influence and paid for by American dollars. Mr. Carnegie is at the head of a conspiracy which is more subtle and dangerous than that of the dynamiters and which seeks to destroy both the Crown and the House of Lords."[2] His calls for death to privilege and the overthrow of the monarchy was like swatting at a bees' nest.

Storey, who had few friends in Parliament as it was, did not expect such virulent language on Carnegie's part, so he suggested to his partner that too provocative of a tone was counterproductive. No apologies offered, Carnegie responded vigorously, "My Dear Friend, You regret that in the published interview I attacked the Crown. What I then said was in reply to the charge of the St. James Gazette that I was engaged in a conspiracy against English institutions. This charge I resented. I am no conspirator; but I am, as you are well aware, and as I would have all the world know, a man who regards the doctrine of the political equality of man as man, as the very soul of politics; the precious root from which spring manly self-respect and all its attendant virtues. . . . Holding these opinions, I should not have been honest had I not admitted that I would destroy, if I had the power, every vestige of privilege in England . . . but at the same time, I would not shed a drop of blood, nor violate a law, nor use violence in any form, to bring about what I so much desire."[3] Carnegie, who adopted the moral-suasionist position of his Uncle Thomas, had never been exposed to such private and public disapproval and fought it off with brave words, but the bloodless revolution contested with pens hurt him more than he expected.

The conservative faction expanded their attack, claiming Carnegie was buying newspapers merely to establish a foothold for his own political ambitions—a seat in Parliament. At first Carnegie denied interest: "I do not think I would care much to enter Parliament even if I were a British citizen. The Press is the true source of power in Britain as in America. The time of Parliament is consumed in discussing trifling affairs, which should be relegated to local assemblies. Members of Parliament sit merely to carry out the plans dictated by the press, the true exponent of the wishes of the people."[4] Yet, he began to entertain the idea, asking his friend James Blaine jokingly, or perhaps half-jokingly, whether he should enter the House of Representatives or Parliament. Blaine said blithely, "If you take a seat in the House of Commons, you will be a greater man in the United States, but, if you enter the House in Washington, you will be a greater man in England." Considering he was a former Speaker of the House and now secretary of state, he certainly knew. Vanity swelling, Carnegie started fanning rumors of political aspirations; he told a friend that the American minister to Britain "had heard I intended to enter public life in England & sometimes I feel it is my mission to do so—but only to give my native land some of the political justice enjoyed by my adopted one."[5]

Any political aspirations were halfhearted, and within a year of founding the newspaper syndicate Carnegie was as concerned with the financial position as the editorial content. In a January 3, 1883, letter to Storey, he recommended higher advertising rates to boost revenue and also said he wanted far more effort put into increasing circulation: "Nothing should be omitted to give it circulation. Money no object as compared with *power*." On the political front, his primary goal for the newspapers was to exert pressure on Parliament to extend the franchise, because in his idealistic world the right to vote was the ultimate power. "I hope you are to be found in the front charging solidly for that one thing—*extended franchise*. . . . ," he exhorted Storey. "I am going out of business but it takes a little more time than I bargained for— that's all. Then I want more papers, so look about you for another at Portsmouth. I'll have ready cash some day you know!"[6]

Suddenly, Carnegie was an expert on all facets of newspaper publishing—circulation, design, and editorial—but if not careful, his overbearing style would undermine his relationship with Storey, as it had with Shinn. More revealing, two of Carnegie's internalized thoughts were exposed in this letter. The first: "Money no object as compared with power." While he was concerned with costs and receipts, he recognized that the receipts equated to circulation, which equated to the volume of his voice, which equated to the power to influence. He was motivated by the attainment of power; it was his Holy Grail, his drug, his ultimate aspiration, and he was willing to pay for it. Such was the case in the iron and steel industry, too; for him it was no longer about money, it was about attaining power.

The second confession: he expressed a desire to retire, an echo from fourteen years earlier. Carnegie was now successfully inventing the life he wanted among literary men and politicians; it was time to exit the brutal world of iron and steel that required his relentless attention. The predicament Carnegie faced was that if he did retire, his income would surely decrease and therefore so would his power. He was trapped. For the moment, however, he could rejoice in feeling himself evolve beyond the nagging mills he forced brother Tom and Phipps to manage.

A decade earlier, Carnegie's social realm of intellects had been confined to Madame Botta's parlor and the Nineteenth Century Club, but now it expanded quickly to encompass Victorian England's most influential poets and critics. Some of these men of letters, like William Black, he met during his ambitious travels. Others he became acquainted with because of his newspaper syndicate and his willingness to fund the radical element that thrust him into the limelight. At a dinner hosted by Yates-Thompson, proprietor of the liberal literary magazine *Pall Mall Gazette*, Carnegie was introduced to Matthew Arnold, an Englishman who was the most influential literary critic of his age. Arnold then introduced Carnegie to his radical friend John Morley, also of great influence and editor of the *Fortnightly Review*. In February 1882, Morley would publish Carnegie's essay "As Others See Us," a glorification of America and a derision of Britain's House of Lords, landed aristocracy, and social snobbery that was based on observations from his 1881 coaching trip. When Carnegie first met Morley, who had thin, graying hair receding straight back and eyes set deep in a dignified, narrow face with a strong chin, the Englishman had already authored eleven books of social and literary criticism and was in his fifteenth year as editor of the *Fortnightly Review*, which he had transformed into the most influential magazine in Britain.

Born in the industrialized city of Blackburn, where old handloom weavers haunted dingy streets beneath towering factory chimneys, Morley discovered he shared a similar childhood with Carnegie, and a lifelong friendship developed between the two kindred spirits. Morley, like Madame Botta, was particularly intrigued by the inherent conflicts between Carnegie's devout allegiance to American capitalism and his radical actions to benefit the British working class. He was a case study, an experiment, to be dissected and analyzed. Carnegie was equally intrigued by Morley, three years his junior. Influenced greatly by John Stuart Mill's *On Liberty* and Charles Darwin's *Origin of Species*, both published in 1859, Morley was very much an independent thinker.

Although a champion of Darwin, he viewed evolution as "nature's appalling law of merciless and incessant destruction." His view darkening with time, he would become convinced Darwinism was being abused "to give brutality a more decent name."[7] Morley placed Darwinism in a negative framework, whereas Carnegie considered it to be a positive epistle of progress. Carnegie admitted he and Morley were opposites when it came to temperament: "We are drawn together because opposites are mutually beneficial to each other. I am optimistic; all my ducks being swans. He is pessimistic, looking out soberly, even darkly, upon the real dangers ahead, and sometimes imagining vain things. He is inclined so see an 'officer in every bush.' The world seems bright to me, and earth is often a real heaven—so happy I am and so thankful to kind fates."[8]

Toward the end of his 1882 stay in Britain, Carnegie heard from Morley that Herbert Spencer was sailing to the United States in August on the steamer *Servia* for a three-month tour of the rapidly evolving country. Always quick to seize an opportunity, Carnegie immediately booked passage on the same steamer and procured a letter of introduction from Morley. When he first caught sight of Spencer on board, the philosopher didn't exude a powerful intellect: the sixty-two-year-old master was bald across the scalp with shaggy gray tufts of hair sprouting above the ears and thick sideburns wrapping under the chin; his facial features were chimplike and he was visibly grumpy; he appeared unapproachable and aloof. That didn't stop Carnegie. It was like a child meeting his hero when he introduced himself to the philosopher early in their crossing, and, to his overwhelming delight, he ended up dining regularly with Spencer and the philosopher's friend, Edward Lott.

One peculiar occurrence on the trip that stood out in Carnegie's mind involved cheese, of all things. After one dinner, the waiter offered a selection of cheeses. Spencer placed his order, but when the waiter returned and placed it before him he peevishly pushed away the plate, exclaiming, "Cheddar! Cheddar! I said Cheddar, not Cheshire! Bring me Cheddar!" Carnegie was flabbergasted; the great philosopher aroused over cheese? This seemingly trivial concern triggered a conversation about meeting famous personalities and whether expectations are met. Bluntly, Carnegie said the flesh rarely lived up to the preconceived legend.

"In my case, for example," Spencer sniffed, "was that so?"

Eyeing the rumpled philosopher intent on his cheese, Carnegie said, "You more than anybody. I had imagined you, the great philosopher brooding over all things. Never did I dream you could become so excited over the question of cheese."[9] Carnegie wanted heroic proportions to meet his illusionary expectations.

Despite the great cheese controversy, Carnegie convinced Spencer to visit Pittsburgh and the magnificent Edgar Thomson steel works, which, according to America's most ardent promoter, exemplified progress. Crumbling under the Carnegie charm and pressure, Spencer agreed. On arriving in New York, Spencer went directly to the Catskills for a five-day respite to rejuvenate after what he considered to be an arduous ocean voyage. He then traveled up the Hudson River and on to Montreal, Niagara, Cleveland, and finally Pittsburgh, where Carnegie waited anxiously. Spencer's evaluation of the city left no room for interpretation. "Six months here would justify suicide," he said to Carnegie.[10] It was not the industrial utopia that Carnegie blindly believed it to be; the smoke, the filth, and the noise disgusted Spencer. Clearly, there was a disconnect between Carnegie and reality; he remained either incredibly naive to America's industrial underbelly or extremely accepting of the natural conditions—the good and the bad—of the Industrial Revolution.

Spurning the fancy Pittsburgh hotel suite an already wounded Carnegie had reserved for him, Spencer accepted Tom's offer to stay at his Homewood house, later explaining, "The repulsiveness of Pittsburgh led me to break through my resolution always to stop at an hotel; and in the evening we drove with Mr. Carnegie to the house of his brother a few miles out."[11] Tom's more affable personality appealed to Spencer, who had quickly wearied of Carnegie's frenetic character. He even invited Tom to join him on the remainder of his tour, but the younger Carnegie declined.

England's most prominent man of letters, Matthew Arnold, was Carnegie's next visitor when the critic launched a lecture tour of the United States in the fall of 1883 to raise much needed personal funds—a career in letters was no match for one in steel. His British colleagues certainly questioned why Arnold, as well as Morley and Spencer, would so readily accept Carnegie's hospitality and eventually his friendship. Morley posed that very question to himself and answered it as he would in critiquing a literary piece:

> His extraordinary freshness of spirit easily carried Arnold, Herbert Spencer, myself, and afterwards many others, high over an occasional crudity or haste in judgment such as befalls the best of us in ardent hours. . . . He is an idealist who lives and works with his ideals, and drudges over them every day of

his life. He maintained the habit of applying his own mind either to the multifarious projects that flooded in upon him from outside, or to elaborating the independent notions that sprung up within him from his observant common sense in union with the milk of human kindness. Rapidity, energy, confident enthusiasm, were the mark of his days. . . . His enthusiasm for Burns and his radiant knowledge and love of Shakespeare are good testimony to his fine gaiety of heart. A strenuous disputant, yet he knows how to keep himself in order by quick, racy, and superabundant sense of humor. A man of high and wide and well-earned mark in his generation.[12]

As for Carnegie's critical evaluation of Arnold, who had bright eyes under heavy eyelids, a sharp nose, pouting lips, and unkempt sideburns that wrapped under his chin, it was reverential: "The most charming man, John Morley and I agree, that we ever knew was Matthew Arnold. He had, indeed, 'a charm'—that is the only word which expresses the effect of his presence and his conversation. Even his look and grave silences charmed."[13] For all his charisma, Arnold was a relatively poor man in 1882. Worrying about retirement, he started plotting a grand invasion of the United States, a country he had not yet visited.

To Arnold, the United States was a country of Philistines—a land of asinine, banal individuals driven by material gain. It was a period in American history dubbed the Gilded Age by Mark Twain, a time marked by conspicuous consumption, a time when not poets and artists but wealth and power fascinated the public. Oil refineries, steel mills, and enormous factories defined the cities, not ornate cathedrals, palaces, and gardens. The dynamo, thanks to Thomas Edison, was a new god for the people to worship. Gaudy advertising hoodwinked the proletarian masses. Women were loud and chatty. Men were boastful, coarse, and relished a fistfight, chewing tobacco, and drinking bourbon whiskey. While Arnold ridiculed the Philistines—a group Carnegie belonged to—he was intrigued, too. America was still a democratic experiment to the British, and, like Spencer, Arnold wanted to better understand this experiment.

Arnold's invasion involved a seventy-engagement lecture tour, during which he would speak on Ralph Waldo Emerson and on the need to balance literature with science. As he made travel plans that included bringing his wife Flu and his daughter Lucy, Carnegie insisted the Arnolds stay with him at the Windsor Hotel while in New York. He accepted, replying he would meet Carnegie at the hotel "and shall look to your kindness to advise us in all sorts of matters."[14] He could count on it. After a transatlantic crossing marked by rough seas, rain, and gloom, the Arnold family arrived in the early morning hours of October 22. "We expected a two or three hours' wait with our baggage," Arnold wrote his sister, "but Mr. Carnegie met us with his Secretary, took all trouble off our hands, and bore us away up to the Windsor Hotel in a carriage."[15] No one was going to come between Carnegie and his prize. The rescue was a welcome surprise for Arnold, who was bombarded by autograph seekers and newspapermen the moment he stepped ashore.

To properly introduce him to New York, Carnegie hosted a lavish reception at the Windsor, with dozens of dignitaries in attendance and the hall decorated with floral wreaths spelling out the names of Arnold's books. "I think the reception I gave him combined more distinguished people than ever before assembled at one time in America," Carnegie boasted to Morley, while Arnold reported to his sister: "The reception last night was magnificent, and Flu and Lucy did their duty splendidly. They will tell you about the reception and the decorations. What I like is the way in which the people, far lower down than us, live with something of the life and enjoyment of the cultivated classes. The young master of the hotel asked to present his steward to me last night, as a recompense for his beautiful arrangements of palms, fruit and flowers in the great hall."[16] Carnegie, in his reverence of Arnold, was willing to overlook the critic's snobbish, condescending view of lower classes.

The great lecture series commenced on October 30 before a crowd of two thousand packed into Chickering Hall. A true celebrity, Arnold's attire didn't escape the press. He wore a black necktie that was wrapped around a pointed, stand-up collar and tied in a loose sailor's knot, along with a black-and-white worsted scarf draped around his neck, a small silk cap on his head, and slippers on his feet. As Arnold took the podium, he struck a critical but not haughty pose, and he talked with his head thrown back, sighting the audience down his nose. The remainder of the tour took Arnold through New England cities and college towns, as well as Philadelphia, Washington, D.C., Richmond, Baltimore, Chicago, St. Louis, Toronto, Montreal, and Quebec. When in Chicago, Carnegie wanted Arnold to visit the stockyards where the slaughterhouses used everything but the pig's squeal—American efficiency at its best—but he refused to enter the Philistine stronghold.

Arnold appreciated the United States for being less class inhibited and striving for stronger education, and he admired the Constitution, the Supreme Court, and the legislative system; however, he ultimately took the same attitude as Spencer toward American culture—unimpressed. "Say what Carnegie will," he wrote, "this is the civilization of the Australian colonies and not of Europe."[17] The opening of the Brooklyn Bridge and the Metropolitan Opera the year he visited did not dissuade his preconceived notions, as the British perceived that America's nouveau wealth made for an anxious nation, one seeking identity and tradition found in European cultures hundreds of years older. But quick to reject all that was European, America cut itself off from its cultural roots, and its industrial might offered nothing in the way of real values on which to build a truly civilized nation. To prove their success, Americans hunted culture, imported artwork and artists, built opera and music houses and museums to house their captured treasures, and trumpeted such efforts, hoping to win Europe's approval. The boastful Carnegie embodied the American angst Arnold witnessed. The rising capitalist was rootless, cut off from his native land, and he was now searching for a unique identity as the Star-Spangled Scotchman. He, too, was apprehensive about his new wealth, and to ease that anxiety he sought approval and love. He sought culture and high society to wear as his emblem of success, and he would build libraries to propagate culture and knowledge across the land.

The investment in Frick, the thrust to become an influential newspaper magnate, and the courtship of Arnold, Morley, and Spencer left little time in the schedule for matters of love. Throughout 1882, Louise and Carnegie's relationship evolved little, continuing to revolve around occasional evenings at the opera or theater and rides in the park. It became a morning routine for Carnegie to send his footman, an Irishman named John O'Hara, to the Whitfield home with a card: "Shall call for you this afternoon hope you can take a drive with me three o'clock."[18] There was little spontaneity; he conducted his courting as efficiently as he did business. On their rides together, Carnegie did speak ardently about his newspaper syndicate, about changing the disenfranchised British laborer's life for the better, and about his new friends, Morley, Arnold, and Spencer. Hearing of the distinguished friends and formal affairs he attended only intimidated Louise, because while sociable, she was not the social animal Carnegie was; even her coming-out party at age eighteen was a low-key affair held in her parents' home. To Louise's dismay, Carnegie also expressed genuine interest in moving to England when he finally retired, an impossibility for her, considering she had younger siblings and a now invalid mother to watch over. Even extended periods abroad were out of the question, so when Carnegie began to hint at marriage, his advances were met with indifference.

Since her father's death, Louise had become more independent. Even as a child, she had given her parents trouble: "I am afraid that they sometimes found me a little difficult; I had a mind of my own."[19] Carnegie now faced the same difficulty, for Louise was not a business partner who could be cajoled with compliments and money; she was a stoic Connecticut Puritan who believed her family needed her more than Andrew Carnegie. But her adeptness around the house, whether cooking and cleaning or brightening the day with piano and song, made her all the more attractive to him. He persistently dropped hints. Why, Louise asked, should I marry a rich man with no worries? What benefit would I be? A struggling man would find me indispensable and appreciate me. Poor Carnegie, who craved approval from everyone, wanted it most from the woman who wouldn't give it.

Another thorn in their relationship continued to complicate matters: Carnegie's mother. Louise was not endeared to Margaret, who cast her shadow over her son, and years later she admitted that Margaret was the most unpleasant person she had ever known.[20] But the matriarch was not the only family baggage. There was also brother Tom's struggle with alcoholism. Many days he would arrive at his Pittsburgh office around 10 A.M., work briefly, and then depart for the local watering hole. "After an hour or so at the office," recalled his lieutenant, William Abbott, "Tom would go to the Pittsburgh Club, have lunch with his cronies, and tank up! About four in the afternoon he would appear at the office again, stay for an hour and then go home."[21] His interest in the business was quickly waning as pressures intensified. "Tom was devoted to his family," recalled Abbott. "His wife was beautiful as a girl, though she became ill proportioned as she grew older. . . . Tom, though not lacking in geniality, was not a social man. He was silent and retiring, the complete reverse of the loquacious Andrew."[22] It was true: bearing nine children had taken its toll on Lucy, but she did not lose her vivacity.

Louise appreciated Lucy's unyielding personality. Lucy, who understood all too well the pressures Carnegie placed on her husband, became known for her tart tongue and frequent spats with her overbearing brother-in-law. There was no estrangement, though. When Tom bought twenty thousand acres on Cumberland Island, off the coast of Georgia, Carnegie often accompanied his brother's family there for vacations. Although he unwittingly placed an inordinate amount of pressure on his brother, Carnegie was extremely protective of his immediate and extended family. He continued to handle investments for his relatives in Scotland and the United States. Learning that his cousin Maria Hogan needed new eyeglasses, he made sure McCandless sent her a pince-nez by the best maker. He sent most relatives $300 cash Christmas gifts, a substantial sum at the time.[23] In 1883, when death struck down another Original Six member, James R. Wilson, who was survived by a wife and several children, Carnegie stepped into the fold, providing financial aid and advising Wilson's widow Callie: "Now my dear Friend put away the notes & draw interest & you have plenty upon which to maintain & educate your children." His reason for helping her, he explained, was that there were "no friends like those of boyhood Callie—later acquaintances never can take their place & now if there is ever anything about which you wish to see me, don't fail to send for me for surely you know there is nothing which I do not wish to do for you."[24] Carnegie would later buy her shares in Frick's company, another unnecessary act of kindness.[25]

When with Carnegie, Louise saw a millionaire man-about-town who acted with such grand motions and exaggerated emotions he appeared almost superficial; she was not privy to his little acts of kindness for family and friends that said more about him than did his radical pronouncements and large bestowals. Lost within his inflated legend was the fact that he was a sensitive, intensely loyal family man, but because he was hard to pin down for an extended period, it was difficult for Louise to perceive any depth to Carnegie's emotional substance.

He was again elusive in 1883 when he spent the summer season in Britain, attending to his newspapers, agitating the upper class, and participating in the grand opening of the Dunfermline Carnegie Library. The ceremonial opening was presided over by Lord Rosebery, whose conservative ancestors had

been relentlessly attacked by Carnegie's Grandfather Morrison. Two generations later found Lord Rosebery to be a Liberal with whom Carnegie could
share a table, and it was Rosebery who introduced the rapacious steel master
to William Gladstone. While cavorting with such politicos, he wrote Louise
frequently, including one July letter she considered memorable enough to
note in her diary as lovely.[26] From the Tremper House in the Catskills, she
returned his favor: "Oh how glad your letter made me! for I was really afraid
this year you would forget all about writing. . . . What a delightful time you
must be having in the society of such congenial people, but I hope you won't
get to like them too well. Rumors are constantly reaching us of the stir you
are creating—and on this side, everybody is talking about your book, *An
American Four-in-Hand in Britain.*" The stir was the result of an uninhibited
Carnegie denouncing the aristocracy to dukes and attacking the parliamentary system to members of Parliament.

Louise also wrote, "We are all very proud of you, and love to think that
you are our friend. I don't like to hear, however, that you have neglected your
health. After a winter in New York, to have a season in London, is more than
anyone could stand. I am afraid you have missed your riding! You must certainly take a good long rest before coming home, or else you will not be able
to ride as much in the fall, and that would be a dreadful disappointment to
me, especially when I expect to have my new riding habit, too!"[27] This last
line was as close as Louise could come to saying she wanted to be physically
appealing to him. She then concluded her letter with this line: "I almost
hope that Scotland may not be quite as kind as usual, in order that you may
hasten your return home." This was as close as she could come to saying she
loved him.

Still emotionally stunted and struggling with how to make a commitment to
Louise, Carnegie gave her a book that meant much to him to express how
much he cared for her. It wasn't *Wuthering Heights* by Emily Brontë, but
Edwin Arnold's *Light of Asia.* The full title given by Arnold was *The Light of
Asia; or, The Great Renunciation, Being the Life and Teaching of Gautama,
Prince of India and Founder of Buddhism (As Told in Verse by an Indian Bud-
dhist).* In this 238-page-long poem, he depicted the life of Siddhartha
Guatama, who founded Buddhism, and his path to Nirvana.

Diametrically opposed to Carnegie's harsh business philosophy, survival
of the fittest, Buddhism is based on four noble truths: existence is suffering;
the cause of suffering is craving and attachment; cessation of suffering is
achieved through Nirvana; Nirvana is attained through the Eightfold Path,
consisting of proper views, resolve, speech, action, livelihood, effort, mindful-
ness, and concentration. Buddhism was not an option in the land of the
Philistines. Could Morgan, Rockefeller, Vanderbilt, or even Carnegie truly
comprehend Arnold's words? Was Carnegie prepared to renounce pleasures,
ambitions, wealth, praise, fame, and conquest? So how could he, who counted

Spencer as his sole master, be interested in the pacifist life of a spiritual leader? Foremost, Arnold's *Light of Asia* was a story of enlightenment that Carnegie believed he had attained, albeit within a different framework. Also, Arnold's work was in vogue.

The *Light of Asia* did serve to bring Carnegie and Louise closer together as the two lovers struggled through the story of Siddhartha, searching for meaning and sharing their thoughts. Watching Louise mark her favorite passages, noting her enthusiasm for the book, Carnegie realized she was the girl for him. In September 1883, Carnegie—tentatively—asked Louise for her hand in marriage. He then argued ardently that she could have a meaningful life with him, that managing a large estate and directing munificence could do the world far more good than her nurturing along a young man just starting in business. Filled with doubt, she consulted her mother, who insisted she accept. She didn't want her ill health to restrain Louise, and she did want to see her daughter, now age twenty-six, married. Carnegie's mother, on the other hand, was hardly so gracious. She made it very difficult for her son, complaining that he was abandoning her. Further complicating matters, Carnegie insisted they keep their engagement secret from friends and acquaintances because he didn't want the newspapers to drag their lives through the mud. This condition of the engagement was difficult for Louise to accept and an emotional strain: one day she would write in her diary, "Had a delightful horseback ride with Mr. Carnegie," and the next she would write, "Am so unhappy, so miserable."

By December, it appeared Louise had accepted the terms and was finally content: "Went shopping in the morning and in afternoon went riding with Mr. C. Glorious sunset. Rode home in the gloaming. Happy at last. . . . Mr. C. came and we went to matinee at the opera. It was *Mephistofeles*. Very grand and lovely. Red letter day." But then, on Christmas Eve, doubts began to surface: "My Christmas task is done. The tree is dressed, the presents set in order. Oh! is this the last time I am to perform this loving labor in my old home? Had a loving note from Mr. C. which made me very happy, but the old ties will pull." On New Year's Eve, her doubts strengthened: "And now we come to the last night of the old year again. What a changed girl it finds me! Life seems so hard. I feel so old and strange. Nothing is certain, nothing is sure. I am striving so hard to do what is right, but I cannot see the light yet."[28] Carnegie, who was under the impression their relationship was evolving into something special and yearned for her, was unaware of Louise's misgivings.

CHAPTER 15

Bleeding Hearts and Bleeding Newspapers

O n New Year's Day in 1884, a forty-eight-year-old Carnegie made his cus-tomary visit to the Whitfield residence, but his feelings this winter day were dramatically different than four years before. This was no social call beginning and ending with gay salutations and in between filled with pleas-ant observations and reflections; tension between Louise and him made for an uncomfortable situation. Carnegie's stories and jokes did lighten the mood eventually, and that night Louise noted in her diary: "Very happy time. Let me record it for it is probably the last."[1] Unable to share Carnegie with his demanding business, let alone his mother, Louise argued in the ensuing days that the relationship was not going to work, that the engagement should be called off. He was not so willing to let go, however, and countered that more time together and a recommitment to each other would permit them to evolve. After hearing him out, on January 6 she agreed to a "cessation of hostilities."[2]

Frequent invitations followed in which Carnegie's desires couldn't have been more transparent: "Miss Florence, Mr Phipps and I going to Theatre tonight. Can we call for you. Want you very much. Answer."[3] What he didn't know, however, was that for three months there was no mention of his name in Louise's diary until finally, on April 1, she wrote, "Mr. C. sent for me to ride—went to painting lesson and then to ride with A.C. Very nice but so tired—quite used up in the evening."[4] The covert relationship, Carnegie's threats to live abroad, his business commitments, and his dynamic, restless personality exhausted Louise. Finally, on April 23, she insisted they break off their engagement. Symbolic of the seriousness of their break, they returned all the letters they had written to each other.[5]

Failure was not something Carnegie was accustomed to and the broken engagement made him miserable. He had wanted her to share in his success, to help manage his affairs, the philanthropy, to be at his side when that spring he donated $50,000 to Bellevue Hospital Medical College of New York.[6] Only now the chance to have the woman who had passed his supreme test was slipping away.

Louise Whitfield's suspicion that their relationship was not of primary concern to Carnegie was apparently confirmed when he departed for Britain in May with the intention of spending the next five to six months overseas. The summer highlight was to be a six-week coaching trip through England's southern counties that would strengthen Carnegie's friendships with his British literary and radical comrades. There were no Gay Charioteers this time as a more serious, contemplative set joined Carnegie, including Edwin Arnold, Matthew Arnold, his wife and his daughter, William Gladstone's son and daughter, Samuel Storey, William Black, and Edwin Abbey, an American illustrator. Upon this arrival in London, Carnegie's first order of business was to extend a lunch invitation to Spencer. Never seduced by the Carnegie charm, Spencer responded wryly with a meticulous, handwritten note in purple pen: "I was glad to get your note, implying your safe arrival. You must excuse me from coming to lunch with you, for it would involve more talking than I just now wish to undertake; but I shall take my chance of finding you when I call in the afternoon."[7]

On June 2, the coaching trip assembled in front of the Grand Hotel and boarded a four-in-hand, their itinerary to cover an average of thirty-five miles a day as they looped toward the rugged, rockbound coast of Ilfracombe. Carnegie, who'd been keeping in touch with Louise, gave her an update: "Many thanks, my dear friend for your kind notes. Here we are coaching once more. Have been out from London for about ten days. Started with William Black, Matthew Arnold, the two charming Misses Arnold, Mr. Edwin A. Abbey, who illustrates for *Harper's*. How delightful it all has been! . . . I hope your summer will be a happy one. I am very sincerely gratified that your picture is voted *good* [she was taking a painting class]. Keep at work but don't forget that after all literature, good literature, is the most important possession for old age. . . ."[8]

On this coaching trip, Carnegie, who declared if he wasn't an ironmaster he'd be a gypsy, quickly discovered his companions were quite intense. While he was apt to exclaim, "By golly boys, there's a great deal in store for us here" when visiting picturesque villages, cathedrals, and castles, he observed that no irreverent word came from Matthew Arnold. Deeply meditative, Arnold's public edicts during the trip included, "The case against miracles is closed. They do not happen."[9] On the lighter side, he was partial to claret and whiskey, even at their midday picnics. Another severe character was William Black, who grew weary of Carnegie and Storey plotting their radical agenda and "proclaiming the glories of the United States."[10] Yet, despite occasional tension, the coaching trip was a success, and Carnegie returned bronzed by the wind and weather.[11]

By the end of the trip, Carnegie had developed a strong friendship with both Arnold families (he placed them on his Christmas list, which meant they would now receive a turkey along with his other friends and close associates), and Edwin Arnold went so far as to present Carnegie with the original manuscript of the *Light of Asia*. He loved to have gifts bestowed upon him, always reacting as though he was deprived boy from a Dickens novel who had just been bequeathed a treasure. Unable to contain his excitement, Carnegie had to share this triumph with someone who would appreciate it— Louise—and the gift gave him the perfect excuse to write her. To his relief, she responded: "My dear Mr. Carnegie, Just a few lines tonight before retiring, to tell you how much I rejoice with you in the possession of your treasure. . . . I always carry the copy of the Light of Asia you gave me, around with me every place I go. I love to pick it up, even if only to read but a few lines, and it always refreshes me, and does me good. I wish I had it, as you have, at my tongue's end, but I have committed a few of the loveliest bits to memory. . . . So now, Good night, my friend; won't you be surprised to receive this! But I hope as well pleased as I was to get yours this morning."[12] Her enthusiastic response gave him hope that their relationship wasn't quite finished.

Plans for an extended stay in Scotland were curtailed in mid-July when Carnegie received reports that his mother's health was poor. Intending to take her to Cresson for some fresh air, he returned promptly. On passing through New York, he walked to the Whitfield's house on Forty-eighth Street, hoping they had come home from their summer house. The windows were dark. From Cresson, he wrote Louise, "Did you see Miss Arnold is engaged to a New York lawyer? Her younger sister is the cleverer, but she isn't pretty. Too bad clever young ladies are rarely beautiful. There are exceptions; I think of one. I spent a night at the Windsor, walked past your house to see it all closed but boasting a span new awning over the door. Not a soul in town I knew, or cared to know that night except did want to find you, and you were gone, too. Just as well, better no doubt, I said, and walked back to the hotel."[13] The image of Carnegie standing before Louise's home offered a glimpse of him as a man, not a legend of mythical proportions. In spite of his extensive network of family, friends, and associates, not to mention his mother's constant companionship, he was a lonely man. Even though Margaret was very ill, once at Cresson she perceived her son's growing desire for Louise, and, realizing she had only a few years remaining at most, she wasn't willing to relinquish him. So, frail and clinging to the life she knew, she exacted a promise from Andrew: do not marry until I pass on.[14]

When Carnegie returned to New York in early October, Louise and he socialized only sporadically, although he did introduce her to James Blaine, the powerful Maine politician who was the Republican candidate for the presidency. In this election year, his opponent was Democrat Grover Cleveland, who did not pander to big business and was considered the antithetical candidate to the ethically dubious Blaine. Whereas Cleveland was indeed a straight shooter who had fought New York City's powerful Tammany Hall as governor of New York, Blaine, in the mid-1870s, had been implicated in railroad corruption that had tarnished his reputation for years. But because he was recognized as the party's most charismatic politician, the Republicans had rehabilitated his image. As for Carnegie, it seemed he always had an attraction to such flamboyant characters who walked a fine ethical line, beginning with his mentor, Tom Scott, which reflected on his own flawed character. "While one is known by the company he keeps," Carnegie wrote in his autobiography (cryptically perhaps), "it is equally true that one is known by the stories he tells. Mr. Blaine was one of the best story-tellers I ever met. His was a bright sunny nature with a witty, pointed story for every occasion."[15] They were good friends until Blaine's death in 1893.

Frankly, Carnegie had little use for politicians who could not be bought, and, true to form, during the campaign Blaine didn't hesitate to ask for funding. "Are you willing to send me $7,500—and let me explain subsequently what I do with it?" Blaine wrote him.[16] Fully expecting Blaine to win the presidency, Carnegie was shocked when he lost, but his failure didn't stop Blaine from asking Carnegie for another $20,000 to help pay off his election debts, reminding the steel master that he remained his most successful friend in Washington.[17] It was true. When Cleveland later acted on his promised initiative to reduce the protective tariff, a prospect that alarmed American capitalists, Carnegie's most powerful friend in Washington successfully took up the battle on their behalf (and asked for a $1,000 donation to aid the fight).[18] The monetary cost was negligible.

Throughout autumn, Carnegie and Louise remained just friends—until an actress came between them. Ellen Terry, an accomplished Shakespearean actress, was in New York playing Beatrice in *Much Ado about Nothing*, and Carnegie, who had made her acquaintance in London, sent her an invitation for a drive, promising the finest trotters in New York. "Oh! Oh!! Oh!!! I could weep," Ellen replied, "for it has become an intense desire of mine to sit, if but for one hour, behind some fast trotters and I have never done so as yet. I cannot come! *and am so sorry*, but a bad cold must not be neglected and I must stay in bed all day for Beatrice's sake and the evening's work. . . . Very truly your Ellen Terry."[19]

It was a small city in those days, so Louise soon heard of Carnegie's interest in the beautiful English actress and expressed her surprise and pain. Carnegie, who was just attempting to escape his anguish over losing Louise, responded, "I only asked her in desire to get someone out of the ordinary. You had to be banished somehow. Now will you go with me at half past two, and let us have a talk. Perhaps this is all wrong, but I do wish to talk to you."[20] Carnegie sent this letter through his loyal footman, John O'Hara, and ordered him not to return until he had a reply—it was time to assume control. Louise agreed to meet with him and, after almost a year of trying to break off their relationship, they wholly admitted their love and became engaged again—this despite Carnegie's confessing his promise to his mother to not marry until she died. All that needed to be done, they decided, was to keep their engagement a secret to not upset Margaret. Considering that Margaret was a complete invalid, Louise knew it wouldn't be long before they could marry, so the arrangement wasn't as unreasonable and farcical to her as the first go-round. Only Mrs. Whitfield was let in on their secret.

A routine resumed between Carnegie and Louise. In the morning he would send his man O'Hara with an invitation for her—perhaps a visit to St. Patrick's Cathedral to swim in the music, or a Nineteenth Century Club meeting, or the theater—and then, at the appointed hour, Carnegie would arrive at the Whitfield residence. They also went for long walks through Central Park; they rode in all weather, with Carnegie on his favorite horse Roderick; they explored the open fields north of Fifty-ninth Street where some colonial houses still stood; they went for carriage rides up into the Bronx, then lush, dense tree groves; and they visited Edgar Allan Poe's old cottage. The constant companionship fed rumors of romance, which they denied despite the occasional slipup.[21]

Never thrilled with Carnegie's now annual pilgrimage to Great Britain, Louise resigned herself to it as summer approached. But because of his mother's physical frailty and his own health weakened by illness and overwork, Carnegie doubted he would make the journey that year. "Mother, I regret to say, is an invalid," he admitted to Morley, "and I fear I must never leave her again. She is one of the grandest characters you ever heard of—a true heroine. My ambitious plans give place to her claims and I shall not desert her. I can't flatter myself that she can ever cross the Atlantic."[22] It was one thing to announce in public his mother was his heroine, but to do so in private letters proved how strongly Carnegie felt for her. He canceled plans for Britain.

Carnegie took his mother to Cresson in hopes the fresh air would revive her. In June, he came down from the mountains to preach at Pittsburgh's Curry Commercial College. The title of his sermon was "The Road to Business Success." From his experiences, he delivered unto them some of his most oft-quoted axioms:

> The rising man must do something exceptional, and beyond the range of his special department. HE MUST ATTRACT ATTENTION. . . . Always break orders to save owners. There never was a great character who did not sometimes smash the routine regulations and make new ones for himself. . . . Boss your boss just as soon as you can; try it on early. There is nothing he will like so well if he is the right kind of boss; if he is not, he is not the man for you to remain with—leave him whenever you can, even at a present sacrifice, and find one capable of discerning genius. . . . "Don't put all your eggs in one basket" is all wrong. I tell you "put all your eggs in one basket, and then

watch that basket." . . . Look out for the boy who has to plunge into work direct from the common school and who begins by sweeping out the office. He is the probable dark horse that you had better watch.

That dark horse was Carnegie, of course. To soothe any painful memories from his struggle to escape poverty, he'd become sentimental about those early years. From his lofty pedestal, however, he failed to explain to the students that it took him a good ten years to put all the eggs in one basket and that he still owned a wide variety of railroad and insurance stocks, among others, as well as land and properties. (He owned stock and bonds in some twenty companies that were not directly related to his iron, steel, and bridge manufacturing, or to his newspaper syndicate.)[23]

Shortly after his visit to Curry Commercial College, Carnegie's plans for the summer changed when he decided to sail for Britain, after all, explaining to Louise, "Mr. Phipps and Mr. Lauder go along and Mother really asked me to go . . . and really my newspaper business demands my presence for a week or two in London. Then two weeks in Scotland is all I have."[24] In fact, there was a very legitimate reason for his going: the newspaper syndicate was very sick, financially speaking.

Louise put on a brave face, claiming she always knew he would eventually go; but then, just a month after his departure, tensions arose, beginning with a letter from Carnegie: "Well, my Dear, here we are in the Whirl. . . . Rather lonely some mornings, at breakfast in my room alone, but I like it some ways. Bachelordom has its advantages! I miss Mother much in such big rooms and wish a certain young lady were only here to brighten them up with her smiles and silvery laugh; but she is having fine hours with many admirers no doubt."

It upset Louise that time and again her Andrew couldn't give her a compliment without mentioning his mother in the same whispering breath. He had great difficulty in ever giving a compliment without it being backhanded. Then Carnegie, who could be extremely insensitive to others' feelings, mentioned a Mary Anderson, who was apparently quite beautiful, and the actress Ellen Terry, which really roused Louise: "I spent last Sunday with the Howards and Clapham Hall and next I go to the Arnolds. Of course Matthew Arnold and Herbert Spencer have been with me here to lunch. Today Edwin Arnold comes and a party of twelve. Mary Anderson couldn't come, unfortunately. (Maybe you are glad.) She is much prettier and younger than Ellen Terry." It did little to soothe her feelings when he told her he was castle shopping in Scotland, but wanted her there to help.[25] So what? Louise decided to inform him she was having a glorious time at a Catskills summer resort hotel, where the weather was glorious, the riding was glorious, the painting was glorious, and, yes indeed, potential suitors inhabited every room.

Louise's letter appeared so buoyant and seemingly indifferent to him that Carnegie exposed his hidden side, the paranoid and insecure man, and he admitted to her he was genuinely pained. Flabbergasted by his childish jealousies, Louise let loose with a good scolding: "My dear Andrew what a goose you are! . . . Shall I tell you the truth of the summer? . . . The summer stretched away such a long dreary space before me and it seemed to me such a sacrilege to even talk about 'having good times,' but I said to myself, 'He evidently enjoys himself just as much with others as he does with me. . . . I will pretend that I enjoy it too.'"[26] Any doubts Carnegie harbored about her commitment were swept away. Meanwhile, because of problems at the newspaper syndicate, his summer in Britain turned out as dreary as hers in the Catskills.

With arguments arising between Storey, Graham, and himself over the editorial content and finances of the newspaper syndicate, Carnegie's dream of owning an interest in a newspaper was becoming a nightmare. At first, the relationship between Carnegie and Storey had been congenial, with Carnegie only occasionally annoying Storey with his stabs at British icons such as Tennyson when he was knighted. "He stands as a miserable example—the highest art of all, poetry, is prostituted to claims of birth," Carnegie wrote Storey. "'A weak old man' is the verdict here. *Barren* Tennyson he has been for years. I don't want to see him now. I think Matthew Arnold would hesitate to accept such a humiliation."[27] His attempts to influence Storey's political agenda, such as voting for home rule for Ireland, were also an irritation.[28]

Two years into the venture, Carnegie's concerns had shifted from Storey's politics to the financial hemorrhaging of the newspaper syndicate, and he proposed a consolidation of operations: "I hope you are ready with your scheme to consolidate all the papers. . . . I do not feel inclined to go on investing more capital at present but of course will pay my share of any assessment made. We would be a strong power were all of our papers merged into one, and could then strike as a thunderbolt, whereas we are now merely showering the enemy with small darts none of which are strong enough to pierce their armor. Even the London 'Echo' should be merged."[29] But the newspaper business was not steel. Editors at the individual papers were highly independent and fought for their autonomy, and the implementation of the "thunderbolt" strategy failed. "Don't be discouraged—I never mounted a horse first time that had go in him which didn't kick," Carnegie, who tried to remain sanguine, wrote Storey. "All our enterprises have gone wrong at first. All came right when reconstructed. You are the sole manager of business matters. Go *ahead.*" But then, immediately after giving Storey his head, he compulsively offered advice: "Put a man at Wolverhampton in *full* charge as you suggest. No divided authority. This is essential. Graham had a good business & profitable one—I agree he lacks the 'go.' Your man should be told he is to have a fair trial. But we know one test only—success. We will change till we get an augur that will bore. . . . We don't know how to give it up."[30] The quality of the man and ensuring he was the right fit was paramount to Carnegie, but pushing Graham to the side didn't resolve the syndicate's financial troubles.

Again, he failed to realize steel and media were two different animals requiring different management skills.

Although the chain of newspapers continued to bleed, some political successes soothed Carnegie's wounds. With the syndicate's support, John Morley won a seat in Parliament as a representative from Newcastle. The trusted man was immediately an influential government player, and the literary community's loss was certainly a victory for the radicals. Carnegie also liked to think the syndicate helped push through the 1884 Reform Act that doubled the electorate, enfranchising most agricultural workers and miners. Just as important to him was the rapport he established with Gladstone.

No other native or British-born American tycoon—Morgan, Rockefeller, or Vanderbilt—was welcomed or enjoyed the inner sanctum of British politics like Carnegie, and the same could be said when he later thrust himself onto the American political stage. Between the influence the newspaper syndicate wielded and the fact that Carnegie donated thousands of pounds to the Liberal Party, Gladstone could not ignore the brash American. When in the Star-Spangled Scotchman's company he certainly couldn't ignore him. Carnegie spoke to Gladstone brazenly—"breezy talk" he called it—about America's superior democratic system and Britain's troubles. Economic statistics spilled from his mouth, offered as proof of America's superiority while he argued Britain was to the United States what Greece had been to Rome—the headquarters of its culture but unimportant materially. The Crown and the House of Lords had to go, he would repeat at each meeting with the prime minister, and Ireland, Wales, and Scotland should be treated as independent states within a larger federal system, like a New York, Virginia . . . and on and on. Gladstone could hardly get a word in, only able to exclaim, "Oh—Ah—How extraordinary—Wonderful—Incredible—Astounding!" Mrs. Gladstone would remark to the audacious Carnegie, "William tells me he has such extraordinary conversations with you."[31]

Once their relationship was established in the mid-1880s, Gladstone was pummeled with almost as many letters as Carnegie's business lieutenants. In an April 1885 letter he informed the prime minister that he had ordered a stick cut from a honey locust tree near George Washington's tomb at Mount Vernon, which was now being cured by Tiffany and Company, as a gift. "I hope you will long be spared to use it," he wrote, "and that you will like to carry it with you, and that it will serve to turn your thoughts at times to your 'kin beyond the sea'—to this giant child of dear old England, who, profiting by the wisdom and labors of her mother, has gone one step further in the upward path of political progress, and founded her institutions on the political equality of the citizen."[32] Just as Carnegie could not express his love for Louise without mentioning his mother, he could not pay tribute to his native land without asserting American superiority, and one can only speculate how Gladstone responded to the backhanded compliment.

Carnegie attempted to set the prime minister's political agenda, everything from his travel plans—recommending a tour that would take Gladstone through Niagara, Chicago, Cincinnati, Pittsburgh, and Washington — to foreign policy:

> Do come over and at a farewell banquet in New York (the only public appearance) stand and proclaim to mankind that hereafter that Nation is morally in the wrong who draws the Sword without first offering to submit to arbitration. *England and America have said it.*
>
> I write this that it may demand your grave and *conscientious* consideration. Depend upon it, Mr. Gladstone you can in no other way so greatly serve man as in doing what I here suggest.[33]

Although Carnegie wanted only what was best, peaceful resolutions to conflict, his presumption was not lost on Gladstone, who never did visit the United States.

When debate over home rule for Ireland reached a climax in late 1885 and early 1886, Carnegie delivered the charge to Gladstone: "Your position upon the Irish question seems to me certain to win and to crown your career with the most important legislation which even you have ever carried. I suggest therefore that you take an early opportunity to refer to the rights of States in the American Union as being the proper position for Ireland. Such a measure will strengthen the bonds of union between Ireland and Great Britain; for America has proved through the federal system that the present self-government of the parts produces the strongest government of the whole."[34] Contrary to Carnegie's rosy prediction, Gladstone's Home Rule Bill was defeated in July 1886. He then resigned as prime minister, a serious blow to the Liberals.

As Gladstone struggled in his final months of office, so did Carnegie's newspaper syndicate, which was under continuous attack from the conservative press. The newspapers Carnegie subsidized began to lose their legitimacy, partly because the righteous steel master was too naive and idealistic in his views that the privileged class could be overthrown. Class was a way of life in Britain, providing structure and stability, as did the church; even those on the lower rungs often embraced the status quo, in spite of Carnegie's exhortations otherwise. There was no time for peasant uprisings; the laboring class was too busy struggling to put bread on the table. Also, the workingmen were not as interested in reading a newspaper spouting Carnegie's political agenda as they were in catching up on the latest football and rugby scores and town gossip.

A bloodless revolution took time and money, but Carnegie had no patience for it. In 1885, he abruptly decided to sell most of his share in the newspaper syndicate to Graham and Storey. Even in failure, good fortune remained on his side. To regain control of his *London Echo,* Passmore Edwards paid $500,000, double what Carnegie and Storey had bought in for, and Carnegie almost broke even on the entire venture.[35] He later said the newspaper syndicate was "one of the forms in which I may be said to have sown my wild oats."[36] That was his excuse, anyway. What he really learned was that a thick skin was needed before climbing on the political stage, where the spotlight was harsh, highlighting and expanding every blemish of character, every conceivable motive, and marking any target susceptible to mudslinging. Because the iron and steel trade papers had always supported him, Carnegie had never before faced such public criticism; in the end, he decided the trade-off of political power versus opening himself up to public attack was not worth it. From now on, he would limit his power plays to using his money to influence the men in high positions who wielded power directly.

Carnegie wasn't finished with attacking the British monarchy, however. During the years he was active with the newspaper syndicate, he was writing what would be his greatest literary triumph, his magnum opus, a 509-page book titled *Triumphant Democracy*. Of the eight books he published, it received the greatest attention. Bound in a flaming red cover—on the front a broken royal scepter, and on the back a royal headband turned upside down—the book was an eye-catcher. The cover's symbolism suggested a damning of Britain's monarchy, and the written words confirmed it. To begin, instead of the book being dedicated to his favorite heroine, his mother, Carnegie dedicated it to his *Beloved Republic*, and it was indeed a grand tribute to America's progress and unparalleled prosperity. "The old nations of the earth creep on at a snail's pace"; he wrote in the preface, "the Republic thunders past with the rush of the express."[37] Armed with eco-demographic numbers and fiery rhetoric to glorify the American democracy and damn the British monarchy, Carnegie discussed, debated, and delivered righteous sermons on the people, cities, occupations, education, religion, crime, agriculture, manufacturing, trade, railways, art and music, literature, government, and foreign affairs, as well as dishing up plenty of his personal reflections in general. No subject was left out. One could hear the drums drumming and the pipers piping as he marched onward. It was promotional literature that couldn't be bested by the greatest of public relations experts.

In celebrating America's many triumphs, Carnegie did not forget the workingman: "As a rule, the American workingman is steadier than his fellow in Britain—much more sober and possessed of higher tastes. Among his amusements is found scarcely a trace of the ruder practices of British manufacturing districts, such as cock-fighting, badger-baiting, dog-fighting, prizefighting. Wife-beating is scarcely ever heard of, and drunkenness is quite rare."[38] Evidently Carnegie had not spent much time with Captain Jones's secretary, a renowned drunk, and had not patronized the saloons around Braddock and Homestead, and was somehow blind to the lines of men on the streets waiting their turn in the brothels. As he did with all things American, Carnegie glossed over the workingman's faults. When one critic asked of his book, "Where are the shadows?" Carnegie wittily answered, "The book was written at high noon when the sun casts no shadows."[39]

Naturally, Carnegie sent copies of the book to his dozens of friends and acquaintances, congressmen, lawyers, editors, historians, competitors, and multiple copies to Captain Jones, who passed them out among the men (Captain Jones had to buy one himself). Letters of thanks poured in, each one carefully filed for posterity and ego's sake. Sales in the U.S. surpassed fifteen thousand within a few months, and a cheap reprint targeting Britain's working class sold forty thousand.[40] While many of the reviews from friends and conservative quarters were glowing, others easily penetrated the book's veneer.

The master, Herbert Spencer, while acknowledging the United States was indeed an economic triumph, discounted the importance Carnegie placed on its democracy and placed emphasis on its prodigious natural resources. He also regretted that there was a cost to American prosperity: "Absorbed by his activities and spurred on by his unrestricted ambitions, the American is, to my thinking, a less happy being than the inhabitant of a country where the possibilities of success are very much smaller; and where, in the immense majority of cases, each has to be content with the hum-drum career in which circumstances have placed him, and, abandoning hopes of any great advance, is led to make the best of what satisfaction in life fall to his share."[41]

Matthew Arnold had a similar response. From Stockbridge, Massachusetts, where he was visiting his daughter, who had married a Yankee, he wrote a friend, "You should read Carnegie's book, *Triumphant Democracy.* The facts he has collected as to the material progress of this country are remarkable, and I am told the book is having great sale, being translated into French and German, etc. He and most Americans are simply unaware that nothing in the book touches the capital defect of life over here [America]; namely that, compared with life in England, it is so uninteresting, so without savour and without depth. Do they think to prove that it has savour and depth by pointing to the number of public libraries, schools and places of worship?"[42] The Philistines would always be Philistines.

Contrary to Arnold's opinion, many Americans did indeed realize Carnegie had glossed over faults. One critic wrote to the proliferator of propaganda: "May I be permitted to doubt 'Triumphant Democracy' and to protest against its bitter disregard, as it seems to me, of fact and circumstance in almost everyone of its assertions, altered so unhesitatingly, about the advance of the United States people. . . . You have no superior in your own estimation—you are to be pitied indeed. Of course a successful business man sees only blessings in increase of business, business, business. . . ."[43] The *Dial,* an American periodical, reviewed the book along the lines of Arnold: "Mr. Carnegie certainly pounds the drum and toots the horn with great skill and volume of sound. . . . The late Mr. Disraeli once referred to Mr. Gladstone as 'a sophistical rhetorician, inebriated by the exuberance of his own verbosity.' One is inclined to fit the coat on Mr. Carnegie, letting it out in spots: 'A sophistical statistician, inebriated by the exuberance of his own statistical fecundity.'" While the magazine acknowledged America's industrial might, it questioned whether Carnegie used the right units—railroad track mileage, dollars, etc.—for measuring true greatness. "The truth is that in America our real tasks have just begun. . . . It wouldn't hurt us if we had less bragging and more books—less show and fuss and more honest living—less pork and more scholars."[44] The Philistines needed more soul.

Liberals like Morley received the book more kindly; the eco-demographic statistics were actually useful weapons in his political party's battle to reform the monarchy. "I congratulate you on your completion of your task," Morley wrote, "and I am much obliged to you for sending me a copy. It is a substantial, well considered and important book. I have not had time to read it all, but I have turned it over pretty carefully, and have got a good idea of it. I do not assent to every word in it, and there are some passages where the sentiment is a trifle too *aggressively* republican, for there is no difference between us as to the roots of things. But that does not matter. The book is a solid contribution on the right side. And it is written in high spirits which give it an attractive literary vivacity."[45]

Triumphant Democracy was indeed infused with literary vivacity. In referring to the Union army during the Civil War, Carnegie evoked powerful images: "Even the vaunted legions of Xerxes, and the hordes of Attila and Timour were exceeded in numbers by the citizen soldiers who took up arms in 1861 to defend the unity of the nation, and who, when the task was done, laid them quietly down, and returned to the avocations of peace."[46] On education, he wrote: "Educate man, and his shackles fall. Free education may be trusted to burst every obstruction which stands in the path of the democracy towards its goal, the equality of the citizen, and this it will reach quietly and without violence, as the swelling sapling in its growth breaks its guard."[47] On art: "If Art be, as she is, a most jealous mistress, she is as just as she is exacting and no respecter of persons. There is nothing monarchical about her."[48] His language was persuasive—too persuasive at times—as he manipulated history.

If critics had known, they would have reserved their severest condemnation for Carnegie's revision of his own personal history portrayed in *Triumphant Democracy*, for his vanity distorted his vision of himself and reality. In a section depicting the invention of the sleeping car and its introduction to the American public, Carnegie glorified himself and evoked T. T. Woodruff's wrath. Back in 1858, Woodruff had brought a model of his sleeping car directly to the attention of Pennsylvania Railroad president J. Edgar Thomson. Not so, according to Carnegie's revised account in *Triumphant Democracy:* "Well do I remember that, when a clerk in the service of the Pennsylvania Railroad Company, a tall, spare, farmer-looking kind of man came to me once when I was sitting on the end seat of the rear car looking over the line. He said he had been told by the conductor that I was connected with the railway company, and he wished me to look at an invention he had made. With that he drew from a green bag (as if it were for lawyer's briefs) a small model of a sleeping berth for railway cars. He had not spoken a minute, before, like a flash, the whole range of the discovery burst upon me."[49] Carnegie claimed that he himself then enthusiastically sold the idea to Tom Scott. The simple farmer type and vigilant young clerk teaming up made for a classic American success story—a classic fictional story, however.

When Carnegie sent a copy of the book—inscribed "To my friend of old T. T. Woodruff. With best wishes of the author"—Woodruff couldn't comprehend Carnegie's arrogance and misleading statements as he read about his supposed discovery of the poor, naive inventor and his stupendous sleeping car. He immediately wrote a letter to Carnegie full of rebuke: "I believe, Mr. Carnegie, that when you penned the said inscription upon the flyleaf of that book, that you then felt all and even more than was expressed by the inscription; but sir, when you were attempting to give the rise and progress of sleeping cars your arrogance spurred you up to make statements recorded in your book, which is misleading and so far from the true facts of the case and so damaging to your friend of old as to merit his rebuke."[50] Woodruff pointed out that he already had his sleeping cars running on other lines and that he had approached Thomson directly, with a letter of introduction from Ohio & Mississippi Railroad president Samuel Barlow. After Scott and Thomson had agreed to create a partnership, in which Andy was given a share, to finance his expanding operations, Woodruff had subcontracted the construction work. "A contract was entered into with Murphy and Allison, of Philadelphia, for the construction of four sleeping cars," he clarified for Carnegie, "which were built and placed upon the Pennsylvania Rail R. Their rank in numerical order was Nos. 22, 23, 24 and 25, the model of which was a full sized car of the finest construction . . . and a little too big for the said green bag in use for lawyers' briefs, to which you allude in that fine spun recollection of events."[51] How confident was Woodruff in his version? Enough to send the Carnegie letter to the newspapers. As mentioned, by 1857 the Woodruff car was on several lines, and when Woodruff found himself on the Pennsylvania's doorstep in early 1858, he found the perfect customer in the forward-thinking Thomson. Also, Woodruff's letter of introduction was from the president of the Ohio & Mississippi, whom Thomson knew well through their price-fixing schemes, which strengthened the inventor's claims of direct contact.

Carnegie's response to Woodruff's charges was lame: "Your letter surprises me. Your error lies in the supposition that I intended to write a history on the 'rise and progress of sleeping cars.' I only mention them incidentally. It is impossible to enter into details in one volume, which aims to give a history of the country as a whole."[52] The tone of righteous indignation in Carnegie's reply was no different than how he had responded more than twenty years earlier to the librarian in charge of Colonel Anderson's books, who "took him to task" over the facts. Carnegie, experiencing a certain arrested development, was like the guilty, sulking boy who never admits his own mistakes—a trait that marked his career. He didn't bother to offer a more specific rebuttal to Woodruff's version of how the inventor came to sell his invention to the Pennsylvania because he knew the inventor was right. Worse yet, in an 1896 essay, "How I Served My Apprenticeship," and later, in his autobiography,

Carnegie stuck to his own green-bag version of the story. Long dead, Wood-ruff could not refute his false claims.

So why the revision besides the wayward vanity? Carnegie wanted to appear more proactive as a rising young man, he wanted to justify the one-eighth interest he was given in the sleeping car business, and he didn't want to acknowledge that a handout gave him his start in business. Come 1886, Carnegie was a true tycoon, a hero to millions in the United States and abroad, and nothing could be allowed to taint his historical rags-to-riches story. And there can be no mistake concerning the importance of the one-eighth interest Carnegie was given in the Woodruff concern: by 1863, it was generating $5,050 in dividends, providing the funds for future investments.[53]

The sleeping car rewrite was not the only instance in which Carnegie dabbled in revisionism. In recounting his very first investment in his auto-biography—the purchase of Adams Express stock—he indulged in wholesale editing. According to Carnegie, when Scott had asked him if he had $500 to invest, he boldly said yes, although he did not. Not wanting to pass up the opportunity, he consulted with his mother immediately. The next morning his mother took the steamer to East Liverpool, and through her brother mort-gaged their house for the $500, which was then given to Scott.[54] His personal papers, carefully archived by him and then his beloved libraries, tell a very different story. The documents show that Tom Scott fronted him the money, and then Carnegie borrowed from others to pay off the IOU to Scott. To enhance his mother's legend and to make him appear more proactive, he had again revised family history.

Carnegie wanted to be the visionary everyone was now making him out to be, the man who allegedly envisioned the day iron bridges would replace wood and the day steel would replace iron. The problem was that his visions involved patient observation, meticulous calculation, aggressive self-promotion, and, to a degree, luck—to being in the right place at the right time. Unfortu-nately, such revisionist indiscretions called all of Carnegie's writing into ques-tion as to its accuracy and truthfulness. What was real? What wasn't? What happened? What didn't? The year *Triumphant Democracy* appeared, Carne-gie also published two essays on labor relations that were hailed as progressive manifestos, but knowing his propensity for self-serving propaganda, one had to question the purpose of these essays.

CHAPTER 16

Patronizing the Peasants

The workmen Carnegie so effusively complimented in *Triumphant Democracy* were not quite as pleased with their progress as their Little Boss was, and in the mid-1880s they began to agitate more vigorously for higher wages and better conditions. The capitalists were not going to be so forthcoming, however; after the economy had peaked in March 1882, a prolonged business contraction had begun and money was tight. Then, in April 1884, a financial panic was set off by a rogue Wall Street speculator, Ferdinand Ward, who had fleeced the prominent Marine Bank, as well as General Ulysses S. Grant. When Marine Bank failed, others followed and visions of the 1873 panic and subsequent depression rattled Wall Street. To survive the volatile market, Carnegie was desperate to cut costs and to solve the wage-related labor troubles that were now plaguing the iron and steel industry.

Prior to 1882, iron and steel industry strikes had been short affairs, a tolerated necessity, almost a game; but with the Amalgamated Association of Iron and Steel Workers' rise in power the stakes had been raised and the conflicts escalated. Certain departments at Edgar Thomson were now union—with men joining the Amalgamated or the Knights of Labor—despite Captain Jones's best efforts to thwart them, and, as David Stewart reported to Carnegie, they were not above using violence: "There was a meeting at Braddock last night and a man by the name of J Arnold from Homestead claimed they could get their advance by Clubs—when they could not by peace."[1] Homestead, despite now being under the Carnegie regime, remained a boiling pot, a source of wider trouble. Jones was so distressed over the Amalgamated lodges now established at Edgar Thomson that he resigned. As individuals, Jones protected his men, but not as members of a union; the union disgusted him because he felt it robbed men of their individuality. To Carnegie, the loss of a genius was far more menacing than the union, and he refused to accept the resignation. It wouldn't be the last time.

It seemed every time he became frustrated with the Amalgamated or the Knights of Labor, Jones quit, at times the resignations coming so fast and furious Carnegie simply ignored them. To his right-hand man Charlie Schwab, the resignations were the stuff of high comedy, especially when the Captain's red-headed secretary, Getty, an enthusiastic imbiber of spirits, shared the stage. A dedicated drunk, Getty was not opposed to spending company money on his liquor. On one occasion when the Captain sent Getty to the train station to purchase a first-class, drawing-room ticket for Philadelphia, the secretary opted to squander most of the money at the bar, saving only enough for a second-class "little red ticket." "When Jones arrived at the station," Schwab recalled, "all Getty could do was to hold out the 'little red ticket' and nod solemnly while Jones fumed and raged." Schwab relished telling the story of how Getty handled Jones's frequent resignations:

> One day a few weeks later, Jones found Getty quite sober, industrially writing at top speed at his desk.
> "What are you doing," Jones asked.
> "Well," said Getty, "I'm writing out a dozen of your resignations so I'll have 'em handy when the time comes."

Schwab and his peers knew "the loss of Bill Jones would mean the collapse of the whole industry," and Carnegie never did allow it.[2]

Another strike threatened in late 1883 as Carnegie anticipated a severe downturn in steel rail prices—in fact, the average rail price would drop from $37.75 a ton in 1883 to $30.75 in 1884, and then to $28.50 in 1885—and wages had to be forced down likewise. Carnegie notified Jones a cut was imminent and, desiring facts as weapons, ordered him to gather evidence for justifying it. "I notice that Vulcan has again reduced wages 10 & 12%," he informed Carnegie, "and while I am naturally averse to stirring up the Devil on this question, yet I feel that our men should readily agree to a reduction here to meet the market. But for fear they might kick I feel like cautioning you to be ready for such an emergency."[3] Carnegie proposed a moderate 10 percent cut and, unless the market improved, another 10 percent in June. The Amalgamated immediately called for a strike, but the Knights of Labor, representing unskilled workers who were largely unaffected, was against it. There was also no financial assistance being made available by the Amalgamated's headquarters in case of a strike, the Pittsburgh Dispatch reported, which would most likely bring "about an amicable adjustment of the existing differences."[4] Both unions held off on a final decision until Carnegie visited Pittsburgh and met personally with the two unions' labor committees.

When Carnegie, or Andy as he was called by everyone, argued his case before the committees, detailing the depressed market and the actions of other firms like Vulcan, the men readily accepted the wage reductions. "With satisfactory evidence of the necessity of a reduction," the Dispatch reported, "caused by the recent decline in steel rails, the workingmen took a conservative and philosophical course in determining to accept lower wages rather than to subject themselves and the community to the loss and sufferings of a lockout."[5] It was better than no work. The paper was clearly on capital's side, but it was also true that the union's leadership realized their men had to meet the market price for labor. It was also a crucial decision on Carnegie's part to personally deal with this labor conflict. His earnest persuasion could win over most anyone, and it was when he stopped dealing with labor conflicts in a personal, face-to-face détente with the workers that he found himself in trouble—as would be the case with Homestead.

His old friend Thomas Miller, who was superintendent of Atlas Works, makers of heavy machinery and castings, congratulated Carnegie and noted, "I know personally from conversations with the leading men in large manufacturing firms with whom we have dealings—all around the country—that you stand head and front over all for your generous treatment of employees—in fact I have heard complaints on that score—!"[6] True, Carnegie had always been quick to capitulate to the men's demands—or, at least, not to cut wages when other chief manufacturers in the industry desired to. But as the unions continued to strengthen and the stakes escalated, his generous attitude would change dramatically.

In late 1884, yet another strike was imminent. This time Carnegie had been keeping in close contact with his Chicago-based sales agent A. L. Griffin, who was monitoring the wages at other mills. "I know we are paying our men too much and if you can get me desired information," Carnegie directed him, "not opinions but *exact figures*, you will do a great service to our firm."[7] Once again he wanted precise information for ammunition, and when both Scranton and Bethlehem cut wage rates by 15 to 20 percent he had the leverage needed to demand further wage reductions.[8] But winning them would not be so easy this time, with the Amalgamated and the Knights of Labor now burrowed in like parasitic moles. As a December chill gripped the mill town, Jones prepared for another battle.

For Jones, it was also an opportunity to purge the Amalgamated from E.T., a prospect Carnegie didn't hesitate to endorse—the union was now becoming a nuisance. In early December, Jones posted a sign at E.T. that stated the works would be closed for an indefinite period beginning December 16, 1884. All employees, unless otherwise notified, would be paid in full and then discharged, which meant throwing as many as sixteen hundred men out of work. The stated reason for the shutdown was for the installation of new machinery to improve the furnaces and the rolling of steel. The unstated reason, of course, was to force out the union and rehire men at lower wages. Quickly realizing only nonunion men would be taken back, many of the men quit the union before the December 16 deadline to better their chances of being rehired.

While the new machinery was installed and the men's families grew hungry, Captain Jones proposed a new wage scale and a return to the double-turn twelve-hour days, which was necessary to trim costs. The labor committees didn't accept the terms, but they had little strength from which to bargain. There was already downward pressure on wages due to the recession; the new equipment made for more efficient production, so a renegotiated wage scale was unavoidable; and the refurbishing eliminated over one hundred jobs, another source of anxiety for the laborers. The rail market was so weak that Carnegie was in no rush to fire up the furnaces, but to increase pressure on the men, the master propagandist used the newspapers to argue his case. In a January 2 interview with the *Pittsburgh Chronicle-Telegraph*, he bluntly stated, "I do not know when they will be started, but not until the rail market improves and we can run and sell at a profit, or until the Amalgamated Association gains control of the other mills in the country and makes better wages in those establishments."[9] The *National Labor Tribune*, considered the workingman's voice, concurred with Carnegie.

By the end of January, in the heart of winter, with the men in need of coal and food, the Amalgamated was broken at Edgar Thomson and disbanded, while the Knights of Labor was simply made impotent because unskilled labor could be had anywhere. In early February, each man signed an individual contract, agreeing to wages slashed by 20 to 33 percent, and the refurbished Edgar Thomson arose like a finely honed, muscular demigod, armed to crush all opposition.[10] As for the double turn, Jones promised it would remain in place only until market prospects brightened and then the triple-turn eight-hour day would be reinstituted.

To garner loyalty in these hard times, Carnegie wisely followed through with his promise to build a library at Braddock and donated $50,000 for the building and other amenities. No union was needed as long as he was a benevolent owner, and Carnegie, feeling sentimental, wrote Louise:

> I gave our Rail Mill men fifty thousand dollars Friday, for Library, etc. Hurrah! That's life. I have not lived before . . .
>   I have been so busy. We have consolidated some of our Works and Interests into one and this has taken my time and thoughts; a new firm organized, but I have had quiet moments and always the hour before sleep your lovely form and voice and oh! such a lovely rippling smile come dancing in upon me to give me such exquisite happiness.[11]

Business and love in the same breath was hardly erotic, but drifting off to sleep with Louise's lovely form and rippling smile dancing in front of him was an impressive expression of sexual arousal from the steel master.

The Amalgamated and wage costs were not the only business issues pricking Carnegie; there was the Pennsylvania Railroad and freight rates to confront if he were to remain competitive. In their war against competitive trunk lines, the railroad slashed rates offered to businesses outside the state of Pennsylvania. Therefore, Carnegie was flabbergasted to discover that not only was his western competition able to ship their products more cheaply to the Atlantic seaboard than he, but it was actually cheaper for his mills to ship their product the short distance to Cincinnati and from there forward it east, with it coming right back through Pittsburgh. It was a preposterous situation. In addition, the Pennsylvania Railroad had a lock on all traffic moving between the coal lands and Pittsburgh. Ever since Tom Scott had died in 1881, it was becoming more difficult for Carnegie to win acceptable rates for shipping. The railroad's president, George Roberts, and vice president, Frank Thomson, nephew of the icon Edgar, no longer considered Scott's Andy a favored son, not after the sordid Texas & Pacific affair they had observed as third parties. In truth, Carnegie had a right to become paranoid over railroad rates.

To break the Pennsylvania's hold on the coal lands and eastern-designated traffic, Carnegie decided to join forces with John D. Rockefeller and William Vanderbilt. Rockefeller, who made millions off railroad rebates and was now operating in the Pennsylvania oil fields, was a natural partner. Both men were puritanically pious in their own ways—Rockefeller a penny-pinching Baptist and Carnegie a penny-pinching disciple of Spencer—both shunned the ostentation plaguing the Gilded Age, and both demanded absolute efficiency in their operations. On the other hand, Vanderbilt, who controlled the New York Central Railroad and joined the industrialists to irk his railroad rivals, was the antithesis of Carnegie's character. Whereas the tightfisted Scotsman lived a relatively simple existence in the Windsor Hotel, the ostentatious Vanderbilt purchased the entire west-side block of Fifth Avenue, between Fifty-first and Fifty-second Streets, for $700,000, and then spent $2 million building twin brownstone mansions for him and his wife and his two married daughters. It took six hundred American laborers and sixty imported Europeans to create what was to many an overly ornate, boxlike architectural abomination. Two of his sons built mansions further up Fifth Avenue, and the span between Fiftieth and Fifty-eighth Streets became known as Vanderbilt Row. Years later Edith Wharton wrote, "I wish the Vanderbilts didn't retard culture so very thoroughly. They are entrenched in a sort of *thermopylae* of bad taste, from which apparently no force on earth can dislodge them."[12] Carnegie himself once said smugly of Vanderbilt, "I would not exchange his millions for my knowledge of Shakespeare." Yes, for a man who prided himself on his taste for culture, he found an unlikely friend in Vanderbilt—but then again, it was an alliance of convenience.

The trio's strategy was simple: build a railroad from Pittsburgh to Harrisburg, where they could connect with more friendly lines, and therefore circumnavigate the Pennsylvania. To finance their project, now called the South Pennsylvania, they set capital at $15 million with each man contributing money.[13] Before construction began, on January 23, 1884, Carnegie made one last appeal to Frank Thomson for fair rates. If the Pennsylvania Railroad refused to comply, he threatened to incite the general public, "whose opinion no corporation these days can successfully withstand."[14] Carnegie had visions of himself as his uncle Thomas—standing before the crowd, pounding his walking stick, and provoking a mass protest against a totalitarian regime. But apparently Thomson was not impressed by the bellicose rhetoric, so grading, foundation work for bridges, and excavations for tunnels commenced. Carnegie expected the line to be completed in the summer of 1885.

Now that construction was under way, the Pennsylvania reconsidered its position and, recognizing Carnegie had to be appeased, offered him acceptable rates. Sensing weakness, in January 1885 Carnegie pressed George Roberts for more: "There remains under your administration only one survival of the previous policy which made every manufacturer in Pittsburgh a bitter enemy of the Penna. R.R. Co. While you have removed every other flagrant case of injustice, I have often wondered why you permitted this to mar your reputation. I allude of course to the charge made on Ore from Cleveland to Pittsburgh and Johnstown. . . . I wish you could find time to give this matter your personal attention not allowing your subordinates to deter you from going to the bottom of it. I know the transporter is suffering equally with the manufacturer and I dislike very much to say to you that we must have lower rates. I can only say, we believe the best policy for both is to meet low rates and run our mills and our tracks full, thus producing lower cost."[15] A master of psychological games, Carnegie tried to manipulate Roberts by alluding to a marred reputation and underhanded subordinates in an attempt to create an atmosphere of paranoia and fear.

As it turned out, the Pennsylvania was not going to capitulate to the Carnegie, Rockefeller, and Vanderbilt alliance so easily. Roberts and Thomson targeted a retaliatory strike on Vanderbilt's New York Central Railroad. One morning, Vanderbilt woke to discover laborers on the western shore of the Hudson River surveying and grading for a line to run from New York to Buffalo, a parallel line to the New York Central. It was a declaration of war. But another railroad war in the midst of a recession was the last thing Wall Street wanted, especially the house of Drexel, Morgan. Over the years, the Drexel family had invested in the Pennsylvania while the Morgans did so in the New York Central, so they had much to lose from the warfare. It was more than coincidence when in May 1885 Pierpont Morgan and Vanderbilt sailed from Liverpool to New York together. During the crossing, Morgan convinced Vanderbilt that a negotiated settlement was best for all. In July, Morgan hosted a New York peace conference. George Roberts, Frank Thomson, and New York Central's president Chauncey Depew met with Morgan on his yacht, the *Corsair*. After a day on the Hudson it was agreed that Morgan would purchase 60 percent of the South Pennsylvania and then trade it to the Pennsylvania Railroad for bonds in another line, giving Roberts control and circumnavigating the state's antimonopoly laws.

Once in control, Roberts and Thomson blocked further construction and the South Pennsylvania never laid a rail over hill or dale. Completely ambushed, Carnegie complained bitterly—and with futility. How important were these rates? Ten years later, Carnegie would gain control of a railroad and force the Pennsylvania to cut rates, saving him a tremendous $1.5 million a year.

Although Carnegie failed to intimidate the Pennsylvania Railroad, his relentless downward pressure on wages and the installation of the new machinery yielded soaring profits, from just over $1 million in 1883 to almost $3 million in 1885.[16] Pierpont Morgan's firm, Drexel, Morgan, on the other hand, was not so fortunate. Earnings dropped from $1.6 million in 1882 to $662,000 in 1883; and the company posted a loss of $41,000 in 1884.[17]

Labor trouble continued to plague Carnegie in late 1885 when the men again began agitating for higher wages and better conditions. Realizing that he was going to earn record profits for the year, Carnegie granted a 10 percent wage increase in January. But the furnace men, who were mostly Irish and more savvy than some of their brethren, were not satisfied; they recalled Jones's promise to return to an eight-hour day once market conditions improved and demanded he grant it. Although the market was exceptionally strong, Jones refused and summarily discharged seven hundred furnace men before a strike could be organized. Enough men were brought in to operate some of the furnaces, but then, refusing to work with the strikebreakers, the converter men walked off the job. Not until April did Jones and Carnegie agree to reinstitute the eight-hour day, which required the hiring of another three hundred men.

Labor trouble also hit Carnegie's vital investment: the Frick Coke Company. The Hungarians who had flocked to the coalfields were tired of being abused and went on strike. Wages were always an issue, but now the men, who were paid on a tonnage basis, accused the company of falsifying coke weights so the men were paid less than they should have been, and old accusations of the company stores fleecing the reluctant patrons resurfaced, too. "The Frick Coke Co. appears to be having a monkey and parrot of a time with the Hungarians," the *National Labor Tribune* reported. By the end of February, enough men had joined the "Huns" that about 75 percent of the company's ovens were cold. Riots followed, inducing Frick to respond aggressively, a position Carnegie concurred with. "I agree these foreigners must learn they can't quit work and riot in this free country," he wrote in a perfect display of hypocritical contradiction. The following month the dispute was settled, and the men returned to work at 1884 wage levels.[18]

On the streets of New York, it seemed as though anarchy reigned, too, as the horsecar drivers and conductors who worked on the Dry Dock Line along Grand Street went on strike, demanding their workday be reduced from sixteen hours to twelve. On March 4, riots erupted when 750 policemen attempted to protect scabs. The next day over 16,000 drivers, conductors, and stable hands refused to work. Carnegie, faced with a paralyzed city, realized there was a disturbing pattern developing in labor disputes—namely, they were becoming incessant. There were an astonishing 22,336 strikes from 1881 to 1886.[19]

When he started his career in iron manufacturing, there had been mutual respect and goodwill between capital and labor, an unspoken agreement that wages would fluctuate depending on market conditions; there had even been picnics that included union officials. Carnegie and the large immigrant population working in his mills shared simple values and traditions brought from their native lands, which created a bond, however tenuous, between capital and labor. But labor disputes had become more violent and lengthy in the 1880s. Carnegie, who wanted to be loved by all, didn't enjoy being the target of the workingmen's ire. It was time to speak out on labor conditions in the United States.

Impulsively reacting to his own and the country's labor troubles, Carnegie wrote two essays on labor relations in 1886, published in the April and August issues of *Forum* magazine, that spurred debate in editorial pages across the country and had serious short-term and long-term repercussions. In these essays, he sought to position himself as the progressive employer, the liberal, even the radical, who would lead the way to industrial harmony. The first humdinger, "An Employer's View of the Labor Question," opened in grand fashion: "The struggle in which labor has been engaged during the past three hundred years, first against authority and then against capital, has been a triumphal march."[20] He then traced victory after victory for the laboring classes in their rise from slavery and serfdom. "Now the poorest laborer in America or in England," he wrote, "or indeed throughout the civilized world, who can handle a pick or a shovel, stands upon equal terms with the purchaser of his labor. He sells or withholds it as may seem best to him. He negotiates, and thus rises to the dignity of an independent contractor." The terms were hardly equal, however; more often than not in the 1880s Carnegie and his fellow capitalists had their way, slashing wages and suppressing the unions. So even as he declared the workingman was rising in dignity and equality, in urban-industrialized America it was the opposite, especially as more foreign workers were flooding the labor market.

Carnegie next addressed strikes and lockouts, which he deemed to be ridiculous affairs. "Whether a failure or a success, it [a strike or a lockout] gives no direct proof of its justice or injustice. In this it resembles war between two nations. It is simply a question of strength and endurance between the contestants." What Carnegie refused to acknowledge was that the massive dismissals during the Edgar Thomson shutdown in December 1884 were akin to a lockout as he tried to expel the union. It was simply a matter of semantics, layoffs versus lockout, but semantics worked just fine for Carnegie as he intellectualized what he did and why, and in the process imagined himself above ridiculous affairs. Sadly, he was unaware of not only his twisted logic, but his naiveté concerning the workingmen's conditions.

At least he realized the relationship between capital and labor had to change. In his essay, he called for arbitration as the best option for settling disputes, a solution highly touted by the press. "I would lay it down as a maxim that there is no excuse for a strike or a lockout until arbitration of differences has been offered by one party and refused by the other," he wrote. While he recognized arbitration didn't solve everything, he concluded, "I consider that of all the agencies immediately available to prevent wasteful and embittering contests between capital and labor, arbitration is the most powerful and most beneficial."

Carnegie then fired off a salvo from the big cannon: "The right of the working-men to combine and to form trades-unions is no less sacred than the right of the manufacturer to enter into associations and conferences with his fellows, and it must sooner or later be conceded." This proclamation was a thorny zinger. Because of it, the *Pittsburgh Dispatch* noted that Carnegie's essay would be greeted most unfavorably by capitalists, and for certain the hair rose on the backs of rabid antiunion men like Daniel Morrell at Cambria, who wanted to hear nothing of the rights of men to form unions. (When the Knights of Labor organized a local assembly in 1886 and recruited members from Cambria, the company's management obtained a membership list and fired every worker on it. More than two hundred lost their jobs.)[21] Carnegie's peers must have scratched their heads as they attempted to reconcile his words with his actions, for hadn't Captain Jones and Carnegie himself forced the Amalgamated from the Edgar Thomson mill in early 1885 by forcing each returning worker to sign an individual contract with the company and renounce the Amalgamated? Did he have a different definition for "trades-unions" that again allowed him to play a game of semantics with himself? Perhaps he just didn't want to accept powerful national organizations like the Amalgamated, desiring instead only small committees who represented his furnace men or his rollers. Perhaps, to keep Jones on the payroll, he had to expel the Amalgamated.

He then blamed much of the labor conflict on "salaried officers, who cannot possibly have any permanent interest in the welfare of the working-men. . . . It is the chairman, situated hundreds of miles away from his men, who only pays a flying visit to the works and perhaps finds time to walk through the mill or mine once or twice a year, that is chiefly responsible for the disputes which break out at intervals." Was Carnegie so delusional as to not realize he was becoming that chairman? It was not his title, but he certainly was chairman in spirit. Beginning in the 1880s, he was spending almost half of the year in Europe, and much of the other time he was either in New York or Cresson. His physical presence at the mills was fleeting, and while it was not an issue for now, with the very competent Tom Carnegie and Harry Phipps in Pittsburgh, what if the situation was to change?

Carnegie concluded the essay with his blueprint for greater harmony between capital and labor, his first tenet being "that compensation be paid the men based upon a sliding scale in proportion to the price received for product." In strong markets, the men would be paid more; in weak times, vice versa. Surely he had shared his prosperity with the men when in January 1886 he granted a 10 percent wage increase at Edgar Thomson. However, the average price of rails would increase 21 percent and Carnegie profits 145 percent for the year—so?[22] He also advised this: "A proper organization of the men of every works to be made, by which the natural leaders, the best men, will eventually come to the front and confer freely with the employers." And he reiterated using arbitration to settle conflicts. However honest and visionary Carnegie believed himself to be in this essay, any perceptive reviewer of his writing (like *Triumphant Democracy*) knew that much of what he said was self-serving and could not be taken as gospel.

The essay did not cure the nation's labor woes. The month Carnegie's essay appeared there was a massive railroad strike initiated by the Knights of Labor, who demanded higher wages for unskilled workers, particularly on lines controlled by Jay Gould, and some 9,000 men went on strike. The strike ended in early May with Gould victorious, but on May 1 organized labor launched a movement for an eight-hour day with an estimated 340,000 plus participating in national rallies and some 190,000 going on strike. In Chicago, the tension was particularly high because of an ongoing strike at the McCormick Reaper Company. The company had brought in nonunion workers and on May 3 the strikers battled with police, resulting in one death and accusations of police brutality. A protest was organized for the next day in Haymarket Square; it was a dull affair until the police moved in to break up the crowd and an anarchist threw a bomb into their ranks. Rioting ensued, and seven policemen and eleven protesters were killed. The bomb thrower was never apprehended, but eight anarchists were arrested, seven of whom were sentenced to death and one to life in prison. Four were hanged and one committed suicide, but in 1893 the Illinois governor, in a measure of justice, pardoned the three survivors.

Shocked by the violence and concerned conservative forces might overreact, in August Carnegie rushed into publication the second essay, entitled "Results of the Labor Struggle." There was indeed an overzealous outcry against the ignorant workingman as the conservative quarter declared suffrage should be restricted to the educated and the masses must be better policed. Carnegie pooh-poohed the alarmists in his article, pointing out that the omnipresent press and the electric telegraph created unnecessary hysteria. For once quite realistic, Carnegie realized the tension would not cease overnight, nor did he blame the unions, the laborers, and their leaders for the trouble, nor did he think anyone should expect the leaders to be offered up as martyrs, stating that "the safety of its leaders is the key of labor's position. To surrender that is to surrender everything." Carnegie even complimented William Weihe, president of the Amalgamated, for his moderate position—although he did spell the name Wihle, a mistake open to interpretation.

Although professing sympathy to the labor movement, he didn't agree with all of their demands such as the eight-hour day, which he didn't believe to be a possibility for firms that were marginally profitable. Instead, he suggested a series of half-hour reductions, and then an evaluation of each change. Because an eight-hour day meant less money and more intense work, for many of the laborers the eight-hour day was not a primary issue. When the men did work only eight hours, the superintendents like Captain Jones felt justified to push them harder for higher production. Reflecting on the switch to an eight-hour day, one steelworker testified, "Previous to that time we did not work so hard." During a twelve-hour day the men took breaks to eat and rest, but now "we stop only the time it takes to oil the engines . . . working more steady and harder right along to produce this tonnage."[23] Many of the laborers were now unskilled immigrants from eastern Europe who preferred taking home more money from a twelve-hour day to send it to their families still living in their native countries. Carnegie understood how important wages were to a man, and for this reason, even in the face of the Haymarket riot, he didn't wholly condemn the workingman who took to violence: "To expect that one dependent upon his daily wage for the necessaries of life will stand by peaceably and see a new man employed in his stead, is to expect too much."

Carnegie then gave labor its greatest weapon when he trumpeted: "There is an unwritten law among the best workmen: 'Thou shalt not take thy neighbor's job.'" This was a statement of biblical proportions, resounding through newspapers across the country, as Carnegie came down from Mount Sinai to deliver the Ten Commandments. There was no mention of coveting thy neighbor's wife, manservant, ox, or ass—it was the job that was sacred. No strikebreakers should ever be used or tolerated. But the use of strikebreakers was becoming a more potent weapon of capital, and his peers were astounded Carnegie took a position against it. While capital cringed, labor applauded. The Brotherhood of Locomotive Engineers made Carnegie an honorary member. Feeling honored, he wrote the secretary of the Brotherhood, W. R. Thompson: "As you know, I am a strong believer in the advantages of Trade Unions, and organizations of work men generally, believing they are the best educative instruments within reach."[24]

There was no doubt the essays were Carnegie's reactions to events in his mills and in the country at large, but there was also another factor at work: he was vain enough to want admiration from all, so, just as he detested the criticism he faced when operating his British newspaper syndicate, he did not want to be the object of labor's ire. He wanted to be the sympathetic, progressive capitalist. But were these sweeping treatises on labor standards he could live up to, or merely self-serving sermons to temporarily assuage his fears that he was not the radical his ancestors were?

All the noble discourse on the labor struggle begged the question: What were the conditions of labor? Had conditions in Pittsburgh evolved for the better in the two decades since Carnegie first became involved in the iron industry? No. The city had a reputation of being "Hell with the lid taken off." As one wage earner observed wryly, he and his comrades were "working aside of hell." It was certainly as hot as hell in Carnegie's steel mills, where water hissed when spilled on floors that slowly burned through the men's wooden-sole shoes. On one occasion, Jones reported it was so hot that "some of the boys stood by their ports till they fairly staggered with weakness."[25] The heat was the least of their worries.

The accidental death rates were much higher at the steel mills than they were at the iron mills, as a potpourri of hazards awaited both the wizened and green worker. Furnaces exploded, molds exploded, and, once natural gas was introduced as a fuel in the 1880s, gas lines and leaks exploded. Chains supporting massive ladles broke and spilled molten death over men caught underneath. Sometimes the men tripped under the strain of their work and fell into molten steel, casting their own mold. Those who only suffered broken legs from falling billets or lost eyes from flying metal ripping through their sockets were the lucky ones. The introduction of faster-moving equipment and machinery contributed to the increase in accidents. Fatal accidents in the steel industry accounted for 20 percent of the total adult male mortality in Pittsburgh; among "ignorant" southern and eastern European immigrants the rate shot to 40 percent.[26] Pittsburgh had one of the highest accident rates of all U.S. cities, and the *National Labor Tribune* asserted there were as many unreported deaths and injuries as there were reported. Sadly, the newspaper observed the list of killed and wounded in a given year was as long as that from a small battle in the Civil War. These laborers were indeed the frontline troops thrown into battle, pushed into a hail of bullets like those at Pickett's Charge. Families were not compensated for the deaths, and old age was forty in Carnegie's mills.

To Carnegie, these men served a function, just as his friends and family did, and these were the natural conditions in the United States. There was no doubt in his conscience that everyday life should or could be better for the laborers (beyond seeking harmony with their employers, of course). Because Carnegie and the other mill owners would do little in the way of promoting safety, the men knew they had to take measures to protect themselves. To deal with the dangers, the men took a fatalistic approach: your time came when it came, and accidents were downplayed to be mere trifles. Newspapers provided graphic descriptions of accidents, which helped to desensitize the men and their families to the hazards. "He was thrown into the pit of the driving wheel," reported the *National Labor Tribune* on one occasion, in describing how an assistant engineer died, "the lower part of which cut through his body tearing away the flesh so that his entrails protruded."[27] To make the deaths more acceptable, the newspapers glorified the men as though they were heroes lost in war, always describing their rare courage as they died bravely. But no death was heroic; the men were reduced to mules. And these conditions were not exclusively Pittsburgh's; the story repeated itself in Johnstown, Steelton, and Chicago, where men died with equal opportunity.

The movement of wages, while keeping an eye on profits, was an excellent gauge for determining living conditions, one that Carnegie, a stickler for facts, used time and again, albeit for a different reason. After he granted the 10 percent wage increase in January 1886, his unskilled steel mill workers earned $300 to $350 annually, a skilled worker maybe over $600 if lucky.[28] The men deserved more, much more. Steel production tonnage using the Bessemer process was increasing dramatically across the country and realized a gain of almost 50 percent that year. The price of steel rails, the barometer of the market, was rising, too, up 21 percent in 1886, and accordingly, Carnegie witnessed profits more than double to $2,925,350.08.[29] Now were the workers on equal standing as he claimed?

Consider that to support a typical six-member family unit (children and grandparents included) and stay debt free in 1886, a man had to earn $600; but many of the eighteen hundred men at Edgar Thomson were making less than $400. An investigation by the Senate Committee on Labor and Education several years earlier had confirmed that the average workingman couldn't afford a "decent maintenance" for their families.[30] Supposing an additional $200 was given to every laborer, bringing everyone close to or above the $600 mark, it would have cost Carnegie $360,000, or just 12 percent of his $2.9 million in profits. (Meanwhile, Carnegie committed over $350,000 to library and hospital donations in the early 1880s.) Life could have been immeasurably better for these oppressed mules, but that wasn't reality in the steel industry. Pennsylvania Steel in Steelton, like Carnegie and Cambria, exerted the same relentless control over its workers, attacked any form of labor protest, and suppressed wages.

Welfare capitalism was not in Carnegie's vocabulary; he only helped those who helped themselves. To his credit, Carnegie did take some interest in the daily lives of his men when several unnecessary hardships were brought to his attention. Because the men were paid only once a month, by the end of a pay period they were forced to buy goods on credit, adding an unnecessary interest expense. Also, the local shopkeepers charged a premium for necessities like coal. To relieve these problems, Carnegie agreed to pay the men every two weeks, and a cooperative store was opened in Braddock, through which the company sold coal at cost. To encourage thrift and prudence, the company served as a bank by taking up to $2,000 of each worker's savings and paying 6 percent interest. Workers could then borrow money from the resulting fund to build their own home.

Although Carnegie offered his men some assistance, he remained an avid disciple of Spencer and was comfortable with the existing situation, convinced the conditions would evolve on their own at the appropriate rate. "The ideologists of capitalism included clergymen as well as tycoons and corporation lawyers. All commonly rested their case on 'laws,' natural and divine," historian Page Smith summed up the time's pervasive attitude. "Darwinism provided them with the model of ruthless competition in which only the 'fittest' survived. It thus followed logically that the richest entrepreneurs were the fittest."[31] All other men, as far as Carnegie was concerned, had an equal chance to become a rich entrepreneur, just as he had, and if they could not they deserved what they had. Yes, it was true, Carnegie could always claim he rose up from the factory floor. Yes, he was once a bobbin boy making a mere

$1.20 a week. Yes, his family suffered. But Carnegie lived a factory life for only two years, not a lifetime with no prospects; and however disagreeable his work was firing the boiler or coating the bobbins in a vat of oil, it was not physically brutal work like that in the steel mills. Once plucked by Thomas Scott, he lived a dream as one of Calvin's chosen ones.

When considering the reality of the worker's conditions, Carnegie was patronizing them with his rhetoric. Meanwhile, his two labor essays gave other capitalists fits. To explain the position he had put them in, Dod told Carnegie a parable: A man was hit by a streetcar, leaving his features unrecognizable. But after the undertaker tidied him up and placed him on display for identification, a woman claimed him as her husband. She ordered a grand funeral for him and the undertaker's eyes filled with dollar signs, but just as the woman turned to leave, the dead man's mouth fell open, exposing a gold tooth. The woman immediately realized the corpse was not her husband and canceled the affair. Severely disappointed, the undertaker chastised the deceased, "What kind of an idiot are you anyway? If you'd only known enough to keep your mouth shut!"[32] While Carnegie understood Dod's message, keeping his mouth shut was a near impossibility as long as he was breathing.

Now two questions remained to be answered: Could Carnegie be a hero to the working class while he continued his relentless drive for profits? And would his words come back to haunt him?

The first to suffer at the pen of Carnegie was Frick. Like cousin Dod, he wished Carnegie knew when to keep his mouth shut about labor issues, but it was too late for that—and tensions were already running high between Carnegie and Frick, anyway. The latest trouble between the two men had originated just months prior to the publication of Carnegie's "An Employer's View of the Labor Question" in April 1886, when Frick pushed Tom Carnegie to give him a share in Carnegie Brothers in exchange for more Frick stock. Before dashing off to Cumberland Island for vacation, Tom replied in a quick pencil note in his self-deprecating style: "I am somewhat tenacious of my opinions—no doubt they are often wrong. I do confess so much. In the matter of your prospective interest with CB and Co. I cannot help but think that you should become a *manager*—I know that you have weighty arguments against it and . . . I wish you to reconsider and submit the matter to AC."[33] Tom was willing to give Frick an interest *if* Frick took on some management duties; however, to date Frick had not been interested in a formal job with Carnegie Brothers, a position to reconsider if it was indeed the only way to win a stake.

Following Tom's advice, he wrote to Carnegie to request a more definitive role in Carnegie Brothers as well as a partnership, again offering to trade Frick Company stock, which would reduce his own holdings to a paltry 4 percent. Carnegie mulled over the matter, waffling at times, but then wrote Frick a letter that was a slap in the face:

Excuse me for saying that in my opinion you propose what would be the mistake of your life. Your career must be identified with the Frick Coke Co. You never could become the *Creator* of CB and Co. Twenty years from now you might be a large owner in it, perhaps the principal, still the concern would not be *your work and you could not be proud of it.* . . . I cannot imagine how your pride permitted you to think for one moment of sinking to an insignificant holder of 4 percent in your own Creation. To think that you could ever be influential in its councils with such a petty interest is absurd. You would merely be the agent of the real men in the concern— . . . officials and the business community generally would look upon you with suppressed contempt. *The idea is suicidal.*

He advised Frick to put every penny into the Frick Coke Company, to buy out the deadwood, to concentrate his energies, and thus make millions. "File this for future reference," concluded Carnegie haughtily.[34]

The next year tension only increased between the two men when Frick's coal miners, along with the support of the Knights of Labor and the Amalgamated Association of Miners and Mine Laborers, started agitating for a wage increase, some men demanding as much as a 20 percent increase. An arbitrator was brought in, just as Carnegie espoused, and Frick and the national labor officials agreed to a negotiated increase of about 10 percent; however, the local union lodges refused to accept the lower increase and struck on May 7, 1887, as did laborers at other coal companies, many of them Hungarians. The usual shenanigans followed: rallies, more negotiations, imported strikebreakers, scab-related violence, and the hiring of Pinkertons.

At the time, Frick Coke controlled five thousand acres of coal land yielding six thousand tons of coke a day, and when that prodigious supply was suddenly choked off, Carnegie's steelworks were instantly affected.[35] Within days of the strike the mills were faced with having to bank the furnaces and shut down, and just as Carnegie had predicted in his letter, Frick's reputation was questioned by customers and comrades alike. Jay Morse, president of Union Steel and a coke customer, condemned Frick for the labor troubles: "I think that the trouble you are having is largely due to the fact that the men have not been used honestly in times past—and the sooner you get on an honest basis the better."[36] Fellow coke operator Colonel J. N. Schoonmaker accused him of becoming a Carnegie puppet and warned him not to submit to the unions' demands—his manhood depended on it.[37] Schoonmaker's fears were on the mark.

Carnegie was insisting that Frick, who was trapped in a very tight position, acquiesce to the workers' demands. But it wasn't just as simple as wanting to ensure his furnaces received their daily dose of coke; complicating the situation were the haunting words from his labor essays, in particular these: "A strike or lockout is, in itself, a ridiculous affair" and "There is an unwritten law among the best workmen: 'Thou shalt not take thy neighbor's job.'" Now that Carnegie personally owned more than 50 percent of the Frick Coke Company, this strike was his first test in applying those declared principles, only Frick wasn't interested in playing along. He had tried arbitration, which failed, and now he wasn't going to listen to any more of Carnegie's blather, especially if it was going to cost his company money. In fact, the conservative press was calling for the cleansing of Hungarians from the coalfields. Frick, an antilabor zealot from the days of the Molly Maguires, concurred.

His reputation as a progressive capitalist at stake and with little patience, Carnegie, who was vacationing at the Kilgraston, a country estate in Scotland, at the time, again demanded Frick settle with the strikers. On May 13, unwilling to capitulate to either Carnegie or to labor, Frick took the only possible course: he submitted his resignation, declaring his own honor was at stake. With the furnaces cold, Carnegie had no choice but to accept Frick's resignation and then settle with the union. In a biting last letter, Frick protested settling the strike and warned it would "only lead to still more unreasonable demands in the near future." After thoroughly objecting to the prostitution of his company, he concluded, "Whilst a majority of the stock entitles you to control, I deny that it confers the right to manage so as to benefit your interest in other concerns at the loss and injury of the coke company in which I am interested."[38] An embittered Frick had lost control of his company. And Carnegie, even though he earned dividends from the coke company, clearly demonstrated that his iron and steel mills would flourish at any cost, including to the detriment of supposed allies.

A dramatic headline splashed across the June 11 issue of the *Pennsylvania Press:* "Coke Men Crushed. Carnegie Thunders from His Castle in the Scottish Highlands. His Bolt Wrecks the Syndicate. Millionaire Operators Mourn and Hungry Hungarians Dance with Glee. President Frick, Overpowered, Resigns."[39] As Phipps now took control and settled with the workers, agreeing to a 12 percent raise (a small sacrifice), the other coke companies' positions— that is, the syndicate's—immediately weakened, and by the end of August they were ready to capitulate. In this first test, Carnegie had made himself some enemies, but his mills were running and he hadn't reneged on the vulnerable principles set forth in his labor essays.

A humiliated Frick put on a brave face, pretending he had better things to do than wallow in self-pity. On July 20, his wife and he left New York City for Bremen, Germany, for a tour of the Continent and then Great Britain. Meanwhile, Carnegie couldn't tolerate having a bereaved partner—especially one of whom he said, "The man had a positive genius for management"—so he summoned Frick for a détente in Scotland.[40] The volatile men smoothed over their differences and on November 5, 1887, Frick was reelected president of the Frick Coke Company. Nevertheless, scars would remain. Frick's influence in the coke industry was diminished, he was constrained by the confounded labor essays, and, due to such ulterior agendas, he knew he could never wholly trust his pard Carnegie.

Lack of faith in Andy was nothing new to Captain Jones, an enduring character in Carnegie's Shakespearean drama. In evaluating Frick and Carnegie, Jones said, "I don't particularly like Frick, nor do I admire him," but at least "you always know where you stand. . . . with Carnegie, it is a different matter, he is a sidestepper."[41] To protect himself, Jones, who was forever tinkering with the mechanics of the plant, began to file patents for his inventions. By the late 1880s, he had more than fifty secured, giving himself a few aces to play if ever his relationship with Carnegie soured beyond salvage. The importance of Jones's innovations could not be overstated, according to James Gayley, who was the superintendent of E.T.'s furnaces under Jones and considered his boss's contributions to steelmaking on par with Bessemer's.[42] Most of them involved laborsaving devices, but one of Jones's greatest inventions was what came to be called the Jones Mixer—literally a metal mixer made from firebrick positioned between E.T.'s blast furnaces that were turning out pig iron and the converters that made steel from the pig iron. The Mixer temporarily held and mixed up to one hundred tons of molten pig iron, from which smaller portions of pig iron were tapped into the converters, making for more uniform steel while allowing a continuous, highly efficient operation.

Carnegie's labor treatise was more severely tested in late 1887 and early 1888. At Edgar Thomson, Jones was again refurbishing his mill and installing new machinery, and as of December 17, 1887, the plant was closed, throwing almost two thousand men out of work.[43] Shutting down in the heart of winter made sense—business was slow because frozen rivers and snowstorms hindered shipments of resources and finished products—but there was also another more devious reason: the loss of work hit the men hardest then. It was difficult for them to find jobs elsewhere in these dull months and there was the added cost of heating fuel, which gave Carnegie leverage when it came time to rehire the discharged men. He would need the leverage because he was planning to demand a 10 percent wage reduction in all departments and institute a new sliding scale for wages based on the prices of steel rails.

This preemptive strategy worked perfectly in his mind: he discharged the workers because of repairs, and then, if they refused to return at lower wages, he could hire outside help to replace them. Because the mills were closed to begin with, there could never be a strike, or a lockout, or scabs; therefore, he could remain in accordance with his labor principles. In essence, it was a matter of semantics, but it enabled Carnegie to justify his actions and soothe his conscience, however twisted his logic. He set the rules for the game and then bent them to the point of breaking, but not quite—that would come later. Meanwhile, the men received quite a Christmas present: summary dismissal.

Less than two weeks after the shutdown, the Knights of Labor, which still had members in E.T, offered a new wage scale effective January 1, but the company simply didn't respond for six weeks, letting the noose tighten. Only now did the union realize this shutdown involved more than repairs. Finally, Carnegie made his demand for a 10 percent wage reduction, which was immediately rejected. Jones volunteered to arbitrate, which the men were

open to *if* it was for an agreement to end June 30, a kinder season to be negotiating in. Jones refused such a demand and talks ended before they started,
but at least Carnegie could say he had offered arbitration, however halfhearted the token effort was. As the days progressed, he hardened his position:
not only would wages be reduced, but he became determined to introduce a
sliding wage scale based on the price of steel, as outlined in his April 1886
essay, and to have the men return to the twelve-hour day. It was to be a three-
year deal, and he wanted it ratified by at least two-thirds of the Edgar Thomson men in a vote—ah, democracy at work. To compete with the other mills
that had always been running on two twelve-hour shifts, the change had to be
made, Carnegie reasoned.

Cold and hungry, the laborers sent a committee to New York City to
meet with Carnegie in March, but neither side would budge. Carnegie did,
however, confirm his position taken in the August *Forum* article, telling the
committee, "We will never try to fill our works with new men, for two reasons: first, we could never get such good men as you are. It is scalawags that
are idle and looking for work when there is a strike. Do not be alarmed. No
one will ever have your places here. We like you too much."[44] He then took
his case public, striking a very resolute posture in an interview with the *Pittsburgh Commercial Gazette*. "The firm unanimously decided not to start the
works until the men agree to give the sliding scale presented a trial," he said.
"This may not be till January next or January, 1890. It makes no difference
when. There will be no strike or quarrel between us and our men. We fully
recognize their right not to accept our terms and they no doubt recognize our
right to run our works or stop them just as we please. . . . The attempt to
make Pittsburgh manufacturers pay more than Chicago must be met and settled now, once and for all."[45] Carnegie had indeed paid about 6 percent more
in daily wages in 1887 than the Chicago mills, but the sliding scale he had
proposed had no minimum like the one now used in Chicago, so if the market became extremely depressed, the workingmen would starve. In fact, rail
prices would fall almost 20 percent in 1888, and Carnegie's profits would fall
more than 40 percent to a shade under $2 million.[46]

The *National Labor Tribune*, voice of the worker, indirectly supported
Carnegie's position by arguing mills such as those in Chicago should increase
wages and reduce hours and by pointing out Carnegie was only submitting to
market pressures.[47] As tensions in the town of Braddock increased, the company employed a gang of Pinkertons to guard the property, which, the *National
Labor Tribune* observed, "adds a peculiarly repulsive feature to the unfortunate lockout which the Edgar Thomson owners have instituted." Pittsburgh's
usually pro-capital newspapers were also against the Pinkertons.[48] Still, the
workers had little support and in May the Braddock men overwhelmingly
voted to agree to Carnegie's terms. While Carnegie had been paying about
6 percent more in daily wages in 1887 than the Chicago mills, after his hard-
nosed negotiations he was paying almost 19 percent less.[49] This result left no
doubt that Carnegie was a tenacious exploiter of labor.

Each returning man was required to sign an individual contract, a situation that surprised the men and the editors at the *National Labor Tribune*, who commented, "It would be interesting to know just what Mr. Carnegie had in pickle when he evolved that idea of individual signing of a long contract." It didn't take long to figure out.

Astoundingly, each man had to pledge they would not join nor remain a member of any labor union (just as they had to in 1884), which was in direct conflict with what Carnegie had written two years prior in "An Employer's View of the Labor Question," when he unequivocally stated, "The right of the working-men to combine and to form trades-unions is no less sacred than the right of the manufacturer to enter into associations and conferences with his fellows, and it must sooner or later be conceded."[50] The side-stepping Carnegie had now reversed himself. What made this reversal even more hypocritical and galling was that Carnegie had just joined an association of his fellows; his firm was now the leader in a rail pool formed toward the end of 1887, which only fifteen of the largest mills were allowed to join. Carnegie was given the top allotment of 13.5 percent, followed by North Chicago at 12.5, Pennsylvania Bessemer Steel at 9.8, and Bethlehem Steel at 9. The pool was powerful enough that wild rumors of an international rail pool spooked the railroads and the public.[51]

Also extremely disturbing was that when the mill reopened, over one hundred men found themselves blacklisted due to alleged union activity; even a Dunfermline native, David Gibson, was told to go elsewhere. He found work with a firm that repaired the stoves at Edgar Thomson and later recalled, "I worked for eight days, when on Tuesday last, I was sent over to the store for some tools and Jones ran against me. He said, 'I thought I told you that you were never to get any more work around here?' I said he never told me anything of the kind. He said he did. I said again he did not. 'Well,' he said, 'it does not matter a ———. You may get the hell out of this.' I said I could go, but I told him I was not working for his firm. He asked me who I was working for. I told him. He said it didn't matter a ———, for he would have me discharged." And Jones did. If any of the blacklisted men found work elsewhere and Carnegie's lieutenants found out, they had the men discharged. Some of these men grew so desperate for work they threatened to kill Jones and his family if he blocked them from getting a job.[52] To retaliate against the blacklisting, the Knights of Labor declared Edgar Thomson nonunion and urged all men to boycott the mill, hoping to dry up Carnegie's labor supply, but the resolution had no effect as the men currently employed had to eat and the influx of immigrants would work anywhere for anything.

Why Carnegie's hypocritical reversal on the progressive labor attitude? To begin, fellow manufacturers had completely ignored his tenets for achieving harmony with labor and conflicts continued unabated, prompting the cynical mind to pose: Why should Carnegie listen to himself if no one else did?

A better explanation originated with the Haymarket Riot, which had turned public sentiment against labor unions and caused many capitalists to consider all labor unions part of an anarchistic element. So there was little popular support for Carnegie's call to recognize unions, and this lack of empathy included his partners. The very month Edgar Thomson reopened, one of Carnegie's partners, William Singer, who had been an investor in Homestead and remained president of Sheffield Steel in Pittsburgh, stated he would run his mill on a nonunion basis only and announced severe wage cuts. The men went on strike, and Singer hired special police to protect the property. Because Singer, unlike Carnegie, was of the old iron aristocracy—an allegedly more civilized class—his aggressive actions were unexpected and shocking. Other members of the iron aristocracy followed Singer's lead in summarily expelling the unions.

The concept of arbitration, by the time Carnegie wrote his 1886 articles, was passé, and, in fact, an 1886 survey conducted by *Age of Steel* discovered that both manufacturers and workers no longer considered arbitration an option by a three-to-one margin. Strikes and lockouts were now unavoidable and only five of twenty-two mill owners considered profit-sharing or some form of welfare capitalism as a means to harmony.[53] So, as it turned out, Carnegie's high and mighty call for labor harmony, while it attracted attention, was completely out of touch with the times. He had not spent enough days in the Pittsburgh trenches to comprehend the situation and was now forced to act in contradiction to his ideals. Also, because Carnegie couldn't afford to lose either Jones or Frick, to a degree, he was acquiescing to their desires to expulse the union. Considering he was submitting to pressures on a number of fronts, his reversal was not a cut-and-dried case of contradiction and hypocrisy.

Not to be forgotten, the Amalgamated and the Knights of Labor were still entrenched at Homestead, but their time would come. In the ensuing years, tension between capital and labor would increase as the workers' conditions in America's increasingly urbanized and industrialized cities deteriorated. The labor problems at Carnegie's mills would be compounded by Carnegie's prolonged absences, during which he became more involved in the cultured life and American politics.

CHAPTER 17

The Pale Horse
and the Gray Dress

The year Carnegie was making a splash as a progressive labor leader, his heroine was extremely ill. He decided to remain in the United States for the summer of 1886, and he again took his canonized mother to Cresson, hoping the mountain air would prove an elixir. While Margaret's tenuous hold on life overshadowed his activities, he did look forward to Matthew Arnold's impending July visit to Cresson—and even more exciting, Louise Whitfield's.

When Arnold returned to the United States in 1886 to visit his daughter, he promised Carnegie, "I have no intention of letting my time in America end without a visit to my friend and last in this country."[1] The Pennsylvania Railroad ran a special train for him to Cresson, and afterward Arnold related the visit to his sister: "We stayed three days. The first day we went down to see his works at Pittsburgh, one hundred miles by rail. The country around Pittsburgh is full of natural gas, which you see here and there towering in the air in a clear flame through an orifice in the ground; this gas they have lately conducted to the works and made to do the work of coal; no more coal is used and there is no smoke. As a consequence, Pittsburgh, from having been like a town in the Black Country, has become a seemly place."[2] When climbing the stairs at a Pittsburgh mill, Arnold suddenly stopped, clutching his chest and gasping for breath, his heart weak. "This will some day do for me as it did for my father," he remarked to Carnegie, who shrugged it off at the time. The great intellect would be dead in two years.

Even though Cresson was blessed with the great Matthew Arnold's presence, Carnegie's mind was on his fiancé. He wrote her during a quiet moment:

> That you are coming on the 29th seems to change the scene. I count the days. The Mountain will seem alive when you are upon it. I have not written to you because it seems you and I have duties which must keep us apart.

Our parents are better, and I have always known what you said recently was true. To leave your Mother: 'you could not think of it' nor could I leave mine . . . Mother seems really better, it is miraculous. I trust yours is also better. Everything does hang upon our mothers, with both of us—our duty is the same, to stick to them to the last. I feel this every day. . . . I wish you were here, but you will be the only belle when you do come and I shall ever be Your Andrew Carnegie.[3]

The fifty-year-old steel master, who could very well have been a grandfather like Arnold or Louise's father, was instead behaving like a love-struck adolescent, full of rabid doubts and blissful dreams.

His days with Louise at Cresson were filled with forest walks and horseback rides, flower picking and cups of tea, and romantic walks under the stars. Wedding plans were made and remade, but always haunted by Margaret's immortality, which had begun to actually frustrate her son. After Louise returned to New York, Carnegie's feelings finally burst out in a letter to her. "What nonsense for us to dwell apart very much longer!" he wrote. "I sometimes feel I can't endure separation."[4] Their love story was taking on an epic quality. Their separation did endure, however, when it was decided Margaret couldn't make the return to New York. They remained at Cresson as sharply chilled autumn weather set in. Carnegie made several rushed trips to New York and Pittsburgh in September and October, dashing from Margaret to business to Louise and back again. Ragged and rundown, he was on one such visit in New York when he started to feel ill. Shaking it off, he took the train to Cresson for a sojourn at his cottage, where he wrote Louise, "Am keeping in the house and hope to be all right in the morning. . . . Yours miserably, A. C."

What Carnegie thought was a mere cold worsened. He took to his bed, but he took time to reassure Louise: "Don't be alarmed. Nothing serious—sure." Two days later he wrote, "I'll be very careful for a few days. Got your letter. Mr. Bridge brought it up—the only one I have been allowed to get for three days. . . . Don't be alarmed."[5] Then, with his health rapidly deteriorating, he summoned a physician who determined he had the dreaded typhoid fever. Unwilling to accept the diagnosis, Carnegie called for his New York physician, Dr. Frederic S. Dennis, who promptly took the train to Cresson and corroborated that it was indeed typhoid. An attendant physician and nurse were hired to see him through the coming battle. As the leaves changed color and dropped from the trees, Carnegie's health deteriorated further. In his weakened mental state, he felt the cold chill of death. His mother, who had been in an enfeebled state for some months, also took a turn for the worse. The gloom deepened when a telegram arrived from Pittsburgh stating Tom had fallen ill with fever. He would soon become bedridden with pneumonia.

Harry Phipps, the Carnegies' primary partner, became frantic and moaned to John Walker, "Tom Carnegie is sick with pneumonia and is going to die. Andrew Carnegie is sick with typhoid fever and is going to die too. That's going to leave Carnegie Brothers in a nice mess. You know our finances are not in any too good condition. We shall be called upon to settle with their estates and it will ruin us." At the time Tom had a 17.5 percent interest in Carnegie Brothers and a 16 percent interest in Carnegie, Phipps and Company, while his older brother held 54.5 percent and 52.5 percent respectively, so Phipps's assessment, absent sympathy for the sick, was correct.[6] The partnership could never buy out the two brothers. "Don't worry," Walker replied matter-of-factly. "Tom Carnegie probably will die for he has been a hard drinker. But Andrew has lived an abstemious and regular life and will probably recover."[7]

After two weeks in bed, Carnegie was beginning to feel better when tragic news reached him: Tom was dead at the age of forty-three. He had been in the office as recently as October 14th, but after three days in bed, on October 19, he had died. Shocked by the suddenness of his brother's death, and with his seventy-six-year-old mother deathly ill, Carnegie suffered a relapse. Again he reconciled himself to his own death. To prepare his estate, he instructed Dod and Phipps to take charge of all his investments and valuables.[8] A cold November and bitter days now swept into Cresson. One night Carnegie felt a presence in his room and he looked up to see Dr. Dennis, who had returned to help. When he asked the doctor what he was doing up so late, he merely replied that Margaret had needed him.[9] The doctor didn't have to explain that such a late visit didn't bode well. Margaret Carnegie died on November 10, almost forty years after bringing her family to America, her job now complete. Because Dennis didn't want to risk her death sending her son into an unstoppable free fall, he had her coffin removed through the bedroom window rather than carried past Andrew's room and possibly alerting him. It would be days before Carnegie was told, but as Louise noted in her diary, "He suspects it. All the partners very anxious about him."[10]

Back where the Carnegie American dream originated, in Allegheny City, Aunt Annie Aitken grieved. In small tense script, she wrote her niece Rachel Pattison: "The death of Aunt Carnegie and Tommy has caused a cloud to [hang] over our mental horizon, that tends to obscure our vision. . . . Poor sister had no pleasure in living any longer, in fact, a few weeks before her death she told Aunt Hazern that every night she wished she might never see another. . . . With Tom it was different, but still the effects caused by bodily suffering were nearly the same and he expressed himself anxious to go."[11] Even though he would leave behind a sizable family, Tom could hang on no longer; life in Pittsburgh's "Hell with the lid taken off" under the command of the Scotch Devil had taken its toll.

"My life as a happy careless young man, with every want looked after, was over," Carnegie reflected mournfully. "I was left alone in the world."[12] He took the deaths of his mother and brother so hard that he had all memorabilia reminding him of them removed from his sight. Letters and postcards were filed away, paintings and miniatures were stored in the attic, and he could not speak of them. Not until years later would a miniature of Margaret and other items slowly begin to resurface. He had so immortalized his mother that he once paid off the mortgage of a complete stranger because she looked like his mother. So often, in front of guests, he had pressed his finger to his mother's forehead, and said, "Here's where Tom and I got our brains."[13] Never again would he say those words. His vivid memories of his mother were a means of achieving consolation.

Emotionally spent and nerves raw from grieving, it took Carnegie weeks to realize there was still a joy in his life. "It is six weeks since the last word was written and that was to you as I was passing into the darkness," he finally wrote Louise. "Today as I see the great light once more my first word is to you. . . . Louise, I am now wholly yours—all gone but you. . . . I live in you now. Write me. I only read yours of six weeks ago today. Till death, Louise, yours alone."[14]

Once emotionally stable, physical recovery still hindered Carnegie's union with Louise. "I am doing so well," he reported to her. "Walked yesterday round the room three different times supported by Drs. Dennis and Garmany, and twice today already. No pain and such sweet waking and such sweet dreaming thoughts of you through the night. You make night itself bright."[15] Sweet dreaming was as close as the prudish Carnegie would ever come to expressing his suppressed sexual needs. In another letter he wrote, "Three months the doctor says I shall be better than for years and stronger. After that, Louise, the soul hunger for your companionship must be satisfied. I'll run back to you and run away with you!"[16] Yes, through all the years of bachelorhood and unconfirmed celibacy, the physical needs had been there. Yet he had devoutly pursued a traditional Victorian relationship based on feminine virtue and masculine honor.

As soon as Carnegie could travel, Dr. Dennis and his wife came out to Cresson. On December 12, they assisted him back to New York, where for weeks he remained under their care. The epic courtship of Louise now entered its final stage. Still, no public announcement of their engagement was forthcoming, as Carnegie felt it would be in poor taste so soon after his mother's death. "The quietness that would surround our union," he explained to Louise, "so appropriate after recent events and the months that would ensue before our return to New York life, would, as I see it, enable us to begin life together so much sooner without violating the properties—think all this over, my love."[17]

It seemed one obstacle after another always planted itself between Carnegie and Louise; this time it was Dr. Dennis's recommendation that Carnegie go south to recuperate.[18] Before Carnegie departed, there was some business to attend to: Phipps's fear of what would happen to the companies on Carnegie's demise. It was a reasonable and practical concern, not callous at all. The partners had documents drawn up that stipulated if a partner died, his interest would be purchased at book value by the company's treasury, to be paid for in installments. In the case of Carnegie, the company was to have fifteen years to liquidate his shares. Also, the partners themselves could acquire the stock of deceased, retired, or expulsed partners, if two-thirds of the partners, in number and interest, voted to do so.[19] Naturally, Carnegie's vote was the final word as long as he lived, and he made arrangements with Lucy to buy Tom's interest over a number of years. The papers—signed by Carnegie, Phipps, Walker, and newly admitted partners John G. A. Leishman, William Abbott, and Clay Frick, on January 18, 1887—were ominously called the Iron Clad Agreement.

Frick had finally been granted what he wanted—a partnership. Brother Tom's death in October 1886 had forced Carnegie to change his position on making Frick a partner because he needed to bolster his management team. On November 1, while he and his mother lay sick in Cresson, he allowed Frick to purchase $184,000 in stock, a premium of $84,000 over the original par value of $100,000, to be paid for by future dividends. At the same time, Frick was given informal management duties within Carnegie Brothers to fill the void created by Tom's death.

Carnegie stayed with his brother's family on Cumberland Island, Georgia, the two-thousand-acre estate his brother had purchased, renovated over the years, and called Dungeness, and together they healed their wounds. He took walks and rides on the beach and played with his nephews. Via mail and telegraph, Carnegie and Louise planned their wedding for April 22, and he returned north that month. Throughout these mad months of illness and absence, Carnegie was fortunate that business took care of itself; the market was strong, and Edgar Thomson had all the orders it could handle.

He did have to deal with one disgruntled customer, which was a blessing in disguise. Collis Huntington, a railroad magnate who was one of the cofounders of the Central Pacific Railroad, complained he was paying too much for rails and not getting the service he deserved. As soon as Carnegie returned to New York, he told Huntington he would not sell rails for under $42 a ton and defended his people: "I hope, by the time this reaches you, you will be in your natural good humor, and satisfied that at all times, and under all circumstances, your alliance with us is under 'the most favored nation clause.' Let us know what we can do for you and it shall be done." He added a postscript: "I had time to take a hurried look at your house as I passed through New York. It would suit me and I would give you cost for it, which you told me was $170,000, adding to this the amount you have expended upon it, paying you $100,000 in bonds of your splendid Steamship line, at par, and the remainder as you wish it, even if we have to give you rails for the remainder of what rails you wish this year at $41."[20] Even though Carnegie had first insisted he would not sell rails for under $42 a ton, he figured a few pennies out of his partners' pockets was negligible if he could buy Huntington's magnificent mansion at Fifty-first Street and Fifth Avenue and present it to Louise as a wedding gift. He pulled it off for $200,000.

As the wedding approached, Carnegie resumed his hectic schedule. On April 14, he attended a talk by Walt Whitman delivered at the Madison Square Garden theater. He also took the time to send Whitman, via a mutual acquaintance, Richard Watson Gilder, money to help support the man who would become one of America's most celebrated poets. Carnegie, a member of New York's Author's Club, considered himself not only a patron of the arts, but a patron of artists—as well as politicians and scientists, among others. His philosophy was that people making vital contributions to society should not have to worry about money so they could focus on their work. Eventually, over four hundred names would grace his private pension list. Whitman, who spent much of his later life impoverished, was touched: "Yours enclosing Mr. Carnegie's magnificent contribution to me (& to the Lincoln memory lecture) of $350 has safely come to hand. I thank AC from my heart—The money, of course will help me every way & practically. It is appreciated for its source in kindest human good will. I thank you, too, dear friend—your faithful heart & voice—I wish this note sent to Mr. Carnegie with my gratitude and love."[21]

He was so busy wrapping up business before his wedding that with just six days to go, he wrote from Pittsburgh to Louise's pastor, Reverend Charles Eaton, requesting he perform the ceremony.[22] He also had a prenuptial agreement drawn up, clarifying that he "intends to devote the bulk of his estate to charitable and educational purposes and said Louise Whitfield sympathizes and agrees with him in said desire and fully approves of said intention."[23] To guarantee Louise's financial health, he gave her a bounty of over $300,000 in stocks and bonds, intended to provide her with $20,000 annual income.[24]

Andrew Carnegie and Louise Whitfield were married on April 22, 1887. The ceremony was held at eight o'clock in the evening at the Whitfield home. Reflecting Carnegie's desire to respect his mother's recent passing, it was a very modest, subdued affair, with no maid of honor and bridesmaids, no best man and ushers, and but thirty guests, all family and close friends, including Dod and his wife, the Phippses, the Kings, and David Stewart. The fifty-one-year-old Carnegie, his trim, spade-shaped beard fully gray, escorted Mrs. Whitfield to her seat, and then thirty-year-old Louise, in an elegant gray traveling gown and on the arm of her grandfather, George Buckmaster Whitfield, walked down the aisle. An hour after the ceremony found Mr. and Mrs. Andrew Carnegie being whisked by carriage away to the North German Lloyd pier to board the steamship *Fulda*, bound for England. Carnegie had arranged to commandeer the captain's quarters and general officers' rooms for their honeymoon suite.

The honeymooners' first stop in England was Bonchurch, a beautiful resort on the Isle of Wight covered with fields of wildflowers and glorious views of the sea. Entranced, Carnegie and Louise started dreaming about the country estate they had leased in Scotland for the remainder of the summer. It was the Kilgraston House, located in the beautiful Highlands' Valley of the Tay, near Perth. "We are already counting on the pleasure of selecting in

London the things we may need for our Scotch home," Louise wrote her mother, "thus having many things ready for 51st Street. I have been so amused, John [O'Hara, Carnegie's footman] has just put tags on my trunks as follows: 'Mrs. Andrew Carnegie, No. 5 W. 51st.' I believe John is as delighted as we all are. Doesn't it seem almost too good to be true?"[25] Was it? Blissfully attendant to her still recuperating husband, Louise left herself no time to consider how good a husband Carnegie would be. There was such a self-serving disparity between his words and actions in the realm of business and social thought; would it be the same for his marriage? Did he love Louise as much as he professed? Would his relationship with his mother continue to haunt them? After all, he would nickname his wife Lou, echoing the perfunctory nickname for his mother—Mag. Carnegie was also not a negotiator, a critical element to a marriage, and he was not domesticated, having always worked in a man's world.

No magnate's honeymoon would be complete without some attention to work and politics. It was at this time that Carnegie's labor treatises were being challenged as strikes in the coke industry strangled Edgar Thomson's supply, and Frick was threatening to resign if he wasn't given a free hand in dealing with the strikers. There was also a continuing conflict with his former newspaper partner Samuel Storey, who owed him money from the buyout, and Carnegie was forced to hire a solicitor to exact payment.[26] While honeymooning, he even took time to read all of the speeches resounding through the House of Lords, and he dashed off a note to his Liberal friend Lord Rosebery, whose home ground was near Dunfermline, declaring his "the very best of all."[27]

Their next stop was London, where they stayed at the Metropole Hotel, to celebrate the Golden Jubilee of the reign of Queen Victoria. "Have met more celebrities than I can count—the poet Robert Browning, and Edwin Arnold, writer John Morley—and spent the day with Lord and Lady Rosebery at their place at Mentmore," Louise gushed in a letter to her mother on June 10. "Sunday we spent with the novelist William Black. . . . Am charmed with all I meet, they are all so delightful, but the constant rush confuses me and I sometimes scarcely know whether I am on my head or my heels. . . . Well, Mother Mine, we are in the whirl, nothing but a rush and a bang all the while. I begin to experience the realities of life now and oh! how I do long for Mother! I am not a bit homesick but I begin to realize how much a man wants and how important it is for a woman not to have any wants or wishes of her own."[28] So it began—the whirl of socializing—and the demands on Louise would only become more intense.

Finally, on June 22, the Carnegies started north, accompanied by James Blaine and his wife. On July 7, before they could settle into manor living, they traveled to Edinburgh, where Carnegie laid the cornerstone for his second Scottish library, the result of his most generous benefaction to date—$250,000—and was presented with the city's Freedom, akin to being given the key to the city. People lined the streets, cheering and saluting, as the Carnegies made their way by coach to the construction site. After the cornerstone ceremony, Lord Rosebery presided over the presentation of the Freedom, an event held in the great Synod Hall, with pipers piping gloriously. Once at Kilgraston, Louise wrote her mother: "Well the conquering hero is once more at home. . . . It is all right enough for Andrew but imagine *me*, who *three* months ago was not known, riding in the carriage with *Mr. Blaine*, who for once had to take a back seat. *I* had to bow right and left in response to the cheers with which we were greeted from thousands who lined the streets. . . . At every station crowds collected and cheered and then pressed up to the car window to shake hands with Andrew, one old man peering into his face and exclaiming, 'Are you the *real* Andrew Carnegie?'"[29] He was fast becoming a legend.

Once fearing her Andrew's desire to live in Britain would separate them forever, Louise herself now fell in love with his Scotland. Particularly taken with bagpipes, she sweetly asked her husband if they could not have a piper at their temporary home, and the doting Carnegie hired one immediately. Over the summer months, visitors trooped in and out of the newlyweds' Kilgraston home; apparently the consummation of the marriage and the honeymooning were officially over. Visitors included the Blaines, Matthew Arnold, and John Hay, among many other friends. Hay reported back to his friend Henry Adams that "we went to Andy Carnegie in Perthshire, who is keeping his honeymoon, having just married a pretty girl. . . . The house is thronged with visitors—sixteen when we came away—we merely stayed three days: the others were there for a fortnight."[30]

Mrs. Blaine, writing her son, captured life at Kilgraston, each day beginning with a gillie in tartan waking them by playing the bagpipes. To serve their needs there were two cooks and twenty servants, some who were rather sly.

> Andrew Carnegie may be little but his hoard and heart are great, and he is a happy bridegroom and rejoiceth as a bridegroom to have his happiness sure, so that we are enjoying, as only pilgrims and sojourners at hotels should enjoy, this oasis of home life. Yesterday we returned from an excursion of two days to Dunfermline. . . . As we drove in at an opposite direction from that on which we started out, we surprised all the servants dancing at the rear of the house. As English servants are always instructed to keep away from the master and mistress, they scurried to cover like rabbits, and when we drove around to the front door, there was the piper marching up and down imperturbably, playing "The Campbells Are Coming!"—the butler, the housekeeper, the lady's maid waiting at the entrance, and all the housemaids carrying hot water to the various bedrooms. It was the funniest transformation scene I ever saw.[31]

Although he would have denied it, Carnegie, whom Mrs. Blaine found to be somewhat autocratic, was living the life of an English lord.

Lady of the house or not, twenty servants or not, Louise did not anticipate the invasion on her honeymoon and was overwhelmed. She felt oppressed, as though she was living a double life, and on July 17 she wrote her mother to "have a little chat" with her: "I miss the old sweet routine and the great change in my life comes over me more then than any other time. Andrew is sweet and lovely all the time but he is so very different from every other human being. There is not the first particle of pretense about him—he is so thoroughly honest." If his wife found him startling at times, Carnegie must have really shocked those not accustomed to his outbursts.

Louise also lamented that the house was filled with fifteen guests: "I really have no actual care but it oppresses me to have so many people around. I see very little of them except at table and while we are driving but it all seems so very sudden; there has been no growth, no gradual transition. I seem to be leading two lives—outwardly I am the mature married woman, while inwardly I am trying to reconcile the old and the new life. I get awfully blue sometimes but I know it is very wrong to indulge in this feeling and above all to write to you, but, Mother dear, I feel so much better for it."[32] Carnegie, on the other hand, relished having so many visitors and began to search for a castle for the summers to come. Playing host to so many would become the one enduring conflict in their marriage.

When the lovebirds left their crowded Scotland nest to return to their spacious new home on West Fifty-first Street, they brought with them the Kilgraston housekeeper, Mrs. Nicoll, who remained with them for the next twenty-five years; the butler, George Irvine; and another servant, Maggie Anderson. The latter two had tenures almost as long as Mrs. Nicoll. The help, to whom Carnegie was relatively kind, found their master far more tolerable than his competitors and partners did.

The next summer, Carnegie leased Cluny Castle in the Highlands. To kick off the season's festivities, he organized a seven-hundred-mile coaching trip from London to Cluny—a coaching trip long due Louise. Even though the United States was gearing up for the presidential election in the fall, the influential Republican James Blaine and his wife, Harriet, again joined the Carnegies. Blaine wanted to escape the coming political maelstrom, the Republican Convention, which would result in Benjamin Harrison being nominated for president and Levi P. Morton for vice president. Also joining them were the Blaines' daughters; author Mary Dodge, who wrote under the pen name Gail Hamilton; Harry Phipps and his wife; Walter Damrosch, who was the dashing twenty-six-year-old conductor of Wagnerian operas at the Metropolitan; Charles Eaton, who had married the Carnegies; and Lord Rosebery. The highly detailed coach, with entwined American and British flags painted on the doors, that greeted them at the Metropole Hotel was a wedding gift from Lucy Carnegie.

A British newspaper described the primary characters as they climbed aboard:

> Mr. Blaine, a gentleman of some sixty years, with whitey grey hair and sallow face, wearing a white hat and blue coat, jumped up to his seat by the whip with alertness of youth.

"The Iron Queen" [Louise] in a blue serge travelling costume, carrying a detective camera and a lovely bouquet of Marechal Neils, was assisted to her place at the back by Lord Rosebery, who, with his close shaven face and spruce attire, his bell shaped hat and the humorous smile which plays about his mouth, is the very ideal of a prosperous comedian.

Carnegie looked the picture of health and happiness, and as chirpy as a cricket, with a little serge suit, a white hat fixed well on his head, a red rose in his buttonhole. Up he climbed to his seat by the side of his charmingly pretty wife, who, like all American ladies, was not in the least ashamed of showing her keen enjoyment of the lively scene.[33]

Carnegie and Blaine's growing friendship was attracting particular attention. They were, after all, two of the most charismatic icons of the Gilded Age, but their relationship also posed ethical questions as critics evaluated whether the politician and tycoon were too tight, and whether Carnegie had undue influence in the capital. The reporters hounded the coaching party every time they entered a sizable town, prompting one charioteer to remark, "We were annoyed by their constant presence, but, when they left us, felt a little lonesome and neglected."[34] Still, they enjoyed their tour northward through the cathedral towns of eastern England, "tracking the Roman roads, sleeping in the rooms of Tudor kings, lunching under yew trees that might have been ones that bothered Caesar."[35]

The approach to Cluny took the charioteers through a pass in the Grampian Hills that was fifteen hundred feet high, and from there the beautiful Valley of Spey spread out before them, home to the turreted, white granite Cluny, a blue smoke of peat curling from the chimneys. A dark forest of larches, fir, and birch, concealing secluded burns and waterfalls, surrounded the castle, and nearby were the caves where Cluny MacPherson—Highland chieftain, Jacobite leader, and fugitive—hid himself for much of nine years. The interior of the castle reflected a violent past; it was decorated with guns, claymores (double-edged swords), dirks (long daggers), and other nasty-looking weapons. The landscape inspired Louise, who was taking an active interest in photography, and she faithfully recorded their time there.

Carnegie relished the fishing and hunting available on the eleven-thousand-acre estate. Demonstrating a certain degree of insensitivity to one of his junior partners' hard work, he wrote William Abbott that "60 trout caught yesterday by one rod in our own Burn—We have splendid grouse shooting also, everything there is Lochs—Burns, Moors and the Spey River all round us. Two trout streams run past the Castle one on each side. Waterfalls, Rustic Bridges over them. This is indeed a gem—I will have you all over in pairs year after year if you are good boys and don't get into Beam Pools at a loss."[36] Although Louise and he hosted a castle full of guests, they did share some intimate moments, depicted by Louise: "From my little sitting room, steps lead right to the lawn, and Andrew's business room opens from my sitting room; so we slip from each other's rooms and out to the lawn with the greatest ease."[37]

The King family, Dr. Dennis and his wife, and John Morley, among others, joined the Carnegies, but one character sorely missed at Cluny was Herbert Spencer, who declined to visit, citing poor health, an excuse he used on many an occasion.[38] Between Blaine, Morley, and Carnegie, boisterous debates were a given, and when Carnegie was too loud or adamant, Louise would preen the front of her dress as a signal, and he would invariably say, "Oh! Lou thinks I'm talking too much."[39] Not the retiring type, he didn't remain quiet for long as the festivities continued into the night. After a meal of roast lamb, cabbage, stewed rhubarb and cream, whiskey and water, and crackers and cheese, Damrosch gave singing lessons and played the piano to candlelight, while Blaine danced the Virginia reel on the front lawn. On July Fourth, flags were flying over Cluny, cannons fired in the morning, spectacular fireworks lit the sky at night, and Damrosch taught Cluny MacPherson, descendant of the Jacobite leader and now the castle's owner, how to play "Yankee Doodle" on the bagpipe for leading them to dinner.[40]

For the next ten years, Carnegie's Scottish home was at Cluny, and because he despised hereditary privilege, it gave the Star-Spangled Scotchman great pleasure to be leasing the historic castle. Like his boyhood hero William Wallace, he had risen from the commoners to an exulted rank and was intent on flaunting it. But some of the more critical American newspapers questioned Carnegie's extended sojourns as well as his patriotism, and argued that he should be spending his money in America, where he made it. Nonplussed, Carnegie responded while making a speech in Inverness, Scotland: "The exile may be excused if his fondness for his native land knows no bounds. Scotland was to me the land of childhood, the fairyland. Here I have never known labor nor struggle, nor any of the trials—the invigorating trials—of life; nor sorrow, nor pain; and across the Atlantic, amid the early struggles— the fierce struggles for success—amid all my cares and throughout every weary hour, there shone upon my path, shedding its beams of poetry and romance, the resplendent star of Scotland. Return to Scotland was ever to me the prize of life."[41] The polemic Carnegie could be quite poetic.

Any critic who questioned Carnegie's interest in his adopted country, the United States, was silenced during the presidential election of 1888. This year marked Carnegie's entry onto America's political stage with the same fervor he had brought to British politics during his involvement with the newspaper syndicate.

CHAPTER 18

Gospel of Conscience

Carnegie's political and social agenda had been confined mostly to Britain until he sold his newspaper interests and President Grover Cleveland made noise about lowering the protective tariff. In 1887, Cleveland, who believed it was time to stop passing along government privileges to businessmen in protected or favored industries, was urging the reduction of tariff levels to save American consumers money. Fortunately for Carnegie, the president left it to Congress to reform the tariff, and his initiative sank in a legislative quagmire. Overall, Cleveland took a laissez-faire approach to big business, accepting the day's conventional wisdom that individual economic freedom equated to national economic progress. Regardless, Carnegie was wary of another four years with the Democrats ruling the capital and desired the business-friendly Republicans back in office. So, during the 1888 election campaign, he threw his full weight behind Benjamin Harrison, as did Matthew Quay, a powerful Pennsylvania senator who was named campaign chairman, and John Wanamaker, the retail genius, who headed Harrison's campaign finance committee.

Carnegie's fellow Republicans were not choirboys, which reflected poorly on his own character. Quay was known to take stock in companies for favors, and it was said he knew how "to keep silent in sixteen different languages"—just the kind of man Carnegie could appreciate—and, needless to say (but said anyway), the campaign was highly funded by powerful businessmen for whom Wanamaker later secured favors.[1] One wide-girthed pipeline for funds was provided by James M. Swank, the hardheaded, Scotch-Irish chief of the American Iron and Steel Association. Since the 1870s, he had lobbied Congress for protective tariffs on behalf of clients like Carnegie and now provided Harrison, who promised aggressive tariff protection, with a bottomless bucket of funds. Some of the money was used in voter-fraud schemes engineered by Quay in Pennsylvania and New York.[2] The Democrats were guilty of fraud, too; it just boiled down to who was willing to pay the most. How much money was donated to Harrison and how much was spent where will never be known, for Quay and Wanamaker wisely destroyed their campaign records. Nevertheless, cash was king, with Harrison winning the Electoral College while Cleveland won the popular vote.[3]

Back at their New York home on Fifty-first Street, where the painters had their oil pots in every room, putting the finishing touches on the redecorated house, Carnegie at once congratulated Harrison, who responded with "sincere thanks for your friendly words and for your manifested interest in the campaign."[4] Yes, Carnegie's interest had been most manifest. Harrison was the first president for whom big business was particularly active in winning the election, demonstrating that the new industrialized order with Carnegie as one of its leaders now ruled American politics on a national scale. Harrison was going to have to contend with the many problems presented by this new industrialized and urbanized America.

In his final message to Congress, in December 1888, Cleveland warned that government had best be wary of showing favor to big business in the Gilded Age or soon all would be slave to the corporation. "The gulf between employers and the employed is constantly widening," he observed, "and classes are rapidly forming, one comprising the very rich and powerful, while in the other are found the toiling poor. As we view the achievements of aggregated capital, we discover the existence of trusts, combinations, and monopolies, while the citizen is struggling far in the rear or is trampled to death beneath an iron heel. Corporations, which should be the carefully-restrained creatures of the law and the servants of the people, are fast becoming the people's masters."[5] Carnegie had no interest in being a "carefully-restrained creature;" however, public opinion did have a profound impact on him.

During the election campaign, caricaturists had a field day with Carnegie and the other industrialists. The enormous wealth of the men now dubbed robber tariff barons, or more commonly just robber barons, the promise of protection against foreign manufacturers, the generous campaign contributions to Harrison, and the relentless oppression of labor made for a plethora of material. In *Puck* magazine's May 1888 edition, there was a widely reprinted cartoon depicting Carnegie in a Highland kilt, hauling a sack labeled "Annual Personal Profits from the Poorly Protected Edgar Thomson Iron Works $1,500,000," which he is about to hand over to James Blaine (who would be appointed Harrison's secretary of state), standing in the doorway of the "High Protection Mill" and rubbing his hands gleefully. The cartoons, as well as song parodies that were circulating, effectively stirred public sentiment against Carnegie and his fellow robber barons, a term he despised.

Fond of applause, Carnegie hardly wanted to be considered a descendent of the medieval feudal lords who engaged in the wanton plundering of their people and land; but in the 1880s, that was the term applied to the powerful industrialists who, in the eyes of many, were exploiting labor and land. The protective tariff Harrison promised, critics argued, was no different than the medieval robber barons' net strung across the Rhein River to capture and pillage the traders' boats filled with goods from other lands; the protection gave them free reign in their own territory. Such an association was distasteful to the Star-Spangled Scotchman, who desired to be regarded as a chief builder of the great Republic, as a progressive leader of a great industrial state. But, as Carnegie sat in his spacious library, looking over his personal ledger of assets amounting to almost $15 million, it dawned on him that perhaps he was a gorged monopolist who needed a dose of tariff reform, or a dose of something—but what?[6]

Carnegie's thoughts drifted back to 1868 when unbeknownst to others, he had written, "Thirty three and an income of 50,000$ per annum. . . . Beyond this never earn—make no effort to increase fortune, but spend the surplus each year for benevolent purposes." It was a heartfelt, honest statement of values, as was a statement he made to Gladstone in June 1887 that he "considered it disgraceful to die a rich man." It was time to be more proactive in beneficence, it was time to take his 1887 statement to Gladstone and use it as a cornerstone around which to construct a logical philosophy on philanthropy. As Carnegie mulled over the matter, his shrewd mind understood that while he would be giving away money, his philanthropy would yield other rewards, such as the respect, power, and glorification he so desired. His benevolence would serve many purposes, including a means to justify and define his existence.

"Half the people of the world are ambitious and seek their happiness in attaining honors," wrote Napoléon. "The love of glory makes them desire positions of power, and take perilous risks, finding themselves enticed by this power of command."[7] So it was with Carnegie, who passed to his newspaper partner Storey these words: "Money no object compared to *power*." Money had bought Harrison the presidency, had bought the life of royalty at Cluny Castle, and had bought influence in the House of Lords. If Carnegie had read Machiavelli's *Prince*, however, he would have done well to recall the warning, "Those who rise from private citizens to be princes merely by fortune have little trouble in rising but very much in maintaining their position."[8]

To date, his major philanthropic projects had included either the establishment of or a commitment to fund libraries at Dunfermline, Edinburgh, Allegheny, and Braddock; the building of the Dunfermline baths; and the funding of a research laboratory at Bellevue Hospital. The giving was notable, but not substantial compared with John Jacob Astor, who, in 1849, had left $500,000 for the Astor Library; or Matthew Vassar, Ezra Cornell, and Leland Stanford, who had founded universities; or the venerable New Yorker Peter Cooper, who had given away some $2 million for public good by 1883, the year he died. Cooper had been and was still a most respected man, a man to emulate, as was his protégé Abram Hewitt. Elected mayor of New York in 1886, Hewitt pushed for public parks, baths, and recreational facilities. It saddened him to report, "On the east side of the city there are boys between seventeen and eighteen who amuse themselves by shooting policemen."[9]

Carnegie was well acquainted with both Cooper and Hewitt, who had made fortunes in the iron industry, among other ventures. Cooper's major philanthropic project was the founding of Cooper Union, the first free adult education school to give the working people training he had never had.[10] He believed intelligence to be the individual's great contribution to civilization, so he wanted more than just a vocational school; he wanted a school that balanced the study of the natural and social sciences with the arts. The stone-and-brick building housed classrooms, exhibition and lecture rooms, a library, artist studios, a laboratory, and an observatory on the top level. Included in the annual budget was $500 to be given to a woman who exhibited great heroism or sacrifice for humanity. By the time Cooper Union opened in May 1858, Cooper had contributed $630,000.

Cooper was not afraid to preach his philosophy. In a well-recounted 1871 address to Cooper Union students, he said, "I cannot shut my eyes to the fact that the production of wealth is not the work of any one man and the acquisition of great fortunes is not possible without the cooperation of multitudes of men; and that therefore the individuals to whose lot these fortunes fall . . . should never lose sight of the fact that they hold them by the will of society expressed in statute law, so they should administer them as trustees for the benefit of society as inculcated by the moral law."[11] These words had a profound impact on Carnegie; as his own ideas became more cohesive on philanthropy, he borrowed directly from Cooper's. Like his model, Carnegie was not afraid to speak his mind, and he now decided it was time to silence the critics who branded him a robber baron.

Carnegie sat behind his library desk, his personal secretary at his side, and in early 1889 penned an essay that would rattle the moneyed roosts more than his 1886 labor essays and deflect the criticism aimed at his wealth. A consolidation of three rooms, the library was the most spacious room in their Fifty-first Street home, taking up the entire front side of the second floor. It was his sanctum for both directing war and meditation. In fact, over the same days he was working on his philanthropic philosophy, he was plotting with lieutenants to force lower wages on the Homestead men—a dichotomy of character that maddened those who contemplated it. In one breath he was telling his lieutenants to slash wages, and in the next he was writing a bold opening to his essay: "The problem of our age is the proper administration of wealth, that the ties of brotherhood may still bind together the rich and poor in harmonious relationship." His treatise on philanthropy was published under the title of "Wealth" in the June 1889 issue of the *North American Review*. Up to that time, Carnegie had been renowned as an iron and steel magnate who epitomized the Horatio Alger rags-to-riches story, but beyond that, the American public was ignorant to any greater Carnegie agenda. Now, before them, he laid out a bold and systematic philosophy for distributing wealth based on a set of values he thought best.

Although the essay was on giving, Carnegie felt compelled first to defend the accumulation of money that was so vigorously being lampooned and criticized. What amounted to a large class gap was acceptable to Carnegie, a given of progress. "It is a waste of time to criticize the inevitable," he concluded, and further justified the concentration of wealth in the hands of the few by stating matter-of-factly that talent is rare, as "proved by the fact that it invariably secures enormous rewards for its possessor, no matter where or under what laws or conditions." Spencer's voice resonated in this essay, as did Calvin's: the blessed were naturally rewarded.

While the first part of Carnegie's essay justified the individual's accumulation of wealth, the second part addressed the question of what to do with the accumulated wealth. He decreed that there were "three modes" for disposing of wealth: leave it to the family; bequeath it for public purposes; and administer it before dying. In evaluating each mode, he quickly dismissed the first as "the most injudicious." Carnegie considered leaving large inheritances to children "misguided affection" that amounted to a curse. (The inheritance tax existed in only six states in 1890, so it was not much of a motivator for dispersing wealth prior to death.) As for the second mode, he believed that many postmortem public bequests "become only monuments of his [the giver's] folly." As a prime example, Carnegie pointed to Samuel Tilden, who bequeathed a share of his estate to a trust to establish and maintain a public library in New York (reportedly $5 million), only to have his family contest his will and tie the money up in court. Not until 1901 would the fruits be realized, when $2,250,000 from the Tilden Trust, amalgamated with the Astor and Lenox Libraries, was used to form the grand New York Public Library on Fifth Avenue. Spicing the essay with a bit of humor, Carnegie concluded his evaluation of the second mode by stating, "Men who leave vast sums in this way may fairly be thought men who would not have left it at all had they been able to take it with them."

The only mode for dispersing fortunes acceptable to Carnegie was for the possessor to take on the responsibility—*before* departing for the hereafter. He was also convinced that "wealth, passing through the hands of the few, can be made a much more potent force for the elevation of our race than if distributed in small sums to the people themselves." By small sums, he meant wages, which, he felt, "would have been wasted in the indulgence of appetite, some of it in excess, and it may be doubted whether even the part put to the best use, that of adding to the comforts of the home, would have yielded results for the race, as a race." Carnegie spoke as though he and other men of capital had been called upon to decide the fate of the people in every aspect. It didn't matter that people were living in slums without plumbing and sewers and might have used the money to better themselves; he didn't give them the benefit of the doubt. He should have. The wives of the laborers were frugal and budget conscious, just as Margaret Carnegie had been, for they, too, wanted a better life for their children. It didn't take exceptional talent to understand there was a better life than that in the tenement.

To Carnegie, "the duty of the man of wealth" was to uphold a thrifty lifestyle and "to consider all surplus revenues which come to him simply as trust funds, which he is called upon to administer in the manner which, in his judgment, is best calculated to produce the most beneficial results for the community—the man of wealth thus becoming the mere trustee and agent for his poorer brethren, bringing to their service his superior wisdom, experience, and ability to administer, doing for them better than they would or could do for themselves." He was certain he could administer wealth better for the community than the community could. This idea of acting as trustee came directly from Peter Cooper and again reinforced the point that Carnegie considered himself a chosen one, per Calvin, or at least a man who walked with the gods, per Channing.

Toward the essay's conclusion, Carnegie, who didn't believe in indiscriminate charity, suggested to whom and what kind of institutions the money should be given. His cornerstone: don't bother with beggars, but only with those who will help themselves. This tenet fell in line with Spencer, who believed evolution was nothing but the "ceaseless devouring of the weak by the strong." It was best that those unable to survive on their own be left to die. As leading examples of philanthropists, Carnegie invoked "Peter Cooper, Enoch Pratt of Baltimore, Mr. Pratt of Brooklyn, Senator Stanford, and others, who know that the best means of benefiting the community is to place within its reach the ladders upon which the aspiring can rise—free libraries, parks, and means of recreation, by which men are helped in body and mind; works of art, certain to give pleasure and improve the public taste; and public institutions of varying kinds, which will improve the general condition of the people; in this manner returning their surplus wealth to the mass of their fellows in the forms best calculated to do them lasting good."

Carnegie concluded his essay with resounding words: "The man who dies thus rich dies disgraced." It was a strong statement considering that the rich and powerful, with whom he had business dealings, preferred to create dynasties. His friend Morley immediately perceived its import, writing, "I found you had guarded the phrase well, but it will stick with you forever as an unreserved condemnation of those dying rich." Carnegie didn't hedge, confirming his position in an 1890 letter to a fellow industrialist: "Mr. Astor dies, in my opinion, disgraced by leaving $150,000,000 to one person, while the Astor Library suffers for want of enough money to make purchases of modern books necessary to hold its position as a first class library."[12]

Lloyd Stephens Bryce, the owner and editor of the *North American Review*, considered "Wealth" the finest essay he had ever read. Bryce, a rich merchant who served in Congress, was biased toward men like Carnegie, however. He encouraged the steel master to write a second essay that more specifically addressed how and to whom money should be given. Intoxicated with praise, Carnegie immediately agreed. Once again he was like Moses, down from Mount Sinai, the people waiting breathlessly for the commandments. After several months of work, he submitted his second essay, "The Best Fields for Philanthropy," for the *North American Review*'s December 1889 issue.

In the opening section, Carnegie reiterated that it was a disgrace to die rich and restated his basic principles for giving, which included being careful to not pauperize the recipients, but rather stimulate the members of the community to further "their own improvement." As for the "irreclaimable destitute, shiftless, and worthless," according to Carnegie, the city or state should shelter, clothe, and feed them. Again, his message was that indiscriminate giving, especially to charity cases, would not help the race as a whole, a position Uncle Lauder heartily agreed with, writing his nephew: "You are right on the subject of giving to the thriftless. The last clothes I gave to a beggar that I knew before he begged was worth 30/-. He sold them for 3/6 got drunk and beat his wife. That cured me."[13]

The most controversial section of the essay now confronted the reader: Carnegie's hierarchical list of worthy causes.

"*First.* Standing apart by itself there is the founding of a university by men enormously rich, such men as must necessarily be few in any country." As examples he cited Cornell, Stanford, Johns Hopkins, and the Vanderbilts, but apparently did not yet consider himself in this pantheon.

"*Second.* The result of my own study of the question, 'What is the best gift which can be given to a community?' is that a free library occupies the first place, provided the community will accept and maintain it as a public institution, as much a part of the city property as its public schools, and, indeed, an adjunct to these."

Third on his list was "founding or extension of hospitals, medical colleges, laboratories, and other institutions connected with the alleviation of human suffering, and especially with the prevention rather than with the cure of human ills." Fourth was public parks, and Carnegie believed the community should pay "graceful tribute to the citizen who presents it" by giving "his name to the gift." (Unlike Rockefeller and Morgan, who preferred to keep their name off buildings and monuments, Carnegie never shied from such recognition and endorsed it.) As a prime example for park giving, Carnegie used his very own partner Harry Phipps, who had donated a conservatory to Pittsburgh. Phipps had also founded the Phipps Cooking School, for which he paid all the expenses and salaries. Not everyone viewed such giving as useful, however. During the 1888 Edgar Thomson shutdown, the proletarian newspaper *Commoner and Glassworker* opined that the two thousand "idle workmen of Carnegie, Phipps, and Company at Braddock don't care much how the cooking is done, but they are greatly interested in knowing where the food to be cooked for them is to come from."[14]

The Carnegie list continued: fifth was music halls; sixth was public baths; and seventh was churches. Placing churches last on his list rankled the clergy, but Carnegie relegated them to that position because he felt strongly that giving to churches was of limited benefit; they were sectarian, serving a small segment of the public. Carnegie concluded this essay with these words: "The gospel of wealth but echoes Christ's words. . . . This much is sure: against such riches as these no bar will be found at the gates of Paradise." Although not a believer, he thought it best to hedge his bets—a wise investment strategy.

To prove to his idol, William Gladstone, that he truly believed what he had said in 1887—that it was disgraceful to die rich—Carnegie had Louise send the proof sheets of the first article to him with a note: "We think we have found the true path—it is the one we mean to tread. If it commends itself to you we shall be so happy."[15] Impressed, Gladstone requested permission to republish the essay in England, which was immediately granted. It appeared in the *Pall Mall Gazette,* whose editor, William T. Stead, renamed it "The Gospel of Wealth," a title Carnegie adored and adopted. The essay was also published in pamphlet form in both the United States and Great Britain.

The next year an inspired Gladstone published his own essay on wealth, which appeared in the November 1890 issue of *Nineteenth Century* magazine. He endorsed Carnegie's gospel but for two points: he placed churches further up on his hierarchical list, and he did not find "the hereditary transmission of wealth" to be evil, an expected British position. In complimenting Carnegie, Gladstone wrote: "This self-made millionaire has confronted the moral and social problem of wealth more boldly, so far as I know, than any previous writer. He may, like the rest of us, have his infirmities; but his courage and frankness, both of them superlative, are among the attendant virtues, which walk in the train of a munificence not less modest and simple than it is habitual and splendid."[16]

Carnegie was the first of his generation to espouse a systematic approach to giving away personal wealth and to damn those who did not. Such rhetoric meshed well with his radical heritage, but so had his epistles on labor relations, and had those been applied? No, they were not pragmatic and failed dismally. One certainty: between the wide distribution of the essays, the publicity from Gladstone's endorsement, and his being the first industrialist to distinguish himself on the issue of philanthropy, Carnegie invited criticism. As the *New York Tribune* noted, "Mr. Carnegie is not only the greatest ironmaster in the world, but also one of the most conspicuous controversialists in social ethics."[17]

Eager to fuel the debate over wealth and its distribution, the editor of *Nineteenth Century* solicited essays from three church leaders—Henry Cardinal Manning, archbishop of Westminster; Hermann Adler, Chief Rabbi of the United Hebrew Congregations of the British Empire; and Reverend Hugh Price Hughes, recognized as a great Methodist divine—which then appeared together as a forum in the December 1890 issue under the title "Irresponsible Wealth." Cardinal Manning and Rabbi Adler had no quarrel with Carnegie.

Not so with Reverend Hugh Price Hughes, who could not dismiss the Scotsman in the "approving way" in which Gladstone did. While Hughes acknowledged that Carnegie was most generous, "when I contemplate him as the representative of a particular class of millionaires, I am forced to say, with all personal respect, and without holding him in the least responsible for his unfortunate circumstances, that he is an anti-Christian phenomenon, a social monstrosity, and a grave political peril." The British reverend was alluding to the protective tariff, considered a monstrosity in his country.

"They have no beneficent raison d'etre," Hughes wrote of Carnegie and his industrial American peers. "They are the unnatural product of artificial social regulations. They flourish portentously in the unhealthy forcing house of Protection, but everything else fades and dies behind them. We prefer fresh air. Millionaires at one end of the scale involve paupers at the other end, and even so excellent a man as Mr. Carnegie is too dear at that price." No matter how generous Carnegie was with his money, according to Hughes, the fact remained that many of his laborers lived in squalor, had not shared in the protective booty that boosted Carnegie's profits, and were becoming poorer while the rich became richer, all making this situation anti-Christian and unacceptable. With a sardonic tone, Hughes contended, "Free trade, free land, and a progressive income tax would relieve him of the greater part of his anxious financial responsibilities."[18]

Always one to get in the last word, Carnegie responded to Hughes in the March 1891 issue of *Nineteenth Century* with an article titled "The Advantages of Poverty." It was a long, rambling response filled with flashy rhetoric. Carnegie's counterattack opened: "Imagine one speaking of 'growing poverty' in the United States! The American, more than any other workman, spends his savings for the purchase of a home." As for being anti-Christian, Carnegie now turned the tables on Hughes. In one body blow, he used a quote from the Parable of the Talents (Matthew 25:14–28), which strongly suggests God blesses those with talent: "It was those who had accumulated and even doubled their capital to whom the Lord said: 'Well done, thou good and faithful servant: thou has been faithful over a few things, I will make thee ruler over many things: enter thou into the joy of thy Lord.'" To serve his argument, Carnegie had put a twist on the parable's story; in the Bible's version, it was those servants who had doubled their talents, not capital, who were rewarded, giving it a more spiritual meaning. To further refute Hughes's criticism, Carnegie used the words of the founder of the Methodist Church—Hughes's church—John Wesley, who preached: "Gain all you can by honest industry. Use all possible diligence in your calling. Lose no time. Gain all you can by common sense, by using in your business all the understanding which God has given you. It is amazing to observe how few do this—how men run on in the same dull track with their forefathers. . . . If then you have an overplus, do good to them that are of the household of faith. If there be still an overplus, do good to all men."[19] As far as Carnegie was concerned, he had shown diligence, common sense, and had used all his god-given talents. And now, he was bent on doing good to all men.

There was, however, one extremely revealing line buried in "The Advantages of Poverty." In discussing the distribution of wealth by the very rich, he stated that "they can, perhaps, also find refuge from self-questioning in the thought of the much greater portion of their means which is being spent upon others." In his mind, philanthropy was, to a degree, a means for cleansing any doubts about how the money was made or class inequities, in spite of contrary claims made by the benevolent rich—including Carnegie himself. The "self-questioning" would plague the Scotsman even in his final years.

Ultimately, Carnegie dedicated so many words to defending the accumulation of wealth, the class gap, and the need for millionaires to act as trustees that his gospel was indeed suspect. Another notable critic, William Jewett Tucker, founder of the *Andover Review* and later president of Dartmouth College, questioned Carnegie's assumption "that wealth is the inevitable possession of the few" and claimed that the issue "begs the whole question of economic justice now before society. . . . The ethical question of today centres, I am sure, in the distribution rather than in the redistribution of wealth."[20] He was addressing the moral issue of fair wages, an issue Carnegie righteously swept aside. The usually supportive Pittsburgh press even took swipes at Carnegie, while the city's most notable journalist, Arthur G. Burgoyne, published a poem about him that ended:

On public libraries he spent
    Of shekels not a few;
A goodly slice to Pittsburgh went
    And to Allegheny too;
But still the loss he doesn't feel,
    It cannot hurt his health,
For his mills keep on with endless zeal
    A-piling up the wealth.[21]

Still, for every critic, there were thousands who would take a Carnegie handout in a flash. Immediately after Carnegie's "Gospel" was published, he began receiving hundreds of letters from people requesting money for statues, memorials, and libraries, among other ventures, both reasonable and madcap. He was also invited to speak before or to join dozens and dozens of organizations looking for a wee dollar or two. Many of the letters were painfully long, always starting with, "I wish to bring to your attention . . ." or "I have tried several times within the last year or two to come near enough to you for a little about a matter . . ." or "Permit me to introduce myself . . ."

For all the criticism, it could not be denied that Carnegie's "Gospel of Wealth" spurred other rich men to incorporate philanthropy into their lives, from which the working class did benefit. His methodical approach to library giving impressed and influenced John D. Rockefeller, for one. By the early 1880s, Rockefeller was a world-famous celebrity who, due to the charges that Standard Oil was a monopoly, had a far more notorious reputation than

Carnegie—for the moment. It was also estimated that his net worth in 1889 was well over $100 million, compared with Carnegie's $15 million.[22] His philanthropy had begun modestly enough; Rockefeller gave away $61,000 in 1881 and $119,000 in 1884.[23] But in the years after Carnegie's essay, Rockefeller's philanthropy accelerated quickly; he gave $304,000 in 1890, $510,000 in 1891, and $1.35 million in 1892.[24] In March 1891, he hired Frederick T. Gates, a Baptist minister, to work full-time on his philanthropy; in the ensuing years, he donated millions to the Baptist Church, its theological seminaries, and the University of Chicago.[25] Although he was the university's prime benefactor, Rockefeller's only involvement was to take part in selecting trustees. His name appeared on no building until the Rockefeller Memorial Chapel was so named after his death.

Like Carnegie, Rockefeller had to become very disciplined in adhering to his precepts for redistributing wealth. Rockefeller biographer Ron Chernow wrote, "Even as he was being reviled as a corporate malefactor in the press, this contradictory man agonized over the judicious application of his money and found it harder to exercise scrutiny over charities than over business."[26] Just as Rockefeller often relied on his wife and four children to study charitable opportunities, Carnegie recruited Louise to assist him. Neither man was timid, nor did they scatter their resources, preferring to focus on big-ticket projects, which is why the pair became renowned for turning philanthropy into a big business.

There was more humaneness to Rockefeller's giving, though. He expressed more concern for the submerged tenth, the downtrodden, encouraging one clergyman he supported to venture into "the midst of the multitudes thronging up and down the Bowery or thereabouts, and settle and stay right there with them, establish a church."[27] In the mid-1880s, he supported an Atlanta school for black women (later named Spelman College in honor of his wife's family), and he even picked out shrubs and trees for a redesigned campus.[28] A thought on the minds of many was that such philanthropy would cleanse the monopolist's degradation. Even one of Rockefeller's advisers, who was soliciting funds for a new university, wrote him: "You have the opportunity of turning the unfavorable judgments of the world at large into favorable judgments—and not only that—of going down to history as one of the world's greatest benefactors."[29] The arm-twisting didn't work in this case, but both Rockefeller and Carnegie had to be cognizant of the relationship between philanthropy and image.

Banker Pierpont Morgan's fortune ultimately didn't match that of industrialists like Rockefeller and Carnegie—although he and his father's combined net worth was about $30 million in 1889—but he, too, was active in public and personal philanthropy. He was not interested, however, in Carnegie's tenet that the wealthy should live modestly and shun displays of extravagance. To the contrary, Morgan relished luxuries and indulged himself and his friends, whether it be bushels of oysters and brandied fruit or taking large parties to the opera or the Patriarchs' Ball. In the 1880s, he once spent $55,000 on jewelry at Tiffany's in Paris.[30] Although Morgan did not publicly articulate a specific program for philanthropy, his interests were hospitals, museums, and the Episcopal Church, giving hundreds of gifts annually in a more haphazard fashion than Carnegie or Rockefeller. He was very active prior to Carnegie's essay, however. In 1887, he gave St. George's, an Episcopal church, over $200,000, and since the founding of the American Museum of Natural History in 1869 he had served as trustee and donated some $10,000 a year. In 1890, he gave the museum $15,000 toward the purchase of a gem collection, but wanted no public recognition, stating, "The less said the better to my taste."[31] The Episcopal Church was his main interest; he gave it millions, donating $500,000 in 1892 alone for an Episcopal cathedral, St. John the Divine, to be built on 112th Street.[32] (Over one hundred years later, it was still under construction.)

The power such philanthropy gave Carnegie was not lost on the media or the laborer. There was a fear within the proletarian ranks that it amounted to social control: Carnegie and others like him were forcing their ideas and values on the masses in an attempt to control their thoughts and actions, to control their behavior by instituting strict conditions for how their far-reaching benefactions could be used. It was antidemocratic, a charge the author of *Triumphant Democracy* abhorred.

To date, the library was the cornerstone of Carnegie's philanthropy, and there was no doubt he respected—even worshiped—books and authors. This reverence came to the fore in 1890 when Carnegie learned that Lord Acton, a renowned British historian who had assembled a priceless personal library of eighty thousand books, had fallen on hard times. At first, the newspapers reported that his creditors were planning to auction the library. Not long after that, a second announcement appeared in the papers: Acton's library was not to be auctioned after all. Apparently a generous but unidentified soul had paid Acton's debts, which amounted to about $45,000, and saved the library from being parceled off. It was Carnegie who played the anonymous hero. On June 13, 1890, he wrote to his go-between, Gladstone, from Cluny Castle: "Now one point. I wish no one to know about this, not even my wife shall know. Lord Granville [Acton's stepfather] should understand that such an arrangement, if known, must make it somewhat uncomfortable for Lord Acton."[33] Although Carnegie loved to be recognized for his good deeds, there were occasions when modesty ruled to preserve a friend's dignity.

The grand opening of the Carnegie Free Library in Allegheny City was anything but anonymous. Back in 1881, flush from the Dunfermline library celebrations, Carnegie had been determined to fund a spectacular public library in Pittsburgh, but here again he encountered difficulties in giving away money. In November, he wrote Mayor Robert Lyon, offering $250,000 for a library building and concert hall on the condition the city contributed $15,000 annually toward operating expenses. The approving newspapers trumpeted

"Andrew Carnegie's Magnificent Offer"; but alas, the city council could not authorize the annual expenditure, and the mayor was forced to reject the offer.[34] Not to be denied, Carnegie turned to his boyhood town of Allegheny. There the town elders accepted the $250,000 at once. It was nine long years before the Carnegie Library opened, but at last he was giving back to a community from which he had taken. Carnegie had added $50,000 to his original $250,000 to construct the Romanesque building of gray granite, which had enough shelf space for seventy-five thousand volumes and housed a music hall with a $10,000 organ.

President Harrison had agreed to attend the opening ceremony, and there were some forty thousand applicants for tickets to the night of speech making and music.[35] When Harrison had accepted the invitation, Carnegie, who was in Pittsburgh, could hardly contain himself and wrote Louise immediately: "I am greatly pleased. You know what 'the President of the United States' means to me. No official in the world compares with him." Carnegie also wanted his wife beside him for the event: "Somehow I begin to picture helpmeet, partner, wife, love, at my side upon the occasion. If you stood on the platform in Allegheny, I should feel the ceremony to be complete—otherwise not."[36] But Louise would not be there.

What should have been a joyous month of preparations was tainted by Carnegie's mother-in-law's death. In January 1890, Mrs. Whitfield died at age fifty-four. Having cared for her mother at the family home on Forty-eighth Street for much of the last four months of her life, Louise was distraught and went into deep mourning. Family was important to her and Carnegie, and both were disappointed they had not produced a grandchild before her death.

The impending opening of the Allegheny library generated so much excitement that a jealous Pittsburgh reconsidered Carnegie's old offer of giving the city a library, and representatives from that city approached Carnegie to ascertain if the $250,000 offer for a library was still good. No, Carnegie said, surprising and embarrassing the men. It must be a million dollars, he added with a grin, provided the city appropriated $40,000 for maintenance.[37] They agreed. The Pittsburgh library would become Carnegie's most ambitious project yet. The plans included a main branch with a music hall, an art gallery, and meeting rooms, among other facilities, costing $700,000, and three branch libraries costing $100,000 each. Carnegie became very involved, selecting the trustees and then assisting them in the selection of the architects, recommending books, buying artwork, even choosing the stone to be used in the construction. As with his business, Carnegie was very hands-on in managing his philanthropic projects.

The Allegheny City Library was dedicated on February 20, 1890. The music hall filled with guests long before 8 P.M., the anointed hour that the pomp and circumstance was to begin. The Mozart Society opened the affair by singing "America." Following Bishop Whitehead's invocation, Carnegie presented the library key to Mayor Pearson. "My wife, or her spirit and her influence, are here to-night," Carnegie said in his dedication speech, and after thanking all involved in the project, he challenged the citizens to make use of a gift that was now theirs. "The poorest citizen, the poorest man, the poorest woman that toils from morn till night for a livelihood (as, thank heaven, I had to do in my early days), as he walks this hall, as he reads the books from these alcoves, he listens to the organ and admires the works of art in this gallery equally with the millionaires and the foremost citizen; I want him to exclaim in his own heart: 'Behold all this is mine.'"[38] Such a noble comment did not stop what became a popular refrain among his critics: oppressed laborers had no time for books. Steelworkers themselves told the *Pittsburgh Survey*, "We'd rather they hadn't cut our wages and let us spend the money for ourselves. What use has a man who works twelve hours a day for a library, anyway."[39]

Such public displays of munificence only caused greater friction between hungry labor and gorged capital. For all the concern Carnegie demonstrated over labor relations in his 1886 essays, he was now less attuned to the problems—dangerously so in the years 1889 through 1892, as he ingratiated himself with the Harrison administration and attempted to influence Washington politics.

CHAPTER 19

Rewards from the Harrison Presidency

There was no doubt that President Harrison had more pressing matters to attend to than a library opening in dirty Allegheny City, but he was indebted to Carnegie for his substantial campaign contributions. After the ceremony, both men traveled to Washington, D.C., where, on February 25, Carnegie hosted a magnificent dinner for the president at the Arlington Hotel. The affair was called the most elegant ever by the *New York Tribune*. The dining room walls were banked with spring flowers, and the tables' centerpieces were mammoth four-leaf clovers of maidenhair fern; the menu was engraved with Carnegie's initials at the top, and the guest's name was blown in glass at the bottom; the bill of fare included oysters, turtle soup, broiled sole, spring chickens from Louisiana, roasted spring lamb from Scotland, and teal ducks from North Carolina; and the wine list featured Château Yquem, Château Lafitte, and a rare Madeira.

Although Harrison enjoyed treating himself to such fine affairs, he was upset when critics accused him of pandering to the capitalists. He was so sensitive that when Carnegie sent him a keg of Scotch whiskey to give him a wee bit of Scotch courage and the gift made the newspapers, he scolded his benefactor.[1] Harrison was especially distraught when he read reports in the papers that stated the party's national chairman, Matthew Quay, had bought him the presidency. To disprove his critics, Harrison was fiercely independent in his selection of a cabinet, but one of its members left Carnegie rubbing his hands in glee—Secretary of State James Blaine. With Blaine in the administration, Carnegie knew he had to take advantage of the situation while he could. Indeed, he would reap benefits that were both political and monetary.

When Supreme Court Justice Bradley died toward the end of Harrison's term, Carnegie realized his most successful coup. At a Washington dinner with the president, Carnegie noticed Harrison looked exhausted and was complaining he needed a worthy Supreme Court justice. "I said there was one I could not recommend," Carnegie recalled in his autobiography, "because we had fished together and were such intimate friends that we could not judge each other disinterestedly, but he might inquire about him—Mr. Shiras, of Pittsburgh." In fact, Carnegie and George Shiras were more than fishing partners; Shiras had been Carnegie's lawyer for many years. Also, Carnegie did recommend Shiras in a letter to Harrison, claiming he was "a Lawyer not a Money-maker or a politician."[2] The Shiras appointment to the Supreme Court paid off, as Carnegie's lawyer proved to be a proponent of big business: In January 1895, in *United States v. E. C. Knight Company*, he voted that the American Sugar Refining Company had not violated the Sherman Antitrust Act, even though it controlled 90 percent of the U.S. sugar-refining industry; in May 1895, he voted against an income tax; and a week later he voted to uphold the injunction the federal government used to break a strike at George Pullman's company. An ally on the Supreme Court was supremely beneficial.

Carnegie had dreamed of Blaine inviting him into Washington's inner circles, and he wasn't disappointed. At the top of Blaine's agenda was economic expansion, and toward that end he organized the first Pan-American Conference, which brought together countries from Central, South, and North America to discuss closer trade relations. Ten U.S. delegates were needed, men with experience in business and diplomacy, and Blaine tapped Carnegie; it would be the steel titan's only political appointment. With his usual enthusiasm, Carnegie delved into Central and South American issues so that he was prepared when the conference opened on October 2, 1889, with a fancy affair at the presidential mansion. The delegates then embarked on a six-week tour of U.S. industrial and agricultural centers, with Carnegie playing host in Pittsburgh.

Now an expert on South American affairs, Carnegie took an interest when rebels overthrew the Chilean government in the spring of 1891. The United States granted asylum to prominent members of the deposed government, which it had supported during the conflict. America became more embroiled when the captain of the USS *Baltimore*, stationed off the coast of Chile, granted shore liberty to 117 seamen. With tensions high between the two countries, conflict was inevitable. On October 16, two naval men were stabbed to death, and seventeen others were knifed, shot, or otherwise wounded. There was a cry for revenge in the United States, but Carnegie, intent on inserting himself into the fray, cautioned Harrison: "Chile very weak and sorely tried. Her giant sister should be patient and forbearing."[3] Diplomacy ruled the day this time. Whenever such crises arose, Carnegie now felt compelled to impose his views via telegrams, letters, and visits to Washington. Arm in arm, he and Harrison would stroll through the streets of Washington, hashing out matters, the president compelled to listen. Never again would Carnegie be a laissez-faire citizen when it came to U.S. politics.

*   *   *

Carnegie was energized by the Harrison presidency, more so than he had been by any past administration. The most obvious reason was that he had helped to buy the presidency and rightly felt his voice should be heard. Another factor was the business-friendly Republican agenda now ensconced in Washington, offering him an opportunity to promote his interests and causing him to shift his focus from British politics—his interest there having waned since his exit from the newspaper syndicate, anyway. He also had a clear channel of communication via Blaine, and several key legislative initiatives caught his attention: the Sherman Silver Purchase Act, the McKinley Tariff, and the Sherman Antitrust Act. As each of these acts took center stage, Carnegie vigorously addressed them, lobbying the president and other politicians, as well as using the media, to both promote and protect his business.

The most controversial legislation was the McKinley Tariff, which raised import duties to an average of 49.5 percent, reinforcing the robber baron image, and was considered the "Mother of Trusts" by its critics. The bill's sponsor, William McKinley, was chairman of the Senate's powerful Ways and Means Committee and was considered the high priest of high protection. For men like McKinley, protection was a patriotic duty that allowed infant industries to mature while inspiring internal competition. The tariff, they said, also created jobs and generated revenue for the government. On the other side of the argument, the free traders, which included a minority of Democratic congressmen and the rest of the world, claimed that the tariff aided and abetted the industrialists and their trusts, while the laboring class allegedly suffered by having to pay artificially high prices for products. Free trade, they believed, would result in more imports, competitive pricing, and thus cheaper products in the stores. Only important goods that didn't compete with American production, such as tea, coffee, spices, sugar, and drugs, were on the free list. Although duties on steel rails were lowered from $17 a ton to $13.40, and lowered on iron and steel structural shapes from $28 a ton to $20.16, the now mature industry considered it the most protective tariff yet.[4] Taking into account that the import of pig iron dropped by more than 50 percent the year after the bill was signed, and that the import of iron and steel products dropped by more than 50 percent within five years, Carnegie and his cohorts were indeed well protected.

Before the president signed the tariff into law in October 1890, there was impassioned debate on an international level. Gladstone, who considered the American tariff barbaric, squared off with the Harrison administration, and tensions between the two nations increased. Carnegie was distraught that the motherland and her successful son were at each others' throats. Any conflict between the United States and Britain nourished his internal conflict—the capitalist versus the radical—which explained why he always sought so fervently to settle disputes between the two nations peacefully. Over the next year, he penned several essays published in prominent journals designed to promote conciliation and to justify the tariff. The first, "Do Americans Hate England?" appeared in the June 1890 issue of the *North American Review*. Britain and the United States are so much alike, he argued, that a rivalry was natural. He wrote that America "'is a chip off the old block,' and means to have his way upon this continent, after the example of his sire in other parts of the world." He believed it was a matter of imitation, not intimidation.

The *North American Review* asked Carnegie to weigh in specifically on the McKinley Tariff in the July 1890 issue, which he did with relish. The result was an extremely long-winded essay titled "Summing Up the Tariff Discussion," in which he supported the American tariff and reiterated the argument that it was necessary for the young country to protect its fledgling industries. To give great weight and respectability to his argument, he quoted such heroes as Founding Father George Washington, who said, "Congress have repeatedly, and not without success, directed their attention to the encouragement of manufactures. The object is of too much consequence not to insure a continuance of their efforts in every way which shall appear eligible." Of course, the antiquated quote was almost a hundred years old, from Washington's final annual address on December 7, 1796. Using a cute analogy, Carnegie did concede, "We gladly admit the charge, however, that protection is entirely artificial—not less so than the protection given by the market-gardener to his young plants, which he covers with a sunshade through the day." He allowed that the tariff should be lowered on some imports, but endorsed a prudent, conservative policy.

A third essay on the McKinley Tariff by Carnegie appeared in the June issue of *Nineteenth Century*, the British magazine. It was simply titled "The McKinley Bill" and designed to explain the tariff to the British in a reasonable, not passionate, manner. He walked through the basics of the bill, concluding that one or two adversely affected British industries were creating, and would continue to create, agitation over the tariff. Carnegie topped the essay off with a rousing cheer for America, Britain, and Australia: "This is the great and inspiring thought of the age as far as our race is concerned, for it secures to it beyond question the future dominion of the world, and that for the good of the world; for the English-speaking race has always stood first among races for Peace, Liberty, Justice, and Law, and first also, it will be found, for 'government of the people for the people by the people.' It is well that the 'last word' in the affairs of the world is to be ours, and is to be spoken in plain English."[5] In coming years, Carnegie would attach himself to the concept of the English-speaking race governing the affairs of the world—otherwise called race imperialism—and would promote it ceaselessly.

Not all industrialists agreed with the McKinley Tariff nor bought into Carnegie's vision of a world dominated by the English-speaking race. New York mayor and ironmaster Abram S. Hewitt, who was sensitive to the working class, took the proletarian viewpoint. Rather than relying on rhetoric, he analyzed the steel industry using census data to determine whether the workers benefited or not from the tariff. In an argument difficult to refute, he concluded that the tariff, "so far as steel rails is concerned, is not to benefit the working classes, who are not paid at any higher rate than they would be paid in any other branch of business, but to take from the community at large at least fifteen times, if not twenty times, as much profit as the general average business of the country will warrant. It is thus that the rich grow richer and the poor poorer."[6]

Passage of the McKinley Tariff did rely on some cozy back-scratching. To win the support of congressmen from newly admitted western states reliant on the mining industry, eastern politicians like Senator John Sherman of Ohio pushed through an act that greatly benefited the mining interests. The Sherman Silver Purchase Act permitted the coinage of larger amounts of silver and required the government to purchase the total production of American silver mines. Because of this requirement, Sherman argued, free coinage of silver would be impossible. That was beside the point, critics countered. They feared that the government's churning out of silver coins would lead to uncontrollable inflation and that a bimetallic standard would lead to chaotic monetary policy. Gold, they said, should be the only standard upon which the dollar is based.

Regardless of the critics, the Sherman Silver Purchase Act was passed in 1890, inciting Carnegie to join the dissenting voices. He immediately began working on an essay titled "ABC of Money," which was published in the June 1891 issue of the *North American Review* and would become the most circulated of all his writings. (In 1896, presidential candidate William McKinley's campaign chairman would reprint 5 million copies for distribution to aid their pro gold cause; the essay was pivotal in helping him win the election.) Unfortunately, the dissertation on monetary policy was hardly spellbinding, but Carnegie successfully put the issue in terms the layman could understand. In plain language, he argued that silver's valuation as a commodity fluctuated too wildly and that a bimetal policy would result in American gold being siphoned off by wary foreigners and result in high inflation. "The good senses of the people will restore the gold basis after a time," he predicted, "and the republic will march on to the front rank of nations."[7] Carnegie's emotionally charged scare tactics provoked no legislation to rescind the act— it would take, instead, a depression that was still over the horizon.

The Sherman Antitrust Act was the third and last piece of legislation in Harrison's tenure that caught Carnegie's attention. On the tariff issue it was a house divided, but the "Antimonopoly" slogan was bipartisan. Trusts involved dangerous conspiracies, charged the Washington demagogues—a view shared by Harrison—and it was the mother of all trusts, Rockefeller's Standard Oil of Ohio, that spawned the outcry.

According to the laws of Ohio, Standard Oil could not own companies outside that state; therefore, to circumvent what Rockefeller considered archaic and unfairly restrictive legislation, he organized a Standard Oil company for every state in which he wanted to operate, each with its own management team and board. The stock of each company, however, was placed in the hands of select group of trustees (i.e., a central board of directors) who oversaw the trust estate (i.e., the Standard Oil companies). As Standard Oil devoured the competition, acquiescing stockholders of the various competing companies turned their shares over to the trustees, and those stockholders then earned interest on their investment, but sacrificed their voting rights. By the late 1880s, Standard Oil controlled 90 percent of the oil refinery business and was the model organization for the other prominent trusts that took root, such as the American Tobacco Company, the Diamond Match Company, the Distillers Trust, the Cattle Feeders Trust, the National Biscuit Company (which controlled 90 percent of the cracker industry), the Sugar Trust, and even a Cottonseed and Linseed Trust. The word *trust* was synonymous with *monopoly* in the public's mind, and an outcry ensued. In February 1888, a New York State Senate investigating committee put Rockefeller, now a mythical figure, on the stand. He kissed the Bible with great enthusiasm and then proceeded to answer questions with the least bit of information and in the most muddled form possible. Still, enough facts came to light that the committee's report stated Standard Oil was "the most active and possibly the most formidable moneyed power on the continent."

With the debate raging, Carnegie reacted with his usual gusto, penning an essay for the February 1889 issue of the *North American Review*, which he titled "The Bugaboo of Trusts." He opened with a witty scolding of fashionable business: "We must all have our toys; the child his rattle, the adult his hobby, the man of pleasure the fashion, the man of Art his Master; and mankind in its various divisions requires a change of toys at short intervals. The same rule holds good in the business world. We have had our age of 'consolidations' and 'watered stocks.' Not long ago everything was a 'syndicate;' the word is already becoming obsolete and the fashion is for 'Trusts,' which will in turn no doubt give place to some new panacea, that in turn to be displaced by another, and so on without end."[8] Of course, no trustlike combination existed in the American steel industry, according to Carnegie; meanwhile, he was participating in such panaceas as rail and beam pools, an iron association, Frick's coke syndicate, and the Bessemer Steel Association, a very powerful force in steel. To be fair, no single steelmaker wielded the power in their industry that Rockefeller did in oil refinery.

In writing the essay, Carnegie was hardly interested in Rockefeller; rather, his ire was focused on the railroads, and he attacked what he considered to be abusive rates and monopolistic behavior. He also took his case before the Pennsylvania legislature. Just two months after "Bugaboo" was published, Carnegie appeared in the chambers of the Pennsylvania legislature to speak on Pennsylvania's industrial and railroad policy. The Little Boss's large voice echoed through the chambers: "My address this evening will be an honest effort to point out those influences which threaten the future of our state, and to suggest remedies for these unfavorable influences." Those influences were the railroad and the excessive rates that he believed were depressing the state's economy. According to him, rates could be reduced by one-third and "still leave the railway companies a fair profit."

Carnegie condemned the Pennsylvania Railroad's monopoly of state traffic and was convinced the people would demand action: "I never fight unless I see the end clearly and know that victory can be won, just as I now know that it is impossible for any corporation to stand which I can show the people of Pennsylvania does not treat Pennsylvania justly." As exhibit A, Carnegie recalled for the legislators his failed 1885 attempt to break the Pennsylvania Railroad's grip on traffic. He also pointed out that the state of Pennsylvania contributed 68 percent of all steel rails made in the United States in 1885, but that number had fallen to only 59 percent in 1888 because, according to Carnegie, the Pennsylvania Railroad was depressing the state's economy. Voice at a fevered pitch, Carnegie wanted blood and was willing to be the executioner, boldly stating that "there will be no difficulty in getting at the truth if you will allow me to conduct the cross-examination of the President and the First Vice-President of the Pennsylvania Railroad Company and one or two others." In support of Carnegie, the Pittsburgh newspapers attacked the Pennsylvania Railroad, while the Philadelphia papers sided with the hometown railroad, sarcastically questioning why the Pennsylvania Railroad should divide its profits with Carnegie: "The thought of a division of profits between Mr. Carnegie and his laborers never entered into his wildest dreams."[9] The battle with the Pennsylvania Railroad would continue.

On July 2, 1890, Harrison signed the Sherman Antitrust Act. To the business elite's delight, the act's language was ambiguous—some wondered if it was not purposefully so to allow for loopholes—and it was sneeringly dubbed the Swiss Cheese Act. Still, in a freewheeling age, it was the first attempt to punish those who restrained or monopolized trade via a conspiracy. According to Section 1 of the Sherman Antitrust Act, Carnegie and a clan of his fellow steel manufacturers were in violation of the law because the Bessemer Association and the various pools conspired to restrain trade. No corrective action was taken.

To have its way with the trusts, the federal government would have to rely on judges sympathetic to the spirit of the law—that is, if the prosecutors' cases ever made it to court. The Department of Justice had a small staff, and Harrison did little to support antitrust enforcement; only seven antitrust cases were initiated, and the government won but once. The next two presidents would witness eight and three cases, respectively. Not until Teddy Roosevelt, who had an ego to match the industrial titans, would the government become more aggressive.

Money had bought Carnegie a voice in Washington's affairs, which intoxicated him. Now came the pecuniary benefit of his lavish campaign contribution—the kickback, so to speak. It involved an orgiastic fit of hypocritical patriotism.

Several years earlier, Carnegie had been offered the chance to bid on an armor contract for the U.S. Navy, but declined it, complaining the navy's specifications for its manufacture were too rigid, there was no money in it, and besides, it went against his pacifist nature. Only Bethlehem had bid on the project in 1887, so it naturally won the contract to deliver three hundred tons of armor by December 1889; but December had come and gone, and there was no armor. Construction of a cruiser, New York, and a battleship, Maine, was delayed, prompting Navy Secretary Benjamin Tracy to approach Carnegie for help—no one else—hoping to entice the proclaimed patriot with a juicy contract for six thousand tons of armor, a bit larger than the original three hundred tons. As Carnegie saw it, the navy was appealing for his help, and how could he, a patriot and a good friend of the secretary of state, allow the construction of a battleship named after Blaine's home state to be delayed? It appealed to his vanity—Carnegie's Achilles' heel—and would lead to scandal.

Before manufacturing the armor, Tracy wanted Carnegie to participate in testing different steel compounds to determine the strongest armor plate, although the navy secretary was already biased toward a nickel-steel, which was yielding excellent results in Europe. Once the tests were finished, the bidding process would begin, a mere formality to satisfy congressional watchdogs. Carnegie relayed William Tracy's desires to Abbott and joyfully predicted, "There may be millions for us in armor."[10] Enthused by the prospect of millions, Carnegie's pacifist traits were trampled under.

Government patronage aside, there were barriers to entering the embryonic armor plate business: building new plant and equipment, finding quality resources, training employees, and passing rigorous government testing, among other issues. Who was to play point man for Carnegie was a real sticking point; it required someone who was diplomatic and unwilling to be bullied by the government. While at times headstrong, opinionated, and callous to others' feelings, Carnegie did understand the duplicitous nature of diplomacy and the potential pitfalls in Washington—a town filled with politicos and vipers—where a wrong word, a miscue, a misplaced trust resulted in political and financial disaster. "It's too harassing to be always dreading one false step which may lead to so great a loss," he complained to Frick. A strong-willed character was needed, so Frick took charge personally.

Throughout the spring and summer, Carnegie wavered on entering armor, at times enthusiastic about the millions and at other times annoyed by government intrusion, telling Tracy they would not participate in the armor testing scheduled for September. Blaine stepped in to coax Carnegie along, whereupon, to give his friend the inside edge, he covertly passed along sensitive information detailing the government's requirements via a naval attaché in London. In June, the attaché, W. H. Emory, forwarded the documents to Carnegie, who was ensconced in Cluny: "Enclosed you will find the thickness of the armor and number of tons to each thickness. Besides, I also give a detailed list of everything composing the hull of the ship except the fittings—as I think they would come under the list of what could be made at your works. . . . In sending this list I have to request that it will only be used by you personally and that the source of your information or anything which would point to me will be carefully avoided. . . . I owe a deep debt of gratitude to Mr. Blaine and I know that he will be gratified to have me place myself at your service."[11]

When securing patents for the latest armor-making technology presented another roadblock, Carnegie again wavered, telling Tracy, "Want to help you out with Armor and will do best possible but . . . Armor making no child's play."[12] Playing a last card, a calculating Tracy threatened to buy his armor from the British, who were a step ahead in its manufacture. Appalled, the vain Star-Spangled Scotchman argued that his company must make the steel plates in the United States because the methods in Britain were suspect. Worried his British peers might catch wind of his criticism, he requested that this strictly personal letter not "go on file in the Department. It is for yourself and Commodore Folger alone; for as you can well understand, I am a steel manufacturer, and do not wish to antagonize any interests whatever."[13] It was the reaction Tracy had hoped for.

Finally, in mid-July, Carnegie sought to purchase a parcel of land adjacent to the Homestead works on which to build an armor-making mill. The city of Pittsburgh owned the 144.48 acres of prime real estate, known as City Poor Farm, which was occupied by the City Poor House and Home for the Insane. Back in March, Carnegie had first eyed the property, writing Philander Knox, the company's legal counsel, that he would be willing to pay $3,000 per acre for City Poor Farm and let the city retain the buildings rent free for up to three years.[14] In a second letter, dated the same day, Carnegie offered Knox an incentive: "In event of purchase being made of City Farm for us, at price given you in letter this date, we will, on obtaining a satisfactory deed for same, pay you the sum of Fifty thousand dollars Commission, and any saving to us under $3,000 per acre, we will divide with you."[15] Three days later, Carnegie offered to pay Knox an additional $25,000 toward expenses in the purchase of the property; what the money was to be used for was not stated, but it could reasonably be suggested it would pass under the table.[16] Knox, with short-cropped hair receding at the temples and eyebrows arched in permanent inquisitiveness, had a weaselly look about him; he would know what to do with the money. Clearly, this was a valuable piece of land, but not until July was Carnegie's interest again piqued.

City Poor Farm was not for sale, however, at least not until the city's Republican leader, Christopher Magee, who looked like a bulldog (to complement Knox the weasel), pressured the city council into authorizing its sale. Bids were accepted and then opened on July 27. Joshua Rhodes, owner of Pennsylvania Tube Works, offered $2,715 per acre; Carnegie, Phipps, and

Company offered $2,805; and Milton Baird, a real estate broker, offered $2,903. It appeared Baird had shut out Carnegie. Meanwhile, a suspicious mayor of Pittsburgh, expecting much higher bids for what was considered a million-dollar-plus property, wanted the deal nullified.[17]

The deal did raise questions, considering that Carnegie and Magee were tight, as was Magee with Baird and Rhodes, as were Knox and Frick with Magee and Baird. The newspapers accused the men of collusion, but Baird claimed he was representing an unnamed party. It appeared he was telling the truth on July 31 when Carnegie cabled Frick to settle with the "interloper" promptly to procure the property's strategically essential flat part along the river. Now, perhaps, the $25,000 he had offered Knox for certain expenses might come in handy. Bought-and-paid-for political connections helped as Magee stepped in and gave Baird an ultimatum: deal with the Carnegie concern or else. Using code, Knox reported to Frick: "Angel [Magee] sent success [Baird] to me demanded dot band fifty con [$150,000] down now to give or take half success [Baird] represents the people we thought am on whole combination are trying to work it from both sides am satisfied attempt will be made Monday or Tuesday to Pittsburgh must act." Baird wanted $150,000 for his troubles, but Knox also had to mollify the unnamed party and work matters from "both sides." Baird finally succumbed to the pressure on August 1, as Knox informed Frick: "Everything fixed Suspend judgment on Angel until you get all facts."[18]

Apparently, the third party had been compensated, for two days later the city councils approved the deal, the speed of the usually rusty government wheels surprising the entire community. The *Pittsburgh Post* reported, "Those who know how the city of Pittsburgh is regularly milked by the professional politicians who acquire their living and their fortunes through its necessities, real or imagined, will not readily discard the idea that there was a job, and a big one, in the poor farm sale and purchase."[19] Fallout continued. In September, one Charles Straub sued the city, Mayor Gourley, Baird, and Carnegie, Phipps, and Company over what he considered to be irregularities in the transaction. A brazen Knox represented Carnegie, Phipps, and Company, *and the city!* Knox won the case before Judges Ewing and White—who were friends of his, of course. Finally, on November 20, the sale was consummated and Carnegie, Phipps, and Company paid the city $370,906 and Baird $125,000. The *Post* concluded that the deal was an outrageous swindle.

Carnegie may or may not have broken laws, may or may not have bribed city officials, but he certainly excelled at manipulating the system. Monetary rewards, whether in the form of campaign contributions or outright bribes, ruled the day at all levels of politics.

Carnegie had friends in Washington, friends on the Pittsburgh city councils, and friends on the bench—how could he ever lose? Armament, he was now convinced, was another winner. The day after the City Poor Farm sale was approved, he extolled the virtues of armor making to Frick from the Royal Hotel in Thurso, Scotland: "No specialty can be had equal to this. Further study of the situation convinces me that we can easily succeed. Lauder shows me that we require little ground for new machine shop. . . . Lauder says it's not half the task I thought. . . . I think we can average a million per year out of this department with ease."[20] Cousin Dod was fast becoming the company's expert on armor and had convinced Naig there were indeed profits to be had. In fact, Carnegie was already thinking about other potential customers such as Russia, as well as dividing orders with Bethlehem Steel. So much for it being a patriotic duty to defend the great Republic; Russia needed a helping hand, too.

In October, the U.S. Navy took bids to supply armor for three "coastline" battleships, the genesis of America's rise as a naval power. Carnegie easily won a contract to supply six thousand tons of the needed nickel-steel battleship armor. The day was nearing when the pacifist would pay for his hypocrisy.

CHAPTER 20

Prelude to Homestead

The year Harrison was elected a changing of the guard also took place at Carnegie Brothers. It was one event in a series of management changes, some by design and some forced by fate, over the next two years that would profoundly affect Carnegie's operations and his legacy. Exhausted from a near-thirty-year battle in iron and steel, Harry Phipps, who had replaced Tom Carnegie as chairman of Carnegie Brothers, retired on October 16, 1888. Nevertheless, he would remain a partner and an active promoter of the firm's interests.[1] Carnegie's longtime friend David Stewart was elected chairman, but then Stewart died unexpectedly. To fill the sudden vacuum in upper management, Carnegie turned to Frick, who, on January 14, 1889, was elected president of Carnegie Brothers. Under him was the Edgar Thomson operation as well as his coke firm, a daunting challenge.

No doubt Frick knew the steel business or Carnegie would never have selected him, but in his first months in office he was tentative and actually admitted to Carnegie that "I have many things to ask you about."[2] Such an admission tickled Carnegie, and he let loose with a barrage of the usual advice on running full, wages, railroad rates, and coke costs. Before Frick had been in office six months, he was compelled to forcibly cut Carnegie off: "I cannot stand fault-finding and I must feel that I have the entire confidence of the power that put me where I am, in a place I did not seek. With all that, I know that I can manage both Carnegie Brothers and Co. and Frick Coke Co. successfully."[3] Carnegie eased off quickly, and the next month he acknowledged Frick's worth: "Let me express the relief I feel in knowing that the important departments of our extended business are in the hands of a competent manager. Phipps and I exchanged congratulations upon this point. Now I only want to know how your hands can be strengthened."[4] These flattering words echoed precisely what Carnegie had written to Shinn a decade earlier—and Shinn's ejection had been a messy one.

Carnegie had good reason for wanting to strengthen Frick's hand. A recent consolidation of steel companies in Illinois presented a forbidding specter, while a new Pittsburgh competitor started rolling out steel rails in March 1889. As for the Illinois threat, North Chicago Rolling Mills, Joliet Steel, and Union Steel merged to form Illinois Steel, which now had a rail-making capacity twice the volume of Carnegie. It was now the world's largest steelmaker and a serious menace. Behind the second competitive threat, the Pennsylvania concern, were some of the same names who had founded Homestead, including William Clark's son Edward, who, in addition to profits, had revenge on his mind. First organized as the Duquesne Steel Company in 1886 and then reorganized and renamed Allegheny Bessemer Steel, the company built a technologically advanced mill across the Monongahela, a stone's throw upriver from Braddock, to purposefully intimidate Carnegie.

With Illinois Steel a hearty enemy he could not immediately crush, Carnegie concentrated on answering the Allegheny Steel challenge. He was particularly worried about this competitor's new method, the direct rolling process, for rolling rails that offered dramatic savings on cost. At Carnegie's E.T., steel ingots were reduced to blooms (steel bars) and then reheated and rolled into rails, whereas at Allegheny they were successfully skipping the bloom stage and rolling rails straight from the ingots. It was efficient, effective, and allowed Allegheny to undercut Carnegie's prices. It was an intolerable situation, so much so that Frick confessed to Carnegie that Allegheny was "a great nuisance." He also apprised fellow steel man Jay Morse, "This Allegheny Bessemer business has been costing us a great deal of money, but I think we are pursuing the right course."[5] The course included a three-pronged attack.

The first prong was obvious: match Allegheny's prices to prevent the company from gaining market share. The next two thrusts were a bit more devious. In an attempt to discredit the direct rolling process and thus Allegheny, Carnegie sent out a circular to the railroads, warning them that Allegheny's methods led to a lack of homogeneity and defective rails, and to incite alarm he implied the rails could cause fatal accidents—an unfounded implication. In his sly use of propaganda, he was careful not to lie outright about his competitor's rails; rather, he selected perfectly suggestive language. Carnegie understood that words, like money, could bring power. The third strategy put into play was to ban Allegheny from participating in the rail pool, forcing the company to chase small, low-profit sales and offer ever-lower prices. Adding to the Allegheny's troubles, it experienced a number of labor disruptions even though the mill was nonunion.

Before its first year of operation was out, Allegheny Steel was feeling the squeeze, and the proprietors were forced to contribute an additional $300,000 of capital. Like a vulture, Carnegie kept an eye on the company, and in the fall, he ordered Frick to approach William Park, a principal partner, about selling. Frick found him receptive and offered $600,000, half of what it cost to build the plant, which was rejected. The next year, there was an economic downturn and rail orders slowed dramatically for Allegheny. Facing bankruptcy, Park had no choice but to approach Frick, who now offered $1 million. It was accepted, and Carnegie and his partners assumed control on November 21, 1890. The purchase became a coup of legend within the industry. Instead of paying cash, Carnegie issued five-year bonds; by the time the bonds came due in 1895, the plant had paid for itself six times over. Never before or after was there such a bargain, and Carnegie again triumphed over Pittsburgh's iron aristocracy.

Once Carnegie took control of the works, Charlie Schwab and J. G. A. Leishman investigated the direct rolling process and agreed it saved time and money without compromising quality. The Duquesne mill, now managed by Thomas Morrison, reputedly a distant relative of Carnegie's, was so efficient, Frick wrote Carnegie, that to keep up "Schwab will have to hump himself."[6] In an ironic twist, Edgar Thomson was modified to make rails using the direct rolling process, the process the devious Carnegie had so vehemently discounted.

The labor troubles that had hampered Allegheny Bessemer Steel also affected Carnegie's competitiveness and were not so easily solved. The Amalgamated had continued to gain strength and now had six lodges entrenched at Homestead; just four years earlier there had been only two. Although there'd been no labor strife since Carnegie conquered Homestead, he feared the Amalgamated's growing strength. Also, by the summer of 1889 he wanted drastic wage reductions in place and the installation of the same sliding scale that had enhanced Edgar Thomson's profitability. Nothing could stand in the way of Carnegie's majestic life at Cluny Castle and his plans to become the most renowned philanthropist the world had known. But Carnegie, who had been focusing so much attention on life away from the mills, was unaware of how hard the fight would be to win significant concessions. It was a fight designed for a man like Frick, but Frick was in charge of the Edgar Thomson side of the business. No, this fight was for another rising star in the company: William Abbott.

Abbott, with full lips, thick, wavy hair, and the looks of a star in the theater, had started with Carnegie, Phipps, and Company as a clerk in the iron mills. In 1888, he succeeded Walker as chairman of Carnegie, Phipps and was given a partnership. Naturally, Carnegie rode Abbott like he would a Cluny saddle horse, demanding weekly reports on the back of which the taskmaster Carnegie scribbled his comments, questions, suggestions, and explosions of temper and exasperation. "I think (if you will excuse me) that for the success of your administration it will be wise for you to let office work go for a while," he opined in Abbott's first year, "and visit every competing works often and get posted about their modes, costs and men if you find a real man anywhere get him in your service—It can never be accepted by your partners that you can't compete with and whip others—This is what our young partners are partners for."[7] Demonstrating his attention to every minute detail, he even critiqued Abbott's letters: "My Dear Boy . . . You did well, and let me say that your letter is creditable as a literary production. Not one superfluous word and all excellent English."[8] In early 1889, he prepared Abbott for the upcoming negotiations with the union and instructed him to get labor figures for Homestead in "proper shape" to justify the wage cuts.[9]

While Carnegie was preparing to crack down on Homestead, on March 30, he presided over the opening ceremony of his Braddock library, a Romanesque Revival structure built with sandstone that would soon turn black with soot. Dedicating his first American library (the Allegeny library would open the next winter) filled him with unalloyed pleasure, and he considered it a very proper administration of wealth. In his speech, he proclaimed, "Believe me, fellow workmen, the interests of capital and labor are one. . . . I am just as much entitled to the proud appellation of 'working man' as any of you, and I hope you will remember this hereafter and treat me with proper respect as one of the great guild of those who labor and perform a use in the community, and who upon that basis alone founds his claim to live in comfort."[10] Within the subtext, there was a clear warning: respect me or else. Here was Carnegie at his schizophrenic best: the hardened chieftain and sentimental benefactor, the man who could growl one minute and smile adoringly the next.

Abbott had the numbers ready in early May 1889, and Carnegie presented his demands to the local union officials. They included a dramatic reduction of wages, amounting to 25 percent for some men, and the institution of the sliding scale in effect over at Edgar Thomson, which meant the wages for the month were to be based on the average price of steel billets during the previous month.[11] The agreement was to go into effect on July 1 and hold until the strategically important date of January 1, 1892—when the men were most vulnerable due to the weather and the accompanying business slowdown—at which time it would be renegotiated. Naturally, the men balked. Before leaving for his annual Scottish sojourn, Carnegie reiterated to Abbott, who was to handle the negotiations solo, that the men had to agree to their proposed scale. "If not it is fight to finish," he wrote, sounding more like Frick than a progressive employer. "There is this to be said for the plan. If they don't agree then our consciences will be easier—We shall have offered *fair* and agreed not to break with organized labor." At this point, Carnegie was willing to accept the union at Homestead.

Before serious discussions could occur between Abbott and the union, tragedy struck Johnstown, Pennsylvania, home to Cambria. On May 31, a dam above the town burst after heavy rains and a forty-foot wall of water roared down the valley and crashed through Johnstown, killing more than two thousand citizens. Captain Jones closed Edgar Thomson and, along with three hundred of his men, rushed to help with rescue efforts and the cleanup. The shutdown cost Carnegie $15,000 a day.[12] He could not complain, however, considering that the dam's purpose was to create a lake for the South Fork Fishing and Hunting Club, an exclusive resort for Pittsburgh's wealthy, in which he was a member. In Paris for the World's Fair, Carnegie escaped the inquisition that followed. The other club members, including Frick and the Mellon family, donated thousands of dollars toward relief, but they never paid a dime for their crimes even though the club was certainly guilty of negligence in maintaining the dam.[13]

After the flood and the scandalous revelations, the Homestead men were in no mood to accept the severe terms Carnegie demanded. They went on strike on July 1. Rumors immediately circulated that workers in other Carnegie-owned mills would walk out in a sympathy strike, so, to keep Edgar Thomson out of the fray, Carnegie instructed Abbott to have Captain Jones order his men to keep clear of the fight until Andy could return home for a chat. As for the Homestead strikers, Carnegie advised Abbott to take no action.[14] Despite this advice, Abbott decided to break the strike by advertising in newspapers for willing scabs and hiring employment agents to secure them. To block any attempt to restart the works, the Homestead men patrolled the perimeter of the mill. Finally, when the first trainload of scabs rolled in, the strikers attacked, threw the scabs out of the cars, and, wielding brickbats, chased them into the surrounding hills. Upping the ante, Abbott brought in the Allegheny County sheriff to protect the strikebreakers; but when the sheriff arrived on July 10 with another trainload of scabs, an army almost two thousand strong blocked his way through the gates. Two days later, the sheriff returned with 125 deputies to take control of Homestead, but the strikers disarmed them, took their coats and caps, and sent them packing. Word then circulated that on July 13, workers at E.T. and the Upper and Lower Union Iron Mills had in fact voted for a sympathy strike.

Pressure mounting, Abbott called for a truce and the sheriff brought the two sides together for negotiations. The union agreed to the wage reductions and sliding scale, while Abbott agreed to a full three-year contract to expire July 1, 1892, a date to keep in mind. Schwab, the Homestead superintendent, played a key role in convincing the men to accept the wage cuts. Much to Carnegie's chagrin, however, Abbott also agreed officially to recognize the Amalgamated as the exclusive bargaining agent for the men; the next year there was an additional Amalgamated lodge in the mill, bringing the total to seven.[15] While the Amalgamated had won this battle in achieving official recognition, the epic war was far from over. Soon to complicate Carnegie's increasingly difficult relationship with labor were two horrific accidents that rocked the steelworks—the first at Homestead and the second at Edgar Thomson. Carnegie's destiny would be forever changed.

September 16, 1889, was just another day at Homestead. The men were under strain, sweating, the droplets hissing on the floor. As lunch hour approached they kept an eye on the clock; then, due to a careless mistake, a stack of structural steel tumbled over. Two men were trapped in its path, their feet crushed, and the ambulance was summoned to cart off the wounded. "It had hardly accomplished this when it was again called out to carry away the victims of the most terrible accident Homestead had ever known," wrote the correspondent for the *National Labor Tribune*. "Just at 2 o'clock the big ladle in the open hearth department boiled over, showering the molten metal over the pit men."[16] One man, Andrew Keppler, was completely embedded in a slab of molten steel. Two of his comrades, Hugh O'Donnell and Robert Dobson, worked feverishly to pull the slab away from the accident area, to where it could be cooled and Keppler's body pried free. Later that night, in the yard, a group of men buried the slab of steel molded around Keppler's body. O'Donnell, who could not stand the sight of Keppler trapped in the molten metal, was a name Carnegie and his lieutenants would have done well to remember. Such accidents and growing frustration would induce him to become a union leader and a pivotal character in the escalating labor agitation. But the more disastrous accident had yet to come.

The very next week, Carnegie was in Pittsburgh to survey the construction of his library project in Allegheny City, which was to open in five months. "Yesterday I strolled out with Henry Phipps and walked over to see the Library in Allegheny," he wrote Louise. "If ever there was a sight that makes my eyes glisten it was this gem. A kind of domestic Taj. Its tower a pretty clock, so musical in tone too, for it kindly welcomed me as I stood feeling—'Yes, life is worth living when we can call forth such works as this!' I saw many people standing gazing and praising and the big words Carnegie Free Library just took me into the sweetest reverie and I found myself wishing you were at my side to reap with me the highest reward we can ever receive on earth, the voice of one's self, saying secretly, well done!"[17] The ability to "call forth such works" justified accidents, deaths, and the other costs of empire building; it kept Carnegie's conscience clear.

The very day Carnegie wrote Louise about his "domestic Taj," the second catastrophic accident occurred. The Friday, September 27 headline of the *Pittsburgh Post* blared:

FATAL FURNACE C
A SHOCKING ACCIDENT AT THE EDGAR THOMSON WORKS
NINE MEN ENVELOPED IN FLAMES
MANAGER W. R. JONES IN THE LIST OF INJURED

The men had been struggling to unplug a clogged tap hole in the egg-shaped converter when Jones arrived on the scene. Then, at about 7 P.M. on September 26, trapped gases ignited and an explosion blasted open the furnace wall, spewing out forty tons of molten iron. Captain Jones was thrown thirty feet down into the casting pit, where molten metal severely burned him. Alive, but unconscious with a severe head wound, Jones was taken by his brother James to Pittsburgh's Homeopathic Hospital.

Two other burned men died by Saturday afternoon. Fearing the worst, Carnegie summoned in his personal physician, Dr. Dennis, but it was too late. Jones died Saturday evening. He was a hero who died with his boots on, a noble end he had anticipated years earlier when he said, "Thank God, when I die, I will die like a man at my post of duty, or whatever helm it is."[18] For the funeral, every Carnegie employee was given the day off, and the streets were lined with ten thousand men, women, and children, hats off, paying tribute to the folk hero who shaped the elements of hell. The town was draped in black crepe and the obituaries were glowing, as the Captain was celebrated for his organizational abilities, his knowledge of detail, his fertile mind, and "always planning new victories and winning them."[19] Carnegie lost more than his Captain; he lost a leader who used baseball games to create an unequaled esprit de corps.

Several days after the Captain's death, Frick visited with his widow, Harriet, to pay his respects and to explain that William Yost, a company lawyer and the Jones family lawyer, would be stopping by to discuss matters.[20] Yost was accompanied by Phipps and Dod, who were intent on discussing more than the family estate. The Carnegie executives were concerned about control of the patent rights to the Jones Mixer, as well as more than fifty other inventions that now reverted to Harriet. The emissaries successfully convinced her to sign the rights over to Carnegie Brothers, which she did on October 24, 1889, for the sum of $35,000. It was quite a bargain, considering that six years later Carnegie would estimate the Jones Mixer saved the company $150,000 to $200,000 per year, and that over the next decade, the company would spend hundreds of thousands of dollars in legal fees to protect its patents.[21] The value of the patents was not in question, but Harriet Jones's compensation certainly was. Jones's son-in-law, Daniel Gage, would pursue the matter in the early 1900s, seeking some monetary retribution. He found no sympathy in the Carnegie quarters. For Carnegie, it was just another savvy business deal. And it can't be forgotten that when Andrew Kloman had died years earlier, the Captain's only concern had been what would happen to Kloman's patents.

Coincidence or not, immediately after Jones's death, Carnegie, who perhaps sensed his companies would never be the same, attempted to sell out to English interests, but the negotiations failed. Harry Phipps, who was in Dresden, Germany, at the time, was pleased with his partner's failure: "I am gratified that we are not to go out of business, and especially to make room for a trust, which is by no means a creditable thing. . . . With Mr. Frick at the head, I have no fear as to receiving a good return on our capital."[22] Frick didn't have the Captain's rapport with the men, but Schwab did, and the onetime grocery store clerk lobbied to replace his mentor as general superintendent of E.T.

Schwab's rise through company ranks had been meteoric and precipitated by an encounter with Carnegie. As he had gained experience under Jones's tutelage more had been delegated to him, including the one job the Captain detested, which was playing messenger to Carnegie, who demanded hand-delivered daily reports when in town. One evening, while waiting for Carnegie, he sat down at the piano in the parlor. When Carnegie heard him playing he was impressed enough that several days later Schwab found himself playing Scottish ballads at a Carnegie party. He had won himself the ultimate champion, for once Carnegie trusted a man he conferred great power on him. Carnegie the positivist also appreciated Schwab's scientific approach to steelmaking, as opposed to the old guard's rule-of-thumb approach, and in 1886 he appointed the young, brilliant Schwab superintendent of the troublesome Homestead works. Always quick with a joke and a cheery whistle, the strapping young man was nicknamed Smilin' Charlie and had the men's confidence. He was given E.T.

With Phipps's retirement and Jones's death, management ranks were thin and, to replace Schwab at Homestead, Carnegie was forced to select a less-than-desirable man in John A. Potter. Schwab had little respect for Potter, suspecting he was "a hand-shaker" with little real interest in the workingman—which, if true, would not sit well with men like Hugh O'Donnell. This change would indeed affect Homestead as tensions there mounted and deft diplomacy was required. Yes, forces were at work that would negatively affect Carnegie's legacy.

There was another factor that was pushing Carnegie on a course for a disastrous collision with his labor force—his own naiveté concerning his men's growing discontentment as he made unilateral decisions to institute the sliding wage scale and to slash wages. He was as much out of touch with the times as he had been in 1886 when he wrote his labor treatises.

Carnegie really believed the sliding scale was fair, as indicated in a November 1890 letter to Gladstone: "We have not reached the ultimate when we pay thousands of workmen so much per day & take profits. The Sliding Scale is in my opinion, the next step. We have it in our principal Works and hope to make it universal."[23] The scale at E.T., however, didn't have a minimum, and as prices for rails became severely depressed in the 1890 downmarket, wages fell to dismally low levels. Completely oblivious to the living conditions in Braddock, Carnegie didn't grasp that his grand sliding scale now amounted to starvation wages.

Frick, still operating out of Pittsburgh, was the first to sense trouble. In October 1890, he asked for an assessment from Schwab, who responded with a sixteen-page typed report in which he summarized the mood and recent labor developments. Frick was shocked to discover that the Amalgamated was trying to retake the mill and that various departments had started submitting requests for a return to the eight-hour day. A blast furnace delegation demanded higher wages and even an end to the sliding scale. Schwab advised Frick that they couldn't simply dismiss the request for higher wages because furnace output had increased 25 to 30 percent while wages had remained the same. He calculated that it would cost the company $2,362 a month, or $28,344 per year, to give the men what they wanted.[24] Considering that Carnegie-owned companies' profits for 1890 were over $4.8 million, it seemed a small price to pay, but Frick had no interested in granting advances. Instead, he suggested sending a committee of furnace men to tour other companies to prove they stood on equal ground. The furnace men had no interest in a tour and announced that unless their demands were met by January 1, 1891, they would go on strike.

Carnegie was ignorant to the mounting tensions at Edgar Thomson as January 1 drew near; he was focused on his latest philanthropy and on his wife, who, in December, contracted typhoid.[25] All too cognizant of typhoid's mortality rate, Carnegie couldn't bear to see Louise stricken and insisted Dr. Dennis personally care for her on a daily basis. She didn't leave the house for almost four months, and there was no commuting to Pittsburgh for Carnegie. Not until the end of March was Louise able to walk around the house, and not until April 3 did she venture outside. She had her strength back not a month too soon, for Carnegie had been busy with his latest philanthropic endeavor, Carnegie Hall, and needed her there for the opening ceremony.

Carnegie wanted to be considered a patron of the arts as well as books, so, in keeping with his "Gospel of Wealth," he was busy planning a great music hall to satisfy New York City's cultural aesthetes and elitists. Since 1878, Carnegie, along with Morgan, Rockefeller, and Vanderbilt, had underwritten the New York Symphony Orchestra, which held its concerts in the Metropolitan Opera House. The conductor, Walter Damrosch, now an intimate of Carnegie, convinced his patron the group needed a home more suitable for orchestral performances; thus, in late 1889, Carnegie offered to foot the cost for what was to be called the Music Hall, later to be rechristened Carnegie Hall. Rather than giving it outright to the city, he formed the Music Hall Company of New York, Limited, which had its own president and board and operated autonomously. On May 13, 1890, with silver trowel in hand, Louise gracefully laid the cornerstone at Fifty-seventh Street and Seventh Avenue. Amid applause, Carnegie stepped forward and delivered a short, compassionate speech in which he claimed that "this is no ordinary structure. It differs from most others in this that it is not erected for gain. Its owners seek not to reap high profits from the community. . . . From this platform men may be spurred to deeds which end not with miserable self; here an idea may be promulgated which will affect the world, or here a good cause may be promoted. The hall may lend itself to do charitable work, only true charitable work, which helps those who wish to help themselves." Carnegie, forever sensitive to charges of being a robber baron, was careful to emphasize the charitable, nonprofit aspects of the hall, and at its conclusion he was given a hearty three cheers.[26]

As Carnegie watched his $2 million investment arise, its architecture reminiscent of the Italian Renaissance, the interior velvet-lined and an acoustical marvel, he knew it needed truly professional musicians to fill the air with splendor. So, with the Music Hall almost complete in February 1891, Damrosch announced that Carnegie had agreed to support the hiring of the city's first permanent orchestra. Opening ceremonies involved an extravaganza that lasted the entire first week of May, at which Damrosch conducted the finest music by Wagner, Beethoven, and Tchaikovsky, among other masters. Pyotr Tchaikovsky was the guest of honor—a paid guest, courtesy of $2,500 from Carnegie. On May 6, Tchaikovsky noted in his diary:

> I had scarcely time to dress and drive to Carnegie's in a carriage, which had to be fetched from some distance, and was very expensive! This millionaire really does not live so luxuriously as many other people. . . . During the evening he expressed his liking for me in very marked manner. He took both my hands in his and declared that, though not crowned, I was a genuine king of music. He embraced me (without kissing me, men do not kiss over here) got on tiptoe and stretched his hand up to indicate my greatness, and finally made the whole company laugh by imitating my conducting. This he did so solemnly, so well, and so like me, that I myself was quite delighted. His wife is also an extremely simple and charming young lady, and showed her interest in me in every possible way.[27]

Another major cultural project was being executed in the winter of 1890–1891 under the guidance of Pierpont Morgan. He had organized a syndicate to build a vast entertainment hall—Madison Square Garden—in which Carnegie invested. Originally it was to be for equestrian use only, but the plans were radically modified to make it a pleasure dome. Built at Madison and Twenty-sixth Street, on the site of an old railroad depot that P. T. Barnum had remodeled as the Great Roman Hippodrome, it was a massive structure of Spanish Renaissance architecture, brick with white terra-cotta trim, Roman colonnades, arched windows, eight domed belvederes, and a 341-foot tower modeled on Seville's Moorish Giralda and crowned by an 18-foot copper statue of the goddess Diana with bow and arrow. It housed restaurants, theaters, a reproduction of Shakespeare's house and the Globe Theatre, as well as an amphitheater for horse, dog, and garden shows. Madison Square Garden opened in November 1891.

Carnegie was also involved with the New York Botanical Garden and was appointed to the finance committee, joining Morgan, among others.[28] A healthy competition had developed between these titans to fund such cultural institutions. For Carnegie, day-to-day business in Pittsburgh was hardly a priority, especially in the winter of 1890–1891, when he was so distracted by Louise's health and New York's cultural vibrancy. While he spent New Year's

Eve at his wife's side, he neglected the situation at Edgar Thomson, where the furnace men were preparing to strike.

To prevent any booze-inspired labor violence on New Year's Eve, the night before the furnace men promised to strike, Schwab considered asking the local saloon keeper, Mr. Wolfe, to close for the night; but unwilling to play Scrooge, he did not. It was a mistake. Late on December 31, the stockyard men unexpectedly walked off the job to join a crowd of fellow Hungarians at the saloon for a night of drinking, carousing, and bitter complaining about wages, and by midnight the men were soused, ready to take their seething frustrations out on Carnegie property.

Shortly after midnight a gang of 60 Hungarians attacked the stockyards, vandalizing the property and beating any men who attempted to stop them. Schwab quickly rallied loyal men, whom he armed with clubs, and organized a defense line around the furnaces, which if extinguished, would paralyze the mill. The battle lasted almost three hours before the Hungarians withdrew. But then, beginning around noon, a gang of 250 drunken Hungarians organized and rushed the furnace department, closing it down. Some men were fatally wounded. Anxious and smarting from the forced retreat, Schwab dashed off a letter to Frick, suggesting they bring in Pinkertons if keeping the mill open was of the utmost concern.[29]

Surprisingly, the man who had been quick to crush violence in the coal-fields by using the Pinkerton detectives was opposed to using them now. If the hated Pinkerton boys were brought in, Frick reasoned, it could enflame the violence and cause more men to join the Huns. He preferred to rely on the sheriff and deputized company men to restore order.[30] So, throughout New Year's Day, Schwab rallied a force of at least a hundred men, twelve of them armed with repeating Winchester rifles. "I understand the 'Huns' intend making another attack tonight," he reported to Frick, "and I can assure you that if they do, they will meet with a pretty lively reception as I am determined to drive them out, no matter at what cost or sacrifices."[31] Schwab clearly shared both Frick and Carnegie's intolerance for labor disruptions and the union.

Although it was New Year's Day, Carnegie soon heard of the violence at Edgar Thomson. He immediately cabled Frick, who responded that it was "not anything more than a drunken Hungarian spree." As he explained, "We are asking for no reduction even in these depressed times, when furnaces all over the country are either banking up or their employees accepting a reduction in wages. A little nerve and patience will certainly bring this matter through all right."[32] Frick, who discussed the matter as he would a shopping trip to Macy's, hoped to downplay the incident and keep Carnegie in New York. At the same time, he prepared his lieutenants for greater violence. Early on January 2, Frick notified his superintendent of the furnaces, James

Grayley, that they had procured about twice as many revolvers as needed and would ship them out on the 12:30 P.M. train.[33] Again Frick cabled Carnegie that day: "All quiet last night and this morning. Think it is working itself out all right. Newspaper reports greatly exaggerated."[34] Unwittingly, Frick was contributing to Carnegie's inability to fully understand the dire labor situation by feeding him false information, especially since there was a distinct concern that Hungarians from Homestead would join the battle.

That night the Hungarians did not mass, their drunkenness dissipated, their energy and anger spent. Relieved, Frick cabled Carnegie that all was quiet.[35]

For the moment, Schwab had regained control, and, by the end of 1891, he had his men beating twenty-four-hour production records at E.T. and rival mills. He did so by taking his best men, putting one in charge of each department, and setting them against one another like roosters in a cockfight. Any such esprit de corps was nonexistent at Homestead, however, where men like Hugh O'Donnell, who had pulled dead comrades from molten steel, harbored venomous resentment toward Superintendent Potter and other Carnegie managers. The Homestead men's disgust with the Carnegie Company's callous attitude toward wages, hours, and accidents was not limited to a group of Hungarians, but had taken root throughout all departments and ethnic groups and was growing like a beast gorging itself, building toward an explosive climax.

CHAPTER 21

The Homestead Tragedy

The year 1892 started pleasantly enough. Carnegie, Louise, and a party that included the president of the New York Chamber of Commerce, Charles Smith, made a monthlong tour of California and Mexico by private railcars. Planning the mid-February to mid-March trip himself, Carnegie relied on his railroad friends to accommodate his private train clear from New York to San Francisco, with George Pullman personally handling Carnegie's travel on the Southern Pacific.[1] Not having lost his appetite for adventure, Carnegie looked forward to San Francisco, a city founded by the Spanish in 1776, but later shaped by business tycoons like Leland Stanford. Its ports, controlling trade from Panama to Alaska, were set in the Bay, a beautiful expanse of water cuddled by the low red hills.

Here, the Carnegies took in the mansions of Nob Hill, dined with millionaires who made their fortune in mining, and made forays into the wine country where the dry, cool climate agreed with the Scotsman. They visited the Beringer Brothers winery, from whom the temperance-minded Carnegie ordered twenty-five gallons of brandy and four cases of white wine. Then it was to northern Mexico and the Baja Peninsula, where it seemed there were as many policeman as churches under the regime of dictator Porfirio Diaz. Louise and he were enchanted by the primitive scenery, the lunar landscapes, the rugged peaks, the copper cliffs plunging into the sea, and the surf crashing into romantic coves. The denigrated Indian population was invisible, however.

Back in Pittsburgh, Frick was pushing to consolidate the various companies and mills under one organization to realize greater efficiencies. The orchestration was simple: the Carnegie Steel Company, its nucleus being Edgar Thomson, would purchase all the other operations, except Frick Coke.[2] Frick was to be chairman and the fallen Abbott shown the door; Charlie Schwab would remain general superintendent of the Edgar Thomson Steel Works and Furnaces, John A. Potter general superintendent of Homestead, and Thomas Morrison superintendent of Duquesne. The capital of the new organization would be an even $25 million, with Carnegie holding $13,833,333.33; Phipps, $2,750,000; Frick, $2,750,000; and Dod, $1,000,000. Nineteen other company men (including John Vandevort) held stakes ranging from $28,000 to $500,000. Carnegie still controlled with an iron fist armored with 55 percent, but at least Frick, who had been permitted to purchase the interest belonging to David Stewart, who had died in 1889, could take comfort that his share had increased to 11 percent, putting him on equal footing with Phipps. Carnegie and Frick planned for the reorganization to take effect on July 1, the day after the company's contract expired with the Amalgamated men at Homestead and the day Carnegie expected to have a new agreement in place.

Winning wage cuts, as usual, were going to be vital because Carnegie anticipated a business downturn while a relentless price war with Illinois Steel continued. The price of the steel billets made at Homestead had plunged from $36 a ton in December 1889 to $23 in March 1892. Also of grave concern, the union had become a major obstacle to efficiency as far as Carnegie and Frick were concerned. The Amalgamated insisted on having a certain amount of skilled men in particular departments, more than were necessary, adding to costs and infuriating the chieftains. And there was the Amalgamated's *Memorandum of Agreement for the Homestead Works*, which included fifty-eight pages of "footnotes" with rules of work for the union men. Not surprisingly, union leaders wielded their power at times just for the sake of it by making unfounded grievances.[3]

The two men held meetings at Carnegie's Fifty-first Street home and focused on three goals to be accomplished in the Amalgamated negotiations: the tonnage wage rate had to be reduced to take into account increased productivity realized through new machinery; the minimum base the men could earn had to be lowered to reflect the depressed market; and the new contract had to terminate on December 31, not June 30. The wage reduction Carnegie sought amounted to about 15 percent, according to him, while the Amalgamated representatives insisted it was close to 18 percent.[4] Regardless of the math, of the 3,800 Homestead employees, 800 were Amalgamated members, and of those only 325 would be affected by the new scale. These skilled workers were mostly Irish, Welsh, English, and German; the common laborers predominantly Hungarians, Italians, and Poles. Such a small number of men would be affected, men the common laborers were indifferent to, that Carnegie anticipated no problems in forcing the new scale on them.

The Amalgamated, which had reached its apex of power with over twenty-four thousand members, had also been making plans, plans stumbled upon by A. C. Buell, a government inspector at Homestead's armor mill.[5] When an Amalgamated member, J. W. Allen, posing as a reporter from the United Press, tried to elicit information from Buell about government armor contracts to use in the upcoming negotiations with Carnegie, Buell recognized him, but didn't let on, and then reported their subsequent conversation to a fellow Navy Department official. Allen told him that the mill men knew there was "a bonanza in armor contracts" and wanted their share of it. "There was much more of the same sort," Buell reported, "but the upshot of the whole was an impression that a great strike is impending in the steel industries. I considered the information I got from Mr. Allen valuable. In fact, it afforded me the first real insight into the workings of the Amalgamated Associations that I have ever enjoyed." He also noted that Mr. Allen was quite sober.[6]

The Homestead men weren't fools; they knew the government's armor contracts meant big money, and they wanted a share of the booty. They were also tired of hearing about jobs lost to new machinery, about wage cuts due to higher productivity. They were tired of the surrounding squalor. They were tired of hearing about Carnegie's great benefactions and tours of Europe. In fact, confident the Homestead negotiations would conclude satisfactorily with Frick in charge instead of Abbott, Carnegie had already made plans for his annual sojourn to Scotland. Louise and he were to sail on April 13, stay at Coworth Park, a lovely estate in southern England, and then head for Scotland.

As Carnegie's departure date approached, Frick left his pregnant wife and their plush Homewood residence for yet another meeting at Carnegie's home in New York. As a soft spring light filtered through the windows, they tackled the prickly issue of how to handle a strike if, in the unlikely case, the men walked out. Carnegie was in favor of shutting down the works and letting the men vote on the new scale by secret ballot as they had done at Edgar Thomson in 1888.[7] Back then the union had been expelled from the works and the same result, he concluded, could be had at Homestead.

The more he mulled over the power the Amalgamated wielded, the more convinced he was that the union had to be vanquished. Therefore, to support Frick's impending hard-knuckled negotiations, Carnegie drafted a memo signed by himself to be posted if necessary. In complete opposition to his righteous 1886 labor essay proclaiming the right of men to organize, he now declared Homestead must run nonunion: "This action is not taken in any spirit of hostility to labor organizations, but every man will see that the firm cannot run Union and Non-union. It must be either one or the other."[8] The inconsistent Carnegie wanted consistency; it was a solid argument. Not only was the Amalgamated a hindrance to efficiency, he reasoned, but it wasn't a true union because it admitted only a small group of skilled workers. It was in its own way an elitist, discriminatory organization that was not worthy of the Republic.

During the crossing to Britain, Carnegie decided the memorandum was too self-condemning, however, and so, fearing for his already tainted reputation as a progressive employer, he gave Frick revised instructions. Instead, he was to post a sign stating that with "a consolidation having taken place, we must introduce the same system in our works; we do not care whether a man belongs to as many Unions or organizations as he chooses, but he must conform to the system in our other works." This system, of course, was nonunion. So a man could belong to a union as long as it wasn't related to Carnegie's steelworks—some good that would do. He concluded his note to Frick by stating, "We are with you to the end."[9] It was mere Carnegie rhetoric, but a haunting conclusion to the letter as it forewarned of a fight. If tragedy struck, Carnegie might not be so quick to stand by Frick and regret those words.

With just a month to go before the current agreement expired on June 30, Frick offered a slightly better wage scale and advised Superintendent Potter to tell his men, "We do not care whether a man belongs to a union or not, nor do we wish to interfere. He may belong to as many unions or organizations as he chooses, but we think our employees at Homestead Steel Works would fare much better working under the system in vogue at Edgar Thomson and Duquesne."[10] Carnegie and Frick were waffling over recognizing the union, when a decisive position was required.

At the same time Frick was offering his fabricated olive branch, he ordered the construction of a three-mile-long fence along the Homestead perimeter. Spaced at regular intervals were portholes five to six inches in diameter, allegedly for lookouts but suitable for putting a rifle through. Barbed wire was strung across the top, and the rumor in town was that it could be charged with electricity at moment's notice. Within the compound, platforms were built and equipped with searchlights. The Homestead men were surprised by the conversion of the works into a very military-looking, turreted complex and quickly dubbed it Fort Frick. Clearly, Frick's words didn't jive with his actions, as he appeared to be preparing for an extended lockout that he apparently expected to turn violent. Tension mounted not just between the union men and Carnegie management, but between all the men coming to work inside the "Fort" and management.

Such an aggressive posture was hard to explain. If only 325 men were to be affected by the new wage scale, why was Frick apparently picking a fight with all 3,800 men? Because he feared another Hungarian rampage like the one at Edgar Thomson. Also spooking Frick was a three-month strike in 1991 that had wreaked havoc in the coalfields. Armed mobs committed arson and murder, blew up mines, and destroyed machinery. In all, seven strikers were killed in gun battles with deputy sheriffs.[11] Influencing his preparations the most was the report from Buell that the men were planning to strike. Yes, Frick expected violence.

Yet, while he prepared for an extended battle, a cocksure Frick, planning to visit Carnegie in Scotland that summer, expected a swift conclusion to any hostilities. So did Carnegie, who, surmising and advising, penned his second letter in three days to Frick: "Of course, you will be asked to confer [with the Amalgamated], and I know you will decline all conferences, as you have taken your stand and have nothing more to say. . . . Of course you will win, and win easier than you suppose, owing to the present condition of markets."

THE CARNEGIE STEEL COMPANY, LIMITED.

NOTICE.

THE FOLLOWING

RULES AND REGULATIONS

WILL BE IN FORCE AT THE

HOMESTEAD STEEL WORKS,

BEGINNING JULY 1st, 1892.

1. No one will be permitted to interfere with the Civil, Religious or Political opinions of the Workmen, and no political notices or posters will be allowed to be circulated or posted on the property of this Association.

2. All employes wishing to absent themselves for a turn, or longer, must first apply to and receive permission from their Foreman; and all persons working on night turn must make their application before 4 o'clock P. M. All persons violating this rule will be subject to discharge.

3. Employes are required to exercise economy in the use of all material, and to keep the machinery and works neat and clean.

4. Any employe, who through gross carelessness or malice, destroys the property of this Association, or is found stealing or carrying away the property of this Association, will be discharged.

5. Any employe, who on account of violation of the Criminal Laws of the Country is arrested, and by reason of his arrest leaves his position vacant, will be discharged and his position filled.

6. Any employe who habitually neglects or refuses to pay his debts will be subject to discharge.

7. The use of intoxicating liquor by any employe, while on duty, is absolutely forbidden, under penalty of immediate discharge.

8. All Superintendents and Foremen must pay strict attention to the rights and privileges of employes. Where a position is vacant, the employe of longest service at the Homestead Steel Works, and in the line of promotion, must fill the vacancy, without regard to his political or religious opinions; provided, however, he is fully competent to fill the higher position.

9. Excepting only where a special contract has been made, as for advice, counsel, etc., every salaried employe of this Association is expected to devote his entire service to the interests of his employer; and while no restriction is sought to be placed upon investments made by any employe, the taking of any active part in the conduct of the business in which such investment is made will not be permitted.

10. Department Superintendents and Foremen shall give hearing and prompt attention to any reasonable complaint or claim for redress, and if unable to amicably adjust the matter, shall refer the same to the General Superintendent.

11. All Department Superintendents and Foremen must see that the above Rules and Regulations are strictly complied with and rigidly enforced.

By order of the Board of Managers.

H. C. FRICK,

PITTSBURG, PA., July 1st, 1892.

Chairman.

(Courtesy of the Historical Society of Western Pennsylvania)

He also ordered Potter to tell the men that if they didn't accept the new wage scale, Homestead would run nonunion.[12] The next week, he reiterated that the Homestead men must be made to understand that if they didn't accept the new wage scale, it meant *"Non-Union forever."*[13] His position was beginning to harden against the union, but Carnegie and Frick's overconfidence and bravado masked what they were really feeling: uncertainty as to how the union men would react to the ultimatum. The uncertainty was evident in the two men's wavering over whether to recognize the union and in the conflicting message sent during negotiations; that is, the offering of small wage concessions while building a stockade fence. It was not like Carnegie, nor like Frick, to be tentative, but Homestead had had a violent tradition of labor strife from day one, and across the nation, guns were settling more and more labor disputes.

One week before the Homestead contract expired, Carnegie departed Coworth Park for Aberdeen, Scotland, where he was to dedicate a library and receive the city's Freedom, the festivities to be held July 5 and 6.[14] Then it would be on to Sir Robert Menzies' Rannoch Lodge, a picturesque country home on Loch Rannoch in the Highlands, where the Carnegies were to spend the summer while Cluny was being refurbished. That same day Frick met with the Amalgamated's national president, William Weihe, and a committee of some twenty-five Homestead men led by Hugh O'Donnell. Frick had promised and Carnegie expected that the two sides would no longer confer, but again demonstrating uncertainty, Frick had decided to meet with the enemy. For his part, Frick conceded $1 in per ton wages for billets, offering $23 as a minimum versus $22, but the Amalgamated wouldn't accept anything less than $24, leaving Frick to advise Carnegie, "We are now preparing for a struggle."[15] Those preparations included Frick hiring a force of three hundred Pinkertons—considered capital's assassins—to protect the company's property.[16] He instructed the Pinkertons to be prepared, equipped, and assembled on July 5 in Pittsburgh, from where they would boat to the Homestead works.

The union also prepared for a fight and created an Advisory Committee of forty men to direct their battle. The committee set up headquarters in a three-story brick building in Homestead proper, a conspicuous American flag hanging over the dirt street, and two men assumed prominent roles: Hugh O'Donnell, who was elected chairman of the committee, and Homestead mayor John McLuckie. A skilled worker making $144 per month, O'Donnell had seen his share of death in the mill and was ready to make a stand against the greedy capitalists. He had short, cropped hair combed straight back and a walrus mustache, the style of the day; he was a thin, hollow-cheeked, plain-looking fellow, except for his large, round eyes, which were all the more intense as they debated the situation. McLuckie, also a skilled worker, was more hot-blooded than O'Donnell, although one wouldn't know it by looking at him. He had slicked dark hair, parted just left of center, a soft face with a curtailed handlebar mustache, and oval glasses that gave him a studious air.

After the Advisory Committee was created, the union men hung Frick and Potter in effigy, amid much jeering as a mob psychology began to take hold. The company retaliated by shutting down the works on June 28, two days before the contract expired. In light of Frick's blockade fence, and the hiring of Pinkertons, the union men realized it was 1889 all over again—war—inducing O'Donnell and McLuckie to issue a brazen declaration: "The committee has, after mature deliberation, decided to organize their forces on a truly military basis." The document all but guaranteed bloodshed. The four thousand men were divided into three divisions, or watches, to guard against strikebreakers. They posted sentries at all mill entrances, set up a spy network extending to Pittsburgh, and chartered a steamboat to patrol the Monongahela. "In addition to all this, there will be held in reserve a force of 800 Slavs and Hungarians," the committee declared. "The brigade of foreigners will be under the command of two Hungarians and two interpreters."[17] Considering the ill-feelings between the skilled and unskilled workers, between the Anglo-Saxons and the Huns, it was a point of interest that the unskilled workers were just as eager to join the imminent fight. That the entire workforce had united was unexpected; Carnegie and Frick had hoped the war would be limited to the union men.

As O'Donnell and the union men anticipated, the company was advertising in newspapers in Boston, St. Louis, and Philadelphia, among other cities, for strikebreakers. If Carnegie didn't already know about it, news of the labor recruiting must have reached him—the man who six years earlier had pledged to take no man's job—for he had good friends in New York, Philadelphia, and Pittsburgh to pass along information. Now acting decisively, on July 4, Frick, who wanted to restart the works as soon as possible, officially requested the Allegheny County sheriff to protect the property. Expecting the sheriff to prove himself useless (which he did), Frick also moved ahead with bringing in the Pinkerton men, on the same day reporting to Carnegie: "We expect to land our guards or watchmen in our property at Homestead without much trouble, and this once accomplished we are, we think, in good position. . . . We shall, of course, keep within the law, and do nothing that is not entirely legal."[18] They were not Pinkerton detectives, not mercenaries, not assassins to Frick, at least not when writing to Carnegie; they were guards or watchmen, a term all company officials were careful to use again and again. On this Independence Day, did Carnegie remotely recall his November 12, 1855, letter to Dod, in which he hoped to never be found upholding oppression in any form? The building tension within the borough of Homestead was obvious as groups of men and women huddled on street corners to gossip, to speculate what the next day would bring.

A grinning Carnegie, his white beard trimmed and decked out in a tailored black dress coat, a white waistcoat, and black, straight trousers, with patent leather button boots on his feet and a silk top hat perched on his head, was looking quite regal when he presented the library to Aberdeen and received the city's Freedom, akin to the American tradition of receiving the key to the city, on July 5. Louise stood next to him proudly, she, too, in a black tailored jacket and a waistcoat, but with a bustle-supported skirt and a hat trimmed with ribbons and feathers. About the time the Carnegies were preparing for a second day of festivities on July 6, the three hundred Pinkerton guards, joined by Superintendent Potter and a deputy sheriff named Gray, boarded two cus-tomized barges at Bellevue, Pennsylvania, about five miles down the Ohio River from Pittsburgh.[19] Their supplies included enough food to last several weeks and boxes of firearms—300 pistols and 250 rifles—which were not to be opened until the men were on mill grounds. The barges were to be pulled to Pittsburgh and then up the Monongahela to Homestead, where the guards would disembark and secure the steelworks.

Closely monitoring the activity, a spy cabled the union's Homestead head-quarters that the barges were on the move. At about 4 A.M., the flotilla was sighted about a mile below the mill. The Homestead men's steamboat blasted a warning whistle and someone launched fireworks; flashing across the water and glowing in the river mist, hissing and exploding in the air, they made for a surreal scene. A crowd rushed to the river's edge to greet the steamboat and the two enclosed barges, which looked much like the low-profile packet boat Carnegie had taken on the Erie Canal exactly forty-four years earlier; there was no deck and but a few portholes, allowing only a handful of Pinkertons to see what was happening. They witnessed ruddy-faced workmen in slouch hats or bowlers, frayed colored shirts and trousers held up with suspenders, and women in blouses and bustle-supported skirts carrying guns and babies, race along the railroad tracks that paralleled the river. Men, women, and chil-dren hurled insults and rocks at the Pinkertons, so spiffy in their banded slouch hats, white blouses, and dark blue trousers with navy stripes. Of course, O'Donnell and his lieutenants immediately lost control of the mob and gun-shots were traded as the flotilla neared the Homestead wharf.

The riverbank crowd, suddenly realizing they had to beat the boat to the dock to prevent the Pinkerton guards from taking the property, ran ahead and broke through Frick's stockade fence, which extended several feet into the water. They gathered on the bluff above the landing, a much better position than that of the Pinkerton men who were now trapped on their barges. Still, they attempted to establish a beachhead, and in the ensuing gunfight it ap-peared as though they would succeed, but the Homestead army rallied and pinned their quarry in the barges. Six Pinkerton guards were wounded and required treatment, so the tugboat, with Potter on board, left the barges for a dock downstream where the wounded could be put on a train for Pittsburgh. The cowardly Potter shouldn't have abandoned the fight; instead, he should have remained to reason with the men.

As the early morning mist burned off, the challenge the Pinkertons faced fully revealed itself: a force now five thousand strong was entrenched in Fort Frick, a massive complex of looming mill buildings and smokestacks, stark against the sky. At 8 A.M., the Pinkertons again attempted to establish a beach-head only to be repulsed, although four Homestead men were killed. The cry of revenge ran through the crowd, and, between exchanges of gunfire, the Pinkertons watched horrified as the Homestead men diligently attempted to annihilate every last one of them. Completely succumbing to their thirst for blood, the workers sent a burning raft downriver, hoping it would crash into the barges and ignite them; but the fire went out before reaching the target. Next the men sent a railroad car loaded with burning barrels of oil at the barges; it stopped short. Undeterred, they pumped oil onto the surface of the river and then attempted to light the slick encircling the barges; it was lubricant oil and would not light. An old cannon was brought up; it kept firing high because it couldn't be sighted downward any further. Dynamite, or "stuff" as the men called it, was the next weapon of choice. The feverish laborers hurled it onto the barge roofs, slowly blowing away sections, until they ran out of stuff. It was a comedy of errors, an entertaining show noir for the audience that had been arriving all morning from surrounding towns. A morbid carnival atmosphere prevailed. By late morning, two Pinkertons had been killed and they raised a white flag—it was ripped with bullets. Back at the union's headquarters, telegrams of support were coming across the lines and the Homestead men realized they were fighting a much larger battle that represented all oppressed laborers.

Frick was kept fully apprised as each hour brought another horror. Later in the day, the company issued a statement that the workers had fired at the boats for a full twenty-five minutes before the watchmen returned a single shot. There was no mention by the company that those watchmen were Pinkerton guards. Meanwhile, the Allegheny County sheriff sent a number of urgent cables requesting help from the governor, who wired back that local authorities must exhaust all measures at their disposal, including deputizing enough citizens to handle the situation. No one was interested in tangling with the Homestead army, however.[20]

Later in the day, O'Donnell regained some control of the men and at 5 P.M. accepted the Pinkertons' surrender. As the Homestead union men herded the Pinkertons, their uniforms disheveled and sweat-stained, through the mill, groups of workers, women, and children rushed forward to throw more insults and rocks, and the Pinkertons suddenly found themselves running a six-hundred-yard gauntlet. Cries went up to "kill the murderers" and the most upright citizens were said to have become a bloodthirsty pack of wolves, clubbing and stabbing the would-be guards—one of whom was clubbed to death. The Opera House proved the best temporary jail; the Pinkertons were held there until 12:30 A.M., when a transport train arrived. O'Donnell expected the sheriff to serve the Pinkerton men with arrest warrants for murder, but none were issued.

After surrendering, the Pinkerton guards were forced to
run a six-hundred-yard gauntlet, during which they were
attacked by men, women, and children.

✳　✳　✳

After a restful night in the Haddo House hotel in Aberdeen, Carnegie could
not comprehend what he awoke to. Newspaper headlines blared A DAY OF
RIOTING: BLOODY WORK AT HOMESTEAD: TWENTY KILLED IN A BATTLE BETWEEN
STRIKERS AND PINKERTON MEN. It was an international event, covered as diligently by the British press as by the American. Frantic, he wired Frick that he
was willing to take the first steamer home. An excitable Scotsman was the last
extra burden Frick wanted; his wife had just given birth to a son, Henry Clay
Jr., prematurely, and the lives of both mother and child were in doubt. Frick
cabled that the company was standing firm and Carnegie should remain in
Scotland. If he returned, it would be seen as a sign of weakness, and now
Frick, fearing for his wife and son and under duress, was determined to crush
the union once and for all. Just before starting for Rannoch Lodge, Carnegie
wired Frick: "All anxiety gone since you stand firm. Never employ one of

these rioters. Let grass grow over works. Must not fail now."[21] His position was clear and yet it wasn't: he didn't want to employ any of the rioters, which could include every Homestead man; but he also didn't want to bring in strikebreakers, preferring to let the works stand idle. The lack of definitive guidance left Frick to pursue his own means.

While Carnegie claimed all anxiety was gone, when an enterprising reporter tracked him down at Rannoch Lodge on July 8 and peppered him with questions, Carnegie became so agitated that Louise thought he was going to have a seizure and was forced to lead him away. The next day, a *New York Herald* reporter tried his luck. Carnegie, having realized he was facing a public relations disaster, made a statement in which he expressed some remorse, heartfelt or otherwise: "The strike is most deplorable, and the news of the disaster, which reached me at Aberdeen, grieved me more than I can tell you. It came on me like a thunderbolt in a clear sky. I must positively decline to enter into any discussion as to the merits or demerits of the case. All I will say is that the strike did not take place in the old Carnegie works, but the difficulty has been entirely in the recently acquired works."[22] The "recently acquired works," however, had been under the Carnegie umbrella since 1883; and the strike was hardly an unexpected thunderbolt, considering Frick and he had been plotting strategy since the beginning of the year. The number of fatalities was the unfortunate surprise. One or two would have passed without notice as they had at Edgar Thomson during the Hungarian rampage, but as many as twenty dead? It was unthinkable.

On both sides of the Atlantic, radical proletarian papers were quick to fiercely condemn Carnegie, as did some of the mainstream publications. On the British side, the *London Financial Observer* opined: "Here we have this Scotch-Yankee plutocrat meandering through Scotland in a four-in-hand, opening public libraries and receiving the freedom of cities, while the wretched workmen who sweat themselves in order to supply him with the ways and means for this self-glorification are starving in Pittsburgh."[23] And the ultraradical *Star* offered: "Mr. Carnegie, who is on this side of the water now, cannot of course be held directly responsible for yesterday's tragedy; but his harsh treatment of his men makes him indirectly responsible, and any way it is a little odd that this enunciator of beautiful sentiments about the blessing of giving, and the rest of it, should be unable to carry on his business without such scenes as reported from Pittsburgh this morning." *Blackwood's Magazine*, a British periodical, didn't find the violence surprising and blamed it on "the evil seed which has been so assiduously sown by Socialist agitators."[24] The magazine did not condemn Carnegie, considering him nothing more than a typical American employer.

On the American side, the *St. Louis Post Dispatch* cut a deep wound in Carnegie's pride with an editorial that was widely reprinted:

> Three months ago Andrew Carnegie was a man to be envied. Today he is an object of mingled pity and contempt. In the estimation of nine-tenths of the thinking people on both sides of the ocean he had not only given the lie to

all his antecedents, but confessed himself a moral coward. One would naturally suppose that if he had a grain of consistency, not to say decency, in his
composition, he would favor rather than oppose the organization of trades-
unions among his own working people at Homestead. One would naturally
suppose that if he had a grain of manhood, not to say courage, in his composition, he would at least have been willing to face the consequences of
his inconsistency. But what does Carnegie do? Runs off to Scotland out of
harm's way to await the issue of the battle he was too pusillanimous to share.
. . . America can well spare Mr. Carnegie. Ten thousand "Carnegie Public
Libraries" would not compensate the country for the direct and indirect evils
resulting from the Homestead lockout. Say what you will of Frick, he is a
brave man. Say what you will of Carnegie, he is a coward. And gods and
men hate cowards.[25]

There was widespread belief that a cowardly Carnegie had purposefully
gone into hiding in Scotland, but that assessment was not quite fair. The
plans had been made long ago. Frick knew where he was, and the British
press tracked his movements. In other reactions, the *Forum*, in which Carnegie had published his enlightened labor essays, also came out hard against
him, one of its authors decrying the work in the mills as tantamount to slavery; the *Pittsburgh Leader* kindly declared Carnegie's progressive labor ideas
expressed in 1886 to be as "extinct as a dodo"; and a handful of prominent
men called him the arch snake of his age, demanding he be extradited for
murder.[26]

As details came out in the press, Carnegie began to have his doubts about
how Frick had handled the conflict, especially in hiring Pinkerton. The question observers would have to eventually answer about both Frick and Carnegie: was the tragedy a result of an error in judgment or malicious intent? One
of Carnegie's biggest concerns was who was in the legal right. If the Homestead men fired first, the Pinkertons, and thus Carnegie Steel, could claim
self-defense and Carnegie could justify everything. But if a Pinkerton man
shot first, then Carnegie Steel and Carnegie himself could easily be censured.
That was how Carnegie's mind worked: because he always considered himself
highly evolved (as proven by his material progress) and on the moral high
ground, he could justify any of his actions as being right as long as no law had
been broken. Anxious to begin that process of justification, he cabled Frick,
questioning who had shot first—a debate also carried by the newspapers.

"There is no question but that the firing was begun by the strikers," Frick
responded on July 11. "All that I have to regret is that our guards did not land,
and, between ourselves, think that Potter was to blame. He did not show the
nerve I expected he would. He was most anxious to accompany the guards to
Homestead, but failed at the critical time."[27] Frick was a little too quick to
drop the gunplay issue and shift the blame to Potter. Carnegie was not so
convinced Frick's account was truthful. Some of the newspapers were offering
pretty clear details as to who shot first and at whom. "The first shot of the
engagement came from the barge," the *New York Daily Tribune* reported on

July 7. "It was aimed at a big Hungarian who stood at water's edge. The ball went wide of the human target, but it was the signal to the Pinkerton men to begin, and for a full ten minutes they continued to fire." Before the congressional investigating committee that descended on Homestead, Deputy Sheriff Gray initially testified the first shot came from the shore, but under cross-examination he admitted shots were fired from the barges before a continuous volley from the shore. Testimony continued to differ, but one fact was certain: it was a Homestead man who was hit first.

Sensing Carnegie's doubts as to the truth, Frick sent him a second letter on July 11, assuring him that once fully acquainted with the facts "you will be satisfied with every action taken in this lamentable matter. The best evidence of the character of the men employed at Homestead is shown by the manner in which they treated the watchmen after they had surrendered, and also, it would not have mattered who the men were that they were in those boats, their treatment would have been just the same. They did not know they were obtained through Pinkerton at the time they fired on them."[28] Again he deflected questions about the facts and pointed Carnegie to how the Homestead men treated the Pinkertons, suggesting the strikers were morally inferior and deserved no due consideration. To believe that the strikers, with their spy network, had no idea Pinkertons were in the barges, was nonsense; after all, a primary reason the Hungarians and the Slavs were so eager to join the Anglo-Saxons was to do battle with the hated Pinkerton men who had gunned down scores of their countrymen over the years. Again, both Carnegie and Frick were desperate to justify the killings.

A quiet tension settled over Homestead during the hot week following the battle, and the burning question was, what would Carnegie Steel do next? To begin, Frick and the sheriff finally convinced the governor to send the state militia to retake the works. On July 11, Homestead knew the troops were on the way, but as to when and where they would arrive was a highly guarded secret. Few slept easily that night. "Morning broke gray and somber," the *Harper's Weekly* correspondent wrote, "and still there was no news. A great red sun rising over the eastern hills was partially concealed by the mist that hung over the limpid waters of the Monongahela."[29] Within a few hours, the rhythmic rumbling of a train could be heard as eight thousand members of the militia arrived in ninety-five cars. The soldiers were impressive in their blue uniforms, guns and knapsacks slung over their shoulders, bayonets flashing, polished boots reflecting the sun as they marched in time, followed by horse-drawn artillery. McLuckie strode down to the tracks to meet them, but he was brushed aside. The townspeople meekly watched as the soldiers pitched their white tents on the side of a black hill overlooking the area and strategically positioned their cannons.

The Amalgamated serenely surrendered the town and works, but the union was resolute in forcing a prolonged strike. Rumors of sympathy strikes soon circulated. Workers at the Union Iron Mills, Duquesne, and Beaver Falls struck for various lengths of time, but not at Edgar Thomson, where Schwab was in complete control. Throughout, Frick was unbreakable. With plenty of scabs applying for work, he pushed ahead with plans to reopen Homestead as soon as possible. He also invited all old employees to reapply for their positions, giving them until 6 P.M. on July 21, or they would be replaced. According to Carnegie and Frick's logic, if the men didn't reapply, then those hired in their place were not scabs. It was a strong-arm tactic with mixed results: by July 17, only 487 men had returned.

Amazingly, Carnegie managed to maintain public silence and supported Frick, but what he said behind Frick's back was another matter. On July 17, dressed in tweeds after some early morning angling, Carnegie sat down to write Dod a letter. It was a tired, resigned letter in which he criticized Frick's management of the tragedy for the first time. "Matters at home *bad*—such a fiasco trying to send guards by Boat and then leaving space between River & fences for the men to get opposite landing and fire—still we must keep quiet & do all we can to support Frick & those at Seat of War." It wasn't the fence that was the issue; it was the space allowing the Homestead men a strategic position. It was an error for which Frick was to blame, and a rift would open between him and Carnegie.

In this letter, Carnegie also exposed one of his own prominent weaknesses: his naiveté concerning labor's conditions. "Men at Upper and Lower Mills and Beaver struck—," he wrote. "This was uncalled for they have no grievance but we must not bother with them just now—Concentrate everything on Homestead. Win there—then talk to these foolish men."[30] With more than an ocean between them, Carnegie was demonstrating his disconnect from the workingman's feelings, otherwise he wouldn't have condescendingly dismissed the sympathy strikes as "uncalled for" and the men as "foolish." The laborer, from his degraded perspective, was fighting for his life.

Just ten days after the violence, with men trickling back to the works and strikebreakers being shipped in, O'Donnell sensed his position beginning to weaken and decided to contact Carnegie. If he could sound out Andy, get a feel for how resolute the capitalist was in no longer dealing with the Amalgamated, then O'Donnell would be able to decide how best to save the union at Homestead. Leaders at the American Federation of Labor suggested he use Whitelaw Reid, the publisher of the *New York Tribune*, a Republican mouthpiece, and the Republican candidate for vice president on the ticket with Harrison, as a go-between. The Republicans had good reason to want the strike settled. Because Carnegie was a prominent Republican and beneficiary of the McKinley Tariff, the party leaders realized no laborer would vote Republican come election day unless there was an equitable end to the strike. Even before the violence, Republican leaders had urged Carnegie not to reduce wages in an election year, but such pressuring only inflamed his independent spirit.

Unbeknownst to his fellow committee members, O'Donnell wrote to Reid, stating the union's position. On behalf of the 12,000 inhabitants of Homestead, he urged Reid to convince Carnegie to simply "recognize the Amalgamated Association," for he had "no hesitation in saying that, when that is done, the end of the strike is at hand." All other demands would be dropped.[31] All he wanted was recognition of the union, recognition that was significant to only 800 of the 3,800 Homestead workers. Reid, who wanted votes from the Amalgamated's 25,000-strong membership and didn't care how the strike was settled as long as the union was happy, took up O'Donnell's cause and assigned his campaign manager, John E. Milholland, with procuring Carnegie's address. When Milholland contacted Frick for the information, the chairman hesitated; he wanted Carnegie left out of it.

The company had no desire to settle; in fact, on July 18, murder and riot charges prepared by Philander Knox were served to the riot's leaders. First on the list was McLuckie, who was thrown in jail with bail set at $10,000. From behind bars, he defiantly declared Frick and other company officials would suffer the same fate. More than one hundred indictments were handed down, but not one went to a Slav or Hun; only the Anglo-Saxon leaders were targeted. To further tighten the noose, Frick personally spearheaded the hiring of strikebreakers. On July 23, he had a 2 P.M. appointment with a New York employment agency representative who claimed to have access to a large supply of men.

When the agent arrived early at the office on the second floor of the *Chronicle-Telegraph* building in Pittsburgh, he was told to wait. The door to Frick's office was open and he could see Frick, a brown-bearded, well-knit figure, sitting at his desk, talking business with John G. A. Leishman, the company's vice president. The agent, a thin, weepy-looking fellow in an ill-fitting, medium gray suit with thin pinstripes, subsequently barged in unannounced. As Frick rose from his chair, the intruder—really an anarchist named Alexander Berkman—lifted a cheap pistol and, concerned Frick was wearing body armor, aimed for the head. The bullet hit Frick in the neck, and he fell to the floor. Berkman stepped forward and again shot Frick, another bullet ripping into his neck. Just as Berkman raised his arm to fire a third shot, Leishman reached him and knocked the assassin's arm upward, the pistol discharging again. The two fell wrestling to the ground, Berkman crawling toward the helpless Frick. Now within reach, the anarchist pulled out a knife and stabbed Frick near the right hip and again near the left knee. By now several clerks had charged into the room and subdued Berkman. But the anarchist was not quite finished with his deed. He started working his mouth, which the men quickly pried open. Inside was a capsule containing fulminate of mercury—enough to blow Berkman's head off, but not enough to blow them all to hell.

Blood was spurting from Frick's wounds, staining his white collar a deep red, and he collapsed. When the doctor finally arrived and prepared to remove the bullets, he offered Frick anesthesia for the pain, but he refused it, bravely claiming that if he were lucid he could help the doctor locate the lodged bullets. His toughness made him a hero to many, while Berkman's attack only hurt the union's cause. As O'Donnell said, "The bullet from Berkman's pistol went straight through the heart of the Homestead strike."[32]

Once the wounds were dressed and bandaged, knowing news of the assassination attempt would spread quickly, Frick apprised Carnegie: "Was shot twice, but not dangerously. There is no necessity for you to come home. I am still in shape to fight the battle out."[33] What should have been a simple standoff, perhaps the shutting down of the works for a few months until the men came to their senses, was spinning out of control. A darkness descended on Carnegie, and his debilitated mental state was reflected in a disjointed cable to Leishman: "Early anxiety his recovery. . . . Close all works until recovery complete. We regard it is necessary something must be done to save Frick anxiety—his recovery before all—if others are willing we can close. Can you see daylight?" His overreaction of wanting to close all the works was extreme, his reasoning imbalanced almost to a point of insanity, but then Carnegie always lived on the edge.

A defiant and unrelenting warrior, Frick refused bodyguards and spent ten days in bed. Meanwhile, Reid's emissary, Milholland, had decided to travel to Pittsburgh to meet with Frick personally. The chairman was in a first-floor bedroom of the Homewood mansion, his head and neck swathed in bandages, a telephone and several secretaries by his side. Upstairs was his wife and son, Henry Clay, born prematurely the day of the Homestead battle and slowly dying. Milholland pursued his mission resolutely, relating how O'Donnell had approached Reid to seek Carnegie's help and how the situation was hurting the Republican Party's standing with the public and thus President Harrison's reelection bid. Frick said he would never deal with the Amalgamated nor settle the strike for Harrison's benefit. Now worked up into a froth, Frick burst out that O'Donnell was a "blood-thirsty villain" and a "red-handed murderer. . . . I will fight this thing to the bitter end. I will never recognize the Union, never, never!"[34] But he did disclose Carnegie's whereabouts.

Several days later, on Wednesday, August 3, Frick's son died. The funeral was held on the fourth, and Frick was back at work on Friday the fifth.

Reid finally contacted Carnegie through the U.S. consul general in London, John C. New, who personally delivered a letter written by Reid in which he stated that he had met with O'Donnell, who was appealing for Carnegie's aid on behalf of the suffering men, women, and children of Homestead. "He assures me that if your people will merely consent to reopen a conference with their representatives," Reid wrote, "thus recognizing their organization, they will waive every other thing in dispute, and submit to whatever you think it right to require, whether as to scale or wages or hours or anything else; and do all in their power to reestablish harmonious relations."[35]

As John New sat across from Carnegie, the steel master appeared quite delighted; like a whimpering dog, the union had come crawling back to its master. It was just the thing, Carnegie pronounced, and New cabled Reid: "Proposition heartily approved here. Send copy of same to Frick and have Elkins and Wanamaker see him at once. Utmost importance."[36] Stephen B. Elkins and John Wanamaker, Republican front men for the presidential election, would still have to negotiate the matter with Frick. At the same time that New sent his telegram, Carnegie, using code, cabled Frick about the meeting. "The proposition is worthy of consideration," he concluded, but he made it clear it was Frick's decision.[37] Evidently, Carnegie was no longer interested in a prolonged struggle and was willing to settle the strike; pressure from the newspapers and now the Republican Party was getting to him. He remained careful to defer to Frick, however.

A week later, William T. Stead, editor of the *Review of Reviews*, tracked down his friend Carnegie in hopes of gleaning the inside story, even enclosing a provocative article with his letter to incite a reaction. Carnegie refused to elaborate on the tragedy, however; instead, he regurgitated what was already known and then began to revise reality: "I hear of events only two days after they take place. It is three years since I retired from the active management, and I have spent the last six months writing a book upon the burning "Questions of Today"—Capital and Labor, Shorter Hours of Labor, Strikes, Cooperation, etc., etc." He then placed the blame squarely on the Homestead men for not accepting the new wage scale.[38] While Carnegie didn't criticize Frick's actions, he did attempt to distance himself from the tragedy by claiming to have been retired from active business for three years. The statement was a lie; the continuous exchange of Carnegie-Frick telegrams leading up to the strike was proof. For Carnegie to suggest he was receiving information too late to act upon was another lie; despite the time difference between the United States and Britain, he was well informed. The revisionism and lies would continue in the months and years ahead.

As September came to a close and there was still no major break in the strike, Carnegie turned his ire on John Potter's management skills. "I am expecting daily to hear that a break has occurred," he wrote Frick. "Believe me, he is a poor manager who has not sufficient influence over part of his men to draw them to him."[39] (Schwab and some of the other men must have wondered if the tragedy would still have occurred if Captain Jones was alive and Schwab superintendent at Homestead.) The beleaguered Potter was a shared source of contempt that brought Carnegie and Frick together; however, while showing public solidarity, they had their differences as the rift widened. Frick wished

Carnegie gave him stronger support publicly, and he had wanted Carnegie to tell Reid in definitive terms they would never again deal with Amalgamated, which Carnegie failed to do or simply refused to do.[40] From Carnegie's viewpoint, he thought all the violence could have been avoided if they had just let grass grow over the works. No doubt the words of Senator William C. Oates, who chaired the congressional investigating committee on the strike, echoed in his own mind: "They did not violate any law of Pennsylvania; but they knew that the hostility to the Pinkerton men upon the part of all labor organizations was calculated to produce a breach of the peace."[41]

To ratchet up the pressure on the Amalgamated, in early October the company's lawyer, Philander Knox, consulted with Chief Justice Edward Paxson of the Pennsylvania Supreme Court and decided it was possible to bring charges of treason against members of the union's Advisory Committee. In an unprecedented move, Paxson himself brought the charges, the first time such charges had been brought against those allegedly inciting labor violence — thus inviting heated criticism from legal scholars and suggesting Carnegie had bought the judiciary.[42] The charges certainly did demoralize the steelworkers as they realized, more so than ever, the officials of the Carnegie Steel Company effectively controlled Pennsylvania's political and legal systems. But the company did not necessarily control the juries that would be asked to convict these men — their only hope. There was also a glimmer of hope for the Homestead men on October 11, when McLuckie's pledge to have his day in court with Frick moved one step forward after a grand jury indicted Frick, Francis T. F. Lovejoy, and other company officers on murder and conspiracy charges.[43] Carnegie was not among those named.

On October 13, Carnegie arrived in London and made a statement to the Associated Press, which was summarized in the *New York Daily Tribune*: "He informed the Associated Press representative that he had been busily engaged all during the spring and summer in preparing a new book treating of the industrial problems of the day." It was a repeat of what he had told Stead. The newspaper also reported that Carnegie stated "he had not heard of the outbreak at Homestead until two days after it occurred, and then meagerly. Since those deplorable occurrences, which had burst upon him like a thunderbolt from a clear sky, he had been unable to work much. They had such a depressing effect upon him that he had perforce to lay his book aside and resort to the lochs and moors, fishing daily from morning to night. . . . For all the deplorable incidents of the Homestead strike his chief regret was that so many of the old men had allowed their places to be filled." It was difficult to pity the fisherman, who was diligently refining his story so as to appear uninvolved and uninformed. And the old men had not simply allowed their places to be filled, but it was so easy for Carnegie to shift the blame to them. Carnegie was *never* at fault; still, he decided it was best not to return to the United States that fall. He wrote a New York friend that he was extending his overseas stay and proceeded to the Mediterranean.[44] (The book Carnegie was working on, incidentally, didn't materialize until 1908, under the title *Problems of To-Day*.)

THE CARNEGIE STEEL COMPANY, LIMITED.

I, ..., employed in the works of THE CARNEGIE STEEL COMPANY, LIMITED, at Munhall, Pa., prior to July 1st, 1892, as ....in the..mill, do hereby apply for re-instatement in the position held by me.

My age is..............years,..................married, have................children.

I was not present on the grounds of The Carnegie Steel Company, Limited, in Mifflin Township on July 6th, 1892, at any time, nor did I take any part in any of the rioting or disturbances occuring in the Borough of Homestead or in Mifflin Township from July 1st, 1892, to the present time, nor do I know of my own personal knowledge of any one who did take part therein.

On July 6th, 1892, I spent the day as follows:

....

....

....

....

....

....

....

....

Sworn to and subscribed before me this..........................day of

....1892.

_____
Notary Public.

The returning strikers were forced to sign both a pledge of allegiance to Carnegie Steel and an affidavit declaring they had not participated in the violence. (Courtesy of the Historical Society of Western Pennsylvania)

*   *   *

In mid-October, Schwab was transferred to Homestead, per Carnegie's rec-ommendation, and Potter was made superintendent of general engineering for all operations, a job that removed him from the spotlight. Schwab worked night and day to endear himself to the men on both turns; nevertheless, to keep attuned to rumblings among them, he organized a spy network. "If you want to talk in Homestead, you must talk to yourself," became the maxim for the rightly paranoid at that plant.

Not until four months after the bloody fight, on November 17, did the workers return en masse and the Amalgamated then call it quits at Home-stead. Those returning were emasculated, forced to sign a pledge of loyalty and a statement declaring that the applicant had not been on company grounds, had not participated in the rioting, and did not know anyone who did. "Our victory is now complete and most gratifying," Frick wrote in a cel-ebratory note to Carnegie, who crowed from Italy, "Life worth living again— Cables received—first happy morning since July."[45] Life may have been worth living again, but after reflecting on the entire experience, Carnegie realized life would never be the same. Writing Frick from Rome shortly thereafter, he was quite subdued: "Think I'm about ten years older than when with you last. Europe has rung with Homestead, Homestead, until we are sick of the name, but it is all over now."[46] There was no gloating.

The Homestead strike was called the most violent in history, but within the context of the times it was not. Yes, thirteen men had died and more than a hundred were wounded, but dozens died as a result of labor strife every year. And what about the 1877 Pennsylvania Railroad strike, in which at least forty were killed? Expelling the union, forcing the men to sign individual con-tracts, using strikebreakers, and hiring the Pinkertons to protect property were nothing new. The difference at Homestead was that it was a Carnegie strike. If Carnegie had kept his mouth shut in 1886, as Dod had warned him he should, and hadn't written his gospel on benefaction in 1889, the extreme negative reaction would never have occurred. All too late, Carnegie perceived the cost of the violent strike and that Homestead would suffer for years.[47] Even Frick was forced to admit to him, "The cost of the strike was, as you say, simply awful." But Frick justified it by saying that "we had to teach our employees a lesson and we have taught them one they will never forget."[48] And it did cost Homestead for years—not in profits, but in destroyed lives. By December, the destitution in Homestead was so bad that the press started a relief fund.[49]

In fact, it was the preexisting destitution that inspired the Slavs, Huns, and other unskilled workers to join forces with the discriminatory Amalga-mated men, and transformed upright citizens into wild dogs thirsting for blood. The town was bleak; the buildings were all framed, dirt-gray structures; there were no paved roads and no sewage system; the inhabitants used outdoor privies just as Carnegie had in Dunfermline fifty years before; alleyways were filled with debris, and garbage blew aimlessly between the buildings; a row of saloons graced Eighth Avenue, and fifty-cent prostitution houses abounded; scruffy children played marbles, women gossiped, and old men smoked pipes and played cards. "Everywhere the yellow mud of streets lay kneaded into sticky masses," wrote journalist Hamlin Garland, "through which groups of pale, lean men slouched in faded garments, grimy with the soot and dirt of the mills. The town was as squalid as could well be imagined, and the people were mainly aged and sullen type to be found everywhere where labor passes into the brutalizing stage of severity."[50]

The men continued to work twelve-hour days, every day but Christmas and July Fourth, with wages ranging from fourteen cents an hour for a common laborer to $280 a month for the most highly skilled, but most skilled workers received no more than $50 a month.[51] The sharp contrast between the laborer and the capitalist's living conditions prompted a populist campaigner in Kansas, Mary Elizabeth Lease, to declare, "You may call me an anarchist, a socialist or a communist, I care not, but I hold to the theory that if one man has not enough to eat three meals a day and another man has $25,000,000, that last man has something that belongs to the first."[52] It was about the fair distribution of wealth argument raised by William Jewett Tucker in criticizing Carnegie's "Gospel of Wealth."

Not just the Homestead laborers were pushed hard; the office clerks were, too. "My eyes bothered me," a clerk named Suter recalled. "At times they dazzled and would not focus probably from constant night work and long hours." He once lost the power of speech and became so fearful for his health he actually transferred to the open-hearth department for arduous outdoor work.[53] Highly prized chemists also suffered, including S. A. Ford, who wrote Carnegie, "I am still comparatively a young man and able to do a deal of work yet I know that my long close confinement in the laboratory is naturally telling upon my health and I wish to make some provision for—such a time—should it come to me—when living constantly amongst the chemical fumes would be no longer possible for me. . . . I ask therefore whether it is possible for me to obtain $1,000 worth of stock in any one of your companies."[54] Besides the fact that Ford was suffering physically from his work, it was a sad commentary that a skilled chemist could save but $1,000 over thirteen years. And if that's all he could save, what of the common laborers?

It was a tolling bell to repeat again and again: the men were paid a pittance for dangerous work. It was estimated that in 1891 there were about three hundred fatalities in all Carnegie-owned and other Pittsburgh area mills.[55] So in July 1892, the Homestead men were brought together by a common cause—to fight capital's oppression and for a larger share of the wealth. As they walked through Homestead, the tenements, the stink, while the Pittsburgh papers trumpeted the privileged lives of Carnegie and Frick, they realized they deserved more. The men had been bent to a breaking point, but they didn't break; they snapped back in a violent reaction.

O'Donnell, McLuckie, and the others who suffered could take some solace in knowing they weren't the only losers: Republican candidate Harrison was crushed on election day. It had been an uphill climb for the president before Homestead. Blaine had jumped ship on June 4, three days before the Republican Convention; and that summer, Quay, who had been given the cold shoulder by Harrison and Wanamaker, supported Blaine for the presidential nomination, fracturing the party. Complicating matters, Harrison's wife had tuberculosis and died on October 25. The McKinley Tariff, considered "the culminating atrocity of class legislation,"[56] was another handicap and mercilessly attacked by democrats. Despite these extenuating circumstances, prominent republicans blamed Carnegie, Frick, and the strike for their loss.[57]

Initially unperturbed by Harrison's loss, Carnegie wrote Frick from Italy: "Cleveland! Landslide! Well we have nothing to fear and perhaps it is best. People will now think the Protected Manfrs. will be attended to and quit agitating. Cleveland is a pretty good fellow. Off for Venice tomorrow." But from Venice he expressed some regret: "I fear that Homestead did much to elect Cleveland—very sorry—but no use getting scared."[58] Carnegie's trepidation was well founded as a backlash against him gathered strength. In addition to the Republican censure, in Britain it was argued he should be ejected from the National Liberal Club; the Labour Representative League and London Trade Council advised rejecting any monetary gifts offered by Carnegie; the Glasgow Trades Council compared him to Judas Iscariot; and a member of Parliament running for reelection took the $500 donated to him by Carnegie and sent it to the Homestead Relief Fund. Such harsh reactions were isolated, however, and he was hardly the leper he was made out to be by historians.

Letters of support came from many quarters throughout and after the strike, and friends were quick to absolve Carnegie of any responsibility. In September, the Scottish Home Rule Association invited Carnegie to a private conference, and Lord Rosebery was generous with his sympathy: "I know nothing of the rights and wrongs of the Homestead case, but I cannot believe that you would ever be illiberal or unjust. And even had you been taken with a sudden fit of those complaints all the more necessity for your friends to stand by you."[59] John Morley, silent during the strike, wrote Carnegie the next spring: "We've had a good deal of tribulation during the last twelvemonth both you and I. . . . As I told you, the world is often harsh to its benefactors. But this philosophic truth does not make me the less angry at the odious line taken about you by English newspapers and Scotch. However, it is past, and by now pretty well out of your memory, I'll be bound."[60] Morley was wrong; Homestead would haunt Carnegie until his death. Uncle Lauder, not exactly sounding like a Dunfermline Chartist, wrote, "I am glad all your troubles are now over at Pittsburgh and will remain so for a long time. This working man question is the question of the day. The more you give them, the more they will take. I see this every day in little things as well as big."[61] Support from Uncle Lauder was very important to Carnegie, who claimed everything he accomplished was to please either his mother or his uncle.

When Carnegie finally returned to New York in January 1893, he was not treated like a leper, either. Abram S. Hewitt, mayor of New York and some-time Carnegie critic, invited the beleaguered steel master to his country home in Ringwood, New Jersey, where he had a good stable and excellent fishing.[62] The editor of *Engineering Magazine* wrote Carnegie to say he thought that "Mr. H. C. Frick . . . has done more than any many man of his generation to re-establish the fundamental principles of property rights."[63] And Thomas Mellon voiced the business community's support; "It was and is the opinion generally expressed by manufacturers and other employers of labor here that the stand taken by your firm was a necessity, forced upon it, and what all will be compelled to take sooner or later. . . . There has been so far no fair statement of the facts and merits of the controversy."[64] Like his peers, Mellon felt the press corrupted public sentiment and promoted anarchy, catering to the worst elements to gain readers and advertising.

Cities even wanted to be named after him. Carnegie was pleasantly surprised when in February 1893 he received a letter from Philander Knox, stating the boroughs of Mansfield and Chartiers, suburbs of Pittsburgh, wanted to merge and rename the new town Carnegie.[65] He approved and even personally wrote the fourth assistant postmaster general to expedite the change—another piece of evidence demonstrating Carnegie did indeed relish his name on a monument, a library, and even a whole town. As he told the burgess of Chartiers, life wouldn't be worth living if people in and around Pittsburgh didn't reciprocate the affection he had for them! On March 1, 1894, the governor of Pennsylvania officially recognized the borough of Carnegie.[66]

Of all the letters and friendly support, Carnegie most appreciated a letter from William Gladstone. When the eighty-two-year-old became prime minister for a fourth time and formed his cabinet in August 1892, Carnegie congratulated him, dubbing him William the Fourth. Responding in September, Gladstone thanked him and offered his sympathy:

> I wish to do the little, the very little, that is in my power, which is simply to say how sure I am that no one who knows you will be prompted by the unfortunate occurrences across the water (of which manifestly we cannot know the exact merits) to qualify in the slightest degree either his confidence in your generous views of his admiration of the good and great work you have already done.
>
> Wealth is at present like a monster threatening to swallow up the moral life of man; you by precept and by example have been teaching him to disgorge. I for one thank you.[67]

The venerable prime minister touched on three themes that marked the letters of support: authors tended to point out they did not know the merits of the case, therefore not completely absolving Carnegie; the press was criticized and held partly responsible for inciting the violence; and Carnegie's philanthropic ventures were noted to strike a positive chord amid the dark times.

Within days of receiving Gladstone's supportive letter, a grateful Carnegie earnestly wrote back as though at confession, although he continued to revise his story:

> This is the trial of my life (death's hand excepted). Such a foolish step—contrary to my ideas, repugnant to every feeling of my nature. Our firm offered all it could offer, even generous terms. Our other men had gratefully accepted them. They went as far as I could have wished, but the false step was made in trying to run the Homestead Works with new men.
>
> It is a test to which workingmen should not be subjected. It is expecting too much of poor men to stand by and see their work taken by others. *Their daily bread.* . . . Feelings had been aroused, the Sheriff's aid had been called in and his Deputies hooted. Then other guards sent for *with Sheriff's approval*. These were attacked and then the military.
>
> All this time I heard nothing until days had elapsed and, as the way *easiest to peace*, going on was then best—returning being impossible, for the State of Pennsylvania could not retire troops until they had established and vindicated *Law*. The pain I suffer increases daily. The Works are not worth one drop of human blood. I wish they had sunk.
>
> I write this to you freely; to no one else have I written so. I must be silent and suffer but after a time I hope to be able to do something to restore good feeling between my young and rather too rash partner and them over at Homestead. . . . Look at me!—hitherto Master, now condemned to inaction yet knowing the right, and anxious to carry it. . . . I have one comfort, self-approval & a second—the support of a wife who is as strong & as wise as she is gentle & devoted—so I shall sail on & let the tempest howl.[68]

The howling tempest alluded to Shakespeare's *King Lear*. The mad King Lear rages, "Thou think'st 'tis much that this contentious storm/Invades us to the skin. . . . Pour on; I will endure."[69] In *King Lear*, Shakespeare played with several themes, including, in part: the universe is indifferent; man is but an animal; life is brutal and meaningless; the contrasting of an unappreciated child and the unwanted aging parent; and, of course, the perilous nature of power. Certainly, Carnegie must have felt as though he was fighting an indifferent storm, fraught with brutality. But more important, he was like King Lear, a ruler who "hath ever but slenderly known himself,"[70] in that Carnegie deluded himself. In 1886, Carnegie had written, "It is the chairman, situated hundreds of miles away from his men, who only pays a flying visit to the works and perhaps finds time to walk through the mill or mine once or twice a year, that is chiefly responsible for the disputes which break out at intervals." What he now failed to recognize was that he had become just such a chairman. He was also deluding himself as to his role in the Homestead tragedy. He claimed he had been retired for several years, but in truth he and Frick were the masterminds behind the campaign to expel the union; he believed he was receiving Homestead information too late to act upon it, but in fact he was in almost continuous contact with Frick via cable; and he believed he did not know Frick was planning to hire strikebreakers, but considering that Carnegie Steel agents were out recruiting men before the violence, word must have reached Carnegie, especially since the agents were recruiting north, south, east, and west. He was starting to believe his version of the events.

Carnegie had lost a realistic perspective on power, as had King Lear. By handing Frick the chairmanship and abdicating the throne by taking extensive European sojourns, but keeping the title of king, Carnegie was setting himself up for betrayal. Frick was the unappreciated child with restive ambitions, and Carnegie the unwanted parent whom Frick wanted out of the way and kept quiet. King Lear proclaimed, "I am a man/More sinn'd against than sinning," but he brought it upon himself by failing to maintain his full authority; so had Carnegie.[71] The abuse of power and the resulting unnecessary deaths at Homestead made for a gripping Shakespearean tragedy.

On returning from Europe in January 1893, Carnegie gathered himself and continued on to Pittsburgh. It was time to start healing the wounds and reconcile himself with the tragedy. On the train to Pittsburgh, he edited and refined a speech to deliver at Homestead. The words were old words, old themes—there'd been no epiphany—and he didn't have the energy or the conviction to imagine a new relationship between capital and labor. He regurgitated what he had written in his 1886 labor essays; specifically, that there could be no winner in a strike or lockout. And he regurgitated his gospel in defending his wealth and asserting he would not die rich. With great conviction, he also told the workers they were the best paid in the world of steelmaking. He then extolled Frick, predicting that "no man who ever lived in Pittsburgh and managed business here will be better liked or more admired by his employees than my friend and partner Henry Clay Frick, nor do I believe any man will be more valuable for the city. . . . I hope after this statement that the public will understand that the officials of the Carnegie Steel Company, Limited, with Mr. Frick at their head, are not dependent upon me, or upon any one in any way for their positions, and that I have neither power nor disposition to interfere with them in the management of the business." Carnegie was distancing himself from Frick and the Homestead violence by claiming he had not the power to interfere. It was a lie, a repeated lie, and Frick and he knew it. The lie continued to grow.

To further purge himself of Homestead, Carnegie wrote that March to Whitelaw Reid, who had briefly played intermediary between Carnegie and O'Donnell. The themes and excuses sounded in this letter echoed those in his letters to Gladstone and Stead months earlier—yet again he was refining his story, embracing it, believing it in full, as he sought pity and to apologize. The letter opened with almost the identical line as that to Gladstone: "This has been the hardest trial I ever had to endure (save when the hand of death has come)."[72] Reid, who lost his bid for the vice presidency, never felt pity for Carnegie and never forgave him; thereafter, he used his *Tribune* to oppose him whenever possible.

Comfortably resettled in his Fifty-first Street home, Carnegie brooded over Homestead. What was done was done; now what could polish the tarnish? Although Carnegie, Rockefeller, Morgan, and other titans would never admit they used their philanthropy to improve their image, in 1893 Carnegie most certainly did, only he would take a different tactic. He knew a sudden announcement of a new initiative would have the cynics jumping down his throat; therefore, he opted for a more subdued and charitable course as he continued to cleanse himself of the Homestead sin.[73] At a notably increased rate, Carnegie gave money to strangers with hard-luck cases, passing acquaintances, old friends, and family.

He aided a mechanic's wife who was sick and overwhelmed with doctor bills; he sent $150 to a woman whose husband was out of work and had had all her furniture taken except her wedding presents; and he spent $99.80 to purchase and ship a loom to one Alice Burns.[74] He sent a check to a Mrs. Henderson whose husband, an inventor, had died, because the family couldn't live off the royalties from his inventions as he had promised.[75] When Sarah Kerr Heistand, a retired telegraph operator who remembered Carnegie when he was at Altoona, wrote to say she was raising money for a new rectory for her church, Carnegie promptly contributed.[76] The nonchurchgoer, perhaps seeking absolution, became very active in giving Farrand & Votey Pipe-Organs, at approximately $5,000 apiece, to various churches. He gave money to his friend William Clark for a soldiers' monument.[77] Carnegie sent $500 to another old friend, William Curtiss, who was unable to work after the untimely death of his daughter.[78] As for the more fortunate, he kindly invested $5,000 for his New York friend Mrs. Alexander King.[79] Carnegie's blood relatives experienced a windfall in the year after Homestead. He gave money to his cousin William Carnegie, who was out of work, and an allowance to cousin Charlotte Carnegie. For his cousin Delia Morris, he invested $6,000, promising a handsome return of 12 percent per year, to be paid semiannually.[80] Late in 1893, Carnegie donated $125,000 to a Pittsburgh relief fund managed by his friend Robert Pitcairn to aid the poor during a bitter economic downturn.[81] Carnegie reported his good deeds to John Morley, who acted like his conscience in replying, "Such handsome and humane conduct ought to wipe out every trace of the mischief of last year—mischief for which you, I verily believe, were no more responsible than I was."[82]

At the same time Carnegie was indulging in charity, he put some effort into suppressing newspapers stories about the company and himself, and hired a press clipping service to keep tabs. To curtail the bad press, he even played with the outrageous idea of paying the newspapers to not print articles, a strategy he shared with Leishman, who promised that "we have done everything possible to prevent articles in regard to our operations etc. from getting into the paper, even to the extent of telling the Superintendents to discharge any man that they found retailing our business to the newspapers. . . . We are so prominent and the newspapers here so hard up for news that it would be a very hard thing to shut them off entirely, and unless we went to the expense of paying different papers to keep us out it would not be possible, and even then I am afraid they would make a slip occasionally in order to cater to the working man's vote."[83] Control of the press was key to a totalitarian regime's success.

Carnegie was not the only one suffering a tainted legacy. The Amalgamated, which had over twenty-four thousand members in 1891, witnessed its membership drop below ten thousand within two years after Homestead, and never recovered from the blow the Carnegie Steel Company delivered with full force. O'Donnell, the deposed chairman of the Advisory Committee, who had been indicted for murder, riot, and treason, was acquitted in February 1893, as was every other Homestead man. The jury could not be bought. O'Donnell left a disgraceful legacy in the eyes of the union, however, for covertly conferring with Reid and offering to drop all demands except recognition of the union. O'Donnell went on to manage a small orchestra and later served as an editor for a weekly Chicago journal.

After McLuckie was acquitted, he made a deal with Philander Knox in which they agreed to drop all criminal charges against concerned parties.[84] The only notable victory scored by the Homestead men was in 1893 when Pennsylvania legislators passed an anti-Pinkerton law designed to prevent the deputizing of nonresidents. Part of the credit went to McLuckie, who, during the congressional hearings, charged that the Pinkerton guards were a "horde of cut-throats, thieves, and murderers . . . in the employ of unscrupulous capital for the oppression of honest labor."[85]

According to the story in Carnegie's rather suspect autobiography, McLuckie eventually fled to Mexico to escape jail. A Carnegie friend and editor of his autobiography, John C. Van Dyke, happened to be in Mexico and stumbled on a penniless McLuckie. "I do not think I told him at the time that I knew Mr. Carnegie," Van Dyke recalled in Carnegie's autobiography, "and had been with him at Cluny in Scotland shortly after the Homestead strike, nor that I knew from Mr. Carnegie the other side of the story. But McLuckie was rather careful not to blame Mr. Carnegie, saying to me several times that if 'Andy' had been there the trouble would never have risen." After returning to the United States, the story continued, Van Dyke relayed McLuckie's situation to Carnegie, who then told Van Dyke to offer the runaway any money he required but not to say who it was from.

McLuckie declined the help. The following year, Van Dyke again met the ex-Homesteader, who was making a good wage driving wells for the Sonora Railway in Mexico and had taken a Mexican wife. He told him the truth about the money offer. Stunned, McLuckie said, "Well, that was damned white of Andy, wasn't it?"[86]

But McLuckie had not disappeared into Mexico never to be heard from again. To the contrary, he remained a thorn the size of a steel plate in Carnegie's side, never relenting in his public attacks. In 1896, McLuckie spoke before a Central Labor Union meeting in Haverhill, Massachusetts, at which he condemned Carnegie's business practices and declared he wanted revenge: "In 1892 the men at Homestead had 300 Winchester rifles; now they have 3,800 and they are ready to use them if occasion requires."[87]

Van Dyke did indeed become involved with McLuckie, but not by mistake. In the 1890s, Van Dyke was advising Carnegie on the procurement of artwork for Carnegie's Pittsburgh library. Sometime around 1898, Van Dyke was in Mexico, where he did come into contact with McLuckie. Then, on June 29, 1898, from Scotland, Carnegie wrote Van Dyke an apparently cordial letter, thanking him for a book and hoping he would visit next year, but in the margin he made two notations in pencil: "Give McLuckie all the money he wants" and "Rub this out." Van Dyke did. But at some later point, for the benefit of future scholars and playing a little game to amuse himself, across the top of the letter he wrote: "This is the letter in which A.C. wrote in pencil to give McLuckie all the money he wanted and to 'rub this out.' See Autobiography p. 237." Almost one hundred years later, a scholar did discover the letter and was able to identify the faint remains of Carnegie's pencil note and quickly discovered that page 237 is Carnegie and Van Dyke's sentimental but fanciful story about McLuckie.[88]

Why would Carnegie want what he obviously considered a condemning pencil note rubbed out? Was his willingness to give McLuckie the money he wanted an admission of a guilty conscience, of outright guilt? Or was the truth that McLuckie was demanding the money to finally keep quiet and it amounted to bribery? There was no reports in the press of McLuckie's movements at the time, but one had to wonder what the agitator was concocting to prompt Carnegie's gift of money to a man sworn to revenge the Homestead tragedy? The only event on the horizon was the opening of the Homestead library to the public on August 1 and then the official ceremony in November. One might surmise that McLuckie had made a threat in connection to the impending opening, but only Carnegie and McLuckie knew the truth. The exact facts and motivation remain a mystery, but Carnegie was again dabbling in revisionist history.

Another character in the story, John Potter, suffered a tainted legacy marked by tragedy. After the strike, the Homestead superintendent was kicked upstairs to become chief mechanical engineer for all the works. Disillusioned, he quit on November 1, 1893. In his resignation letter, he admitted that "about the time the strike was ended and our victory won, my career of usefulness also ended, and I was removed to a new field of labor. The cause for the sudden change is still as great a mystery to me as it was at the time it was made."[89] An oblivious Potter didn't realize his shortcomings—not yet, anyway. Eventually, he moved to Latin America, where he remained until returning to Los Angeles in 1914. In 1925, he received an invitation to attend the twenty-first annual meeting of the Carnegie Veterans. On December 18, the day the meeting started, he walked to Carnegie Street in Los Angeles and shot himself in the head.[90]

CHAPTER 22

The Great Armor Scandal

As if the Homestead strike aftermath wasn't enough to contend with, Carnegie and his men were faced with national economic chaos and another scandal at Homestead. The country's gilt and glitter was stripped away when, in March 1893, a financial panic hit Wall Street, which was, in a large part, blamed on America's schizophrenic money policy embodied by the Sherman Silver Purchase Act of 1890. Wall Street believed that foreigners had little confidence in a country that backed the dollar with silver and gold, and indeed the Europeans had been cashing their investments and insisting on taking only gold with them. As the gold reserve was drained, the dollar weakened and the economy became vulnerable. Then, in February, an overextended Philadelphia & Reading Railroad failed. The next month, panic selling on Wall Street ensued.

In Washington, President Cleveland attempted to reassure investors by announcing the government would pay its notes with gold, but Carnegie still feared the worst and felt compelled to advise the new president, "Unless all doubt is put to rest, there is still great danger of the country being drained of gold. . . . All excitement can be allayed and the crisis safely passed by the simple declaration from you. If I might suggest, somewhat like the following: 'As long as I am President of the United States, the workingman is going to be paid in as good a dollar as the foreign banker is.' I think this would also be good politics."[1] Like a chameleon, Carnegie the ardent Republican had already ingratiated himself with the Democrats; the only loyalty he served was in the name of material progress. In spite of Homestead, Carnegie's knowledge about markets was respected. He also remained influential, for the next day Cleveland did indeed issue another statement in which he assured the public the government would do all in its power "to maintain the public credit and to preserve the parity between gold and silver and between all financial obligations of the Government."[2] Not exactly Carnegie's words, but he did calm the financial markets temporarily.

In May, however, there was another stock-market drop, and by the end of the summer 141 banks had failed. Congress hoped to bolster the economy by rescinding the Silver Act in November and paying all its obligations in gold, but it was too late. By year-end, sixteen thousand businesses had shuttered their doors and a four-year depression was well under way, with the iron and steel industry hit particularly hard. Prices were severely depressed, making profitability near impossible. In the first six months of 1893, there were thirty-two failures in the sector, including the once-feared Pennsylvania Steel Company and Oliver Iron and Steel Company, owned by Carnegie's old Allegheny City acquaintance, Henry Oliver.[3]

Throwing the steel market in further disarray, the rail pool collapsed, which was prone to happen when manufacturers were unable to maintain price levels and struck out to save themselves. Carnegie was actually pleased with the pool's dismemberment; in some years it had cost the members up to a million dollars to pay other firms to stay out of the business, a cost that irked him. Also, he had never trusted their biggest rival, Illinois Steel, which had snaked some orders in Carnegie territory in 1891—although there was always some poaching going on by both sides. Now he could strike back without hesitation. As the *Pittsburgh Dispatch* reported, "Carnegie has cut the price for steel rails about $5 a ton and proposes to knock out competition and make Pittsburgh the steel rail center of the world."[4] While the market contracted, Carnegie intended to thrive. In 1894, Carnegie controlled one-fourth of the nation's steel output and could easily scoop a depressed market at his will.[5]

There would be an attempt to reestablish the rail pool in December, with Frick handling the negotiations, but after he made preliminary agreements Carnegie, who was contemptuous of the competition, announced he wanted no part of it. "I do not think any one can stand in our way. . . . I get no sweet dividend out of second fiddle business, and I do know that the way to make even money *is to lead*. . . . we needn't hesitate, take orders and run full, there's a margin."[6] John "Bet-a-Million" Gates, who became president of Illinois Steel in 1894, later recalled, "Well, in those days we used to have a few agreements. The boys would make them and Andy would kick them over. . . . I know that if Frick and I would agree to anything in the forenoon, as between our two companies, he might tell me in the afternoon that Carnegie would not stand for it. In other words, no one in the Carnegie organization controlled Mr. Carnegie, but he controlled every other man."[7] For now, a price war ensued between Carnegie and Illinois Steel. As a result, Carnegie Steel forced drastic wage cuts on its men so the firm could push down prices and remain profitable.

Frick and Charlie Schwab kept an eye on Homestead for a reaction, particularly when a picnic to mark the first anniversary of the tragedy was organized and rumors of another violent strike circulated, but a large police force presence and lurking spies subjugated Homestead quite nicely. The extensive spy network managed by the company's Bureau of Information proved extremely potent. When the Amalgamated attempted to penetrate Homestead again by secretly forming a lodge in 1895, the company suddenly fired every man who signed on, taking them completely by surprise. The Amalgamated would eventually come to the conclusion that one out of ten men was a spy.

While the depression deepened that summer and autumn, there was one bright spot for Carnegie: before returning from Scotland in October, the Edison Electric Illuminating Company wired his New York home with electricity.[8] The bright lights did little to help Carnegie's image, however. In the winter of 1893–1894, a new Carnegie scandal erupted.

When Carnegie Steel had signed the contract to supply armor to the U.S. Navy in the autumn of 1890, Carnegie had no idea the toll such an agreement would take on his company. It was as though he had signed a pact with the devil—and perhaps the self-proclaimed pacifist had. The armor-making crews, from Frick right down to the workers in the press shop, were pushed hard to fulfill the company's first contract, armor for the monitor *Monterey*. Now, in the wake of the Homestead strike and lost production time, the company had to drive the men harder to meet the scheduled armor deliveries, as well as to please Secretary of the Navy Hilary Abner Herbert, a vigilant southern lawyer who was suspicious of the North's industrial titans. The continuous pushing of men, haphazard tests, secrecy, and, in particular, a dragging current of ill feelings still running through Homestead made for a volatile situation. From the beginning, questions had been raised about the quality of various batches of armor; those concerns came to the fore in the autumn of 1893, when a Pittsburgh attorney knocked on Frick's door.

The attorney claimed he represented four Homestead men who had information about fraudulent activities connected to the armor making, and said that for a price, he would divulge that information. Frick considered this offer blackmail and summarily dismissed the lawyer. He also took the threat of irregularities seriously and notified Schwab that enforcing quality control was paramount and to guard against sabotage.[9] Inspectors were alerted, too.

Unbeknownst to Frick, the Pittsburgh attorney won an audience with Navy Secretary Herbert and the two came to an understanding: the government would pay the four men 25 percent of any fine levied against Carnegie Steel for fraudulent or criminal behavior. The zealous Herbert created a three-man board of inquiry, which then conducted what has been characterized as a "speedy *sub rosa* investigation."[10] The board of inquiry relied completely on the testimony of the four informants and did not enlighten Carnegie Steel of the investigation until *after it was completed*. In early December, Herbert summoned Frick to Washington and leveled a dozen charges against the company, of which the board of inquiry had already found the company guilty. Several, in particular, were serious. As Herbert reviewed the charges, Frick answered each in turn.

The first serious charge involved the company's practice of filling in blowholes in the surface of the plates. All armor plates had blowholes, Frick explained, and filling them in was considered cosmetic and a common practice, which was true. However, Herbert pointed out, the company failed to follow agreed-upon manufacturing procedures, a breach of contract. This Frick could not deny. From the beginning of the contract, Carnegie Steel had fought the government over strict processes the company considered impractical. As long as quality results were delivered, Frick reasoned, any dispute over methods was negligible. Herbert now leveled a more serious charge: the company had falsified the results of certain ballistic tests. In a demonstration of arrogance on the company's part, Frick claimed some of the tests were irrelevant to the type of armor being made; moreover, in some cases, the tests were inexact. Such arguments could not dismiss the fact that the tests had been falsified, however, and that fraud had been committed. As for the most devious behavior on Carnegie Steel's part, Herbert accused the company of secretly removing six plates selected for testing and adding a treatment to strengthen them. Frick claimed his men were merely exploring ways to further strengthen the plates, but his answer reeked of deceit. Herbert did concede that none of the plates were defective. Still, the company was guilty of fraud and breach of contract. Herbert set the fine at 15 percent of the value of all armor plate delivered to date, which amounted to $210,734. The four informants were to receive $52,683, quite a bounty for mill workers.

Carnegie, who was outraged by the lack of due process, knew that he would be crucified if the allegations were made public. On December 17, he, along with Frick and his assistant Millard Hunsiker, Schwab, and the company's attorney, Philander Knox, traveled to Washington to meet with Herbert and President Cleveland. In hopes of keeping his visit inconspicuous, Carnegie checked in at the Shoreham Hotel instead of his customary favorite, the Arlington. A vigilant *Washington Post* reporter discovered Carnegie at the Shoreham and tracked the titan's movements: "Shortly before 3 o'clock yesterday afternoon Mr. Andrew Carnegie, accompanied by Mr. Millard Hunsiker, of Pittsburgh, and another gentleman, arrived at the White House, and were ushered into the President's room. A few minutes later Secretary Herbert and Mr. H. C. Frick, superintendent of the Carnegie Works, came over together from the Navy Department and joined the party."[11] While in Washington, Carnegie let it be known that he was feeling ill and not available for interviews. He also claimed he was there to discuss a new tariff bill being proposed, the Wilson Tariff, nothing more—even though he'd met with Herbert.

On the train home, however, the true purpose of the visit was revealed in a letter Carnegie wrote to the president, in which he poured out his feelings on the armor dispute: "We have been accused, tried, found guilty & sentenced without ever having been heard—The vilest criminal has always the right to be heard in his defence—The Secretary of the Navy even condemned us & after notifying Mr. Frick that he had approved the finding of the so called Board (which was not a Board but only one man with two assistants upon whom he might call to aid him if necessary) & then allowing us to say what we had to offer in defence—monstrous this." He then accused Herbert of overzealousness and threw in some guilt for good measure: "Spent millions, subordinated every other Branch of our business to the Govt's needs, succeeds—& then upon the testimony of spies we are charged with irregularities & our men with fraud." Carnegie concluded: "No one, not even Mr. Frick knows of this letter, it is between you & me alone—I keep no copy."[12] (Both Carnegie and Cleveland kept a copy.)

Over the next week, Carnegie armor plates successfully passed more government tests, and on December 27, Carnegie sent a gloating letter to the president: "I told you that fifteen thousand dollars of the Government's money was to be wasted this week. . . . This is 'Inspection' run mad, caused by the hasty, over zeal of an inexperienced Secretary who charges 'fraud' upon people (Mr. Schwab & others) quite as incapable of attempting to defraud the Government as the Hon. Sec'y himself." He asked for an impartial board to be convened for a retrial of the company.[13] Cleveland refused the request; unlike Carnegie, the president understood the importance of not disrupting the chain of command and undercutting his navy secretary. Besides, even though Carnegie made valid points, Cleveland could not appear to be pandering to big business. Also, the president was entertaining a somewhat devious idea to boost his agenda that played out in the coming weeks.

Shaken by the armor charges and now taken with a case of the grippe, Carnegie spontaneously planned a vacation in Egypt, where he hoped to regain his health in the arid climate. Departure was set for January 4. As Carnegie shuttled about New York, tying up loose ends and buying a wardrobe suitable for Egypt, the breadlines and destitution were unavoidable. Unemployment was rampant in New York City; in January, when the mayor ordered the police to canvass the city to assess the depression's impact, it was discovered that approximately seventy thousand were unemployed and twenty thousand homeless. Unionists, socialists, and anarchists protested in the streets. Emma Goldman, who had inspired Alexander Berkman's assassination attempt on Frick, told those who would listen: "If you are hungry and need bread, go and get it. The shops are plentiful and the doors are open."[14] The *New York Times*, fearing riots would erupt from the foreign quarters, called for a halt of immigration. Other newspapers promoted food and clothing drives. J. P. Morgan, while snapping up and reorganizing near defunct railroads and making millions in the process, formed the Business Men's Relief Committee to alleviate the suffering.

Back in his library, on the eve of his departure, Carnegie penned a shocking letter to the editor of the *New York Tribune*, which was published on January 8, four days after he left for Egypt. To the astonishment of his fellow Republicans, he urged the passage of a new tariff bill under consideration, the Wilson Tariff Bill, which Cleveland was championing and which would *reduce duties.* For those who wanted to interrogate Carnegie over his sudden reversal on protection and apparent heretic behavior, they would have to wait; he was aboard the Hamburg-American steamer *Columbia* bound for Algiers, Naples, and Alexandria.[15] The Carnegies were accompanied by a manservant and a maid, as well as their friend Henry Van Dyke.

Egypt had become a popular destination for travelers, its mystique and allure enhanced in the early 1890s by the excavation work of Egyptologist William Matthew Flinders Petrie, who had recently discovered information about the heretic pharaoh Akhenaten, who renounced the old gods and introduced the worship of Aten, the sun god. Akhenaten was a pharaoh after Carnegie's heart, and by the time his group landed at Alexandria, on the Nile Delta, he was anxious to proceed upriver by boat and visit the magical ruins. Although Carnegie had visited the country some ten years before, he was still impressed by the contrast between the lush Nile valley with its sweet scent of citrus trees and the arid land with its sands sweeping over the ruined temples. "We are tanned like Indians by the hot sun," he updated Frick. "Nights and mornings and in the shade always cool and truly the Nile trip is a treat in store for you, only you of all men will be bored by it at first such beggars, such dust and squalor I never saw but the temples are great and the blue sky, green crops always the banks and the sunsets are all unequalled elsewhere. We take no interest in anything not at least 3000 years B.C."[16]

Meanwhile, in Washington there were some intriguing developments in the armor case. Cleveland decided to reduce the Carnegie fine from 15 percent to 10; moreover, on January 10, he explained to Herbert that while he agreed that a large portion of the armor was substandard, he believed the facts establishing fraudulent activity were murky and considered the company guilty of bad management, but not of criminal behavior. Also, the story of the scandal, so far suppressed, finally broke in the papers in March, courtesy of one of the informants who was displeased with his share of the prize, had a little too much to drink, and did a little too much talking. As news spread of Cleveland's decision, no one was happy. Democrats considered Cleveland's actions cowardly, while Republicans like Whitelaw Reid, who still blamed Homestead for Harrison's loss, called for a full-scale investigation. As the series of events were pieced together, Reid didn't like what he saw. The president's mild scolding of Carnegie Steel and reduction of the fine on the heels of Carnegie heretical support of the Wilson Tariff smacked of political shenanigans. On March 2, the *New York Tribune* reported, "The discovery by the Navy Department early in November of startling irregularities in the execution of the contracts between it and the Carnegie Steel Company for the supply of armor plates may, in a measure, explain Mr. Carnegie's subsequent attitude of friendliness to a bill that must work serious injury to his own interests and means all but destruction to the interests of his rivals in business."[17] Cleveland's actions were also questioned: "Indeed, one is rather mystified at the ease with which Mr. Carnegie made his escape. Mr. Cleveland has the reputation of driving pretty hard bargains with Senators and Representatives who exchange their votes for pelf and plunder in the shape of offices. He might perhaps have obtained so much more from Mr. Carnegie than that letter if he had tried." The *Tribune* then related the series of events leading up to President Cleveland's decision.

Foremost, the paper pointed to Carnegie's suspicious behavior. When he arrived in Washington on December 17, why had he taken a room at the Shoreham Hotel instead of the Arlington, his choice for years? Why did he claim to be talking tariff only with Cleveland while it was known Frick and Herbert were in on the meeting? Why did he claim he was ill, even an invalid, when he was seen bounding up the executive mansion's stairs? Why did he change his mind on the tariff, as evident in his January 3 letter to the *Tribune* editor? Was it coincidence that Carnegie left the next day so that he would not to have to explain himself? Was it merely coincidence that two days after Carnegie's letter appeared in the *Tribune*, Cleveland reduced the Carnegie Steel fine? And why were the government's charges never made public? The *Tribune* surmised that Carnegie's 180-degree reversal on the tariff bought a reduced fine and the government's silence. Only a damn drunken knave from Homestead had blown their covert agreement. The *Tribune's* claims were circumstantial, but they set many a mind thinking.

Carnegie Steel countered the accusations with a propaganda campaign of its own. Through the *Pittsburgh Times*, the company's mouthpiece, Carnegie Steel claimed that it was the victim of a conspiracy concocted by bitter Homestead men, a position the company never deviated from. But Frick had already admitted to some of the irregularities, so the company's claims of conspiracy were suspect. The hot issue now was whether Carnegie had indeed changed his position on the tariff to escape the government and public's wrath, as well as to ensure future lucrative armor contracts? To determine the answer, it was necessary to track his view on the tariff and to discern whether it did suddenly change in January.

In a May 1893 interview, Carnegie had said, "The robber baron has ceased to rob and is now being robbed"; he also claimed no money could be made in steel, so he was certainly for highly protective duties.[18] On December 6, Carnegie wrote a friend that steel is in "positive distress. . . . What the United States manufacturer needs most is, to be saved from the foreigner dumping his surplus into this market in times like the present extreme depression."[19] His position couldn't be clearer: he wanted a high tariff to prevent dumping. The next month was another story. In addition to the *Tribune* letter, he also wrote on January 2 to Arthur P. Gorman, an influential senator who was working on the Wilson Bill. Instead of unilaterally demanding protection, he made suggestions as to how much of a duty cut might be acceptable, and concluded, "I wish to see the 'Robber Baron' completely exterminated."[20] He had turned traitor.

* * *

While his management team remained under severe duress in Pittsburgh, Carnegie indulged in Egypt and then traveled to southern England, to Buckhurst Park, a luxurious estate, where Louise and he stayed for three months before moving on to Cluny. (Cluny was not heated, so before proceeding north they always waited until the sun warmed the Highlands.) While at Buckhurst, he contacted his friend Andrew White, who had been president of Cornell and was now the U.S. ambassador to Russia, to gauge if there was any "prospect of being allowed to furnish some armor for Russia."[21] For all the hassles, there were obviously millions in armor.

Frick and Schwab were hardly sanguine about armor, however. Anxiety levels in Pittsburgh were rising as the House of Representatives' special subcommittee of the Committee of Naval Affairs opened its investigation of the armor scandal. Witnesses included the four informants, William Corey, who was in charge of the armor department, Frick, and Schwab, among others. When Corey took the stand, he said Schwab knew of the irregularities; and when Schwab took the stand, he contradicted Corey. Fingers were pointing in all directions. When the congressional investigation confirmed the navy's findings in a report published that summer, asserting "no fine of mere money compensation is an adequate atonement for such wrongs," Carnegie, Frick, and Schwab all came under fire in the press. It didn't matter that none of the plates were in fact defective. "In palming off those defective and inadequate armor plates upon the government," the New York Daily Tribune accused Carnegie and Frick, "they were imperiling the lives of thousands of our seamen and jeopardizing the nation's honor and welfare, but they were making money. It is an appalling conclusion. One shrinks from believing a thing so monstrous." The roast continued, "The expenditure of money in ostentatious charity and beneficence will not excuse the shameful means by which that money was acquired."[22] Carnegie was lampooned, depicted by one cartoonist as cowering behind an armor plate, shouting, "Don't shoot, I made this plate."

To capitalize on Carnegie Steel's gaffes and stir up trouble, John McLuckie returned to Homestead. He and onetime fellow Advisory Committee member Elmer Bales attempted to incite the town's populists to protest against the steel company.[23] Enthusiasm was lacking, however. Carnegie Steel had spies everywhere, and with the depression destroying families, no one wanted to risk losing his job.

Carnegie didn't return to the United States until November 3, later than usual and months after the president signed the new tariff bill, then called the Wilson-Gorman Bill, into law on August 26, 1894. When he arrived at the port in New York, a gaggle of reporters were waiting and pelted him with questions about armor and the tariff. Before being whisked away by carriage, he praised the new tariff, but he had nothing of substance to say on armor. He had spent just two months in the United States in 1894, driven away by scandal and criticism and his traitorous politics. National politics took its toll on Carnegie, who wrote a friend, "Like yourself I grow less and less keen about politics, which are upon the surface of things only. In the United States the ablest people have already discovered that there are matters of much greater importance; therefore, our best men are not politicians."[24]

Turmoil and dissension among Carnegie lieutenants marked the years immediately after the armor scandal, with each man suspecting the other of negligence or meddling or disloyalty. During this period, two of Carnegie's more disagreeable traits, vanity and paranoia, commanded his actions. At first oblivious to any internal company conflicts, Carnegie told Frick in September 1894 that he was "sanguine that we are now entering upon smooth waters and will make a splendid record for years ahead. The only weak department is the armor department, which may have to close."[25] Frick responded with a stab at Schwab: "This armor mess handicaps us in many ways, as the Navy Department are anything but friendly to Schwab, and have no confidence in him."[26] Instead of directly confronting Frick's apparent doubts about Schwab, Carnegie, who had unshakable trust in the young superintendent, chose to avoid any confrontation. As blindly as he worshiped heroes, Carnegie, unwilling to accept he may have erred in promoting a particular man, faithfully believed in lieutenants he deemed to be geniuses. Three months later, he paid the price for not recognizing Frick's discontentment with the armor mess.

It was the week before Christmas. The crisp air carried the sound of jingling bells. Holiday decorations graced storefront windows. Thanks to Thomas Edison, colored globes shone on Christmas trees. Crowds scurried through the streets with armfuls of presents. It was a time of goodwill for all men. Carnegie was enjoying the holiday season at home when a letter from Frick arrived. As his eyes traversed the page, his face turned as white as his Santa Claus beard. Frick was resigning, effective January 1. "The affairs of this association are in splendid shape as you know from examination made during your recent visit here," Frick wrote matter-of-factly. "In every way better than at any time in the past and the outlook for the future very bright, otherwise I should not think of retiring now. The past six years have been trying ones to me, and my mind from necessity has been so absorbed in looking after the interests of this great concern, I have had no time for anything else and feel now that I need such a rest as is only obtained by almost entire freedom from business cares."[27] Flabbergasted, Carnegie couldn't comprehend how Frick could act so cruelly as to resign suddenly in the midst of the holiday season. He also couldn't afford to lose Frick, the man who did his dirty work, who brought a strong hand to everyday management, who generated a superlative $4 million in profits in 1894 despite the depression. But Carnegie had brought it upon himself by acting vainly and infringing on Frick's responsibilities during two recent episodes—one dealing with armor sales to Russia, the other with consolidating the coke industry—that resulted in a serious breach of trust between the two men and precipitated the resignation.

Despite his pessimism about armor, in the fall of 1894, Carnegie was still in the hunt for a very profitable order from Russia and sent his salesman Millard Hunsiker overseas in an attempt to win the contract. In October, stories that Carnegie Steel was seeking the Russian armor contract, as well as what would be required to secure it, made the newspapers—this despite the fact that all of the partners had agreed to an absolute code of silence concerning all aspects of business. Frick, knowing the stories would hurt Hunsiker's chances, unleashed his potent anger. "To my mind," he wrote Lieutenant C. A. Stone, the ex-navy man they astutely hired to be their representative in Washington, "this could only have reached the public through one source (through our leading stockholder) who, it seems, is not able to contain himself at any time or under any conditions. I will have this traced and ascertain. If it was an employee of this company, we would have no further use for his services."[28] Unafraid to level his criticism at the guilty party, Frick wrote the compromised Hunsiker: "It is unfortunate of course that our leading stockholder is a little injudicious at times, but we cannot have everything as we should like it."[29] Regardless of what the "leading stockholder" had leaked, Frick was treading on dangerous ground; Carnegie didn't tolerate backstabbing when it was he who suffered.

As Frick feared, in December, Bethlehem won the Russian contract by bidding a much lower price. Surprised by being undercut, Carnegie suggested to Frick that he visit Bethlehem's president Robert Linderman and find out the whys and hows of Bethlehem bidding so low. Partly appalled and partly outraged, Frick responded, "As I told you (and you seem to have forgotten it), I happened to be with Mr. Linderman when he received news of their success in Russia, and, of course, congratulated him most heartily. Bethlehem, as you say, is certainly a lively competitor, made more so from the fact that they were told by you, *before they put in their bid*, if they took the contract they would have to take it at a very low price. They entered the race with some other advantages over us, most unfortunately, which it would be well for you not to forget."[30] Carnegie, by bragging about how low his supremely efficient company could go and how low Bethlehem would have to go, had lowered himself into rather hot water.

Adding to Frick's exasperation, in one last scrape that brought their conflict to a climax, Carnegie alone had approached the Frick Coke Company's archrival, W. J. Rainey and Company, to discuss a possible consolidation. Under the guise of solicitude, Carnegie had broken the chain of command and compromised Frick's authority. For years, Frick, who considered his rival a thief, and Rainey had battled each other over pricing and territory. Nonetheless, there was now an ongoing dialogue between Carnegie and Rainey, with the former suggesting the consolidation be renamed the Frick-Rainey Company and promising Rainey executives excellent management positions.

Frick was outraged that Carnegie, who was either oblivious to or indifferent to his partner's feelings, would consider such a consolidation without consulting him. Unfortunately, when Carnegie took hold of an idea, he charged ahead like a bull, head down. The more Frick mulled over recent events and his contentious relationship with Carnegie, the more incensed he became. At his wit's end, he submitted his resignation letter on December 18.

If Frick thought Carnegie was just going to let him walk away, he was a damn fool, because no man was going to impose chaos on Carnegie's well-ordered empire. After Carnegie read the letter, with the most unacceptable termination date of January 1, he composed his thoughts and drafted a response that was both pleading and castigating. He protested Frick's intent to retire "without proper notice to your partners and friends"—a valid ethical point that was also a play for time—and he asked Frick to stay on for another full year, which would be "ample time to adjust matters." As he had done with William Shinn years earlier, Carnegie also dangled an irresistible carrot: "I have told you of my desire to sell to you and my partners and that I only waited until our affairs were in order when such a proposition could be made without adding to your cares. It is I who should be relieved My Dear Friend not you. . . . You are yet young and should be my successor as chief owner a post I have told you I aimed at your being and left it to you to say when you felt the Company was ready to take my interest." But then, in a postscript, Carnegie wrote, "You are not well my Friend you are not well. You would never never have done me this injustice were you well."[31] How was Frick to interpret such a mixed message? It was a sugarcoated, bitter pill that reflected Carnegie's childish spitefulness and was difficult to swallow. Carnegie's inconsistent message also reflected his anxiety in managing a man as strong in character as himself.

Carnegie decided to play up Frick not being well in a second letter that day, in an attempt to convince him all he needed was a respite to rejuvenate himself and advised a vacation to Egypt.[32] The strategy would backfire. At the same time, Carnegie cabled Phipps to return at once from Knebworth, a luxurious estate in southern England, in hopes that Frick would take no further action if he knew Phipps was on his way. The next day, Frick received Carnegie's letters at his office. Realizing his responsibility to the other partners, Frick responded with a hint of conciliation by offering "to advise my successor in every way that I can when he may deem it necessary or until he gets everything well in hand."[33] Who would be the successor? the panic-stricken chorus sung.

Roused from his retirement, Phipps became distraught when he read Carnegie's cable and realized the company was about to lose its profit maker. Three days before Christmas, he cabled Carnegie: "Mr. Frick is first and there's no second, nor fit successor, with him gone, a perfect Pandora box of cares and troubles would be upon our shoulders." Blubbering with self-pity, Phipps claimed he was too old and weak to take on the "Herculean tasks"

Henry Clay Frick, at age forty-five, shocked Carnegie by submitting his resignation. It was a mistake to think Carnegie would just let him walk away. (Courtesy of the Carnegie Library of Pittsburgh)

Boyhood friend and long-time business partner Harry Phipps turned against Carnegie.

before them and concluded that Carnegie, Dod, and he should sell the company within the next year or two.[34] That same day, both Carnegie and Frick were in Washington to meet with Navy Secretary Herbert to discuss armor, an awkward situation for all parties for varying reasons. Before the two partners parted ways, Carnegie pleaded with Frick to put off his termination date until later in January, so he could arrange for the buying of Frick's interest and secure a new chairman. As an alternative to consider, he again pitched the idea of Frick buying his shares and ascending the throne, which would at long last free Carnegie to pursue his philanthropy, a vague dream since 1868. Desperate for a glimmer of hope, Carnegie thought Frick was interested in taking the crown and followed up with a letter confirming the plan.[35] Frick slammed the door, however: "Yours of 23rd rec'd and carefully noted and is not—speaking for myself—satisfactory, as I do not desire to purchase your interest or any part of it."[36]

As Carnegie, who was committed to promoting from within, reluctantly evaluated his executives for the presidency, he immediately determined that Vice President John Leishman, next in the line of command, was his only choice. Born in Allegheny in 1859, Leishman had been orphaned and forced to support himself as a boy, which had endeared him to Carnegie when the scrappy character joined the steel company in 1886 as a salesman. It was Leishman who saved Frick from imminent death during the Berkman attack. But it was now brought to Carnegie's attention that Leishman had speculated in pig iron, committing the company to buying and selling substantial amounts at prices that might fluctuate radically and cost them tens of thousands of dollars.

On Christmas Eve, distraught that his choice for succeeding Frick was a speculator, Carnegie wrote Leishman a long, punishing letter, a vein of hysteria running through his words. He lashed his lieutenant for making "tomorrow a sorry Christmas for me and for Mr. Phipps from whom I have heard" and for having "kept silence and deluded me." Carnegie concluded with a postscript designed to fill Leishman with guilt: "This will not be sent until your Christmas day is over. I would make it less sad than mine."[37] Carnegie always took his lieutenants' mistakes and indiscretions as personal attacks on himself. Realizing Frick was clearly a superior leader to any other partner, he quickly returned his attention to him, hoping to salvage their relationship.

The day after Christmas, Carnegie, who was apt to see only what he wanted to, expressed genuine surprise that Frick rejected his plan to purchase his interest. "Well, let's have your plan!" Carnegie wrote. "You seemed delighted in Washington with idea of my going out and giving you plenty to do, and I'm sure I was happy believing my aim was so near realization. . . . Won't you please sketch it for me, that I may know just what it is you *do* desire."[38] In these waning days of 1894, paranoid and compulsive behavior got the better of Carnegie.

Instead of Frick being the one who was sick and in need of rejuvenation, it was actually the Scotsman. He was manic, trying to woo Frick while torturing him with Rainey, and considering Leishman a worthy successor while attacking him mercilessly. Also heightening Carnegie's anxiety was the unavoidable fact that the labor contracts at all Carnegie works expired on December 31: due to both the continuing depression and recent productivity increases, the company was demanding wage reductions ranging from 25 to 45 percent for skilled workers. He didn't know how they would react, especially at Homestead. Taking in all of this conflict at once was as perplexing as watching a number of vignettes performed on stage simultaneously. The topping cherry in the midst of all this madness: Carnegie pressed his men to secure lower freight rates from the Pennsylvania Railroad.

Now a letter Carnegie had written to Phipps, after his initial cable, concerning Frick's alleged poor health sabotaged any hope for reconciliation. In the letter, Carnegie had made the mistake of overdramatizing the situation, as he was apt to do, by telling Phipps that he had to instruct Frick to "keep cool or I will have to treat you as a 'disordered man.'" It was an error to confide in Phipps. While Carnegie had great loyalty to Allegheny City childhood comrades, Phipps did not, and he forwarded the slanderous letter to Frick. On New Year's Day, while the men at all Carnegie works meekly agreed to wage reductions, the king of coke exploded: "It is high time you should stop this nonsensical talk about me being unwell overstrained etc and treat this matter between us in a rational business like way. If you don't I will take such measures as will convince you that I am full competent to take care of myself in every way." Following the veiled threat, Frick divulged his real reasons for leaving in a scalding assault:

> I desired to quietly withdraw, doing as little harm as possible to the interests of others, because I had become tired of your business methods, your absurd newspaper interviews and personal remarks and unwarranted interference in matters you knew nothing about.
>
> It has been your custom for years when any of your partners disagreed with you to say they were unwell needed a change etc.
>
> I warn you to carry this no farther with me but come forward like a man and purchase my interest, and let us part before it becomes impossible to continue to be friends.[39]

Yes, it could be said that Frick was fed up with Carnegie's vanity and deceit, his lies to the press about being retired during the Homestead crisis, his recent bragging to the press about armor contracts, his traitorous position on the tariff, and his meddling in the coke business.

Although Carnegie would not admit his mistakes—he never did—he attempted to explain his letter to Phipps, but on his heels and off balance, he made a disjointed, rambling mess of it:

> Of course some mistake has happened about letter to Mr. Phipps. . . . What I scribbled I don't know, but still, my friend, I do know you will recognize in it one who likes you and values you. . . . This is not the first you have resigned. . . . Well, you resign again and I have tried my best to be your friend again. It is simply ridiculous, my dear Mr. Frick, that any full grown man is not to make the acquaintance of Mr. Rainey, or anybody else without your august permission—really laughable—but I did not do it till you had given approval. . . . No one values you more highly as a partner, but as for being Czar and expecting a man shall not differ with you and criticise you, No. Find a slave elsewhere, I can only be a man and a friend.[40]

Carnegie's contemptuous ego could be intolerable and his sanctimoniousness repulsive, but his persuasiveness could also be irresistible; and so Frick, having second doubts about his decision, agreed to meet with him in Pittsburgh. It appeared Frick also put dollars before ideology. Meanwhile, Phipps cabled Carnegie that he would take his money and retire completely from the business if matters weren't patched up with Frick. In an attempt to bring both men to their senses, Phipps also urged Frick to remain with the company.

There may have been a mutual distrust and dislike, but there was also a mutual need that boiled down to the fact that Carnegie financed the operation and Frick did the dirty work—and both reaped profits. At the tête-à-tête on January 5 in Pittsburgh, Carnegie was surprised when Frick expressed a desire to remain president of the company. He had already offered the presidency to Leishman, so Frick, who wanted less involvement with the daily management anyway, suggested he be made chairman of the board of directors. He would save face; Phipps would be mollified; and Carnegie would still have a powerful figure guarding his profit machine. Carnegie agreed on the condition that the chairman's duties be strictly limited to presiding over the meetings of the board, which, he should have known, would be difficult for Frick to adhere to.[41] Ah, if he'd only read Machiavelli, who warned, "An Army should have but one chief: a greater number is detrimental." More chaos and dissension would ensue.

Phipps summed up the situation to his son Jay: "This Christmas to me has been marked by a series of serious cables from A.C. in regard to the Chm. leaving us; of course it is the egotism and bad temper of the one who is not unknown for his exhibitions. It looked on the 21st as tho' I must at once go home, and the strain has more or less continued until this morning when a cable from Mr. Frick said 'Everything arranged satisfactorily.' It seems A.C. must have climbed down a very long and steep way; in fact I went so far as to cable that unless something was done, I intimated I wished to retire. A.C. was awful hot at HCF who was the wronged one and had my sympathies and best support."[42] The truth was that both Carnegie and Frick had climbed down off their pedestals. And both were guilty of bad behavior, Frick for backstabbing and quitting with little notice and Carnegie for bragging to the press and emasculating his chief by dealing with Rainey. The curtain fell, but the most contentious act was still to come.

For now, Frick, the temperamental coke king, was brought in line—even broken, it seemed. He sold almost half of his 11 percent interest back to the company; the next month, he met with Rainey at the Duquesne Club, afterward claiming he "had quite a pleasant chat with him."[43] Carnegie continued to push hard for the consolidation, but, in the end, despite all the encouragement, time, money, and the fight with Frick, the untrustworthy Rainey demanded too high a price and the deal was never consummated.

Late in the spring of 1895, the steel market began to improve and the Carnegie Steel men, who had suffered repeated wage cuts, started grumbling for an increase. When the board of managers discussed an upward adjustment to the sliding scale, Carnegie, in repose in southern England, quickly voiced his objection. Nothing but a severe crisis should alter the wage scale, he declared, and suggested giving the men a bonus based on a percentage of their wages.[44] The advantage of giving the men a bonus was clear: it was a one-time deal. Frick was given the honor of announcing a 10 percent bonus on wages.

Profits would jump 25 percent to $5 million in 1895, money needed for Carnegie's big expansion plans; he was determined to take advantage of the still depressed economy and prices, as he had done in the past, by making improvements and expanding operations. These plans included four new furnaces, a major capital expenditure. Frick, for once, concurred with his philosophy; but Phipps, hungry for dividends to support his lifestyle, that of a country squire, was most disgruntled and now threatened to incite a mutiny. "Would much prefer increasing our cash capital and have it ready to pay retiring Partners," he wrote Carnegie. Hoping to strum a chord of guilt, he pointed out that John Vandevort, Carnegie's old traveling companion, was in need of money, too. "I know it must annoy & bore you my giving opposite views — have not hesitated much when it seemed duty. . . . We get in sight of div'd. then like Phillip Nolan ('man without a country') he sees his native land — then a new ship, a new voyage — and never lands, each time a new & deeper disappointment, so with our divd's."[45]

To pressure Carnegie, Phipps enlisted Dod's help, urging him to study the firm's books. After reviewing the finances, Dod joined the mutiny:

> I have a long communication from Harry on the question of dividends v. improvements. His position seems to me unassailable.
> But apart from all urges, I cannot see why you do not make dividends. In the first place it would only take what money Harry needs out of the firm and that I suppose he will have to get anyway . . . . Lovejoy [the firm's secretary] has just been shewing me a statement that shews we are in a better condition financially than we have been since 1888. . . . If I am not right about this I would like to know it. If I am, why do you not make dividends?[46]

Carnegie's policy had been to take 25 percent from profits for dividends, the remainder to be plowed into plant and equipment, and he had no intention of swerving from this course. So, from the impregnable Cluny Castle, the tightfisted Scotsman's answer was: we're going to build. Despite all the trouble over the previous two years, Carnegie remained relentless and ruthless.

To dominate the local pig iron market, Carnegie insisted that his men build the four furnaces in double time. In August, he instructed Leishman to publicize the expansion to dissuade other firms from thinking of entering the market.[47] On the steel rail front, Carnegie, fearing there was overcapacity unless railroad building "heats up," was also on the attack and negotiated a dominant piece of the latest rail pool. The allotments: Pennsylvania and Maryland Steel, 15.74 percent; Lackawanna, 15.74 percent; Cambria, 7.87 percent; Bethlehem, 7.87 percent; and Carnegie Steel, 52.78 percent.[48] Carnegie was so confident of their grip on the market that he wrote Leishman, "I do not think you need pay outsiders very much to keep out of the rail business next year, especially if you arrange with them soon, as you are very wisely trying to do."[49] He forged a profitable armor pool agreement with Bethlehem, as well.[50] Ultimately, Carnegie's unilateral demand for improvements, expansion, and aggressive tactics would prove insightful as profits mushroomed in the coming years. He was the steel industry's undisputed Napoléon; he just had to avoid his Waterloo.

*   *   *

As the general, emperor, and absentee partner inspected his troops, he realized his lieutenants were restless and greedy. Frick wanted power, Phipps and
Dod wanted money, and Leishman was a gambler. To suppress these errant
impulses, more control had to be exerted, which required continuously gauging the attitudes, opinions, and character of his entire board of managers in
Pittsburgh—a very challenging task while he resided in New York and Scotland. Carnegie solved this management quandary by insisting on more
detailed minutes of the weekly board meetings. Moreover, shortly after Leishman took the helm, Carnegie insisted "that the votes of each member, pro
and con, in the board shall be recorded" and that no new projects or methods be undertaken except by a two-thirds majority vote of the total number of
the board.[51] By requiring a vote, Carnegie could track who voted how—a simple and effective method of control. Later in 1895, Carnegie extended the
purpose of the minutes. "My idea is that there should be a permanent record
of every vote of every voter," he wrote Leishman. "This is provided for; but
there should also be recorded the reasons given for any vote which a voter
may ask to have recorded. The idea is this: The shareholders should be able
to read a record of proceedings which would enable them to judge of the
judgment displayed, good or bad, by every manager. I do not see how we can
in any other way form a correct judgment of the ability of our managers."[52]
He also notified the company's secretary, Francis Lovejoy: "The Minutes . . .
should record every reason or explanation which a member desires to give. If
this were properly done then any of us looking over the Minutes would be
able to judge of the judgment displayed by the voter, which of course would
affect his standing with his colleagues. It would bring responsibility home to
him direct. The Minutes cannot err in being too full, the fuller the better.
They can err in being too much curtailed."[53] It was all about Carnegie's
obsessive need to control and to judge: Who wanted money? Who made slapdash recommendations? Who didn't provide facts? Who was too hesitant?
Who was too optimistic? After digesting the minutes, he would write critical
comments, which he called "Thoughts on Minutes" or "Notes on Minutes,"
on the back and then send them to the appropriate person. If you weren't
catching hell from Carnegie's pen, that was a compliment.

The greatest tool for controlling his partners, especially the junior partners, was the Iron Clad Agreement. It was used to eject as well as to buy back
the interests of fifteen partners over thirteen years beginning in 1887. While
quick to expel those who didn't perform, Carnegie was equally enthusiastic in
promoting those with potential. As he told Frick, "Every year should be
marked by the promotion of one or more of our young men. I am perfectly
willing to give from my interest for this purpose, when the undivided stock is
disposed of. . . . We cannot have too many of the right sort interested in profits."[54] Always on the lookout for the next Frick or Charlie Schwab, Carnegie
once divulged to Charles Scribner, "I do not believe it possible to found a

really great business except upon the Napoleonic plan: every soldier carried in his knapsack a possible Marshal's baton. To bring an outsider in over the heads of men in service is unjust and should create a revolution. . . . Promotion from the ranks should be the motto."[55] True to his word, over the years, thirty of thirty-three superintendents rose through the ranks, and a derisive comment Carnegie enjoyed repeating over the years was "Mr. Morgan buys his partners, I grow mine." He was more than willing to give a man "a trial. That's all we get ourselves and all we can give to anyone. If he can win the race he is our racehorse; if not he goes to the cart."[56] It was survival of the fittest in the Carnegie ecosystem, a constant feeding frenzy as each man fought to beat the other to avoid the cart and being shackled by the Iron Clad. In this jungle, average men became superlative, for as William Abbott observed, "Most of Carnegie's partners were ordinary men. . . . Yet Carnegie could take this commonplace material and make out of it a truly great organization."[57]

Now, as an increasingly paranoid Carnegie sought to solidify his power in the wake of Frick's threatened resignation, the Iron Clad was more important than ever. Since the last fully executed agreement dated back to 1887, Carnegie pressed Lovejoy to update the document: "It is highly important that every shareholder shall sign that, just as he has signed these By-Laws, because we do not know what day someone may 'fall from grace,' or do something which will require the interests of the firm to sever connection with him."[58] But not until September 1, 1897, was a revised Iron Clad submitted for every partner's signature. Of particular interest were the clauses stating that upon the demand of three-fourths of the partners in numbers and interest, a partner could be ejected, and that upon ejection or death, the company's treasury would purchase the former partner's interest at book value. The company's current total value was $45 million, putting Carnegie's share at over $26 million.

When the agreement was mailed to Phipps, Carnegie sent an explanatory note: "My Dear Squire—A small interest now in our firm amounts to so much that the first agreement has to be changed, certainly. . . . My suggestion is that we should not agree to pay cash for our interests at all, but long time certificates bearing interest, which is as good an investment as any one should get."[59] If Carnegie were to die, according to the new Iron Clad, the partners were given fifty years to absorb his shares, while paying 5 or 6 percent interest.

As Phipps mulled over the Iron Clad, it dawned on the retired man that if he signed the agreement he was subject to the whims of Carnegie and the junior partners and could be ejected from the firm and bought out at a less than desirable price. He declared the document illegal and refused to sign it.[60] Carnegie was deeply hurt. His boyhood friend, who had already stabbed him once by siding with Frick during the 1894–1895 resignation dispute and who was forever quibbling over dividends, stood against him once again. Most appalling to Carnegie was the fact that when he had almost died in 1886, it was Phipps who so desperately wanted the Iron Clad to protect himself. His unabashed, self-serving greed was painful to confront. Even so, it was

Carnegie who sought to smooth Phipps's ruffled feathers. To do this, he enlisted Frick's help, warning him that Phipps "seems unduly alarmed about matters."[61]

At an October 1897 board meeting, Frick dispelled Phipps's claim that the Iron Clad was illegal and said he believed Phipps would "withdraw his objections after he has talked the matter over with Mr. Carnegie and with the members of the Board." If Phipps persisted in his refusal to sign, Frick continued, there was always the 1887 agreement that "we believe to be legally operative until this revision has been signed, as the only changes made, other than the extension of the stipulated terms of payment, are for the better understanding and carrying out of the details."[62] Harry Phipps Jr. never did sign the Iron Clad, the consequences to be realized in good time.

Between the board meeting minutes, the Iron Clad Agreement, suppressing stories to the newspapers, and spying, Carnegie's current regime embodied totalitarianism. But for all the control he exerted, his world continued to experience upheavals, in both business and politics, and over the next several years he would find himself involved in escalating battles on multiple fronts.

CHAPTER 23

Seeking a Measure
of Peace

A t the very time Carnegie was exerting greater control over his men, he witnessed the realization of his greatest benefaction to date and inserted himself as a peacemaker into an international dispute between the United States and Britain. His desire for munificence and peace on a grand scale was to compensate for the Homestead tragedy, the armor scandal, and oppression of the working class; it was, he hoped, to bring him a measure of internal peace as he sought to reconcile himself with his ruthless business tactics. This dichotomy of behavior, which brought public denunciation and praise, would prompt B. C. Forbes, founder of *Forbes* magazine, to observe of Carnegie, "He has been invested with all the virtues of a saint—and condemned as a bloodstained tyrant and slave-driver."[1]

Saintliness took time to buy. But Carnegie was patient and, over five years, built a cathedral of knowledge that took the public's breath away. On November 5, 1895, he dedicated the Carnegie Library of Pittsburgh, which included a science wing, an art gallery, and a music hall, all part of what would soon become the Carnegie Institute.

After Pittsburgh had accepted the million-dollar gift in 1890, Carnegie's first order of business was to handpick William N. Frew to lead the Carnegie Free Library Commission, which was to oversee the construction. They then had to settle on a location. Downtown Pittsburgh was too congested, but three miles to the east was Oakland, an outlying village perched on a high plateau of limestone terraces. The city was evolving toward Oakland, connected by cable car and trolley, and it was the best location for creating a center of culture. There, Carnegie's partner Harry Phipps had already built a magnificent and dreamlike conservatory, which, at the time of its dedication in 1893, was the largest enclosed botanical garden in the country. So Carnegie wrested twenty acres of Oakland property from the city, and then his

Library Commission, in what became a heralded national competition, invited architectural firms to submit their ideas. The winner was Longfellow, Alden and Harlow, a Pittsburgh firm.

One of Carnegie's few prerequisites was that the building was functional, without ornament; therefore, to dress up a rather plain exterior, it was decided to carve in the entablature the names of great authors, musicians, and painters. But when Carnegie, who was very active in overseeing the entire project, read the proposed names in the *Pittsburgh Dispatch*, he immediately protested: "I cannot approve the list of names published in the Dispatch of the 10th instant as those selected for the cornice decorations. Some of the names have no business to be on the list. Imagine Dickens in and Burns out. Among painters Perugini out and Rubens in, the latter only a painter of fat, vulgar women, while a study of the pictures of Raphael will show anyone that he was really only a copyist of Perugini, whose pupil he was. Imagine Science and Franklin not there. . . . As I am to be in Pittsburgh very soon, I hope you will postpone action in regard to the names."[2] To call the Flemish painter Rubens, best known for his intricate detail, his dynamic use of light and color to dramatize action, and his decorative works for churches and palaces, a mere painter of fat, vulgar women displayed both Carnegie's ignorance of art and his squeamish prudishness.

Carnegie was also very vocal about the commission's criteria for selecting trustees for the Institute. He wasn't interested in having experts in letters and arts serve on the board; instead, he wanted men who would efficiently run the institute like a business. "Besides this," he added, "I wish a larger number of officials directly from the people in the committee, as I am satisfied that unless the institution be kept in touch with the masses, and therefore popular, it cannot be widely useful."[3] He was determined to be pragmatic in uplifting the masses. For what it was worth, Frick was appointed treasurer of the board of trustees.

As the construction neared completion, Carnegie selected November 5, 1895, for the grand opening. (November 5 was his favorite day to flaunt his success because it was Guy Fawkes Day, the day the British celebrated the capture and hanging of Guy Fawkes, who had planned to blow up Parliament in 1605. Carnegie paid tribute in a slightly different manner.) He invited President Cleveland, Governor Hastings of Pennsylvania, Mayor McKenna of Pittsburgh, fellow capitalists Alex King, Enoch Pratt, and Russell Sage, as well as his cousin Maria Hogan and Lucy Carnegie, among many others.[4] Naturally, the press was notified, and four days before the dedication Carnegie the egoist gave Frew an advance copy of his speech so it could appear in the local newspapers in full and go out to the Associated Press and the United Press.

Carnegie, who had been in Pittsburgh since the middle of October to oversee opening-day preparations, wanted everything to be perfect and was therefore shocked when he realized they had overlooked one detail—a naked statue on exhibit in the library's art gallery. Just a day before the grand opening, he dashed off a note to Frew: "I strongly recommend nude draped since

It was estimated that Carnegie sunk $25 million into his cathedral of civilization, the Carnegie Library of Pittsburgh.

question has been raised. Remember my words in speech. We should begin gently to lead people upward. I do hope nothing in gallery of hall will ever give offense to the simplest man or woman. Draping is used everywhere in Britain except in London. If we are to work genuine good we must bend and keep in touch with masses. Am very clear indeed on this question."[5] Apparently nude statues were not going to raise the consciousness of the provincial masses, he arrogantly concluded.

As guests arrived on the evening of November 5, whatever biases they might have had against Carnegie were forgotten as they walked the length of the three-story, 303-foot-long, gray sandstone edifice built in the Italian Renaissance style, and entered through the main doors into a spacious hall. The middle section of the building was dedicated to the library with shelving capacity for 250,000 volumes, the stacks made of iron and surrounding structure fireproofed. Housed in the northern wing was the music hall, a semicircular design, with the ceiling an elliptical dome for optimal acoustics. It could accommodate twenty-one hundred guests, and the hall would be home to the Pittsburgh Symphony Orchestra for the next fifteen years.

The southern end of the building was the science wing, which included lecture and museum rooms and, on the third floor, six art galleries that provided the most stunning spectacle that night. John W. Beatty, secretary of the Pittsburgh Art Society, had pulled together a magnificent collection of 231 paintings, including works by Diaz, Mauve, Monet, Tadema, and Rembrandt, among many other European masters and contemporary American painters. It was a magnificent feast never before encountered in Pittsburgh, and it marked the end of the dark ages for the culturally deprived city. Over the years, Carnegie would continue to put great effort into procuring the best for his institute, whether it be Egyptian mummies, stuffed alligators, books, or paintings.

Carnegie was proud and erect as he took center stage of the music hall and bid everyone a hearty welcome. In his dedication speech, he reiterated his philosophy for philanthropy—help those who help themselves—and promised to expand the Pittsburgh library's art gallery and museum, which would include endowments, too, so as not to further tax the city. He also declared he would embark on building libraries at Homestead, Duquesne, and Carnegie, the newly created township named in his honor.[6] Louise looked on lovingly as her husband received a standing ovation.

The peanut gallery voiced its opinion, too. Thomas Crawford, who had replaced Hugh O'Donnell as chairman of the Advisory Committee toward the end of the Homestead strike, never stopped mocking Carnegie, and his libraries were a favorite target. "I have always hoped to educate myself," said Crawford. "But, after my day's work, I haven't been able to do much studying. . . . After working twelve hours, how can a man go to a library?"[7] For years to come, his sentiments were echoed by the working class, while others sniped that it was better to pay higher wages than build libraries. Carnegie never took criticism silently. When an article in *Outlook* took aim at his libraries, Carnegie refuted the author's criticisms that he should pay higher wages instead of building libraries: "You see, Mr. Editor, I differ from him in toto, but perhaps he will be surprised to know that we do pay the highest wages in the world. Every man employed at Homestead last year made two dollars and ninety cents per day average."[8] That amounted to a shade over $1,000 in annual average income for both skilled and unskilled workers, assuming no work stoppages or illness, while the firm generated $5 million in profits.

Philosophical differences aside, the critics raised pertinent questions: Did anyone benefit from the libraries? Were they used by the working class? Did they help elevate the status of current or future generations? Over the next ten years, the Pittsburgh library system would include five branch libraries and an outreach network comprised of thirteen deposit stations, fifty-six school stations, thirty-one home libraries, and twenty-two reading clubs, among other programs to encourage reading and learning. And one day the library would hold 2.5 million volumes.[9] The expansion certainly suggested strong usage, but the true beneficiaries were several generations removed from the men who gave their sweat and blood at Carnegie's profit.

The previously opened Allegheny and Braddock libraries offered a better gauge of current usage, and, in October 1895, *Review of Reviews* magazine published a study on the libraries. The Carnegie Free Library of Allegheny, opened in 1890, now had 30,000 volumes filling shelves with capacity for 75,000. The prior year's circulation reached 125,000 volumes, and 160,000 books and periodicals were used in the reading room. The total capitalization for the library was now $850,000, a healthy increase from the $300,000 Carnegie gave. All this stood as a testimonial of its use and solid standing as part of the community.[10] In Braddock, home to the Edgar Thomson workers, the population was about 16,000, of which one-third were considered regular readers. The library, opened in 1889, contained 10,000 volumes and total circulation for 1894 was 49,013, which the magazine considered encouraging, as did Carnegie, who subsequently funded a music hall with seating for 1,100, which was completed in 1894. He also built a large gymnasium, a swimming pool, bowling alleys, and billiard and card rooms, but to use the sports and leisure facilities, you had to join the Carnegie Club, which cost $1 for three months. It was estimated that between five hundred and six hundred men and boys belonged, mostly of the skilled-worker class. Clearly, class had much to do with usage: the majority of Carnegie's workers didn't know enough English to use the library; or, as immigrants, planned to return to their native countries and were apathetic; or, as menial laborers, were indeed too damn tired.

Regardless of the critics' barbs, Carnegie pursued his library building as fervently as Ramses II built temples. It was estimated that in the early 1890s, Carnegie spent more than $3 million on libraries and associated concert halls, museums, art galleries, and lecture rooms.[11] In addition to the Pittsburgh-area libraries, he had opened libraries in Edinburgh, Ayre, and Jedburgh, Scotland, and in Johnstown, Pennsylvania, and Fairfield, Iowa. It was just the humble beginnings for a man who would build almost three thousand. As he indulged further, he developed a basic formula for giving: he would donate the building while the respective community would provide the land and pay 10 percent of the building cost annually to maintain the library. His one other standard request was to have "Let There Be Light" carved over the entrance. Reportedly, Carnegie didn't insist on his name being carved into the edifice, but he certainly rejoiced when it was; it was the easiest way for a community to endear itself to the philanthropist. And if requested, he was always happy to send a photo of himself to be hung in the lobby.

Just days after the Pittsburgh dedication, Carnegie visited Homestead and formally announced his intention to give $400,000 to build a library, a music hall with organ, a gymnasium, a swimming pool, and club rooms.[12] This complex would be one of the few to benefit from an endowment; the community did not have to fork over $40,000 annually per the formula. Apparently, Carnegie's guilt now worked to Homestead's advantage. Interestingly enough, the chosen site for the library was right where the state militia had encamped in 1892.

While the papers announced a $400,000 building project, in January 1896, Carnegie gave Charlie Schwab alternative instructions to have plans prepared for a library not to cost more than $200,000.[13] Perhaps the other $200,000 was to be used for the endowment, but this wasn't specified. Regardless, Schwab not only jumped on the idea, but, to further improve relations with the community, he suggested the construction of an industrial training school. "I wish you would show this letter to Mrs. Carnegie," he wrote Carnegie. "I am sure she would think well of it, as she has ever evinced such an interest in Homestead affairs."[14] After witnessing the effect of the assaults on her husband's character as a result of the tragic strike, Louise was attuned to any opportunity to rehabilitate and improve his image.

As a sign of his dedication to uplifting the masses, Carnegie committed his entire current supply of surplus wealth to these libraries. When, in February 1896, W. W. Sage of Cornell University approached Carnegie for a donation, he replied, "You notice in reading the proceedings of the Opening of the Pittsburgh Library, I have spent five millions in and around Pittsburgh. I have yet two millions of that to make because I have not accumulated a dollar since I gave up daily attention to business. When it is made and spent I shall hope to see clearly the next field which it is my duty to take up."[15] More so than ever, Carnegie felt it was his *duty* to aid humankind, and, like a prophet, he would wait for a guiding vision. In the meantime, he would drive his men for more profits so that when the vision was delivered, it could be realized.

Even though the large benefactions intoxicated Carnegie, he still didn't forget his old friends and how much a small act of charity was appreciated. When a rather dated letter from a cousin, Ann MacGregor, found him that glorified November of 1895, he took the time to respond promptly: "An old letter of yours turns up to-day, and reminds me it is long since I wrote you. I should like to hear how you are getting on. I send you a paper showing what we have been about in Pittsburgh. I beg to send you a draft, which please use as a Christmas gift."[16] On the same day, he sent $5,000 to a school friend from the Dunfermline days.[17] Carnegie sent $400 to another chum who was ill and pressed financially; he sent money to J. H. Linville, his early partner from Keystone Bridge, who had fallen on hard times; and when his old telegraph comrade William Holmes died, Carnegie insisted his widow accept an allowance for her lifetime.[18]

There were also those who were turned away. That generous November, Ella Newton, a missionary in Foochow, China, whom Carnegie had met years ago while traveling there, requested money for her work, but Carnegie said no: "I think that money spent upon foreign missions for China is not only money misspent, but that we do a grievous wrong to the Chinese by trying to force our religion upon them against their wishes."[19] How correct he was; in three years, the Chinese Boxer Rebellion would terrorize the missionaries and other foreign visitors. China was not the only place where trouble between nations was simmering.

For a century, Great Britain had been in an ongoing dispute with Venezuela over the boundary between Venezuela and British Guiana, and in 1895 it heated up to a degree where Venezuela appealed to the United States to assist in its resolution. So, in July 1895, Secretary of State Richard Olney sent a belligerent note to Prime Minister Lord Salisbury, defending Venezuela and invoking the Monroe Doctrine. Salisbury refused to recognize the Monroe Doctrine, which forced President Cleveland to take a more aggressive posture. On return from a two-week duck-hunting trip in December, President Cleveland delivered a shocking message to Great Britain, declaring that Great Britain's shifting of the boundary was akin to acquiring more territory, which was, in the eyes of America, a violation of the Monroe Doctrine. Therefore, he said, Britain must arbitrate with Venezuela or the United States would do what was necessary to protect its interests. This announcement was immediately followed by a special message to Congress, in which he requested funds to create a boundary commission and then implement whatever recommendations the commission made, implying that force might indeed be necessary. The public assumed war.

The day after Cleveland's message, the stock market plummeted, and a cry rose up on Wall Street denouncing any aggression toward Britain. The pro-Cleveland *New York Times* roundly criticized the "patriots of the ticker," declaring, "If they were heeded, American Civilization would degenerate to the level of the Digger Indians, who eat dirt all their lives and appear to like it." Over at the *Tribune*, the paper published comments by city icon Abram Hewitt, who considered Cleveland's message to Congress needless, arrogant, and dangerous.[20] As for Carnegie, as he read the papers, digesting the news and mulling the possible consequences of Cleveland's announcements, he felt as though he was being torn in two, as though he was the sewn-together Union Jack and Stars and Stripes, which he flew over Cluny to symbolize his love for both lands, being ripped apart one stitch at a time.

The situation was also particularly distressing because for the last several years he had been avidly promoting an economic and political reunion between the United States, Canada, and Britain. It appeared to be a far-fetched, even ridiculous idea, but then Carnegie lived on an imaginary island, it seemed at times, sharing a kinship with Prospero from his beloved Shakespeare's *The Tempest*. An artist-king and island-ruler, Prospero used the powers of illusion in seeking peace, as did Carnegie with his persuasive commentary and grand gestures. He had attached to the idea of a reunion in the wake of the conflict over the McKinley Tariff, which had pitted the countries against each other.

Carnegie's first public expression supporting the concept emerged in the newspapers in December 1891 and set off a minor furor. It was initiated when he wrote John Patterson, a business associate in Canada: "When the foreign colony of Canada recognizes its destiny and becomes a part of the American Union, it will be time enough to consider the investment of capital there by Americans. This natural union of the English-speaking people of the American Continent would double the value of everything in Canada, including the men of Canada."[21] Taken aback by the callous and supercilious dig at Canada, Patterson passed the letter on to the newspapers. While the *New York*

Daily Tribune considered it a shrewd observation, the men of Canada were justifiably offended. But as it turned out there was a small movement in Canada in favor of a union, and Carnegie again wrote Patterson, "It seems to me little less than criminal to remain apart."[22] The idea of a union soon evolved into a grand reunion, a vision of race imperialism.

As Carnegie walked the streets of New York, mulling over the reunion of English-speaking races, what he witnessed there made the idea of race imperialism all the more appealing to him. Foreign populations carved out their own neighborhoods, filled with squalor and pestilence. It was these neighborhoods, quarters, towns within a city that pushed Carnegie into believing that race imperialism would educate the less evolved, banish war, and, generally speaking, save the world.[23] There was the Italian quarter west of the Bowery—Mulberry Bend—considered the most squalid and lively foreign colony, with Italian laborers comprising 75 percent of the menial labor market, whereas ten years prior the number had been 15 percent.[24] Italian women wore peasant clothes with red bandannas and yellow kerchiefs, with men also remaining in traditional garb, refusing to assimilate. Between the Bowery and the East River was the Jewish ghetto, the most densely populated section of the city, filled with Russian, Polish, and Rumanian Jews. Here, men wore skullcaps and long-skirted caftans, and married women shaved their heads and wore the traditional wig. Yiddish was spoken on the streets. Silent and sullen, Chinatown was established between Pell and Mott Streets, where the inquisitive found old men in traditional costume and pigtails, their blank stares unnerving intruders. No women were visible—they were scattered through the city working as house servants. Southeast of Chinatown was a section dominated by Greeks. There were also German, Turkish, and Arab neighborhoods, and the riotous Hungarians in Little Hungary with brightly lit cafés and Gypsy musicians.

As destitute as the ghettos were, New York was evolving favorably as a city—material progress was proof of that. The most conspicuous piece of evidence was the rising skyline that carried the populace closer to the heavens. It was the dawning of the age of skyscrapers, the manifestation of grandiose visions and, to Carnegie's benefit, the necessitation of steel cage support structures. When the first steel skeleton building, the eleven-story Tower Building at 50 Broadway, was built in 1888–1889, it was a startling sight. Now the majestic beacon of the Trinity Church spire was barely discernible on the skyline as the towering buildings for the Manhattan Life, Union Trust, Western Union, and the New York Times companies took to the sky. But as Carnegie surveyed the New York landscape and mulled over the race question, it wasn't the skyline that struck him; it was the accomplishments and failures of the various races. He couldn't help but realize that the Yankees, the Puritans, the Englishman, the Scotch, the Irish, and the Scotch-Irish controlled the capital, and that the Irish and the Germans dominated the skilled labor jobs, while the other races took the unskilled jobs, were coarse, and inhabited neighborhoods known as the "typhus ward" and the "suicide ward," among other choice nicknames, where base entrepreneurs sold sleeping spaces for "Five Cents a Spot" and hawked their wares at the "Pig Market." Such people, stereotyped for sure, deserved no leadership position in the world, according to Carnegie.

In a revised version of *Triumphant Democracy* that appeared in the spring of 1893, Carnegie added a new chapter promoting the reunion scheme. In April, he divulged his desire to Morley to restore "the Union between the Old and New Lands" that would make "Britain permanently prosperous" without the nuisance of debilitating tariffs.[25] "A Look Ahead" also appeared as a stand-alone essay in the June issue of the *North American Review.* Carnegie opened his argument by stating he believed the separation of the United States and Britain was unnecessary and injurious, and that today Britain regretted forcing the Revolutionary War on America. As for the Yankee rebels, Carnegie was certain George Washington and other delegates to the First Continental Congress had not desired separation. Against this backdrop, Carnegie considered a reunion desirable to many, and, although highly utopian, he believed one day it would be a reality.

The first logical step was the union with Canada, so Carnegie, along with others, now took concrete steps toward that goal by forming the National Continental Union League and circulating petitions. Notable figures signed in support, including Chauncey Depew, Elihu Root, John Jacob Astor, Theodore Roosevelt, Collis Huntington, and Charles Tiffany. On the British side of the Atlantic, enthusiasm was lacking, to say the least. In an attempt to win support from powerful editors who held sway over public opinion, Carnegie wrote his friend William Stead, the brilliant and influential editor of *Pall Mall.* "The destiny of the Old Country seems to me very plain," he argued. "You will be the family seat of the race. Your manufacturers will go, one after the other, but you will become more and more populous as the garden and pleasure ground of the race, which will always regard Great Britain as its ancestral home."[26] According to Carnegie, Britain would have to dedicate all its resources to become one large farm to feed its people; or the United States, with its infinite resources, could come to Britain's rescue by the countries jointly creating a magnificent Anglo-Saxon Commonwealth.

As Carnegie's vision evolved, he determined that the capital of this consolidation would be Washington, D.C., and that the U.S. Constitution would be the empire's guiding light. It also became apparent that this grand illusion was a means of fulfilling his youthful desires to destroy the monarchy. Of course, there was no way Britain would accept Washington, D.C., as the capital of the union, among just a few other reasonable objections to a reunion. One had to wonder if Carnegie was so very naive to political complexities. The argument for years has been yes. But the answer is no. He was well aware of just how complex relations were between countries; he just had no tolerance for those complexities. As with business, when he was dreaming, formulating a strategy, and then campaigning, he refused to be caught up in the minutiae, to recognize the many obstacles to success.

Stead was unconvinced, of course; he was adamant the two countries could never be united. More hurtful to Carnegie, who was wide open to criticism after Homestead, were the personal attacks in the press. American detractors began to question his loyalty, while the Democratic nominee for governor of Ohio, Lawrence T. Neal, accused Carnegie of not being a U.S. citizen. Carnegie responded by sending a letter to the *New York Daily Tribune* refuting the charge, and he sent a copy of his naturalization papers to Neal directly.[27]

Despite the criticism, Carnegie's conviction did not waver; he was certain "the Brotherhood of Man, the Federation of the World" would be realized.[28] And he did have some supporters on both sides of the Atlantic. The *Westminster Review*, for one, considered his essay "A Look Ahead" courageous and "a truly grand conception," so perhaps Carnegie had not completely lost his grasp of reality. His master, Herbert Spencer, also encouraged the idea of union, which spurred Carnegie onward.[29] The grand conception intoxicated Carnegie, made him feel euphoric, and it would remain a passion he would continue to pursue. From it would germinate his most ambitious endeavor—a campaign for world peace.

But now the conflict over Venezuela dimmed Carnegie's illusions. In the wake of President Cleveland's bellicose rhetoric, it was turning out to be another depressing Christmas season at Fifty-first Street—not only due to the political situation, but because both Louise and her sister Stella were sick and under a doctor's care. Even so, as he invariably did, Carnegie threw himself vigorously into the Venezuela dispute. On December 23, he cabled the London *Times* a brief letter in which he called for arbitration, the honorable course for settling disputes. Also, he immediately went to work on a lengthy essay, "The Venezuela Question," which was published in the February *North American Review*. After reviewing the situation, Carnegie concluded, "There will be no war between the United States and Great Britain either upon the Venezuela question or upon any other, because the first has already planted itself upon the rock of arbitration, and the other is slowly but steadily moving toward its acceptance."[30]

At the same time, Carnegie did alert his British political friends that war was not out of the question. "The Monroe Doctrine is the 'red rag' to the American people," he informed the duke of Devonshire the day after Christmas, "as 'the right of asylum' is to the British. Any President can rouse the people and carry all classes with him. Those of us who have done our best to allay the present excitement are not deluded upon this point."[31] There was little opposition to Cleveland, he warned, and hostility toward Britain would only build. Toward his friend Morley, Carnegie took a more biting tone in questioning why Morley had not come out in support of arbitration: "If Mr. Gladstone were only your age, we should have the Liberal Party back to power on the issue, Arbitration. If I were in your place, I should demand a day to discuss Lord Salisbury's refusal to arbitrate; denounce it; offer a resolution that this house disapproves Lord Salisbury's refusal to carry out the agreement to arbitrate made in 1885."[32]

The tension in the Carnegie house did little to help Louise's health, so in February Carnegie took his wife to the Florida spa town of Palm Beach, which, along with Poland Springs, Newport, and White Sulphur Springs, was considered the most exclusive and catered to an elite crowd. By mid-month, Carnegie was able to write Frew, who was now president of the Carnegie Institute, which managed the Pittsburgh library and associated programs, that "Mrs. Carnegie's much better. We are just off for a swim in the great bath, both taking lessons. Frog movement seems the ideal—the legs, not the arms, propel us."[33] They remained in Palm Beach until the last week of February and then traveled north to Dungeness, Lucy Carnegie's winter home on Cumberland Island.

Refreshed, the Carnegies returned to New York City, where he rejoined the Venezuela battle. A conference in Washington was organized with the aim of establishing an International Tribunal of Arbitration. Carnegie couldn't attend, but he wanted his name prominently identified with the movement and therefore forwarded a check for $1,000 to ensure recognition.[34] His pacifist friends would have been deeply disappointed to know that the day after replying he couldn't make the arbitration conference, he wrote J. G. A. Leishman: "I have considerable confidence that you can put the gun-forging department in splendid form by visiting Washington and conferring with Secretaries Herbert and Lamont. Naturally, both of these would like to have us go into the business, and you can probably arrange that bids shall be asked by both simultaneously, which will in the aggregate justify us undertaking the matter."[35] Guns were not defensive like armor, but once again profits ruled over ideology—unless Carnegie reasoned the best defense was an offense, which was entirely possible.

One man who easily pierced Carnegie's self-serving hypocrisy and attempted to keep him honest was his friend, the British author William Black, who abhorred the steel master's moralizing from his castle in the air during the Venezuela dispute: "I see you are still calling out for arbitration. Is there no sense of humour left on your side of the water? Of course everyone understands why the United States should clamour for arbitration on every possible point: it is because they alone among the nations of the world know how to manipulate it to their favour." Black was alluding to a territorial fishing dispute between the United States and Canada that was arbitrated in Canada's favor, only to have the U.S. Congress vote against paying the fine.

The prior summer Black had also criticized Carnegie, a self-avowed radical, for cavorting with so many members of Britain's privileged class, and he wrote Louise in hopes she could influence his wayward friend: "It has considerably grieved me of late to see that you and your husband have been frequenting the pernicious society of Princesses, Peers of the Realm, and people of that kind. I tremble to think of the destruction of your loyal republican principles; I hope you will withdraw from the brink of the fatal precipice while there is yet time."[36] While Carnegie railed against privilege, he was intoxicated when in its presence. As Mark Twain said, "He says he is a scorner of kings and emperors and dukes, whereas he is like the rest of the human race: a slight attention from one of these can make him drunk for a week."[37] However, Carnegie's cavorting with lords paid dividends in the summer of 1896.

First, the Carnegies embarked on a grand tour of Europe. Late May found Carnegie, Louise, and her sister, Stella, landing in Naples, Italy, and then continuing to Venice. There, they strolled across the Rialto Bridge, gazed in wonder at the thousand-year-old cathedral of St. Mark, toured the Palace of the Doges, and enjoyed romantic gondola rides through the canals intertwining the city's 118 islands (although the water smelled a bit ripe). The only missing gem from their fortune was a child, and what more romantic place to conceive a baby than Venice. Now age thirty-nine, Louise had grown desperate, and watching Lucy's children grow made it all the more difficult. The sixty-year-old Carnegie, who loved his extended family, would have spent a fortune to see his wife with child.

After a week in Venice, the Carnegies traveled north to the Tirol, then an Austrian province dominated by the Alps. They stayed in the resort towns of Cortina and Innsbruck, and as Carnegie and Louise walked Innsbruck's cobblestone streets lined with rose bushes and baroque facades, the ring of mountains beyond, they were breathless. There was the sixteenth-century Franciscan Hofkirche; the fifteenth-century Furstenburg, the castle with the famous copper-roofed balcony; the grand Hofburg, the imperial palace; and the fourteenth-century Stadtturm, the city's tower, which could be climbed for a stunning view of the city.

That summer at Cluny, the dominant topic of conversation was the continuing conflict over Venezuela—if still in dispute as the 1896 presidential race heated up, there was a concern that both parties would use it to demonstrate their bravado and inadvertently incite war—and Carnegie continued to actively lobby for arbitration, chatting up visiting British dignitaries, and writing letters to Morley and Gladstone. In providing America's resolute sentiment, President Cleveland's in particular, he was instrumental in convincing Britain to arbitrate. Although heavy-handed and prone to callous public outbursts—Carnegie never did recognize the strength of subtleness, whether in business or politics—the rapport he had established with Britain's ruling class—much to Black's chagrin—yielded positive results, as it would in future political conflicts.

On the business front in 1895 and 1896, Carnegie would also seek to negotiate conflicts, but there would be no arbitrators as he jousted with two very formidable opponents: the Pennsylvania Railroad and John D. Rockefeller.

CHAPTER 24

Illegal Rebates and
a Fight with Rockefeller

T he captains of the railroads behaved like monarchs, and Carnegie had no tolerance for them. So, while the United States and Britain dickered over Venezuela, Carnegie found himself in heated battle with a supposed ally, the Pennsylvania Railroad. The prior winter, when Frick was threatening to resign, Carnegie had questioned the Pennsylvania Railroad's freight rates, but the issue was never resolved. Now, even with the market depressed, the company was expanding, shipping more coke, iron ore, and steel, so freight rates took on greater importance. In no uncertain terms, Carnegie told Frick, they must have lower rates, "peaceably if we can, forcibly if we must; but competitive rates we shall have."[1] It was a battle between the state of Pennsylvania's two colossi—with millions of dollars at stake.

Carnegie opened his campaign in December 1895, in Cleveland, where he gave a speech to the city's businessmen. He was blunt, proclaiming (with semiconviction) that Pittsburgh was no longer an advantageous location for business and delivered a veiled threat to abandon the smoky city for a Lake Erie location.[2] Many of the industrialists in the audience were sympathetic— they were also fed up with discriminatory freight rates—but there were enemies, too. Wherever Carnegie went, he aroused the spectrum of emotions, including those of Cleveland's most respected businessmen; two months after his speech, members of the Cleveland Chamber of Commerce denounced him as an oppressor of the poor and blackballed him from ever becoming an honorary member.[3]

The next step in the escalation of Carnegie's war with the Pennsylvania Railroad was to develop transportation alternatives. One possibility was to convince the state legislature to build a canal from the Ohio River to Lake Erie, because from Lake Erie Carnegie Steel could ship east and west, thus breaking the Pennsylvania Railroad's stranglehold. Another option was to build an independent railroad to Lake Erie to access the cheap shipping; but this was considered a drastic measure initially, considering the 1885 debacle when Carnegie joined with Rockefeller and Vanderbilt to build a line east, only to be outsmarted by Morgan. Still, when the general counsel for the Pittsburgh, Monongahela & Wheeling Railroad, James H. Creery, suggested that constructing an independently owned line to the lake would prove to be more timely and advantageous than waiting for a canal with all its associated problems, Carnegie decided to explore the possibility.[4] Fearing the Pennsylvania Railroad would crush them if angered, his partners balked at the idea, but Carnegie assured them he was acutely aware of the power the Pennsylvania wielded. As a precaution, he informed the railroad executives that if they disrupted Carnegie Steel in any manner, he would organize a massive protest.[5]

There was a railroad line already serving part of the proposed route to Lake Erie, the Pittsburgh, Shenango & Lake Erie Railroad, which ran from Butler, about twenty-five miles directly north of the steel mills, to Conneaut, a small Ohio village on the lake with a modest port. A Colonel Saul B. Dick, president of the railroad, had already looked into the possibilities of extending his line to Pittsburgh, but the railroad was run down and had no financing. In stepped Carnegie with the promise of guaranteed freight if he connected with Pittsburgh. Eager to please, Dick confidently told Carnegie that he could organize a syndicate of wealthy Boston men he knew to finance the extension to Carnegie Steel's Union line, which looped through the mills. "After the syndicate is formed and the Agreement made," a very confident Carnegie told J. G. A. Leishman, "the other lines will simply make the best of it, and you may be certain they will do far more for us thereafter, than you can possibly get them to do now."[6] His partners were still wary, however.

As a less aggressive alternative, Frick explored the possibility of buying their own trains to run on the Pennsylvania Railroad's tracks. The railroad's president, George Roberts, was open to this suggestion and negotiations ensued, but Carnegie put an immediate stop to them, cabling, "Board is not free to negotiate with the Pennsylvania Company. . . ." He was intent on dealing the Pennsylvania a serious blow no matter the cost.

The cost to extend Dick's line to Pittsburgh was put at $600,000, a serious investment; but if millions were saved over the coming years, then it was well worth it. There was just one problem: Colonel Dick failed to come through with his syndicate. Publicly committed to the project, Carnegie had to scramble to find financing for what was to be a newly organized railroad company with $3 million in capital. He was forced to do something he had not done in years and had piously warned against: he attempted to take out a personal loan of $1 million from the United States Trust Company of New York. Money was tight during the depression, so, in writing to the bank's president, John Stewart, he concluded his letter with an incentive: "You would also have something quite unique—my note. It is many years since I have had a personal obligation, and I have none now, nor do I intend to have any but this, which I would be about one million for 12 mos. $80,000 each mo. 1 year."[7] For a year, Stewart would have bragging rights that he owned a piece of Carnegie. It worked. The $1.5 million in Frick Coke Company bonds Carnegie put up for collateral helped, too. Colonel Dick was put in charge of extending the line and refurbishing the existing road, now called the Butler & Pittsburgh Railroad Company. The steel master wasn't finished, however. To ratchet up the pressure on the Pennsylvania, Carnegie turned his eye toward building a line to Connellsville, heart of the coke region.

From their Philadelphia offices, the Pennsylvania Railroad executives had seen and heard enough; they knew they could indeed make a profit at lower rates and could *not* afford Carnegie's agitation. In April, they indicated they were prepared to make serious concessions, and Carnegie crowed to Dod that it "seems really as if we were going to save *one cool million* per year in Freights."[8] He was so overjoyed that he told Dod, who was planning a summer yachting trip for them, not to limit the size of the boat. For his old railroad comrades at the Pennsylvania, George Roberts and Frank Thomson, he ordered a cask of fine whiskey. That was April 29. The first week of May brought a different story.

Carnegie Steel lost a bid to Illinois Steel to supply ship plates bound for Newport News, Virginia, and while investigating the matter Carnegie discovered that the reason their Chicago rival was able to undercut his price was due to lower shipping costs. The Pennsylvania Railroad was to blame, and, on May 5, he unleashed his frustration with the conniving and apparently remorseless Thomson:

> I think the great Pennsylvania Railroad has come to a sad condition, when it is only not willing, but not anxious to stand behind its own customers, and give equal rates per ton per mile to those which its competitors receive. . . .
> If the thousands of idle men in Pittsburgh to-day knew that this was one reason for its idleness, I would not give much for the receipts of the Pennsylvania road in and around Pittsburgh after a month or two. Even if you do not arrange with us, something must be done soon, or an explosion will take place.
> I send the enclosed contract to you personally and not as an official of the Pennsylvania Railroad, and I depend upon you returning it by messenger, and not taking a copy. Any notes you may desire for your personal use, of course, are all right.[9]

Enclosed was a contract for secret rebates, a contract Carnegie would guard alone.

Thomson conferred with Roberts as the reactionary Scotsman moved rapidly ahead with the Lake Erie connection. His threat to also build south had to be taken seriously, and so, realizing they had pushed Carnegie too far, Thomson politely requested a meeting in Philadelphia. To prepare for the meeting, Carnegie ordered his freight agent, George E. McCague, to obtain the rebates offered to his competition—they were the decisive weapon. "You must obtain them," he demanded. "How you are to get them I don't know and I don't care. But I must have them." As McCague started for the door, Carnegie left him with a line from *Richelieu*, one of his favorite plays: "From the hour I grasp that packet, think your guardian star Rains fortune on you!" The singsong voice had just given the freight agent carte blanche—cash payment, bribery, whatever necessary—to get the rebate information, for which he would be rewarded.

When, on the anointed day of May 11, Carnegie bounced into President George Roberts's office, he found Roberts and Frank Thomson sitting together, a united front. From their perspective, Carnegie was the son who'd long ago forsaken his father, the railroad, only to return again and again demanding gifts, rebates, money. Damn ungrateful. The Little Boss could be very childish, an ego prone to tantrums laced with fancy, multisyllabic words, always telling everyone how to run their business. He thought he was above everyone else, and in many aspects he was. Roberts and Thomson hated to acquiesce to Carnegie's demands and did their best to take advantage of Andy—it was a game—but ultimately, Carnegie was an economic force to take quite seriously.

"How are you, Andy?" said Roberts.

"How are you, *Mr.* Roberts? How are you, Frank?"

There the cordialness ended as Roberts questioned why Carnegie was fighting the Pennsylvania. In response, Carnegie simply threw a package on the table containing the secret rebates given to his competition. The railroad men were cornered, and Thomson said resignedly, "Well, tell us what you want."

"I don't want anything. I did not ask to see you. You asked to see me." It was a jab meant to humiliate.

"Don't talk that way. What do you want?"

All Carnegie wanted was competitive rates. Well, the railroad men said, you'll have to stop building that line to Lake Erie. No, that could not be stopped, he was obliged and committed, but he did agree to halt any plans for building the spur to Connellsville. When they signed a secret agreement five days later, Carnegie was the victor, reaping rebates on shipping coke, ore, and various steel products. He estimated that from these rebates the company *saved $1.5 million a year*, which would immediately boost profits by 25 percent.[10] He won rebates over which muckraker Ida Tarbell would crucify John D. Rockefeller; he won rebates that had been made illegal by the 1887 Interstate Commerce Act. As long as there were no enforced reforms in regulating the railroads, Carnegie would benefit from the inequities.

Carnegie's railroad line to Lake Erie met with mixed results initially. Colonel Dick turned out to be more interested in nightcaps in the smoking room than talking business during a July 1896 visit to Cluny, and the cost to refurbish the old line rocketed to almost $2.5 million. Despite the rising costs, Carnegie was so pleased with his triumph over the Pennsylvania Railroad that he wrote playfully to Frick about their railroad's physical ailments: "Her case is respectfully submitted to the attention of Dr. Henry Clay Frick, Surgeon and Physician (amputations may be necessary)."[11] Work on *her* moved forward, and by the end of the year Carnegie could claim to his partners that Pittsburgh was a lake port.

The triumph was somewhat offset by deteriorating business conditions as the presidential election approached. Since the onset of the depression, Cleveland's administration had failed to restore confidence. The Treasury's gold supply was drained to dangerously low levels several times, as U.S. and foreign investors withdrew the money from American markets and companies. Disillusioned with Cleveland, in July the democrats nominated William Jennings Bryan, who preached monetary revolution and supported the unlimited coinage of silver. Republican candidate William McKinley, on the other hand, offered no definitive leadership on monetary policy, prompting an irate Morgan to say McKinley had a "backbone of jelly" and that his waffling was "nauseating." Reflecting the political and economic uncertainty, the Dow Jones Average, created by *Wall Street Journal* cofounder Charles Dow in 1884, fell from 40.94 on May 26 to 28.28 at the end of August, more than a 30 percent drop.[12]

On the eve of 1896, Carnegie had known business would be slow, but the degree of deterioration he now witnessed was unexpected. There was talk of cutting wages and ending the bonus, which had been instituted in the prior year. "There is a very easy way to stop bonus," Carnegie wrote to Leishman, in his "Thoughts on Minutes." "When mills stop for a time, as they must, before starting them, let the men be told quietly that the firm regrets it cannot go on paying bonus under present conditions. The men will agree to start without bonus; if not, you can wait."[13] More telling of just how bad business was, on August 6, he ordered a halt to the construction of the Carnegie Library of Homestead and warned his board of managers of a coming economic storm "the like of which we have not seen in our days" and the need to break pooling agreements. "There is one way to secure safety, but to pursue that, we must be free. . . . We should play for safety not profit."[14] The specter of a greater threat than the depression now took shape, however: John D. Rockefeller.

John D. Rockefeller had been using the depression to wrap his hands around the weakened iron ore industry in a stranglehold, his plan to dominate ore as he did oil refining. Despite repeated warnings from Frick and other comrades in steel, Carnegie ignored the challenge—until he began to gasp for air.

One Rockefeller investment that appeared to have unlimited potential was the Minnesota Iron Company, operating in the Mesabi mountain range of northern Minnesota. The range rose unexpectedly above the surrounding land, inspiring the Native Americans to name it Mesabi, loosely translated as "Daddy of Them All." This remote area had been ignored for years until 1856, when the Merritt family settled in Duluth, a frontier post, and heard stories about strange red sand in the Mesabi Range. After a few incursions into the remote area, the Merritts were convinced a rich ore supply lay on the surface and immediately bought large tracts of land. Leonidas "Lon" Merritt knew high-quality ore remained a crucial element in the mix of steel, so, in the spring of 1891, he traveled to Pittsburgh to entice Frick into building a railroad from Lake Superior to the range. Surely, Carnegie Steel would want this ore, but when Frick looked over this coarse pioneer from the Minnesota backwoods, he dismissed him high-handedly. "Frick did not use me like a gentleman," Merritt recalled, "and cut me off short and bulldozed me."[15] Mesabi simply wasn't strategically located, as far as Frick was concerned. Meanwhile, there was still plenty of ore easily accessed in West Virginia and other nearby locales.

Next to attempt to entice Frick was Carnegie's boyhood chum Henry Oliver. Oliver served as a delegate to the National Republican Convention at Minneapolis, and while there he heard of a rich ore field discovered in the Mesabi Range. On investigating the Merritt's property, he was immediately convinced of the ore's quality and gave Lon Merritt a $5,000 check to lease one of the family's large mines. Later in the summer, Oliver took a shot at interesting Carnegie Steel, but when he offered an interest in his newly created firm, the Oliver Mining Company, Carnegie was as equally shortsighted and biased as Frick had been. "Oliver's ore bargain is just like him—nothing in it, . . ." he wrote Frick in August 1892. "If there is any department of business that offers no inducement it is ore. It never has been very profitable, and the Mesabi is not the last great deposit that Lake Superior is to reveal."[16] Granted, at the time, Carnegie was a little preoccupied with Homestead.

Back at Mesabi, the Merritts continued to develop their tracts of land, albeit recklessly, borrowing heavily, and even embarked on the construction of a railroad to carry the ore to Lake Superior. The 1893 panic quickly curtailed their activity, and Rockefeller now stepped in. He loaned them $100,000 and formed a holding company, Lake Superior Consolidated Iron Mines, to manage his iron ore assets and theirs. Before the year was out, the loan ballooned to almost $2 million. Carnegie, assuming the powdery ore simply could not be of good quality, arrogantly ridiculed Rockefeller's extensive purchases.

Frick was the first to recognize their blunder. In the spring of 1894, he arranged for Carnegie Steel to advance $500,000 to Oliver, whose finances had been crippled by the depression. In return, they received a 50 percent interest in the Oliver Mining Company and a new source for ore now proven to be of excellent quality. Reluctantly, Carnegie agreed, but he still insisted the venture "will result in more trouble and less profit than almost any branch of our business. . . . I hope you will make a note of this prophecy. . . . If Massawba ore requires special form of furnaces, it will add force to my instinctive aversion to making investments hundreds of miles away."[17] His intentional misspelling of Mesabi was his way of poking fun at what he considered a backward and second-rate mining operation.

Meanwhile, the Merritts' bad luck—or rather, bad management—was never reversed, and in 1895 they were forced to turn all of their holdings over to Rockefeller. Suddenly, there was a justifiable fear that the Caesar of oil would soon dominate ore. Carnegie, who had failed to seize the opportunity, was now subject to Rockefeller's whim.

Frantic to establish himself in iron ore, Carnegie behaved compulsively and impulsively as he became determined to monopolize what he believed to be unlimited supplies of quality ore in West Virginia. Carnegie had one of his flashes—here the next battle would be fought, and he would triumph—so he ordered his furnace manager to "get options upon all available properties before we are known in the matter." Secrecy was crucial to outflank the competition; and, for once, Carnegie kept his mouth shut. He ridiculed the high prices "Rockafellow" was paying for ore land and found it "amusing, in view of what we know is coming."[18] What was coming, Carnegie assumed, was a bonanza of cheap ore from West Virginia that would depress prices and hurt poor old "Rockafellow," whose name he knew how to spell without a doubt. But the very next month, Carnegie was forced to pay his respects when he realized he didn't have the strength to go it alone and joined an iron ore pool at Rockefeller's behest. If the company refused, Carnegie explained to Leishman in January 1896, "we should lose the friendship of Rockefeller. . . . I think Rockefeller is the coming man in ore and it will be to our advantage to stand in with him. As his ownership in ore lands will be very large, I believe it will be more to our advantage to mine ore in his territory, paying him a royalty, than to attempt to purchase ore property for ourselves."[19]

Carnegie, who had been battling with the Pennsylvania Railroad, quibbling over Venezuela, and touring the Continent, failed in his West Virginia iron ore endeavor. There was no bonanza; but, in seeking a silver lining, he concluded, "It is well worth knowing just what was there. Lake Superior, after all, is to be our source of supply."[20] Just as Carnegie was preparing to approach Rockefeller about buying his ore in the Mesabi, the situation darkened: rumors circulated through the press that Rockefeller was planning to build a major steel mill in either Cleveland or South Chicago to rival Carnegie Steel. Such a move would set up a clash between the two undisputed titans of the Gilded Age—two ruthless businessmen who crushed their competition by scooping the market, reinvested profits to achieve ever-greater efficiencies, and drove their men mercilessly. This was to be a battle of the ages, and their critics relished the idea of the two despots—one of oil, the other of steel—destroying each other.

Instead of retaliating with threats, Carnegie and his men had to devise a plan to dissuade Rockefeller from entering steel, which, they realized, would be most easily achieved by becoming his greatest customer. The Carnegie men offered to buy all their ore from Rockefeller if he kept out of steel — and not only that, but Carnegie Steel, as well as Oliver Mining, would promise to halt its own mining forays in the Mesabi Range. Rockefeller could reign supreme. In early negotiations, Leishman sat down with one of Rockefeller's top lieutenants, Frederick Gates, but they failed to make any progress. Carnegie realized he would have to approach Rockefeller personally, and, although coming from the weak position, he would have to find a way to do so on equal footing. He took comfort in knowing Rockefeller admired him and, in particular, his philanthropy, so he decided the best approach to take with the reclusive titan was to write an honest letter. He admitted that Leishman and Gates had failed in their negotiations, but he said their differences weren't

> too irreconcilable, if both parties realized as I do, the mutual advantage of such an alliance, and were prepared to meet each other halfway.
>
> When Mr. Gates submits the matter to you, as I suppose he will, and you concur in this, I believe you and I could fix it in a few minutes, and I shall be very glad to go and see you if you think it worth while to take the matter up.[21]

Carnegie's willingness to go to Rockefeller was an acknowledgement that the oilman was the ruling power and a sign of humility that Rockefeller appreciated. The two parties struck a fifty-year agreement in which Carnegie would purchase at least six hundred thousand tons of ore a year at a rate Oliver calculated would initially save Carnegie about $1.50 a ton, almost another million in savings on top of the railroad rebates.[22] In addition to the six hundred thousand tons the company agreed to purchase a year, Carnegie Steel also had to ship another six hundred thousand tons of ore from its own mines via Rockefeller railroads and steamships, and Carnegie had to agree to not invade any more territory in the Mesabi Range for the next ten years. For Rockefeller's part, he had to vow he would never enter the steel business. Many years later, Carnegie would crow, "Don't you know, it does my heart good to think I got ahead of John D. Rockefeller on a bargain."[23]

He was talking cocky now, but it had taken several years for Oliver and company to drag him into the "Rockafellow" ore deal. He was no visionary this time. At least, even though Carnegie wouldn't have acknowledged he was eating crow, he did pay Oliver a tribute: "Harry Oliver was a man who saw far ahead. He could not carry all the game he had captured, and he appealed to the Carnegie Company to join him. It did, and carried the treasure safely through with its money and credit."[24] The foresight of Oliver saved Carnegie Steel millions of dollars, and, with the company's supply chain complete, observed *Iron Age*, it gave Carnegie "a position unequalled by any steel producer in the world."[25]

The deal with Rockefeller depressed the iron ore market, and as other mining operators lost money and folded, Carnegie and Rockefeller realized more opportunities to utterly dominate the entire market. Under Oliver's fervent leadership, Carnegie Steel secured three Lake Superior area mines: the Pioneer in the Vermillion Range, and the Norrie and Tilden mines in the Gogebic Range.[26] Carnegie agreed to lease the Tilden and Pioneer mines and to purchase the Norrie mine. When news of these latest ore triumphs reached the press, the New York Daily Tribune unabashedly announced: "Andrew Carnegie has perfected the largest iron-producing combination in the world. . . ."[27] And Carnegie admitted to Frick, "I am happy that we are now in our ore supply; it was the only element needed to give us an impregnable position."[28]

On New Year's Eve, Carnegie reflected on his triumphs. Despite the challenges, profits had increased from $5 million in 1895 to $6 million in 1896, thanks to the historic ore deal, armor contracts, and pools. He heartily congratulated his board of managers: "Let me wish you all the best of New Year's, and congratulate you upon the prospects of THE CARNEGIE STEEL COMPANY, and also THE FRICK COKE COMPANY. You have read the paragraph in to-day's 'Iron Age,' . . . which does not exaggerate, I think, what the company is to do, but which is slightly premature. . . . All hail 1897! No New Year in the history of the Company so heavy with result ensuring our preeminence." He concluded with a commanding flourish: "Our policy should be, THE FRIEND OF ALL, THE ALLY OF NONE."[29]

The most immediate reward of the Rockefeller iron deal, in addition to cheap ore, was that Carnegie could sever all alliances with his competition and go to war against them. The sixty-one-year-old remained a formidable Scotsman, as bold as William Wallace, who confronted, pummeled, and pillaged the armies of England, and as politically manipulative as the Robert the Bruce, who negotiated truces and alliances with the clans of Scotland and then shattered them when no longer convenient, a necessary strategy to win Scotland's independence. Carnegie, with a hard line to his mouth and white-bearded chin, struck a hostile pose. His battle cry: "THE FRIEND OF ALL, THE ALLY OF NONE."[30]

The relationships between the rail pool members had already been particularly chilly during the depression. The pool had collapsed in 1893; then was resuscitated; and now, in February 1897, was shattered. On Friday, February 5, Lackawanna Iron and Steel cut its rail price to $20 a ton, signaling a willingness to go it alone, and an emergency conference of the pool members was immediately scheduled for the following Monday in Pittsburgh. Carnegie, whose firm had been given a 53.5 percent share of the pool, saw no reason to cooperate with the others, however, and by Tuesday afternoon he was selling rails for $17 a ton. As he told Frick, he was going to teach them a lesson, and he expected Pennsylvania Steel to fail, if not Illinois Steel.[31]

The other steelmakers recognized that Carnegie had an opportunity to destroy them, and they were soon running scared. The very month Carnegie Steel bought the Norrie mine, September 1897, Illinois Steel president

Bet-a-Million Gates wrote Frick a "strictly personal and absolutely confidential" letter in which he urged the consolidation of his company and Carnegie Steel. "If the concerns are all in one company," he argued, "there will not be the temptation to hammer the price of soft steel down to such a point that there will be practically no profit left to the maker."[32] Gates should not have shown weakness. Frick passed the message on to Carnegie, who merely chortled at the thought of bringing one of his top rivals to his knees. The letter was filed away for posterity's sake.

Desperate for an alliance, Gates now suggested reestablishing the rail pool; however, Carnegie was extremely wary of cooperating with him. Even Charlie Schwab, who occasionally played poker with Gates, considered him as crooked as they came without breaking the law. In addition, pools weren't so easily arranged anymore with more stringent commerce laws being passed; and, as Schwab recalled, they had to start meeting in New Jersey instead of New York.

> On one such occasion, John Gates and I were going across on the ferry, I was very perturbed about something or other we had agreed upon, and John said to me, "Now you just leave this to me. I'll straighten it out. I have always been able to explain everything—everything except one thing, and for that I never could find any excuse whatsoever."
>
> I asked him what that one thing was and he said, "Well, a while ago my wife took a little vacation, and then, thinking I'd be lonesome, came home without telling me she was coming. She thought she'd like to surprise me. Well, I wasn't home when she arrived, and after she sat up a while and waited, she went to bed. But when two or three o'clock came and I hadn't shown up, she became worried and went down to her maid's room to see whether the girl knew anything about my coming in or not. Well, she found me in bed with the maid, and I couldn't think up any really adequate excuse for being there."[33]

Gates could not be trusted.

"I would not have anything to do with Illinois Steel Company under present management. . . ," Carnegie advised Frick. His opinion of Gates was rather low; as a businessman he considered him "dull of sight" and as a person he despised him for gambling.[34] Carnegie wanted "to stand by ourselves alone" and, in his letter to Frick, continued: "You began a great struggle wisely; it has been fought vigorously and we have triumphed. Now you are a good fighter, but there is something that comes after the fight is over, namely reaping the rewards of victory. Very few commanders have been able to do this. They fight well but are poor reapers. Now let us see that you can not only win victory, but also know how to gather in the fruits."[35] The tone was sharp; Carnegie's independence was flaring, and he demanded absolute victory.

Carnegie's assessment concerning Illinois's vulnerability was on the mark. When, in December, Carnegie Steel quoted rails at $18 to Illinois's $20, Gates panicked and cheerfully reiterated he hoped they could again cooperate, but no agreements were immediately forthcoming.[36] Flush with bringing Illinois Steel to its knees, Carnegie exulted to Frick: "Lauder writes our business never in such fine form and all pulling together. Let us . . . defy the world."[37] The hunger was never satisfied. This sparring with Illinois Steel would ultimately result in a final showdown, a last gunfight at the Carnegie Corral.

From the battles with the Pennsylvania Railroad and Rockefeller, there emerged one prominent casualty in the Carnegie regime—President John Leishman. The strain of being under Carnegie's thumb was crushing the life from him. The flogging had started from the time of his nomination for the presidency of Carnegie Steel and had never stopped. And even though he had taken a severe beating for speculating in pig iron in the winter of 1894–1895, Leishman continued to involve the company in risky ore deals. Making matters worse, he was using his own money to speculate on iron ore and stocks. He had become caught up in the Gilded Age; he had gambled to attain riches beyond his means. The odds were against him, especially during the depression. His personal debts mounted, and by January 1896 stories reached Carnegie at his Fifty-first Street home.

Despising Wall Street, its trappings, and those who become trapped, Carnegie, who was extremely sensitive to the firm's image in light of the prior scandals, lashed out with a venomous tongue:

> When a President has left business methods and brought a great concern into disrepute many tongues wag which other wise would remain silent. . . . Now there may be other complications in your private affairs. *You conceal,* keep silent, when no man can obtain firm standing with partners who keeps any business investments from them. Our President should have reputation, hence influence and financial strength, if not from capital, yet from *character.* The Carnegie Steel Co. is daily compromised by its President owing private debts. I am told of an instance where you borrowed from a subordinate. This is madness. . . . Every dinner you attend, every lunch at the Club at which you may linger, every act affects the Company; every word you speak; but every financial step in your private affairs has serious consequences.[38]

For once, it appeared his tone of righteous indignation was justified. Suspecting the worst, Carnegie had his trusted financial secretary Robert Franks investigate Leishman's account with Carnegie Steel: What did he owe for his interest in the firm? Had he borrowed more for personal reasons? Was he indebted to anyone who might make claims on the company?

Carnegie himself traveled to Pittsburgh to meet with Leishman, who considered the attack unfair and unsubstantiated. At his office in the Carnegie Building, Leishman admitted to buying some stock in phonograph, gas, and ore companies, but only on the advice of company attorney Philander Knox, Phipps, and Frick, who all had investments, too. Carnegie appeared to accept the explanation and promised to not discuss it again. But he did—with Schwab, Gayley, and even Frew over at the library, among others.

Deeply hurt, Leishman protested: "And to make matters worse, although you promised me on the Sunday morning after your arrival that you would say nothing further about it—you have spoken about it to a number of my subordinates in a way that had a decided tendency to belittle me and lessen my influence and standing and I have now heard outside that you have spoken very unkindly if not harshly to Frew and others—and you know that any unfriendly statement coming from you is not only very humiliating but calculated to affect my standing."[39] It didn't matter what Carnegie, who could be exceptionally spiteful despite his claims otherwise, had said or promised in their meeting, he was determined to eject Leishman from the company, and he continued his assault just as he had on William Shinn years earlier, sneering he couldn't "have the Carnegie Steel Company degraded to the level of speculators and Jim Cracks, men who pass as manufacturers, but who look to the market and not to manufacturing, and who buy up bankrupt concerns only to show their incapacity."[40]

Frick suggested that Leishman, who had become a physical wreck under the strain, take a vacation. This option didn't strike Carnegie favorably at all—a vacation was the last thing Leishman deserved—and he thrashed his president again over his management skills, concluding, "Frankly, I must say, that if you do not look out, you will bring even our firm into serious trouble. . . . I scarcely know what next to expect. These things cause me great anxiety."[41] To relieve the anxiety, Leishman resigned on February 12. Because Carnegie had handpicked Leishman, his own leadership had to be called into question. Leishman's tenure as Carnegie Steel president was two years. Before him, there had been Frick, Stewart, Walker, Phipps, Tom Carnegie, and Shinn—a veritable graveyard of destroyed chairmen, presidents, and managers.

Next up was wonder boy Charles M. Schwab. Unknown to his patron Carnegie, Schwab had secrets, too. He engaged in extramarital affairs; and, while not a stock speculator, he enjoyed gambling at cards and roulette. Schwab was well aware that he would have to hide these sins from Carnegie's prudish Victorian sensibilities. For now, the oblivious Carnegie couldn't compliment his new president enough, writing Frick: "You are no doubt feeling as I do that a great load is off your shoulders. We have got the man, and having him, there is no reason why we should hesitate about going forward and keeping the lead."[42] He had been equally effusive about Shinn, Abbott, and Frick, and one can't help wondering if Carnegie was talking himself into feeling so positive about Schwab. To ensure Schwab's loyalty, he boosted his interest in the firm from 1 to 3 percent.

Throughout the triumphs of and upheavals at Carnegie Steel, the depression remained severe. If Republican presidential candidate McKinley didn't win the 1896 election by a landslide, Carnegie was certain a severe panic on Wall Street would ensue and the country's economy would be devastated. Unfortunately for the Republicans, William Jennings Bryan was a great orator and took the early lead in the public's eye. Bryan, flashing steel-blue eyes and well-kept teeth, vowed to fight the money kings of Wall Street and wholly supported unlimited coinage of silver.

McKinley's campaign manager, Mark Hanna, a wealthy Cleveland businessman, undertook the Herculean task of educating the American public on the critical money question and of portraying Bryan as a crackpot economist. As part of the propaganda campaign, Hanna dug up Carnegie's 1891 essay, "ABC of Money," and had millions of copies printed. "It required but a moment for us to see that the leaflet was admirably calculated to make the money issue of this campaign clear to the simplest mind," Hanna wrote Carnegie. "We therefore printed and have circulated more than 5,000,000 copies of the leaflet, and the demand for it was as great as for that of any document we have issued. This of itself is evidence of its worth, but the scores of letters we have received commending the paper, attest its value, and the powerful influence for good we feel it has exerted. . . . and at this late day, I want, in the name of and on behalf of the National Republican Committee, to thank you for your work, and assure you that we appreciate the service you have rendered the party and the country."[43] Nothing could have pleased Carnegie more, and he donated generously to the campaign—as did Rockefeller's Standard Oil and J. P. Morgan, with commitments of $250,000 each. Bryan, whom Carnegie characterized as a "light-headed-blathering demagogue," had to be defeated for the good of the country.[44]

CHAPTER 25

A Point of Disruption and Transition

On November 5, Election Day, McKinley won the Electoral College and took the popular vote by a larger margin than any president since Grant. The weather was fair, unseasonably warm for November, a sign of better times to come, Carnegie hoped; but during the McKinley presidency Carnegie would reevaluate his priorities as there were significant changes in his personal life and the country went to war. While dealing with personal and political disruptions, he would also have to conduct his own war in business as new powers arose to challenge him. At least for now, he could rejoice that the Republicans were back in power and order in his political world was restored.

During the last Republican administration under Harrison, Carnegie had enjoyed a favorable status, especially with his friend James Blaine serving as secretary of state. By contrast, during Cleveland's term, he had suffered a series of attacks from Navy Secretary Abner Herbert, Attorney General Richard Olney, and sundry congressmen. Now it was time to take immediate advantage of McKinley to protect his company's flank, and it was Frick who proposed the most opportunistic idea. Knowing the company's attorney, Philander Knox, and McKinley were friendly, Frick thought Knox might just have a chance at being appointed McKinley's attorney general. How better to protect the company's interests than by having the country's top legal eagle in the bag, so, on December 16, Frick submitted the idea to Carnegie: "Am satisfied you could secure the selection of Mr. Knox for this position, as I know the President-Elect would do almost anything you asked."[1]

Considering Carnegie's financial support of McKinley, Frick's observation was quite correct. The next day, Carnegie wrote McKinley, opening with a humble apology:

> If there was one thing which I had resolved upon, it was that you should never be troubled by me about appointments. I pity you too much. . . .

I cannot refuse, however, to comply with Mr. Frick's request to say a word about Mr. Knox, who ranks with me as the best lawyer I have ever had for our interests, a veritable "little giant," and one of your *real* friends from the start.

However, in calling men into your "official family," I think you entitled to consider their "Congeniality" to yourself, as the Father of the family. Should you like to adopt Mr. Knox as one of your "happy family"—which I hope is to be—I for one will rejoice.[2]

There was no hesitation on McKinley's part to appoint Knox, who would indeed protect big business.

The planets had aligned with the moon, and the goddess Fate blessed Carnegie with good fortune and cleansed his conscience of doubt. The most incredible piece of evidence that Carnegie was a chosen one lay inside his wife. Louise was showing—she was pregnant! Shortly after their romantic stay in Venice, somewhere in the Tirol, perhaps, the sixty-year-old Carnegie's seed had taken. What had been accepted as impossible had happened. Louise would be turning forty in March 1897, the month their baby was due; and while that was old for a first birth, this was no time to worry about physical limitations, this was a time to celebrate. But then the harsh winter weather, compounded by business concerns and the excitement of impending fatherhood, took its toll on Carnegie.

In late February, he fell ill with pleurisy, stricken with a fever, a cough, and labored breathing. With the baby due in March, a trip to Florida to regain his health was out of the question, so Louise, Stella, and he went to Lucy Carnegie's home in Greenwich, Connecticut, to escape New York City's smog, thick with winter stoves burning. As the time neared for the birth, Louise returned to the Fifty-first Street mansion to be attended to by the best doctors, while Carnegie remained in Greenwich, under Stella's care.

On March 30, Louise gave birth to a daughter, named Margaret in honor of Carnegie's mother. The next day the *New York Daily Tribune* announced: "Andrew Carnegie had double cause for rejoicing to-day. He received news of the birth of a daughter in New York, where Mrs. Carnegie went several days ago, and he was also able to be out of doors to-day for the first time since his attack of pleurisy developed about five weeks ago."[3] Within days of the child being born, Carnegie took the train into New York and a coach to the Fifty-first Street mansion to visit with his little miracle. The strain of the journey and the excitement of seeing Louise and Margaret left him pale and shaken—hardly the man who had recently declared unbridled war on the competition. He didn't stay in New York long.

Immediately after returning to Greenwich, he wrote Louise a letter, reassuring her that he was becoming stronger. In it he expressed his amazement with their daughter: "Now since I have seen you and the Little Saint I seem always with you. Before this all was glamour—like a dream. Now as real as ever. Margaret a little 'uncanny' yet—fresh from heaven and not just earthly like ourselves. . . . I do so much wish to be well to welcome you. Only six days more after this. Hurrah! A kiss for Margaret and twenty for her mother. Ever, darling, your own Andrew." The six days were too long in passing, and Carnegie wrote again, "Oh Lou, may this be our last separation. I hope many, many long years together are to be ours with the little Darling closer and closer to us. Ever your own, A.C."[4] When witnessing Carnegie in loving repose, it was difficult to reconcile the gentle family man with the fierce businessman. It simply wasn't possible. Behind each mask was a distinctive personality.

Now that they had a child, Louise wanted more stability in their lives, especially during the summer season in Scotland. She wanted a place to make home—their own home, not a leased property where they were at the whim of the owner, such as MacPherson, who owned Cluny. He was to marry and would most likely take back his ancestral home. The subject of buying their own Highlands estate had been broached, but now it took on more weight. Louise also wanted her husband to reconsider his priorities, and, to prompt a reevaluation, she elicited Stella's help: "Please tell Andrew the most patriotic duty we can perform to our country—better than making armor plate—is the taking care of our wee Margaret so that she in turn may grow up a strong healthy woman and become the mother of men . . . therefore please urge him to take good care of his health, not only for our sakes, but for our country."[5] Apparently, Carnegie was more likely to listen to the earnest younger sister than the nagging wife.

And so, the birth of Margaret initiated a transitional phase in Carnegie's life. He had to think more of the family and how his actions might affect his child's life, an added and weighty responsibility. And now he had to learn to share Louise's affections with Margaret, and how to divide his attention between the two of them. Many doubts flashed through his mind. How would fatherhood affect him? How would it affect his leadership of Carnegie Steel?

The ocean crossing that June did not have the usual soothing effect on Carnegie's nerves, as the presence of Margaret, not yet three months old, added a certain tension. The crying, the nursing, the cloth diapers were completely foreign to the titan. And then there was the prospect of losing Cluny. As the Carnegies coached through the wild mountain land of the Grampian Hills and passed into Spey Valley, their eyes searching for the white granite turrets, they feared it would be their last journey to this raw paradise. Once settled in Cluny, Carnegie, determined to make Louise happy, approached MacPherson about purchasing the castle, but MacPherson was equally determined to return with his bride to his ancestral home and would not sell. The search for a new summer home commenced at once.

Carnegie had three criteria: a view of the sea, a trout stream, and a waterfall. To fulfill his quest, he enlisted the help of Hew Morrison, the resourceful librarian at Edinburgh Library, who was well acquainted with the historic homes of Scotland. The first estate that came to Morrison's mind was Skibo, a Highland castle on the east coast overlooking the Dornoch Firth, and he brought maps, plans, and the deed to Skibo for Carnegie's review. Because the castle itself was too small, had fallen into disrepair, and there was no waterfall, Carnegie dismissed Skibo. The duke of Sutherland had several magnificent estates that sounded promising, however, and a two-week coaching trip was organized to investigate the prospective properties and visit friends. Louise and baby Margaret did not join the charioteers.

While Carnegie was traipsing across the countryside in search of a castle to conquer like one of King Arthur's knights (or, perhaps, Don Quixote), a lonely Louise anxiously wrote her husband: "We now want to take root. We haven't time to make mistakes; as many playthings and play places as you like and yachts galore, but a *home* first *please*, where we can have the greatest measure of health. . . ."[6] Health, especially that of her aging husband, was of a foremost concern now that they had a baby. Meanwhile none of the Sutherland's estates proved worthy; they were too far inland, and Carnegie wanted access to the sea.

The coaching trip now brought them to Bonar Bridge, on the coast of the North Sea and within eight miles of Skibo Castle. Again, Morrison suggested they look at the estate. Carnegie relented, but refusing to further inconvenience his fellow charioteers in what had turned into a wild goose chase, he insisted they go alone. Morrison and he rented a wagonette and driver at Bonar Bridge and set out for Skibo along a winding coastal road that passed through picturesque hamlets and deep woods of bracken, oak, birch, and larch. The beauty did not escape Carnegie as they approached the Dornoch Firth, where the air was strangely mild and embracing, like the northern Riviera. The prevailing winds and sea gave the area its own unique climate zone, Morrison explained; the place was still lush in mid-October, and in some years the rhododendrons bloomed in January. Carnegie began to sense that he was entering a romantic and magical realm, rich with history. In fact, Skibo was the simplification of the name originally given the castle in the year 1225, Schytherbolle, which, depending one whether one was Norse, Celtic, or Gaelic, was loosely translated as either a place of peace or a fairyland.

The wagonette turned onto an unpretentious, narrow avenue that opened into the castle's main drive, lined with ancient beech trees and yews. They came to a halt in a circular drive before the white sandstone castle. Although abandoned, Skibo was impressive in its Scottish baronial style, with ornate bay windows and third-story cupolas, gabled roofs, and a circular turret. As they walked the stone terrace, covered with lichen, Carnegie had a commanding view of the countryside: the sparkling firth, the blue hills, the rocky streams, the woodland, and the pasture. It was not the rugged yet enchanting terrain of Cluny; it was a magnificent, bucolic panorama. The castle's park-like grounds encompassed twenty-two thousand acres, about four thousand under cultivation. There was plenty of wild game; the region was renowned for delicious grouse and herds of roe deer. The fishing was excellent, too, for both salmon and trout, and the firth, shining silver beneath the hills, was ideal for a yacht. But there was no waterfall. That can be built, Morrison suggested slyly.

When the two men entered through Skibo's main doors, they stepped into a great hall with a sweeping, circular staircase that a king and his queen might descend with great pomp and circumstance to greet their guests. The musty smell of the wood, the stone fireplaces, the long cast of sunlight through tall windows and still air stirred Carnegie's imagination. History was alive here. In the thirteenth and fourteenth centuries, Skibo had been home to the bishops of Dornoch Cathedral, four miles distant. It then became a clan fortress and passed through a number of owners and families who couldn't seem to keep it due to death or bankruptcy. In 1882, Ewen C. Sutherland-Walker purchased the castle, then enlarged and renovated it. He had to borrow heavily; thirteen years later, he was forced to declare bankruptcy and was expelled from the premises. There was an evil spell on the castle, according to the locals, who pointed to the fact that for the last 150 years, no family had possessed the lands for more than one generation. Regardless, the rich history enraptured Carnegie. He was enchanted. He had found his heaven on earth, as he would lovingly refer to Skibo.

When Carnegie returned to Cluny, he overwhelmed Louise with his enthusiasm as he described Skibo, the grounds, its location. It was four miles from the parish of Dornoch, which had its own castle, as well as an eleventh-century cathedral and a renowned golf course, second in reputation only to St. Andrews. And ten miles away lay Macbeth's castle—Macbeth—Shakespeare—all signs. She had seen this semicrazed look and behavior before, impetuous and headstrong; and, like his business partners, she reigned him in. A deep breath was needed, as the cautious Harry Phipps would say. They discussed the fact that Louise had not seen Skibo, nor would she that summer, and agreed it would be better to lease the estate for 1898 with an option to buy.

Carnegie had wearied of the business merry-go-round—tariffs, mill renovations, wages, and bickering over dividends—and he made it known he was considering selling out. The closest he would come to it that summer was a rumor circulating through the papers in July, a yarn about the Russian government being interested in buying his steelworks. With Carnegie and Frick overseas, the story couldn't be confirmed, but it wasn't bloody likely the Star-Spangled Scotchman would sell out to Russians. One Cluny guest that summer, Charles Flint, who had made a fortune in South American trade, noticed that the only time his host turned dour was in dealing with "that base and common drudge 'twixt man and man"—business. Such was the case when Schwab proposed major additions to Homestead and renovations to Duquesne. After reviewing the proposals, Carnegie cabled "No." Schwab cabled back, "I'll guarantee it'll be a success." With a twist of humor, Carnegie replied, "Who guarantees the guarantor?"[7]

Schwab convinced the rest of the board to approve his proposal, anyway, forcing Carnegie to respond with a stinging "Notes on the Minutes," in which he questioned how such a large project could be passed unanimously.[8] Disappointed that Schwab had not provided a detailed analysis to justify the work, Carnegie blasted him in a blunt letter: "Show us why the blooming mill at Homestead is one of the best expenditures we could possible make. You must have arrived at this opinion from some data. You have not founded it upon nothing. Why do you keep this data from your Board and partners?"[9] He had no tolerance for slapdash proposals and, clearly, fatherhood had not mellowed him. Quick to appease his master, Schwab wrote two lengthy letters full of data. "You are a hustler!" a satisfied Carnegie fired back, but he also realized he would have to closely monitor Schwab's activities.[10]

In late August, Carnegie and Louise, along with a party of friends, went yachting among the striking Hebrides, a group of five hundred islands off the west coast of Scotland. (Only now, with Margaret almost six months old, was Louise willing to leave her with Aunt Stella and a nanny.) It was a last summer hurrah, a weaning from Cluny. But the dramatically carved islands did little to assuage their melancholy over leaving the Spey Valley. Perhaps it was mere coincidence, but on the eve of departing Cluny, Carnegie again became quite ill. The family went straight to London to consult with the best doctors, who advised them not to return to New York, where, during the harsh winter, he would be susceptible to pneumonia, putting his life in danger. Instead, they rented the Villa Allerton in Cannes for the winter. Poor health was beginning to nag at Carnegie.

In hopes of restoring his robustness, Carnegie inhaled the Mediterranean air, his elixir, during walks on the beach and through the town, which entertained an old section with sixteenth- and seventeenth-century churches. Venerable William Gladstone was there, too, that winter, hoping the Mediterranean might give his eighty-eight-year-old body another breath. (Gladstone would die of cancer of the palate on May 19, 1898, and would be buried in Westminster Abbey.) There was an enclave of British dignitaries in Cannes with whom the Carnegies socialized and with whom Carnegie debated the day's issues. In particular, they were concerned with the American jingoists ranting for war with Spain.

For several years, Cuban nationalists had been engaged in a bloody insurrection against their Spanish occupiers, who had oppressed them for some five centuries. Due to war-hungry William Randolph Hearst and his fellow yellow journalists' vivid stories, a wave of passion supporting the Cubans now swept the United States. As for the less sentimental expansionists, including Assistant Secretary of the Navy Teddy Roosevelt, who carried a smoking Manifest Destiny, Cuba was ripe for the taking to strengthen the U.S. presence in the Caribbean. Then came the eruption of violence. On the evening of February 15, 1898, an explosion rocked the American battleship *Maine* in Havana harbor, where it was stationed on a courtesy visit to protect Americans. The forward section was shattered and quickly sank into the mud. Of the 354 men on board, 266 were killed. Hearst's *New York Journal* headlines blared: DESTRUCTION OF THE MAINE BY FOUL PLAY.[11] A black, calamitous mood gripped Washington as debate immediately erupted over what had caused the explosion—accident or treachery? Secretary of the Navy Long believed it to be an accident; whereas Roosevelt, who supported the accident theory publicly, raged for war in private. McKinley resisted the war fever initially, but the irresistible slogan To Hell with Spain! Remember the Maine! would wear down his convictions.

Cables reached Carnegie on February 16, announcing the *Maine*'s sinking, and later in the day, while holding court with his companions—"distinguished men of European nations"—he relayed how his company had bid to provide the armor for the *Maine* years earlier. The old men deliberated over the circumstances of the explosion and who would win if war were declared. "The opinion was universally held by them that for a time the Spanish Navy would be master over us," Carnegie recalled, "although it was admitted the superior resources of the United States must eventually ensure victory."[12] For his part, the ever-fervent Republican boasted that America's ships were more modern, better armed, and manned by superior men, and would send the Spanish war ships to a watery grave. February came to an end and March passed, and still there was no declaration of war from McKinley.

On April 4, Carnegie received an update from Frick: "Business holds up remarkably well, considering excitement regarding Cuba. Have urged all Congressmen and Senators with whom I am acquainted to stand by the President, and let him handle the matter in his own way."[13] A week later, McKinley requested that Congress grant him the power to end hostilities between Spain and the Cuban nationalists, which amounted to declaring war; and, on April 25, a declaration of war was passed. The United States was intent on expelling Spain from Cuba and Puerto Rico, as well as in the Philippines, where the nationalists were also fighting the Spanish. To Roosevelt and the expansionists' chagrin, an amendment to the war declaration prevented the United States from annexing Cuba, assuming she won, but the fate of the Philippines and Puerto Rico remained up for debate.

A naval blockade was imposed on Cuba, and there was a call for 125,000 volunteers to swell the ranks of the regular army, which numbered a mere 28,000 men. Among those who answered the call was Roosevelt, who requested a commission in the army. He was made a lieutenant colonel and was assigned to the First U.S. Volunteer Cavalry, nicknamed the "Rough Riders."

Although Carnegie considered the blowing up of the *Maine* to be an accident, the pacifist was strangely silent in protesting the war, especially considering his fervor in calling for arbitration of the 1895 Venezuelan dispute. The reason for his silence: he was caught in a profitable quandary. As the United States and Europe's colonial powers armed themselves, Carnegie realized a boon in profits, and he was intent on taking further advantage of the situation. Just six months before, when the navy was aggressively attempting to procure lower tonnage rates on the armor plates, Carnegie had beaten the government into submission by offering to sell the navy his armor mill. Run it yourself, Carnegie had challenged.[14] No one accepted the offer, and now Carnegie was getting $400 a ton for armor versus the $249 Bethlehem was paid by Russia. Net income for March 1898 was an unparalleled $791,302.13—a pace that would give Carnegie record profits.[15] If he denounced the war, he would be attacked fiercely, be labeled a hypocrite, and risk the profits that were to fuel his philanthropy. Besides, he didn't think the war would amount to much killing; as he told Frick, "I am not alarmed, much as I regret war."[16] Carnegie subscribed to the accepted public opinion: "It was a splendid little war."

The lack of guns and ammunition for American armed forces was no secret, and in May Carnegie urged his board of managers to build a mill for forging guns. *Guns.* Like an evolving criminal who commits increasingly heinous acts, the self-proclaimed pacifist, cloaking himself in patriotism, had now taken the next step as profits easily trounced ideology. When the board took up the issue of making guns, Dod Lauder made an alternative proposal based on the soundest of logic: "Projectiles might pay us better than forgings. Guns fire many times their own weight in projectiles."[17] Going into guns involved a large investment, too, so Carnegie took Dod's advice, and soon they were busy making projectiles; it was his patriotic duty, of course.

Amazingly, in the heat of war, at the very time Carnegie was championing guns, Frick and Carnegie actually exchanged a series of congenial letters. The letters demonstrate the complete and distinct separation of the business personality and that of home life. In a postscript to one business letter, Frick wrote, "I look forward to the time when you will receive as much pleasure from association with your little daughter as I do from mine."[18] When Carnegie worried that baby Margaret appeared more attached to Louise, Frick consoled him: "My experience is that little girls show their mamas preference until they are about three years old, and then the papas seem to be really appreciated."[19] An appreciative Carnegie observed, "I think when Helen and she are seen together the people will vote them a prize pair."[20] He even invited Frick to Skibo, but Frick had already made plans to summer at the health resort of Aix-les-Bains, in southeastern France, where his wife could enjoy a completely relaxing vacation. (Frick the machine could be compassionate at times.)

Just before leaving Cannes for their first summer at Skibo, Louise wrote in confidence to her New York pastor, the Reverend Charles H. Eaton: "The giving up of Cluny, with all its tender associations, has affected my sister and me deeply, and we cannot look forward to Skibo with the delight that

Mr. Carnegie does, but when we have seen it and have lived there no doubt we shall grow to like it, particularly if it suits Mr. Carnegie and Margaret."[21] Her husband's needs always superseded her own. Like Carnegie's brother, Tom, Louise internalized much of her emotions, but instead of liquor being her outlet, she had her diary and Reverend Eaton. For an uncertain Louise, the one sure saving grace about Skibo was the organ in the great hall. She decided to surprise her husband by hiring an organist to greet them, and relied on the resourceful Edinburgh librarian Hew Morrison to make arrangements.[22] The prerequisite was knowing Carnegie's favorites: Beethoven's Fifth Symphony and Handel's Largo. He also appreciated oratorio music and choral works with religious themes that set a glorious tone for his daily life.

The Carnegies arrived at Skibo on May 31, and, as they stepped across the threshold of their new home, the swelling tones of the organ greeted them. The organist played Beethoven's Fifth Symphony, an extremely popular work that aroused feelings of heroism—the first movement intense, built on a pounding single four-note figure, then giving away to rhythmic grace. After the rousing welcome, five names were signed into the guest book: Andrew Carnegie, Louise Carnegie, Margaret Carnegie, Estelle Whitfield, and James Bertram, Carnegie's personal secretary.

Every morning the organist played music, which, for Carnegie, was a fine substitute for family prayer. It also became a Sunday night tradition for all— family, guests, neighbors, and servants—to gather in the great hall and sing hymns. That summer, there was no revolving door for guests, for the simple reason that there were no accommodations for them. The Dunfermline relatives visited—Uncle Lauder and Lisa Lauder arriving on June 4—along with Hew Morrison and a John Beatty of Pittsburgh. Frick, Phipps, Dod, and Henry Curry visited in July.

It did not take Louise long to agree with her husband that Skibo was indeed their heaven on earth, and Carnegie paid $425,000 for the property. His Dunfermline solicitor, John Ross, handled the transaction, and Carnegie hired an architectural firm in Inverness on Loch Ness to draw up plans for renovations and an elaborate addition. He was intent on transforming the run-down estate into a true castle to firmly establish his reign, to show the lords who was king. But it was also to be a warm home, not a gaudy palace filled with priceless treasures in which Margaret and her young friends would fear to play.

Louise flourished at Skibo as a mother and a business manager—she worked closely with the architects and became known as the power behind the throne—and she expressed her exuberance in another letter to Reverend Eaton: "To show you the unique range of attractions, yesterday Mr. Carnegie was trout fishing on a wild moorland loch surrounded by heather while I took Margaret to the *sea* and she had her first experience of rolling upon the soft white sand and digging her little hands in it to her heart's content, while the blue waters of the ocean came rolling in at her feet and the salt sea breeze brought the roses to her cheeks. She is strong and hearty and so full of mischief—a perfect little sunbeam."[23]

Carnegie was equally fascinated with Margaret's mischief making and even wrote his British friends about her, worried she needed a firmer hand. Cranky Herbert Spencer actually weighed in: "I hear that your little girl is very precocious and that you are keeping her back. Quite right. But you may very safely expend her energies in the cultivation of the perceptions—the examination of things, especially natural products. That is the normal activity in all children, and would be encouraged if parents were not so intensely stupid as to ignore it. That kind of mental activity you may encourage without any danger of injury from precocity."[24]

Although in heaven, Carnegie had to keep his attention on the affairs of the world and his steel company. The day after arriving at Skibo, he wrote to Dr. Adolf Gurlt, a peace activist in Bonn, Germany, who had questioned why Carnegie was not speaking out against the war. "No power on earth can stop the American people doing what has now become their duty—Cuba must be freed from Spanish oppression," Carnegie explained. "When Spain realizes this there will be peace, but not till then. Knowing this as I do I remain silent. When the proper time comes, when I can urge liberal treatment of Spain and the surrender of the Philippines, believe me, you shall again find me, as you say you did before, pleading the right in the North American Review and elsewhere."[25] In his next breath, Carnegie was telling Dod: "Business is great. War bound to end—probably before this reaches you negotiations will be begun. Spain is done."[26] Carnegie relished the fact that the United States was beating an old-world power, just as he had beaten the iron and steel aristocracy time and again. The war so enthralled Carnegie that he couldn't remain silent; only instead of promoting peace, he decided to give military advice to the commanding general in the Caribbean arena.

On May 8, Major General Nelson A. Miles had been ordered to capture Havana and was given 70,000 men with limited firepower to accomplish his task. Less than enthused, he pointed out to President McKinley that he would be facing a Spanish force of 125,000 with heavy guns in fortified positions. In Britain, Carnegie's network of British dignitaries again served him and the United States when he learned through them that the Spanish did indeed want the United States to attack Havana. He promptly cabled Miles: "Believe you wise bold enough withdraw Santiago. Proceed full force Porto Rico. Object Santiago expedition attained. Town worthless. Capture Porto Rico would tell heavily Spain and Europe."[27] It appeared incredibly presumptuous, but Miles was actually thankful. Carnegie's cable arrived when Miles was trying to convince the president and his advisers that a direct assault on Havana would result in needless death, and in his memoir, *Serving the Republic*, Miles acknowledged Carnegie's timely advice: "Porto Rico and the eastern half of the island of Cuba were the objective points, in my judgment, for the active operations of our army. While I was advocating this I received a cablegram from Europe, signed by Mr. Andrew Carnegie, saying that the Spanish officials were anxious that we should attack Havana, knowing it to be heavily fortified and defensible. In the same dispatch that patriotic philanthropist advised the taking of Porto Rico first, for its effect in Europe. I laid this before President McKinley and his cabinet."[28] Havana was not attacked.

Not until June 22 did 16,000 U.S. troops land in Cuba and move toward Santiago de Cuba. Along with the regular army were the special volunteer regiments, the most famous being the Rough Riders, led by Leonard Wood and Theodore Roosevelt. After successfully seizing the Spanish fort at El Caney and storming the strategic heights of San Juan Hill—attacks that left 205 Americans killed and 1,180 wounded, as well as 215 Spaniards killed and 376 wounded—it was only a matter of time before the war was won.[29] On July 26, Spain sued for peace. Admiral George Dewey, late in receiving the news of the surrender, besieged and took Manila by force. Assisting him was exiled Filipino leader Emilio Aguinaldo, who was under the assumption the Philippines would become an independent republic. The U.S. government had other plans, however, and set about organizing a colonial regime.

Before the war was even over, Americans had been debating what to do with the war booty—Puerto Rico and the Philippines. Talk of taking possession of the Philippines thrilled empire-minded Roosevelt while it distressed the antiexpansionists, who argued for the islands' political independence. But there was a duty to civilize the people, argued righteous ministers and politicians; a duty to educate, uplift, and Christianize them. To the would-be empire builders and capitalists, the Philippines was a means of establishing a military and economic power base in the Far East, a stepping-stone to China and other exploitable markets. In another ominous sign that the U.S. government had imperialistic designs, in August, the United States annexed Hawaii, further securing the country's presence in the Pacific.

As an active member of the New England Anti-Imperialist League since April, Carnegie now protested American imperialism, just as he promised Dr. Gurlt he would. Ensconced at Skibo, and working with his secretary, James Bertram, he wrote "Distant Possessions—the Parting of the Ways," which appeared in the August *North American Review.* He posed the significant question of the day: "Is the Republic, the apostle of Triumphant Democracy, of the rule of the people, to abandon her political creed and endeavor to establish in other lands the rule of the foreigner over the people, Triumphant Despotism?" Carnegie anticipated the United States remaining in the Philippines and warned that the Filipinos would soon revolt. He pointed out that the European nations were all squabbling over their distant possessions, a tinderbox the United States should avoid. To make his point, he used his favorite battle cry: "To-day the Republic stands the friend of all nations, the ally of none . . . she stands apart, pursuing her own great mission, and teaching all nations by example."[30] The Philippines must be set free. His anti-imperialistic ideas were no different than those he had expressed to his cousin Dod over forty years ago, in 1854, when they debated the Crimean War.

John Hay, appointed ambassador in London that spring, read his friend's article intently and reacted favorably, writing Carnegie: "I am not allowed to say in my present fix how much I agree with you. The only question in my mind is how far it is now possible for us to withdraw from the Philippines. I am rather thankful it is not given to me to solve that momentous question."[31] His thankfulness was brief. Shortly thereafter, Hay was appointed secretary of state and would have to deal personally with the question. It would become an extremely sticky issue as potent anti-imperialist forces continued to organize. By September, it was more obvious that McKinley was not going to return the Philippines to native rule; and Carnegie, whose anti-imperialist rhetoric would reach a fevered pitch, would discover his friend Hay was his most bitter enemy.

While McKinley and his cabinet had been conducting a two-front war, one in the Caribbean, the other in the Pacific, Carnegie was suddenly faced with a similar strategic challenge. In business for over thirty years—almost twenty-five in steel—he had yet to meet the challenges he would now. It would be far more complicated than in the past, when the Pittsburgh iron aristocracy's attempt to defeat him with Duquesne and Homestead had been met, the competition conquered, and absorbed as easily as uttering *veni, vidi, vici*. And the complications were exacerbated by the fact that Carnegie had to conduct his efforts from first Cannes and then Scotland.

CHAPTER 26

The Crusades

B eginning in 1898, the wave of the Industrial Revolution Carnegie had ridden so easily was cresting—and he was about to be caught underneath. It was time for the industries driving the Industrial Revolution—steel, ore, railroads—to evolve to the next phase, to weed out the weak, to become more vertical, to consolidate, to mature. There was to be no place for radical individualism in the new order, but Carnegie thought otherwise. To meet the looming challenge, he would have to fight a multifront war requiring massive resources and deft generalship. On the western front there was Illinois Steel, and on the eastern front there was a new menace in the formidable persona of Pierpont Morgan, who was as intent on consolidating the steel industry as he had been with railroads. Carnegie's energy and tenacity could not be overestimated—but at age sixty-two, did he have the stamina? Could he win victories on both fronts? Or should he take a defensive posture on one front while attacking on the other? A defensive strategy did not agree with his nature, but lately Carnegie had been ambivalent about business, and he would waver between fighting and selling.

Some harmony was briefly restored with Illinois Steel and the other steelmakers when the rail pool was reestablished in February 1898, but any mood of cooperation was subsequently poisoned when just ten days later Schwab notified Carnegie that John Gates's company was not "conscientiously" keeping to the agreement. And then he added ominously that there were rumors about the possible organization of a steel wire monopoly capable of dictating what it would pay for steel—including Carnegie's steel.[1]

Behind the rumors was Bet-a-Million Gates, who was fed up with Carnegie's bullying. It was time to strike back. As for Gates's undercutting their rail pool agreement to garner some additional orders, that was akin to sending out a company of soldiers to test his enemy's picket line. When there was no immediate retaliation from the Carnegie troops, it signaled weakness, and Gates decided now was the time to forge his steel wire monopoly. It was the first in a series of consolidations in the industry that would attempt to break free of this reliance on Carnegie's raw steel and to wound the Scotsman.

Rain was falling as Gates and his partner Ike Ellwood took a train from Chicago to Pittsburgh, a tiresome journey. To pass the time, the two picked raindrops on the window, betting $1,000 on which would reach the bottom first. Gates, who subsequently won $22,000 on the trip, was still in a gambling mood when he reached Pittsburgh and repaired to the Duquesne Club, stronghold for the city's iron and steel men. There he met a number of men who owned steel wire mills similar to his up the Monongahela River in Rankin, Pennsylvania, and to each he made a proposal to buy them out. Word of Gates's visit spread rapidly. As Carnegie was digesting what had transpired at the Duquesne Club, a more potent piece of news reached him. Gates had sought the backing of Pierpont Morgan, who was already reviewing the financial status of the companies agreeing to sell out to Gates and those the gambler proposed to include.

Due to the impending war with Spain and the shaky financial markets, Morgan withdrew from participating, but he was intrigued with the concept of consolidation in the steel industry. It was the "Era of Finance Capitalism" that once the Sherman Antitrust Act proved impotent, witnessed the creation of trusts and consolidations in every industry from typewriters to sugar. Between 1897 and 1904, 4,227 firms would consolidate into 257. Steel was ripe to join the unstoppable trend because the industry met a prime condition for consolidation—overcapacity.[2] Morgan would enter the fray in due time.

Gates pushed forward with his monopoly, and on March 18, less than two weeks after Schwab warned Carnegie, he formed the American Steel and Wire Company of Illinois, which controlled 75 percent of the country's wire products.[3] While not in direct competition with Carnegie Steel, but with plants in Pennsylvania, Indiana, and Ohio, the new company could purchase raw steel from any number of producers; thus, Carnegie could be locked out. Sure enough, two weeks later, Frick warned Carnegie, "Gates seems to have it in for us, but Illinois crowd may find, some of these times, a formidable competitor alongside of them, on Lake Michigan."[4] Roused from the languorous Mediterranean life, Carnegie agreed wholeheartedly that the battle had to be taken to Gates's home ground of Illinois, but instead of building a plant there, he proposed using a different tactic: to find cheaper avenues for shipping their product to Illinois and dumping it on the market at cutthroat prices.[5] Profit margin meant nothing to Carnegie if he could destroy his enemies.

To secure a cheap supply line west, Carnegie once again turned to the Pennsylvania Railroad, which the year before had given him major rebates. While the Pennsylvania offered excellent freight rates for rails, it still cost more to ship beams, structural steel, and other products on a tonnage basis. Frank Thomson had just been elected president of the colossus; before he could settle into the new position, Carnegie pressed him by making the usual threats to take his business elsewhere unless given rebates for structural steel products that competed directly with Illinois Steel.

Thomson came into line without a fight and agreed to lower rates. "This understanding is meant to bring the PRR and the CSCo. into close alliance," their agreement stated, "and is never to be referred to, except to the parties hereto. It is in noise intended to be a legal document, on the contrary, it is not. It is however an honorable understanding between the parties."[6] It was an illegal rebate at its best. Although Carnegie was again breaking federal and state laws, he didn't recognize his agreements as such; he was too enraptured with defeating the enemy at any cost. Armed with exceptionally competitive rates, Carnegie now had the weapon to cut the legs out from under Gates and Illinois Steel. The enemy on the western front was about to be fully engaged.

The Spanish-American War inspired Carnegie. He became more militaristic in his business affairs. No longer was it enough to cut prices to crush the competition; now more sophisticated strategies were called for, especially when a formidable enemy emerged on the eastern front. Illinois Steel's general counsel Elbert H. Gary, who had drawn up bankruptcy papers for his company more than once, knew the only way to compete with Carnegie was to surpass the vertical integration the canny Scot had—iron ore to finished products—they would do so by merging with other companies. Gary, who always dressed in dark suits and spoke in a quiet, pious voice, came across as a Methodist minister, but he was usurping power from the philanderer Gates. It was Gary who put together a plan that proposed the amalgamation of Illinois Steel, the Minnesota Iron Company, the Lorain Steel Company, the Johnson Company, and two railroads operating in the Chicago area. And it was Gary who traveled to New York and presented his plan to Morgan, whom he knew had been enticed by Gates's proposal to consolidate the steel wire industry. Morgan did indeed endorse the plan.

To follow these ominous developments, Carnegie Steel employed spies, including John A. Potter, the ex-superintendent of Homestead. Still alive and well in 1898, he visited the Illinois works in June and reported to Schwab that the company's operations continued to lose money, but that its rail mill was busy.[7] It took three months for Gary and Morgan to work out the details with all of the companies, but both men were patient; they knew they needed a critical mass to be able to effectively strike at Carnegie. On September 9, the $200 million corporation, christened Federal Steel, issued stock, half preferred, half common, and Carnegie's most dangerous enemy yet was fully operational. Morgan appointed Gary president, while Gates was left out in the cold—almost. Once Federal's stock was listed, Morgan's cronies, including the former governor of New York, Roswell Flower, bulled it and made a killing on Wall Street. Gates, who held a sizable stake, won a prodigious booby prize. It also prompted Carnegie to write Dod, "I think Federal the greatest concern the world ever saw for manufacturing stock certificates—we are not in it—but they will fail sadly in Steel."

His breezy dismissal of the new rival was premature. Federal was a legitimate threat, with plants strategically located in Illinois, Ohio, and Pennsylvania, booking almost as many rail orders as Carnegie Steel, and throwing any past pooling agreements into uncertainty. The *New York Commercial* trumpeted: "The completion of the consolidation of these ore and steel interests is the beginning of one of the greatest contests for supremacy that the world has ever seen. It is a fight between the new concern and the Carnegie interests, both backed by almost unlimited capital, and each holding patents for many similar articles manufactured from iron and steel."[8]

While Carnegie was having a good laugh over his stock-watering joke, Morgan was working on his next consolidation in the steel industry, which would be called National Tube and eventually combine nineteen companies making steel pipe and tube, many of them Carnegie customers that would soon be former customers.

Morgan was intent on creating fully integrated organizations that sold a wide spectrum of finished steel products. In this way he would outflank Carnegie, who sold raw steel, rails, beams, armor plates, and projectiles, but no other finished goods. Adept at the art of war, Carnegie anticipated the maneuver, envisioning the day orders for his steel declined as huge consolidations did indeed become independent. It was time to fully engage his troops on both fronts; he would take the battle to New York, to Morgan himself, in his plush office surrounded by fine artwork and his latest mistress, tumors of the Gilded Age. Even though Carnegie had had an amicable relationship with Junius Morgan, he perceived the blue-blooded Pierpont as a degenerate. For him, it would always be the Scotsman against the Yankee, his boys and him against Wall Street. Good against evil. As early as July, Carnegie prepared his board of managers for the upcoming war when he advised them, "There are three stages in the development of manufactures; we began in the middle making Iron and Steel and buying our Pig and Raw materials. We have now our Raw materials. The third stage, which is coming, is at the other end; we have to put our Iron and Steel into finished forms. . . . We can get as much ahead of competitors as we ever have got by first accepting the truth that eventually the manufacturer of Steel must also be the manufacturer of Finished Articles. At all events the concern which does this first will remain first."[9]

Two weeks later he wrote another letter, reiterating his point: "I am convinced we should turn our attention to finishing certain articles. Suppose we made Steel Cars for instance. No one could stand against us."[10] If Carnegie was consistent in one trait, it was persistence. He was determined to push his men into the finished products arena, and for each product he would do to the competition what he had done to them in rails—bring them to their knees. Carnegie's call to arms had the desired effect on his lieutenants, who declared in a joint letter they were all for "whipping Illinois Steel into line, and better controlling the markets."[11] Now it was a simple matter of deciding what finished products to manufacture. But before definite plans were made, Carnegie was again stricken with doubts. He had to decide whether to continue the war, to meet the competition head on, or to sell out and enjoy retirement at Skibo with his family. The voice of the fiercely competitive businessmen told him to meet Morgan and the others head on; the voice of the father said sell.

When Carnegie returned to New York City in October 1898, Theodore Roosevelt was running for governor of New York on a war-hero platform. He would win and, two years later, become McKinley's vice presidential running mate. America, now a world power, was also enjoying a coming-out party. Carnegie didn't join in the euphoria. In the postwar world of consolidation and expansion, New York City didn't appear the same to him. It was claustrophobic—both the skyscrapers made with his steel and the people encroaching on his Fifty-first Street home oppressed him. To escape the long shadows, he searched uptown for property to build on and purchased two blocks, comprising thirty lots, between Ninetieth and Ninety-Second Streets on Fifth Avenue, across from Central Park. "As for building a grand palace," Carnegie told inquiring reporters, "that is foreign to our tastes."[12] The new home would be palatial, however, and construction took several years.

Carnegie's growing desire to escape not only the crush of New York but the rigors of business was reinforced in the first week of November when Louise and he traveled to Pittsburgh. On November 3, they, along with Henry Phipps and William Frew, attended the annual Founder's Day celebrations at the Carnegie Library of Pittsburgh, a nifty ploy to pay tribute to the benefactor, who naturally appreciated the attention. The audience wasn't disappointed, either. After congratulatory telegrams from McKinley and other dignitaries were read, Carnegie rose to speak, but thunderous applause prevented any words for several minutes. Then, in his speech, Carnegie announced that the library, now also called the Carnegie Institute, would be enlarged. Wings would be added to permanently house the art and museum exhibits, to which he would commit millions more.

Carnegie's plans to expand the institute were indirectly underscored when, later in November, he was reading the New York Journal and his attention was grabbed by a headline: MOST COLOSSAL ANIMAL EVER ON EARTH JUST FOUND OUT WEST! On the article, Carnegie scrawled a note to William J. Holland, who had been appointed director of the Carnegie Museum of Pittsburgh (a division of the institute), to "buy this! For Pittsburgh." He enclosed a $10,000 check.[13] All that had been found was a single eight-foot bone belonging to an *Apatosaurus*, but Holland sought out William Reed, who had made the discovery, and signed him to a one-year contract. The investment paid off when, on July 4, 1899, the most complete *Diplodocus* to date was discovered, and in the patron's honor it was named *Diplodocus carnegii*. Carnegie had plaster copies made of the dinosaur, which were shipped to other museums to both tout and share the discovery. Everything Carnegie touched seemed to turn to gold.

The day after Founder's Day, the Homestead library was dedicated. The carriage brought Carnegie and Louise up the rising ground where the state militia had camped six years earlier, and which was once part of Pittsburgh's City Poor Farm property that Frick, Christopher Magee, and he had purchased at a good price. Although no one else was aware of it, for Carnegie, the proceedings had been somewhat tainted more recently, for it was that prior June that Carnegie had written the enigmatic instruction to John Van Dyke to give John McLuckie all the money he wanted. Despite all the sordid history associated with this piece of land, Carnegie was a picture of poise as he took the podium and announced to the townspeople it was a day he had long looked forward to. The men in the past had been difficult to deal with, he explained, but today they were blessed to have good men. "The building has rightfully in the center as the focus 'The Library'—Music Hall upon the right and the Working Man's Club upon the left," he said with great flair. "These three foundations from which healing waters are to flow for the Instruction, Entertainment and Happiness of the people. Recreation of the working man has an important bearing upon his character and development as his hours of work." He was at his dramatic best, sighing at appropriate moments, looking stern at times.

The Pittsburgh library expansion and the Homestead library dedication reminded Carnegie of what he would prefer to be doing: casting his benevolence and promoting goodwill among men. To sell or not to sell, that was the burning question in November and December.

Whether to sell was a wrenching decision to make, but it appeared fatherhood was winning. In the fourth week of a rather busy November, Carnegie and Harry Phipps, who still promoted the company's interests, rendezvoused at the Arlington Hotel in Washington. Carnegie's main purpose in going there was to meet with the politicos and argue for giving the Philippines its freedom, but he also talked business with Phipps. After a Tuesday dinner out at a restaurant, they strolled along the boulevards, Carnegie's arm around Phipps's shoulders. Despite his prior biting comments about Federal, Carnegie intimated he was willing to sell to that company. The next day, he gave Phipps an outline of the terms for sale, putting the price at somewhere between $200 and $250 million. Phipps, who was astounded by Carnegie's unexpected decision, excitedly wrote Frick, "It is a chance of a life time—comes to but few and is rarely repeated."[14]

Once Carnegie was back at the Fifty-first Street house, Dod visited to talk the matter over with his cousin. During the intense discussion, Louise happened to enter the library, unwittingly provoking an ugly scene. Dod subsequently reported to Phipps: "Louise came in and sat down, he turned to her and told her what we were talking about, his thoughts were running favorably to the sale at the time—she remarked that when it was done she 'would be the happiest woman in America'—He immediately turned on her quite savagely and went into a tirade on men who retired from business dying etc. etc.—that he would be laying down a crown etc. etc., so I judge the matter will make the most progress by being let alone as much as possible—He is in a considerably excited state about the Philippines anyway and this coming on the back of it may have had physical effects I fear."[15] Dod, perceiving that if one pressured Carnegie too much it would have the opposite effect, warned Phipps to drop the subject of selling for now.

After a brief cooling-off period, in early December, Frick gingerly took up the discussion of the merger of Carnegie and Federal. To make it easier to sell the company, Frick recommended a reorganization of their interests into a holding company, the Carnegie Company, Limited, with its capital to be $250 million.[16] Now leaning toward selling and looking to convince himself that merging with Federal was the proper course, Carnegie penned an article for *Iron Age*, "Iron and Steel at Home and Abroad," in which he wrote: "The consolidation of the iron and steel interests is a natural evolution. If we are going to sell 3 pounds of steel for 2 cents, it must be made by the millions of tons. It is a tight race for the best concerns." He was careful not to annoy Morgan, Gary, and other potential suitors in explaining: "Do not understand me as reflecting on the management of these concerns. Very far from it. It is not the management but the situation."[17]

Frick tested the waters by discreetly shopping their respective companies to Morgan and Gary at Federal Steel, as well as to Rockefeller, but the asking price of $250 million was too rich. With mixed feelings, Carnegie wrote Dod, "Mr. Rodgers, Standard Oil, and Federal, said truly, 'Too big a dog to be wagged by so small a tail.'"[18]

The reason Morgan couldn't arrange the financing was because he was in the final stages of organizing the National Tube Company, his latest amalgamation, which initially controlled 75 percent of the tube and pipe industry. It was incorporated on February 17, 1899. Another formidable consolidation, the National Steel Company, was formed on February 25 and included eight iron and steel firms in Ohio and Pennsylvania. In size, it ranked third after Carnegie and Federal. Behind National Steel was the flamboyant financier William H. Moore, a former judge who was no stranger to the merger game, having formed the Diamond Match Company and the National Biscuit Company, trusts in the matches and baking industries. He had also created the Tin Plate Company in December 1898, an amalgamation of thirty-eight firms; and, in April 1899, he would organize thirty companies into the American Sheet Steel Company and nine companies into the American Steel Hoop Company. The natural alliance between National Steel, Tin Plate, American Sheet, and American Hoop was akin to a vertical organization well beyond

Carnegie Steel, as was the tight relationship between Morgan's Federal Steel and National Tube. The two-front war had suddenly escalated, and Carnegie was in grave danger of being boxed in.

To hell with selling out, to retiring to the grave—Carnegie had plenty of fight in him. Carnegie Steel profits for 1898 had jumped to $11.5 million, up from $7 million the prior year, and Carnegie's personal take from company profits and other investments for 1898 was $10 million. He estimated the company's profits for 1899 would leap to $20 million even in a soft market, and apprised Dod: "I favor holding on for two or three years. No question but we can sell. . . . Why then not wait."[19]

Even as Frick continued to seek a buyer, Carnegie was preparing for a frontal assault on the consolidations, which he viewed as weak bullies. "We should look with favor upon every combination of every kind upon the part of our competitors," he wrote company secretary Francis Lovejoy; "the bigger they grow, the more vulnerable they become. It is with firms as with Nations, 'Scattered possessions' are not in it with a solid, compact, concentrated force." Since naming the Union Iron Mills in the 1860s to memorialize the end of the Civil War, Carnegie always linked his business with the country, and now the same anti-imperialistic fervor he felt over the United States possessing the distant Philippines he transferred to the consolidations. He was still open to pooling arrangements—but only on his terms, and only if it was definitively more advantageous. "Here is a historic situation for the Managers to study— Richelieu's advice: 'First, all means to conciliate; failing that, all means to crush,'" he explained to Lovejoy.[20] When Schwab and Frick favored a new rail pool with Federal, however, Carnegie vetoed it without any considera- tion.[21] That was one company he was intent on crushing, and with that in mind he continued to rally Schwab around the company's penetration into finished products: "We want to sell finished [railroad] Cars as soon as you can do it. We shall want to make Wire, and I think nails, as soon as we can. . . . The concern that sells articles finished, will be able to run all weathers and make some money while others are half-idle and losing money."[22]

For a year, Carnegie had talked of entering the steel railroad car business; he now became resolute. The first all-steel cars had been made in 1897 and were initially used for shipping coal and ore, but he envisioned a day when steel would be used for all cars and, therefore, be a very profitable business. Carnegie was not dissuaded by the newly formed Pressed Steel Car Com- pany, yet another consolidation of several companies, but his vice president of sales, Alexander Peacock, was. Peacock, a slick Scotsman who sported a han- dlebar mustache and had a propensity for drinking, argued, "We have sel- dom, if ever, gone into any business unless we are in shape to control it, but that would not be the case with Steel Cars," and he pointed out that the com- pany would have to rely on suppliers for springs, buffers, wheels, and brakes.[23] The board agreed and voted against steel cars. "Now to give up this business is pretty bad," Carnegie, in a tantrum, bellowed at his lieutenants. "I should be sorry indeed, and would want a pretty big reward."[24] The reward he alluded to was not only a healthy sales contract with Pressed Steel Car, but a payoff not to enter the business. The company's president, Charles Schoen, did indeed agree to pay Carnegie Steel $100,000 a year to stay out of the business; moreover, despite the bullying, Carnegie Steel also successfully closed a ten-year, $144 million deal to supply Schoen's company with steel plates.[25] Clearly, Carnegie still held great power over the industry. Peacock, incidentally, would not last much longer with the firm, even though he hailed from Dunfermline.

During the great steel car debate, junior partner Daniel Clemson had casually suggested there was money to make in tubes, too, and Carnegie heartily concurred. Just four days after National Tube was created on February 17, a letter from Carnegie was read at a board meeting, in which he strongly suggested the company push into steel pipe. He relished the idea of going head-to-head with the Morgan concern and enthusiastically concluded, "I have not heard of anything which strikes me so favorably—from ore to pipe."[26] Other members of the board again dissented, with dividend-conscious Phipps most vehement in his objections and demanding postponement.[27] It was postponed, but only until National Tube built its own furnaces and stopped buying steel from Carnegie.

While Carnegie was pushing the expansion of his empire, he was adamantly opposed to the United States expanding hers. The imperialistic tone in his 1893 essay "A Look Ahead," in which he promoted the union of the United States, Canada, and Great Britain, was now gone as the reality of the United States as a world power struck him differently. Negotiations with Spain were still ongoing in the autumn of 1898, but it now appeared President McKinley was leaning toward possessing the Philippines, a decision Carnegie was certain would result in American bloodshed and war with the European colonial powers. The Spanish war had already cost 379 lives and 1,600 wounded in combat, while more than 5,000 Americans were dead from yellow fever, malaria, or typhoid—and counting.

Now determined to shoulder the White Man's Burden, so called after the Rudyard Kipling poem that romanticized imperialism, in October McKinley went on tour of the Midwest, alluding to America's duty and destiny, building support for taking the Philippines, but not yet saying so definitively. Whitelaw Reid, who was spearheading the treaty work with Spain, also took to the road, arguing that the United States was bound to assume responsibility for Cuba, Puerto Rico, and the Philippines. He advocated a civil service administration for the new possessions. The anti-imperialists contended that the U.S. Constitution was being violated, that these foreign peoples were not being given the right of self-government, that they were not being given the same rights under nor same access to the laws of the United States, and, less tastefully, that the people populating these possessions were unsuited for assimilation into American society.

Carnegie, a vice president of the Anti-Imperialist League, took to the press to promulgate his views. As one quixotic solution to the Philippines question, he suggested giving the islands to Britain in exchange for British possessions in the West Indies; at least the Philippines wouldn't be America's headache.[28] And when Carnegie heard that one of the terms of the proposed treaty was for the United States to pay Spain $20 million for the Philippines, he offered McKinley $20 million to buy the islands' independence. It was a stunt P. T. Barnum would have been proud of, even though Carnegie was quite serious. The Filipino nationalists were even more resolute about taking back their country, and as soon as it became obvious to them the United States was there to stay, Filipino leader Emilio Aguinaldo, who felt betrayed, organized his nationalist army in the jungle. Skirmishes with American troops soon broke out.

Fears of escalating violence were confirmed when the newspapers told tales of colonels, foot soldiers, and nurses dying of yellow fever and of battle wounds. A Colorado regiment complained that 15 percent of its men were sick and that rations were insufficient, and that it had no desire to remain as a garrison. The noise about dissatisfied American troops and soldiers being tortured by Filipino nationalists roused Carnegie and the anti-imperialists to another level of fervor. (The civilized Americans were perfecting the water torture during their own Filipino prisoner interrogations.) A distraught Carnegie wrote a scathing letter to the *New York Tribune* that opened with a confusing burst of rhetoric: "It is glorious. The light has broken. Imperialism has received its first blow—I think its death wound; the Republic may yet be saved." It was the soldiers, like those of the Colorado regiment, who would save the Republic by voicing dissent. The president had erred if he thought volunteers could be induced to do the dirty work of the imperialists, according to Carnegie, who urged the soldiers to express how they had been taken advantage of by the president.[29] The propaganda escalated to a hysterical pitch as Carnegie, egged on by letters he received commending his heroic stand against imperialism, became more brazen in his condemnation of President McKinley in the press and personal letters. The steel titan was inflicted with pomposity.

To his old friend and new enemy, Secretary of State Hay, he roundly criticized President McKinley for being a "Mr. 'face both ways'" and compared him to a blubbering "jelly-fish" for not taking a more definitive position on imperialism. "I am so sorry for the President—I do not think he is well," continued Carnegie, who was obsessed with McKinley's mental health, just as he had been with Frick's. Again, Carnegie's obsession with mental stability was mostly likely because he harbored doubts about his own. He signed the letter with this maddening line, "Bitterly opposed to you yet always your friend Andrew Carnegie," and in a postscript added, "How I wish I could stop all this stirring up of the President in the newspapers but he gave me no hope that he realized how he was drifting to the devil."[30]

From Washington, D.C., Hay updated Whitelaw Reid, who knew Carnegie's ego all too well, on the latest tirade:

> There is a wild and frantic attack now going on in the press against the whole Philippine transaction. Andrew Carnegie really seems to be off his head. He writes me frantic letters signing them, 'Your Bitterest Opponent.' He threatens the President, not only with the vengeance of the voters, but with practical punishment at the hands of the mob. He says henceforth the entire labor vote of America will be cast against us, and that he will see that it is done. He says the Administration will fall in irretrievable ruin the moment it shoots down one insurgent Filipino. He does not seem to reflect that the Government is in a somewhat robust condition even after shooting down several American citizens in his interest at Homestead. But all this confusion of tongues will go its way.[31]

Hay must not have known Carnegie that well, for he had no intention of allowing the anti-imperialist movement to "go its way," and, audacious as ever, he wrote McKinley a presumptuous letter:

> The true friend not only warns a friend of what he sees to be dangers that surround him, but he ventures to counsel him as to what he should do in the crisis.
>
> Were I President of the United States I should announce in my message to Congress that I demanded the Philippines from Spain that I might give to them the Independence which every people can claim as a God-given right, that I had no idea of holding them in subjection, but I would do with them as I did with Cuba, helping the people to establish a suitable government.[32]

It was too late to withdraw from the Philippines, however. To do so would show weakness. More significant at this point in time, despite the efforts of the two camps—the expansionists and the anti-imperialists—the United States couldn't avoid becoming a world power.

Carnegie himself had pointed out the United States exported more than any country, which made it a major player on the world's stage, like it or not. He was even guilty of an expansionist policy without realizing it, because for the last year he had been calling for a major port in New York City for shipping and receiving goods around the world.[33] His own company's growing exports contributed to America's global power, too; in 1898, Carnegie Steel was making two hundred thousand tons of steel a month, and Schwab prophesied that soon one-third would be shipped overseas. In the new industrial order, economic power equated to political power. Men like Hay and Reid accepted America's more prominent position without regrets. They dealt with reality, while Carnegie pursued idealism.

On December 10, 1898, the president signed the treaty with Spain, which formally handed over the Philippines, Puerto Rico, and Cuba. McKinley let it be known that Cuba would be granted self-government as soon as the political climate stabilized. The president's "grand position as to Cuba makes me a happy man," Carnegie wrote Hay in a conciliatory tone the next day. Even in complimenting, Carnegie could be condescending, for he continued, "I see daylight out of our danger cloud and have nothing but praise for the President since he took his rightful place, *that of Leadership*."[34] The Philippines was another matter. The Senate, which would have to ratify the treaty with a two-thirds majority vote, expected to vote on it in February, giving Carnegie and the Anti-Imperialist League time to lobby for the island's freedom. They stepped up their campaign to rally public support through public meetings and the distribution of literature.

Carnegie wrote two lengthy essays, "Americanism versus Imperialism" and "Americanism Versus Imperialism II," for publication in the *North American Review*, in which he dealt with the issues systematically. He despised the fact that one American general was calling for thirty thousand troops in the Philippines because the nationalist rebels may have to be "licked," and he also took aim at the righteous claim it was America's duty to civilize the Filipinos. Carnegie, who never feared offending or shocking others, no matter who they were, even attacked church bishops as contemptible examples of misguided missionary fervor.

Carnegie, who was adamant in his argument that the Filipinos should be permitted self-government regardless of the consequences, concluded the second essay by invoking Lincoln:

> It seems as if Lincoln were inspired to say the needful word for this hour of strange subversion of all we have hitherto held dear in our political life. Our "duty" to bear the "White Man's Burden" is to-day's refrain, but Lincoln tells us:
>
> > "When the white man governs himself, that is self-government; but when he governs another man, that is more than self-government, that is despotism."

Despite his fervent rhetoric, Carnegie found no support from within the Republican administration, so he turned to the Democrats—once again, like Robert the Bruce, he was willing to align with old antagonists to achieve victory—and in December, he secretly met with William Jennings Bryan. The newspaper reporters managed to catch wind of the meeting, which Carnegie refused to confirm, indicative of just how sensitive he was to being publicly criticized for desiring to join forces with Bryan, the proclaimed champion of the working class. The *Tribune* noted the unusual picture of the once bitterest of enemies coming together, the strangest of bedfellows.[35]

Bryan was also wary—of Carnegie. When rumors reached him that Carnegie was planning to make a statement to the press about their meeting and endorsing a Bryan presidential bid in 1900, he warned Carnegie the hoopla would hinder their antiexpansionist battle. Bryan feared that if his alliance with Carnegie was dragged through the mud by the press, he would be discredited, and it would hurt his chances to convince Democrats to vote against the treaty. (Frick knew all too well that Carnegie's appetite for publicity often exposed their strategies and compromised their position.) Bryan was so anxious that from Lincoln, Nebraska, he cabled Carnegie on Christmas Eve morning to request his silence, incisively noting: "You and I agree in opposing militarism and imperialism but when those questions are settled we may find ourselves upon opposite sides as heretofore. Let us fight together when we can and against each other when we must, exercising charity at all times."[36] That same day, Bryan followed up with a letter further explaining that he feared cavorting with such a prominent Republican as Carnegie because it "might embarrass me," and he reiterated that their work together would in no way compromise his belief in unlimited coinage of silver and restraining big business.[37]

Carnegie chided him for talking so foolishly about money, which forced the Cornhusker to make it clear to the steel master that this was an alliance of convenience, giving Carnegie, who entered and exited pools at his whim, a taste of his own medicine: "I believe that the gold standard is a conspiracy against the human race. I am against it. I am against the trusts. I am against bank currency. Just now I am talking against imperialism not because I have changed on the other questions but because the attack of the imperialists must be met *now or never*. The lines of the next campaign cannot be seen at this time but you need not delude yourself with the idea that silver is dead."[38] Their relationship had soured quickly—a passing in the night.

Through January and early February, Carnegie made a number of trips to the Executive Mansion, boldly prophesying to McKinley that he was going to have to shoot Filipinos to keep the islands and that it spelled the Republican Party's doom. In a particularly black mood one week before the Senate was to vote on the treaty, Carnegie lashed out at McKinley in a January 30 letter to the editor of the *New York Journal* (his New York mouthpiece after his falling out with Reid at the *Tribune*). "President McKinley, our 'War Lord,'" he raged, "is beginning to see that he can agree to pay twenty millions for an opportunity to shoot down people only guilty of the crime of desiring to govern themselves."

It went down to the wire, but the Senate approved the treaty in a close vote on February 6. Disillusioned but still a faithful believer in the Republic, Carnegie summed up the bloody political scene for his friend Andrew White, now ambassador to Germany: "We are mad over here just now. Passions, always inflamed by war, must have their fling; but of the ultimate result I am certain. Our party is doomed next election. The masses of the people are not with the leaders."[39] So self-absorbed was he in his own vision of political righteousness, Carnegie was losing contact with reality. The masses would vote McKinley to a second term, the incumbent trouncing Bryan.

The very month—March—Carnegie published his second essay on anti-imperialism, in which he quoted Lincoln—"When the white man governs himself, that is self-government; but when he governs another man, that is more than self-government, that is despotism"—Schwab proposed discharging a few men in the mills simply to make an example of them to keep the others in line. A potential revolt was simmering.

The embittered workingmen remained raw material—exploited, oppressed, and subdued. Despite advances in technology, they were still working seven-day weeks. Living and working conditions had not evolved for the better. Although Homestead workers were making enough money so that one-quarter of the families owned their own homes, Carnegie Steel held most of the mortgages, which gave the company even more power over their workers.[40] And it was the men's failure to make good on their debts that prompted Schwab to make examples of a few. In March, the company posted signs in the mills stating that employees must pay their debts and that those habitually neglecting them would be fired. Carnegie was permitting and practicing despotism by assuming the deadbeats were troublemakers and discharging them. Meanwhile, he, Schwab, and the other executives had no idea why these men couldn't make their payments. They might have had sick family members, which meant unexpected doctor bills; they might have had to buy more coal than anticipated to heat their drafty houses; and yes, they might have piddled their money away at the tavern.

It was not the ideal time to ratchet up the pressure, either. The company had recently completed its line to Lake Erie, now called the Pittsburgh, Bessemer & Lake Erie Railroad, and the railroad workers were well-organized union men. There was the possibility that from direct contact with the union railroad men, the mill workers, like contracting a disease, might be inspired to organize a lodge. When Schwab learned the railroad union was considering establishing a headquarters at Braddock, he notified "the Superintendents to consider carefully the possibility of labor organizations securing a foothold at our works . . . " and made it clear that no Superintendent could "permit any Union labor at any cost, or under any circumstances, but that this was a delicate question and would have to be handled carefully."[41]

As Schwab suspected, in May and June, about three hundred Homestead men joined the Amalgamated Association of Iron and Steel Workers, and the union then tried to arrange a conference with Frick, who refused.[42] Shortly thereafter he sailed for Britain. Carnegie was already in Britain, making several benefactions before proceeding to Skibo, where an update from a nervous Schwab reached him: "Labor seems to be giving us some little trouble in all directions. This week at Homestead there was an effort on the part of some men to reorganize a union. We promptly took action and discharged a half dozen of them yesterday and will do the same to-day. I feel this will nip the move in the bud."[43] The movement was not nipped, however, and, with the seventh anniversary of the Homestead strike fast approaching, there were rumors of an impending strike.

How to handle the Amalgamated consumed the board meeting held on June 13, the aggressive attitude of Schwab and the other officers making for an explosive atmosphere. The consensus was to stop the union from getting a foothold "at any cost, even if it should result in a strike," and Lovejoy went so far as to say, "I would rather see the Works blown up with dynamite than turned over to the control of those scoundrels." Only Dod hedged, preferring to hear from the absent partners—that is, Carnegie—and he warned, "You may do something you will be sorry for afterward."[44]

After reviewing the minutes, Carnegie, Frick, and Phipps, all together at Skibo, issued a joint statement supporting the board's aggressive posture: "We heartily endorse views of Board of Managers with regard to Amalgamated Association. Stop Works if necessary to hold present position."[45] In a follow-up cable to Schwab, Carnegie instructed him to post a sign that the company would never recognize the union and that the mills would be shut down if the agitation persists.[46] In spite of the Homestead tragedy and obscene profits, Carnegie remained resolutely opposed to organized labor. He interpreted the effort to organize as a personal affront: the Homestead men and the Amalgamated were trying to humiliate and embarrass him; they were ungrateful curs considering he had just dedicated the Homestead Library and had given millions to his Pittsburgh institute—for their benefit. Now they wanted to take what was his.

Schwab took Carnegie's advice and posted a warning, after which forty men were summarily dismissed. A group of men who went to Homestead Superintendent William Corey demanding the fired workers be reinstated were themselves fired. The Amalgamated placed pickets at the gates, and more than fifty men went on strike. The number grew to eighty-eight. More men were fired. On July Fourth, the Homestead lodge, realizing it was futile, abandoned their efforts to organize the men. Two days later, Schwab reported to Carnegie that "we have completely knocked out any attempt to organize Homestead workmen."[47]

In addition to their hatred for unions, another reason Carnegie and his men were so eager to quell any labor uprising was a suitor had come calling to purchase Carnegie Steel. In late March, a potential buyer, who wished to remain anonymous to Carnegie, approached Frick and Phipps. The subsequent negotiations would carry into the summer, right through the labor upheavals.

When the partners informed Carnegie of this interested party, he guessed it was either Morgan, Rockefeller, or the Mellon family. Pledged to secrecy, they would not divulge the name. Suspicious, Carnegie demanded a nonrefundable $2 million payment for the option to buy the company, and he also insisted that Frick and Phipps represent the unnamed party, thus becoming part of the syndicate behind the proposed buyout.[48] The purpose of the latter request was more for appearance's sake: in case the syndicate involved unsavory men, Carnegie could claim he was selling to his partners. As negotiations opened, the board halted expansion projects and agreed to price Carnegie Steel at $250 million and Frick Coke at $70 million. Again, it proved too rich, but the suitor subsequently proposed buying only Carnegie's share. If the deal was consummated, the company would be taken public, and the other partners would be able to do as they wished with their shares.

Now Carnegie panicked. He realized he might have created a problem by having just mailed a nasty letter to the editor of *Iron Age*, lambasting the "present craze for consolidation," which could easily be construed as an attack on Morgan, Rockefeller, or any number of potential suitors. (His attitude had apparently changed from the prior year when he stated, "Consolidation is wise and necessary.") Always willing to contradict himself if it served his best interests at the time—again, profits over ideology—Carnegie immediately wrote a second letter to *Iron Age* retracting the first.[49] Frick, knowing the suitor would indeed be insulted, also cabled the *Iron Age* offices, urging the letter not be printed.

On the very day Carnegie wrote his retraction, April 24, he signed an agreement with Frick and Phipps that gave them and the anonymous buyer an option to purchase Carnegie's interest in the company for $157 million—$100 million in 5 percent gold bonds and $57 million in cash—to expire on August 4. The nonrefundable deposit was now set at $1,170,000, but the suitor was willing to front only $1 million; so, after some haggling, it was agreed that Frick and Phipps would add another $170,000, giving Carnegie what he demanded.[50] He assured his partners that if the deal fell through, he would refund them their $170,000 (but certainly keep the $1 million as per the agreement). The suitor and his syndicate now had until August 4 to arrange financing and close the sale. Confident that the option would be exercised, Carnegie sailed for Britain two days after signing the agreement.

There was more to the picture than met the eye, however; rumors were circulating in the press about Carnegie Steel combining with Gates's American Steel and Wire and with Moore's recent amalgamations to create a trust designed to destroy Morgan's Federal Steel. Gates confirmed the rumors while Frick immediately denied them, the denial suspect considering he had been spotted at New York's Holland House in deep conference with Gates and Moore.

Carnegie, who was in London visiting the House of Commons to hear the debates and to visit friends, was caught off guard by the story. When an Associated Press correspondent confronted him with the rumors, he could only furnish a lame prepared statement that he had "given his young partners the terms on which he would be willing to sell and retire from business." Two days later, when asked if he had sold out because he was afraid of the trusts, he replied smartly, "The trusts have never frightened me, and the Carnegie Steel Company has no occasion to be afraid of them, as it is the greatest property of its kind the world has ever seen or probably ever will see."[51] Inside, he was seething over the fact that the anonymous suitor was Moore and that the syndicate included Gates, both of whom Carnegie derided as gamblers and the "Chicago Adventurers." If he'd known they were involved, he would never have granted an option.[52]

Nothing could stop the process now, however; the option papers had been signed. Frick applied for new charters for Carnegie Steel in Pennsylvania and New York, and Moore lined up the Wall Street financing, which included the notorious manipulator Roswell Flower, who had been instrumental in promoting Federal Steel. But then, on Friday, May 12, Flower died unexpectedly, which scared off others willing to finance the syndicate and immediately threw the sale into doubt. With a million dollars at risk, Moore and his conspirators had to salvage the buyout. They still had until August 4, but with the syndicate unveiled, they could expect no help from Carnegie.

The Carnegie family went about its business in London—Carnegie refusing to discuss business with reporters, and Louise partaking in a shopping spree to prepare for Skibo. They stayed at Louise's favorite hotel, the Connaught, where their rooms were always brightened with flowers sent by friends. They attended the theater and visited with the Yates-Thompsons, who had introduced Carnegie to Matthew Arnold years before. In early May, Carnegie offered $250,000 to the University at Birmingham, England, provided it be used for the development of the school's scientific education program and the "scientific school be made the principal department." His proviso raised some objections, but on May 12 the school accepted.[53] After a four-year lull, Carnegie's philanthropic activity, outside of Pittsburgh, picked up considerably in 1899, mostly due to the fact he had pocketed $10 million the prior year.

On June 7, the Carnegies arrived for their second summer at Skibo, their first as its owners, and as the coach passed through the villages within the estate, the family was greeted by homes and shops decorated with glass and bunting. Children were dressed in their Sunday best and bagpipe bands played. At the castle's gate, the oldest tenant on the estate, nearly ninety years of age, officially presented Skibo to its new laird. An emotional Carnegie responded by pointing at Louise and saying, "Here is an American who loves Scotland." He then pointed to himself and said, "And here is a Scotchman who loves America, and"—now pointing at Margaret—"here is a little Scottish-American who is born of both and will love both; she has come to enter the fairyland of childhood among you."[54]

The castle had looked better, however, considering it was now undergoing major reconstruction. As the family settled in one protected wing and the servants in a cottage, work on the castle pushed ahead rapidly. Hundreds of men were hired, barracks built for them, and a 120-foot bridge was built across a ravine at the rear of the castle for bringing in the steel beams, marble, and stone. Carnegie made sure enough meat was supplied to the men to keep up their strength, and he offered to pay 10 percent more in wages to every man who abstained from drinking. The only griping was from some of the locals who mourned the cutting down of many old-growth trees that had stood on the property for generations.

The vastly enlarged sixteenth-century Scottish baronial style home with added square turrets soon took shape. The great hall was expanded to give it noble dimensions; it included marble columns, an elaborately paneled ceiling, a staircase of Sicilian marble, and stained-glass windows with scenes depicting Carnegie's childhood voyage to America, his rise from bobbin boy to titan, as well as others with scenes depicting the history of the castle. There was a gun room with a separate entrance for the gillies and gamekeepers, a billiard room, a smoking room, and a dining room with an immense table that could seat thirty or more. (Carnegie's chair was two inches higher to improve his stature.) Carnegie insisted on a spacious library, and off the library was his office, in which there was a custom-built set of drawers, each drawer affixed with a label: Carnegie Steel Company Reports; Correspondence about Libraries; Pittsburgh Institute; Grants and Other Donations; Applications for Aid; Autograph Letters to Keep; and Skibo Estate, among others. Several maps were always on the wall, little flags marking arenas of action. This was his war room—his coat of arms was a blank shield.

Louise decided a series of large greenhouses would help in maintaining the gardens and allow them to grow more exotic plants and flowers. Carnegie agreed: "If the greenhouses give you pleasure, that is a wise move, a purchase of satisfaction. I believe we shall find them a great satisfaction; and Baba [Margaret's nickname] will, that's certain, and they must foster in her tastes which will remain all her life. Organ, flowers—I tell you we are showing what *Home* means."[55] On occasion, Carnegie did too much for show, and not enough for his own private contentment.

Amid the chaos of construction, Louise was very careful to make time to play with Margaret and not depend wholly on their Scottish nurse, Nana. She read to her, played in the garden, and went for carriage rides. Carnegie, while playing tough with the Amalgamated and the Moore syndicate, was also drawn to his wee Baba, who represented the miracle of life to him and an innocence he couldn't remember having. When Louise was away from Skibo, he updated her: "How grateful for being here at home! Baba has just had her bite with me at breakfast and jelly on it! When you are away I find myself going to her as the connecting link, as indeed she is, part of both which makes us more truly one!"[56]

One of the few guests that season was Rudyard Kipling, whom the Carnegies found to be of simple manners and unaffected. Another was Sir Swire Smith, an advocate of education associated with England's Keighley Institute, a technical school, who found himself on the receiving end of Carnegie's acidic humor. After a round of golf—the laird beating him soundly—the two talked about the school, and Carnegie asked if the town of Keighley had a library. When Smith replied no, Carnegie offered $50,000 to build one, to be his first library in England. More importantly, he offered to give Smith a stroke a hole in the next day's golf round. Because Carnegie had offered the library so casually, so off the cuff, Smith worried the philanthropist would forget or change his mind. The next day his hopes did indeed sink when Carnegie turned to him and said, "I have repented me of the offer I made yesterday." Considering Carnegie had yet to give a library to an English town, Smith shouldn't have been too disappointed. But then, with an impish grin, Carnegie added, "You will have to play me even."[57] It was always a pleasure to toy with people, a component to Carnegie's twisted humor.

*   *   *

Shuttling between Pittsburgh, Chicago, and New York, Frick, Phipps, and Moore now scrambled to create a plan for financing the buyout. The three decided to charter a new company with capital of $250 million, divided into 2.5 million $100 shares. Once the stock was sold, they would buy Carnegie's shares in the steel and coke companies by issuing him $100 million in 5 percent gold bonds and $57 million in cash. Of the $250 million raised, Frick and Phipps informed Carnegie, $15 million would go into the treasury as working capital and a second $15 million to be divided among the buyers to cover expenses and to provide bonuses, with one-third of it going to Moore, one third to Frick and Phipps, and one-third to be used "for deserving young men."[58] So Frick and Phipps stood to reap a hefty bonus of $2.5 million each minus some expenses. Frick then presented the new plan to the board of managers, making them aware of the $15 million for expenses and bonuses, and it was approved.[59]

Reading over the letter and the board meeting minutes, Carnegie was appalled by the fact that Moore stood to receive what would amount to almost $5 million, and Frick and Phipps almost $2.5 million each. It appeared the triumvirate was pulling a fast one—not so much on Carnegie, but on Schwab and the junior partners who were intoxicated by the thought of the firm going public. But again, there was little he could do; the partners had voted.

The June issue of the *American Monthly Review of Reviews* announced "the retirement of Mr. Andrew Carnegie from the business of making iron and steel. Mr. Carnegie was the head of a system of closely connected establishments, with headquarters at Pittsburgh, which had become the most extensive and probably the most complete and perfect plant in the whole world for the supply of iron and steel in large quantities."[60] It was a glowing epithet that also lavished praise on Frick, who was to become the head of the amalgamated companies of Carnegie and Frick. Congratulations poured in. Dazzled by the riches Carnegie was about to bank, his literary friend William Stead immediately published a pamphlet: "Mr. Carnegie's Conundrum: £40,000,000. What Shall I Do with It?" Stead reviewed the Scotsman's benefactions to date and speculated as to what philanthropic course Carnegie might take next.

The effusive congratulations and tributes were premature.

Moore again had trouble arranging a syndicate to back the financing of the new company, and there was now serious doubt as to whether the August 4 deadline could be met. Frick sailed for England on June 6 to reconnoiter with Phipps, and then the two traveled to Skibo castle to present their case before their king. Their only hope: an extension of the deadline.

Carnegie took a hard stand and refused to extend it, which Frick and Phipps expected now that their partner knew Moore was behind the deal.

Carnegie did mollify them somewhat by assuring them the company would realize $40 to $50 million in profits the next year, profits that could be used by the partners to buy the company, as well as fattening everyone's wallet. Frick and Phipps apprised Moore and then cabled the board of managers: "Pleasant interview at Skibo. Will not extend or modify present option. Have advised Chicago."[61] A triumphant Carnegie cabled Dod: "HP and HCF came & told me Moore wished an extension. I said not one hour." It felt good.

Phipps now traveled to Beaufort Castle, in the Highland town of Beauly, sixty miles from Skibo, which he had rented for the summer season. All seemed amicable among the partners when in mid-July the Carnegies visited for two days. "Andrew was made happy by catching two fine salmon—17″ to 18″ long—hooked and landed them unaided—his first salmon," Phipps wrote Frick. He also reported that Mrs. Phipps thought Carnegie was very anxious to sell, and he hoped Frick would have some good ideas on the subject when they next met, indulging his partner by adding: "Your opportunities and abilities are superior to Carnegie's and mine." Phipps did acknowledge one major catch to selling Carnegie Steel, or even Carnegie's share of the company: it would require the movement of so much money within the market that it could touch off a financial panic.[62] Carnegie had created a monster that could not be slain.

The August 4 deadline came and went. Moore failed and lost a cool million. As Carnegie had promised, it was time to return the $170,000 option money owed his pards; but when Phipps pressed him on the matter, Carnegie refused. Such was business, he explained; nothing personal. It had become personal, however.

Carnegie was livid that he had indirectly been involved with three gamblers, Gates, Moore, and Flower, the latter fortunately meeting a timely death, and he was embarrassed by the deal falling through. Also angering him were Frick and Phipps's plans to siphon off $5 million for Moore and $5 million to split between themselves. Carnegie was feeling spiteful, and to discredit his partners in the eyes of history he later wrote on the back of the June 27 board meeting minutes: "Frick and Phipps. Secret bargain with Moores to get large sum for obtaining option. Never revealed to their partners."[63] Carnegie did take comfort in being $1,170,000 richer, which, coincidentally, was almost the exact cost of buying and completely renovating Skibo. The castle, he enjoyed joking, was "Just a nice little present from Frick!" Yes, there was definitely a malevolent streak to his humor.

By the end of August, Phipps was extremely embittered with Carnegie, too, setting the stage for future conflict. When he entertained the newly appointed U.S. ambassador to Great Britain, Joseph H. Choate, who had just seen Carnegie and now relayed to Phipps that the steel king was truly anxious to sell, Phipps passed the information along to Frick in a most acidic tone: "A visitor says the Senior is desperately anxious to sell. An obvious fact. If it had not been for you and me AC would never have gotten his $1,170,000. Mighty little thanks we get for our part."[64]

CHAPTER 27

UnCivil War

The first board meeting following Frick's return from Skibo was tense. The junior partners were well aware of the conflict between the trio of Carnegie, Frick, and Phipps over the failed sale and of the riches they had come so close to winning. The September 11 meeting began with the usual review and approval of the last minutes, but this time, before approval was given, Francis Lovejoy read a letter from the absent Carnegie. Displaying his disgust for Moore and his ilk, he demanded a section from the last minutes "be expunged" because it discussed doing business with speculators. "We do not need to take up with speculators," he ranted, "or adopt unbusiness methods—besides there is only loss and disgrace probably from doing so."[1]

Carnegie also unilaterally demanded the cancellation of specific rail contracts he deemed having too small a profit margin. Frick had heard enough. Just waiting for an excuse to lash out at the absent partner, he attacked: "These contracts have been made, and we must live up to them. If Mr. Carnegie wishes to review past actions, we have as much right to review other things. . . . I think we have blundered about in proportion to our interests in the concern." So, in translation, Carnegie blundered 58.5 percent to Frick's 6. Frick was taking issue with Carnegie on two points: the first was that the prior fall Carnegie had insisted the company contract with their customers to provide rails at below-market prices in his overzealous hopes of knocking out the competition; and the second was that Carnegie had refused to join an industry-wide pool that would have protected their market share and supported prices. The two moves were particularly bad because the rail market had strengthened, with orders and prices on the rise.

When Carnegie read the September 11 minutes, he was embarrassed and angered by Frick's brazen attack. "The Chairman says that we all have blundered," Carnegie wrote the board, shrewdly including them in his collective *we*, in a psychological game to promote animosity toward Frick. "True, and always will blunder; no one is infallible, but suggestions of a change do not imply personal reflections. It is simply a business question as to what is best, and experience should teach us to change when thought best." As for the rail contracts signed at below-market price that he insisted on to crush the competition, he admitted his mistake had "cost us a great deal of money."[2]

In truth, not only had he cost the company money, but Carnegie's multi-front war against the consolidations had bogged down; for all the bellicose posturing and talking, there were no pipe mills or other finished-product mills bringing the Morgan and Moore consolidations to their knees. There was a mutual loss of respect between the three senior partners—Carnegie, Frick, and Phipps—and, sadly, September 11 marked the beginning of the end for more than just their relationships. Battles between the partners would now escalate dramatically, as did those between the American and national armies in the Philippines. And the innocent suffered.

The newspapers were filled with graphic stories of horribly mutilated bodies of the American dead and of merciless American soldiers putting torches to entire villages. The U.S. Army's policy was to take no prisoners—and with a killed-to-wounded ratio of five to one, the inverse of what might be expected in a war, the policy was working.[3] At least New York had a reformer in its midst. Former war hero and now New York governor Teddy Roosevelt, with his trademark zest, was dueling with New York City's Tammany Hall over reforms, corporate greed, and political graft. Thoroughly disgusted with Roosevelt, Tammany Hall boss Tom Platt said, "I want to get rid of the bastard. I don't want him raising hell in my state any longer. I want to bury him."[4] When Carnegie returned to New York in October, he was in the same frame of mind concerning Frick.

"*No Contract. Declaration of War,*" Carnegie wrote across the top of his copy of the October 25 Frick Coke Company board meeting minutes. This latest conflict would become known as "the Clash of the Steel Men"—and it featured a perfect Machiavellian plot, driven by ego, money, power, and innuendo.

It was precipitated by Carnegie's conviction that he and Frick had made an oral contract for the Frick Coke Company to supply Carnegie Steel with coke at $1.35 a ton, but at the October 25 meeting Frick denied any such agreement existed. Disputes over what Carnegie Steel paid the Frick Coke Company for coke were frequent, even though the very same investors controlled both companies. It was a clash of egos, with the respective company's managers mimicking their respective bosses' distrust for each other. Understandably, Carnegie wanted to make sure his mills were paying less than other Frick Coke Company customers, while Frick wanted to get what he could from every customer for those shareholders in his company who were not invested in Carnegie Steel. The current situation was unacceptable to Carnegie, but because Frick men outnumbered Carnegie men on the Coke board, he couldn't simply demand a vote to secure the $1.35 price. He did the next best thing: he ordered his men to stop paying the coke bills. Regardless of whether there was an oral agreement, the next month the issue remained unresolved, with Carnegie and Frick on a collision course that would captivate the public.

Three weeks after the Frick Coke meeting, on November 15, Carnegie arrived in Pittsburgh to review the architect's plans for his institute's expansion. He also dazzled both supporters and detractors by finally committing $1,750,000 to enlarge the building to three and a half times its current size, with the new art and science wings and a larger library. Including this benefaction, the *Library Journal* estimated that in 1899 Carnegie promised or gave $3,503,500 to thirty-four American libraries in fifteen states. There were donations of $350,000 to Washington, D.C.; $50,000 to Dallas; $50,000 to Oakland, California; $4,000 to Prescott, Arizona; and even $500 to Bucyrus, Ohio.[5] Many of the libraries Carnegie gave to in 1899, as before, were strategically located; they were in places where he desired to develop goodwill among the laborers who were key to his success, such as Connellsville, McKeesport, Beaver, and Oil City in Pennsylvania, and Conneaut, Steubenville, and Sandusky in Ohio. East Liverpool, home to relatives, received $50,000. His gospel was slowly coming to the fore.

While in town, Carnegie also reviewed his business operations. In particular, he was still concerned about the slim profit margin for rails, the rail contracts he had wanted to break back in September, and, of course, the October 25 Frick Coke Company board meeting. In reviewing the proceedings with Dod and Schwab, Carnegie masked his own anxiety about the rather sketchy contract he claimed to have made by calling Frick a coward for not taking the matter up directly with him. As he had with Leishman, he was talking behind Frick's back, stabbing him and undercutting his position. If Frick heard of it there'd be hell, and he invariably did when either Schwab or Dod gossiped with the other junior partners.

When the Carnegie Steel Company board convened five days after Carnegie reviewed plans for his "great gift" to Pittsburgh, Frick stood before them, his face flushed. He again lambasted Carnegie for involving the company in unprofitable rail contracts, and then he addressed Carnegie's charge of "cowardice in not bringing up question of price of coke as between Steel and Coke Companies." According to Frick, neither he nor Carnegie had the power to make such a contract, which was technically true. "The Frick Coke Company has always been used as a convenience," he countercharged, and then blurted, "Why was he not manly enough to say to my face what he said behind my back?" No one else said a word as Frick concluded, "Harmony is so essential for the success of any organization that I have stood a great many insults from Mr. Carnegie in the past, but I will submit to no further insults in the future."[6]

Lovejoy quietly adjourned the meeting.

The compelling question was how would Carnegie, who was of course absent from the board meeting, react to Frick questioning his manhood? The day after the meeting, as soon as he had been debriefed, Carnegie did not parry with his double-edged sword, but rather took a defensive posture in replying to Frick's charges. "If I have insulted you I have known it not. . . ," he wrote Frick. "When you get your usual calm and if you come to me, I shall tell you all the circumstances just as they occurred and you will be sorry for your hasty outburst to your partners. I am not guilty and can satisfy you of this, also of the folly of believing tale bearers, a mean lot."[7] The sidestepper denied backstabbing Frick and attempted to shift guilt to the unknown talebearer.

While playing innocent with Frick, two days later he told Dod that he was pursuing other coal lands to render the Frick Coke Company expendable.[8] His cousin, who considered Frick a troublemaker, replied with an insight worthy of Machiavelli: "Now the question keeps intruding itself into my mind all the time: would any possible sacrifice that could be entailed be much in order to cut loose from such a disturbing element? I am well aware the steps to be very grave but an enemy outside your lines is always less dangerous than inside no matter what the apparent sacrifice may be in putting him there."[9]

"You voice my views exactly—" Carnegie answered. "Frick goes out of Chairmanship of Board next election or before. . . . He's too old—too infirm in health *and mind*. . . . My birthday—never better or happier especially since I decided to tell Mr. Frick in kindest manner that I mean divorce under 'Incompatibility of Temper.'"[10] Carnegie and Dod, allies from the days they fought the English with wooden swords, remained blood brothers, and together would fight a man they genuinely considered to be mentally unbalanced.

But was Frick as disruptive of an element as Carnegie and Dod claimed? Or was he simply not a yes-man? Was the "Incompatibility of Temper" reason sufficient? Was Frick's mental constitution faulty? No more than Carnegie's. Closest to the truth was the argument that both men were alike in too many ways; they were aggressive, intolerant of opposition, and driven by egos that refused to accept second place to anyone. Their mutual friend, John Walker, appraised the conflicting personalities:

> [D]on't ever forget that Carnegie was the Napoleon—that is the commander and intuitive genius, who planned campaigns and executed them with a rapidity and boldness that swept all enemies from his path; while Frick had the calm qualities of a von Moltke—long-headed, deliberate, a great tactician,— a man who acted from carefully reasoned premises, while Carnegie struck out boldly, burning all his bridges behind him, not necessarily knowing himself the stages of reasoning by which he reached his results. In fact, he didn't reason much—he acted on impulse; but his impulses were usually far more accurate than others' logical processes. But both were very big men—too big to enjoy each other's presence in the same organization.[11]

It was astonishing they had survived this long together.

To eject Frick from the firm, Carnegie would need a three-quarters vote in partners and in interest. If Harry Phipps, Harry's nephew Lawrence, and Lovejoy, whom Frick had hired and promoted, aligned themselves with Frick, their voting power amounted to 20 percent. There were nine other partners carrying interests ranging from 3 percent to 0.5 percent—enough voting power to block Carnegie if a handful sided with Frick and Phipps, which was not out of the question if the latter two men promised monetary rewards to long-suffering junior partners. The easiest means of guaranteeing victory was to win over Phipps, so he wrote his oldest pard, hoping to appeal to his good reason in explaining, "It is a clear case of 'Incompatibility of Temper,' always sufficient cause for divorce." While threatening to vote Frick out of office, Carnegie also told Phipps there was an alternative, which was for Frick to resign, thereby saving face. "I must beg you in laying this before Mr. Frick to say that the question of adjusting this in any other manner than that I indicate be not raised," Carnegie wrote. "It would be useless."[12]

To shore up support among the junior partners, Carnegie worked feverishly behind the scene. On November 26, he wrote a confidential letter to Schwab apprising him of his plans to eject Frick in which he expressed outrage over "Mr. Frick's partnership with Moore by which he was to make millions—It was a betrayal of trust."[13] The letter served several goals. He confided in Schwab to strengthen their relationship; but in case Schwab was entertaining any thoughts of siding with Frick, Carnegie added in the biting piece about Frick's betrayal of trust in scheming to personally make millions in the Moore deal. He also discredited Harry Phipps by implying he was ill and not fit for decision making, and he reminded Schwab that Lawrence Phipps could be won over because he had been given the vice presidency, the number two spot if Frick was voted out. No vote should be taken, Carnegie advised, unless all of their friends on the board were present.

On the same day, Carnegie wrote the board of managers to explain his position on Frick and to discredit him by intimating that Frick had been attempting to usurp power from Schwab, and that it had been a mistake to split power between a chairman and a president. "There is another reason why Mr. Frick's retirement from office is in my opinion desirable today. His name as chairman means to the public no decided break in the chain of discredit which all failures in the stock exchange world entail. The Carnegie Steel Co. has been less considered recently for its triumphs in manufacturing and for conservative and non-speculative traditions than for its connection with professional speculators. It needs to be brought back to its legitimate business career which steadily pursued means far greater triumphs than any yet attained." Frick had soiled the company's reputation, he believed. Carnegie concluded his propaganda piece with a calculating warm embrace: "One of the chief sources of my happiness in life has been the feeling that my associates in CS Co. have grown to be friends first, partners second."[14] He was playing a well-orchestrated game.

But at the next board meeting, Frick calmly chaired the proceedings as though there were no extenuating circumstances. He appeared quite content with no apparent intent of resigning, and not one of the junior partners mentioned Carnegie's letter nor asked Frick if he planned to resign.

That day Schwab wrote Carnegie: "Believe me, Dear Mr. Carnegie, I am always with you, and yours to command. I want to be straightforward toward all. I believe the great majority of important partners feel as I do." However, Schwab then made it clear to Carnegie that he would have to take Frick on alone. The junior partners feared Frick, he explained, and "The only way for you to do is to take *decisive action yourself first*."[15] Schwab feared him, too. Would he waver in picking sides in the battle? Just two months ago, in September, Frick had given him a fine painting as a gift, which Schwab acknowledged with a loyal pledge: "Working with and for you is a great pleasure, and I am yours to command always. I do not write this as a formal and set letter but as a spontaneous expression of my true feeling."[16] *Schwab was his to command*—words echoed to Carnegie just two months later.

Between his campaign to oust Frick and his increasing involvement in the anti-imperialist movement, Carnegie entered another manic phase in his life, very similar to the winter of 1895–1896 when he was embroiled in Frick's resignation, flogging Leishman over ore speculation, and fighting the Pennsylvania Railroad. His condemnation of the American presence in the Philippines became more acute as Britain became embroiled in the Boer War, which erupted in October 1899. It pitted the Boers, settlers of Dutch ancestry living in South Africa and the Orange Free State, against the British, whose significant presence the Boers detested. The British suffered serious casualties in the first months of the conflict and would eventually deploy 450,000 men— 22,000 never to return home. Such an escalation, Carnegie feared, would occur in the Philippines, and already had to a degree.

His master, Herbert Spencer, loathed the Boer War, which further fueled Carnegie's anti-imperialist activities. Spencer's anger and anxiety over the human condition spilled into a burst of letters to Carnegie, more than he had ever sent before. "No one can more fully agree than I do with your denunciations of the doings of our race in the world," Spencer wrote in October. "And not only our race but of all races."[17] In another letter, he suggested money might buy peace: "I very much wish that you would spend some few thousands out of your millions in employing a few capable men in the United States and Great Britain to war against war. . . . The mass of people do not in the least understand that if they advocate militarism and war as its concomitant they necessarily lose their liberties. That perhaps would be the strongest point continually to make, and a point abundantly illustrated by all human history."[18] Money, Carnegie well knew, could influence the politicians' votes, but as for money having a more definitive role in fighting a war on war, he was skeptical and demurred.

Carnegie was outraged when, in late November, Whitelaw Reid sent him an invitation to a party celebrating the first anniversary of President McKinley signing the treaty with Spain. Aware as Reid was of Carnegie's opposition, it was a mean-spirited stab. Even when they had knocked heads during Homestead, Carnegie had considered Reid a kindred spirit, since he had a little Scottish blood in him, and was fond of saying there was a "wee drap blude between us." The blude, however, didn't stop his temper from flaring when he declined the invitation: "Unfortunately I shall be in Pittsburgh the evening of your reception to the signers of the *War* Treaty with Spain, not the Peace. It is a matter of congratulations that you seem to have finished your work of civilizing the Filipinos. It is thought that about 8000 of them have been completely civilized and sent to Heaven. I hope you like it."[19]

Fighting the insurgents was not near over. Pockets of well-armed nationalists were entrenched in the islands' rugged terrain, with commanding positions along steep and narrow trails cutting through the countryside. The hunt for Filipino leader Aguinaldo was dogged and frustrating. As the United States remained entangled, Carnegie stepped up his attacks on McKinley, writing Secretary of State Hay, "We need more backbone in the President, that is all."[20] His criticisms couldn't get much more blunt or unproductive, but his colorful commentary did fill the newspapers, offering insight and entertainment. In a letter published in the *New York Daily Tribune*, he shrewdly used a metaphor every person could understand: "I know many, poor households far behind me in knowledge and civilization as the Filipinos are behind us. I don't think I should be good by attempting to govern any other household than my own."[21]

An anti-Carnegie movement fired off a few salvos of their own. In Pittsburgh, two authors self-published a ninety-page book entitled *Anti-Carnegie Scraps and Comments*. "Does Andrew Carnegie stand by the flag of this country?" they wrote in the preface. "He has expressed sympathy for and given encouragement to the armed bands of Filipinos, but he has neither for our American soldiers who are now engaged in the final conquest of the Philippines, to prevent our flag from being 'hauled down' from where it has been planted." They accused him of being an extremist who was acting on behalf of the European nations to keep the United States out of the Philippines, and they perceptively exposed his hypocritical streak: "Andrew Carnegie calls himself an anti-imperialist. But Skibo Castle and the town of Skibo belong to him by purchase; he imitates in every way what he condemns and buys all he can of it."[22]

Such attacks did not dampen his enthusiasm. Due to his unrestrained criticism of the McKinley administration, Carnegie was offered the presidency of the Anti-Imperialist League. He declined; it demanded more time than he had to give, considering there was Frick to contend with.

❊   ❊   ❊

That the Anti-Imperialist League had turned to Carnegie for leadership swelled his ego and confidence, as did Schwab's stated belief that only he could take on Frick, *mano a mano.* Now resolved to face his enemy, on Sunday, December 3, Carnegie took the train to Pittsburgh, prepared for a showdown the next morning. Tense but relieved the moment had finally come, on Monday Carnegie marched into Frick's office and simply demanded his resignation. It was an anticlimactic moment, for Frick, who had been expecting him, did so quietly.

Now that Carnegie had his resignation, he wanted his stock. The simplest solution, according to Carnegie, would be for Frick to exchange his Carnegie Steel shares for shares in Frick Coke owned by Carnegie. It would be based on book value, with any imbalance settled with cash, and Frick could then take control of his old company. But what both men knew was that the book value of the Carnegie Steel shares were worth far more if the company were sold or taken public, so Frick balked at the seemingly generous but duplicitous offer. Frick also contended he had no interest in returning to the everyday management of the Frick Coke Company; he wanted a clean break from Carnegie, and, besides, he had other pursuits in life to explore.

Carnegie also still faced the conflict over coke pricing, and he now threatened that he would expel Frick from his own coke company unless the $1.35 contract was accepted. "He can't repudiate contracts for any company which myself and friends control—" Carnegie bragged to Dod, "we are not that kind of cats."[23] The threat failed. In a brazen display, he now had the gall to appeal to Frick's compassion: "Give me a settlement permanent on coke and I'll bless you. . . . We never had friction before—it annoys me more than dollars—even than Philippines."[24] Again Frick refused. Patience spent, Carnegie lashed out with one of his tantrums: "Excuse me, I have no time to waste upon the Prest. of the F.C. Co. who begins saying he didn't know the bargain—that's all I read—It's gone to waste basket." He then insisted Carnegie Steel was going to pay $1.35 permanently—no negotiations—and finished with another stab: "My friend, you are so touchy upon F.C. Co. (fortunately the only point) you are, and we all have our 'crazy bones'—you know where Roslander, thanks to you for him, gets his finger sometimes and oh it hurts, doesn't it?"[25] When Carnegie entered into these manic phases, it was he who appeared to become somewhat unbalanced mentally. He was brilliant, no doubt, but arrested in an adolescent's emotional state, moving in and out of an illusionary world in which he imposed his vision of order and righteousness. When told no, he kicked and screamed.

To date, even though Carnegie and his allies owned a majority in Frick's company, the board had been controlled by Frick men, but the situation was about to change. It was time for Carnegie to take control of the Frick Coke Company board, and then there would be no question on coke rates. To mask his play for the company, on December 19, Frick's fiftieth birthday, Carnegie sent him a birthday greeting, suggesting a desire to reconcile: "Mr. and Mrs. Carnegie cordially wish you many happy returns. Yours is a great record to date which they hope and believe the future is still to enhance."[26] At the same time he was making arrangements to transfer one hundred shares of Frick Coke stock to each of his loyal junior partners to make them eligible to sit on the board.[27]

Frick, who quickly realized he had been outsmarted and blindsided, capitulated control. He humbly wrote Thomas Lynch, his top man, "You are to be President and there will be no Chairman of the Board. . . . I have dictated this in the presence of Mr. Schwab."[28] At the same time, Schwab crowed to Carnegie: "Frick left yesterday for 10 days in the South. Before leaving arranged Coke Board matter with him: to be 7 members of the board, he to name 2 and we to name 5. He named himself and Lynch."[29] When the Carnegie men were officially elected at the next Frick Coke Company board meeting, Frick walked out in protest.

Carnegie had Frick on the run. There remained Frick's interest in Carnegie Steel, but the Iron Clad would take care of that.

Upbeat as the year came to a close, Carnegie wrote Dod:

> So well and all so happy, business an unalloyed pleasure as I think of every partner now—no rift in the lute.
> Played 14 long holes of golf yesterday and same Christmas—60 years younger already.[30]

As a further testament to his good mood, Carnegie donated $300,000 to Cooper Union to help establish a daytime school program to match the evening program. (Six months later, he would contribute another $300,000 to what was one of his models for philanthropy.) And the loyal son gave Dunfermline a Christmas gift of $100,000 for new swimming baths and a gymnasium.[31]

To fill the void created by Frick's ejection, Carnegie decided to take a more active role in daily management. "I have had to take general charge of the business for next year," he wrote John Morley with confidence and conceit. "Some means to be made to meet these huge Combinations which are really at our mercy. But my being at helm makes victory easier. So thought my partners, but it is only a short postponement of withdrawal. Ashamed to tell you profits these days. Prodigious."[32] Indeed they were: $21 million for the year.

The *New York Times* rung in the New Year with a rosy editorial: "The year 1899 was a year of wonders, a veritable annus mirabilis, in business and production. To paraphrase a celebrated epitaph, prosperity left scarcely any of our industries untouched, and touched nothing it did not enrich."[33] The

United States had surpassed Britain in iron and coal output in the mid-1890s and was now a premier economic power, with Carnegie Steel one of the companies setting the pace for industrial development and innovation. Other firms were emulating the Carnegie template for management, which he had adopted from his railroad days. It was highly controlled and coordinated, while at the same time offering incentives to managers and foremen to break old methods and to innovate. His drive for modern equipment and facilities brought riches, and, by inspiring other industrialists, contributed to America's rise as the preeminent economic power in the heat of the industrial revolution.

Mild weather prevailed in the first days of January, followed by increasing clouds bringing snow and rain. Under the cover of this poor weather, Carnegie slipped into Pittsburgh for a January 8 secret meeting of the board of managers, at which he moved that the company invoke the Iron Clad to eject Frick and purchase his interest at book value. The move was seconded and approved.

There was no hiding in Scotland during this conflict; on Wednesday, January 10, Carnegie strode boldly into Frick's office and delivered the news. The Carnegie Steel Company would buy coke for $1.35; and furthermore, he said, the board had voted to enact the Iron Clad and the transfer of his stock would be made at the close of business on January 31. He would be paid book value.[34] The book value of the company, Carnegie claimed, was $25 million, giving Frick a mere $1.5 million for his 6 percent interest; whereas from Frick's viewpoint, the company's real value was at least $250 million, last year's agreed selling price, which would make his interest worth $15 million. As Frick considered this *little* discrepancy in value he felt as though a sword was driven through his back. A fit of anger gripped him and his eyes blazed. Anticipating violence, Carnegie backed away. Coming around his desk, Frick yelled, "For years I have been convinced that there is not an honest bone in your body. Now I know you are a god damned thief. We will have a judge and jury of Allegheny County decide what you are to pay me."[35]

After his verbal spanking of Carnegie, Frick went to John Walker's office to cool off and discuss the situation. Walker, a top executive at Frick Coke, was one of his few allies. "John, I lost my temper this morning." "Well," Walker replied, "I knew you had one to lose." He then agreed with Frick that Carnegie could not force the $1.35 contract on the company and that Frick's interest in the steel company had to be bought out at a fair valuation. Phipps, yet again disappointing Carnegie, supported Frick. The battle lines were drawn, and that same day Frick notified Carnegie Steel that the company was not authorized to sell or to transfer his stock.[36]

Regardless, Carnegie pressed ahead with his unrelenting campaign against Frick. At the January 24 Frick Coke Company board meeting, a resolution was passed stating the company would supply all the coke Carnegie Steel required for the next five years at $1.35 a ton, retroactive to January 1; at the time, coke was selling for about $3.50 *a ton* on the open market.[37] Also, the board voted that the overbilling of the last year, amounting to $596,000, was to be refunded. The vote on both issues was five to two, Frick and Lynch dissenting.

As the battle became more heated, the Carnegie-Frick conflict shook the company like an earthquake, and a great, jagged fault line ruptured as men chose their sides. The first victim to fall into the great crevasse was Lovejoy. Not wanting to lose Carnegie as a friend, but also feeling an allegiance to Frick, who had hired and promoted him years earlier, he resigned rather than pick sides. An unrecognized casualty of the war was Louise. She and Adelaide Frick had become good friends, but now with what appeared to be the final, climactic fight, their friendship was destroyed. Carnegie was ambivalent about their relationship. Frick had married into Pittsburgh's upper class and had been immediately accepted, while Carnegie had always been considered an outsider, and for that, he held a grudge against Frick and the upper-class families. The most prominent and predictable defection to the Frick camp was, of course, Phipps. As early as Christmas, Phipps had anticipated the fight would be taken to court and began to organize his papers on the Iron Clad. He claimed he sided with Frick as a matter of principle, nothing more, as Frick deserved to be paid a fair market value for his stock, just like he himself would want.

It was now January 29, just two days before the company would seize Frick's share. Frick, willing to submit to the decision of three disinterested businessmen, requested arbitration to determine the fair value of his interest.[38] Carnegie, in spite of being a proponent of arbitration, rejected it this time and instructed Schwab to transfer Frick's interests to the company's treasury. As Frick had said, an Allegheny court would decide the matter.

The first lawyer Frick hired was D. T. Watson, the man who had drawn up the original 1887 Iron Clad agreement: who better to penetrate the Iron Clad's weaknesses? Between them, the two titans had some of the best lawyers in the country in their respective stables, and each man was convinced he could win. Both were willing to fight to death 'til they parted. The impending case hinged on two simple questions: Was the Iron Clad legal and binding? And what was the real value of Carnegie Steel? The answers were not obvious. Both men and their legal teams spent the first two weeks of February formulating their battle plans.

The publicity that would be generated was the one underrated factor in the case. The first hint of trouble in the Carnegie realm reached the newspapers on February 2, when rumors circulated that Schwab was about to resign. Reporters flocked to 5 West Fifty-first Street and tried to confirm the story, but Carnegie wouldn't talk. In Pittsburgh, Schwab denied the report but refused to make any further comments. Seven days later, Frick's intention to file suit against Carnegie and Carnegie Steel made the front pages. The revelation of the impending lawsuit caused an immediate sensation, rippling through the press, as well as Carnegie's friends and business associates.

Soon afterward, Carnegie heard that Caroline Wilson, widow of Carnegie's boyhood Original Six pal James R. Wilson, was worrying about the Frick suit. Although her husband had died years ago, she still owned his shares in the Frick Coke Company and relied on the dividends. Not wanting her to worry needlessly, Carnegie took the time to reassure her:

> Do not believe that Mr. Frick did not look after the interests of the Coke Co. He always did . . . My Dear Friend your interests will be as zealously guarded as my own in the Company. I, with sister Lucy own more than half of the Co. and faithfully as I guard hers and mine I shall yours.
>   Callie Carpenter the girl of my boyhood & the wife of one of mine dearest friends is & always will be my charge through life when she needs my services.[39]

Thirty-five years removed from Slabtown had not diminished Carnegie's loyalty to his boyhood friends—again, one of the more poignant pieces of evidence for judging Carnegie's character.

The country's other capitalists were more worried than Carnegie about a dirty court case that might expose the inner workings of industrial America. When a Philadelphia businessman and friend, A. B. Farquhar, read the news, he wrote Carnegie that he hoped the case would be settled out of court and warned, "A lawsuit is war, and war is always bad."[40] George Westinghouse also expressed concern: "I have just seen in tonight's Chronicle that a suit is to be filed by Mr. Frick against you or the Carnegie Company to determine the value of his interest. I believe such a step will be almost a calamity by reason of the fact that the private affairs of your company will undoubtedly be made public. . . . Will you allow me to say, at the risk of being considered officious, that this matter is looked upon by mutual friends as not only very harmful to your own interests but to Pittsburgh generally. Your invariable friendliness toward me must be my excuse for troubling you about your own matters."[41] Before writing, Westinghouse was so anxious he had tried telephoning, only to discover Carnegie had left for Lucy Carnegie's Dungeness estate to escape the media circus.

On February 14, he and a group went to the island's north end to play golf and stay at a rustic lodge, while newspaper reporters gathered at the estate's main gate, clamoring for an interview. Frick had finally filed his suit in the Allegheny courthouse the day before. The island's manager issued a statement from Carnegie that simply said, "I am playing golf and that I broke my record yesterday."[42] Golf had become an obsession which he now jokingly called the only "serious business of life."

There was no mincing of words in Frick's suit, which decreed the transfer of his interest null and void and requested an injunction restraining any interference with his interest, claiming the Iron Clad had been abandoned and was no longer binding. Frick also demanded a market value be set for the company, along the lines of the $250 million Moore had been willing to pay, not the paltry $25 million currently on the books. The suit included an attack on Carnegie's character, too. Frick charged that Carnegie's animosity toward him had grown since he failed to sell the company the prior year, that Carnegie came to his office and "endeavored to frighten me into selling my interests in the Steel Company at much below their value," and that Carnegie had domineered, dictated policy, and coerced the junior partners to help him force Frick from the company by threatening to take their jobs and interests.

Meanwhile, on behalf of the minority shareholders in the Frick Coke Company, Lynch and Walker filed a separate suit against Carnegie to annul the alleged coke contract; but Carnegie, who returned from Florida energized and confident, dismissed its importance and focused on Frick.

Carnegie's response to the suit, filed on March 12, promised a good ol' fashioned, bare-knuckle scrap. He asserted the Iron Clad was legal, and he countercharged that Frick was "of imperious temper, impatient of opposition and disposed to make a personal matter of any difference of opinion, even on questions of mere business policy. At times, moreover, he gives way to violent outbursts of passion, which he is either unable or unwilling to control. He demands absolute power and without it is not satisfied. . . . His time has been largely employed in various speculative schemes for placing the property of the Association in the hands of promoters to be floated in marketable securities on the public."[43] Certainly some of the charges concerning Frick's temper were true, but he hardly spent his entire 1899 in Wall Street backrooms colluding with gamblers. The final battle in a twenty-year war had begun.

Carnegie's assertion that the Iron Clad was legal and binding appeared airtight strictly based on the evidence of its use; it had been invoked to purchase the shares of some fifteen partners over thirteen years. More recently, at the May 18, 1897, board meeting, Frick had invoked the Iron Clad Agreement to purchase the 2 percent interest of H. W. Borntraeger, who had recently died, *at book value*. Just one year before, the Iron Clad was used to purchase John Pontefract's 0.5 percent interest when ill health forced an early retirement.[44] "The Contract does not mean one thing for the Company and another for the partner," company lawyer Gibson D. Packer now explained to Carnegie, "and when the officials of the Company have by acting under it, and in various other ways, given it one construction as against outgoing members, they cannot face about, and say it means an altogether different thing as to them individually."[45] And when Phipps had suddenly reversed his position in 1897 and refused to sign a revised agreement, Frick said to the board, "The old agreement we believe to be legally operative until this revision has been signed, as the only changes made, other than the extension of the stipulated times of payment, are for the better understanding and carrying out of the details."[46] As old hand William Singer put it to Carnegie, Frick has "convicted himself."[47]

But perhaps Carnegie didn't recall a letter from Frick over a year ago, when he wrote, "The fact is that the present Iron Clad Agreement (which I believe is signed now by all juniors, excepting those lately admitted) is not binding on any one of them, nor on anybody, and never has been, Mr. Vandevort never having signed it, and while we have acted under it up to date, purchasing interests of deceased partners under it, if there had been any objection raised on part of their estates, it could not have been enforced."[48] Frick drew this conclusion after consulting with one of the company's attorneys, who also said that a revised version would be binding if signed by everyone in the firm, which never happened. Also, Phipps had discovered a pattern in the use of the Iron Clad, a pattern that could neutralize every shred of Carnegie's evidence. For junior partners who were in debt to the company at the time of their departure, forced or otherwise, they were paid book value for their share and took to the bank whatever they didn't owe the company. For partners fully vested, as William Shinn and William Abbott were at the time of their exits, they were paid a healthy sum over the book value. Based on this pattern, Frick had to be paid a fair premium.[49]

The court filings were an ugly display that for the first time truly opened the company up to public scrutiny, and the public drooled at the thought of seeing how the Santa Claus Carnegie really managed his business and how much he was actually worth. "The suit is regarded as the most important ever filed in connection with the steel business," the *Tribune* declared, "and it is said more money is at stake than in any legal proceedings ever brought in this country to which all the parties were simply citizens."[50] The *Review of Reviews* observed, "Whatever the final outcome of the Frick-Carnegie litigation, certainly the industrial world has not, since steel became an armament of warfare, witnessed a dispute so notable as this between the multi-millionaires who built up an industry international in its operations. . . . Already enough has been told to whet curiosity. Should a compromise be effected, it will undoubtedly be because of what is still to be told." In mulling over the Iron Clad Agreement, the *Review*'s reporter noted, "Since Mr. Carnegie, during the Homestead Strike, disavowed any direct connection with the workings of the concern, it seems rather curious that now should be revealed the fact that all times he held the controlling lever in his hands."[51] The *New York World*'s coverage was laced with sarcasm, especially concerning the company's profits and the need for a protective tariff: "Surely there is something wrong when capital must go dragging for a pitiful return of less than 200 percent. Plainly, Mr. Frick has revealed deserving industry's great need for protection."[52]

Within a few days of Carnegie filing his answer to the suit, both sides realized they were not necessarily guaranteed victory, but it was definitely Carnegie who had more to lose as his company's skeletons tumbled from the closet. At the time, the company was involved in legally dubious pools for angles, beams, channels for steel and for iron, and tees, respectively. The company also belonged to billet and pig iron associations to support prices artificially, and there was a similar arrangement with plate makers.[53] And then there was the extremely profitable armor making, which was open to accusations that Carnegie Steel was taking advantage of the government. Did Carnegie want all of these facts splashed across the front pages? No.

The words "out of court settlement" had been on everyone's lips from the moment Carnegie Steel seized Frick's interest; it was just a matter of letting the egos run their course. With public scrutiny intensifying, Carnegie finally started working through Schwab—and Frick through Phipps—to initiate negotiations. "It is useless now to talk about anybody buying or selling," Frick wrote Phipps. "The fair thing to do is to make the consolidation of the two companies upon the terms agreed to by everybody a year ago before the Moore offer was received. That will solve the whole problem justly and honorably. I am willing."[54] As he had before, Frick suggested merging the two companies, and said he was willing to accept a value of $250 million for Carnegie Steel and $70 million for the Frick Coke Company. At the appropriate time, he would then sell his interest in the new company.

Over several meetings held at Carnegie's New York home and at Atlantic City, Frick's proposal was agreed to; on April Fool's Day, the consolidation was official, christened the Carnegie Company.[55] Capital of $320 million, half in stock and half in bonds, made it the largest capitalized company in the country—three times larger than Standard Oil. "Settlement made," Frick crowed to a friend. "I get what is due me. All well. I, of course, have not met this man Carnegie and never expect nor want to. It is not my intention to be officially connected with the reorganized concern."[56] Frick's interest in the new $320 million consolidation was $31,284,000, to Carnegie's $174.5 million. The settlement covered the coke dispute, too, with both parties accepting blame and Carnegie Steel's outstanding bill cut in half.

As the fallout from the Frick suit subsided, both men received letters of congratulations and support. "As you know I can not be accused of flattery," steel magnate James Laughlin wrote Carnegie in a letter not meant for posterity's sake or publication, "I am pleased to say that I have long felt, and so expressed myself to your credit, that the iron interests of our country and the consumers of the world, cannot appreciate how much is due you personally for the advance that has been made in manufacturing during the past twenty years, for with no 'can't' in your vocabulary, and carrying out the fact that, like causes produce like effects; and that what has been done once can be done again, the present attainment in output and cost of production has been reached; and Pittsburgh stands as the wonder of the world."[57] Carnegie's soother of conscience, John Morley, blessed him: "I cannot tell you how much I rejoice at the end of your break with Frick. I know your horror of the waste of life in lawsuits and the like, and felt sure that somehow your active mind would find a way out."[58]

Businessmen also gathered behind Frick. F. W. Haskell, a comrade from the old coke days now living in Buffalo, wrote Frick that he still received Pittsburgh papers and was reading the articles "containing various allusions to the relations between yourself and the great Egotist."[59]

As for Frick and Carnegie's relationship, they would have only sporadic contact over the next couple of years and then were completely estranged, even though they moved in the same circles and lived within walking distance of each other on Fifth Avenue. Toward the end of his life, Carnegie sought to reconcile their old grievances and via an intermediary requested a meeting. Frick's response was blunt: "Tell Mr. Carnegie I'll see him in hell, where we both are going."[60]

Once again intent on external competition, Carnegie laid plans to sell a large portion of his company's newly issued bonds in Europe to raise money for unheralded expansion. Rumor had it the company would build new mills and start making all the products produced by the Moore and Morgan steel companies. An aggravated Morgan immediately beckoned Schwab to New York for a meeting. Considering the sensitive nature of the events surrounding the last few months and the fact that Morgan's Federal Steel presented serious competition, Schwab should have declined. He did not and booked passage on an overnight train. Before leaving Pittsburgh he informed Carnegie, who, jealous and apprehensive, insisted Schwab visit him, too:

> I was pained to get your wire that you were going to travel all night and per-haps tomorrow night also, & for what?
>
> Mr. Morgan has no business with you to call you to do this, these days when you know how much depends upon your having rest. . . .
>
> You say you are to come up in the afternoon. Please let me know about when—of course if you are going home Saturday night I am anxious to see you—come soon as you can—[61]

Carnegie had good reason to be apprehensive. He would not be notified of the next meeting between Schwab and Morgan.

CHAPTER 28

The World's Richest Man

C onfirming my wire upon the situation let me say that all is coming just as expected. There is nothing surprising; a struggle is inevitable, and it is a question of the survival of the fittest."[1] It was not melodramatic rhetoric; entering the summer of 1900 the market for steel was flat, competition was intense, and Carnegie was putting Schwab on notice. When Carnegie, Louise, and Margaret boarded the American liner *St. Louis* on May 2, bound for Britain, he had no doubt the battles with the Morgan and Moore consolidations would intensify. He was scheduled to speak at the Iron and Steel Institute's meeting at the Hotel Cecil in London on May 9, and he would meet with Morley and Spencer—all three together for the first time in years— but Carnegie planned no other engagements. There would be no time for excessive socializing this summer, no six months of bliss in his heaven on earth.

Although Carnegie had lost his fight with Frick, it was the catalyst for a rebirth of Carnegie as a leader. Now that Frick was gone, there was no hesitation, no waffling, and no ambivalence on Carnegie's part as he now focused on Morgan and Moore. His inability to share power was a fault, perhaps, but he was a much stronger and decisive leader when recognized as the undisputed force in his company. He was almost sixty-five, an age when most men would be retiring, yet Carnegie was thrusting himself back into the heat of battle to fill the breach caused by Frick's expulsion.

"A nation should never make war except to repel invaders," Carnegie once said. As he surveyed his empire, he identified several forces intent on raiding his territory and pillaging his profits. In addition to reenergizing the counterattack on the Morgan and Moore consolidations, which were buying less and less steel from the Carnegie Company, he quickly surmised he had to contend with John D. Rockefeller, who had iron-fisted control of shipping on the Great Lakes and was threatening price increases; and he had to again confront the Pennsylvania Railroad, which had a new president who was refusing to recognize past rebate deals. A hardened veteran, Carnegie was on familiar ground.

Carnegie signaled his willingness to fight in "Popular Illusions about Trusts," an article he penned for the May issue of *Century Magazine.* He again criticized trusts as the panacea of the moment, and he envisioned a line of dead trusts like the ghosts of Macbeth's victims, only much longer. As an "evolutionist," Carnegie believed all businessmen would eventually return to what was best—spirited competition. The month after the article was published, he informed Dod every pool agreement was up for review. If not favorable, the company should break them and "take the business & run."[2] On June 4, he charged Schwab with the same rallying cry he had used for the last twenty-five years: "The sooner you scoop the market the better. It has never failed that the lowest price given has proved to be a high price at time of delivery on a falling market. When you want to capture a falling stone, it won't do to follow it. You must cut under it, and so it is with a falling market."[3] The strategy had been successful against smaller firms without deep pockets, but would it work against Morgan and Moore? Displaying his wicked sense of humor in the time of crisis, Carnegie added, "All very well here and Skibo finer than expected. Tell any of the managers that in case of a collapse they can be cured here upon most reasonable terms."

At the same time Carnegie questioned any pool agreements, he plotted an all-out invasion into National Tube's territory. It was absolutely necessary because Morgan's tube consolidation had built its own furnaces to supply its steel, and whatever additional steel it required was ordered from its sister company, Federal. Once a large supplier, Carnegie was now completely choked off in a quickening race for total domination. To ensure Schwab had support, he informed Dod of his intentions: "We ought to go into tubes because we have a combine at our mercy and lost trade we used to have before National Tube left us. We can spend a few millions (no blast furnaces at present) and divide with the Trust. It is clear sailing." Regardless of the potential for overcapacity, Carnegie was confident Morgan's tube trust would cooperate when faced with cutthroat competition.

Carnegie's unilateral decision to forge ahead was dictatorial and autocratic, but his ability to make instantaneous decisions in the field gave him an advantage over the trusts. Morgan and Moore's lieutenants had to worry about presenting plans to committees, boards of directors, and major stockholders, while Carnegie did not. And Carnegie could postpone dividends, reinvest profits, and spend several millions without fretting a backlash from shareholders, Harry Phipps aside. "It was a contest between fabricators of steel and fabricators of securities; between makers of billets and makers of bonds," Carnegie said.[4] It was survival of the fittest.

The cables from Schwab brought bad news, however. Gates's American Steel and Wire, which had ordered as much as 14,000 tons of billets each month, cut its orders to just 6,000 tons a month and then canceled all

In his sixties, when most men would be considering retirement, Carnegie reigned supreme in steel. (Courtesy of the Carnegie Library of Pittsburgh)

Smiling Charlie Schwab was made president of Carnegie Steel at the tender age of thirty-six. He would become caught in the middle of Frick and Carnegie's bickering. (Courtesy of the Carnegie Library of Pittsburgh)

contracts. Moore's American Steel Hoop, once a customer requiring 15,000 to 20,000 tons a month, had cut its orders to 3,000 tons.[5] Such behavior was unacceptable, and Carnegie ordered Schwab to either recapture the lost orders or to go into direct competition with American Steel Hoop.[6] In a letter to the board, read at the June 22 meeting, he declared that building mills to compete directly with American Steel Hoop "will not only give them but others a lesson, which I am sure we will have to give sooner or later."[7]

Carnegie was quite prepared to raise the stakes, his old motto "The friend of all; the ally of none" was about to be reduced to "The ally of none." He boiled the situation down to one blunt issue, which Schwab relayed to the board: "You are face to face with the great question, the parting of the ways; the country cannot take the product of the steel works. Are we to decide that we will take the business at the best price possible and run the works full, independent of all other concerns, managing our business in our own way, or are we to take percentages of the business with these and try to maintain prices."[8]

Carnegie enjoyed singing the Scottish ballad "Wha Daur Meddle wi' Me?" and it became the refrain for a tempestuous June.

Consumed by business, Carnegie had little time for family, but on July Fourth he hosted a fete for the inhabitants of the entire Skibo estate, a tradition that would continue for the next fourteen years. The event began with the children attending the five schools within the estate, along with their teachers, parents, and friends, numbering anywhere from a thousand to fifteen hundred, assembling at the front gate lodge. Led by brass and pipe bands, they marched up the drive to the castle, where Carnegie greeted them and made a little speech. Joined by Carnegie, Louise, Margaret, Stella, and houseguests, the parade continued, descending the terrace steps to a bright green field where they played games. For the footraces, Carnegie, brandishing a pistol, served as starter. Under a great tent, refreshments were served and cash prizes handed out. Overhead, the Stars and Stripes and the Union Jack fluttered.

Two days after the festivities, Carnegie, exhibiting a growing sense of urgency, again spurred on Schwab: "My recent letters predict present state of affairs; urge prompt action, essential; crisis has arrived, only one policy open; start at once hoop, rod, wire, nail mills, no half way about last two. Extend coal and coke roads, announce these; also tubes. . . . Never been time when more prompt action essential, indeed absolutely necessary to maintain property. . . . Spend freely for finishing mills, railroads, boat lines. Continue to advise regularly by cable."[9] Bolder than most of the other junior partners, Schwab was eager to comply in this high-stakes poker game.

One of Carnegie's favorite weapons was to threaten competition, which had worked so well against the Pressed Steel Car Company, and he hoped it would again to bring the consolidations back into the fold as customers, but if not, he was convinced he would best them in price. The real pressure was on Smilin' Charlie Schwab, who was going to have to play the heavy. Although Schwab had battled the Huns with clubs and guns, this fight was more sophisticated, with millions of dollars at stake, and Carnegie questioned whether he would snap under pressure as Abbott and Potter had. On July 11, Carnegie wrote him an inspirational letter: "Briefly, if I were czar [which he was, Schwab must have noted with a wry smile], I would make no dividends upon common stock, save all surplus and spend it for a hoop and cotton tie mill, for wire and nail mills, for tube mills, for lines of boats upon the lakes. . . . You have only to rise to the occasion, but no half way measures. If you are not going to cross the stream, do not enter at all and be content to dwindle into second place. Put your trust in the policy of attending to your own business in your own way and running your mills full regardless of prices and very little trust in the efficacy of artificial arrangements with your competitors, which have the serious result of strengthening them if they strengthen you. Such is my advice."[10]

Presiding over the board meetings was another duty Schwab had assumed; it was not always pleasant, for although the disruptive Frick was gone, harmony did not reign. At the July 16 meeting, the men were sharply divided over expanding into finished goods, as they debated building the wire and nail mill Carnegie demanded to strike back at Gates. "This is a very dangerous time in our history," said a tentative Dod, and he voted against "further expenditures." Schwab immediately criticized him for always being against expansion, an assault that was construed as personal by Dod, who then called for a delay until his cousin returned in the fall.

Annoyed by the stonewalling when he already had Carnegie's blessing to attack, Schwab said resolutely, "If we want to drop back into an old-fashioned way of doing business, I want to be counted out of it." His threat was taken seriously; the board approved $1.4 million for rod, wire, and nail plants to be built at the Duquesne Steel Works.[11] Finally they were taking the fight to the competition. When Carnegie received the July 16 board meeting minutes, however, he immediately sensed the tension between Schwab and Dod. It would not do—one civil war was enough—so he beckoned Dod and Schwab to Skibo for a conference.

The sudden absence of Dod and Schwab raised eyebrows in Pittsburgh and ignited rumors that Carnegie Steel was in trouble. On September 5, the *New York Daily Tribune* reported: "The facts about the trouble in the Carnegie Steel Company are gradually coming to the surface, despite denials of the officials of the company who are not at Skibo Castle. It is learned that the officials who took charge after H. C. Frick was ousted have been too light for the places they occupy, say those who are interested in the fight. They want H. C. Frick back at the head."[12] Lawrence Phipps first raised questions about management's abilities, according to the *Tribune*, and Harry Phipps was allegedly supporting Frick's return.

Frick's criticism of the Carnegie Company was the source of the innuendo. Still a major stockholder in the company, he analyzed management's every move, and in August he leveled some sharp criticism at Carnegie, which he undoubtedly shared with others. "You being in control," Frick cabled Carnegie, "stockholders and public look to you to see that the great Carnegie Company is managed successfully and honestly." He warned Carnegie to not let his men "hide things from you. You cannot trust many by whom you are surrounded to give you facts. You need commercial rather than professional ability to cope with the concerns managed by brainy and honest men trained to the business. You are being outgeneraled all along the line, and your management of the Company has already become the subject of jest."[13]

Appalled when he heard of the cable, Phipps reproached his ally: "If any good is to be accomplished at this stage it is by patient and gentle methods, and in view of policy I was very sorry that you sent the cable you did to Mr. Carnegie."[14] Yes, it appeared as though the newspapers were correct—a movement was afoot to reinsert Frick. But considering profits would leap to $40 million in 1900, up from $21 million in 1899, Frick's criticism was more mean-spirited than justified.

That summer Morley wrote Carnegie an appropriate and insightful note: "I thought of you t'other day when I came across a line of Wordsworth,—'a man of cheerful yesterdays and confident tomorrows.' Quite right, too. That's the temperament that wins. Only it does not win everything, recollect. There is a crumb or two for people of the other sort, who like to see things as they are, such people as Your friend J.M."[15] It was a gentle caution: Carnegie should not expect to win everything.

It was a tumultuous year in business and in politics, with Bryan again pitted against McKinley in the presidential race and the Philippine War still raging. Although American generals kept on insisting the Filipino nationalists were hemmed in and their defeat imminent, the war dragged on. It was the anti-imperialists' fault, claimed the expansionists, because they gave Aguinaldo and his rebels hope. One of the most outspoken and harshest critics of the war was Mark Twain, an impressive orator for the cause, a striking figure on stage with his white suit, his luxuriant tangle of white hair and mustache, and cigar. Twain's bold commentary endeared him to Carnegie, whom he'd become acquainted with in the early 1890s. They were now drawn closer together by a common cause.

To be sure, Twain had fun with Carnegie's riches, forever scheming to swindle a dollar or two. In one of his more unabashed jabs, in May 1900, he wrote little Margaret a letter instructing her to give her daddy "five or six fingers of Scotch, and then talk. This will mellow him up and enlarge his views, and before he solidifies again you will *have* him. That is to say, you will have his cheque for £500, drawn to order of 'Plasmon Syndicate, Ltd.' which you will send to me, and you and I will be personally responsible that the money is back in his hands in six months, and along with it 500 shares in the Plasmon Company, all paid up. P.S. Don't let your papa get hold of this—he'll sell it for ten dollars. Mark."[16] It gave Carnegie reason to laugh in what was an earnest and taxing year.

The New England Anti-Imperialist League supported Bryan for president, but not Carnegie, who was convinced McKinley would ultimately reverse course on the expansionist policy. His only concern was the aggressive views of McKinley's running mate, Teddy Roosevelt. "I had hoped you would be Vice-President instead of Roosevelt," he wrote Andrew White in June. "He is a dangerous man."[17] He was not the only Republican who felt that way about Roosevelt, for Ohio senator Mark Hanna would warn, "Don't any of you realize there's only one life between this madman and the Presidency?"[18]

The Boxer Rebellion in China, which climaxed in August 1900, reaffirmed Carnegie's fears that friction in the colonies and imperialistic desires would lead to warfare. In hopes of ridding the country of foreign influences, Chinese militia units had staged a series of attacks on foreigners and missionaries, and in the summer of 1900 laid siege to the foreign legations in Peking (now Beijing). To rescue the diplomats and suppress the militants, an international force of soldiers contributed by the United States, Britain, Russia, France, Germany, Austria, Italy, and Japan fought their way to Peking. It was an exotic sight with the French Zouaves in their red and blue, the blond Germans in pointed helmets, the Italian Bersaglieri in tossing plumes, Bengal cavalry on Arabian stallions, and turbaned Sikhs. Each country had a vested economic interest in China, and in August, the siege was lifted. One estimate put the death toll of Chinese and foreign Catholics at thirty thousand or more, and the international force retaliated in kind, slaughtering men, women, and children, prompting journalist George Lynch to note, "There are things that I must not write, and that may not be printed in England, which would seem to show that this Western civilization of ours is merely a veneer over savagery."[19]

American participation in China was mostly limited to action in Peking, a policy Carnegie agreed with, and he complimented McKinley and Hay for taking a more righteous position than the British, French, Germans, and Russians, who were aggressively protecting and carving out their domains. In a letter to the Associated Press, he warned that if the "United States should be drawn into joint action with them, the Washington Government may even find itself pledged to go forward into a campaign against China which would be hopeless, or may ultimately see the Powers at war with each other."[20]

Andrew White, a devout peace activist, wanted more than rhetoric from Carnegie. He thought Carnegie's millions might aid the cause for peace, and in June he suggested the building of a peace temple at The Hague for the Permanent Court of Arbitration—later to be called the International Court of Justice—which was to arbitrate international conflicts. He attempted to entice Carnegie by suggesting "that it would render the man who makes the gift a benefactor to every nation and to all mankind—acknowledged as such through all time."[21] A peace temple was outside the parameters of his gospel, for the moment; but more poignant, with the Philippine and Boer Wars raging, the idea appeared futile to Carnegie, who bitterly observed "it is a sad commentary on its labours, that the two branches of our race are the only ones who are attempting to deprive distant peoples of their liberties and shooting them down remorselessly because they wish to govern themselves."[22]

In September, his literary friend William Stead also requested financial aid from Carnegie for peace efforts. He was to attend a peace congress in Paris and explained, "The first question they will ask me, I am well aware, is what prospect is there of securing any additional financial support for an attempt to promote arbitration; and I wish very much to be in a position to say definitely whether you feel disposed to help."[23] Stead received an adamant no. "I am not a 'peace at any price' man much as I should like to be," Carnegie explained. "I believe it was my duty to be on the field at Bull Run." He also didn't think another peace congress or related organization was needed in addition to the arbitration court at The Hague; in his pragmatic business mind, it was a duplication of effort. "Of course, I may be wrong in believing that but I am certainly not wrong in believing that if it were dependent upon any millionaire's money, it would be an object of pity, and end as one of derision. I wonder that you do not see this. There is nothing that robs a righteous cause of its strength more than a millionaire's money—especially during his life. It makes a serious, holy cause simply a fad. Its life is tainted thereby."[24] So there were limits to Carnegie's ego; he had come to understand that in some arenas—the noble ones, such as peace work—modesty reigned and excessive monetary aid was disdained.

Three days after Stead's request, Spencer weighed in with a unique proposal. He advised Carnegie to spend money on relieving the misery of the Boers, who were watching their farms and villages burn at the hands of the English. "The act would be a grand one and it would be unique in all history," concluded Spencer.[25] Carnegie echoed the fear expressed to Stead that any offer of help to the Boers would be "resented" and considered "most impertinent," but Spencer didn't accept his logic and responded sharply, "You do not apparently distinguish between giving money to the Boers and assisting the widows and orphans of those who have been killed."[26] The rash of letters from White, Stead, and Spencer, among others, was dire evidence of how fearful these men were of world war.

Greater, and more tangible, glory was to be had in building cathedrals of civilization than chasing ghostly dreams of peace. When Carnegie came to Pittsburgh in November to attend a dinner given by William Frew to honor him, as well as for the city's mayor, W. J. Diehl, and other prominent citizens supporting the institute (the library and museums), the city was abuzz with rumors that Carnegie was planning a major endowment for a technical school. Once again, he did not disappoint. At the dinner, he formally offered to build Pittsburgh a polytechnic school in connection with his institute and endow it with $1 million, provided the city supplied the site. For Carnegie, to have the library and museum alongside the school, to have leisure alongside work, represented harmony, and the price was worth it. In his dinner speech, Carnegie said he was moved to make the offer when Pittsburgh's board of education requested $100,000 to begin a technical school, an amount he deemed hardly adequate.[27] His offer was accepted with alacrity, and the technical school would eventually evolve into the renowned Carnegie Mellon University.

That autumn, Carnegie also traveled to Buffalo, Cincinnati, Chicago, and Philadelphia to present libraries, make speeches, and attend dinners. When Louise and he went on these brief trips, Margaret was left in Stella's and the nanny's care, although Louise disliked leaving her even for a short time. Well cared for, Margaret would grow up without a want in the world, would attend excellent schools, but would not have the important influence of her father in her life.

The most important dinner of the season was for Charlie Schwab, now a major player. Carnegie proposed a dinner to introduce Schwab to New York's business elite, and bankers J. Edward Simmons and Charles Stewart Smith agreed to host it. The black-tie affair was held on December 12 at the

University Club in New York, with attendees including Morgan, E. H. Harriman, James Stillman, William Vanderbilt, Chauncey Depew, Jacob Schiff, and H. H. Rodgers, president of Standard Oil. Carnegie was there only briefly, and then went to the Waldorf Astoria for the annual dinner of the Pennsylvania Society of New York, where he was committed to speak before the three hundred people in attendance. It was surprising that Carnegie, who was so diligent about rubbing shoulders with powerful men, would have such a conflict in his schedule and miss Schwab's coming-out party.

As the guest of honor, Schwab spoke for twenty minutes on the future of the steel industry. Although plain-looking, broad-shouldered, and a workingman's man, Schwab was an eloquent orator said to be able to "talk the legs off the proverbial brass pot," and he presented a glowing future for steel, predicting that an age was at hand when a new species of corporation, a massive consolidation, a utopia of efficiency, would be created to compete on a global scale. Playing unconsciously with an unlit Havana cigar, Morgan was the most rapt listener in the audience. Consolidation and stability was the kind of talk he appreciated, and he considered whether Schwab could be won over as an ally in his war against Carnegie.

After the dinner, Morgan drew Schwab aside to the privacy of a window seat. They quickly exchanged pleasantries, Morgan complimenting him on his fine talk, and then Morgan invited Schwab to stop by his office for a visit, to discuss the steel industry's future in more detail. Schwab hesitated to accept, explaining he'd prefer not to for it might suggest disloyalty.[28] The steel war was only going to get worse, Schwab knew, so he had to be careful.

Morgan was not the only one with an agenda that involved Schwab as the fulcrum. "Schwab dinner here remarkable," Carnegie reported to Dod. "Mr. S tells me every one invited accepted & really the biggest man in N York. He is favorite indeed & this makes him more valuable to us."[29] It was an innocent note, but the last line hung in the air, suggesting Carnegie had some scheme in mind in which the dinner played a role.

The gloating tone in his note was certainly not without reason: despite the loss of business to the trusts, in 1900 his company generated record profits of $40 million. To ascertain precisely where he stood against the competition, Carnegie asked Schwab to pull together some comparative figures. Combined, Schwab told him, American Sheet Steel, American Steel and Wire, Federal Steel, National Steel, and National Tube made but 84.5 percent as much crude steel as the Carnegie Company, which was also making half of the country's structural steel and armor plate. While the nation's total steel production fell 4.2 percent in 1900, Carnegie's market share increased from 25.03 percent to 29.15 percent, and he had yet to enter the manufacture of finished products.[30] For all his maneuvering, Morgan had to recognize Carnegie was impregnable.

The business landscape became more treacherous for Morgan as Carnegie's plans for a tremendous tube mill jelled. As Carnegie reviewed the blueprints, he asked Schwab, "How much cheaper, Charlie, can you make tubes than the National Company?"

"Not less than ten dollars a ton."

"Go on and build the plant."[31]

On January 8, 1901, Schwab announced the company's plans to invest $12 million to build the largest pipe and tube mill in the world on five thousand acres the company had purchased at Conneaut, Ohio.[32] Due to the Lake Erie location, the company expected shipping the finished products to cost one-third to one-fourth of what it would be by rail in Pittsburgh. Once this news hit the wires, National Tube stock broke badly, and Morgan was at his wit's end. Carnegie's friend Charles Flint happened to be in Morgan's office as the banker mulled over his response, and he asked Flint to call on Carnegie and to attempt to ascertain what Carnegie's intentions were in building the tube mill. Flint went up to Fifty-first Street. As he sat facing Carnegie, he thought poking some fun at Moore might ease them into a discussion on tubes and the future. "How difficult it must have been," he said, "for Judge Moore to have kept up a smile when he sat opposite you at dinner at my home, having so recently kissed goodbye to a million dollars, as the option which he had purchased on your steel properties expired."

"Under the circumstances," said Carnegie, "it was certainly much easier for me to smile than for the Judge, but that option which I gave him was cheap at a million dollars; I wouldn't renew it now for ten millions." Over the next few hours, he divulged all his plans for the tube plant at Conneaut and other expansions designed to scoop the market from Morgan and Moore's trusts. Flint was surprised by his forthrightness and promised not to tell anyone without Carnegie's approval (although he was there on Morgan's behalf). "What I have talked to you about," Carnegie answered, "is a matter of national interest, and you are free to repeat anything that I have said."[33] And that was exactly how Carnegie viewed his steel empire—it was a matter of national interest.

Another war coming to a climax involved the Pennsylvania Railroad. During the second week of January, Carnegie was in Pittsburgh to host a lavish dinner at the Schenley Hotel for his managers to celebrate the company's success. It was not all pleasure. While in town, he learned the Pennsylvania Railroad was again playing games with shipping rates. Back in the summer, Carnegie had been notified any rebates the Carnegie Company had enjoyed from the Pennsylvania Railroad were to be eliminated, snatching away the cool millions in profits. The railroad's new president, Alexander Cassatt, despised the rebates, so when he had taken the reins after Frank Thomson's premature death, he systematically reviewed each customer's rate schedule. Before he could cut out rebates, however, he needed the support of other railroads to prevent his customers from defecting to other lines. He turned to William Vanderbilt, who controlled the powerful New York Central, to jointly create "a community of interest." The benign-sounding term actually involved the two mammoth railroad companies in buying controlling blocks of stock in smaller lines and then dictating rates.

Once back in New York in the fall, Carnegie went on a crusade as he challenged the legality of the "community of interest," planned meetings of the Pittsburgh Chamber of Commerce and for the public to incite outrage, and announced to Schwab, "The deliverance of Pittsburgh is my next great work, and this time it will be thoroughly done, once for all, if I live."[34] Such revolutionary bluster was just rhetoric. There were other pressure points to be exploited with far more effectiveness; namely, once again aggressively pursuing alternative shipping routes. Ever since Carnegie had connected to Lake Erie via the Pittsburgh, Bessemer & Lake Erie line, he had proven his ability to carry through with such a threat. To bring immediate pressure to bear on the Pennsylvania, he decided to build a fleet of steamships and barges for the Great Lakes based in Conneaut that would permit him to ship east and west, and subsequently placed an order for five steamers, made almost completely of steel and among the largest ever built for the lakes. (The fleet would also break Rockefeller's hold on shipping and fears of price gouging.) The deciding blow in Carnegie's previous fight with the Pennsylvania had been the combination punch of connecting his own line from Pittsburgh to Lake Erie and threatening to build a line into the coke region. Such a tactic would have to be used again, however expensive. Carnegie sent surveyors into the field to determine the best routes into the coke region and to the East Coast. Cassatt relented.

But the rate cuts Cassatt promised proved to be marginal improvements at best. Carnegie then demanded a return to the old rebates, which brought the railroad's legal counsel, Wayne McVeagh, into the fray. McVeagh explained to Carnegie that he had warned Cassatt that "he could not safely violate the law prohibiting secret rates or allowances."[35] Carnegie objected to the idea that his prior discounted rates were secret or unlawful, which prompted McVeagh to chide him for his jaded view: "You fail to give proper weight to the fact that the rebates you were getting were not only unlawful but if he had continued them after he knew all about them, he would have been committing a criminal offense while you in taking them ran no risk whatever of that kind. Of course you may reply that your steel rail pool is equally unlawful & yet it is maintained; but in maintaining it you are not committing a criminal offense; and that is a serious difference."[36] According to McVeagh's interpretation of the laws, Carnegie was not behaving criminally, which was crucial to Carnegie being able to excuse his ruthless actions. Still, there can be no doubt he was guilty of breaking the Sherman antitrust laws and the Interstate Commerce Act.

Carnegie elected to find a new ally in railroads, and Jay Gould's son, George, who had been bequeathed a railroad empire and Western Union, was an ideal choice. George Gould was attempting to pull together a transcontinental line that ran from Baltimore to San Francisco, and he appeared to be the only man bold enough to strike at the Pennsylvania. He also controlled the Wabash Railroad with its strategic lines in the West, including Chicago, a town Carnegie naturally wanted to reach as cheaply as possible. The two met, and Carnegie presented his scheme. If Gould extended his western line to Pittsburgh and offered the same prevailing rates given other customers, Carnegie would give him one-third of all his business, and then jointly they would construct a line east. Gould agreed and plans were immediately drawn up. It could prove a major coup, but Carnegie expressed fears of reprisals to Dod: "It seems almost too good to be true and I am not without fear that allied PR interests here and Morgan may frighten him from going to work. We shall see. If he does come to Pittsburgh, the Eastern Line is next step—but that's another story."[37] When word of the Carnegie-Gould alliance and their plans to build east reached Morgan, he groaned, "Carnegie is going to demoralize railroads just as he has demoralized steel."[38] Cassatt was equally distraught because Carnegie was yet again moving ahead with plans to build a line into the coke region. As the industrial war raged, Willis King, an executive with the Jones and Laughlin Steel Company, observed from the sidelines—until beckoned by the beleaguered Cassatt.

King, who had both begrudging respect for the Scotsman and a desire to see him knocked down a notch, recalled of Carnegie:

> He had the reputation of being "canny," and was inclined to take his own way without regard to the interests of his fellow manufacturers, and was a vigorous competitor.
>   Almost to the point of ruthlessness he demanded and received rebates and other favors from the railroads, denied to his competitors, and these demands finally culminated in a threat to build a railroad from Pittsburgh to the Atlantic seaboard, and to construct the largest tube works in the world at Conneaut on the Lake.

Having known Carnegie for years, King was an ideal person to advise Cassatt, who sent his private rail car to pick up not only King, but Carnegie's old friend Robert Pitcairn, superintendent of the Pennsylvania's Pittsburgh Division, and bring them to Philadelphia to discuss the Carnegie-Gould threat. At the meeting, King confirmed that an officer of Carnegie Steel had told him in confidence the company planned a railroad east. "Mr. Pitcairn, who was present, said that a new road would never pay," King recalled, "and that Carnegie could not run it. Mr. Cassatt, who was walking up and down the office with his hands in his pockets, stopped before Pitcairn and said very abruptly, 'Nonsense, that is beside the question. If the road is well started or finished, somebody will be found to run it.'"[39]

(As it so happened, Gould's Western Union, by prior contract, had been allowed to locate its poles along the Pennsylvania Railroad right-of-way; but now, in a first act of retaliation, Cassatt refused to renew the contract and ordered his men to cut down the poles from one end of the railroad to the other.)[40]

Morgan took the threat to build the railroad east just as seriously, and, in combination with Carnegie's announced plans to build the biggest tube mill ever, he had had quite enough of the canny Scotsman. Just as Cassatt had summoned King and Pitcairn, now Morgan summoned Bet-a-Million Gates. Although Gates was persona non grata at Federal Steel, Morgan knew Gates was on relatively good terms with Schwab, for the two played bridge and poker together—and Schwab was, perhaps, the key player in eliminating Carnegie. He asked Gates to arrange a secret meeting with Carnegie's trusted lieutenant, who had so impressed Morgan at the December dinner.

When the formidable J. P. Morgan beckoned, it was extremely difficult to resist; therefore, as Schwab considered Morgan's invitation to a clandestine meeting in New York, he felt compelled to attend, against his better judgment. Perhaps only his boss, Andrew Carnegie, and John D. Rockefeller had the guts to spurn Morgan, a bulky figure who tended to brandish his cane at photographers on the street. He was particularly uncomfortable about accepting the overture because Carnegie wasn't to know of it. Sensing his ambivalence, Morgan's messenger, Gates, suggested an accidental meeting on neutral ground in Philadelphia. "But suppose you should happen to be in the Bellevue Hotel Sunday evening," he said quickly, "and Mr. Morgan should *happen* to be there?"

"I might be there Sunday evening," said Schwab coyly."[41]

The topic of discussion was to be the consolidation of the steel industry on a scale never before imagined—a future that was not to include the undisputed king of steel, Carnegie.

While an oblivious Carnegie went about his business in January 1901, Schwab took a train from Pittsburgh to Philadelphia. On arrival at the Bellevue Hotel, he was handed a message from Gates stating that Morgan was ill in bed, and Schwab should come to New York later in the week. Matters were already becoming disturbingly complicated, as he would now have to contend with Morgan on the banker's home turf.

When Schwab entered Morgan's lavish mansion at 219 Madison Avenue and was ushered into his mahogany-paneled study, he found himself surrounded by a forbidding trio that included Morgan, his partner Robert Bacon, and Gates, a dangerous speculator who once bet a million dollars on a poker hand and who possessed a few key cards in the steel game. Still relatively young at thirty-nine years of age, but a strapping man with a barrel chest, Schwab remained composed under Morgan's glare. In fact, he couldn't help but return the stare because of Morgan's large and deformed nose, a grotesque attraction resulting from rhinophyma. Embarrassed by the disease, the banker conscientiously avoided the camera lens, but right now his much larger concern was Carnegie, the fiercely independent titan.

To kick off the clandestine meeting and to put Schwab at ease, he asked the younger man to elaborate on his December speech; specifically, to detail what companies should be included in such a consolidation. Naturally, there were the Morgan, Moore, and Gates properties—Federal Steel, National Steel, National Tube, American Steel and Wire, American Tin Plate, American Steel Hoop, American Sheet Metal, and American Wire—among others. It had to include the Carnegie Company, of course, for as one observer later put it, the cooks may have been "ready to bake the finest plum pudding ever concocted, but that Mr. Carnegie had all the plums." It was then intimated by Morgan that if such an amalgamation were to occur, Schwab would be expected to head it. The wily banker was setting the hook, and before Schwab stepped into the cold night, Morgan had one last, all-important question. He turned to the young man and, with piercing eyes set behind his bulbous nose, asked in a terse voice, Would Carnegie sell? Schwab didn't know, but he would find out. "Well," Morgan said, "if you can get a price from Carnegie, I don't know but what I'll undertake it."[42]

As early as January 13, rumors started circulating in the press that Morgan would buy out Carnegie; but in letters to Carnegie, Schwab gave no indication of his role in the matter. On January 24, he forwarded earnings statements and claimed, "I shall not feel satisfied until we are producing 500,000 tons per month and finishing same. And we'll do it within five years. Look at our ore and coke as compared with the others. If you continue to give me the support you have in the past we'll make a greater industry than we ever dreamed of. Am anxious to get at Conneaut. Are finishing plans rapidly & will be ready for a stand in the spring. Hope to see you next week."[43] On the same day, Carnegie wrote Dod: "There is no substance in the reports anent great combination—some talkee, talkee. . . . This years business is secured— 30 millions or thereabouts—we are all right." Carnegie was talking about future profits, not selling, and Schwab was planning the next five years of his career, but someone had leaked the story.

Schwab was faced with a dangerous dilemma. Carnegie didn't know of his meeting with Morgan, so he was hesitant as how to broach the topic of selling without getting himself fired for traitorous behavior. He did know that Louise, who was good friends with his wife, Rana, was eager for her husband to retire, so he approached her first. She suggested a golf outing at St. Andrews in Yonkers, New York, to relax her husband before raising the subject. If Schwab handled it clumsily, it would cost him his career and millions of dollars.

Carnegie and Schwab, wrapped in warm garments to ward off the late January chill, played golf and then repaired to Carnegie's fairway cottage for hot drinks and a bite of food. Finally, Schwab found an opening in the discussion. "I talked quietly to him," Schwab recalled, "suggesting that the time had come to make some disposition of his business that would guarantee its perpetuation and that would gratify his desire to put his wealth in such liquid form that he could do as I knew he wanted to do with it." He then divulged his conversations with Morgan, and relayed that the banker was prepared to buy Carnegie out. After remaining silent for some time, his eyes glazing over as he looked out on the bland green fairway, Carnegie told Schwab he would think about it and Schwab should come by the house tomorrow.

The next day, when Schwab arrived at 5 West Fifty-first Street, Carnegie handed him a piece of paper with a series of numbers jotted down in pencil and said, "That's what I'll sell for."

Schwab took his carriage down to 219 Madison Avenue and handed Morgan the piece of paper. "I accept," said the banker simply. And so the transaction was agreed upon, with no haggling and no platoon of lawyers. On the slip of paper was an asking price of *$480 million*. Carnegie had broken down the means of payment: $160 million was to be in gold-backed 5 percent bonds; $240 million in stock in the new company; and $80 million in cash. Carnegie's take was $225,639,000—enough to buy a few books—paid in 5 percent gold bonds and cash only.[44] He wanted the safe haven of bonds to carry on with his philanthropy independent of worrying about fluctuations in the volatile stock market. Morgan was only too happy to oblige because if Carnegie took stock, he would have a voice in management—a meddling voice.

Well, Morgan had his plums, which included the Carnegie steelworks at Braddock, Duquesne, and Homestead, the Lucy and Carrie blast furnaces, the Upper and Lower Union Mills, the H. C. Frick Coke Company, the Oliver Mining Company, four small railroads, a natural gas company, the Pittsburgh Steamship Company, and a limestone company, among other morsels. Equally important, a disruptive force had been eliminated. (Incidentally, in a parallel story, rebel Philippine leader Emilio Aguinaldo was captured in March, the month the rebellious Carnegie would officially abdicate.) With Carnegie in the fold, Morgan could now go after the other companies Schwab had fingered to create U.S. Steel, the greatest amalgamation the world had ever known.

Carnegie's first order of business was to triumphantly inform his board of managers, who immediately lavished praise on him in a formal letter: "Whatever pecuniary benefits we may derive from a new organization such as outlined, our first and most natural feeling is the keen regret to all of us in the severance of our business relations with you, to whom we owe so much. Your sound judgment and profound business sagacity have been the foundation stones on which has been built the fabric of our success. No expression, however sincere, can adequately voice our deep personal loyalty, and, with you, it is hoped the friendship of the past shall know no change."[45] The day after notifying his board, Carnegie bragged about the sale to John Morley: "I could as well had 100 millions stg. [$500 million for himself] in a few years, but no sir. I'm not going to grow old piling up, but in distributing."[46]

"Well, you are the industrial Napoleon—and no mistake," Morley replied. "I am rejoiced that you are trying to draw out of active trade, but I should rejoice far more confidently, and heartily if you had ½ or 1 million, instead of 40 or 50. Still you make the best of the burden, and nobody who knows you will doubt that you will do your best to diffuse happiness & to spread light."[47] Some burden.

Two days after he wrote Morley, it was time for an exultant letter to Dod, but he warned his cousin not to talk in case the deal didn't go through.[48] Meanwhile, Carnegie was telling everyone.

A few weeks later, Morgan telephoned Carnegie to invite him down to Wall Street for a celebratory chat, but never one to submit, Carnegie replied,

"Mr. Morgan, it is just about as far from Wall Street to Fifty-first as it is from Fifty-first to Wall. I shall be delighted to see you here any time." Shortly thereafter, Morgan appeared at his doorstep. The meeting lasted precisely fifteen minutes—Carnegie's secretary James Bertram timed it—and as Morgan stood to depart, he grasped Carnegie's hand: "Mr. Carnegie, I want to congratulate you on being the richest man in the world!"

Legend has it that the two titans were aboard the same transatlantic steamer a couple of years later, and in the course of one discussion Carnegie said, "I made one mistake, Pierpont, when I sold out to you."

"What was that?"

"I should have asked you for $100,000,000 more than I did."

With a sly grin, Morgan said, "Well, you would have got it if you had."[49]

After the official announcement in the newspapers on March 3, informing the stockholders of the affected companies that their stock was to be exchanged for U.S. Steel stock, it dawned on the public this was to be a billion-dollar concern—the *first* billion-dollar concern. To be exact, the capital of the company was set at $1.1 billion in common and preferred stock and $304 million in bonds, bringing the grand total to $1.4 billion. At the time, no one thought in billions or could even comprehend the magnitude of the company, and the uneasiness soon gave way to fear. In the April *Cosmopolitan*, author John Brisbane Walker published a piece entitled "The World's Greatest Revolution," full of dramatic rhetoric as he evaluated the impact of U.S. Steel on the world: "This momentous event did not concern itself with princes or even so-called statesmen. The world on the 3d day of March, 1901, had ceased to be ruled by such. True, there were marionettes still figuring in Congress and as Kings, but they were in place simply to carry out the orders of the world's real rulers—those who control the concentrated portion of the money supply."[50] Other critics screamed MONOPOLY and assumed price gouging would commence at once.

The public had good reason to fear U.S. Steel. Its capital was twice the amount of the capital stock for all the national banks in the United States combined and amounted to 7 percent of the nation's GNP. In one fell swoop, Morgan had captured two-thirds of the steel market, and Schwab confidently predicted they would soon own 75 percent of it. The company employed in its 170 subsidiaries more people than were living in Maryland at the time. It owned or controlled some 150 steel plants producing more steel than Britain or Germany, 115 steamships on the Great Lakes, 6 sizable railroad lines and several smaller ones, 80 percent of the quality iron ore found at the head of Lake Superior, over 75,000 acres of coal land, 18,309 coke ovens, and 98,000 acres of leased natural gas lands. Despite the tremendous assets, well-founded accusations of stock watering started ringing through Wall Street. Morgan was undeterred; nevertheless, to guarantee success, he hired a certain Mr. Keene, a stock promoter, or rather manipulator, extraordinaire, who would be responsible for bulling the stock so the Morgan syndicate could reap its millions.[51] Considering common shares opened at $39 and within a month were at $55, Mr. Keene was doing his job. What would happen in subsequent years was yet to be seen.

Carnegie appeared to be unperturbed by the hoopla and cabled Dod: "All seems right about Steel matter—no hitch—so be it."[52] To Phipps, he offered a more reflective letter:

> My Dear H. P.
>   Mr. Stetson has just called to tell me it is closed, all fixed—big times on Stock Exchange tomorrow.
>   Well, this is a step in my life—a great change, but *after a time*, when I get down to new conditions, I shall become I believe a wiser and more useful man, and besides live a dignified old age as long as life is granted, something few reach.
>
> > Yours,
> > A.C.

For Phipps, as it would for Carnegie, it took time for the magnitude of the transaction to sink in. "When I received this word I did not feel like cheering or hurrahing," Phipps recalled. "It was so impressive that it did not seem possible to be true, and it took weeks and months to have a full realization of it."[53]

One question tantalized observers and students of Morgan's buyout: did Carnegie surreptitiously engineer the sale? While Morgan's son-in-law, Herbert Satterlee, denied Morgan was scared into buying Carnegie Steel, Charles Flint and Willis King disagreed with that conclusion.[54] In recalling his meeting with Carnegie, during which he had fished for information for Morgan, Flint wrote: "He then spent several hours describing to me his plans for increasing his production and fabrication of steel; Carnegie knowing my pleasant relations with J. P. Morgan & Co. may have shrewdly divined that I was gathering information in their interest. I cannot explain in any other way why he gave me so much detailed information about his business."[55] King also assumed Carnegie's aim all along was to persuade Morgan to buy him out: "I believe fully that this fear of a competing railroad induced Morgan to undertake the putting together of the Steel Corporation, and am inclined to think that the final result was exactly what Carnegie was aiming at."[56] And then there was the December dinner to honor Schwab. Was it actually part of Carnegie's plot to sell the company without even Smilin' Charlie himself knowing? Carnegie had indicated to Dod that Schwab's favorable impression at the dinner made him more valuable to them—more valuable for what? *Selling the company.* Carnegie's threats to go into finished products were all calculated bluffs on his part, considering his profits were soaring despite the competition from Moore and Morgan's consolidations. No one else was made privy to his intentions lest he gave it away. It was a brilliant game of poker for a man who didn't play cards.

But Carnegie was hardly dancing with self-satisfaction. Yes, he had his millions, his castle, his dear four-year-old daughter, and a loving wife, but none of that mattered. For almost forty years he had been building an empire; he had survived tragedy and scandal, and then, with the flash of a pen, a signature, it was gone. Emotionally, it felt as though his child had been ripped from his arms; for a time, the hardened warrior was severely depressed. He wrote a memorandum to himself, more of a diary entry really: "Trial bitter— father bereft of his sons—abandoned & alone—no more whirl of affairs, the new developments in—occupation gone. Advise no man quit business— plenty retire upon nothing to return to—misery. Reading Scotch Am selections—the gods send thread for a web begun."[57]

CHAPTER 29

Tainted Seeds

P ray sleep soundly—all is fixed—your Bonds and mine go as our partners' go—into vaults," Carnegie wrote cousin Dod.[1] The vault, built specifically for their stacks upon stacks of almost $300 million in bonds, was located in friendly Hoboken, New Jersey, out of the New York City taxman's reach. It was in a building that also housed the Home Trust Company, essentially a private bank Carnegie created to handle his financial interests—including the disbursements for his munificence, from major endowments to small pensions—all managed by Robert Franks, his trusted financial secretary since 1883.

Although Carnegie visited the Home Trust building several times, he never laid eyes on the mountainous stacks of bonds. He preferred to be the monkey who heard no evil, saw no evil, spoke no evil, because while money was power, it also had an odious element. He rarely carried cash with him, relying on James Bertram and Franks to handle any transactions. Once, he was even tossed from a London bus for not having the fare; and he was heckled by Mark Twain for years for borrowing a quarter from the author when Twain himself was in dire financial straits. He liked to consider himself above the dirty stuff, yet the very act of rejecting its physical presence gave him a sense of control over money, a need dating back to his family's hungry days.

Now came the penultimate challenge of giving away his accumulated wealth, all $360 million plus. Morley didn't envy him and warned him that he'd have some difficulty "in adapting the principles of accumulation to the business of distribution."[2] Carnegie, however, was confident: "Thousands of clippings from eleven thousand daily papers reach me. I read them to get my bearings in the new Line of Trade. Some are really strengthening. . . . Tenacity and steady sailing to the haven we clear for—supreme confidence in one's own ideas, or conclusions rather, after thought—and above all, placing *use* above popularity."[3] He knew he'd come under criticism, but would persevere as he always had. His first benefaction on retiring, he was certain, was impervious to slander.

"I make this first use of surplus wealth," he wrote proudly in an open letter to the Carnegie Steel men on March 12, announcing the creation of the Carnegie Relief Fund to provide pensions for the retired, as well as aid for the injured and families of those who died in Carnegie mills, "four millions of first mortgage 5% Bonds, upon retiring from business, as an acknowledgement of the deep debt which I owe to the workmen who have contributed so greatly to my success."[4] The Relief Fund, with its $4 million endowment of U.S. Steel bonds, was modeled after similar funds created by the Baltimore & Ohio Railroad and the Pennsylvania Railroad. Once again, Carnegie borrowed an idea and expanded on it. *Harper's Weekly* called the pension gift the work of "a good magician," but why did he wait until now to create a pension for the workers?[5] How many who could have benefited were long since dead? Thousands, perhaps tens of thousands. Even so, Carnegie was becoming a pioneer in pension funding, although he didn't realize it at the time.

Total relief disbursements for 1902 were $48,213.80, of which $19,700.90 was for accident benefits, $16,316 for death benefits, and $12,196.90 for pensions. Men disabled by accidents received 75 cents a day if single, $1 if married, and an additional 10 cents for each child for one year, and then the rates were cut in half. In the case of death due to an accident or heat prostration, the widow received $500 and an additional $100 for each child, the total not to exceed $1,200.[6] Two years later, almost $242,000 was disbursed, including benefit payments for 230 men killed—quite a few more than the number killed during the Homestead strike—but there was no furor and the obliged Homestead men even thanked him: "The interest you have always shown in your workmen has won for you an appreciation which cannot be expressed by mere words. Of the many channels through which you have sought to do good, we believe that the 'Andrew Carnegie Relief Fund' stands first."[7]

Carnegie also set aside $4,250,000 for his private pension list, the income used for annuities given to relatives, friends, Dunfermline schoolmates, Dunfermline postmen from his youth, fellow choir members in the Swedenborgian church, former associates, renowned artists, scholars, statesmen, and even strangers who, for some reason, had made the grade. These pensioners were subject to his code of morals: one friend that Carnegie knew to be a drunkard was rejected, but then, feeling a twinge of guilt, he made him sign a pledge of sobriety and put him on the list. Eventually, 409 names would be on his private list with about $250,000 distributed annually, the amounts ranging from $25 a month to $10,000 a year. He wanted friends and strangers alike to enjoy deserved retirement. For the valuable contributors to society, he wanted to relieve their daily anxiety over money getting so they could fully dedicate themselves to their chosen fields and benefit mankind.

The day after Carnegie announced the Relief Fund, he sailed for the Mediterranean, his first port of call Genoa and then on to the Antibes and Aix-les-Bains.

Although a new life awaited, he remained tied to the last. "I sailed soon for Europe," he recalled, "and as usual some of my partners did not fail to accompany me to the steamer and bade me good-bye. But, oh! the difference to me! Say what we would, do what we would, the solemn change had come. The wrench was indeed severe and there was pain in the good-bye which was also a farewell."[8] The spa town of Aix-les-Bains, in the French Alps, would help heal the melancholy.

While Carnegie sailed the Atlantic, announcements of his initial beneficence emblazoned the front pages of newspapers. The hoopla, the speculation, the critical commentary surrounding these first activities of retirement, he knew were best to be avoided. Still, the sale of the Carnegie Company thrust the entire family onto center stage, a role Louise found painful. She was profiled in *Harper's Bazaar*, along with one of the leading stage actresses of the day, Ethel Barrymore, and Queen Olga of Greece. "Mrs. Andrew Carnegie is comparatively little known in New York outside of her circle of personal friends," the magazine observed. "Her tastes are simple, and do not incline to the brilliant social life which it would be easy for her to lead." For their immense wealth, the Carnegies' tastes were relatively simple, typified by the fact they never owned a private box for the opera nor indulged in acquiring priceless art nor cruised aboard a 241-foot, steel-hulled, steam-powered yacht, as did Morgan on his *Corsair*. *Harper's* also noted, "She shrinks, however, from publicity, and is glad to slip behind the protection of her husband's prominent and strong personality. She is in sympathy with Mr. Carnegie's munificence and schemes for public benefaction."[9] To be sure, requests for aid were now unrelenting. "The Lord has got tired of beggars," Carnegie would say as he looked over the mounds of letters. "I know just how He feels." One of those letters included a humorous solicitation from Mark Twain: "You seem to be in prosperity. Could you lend an admirer a dollar and a half to buy a hymn book with? God will bless you. . . . P.S. Don't send the hymn book, send the money; I want to make the selection myself."[10]

The greatest question of the day was how Carnegie would spend the $360 million. The makers of Mother's Seigel's Syrup, a British firm, sponsored a competition called "How Mr. Carnegie Should Get Rid of His Wealth." Any contestant whose suggestion was used by Carnegie was to win a gold sovereign, and some forty-five thousand answered the call. Over twelve thousand respondents wanted his money for themselves. Another five thousand plus wanted it used to subsidize the free distribution of Seigel's Syrup. All of thirty-six hundred said he should give it to churches or the poor. Other suggestions included bequeathing it to little Margaret and paying off the national debt.[11] Under constant scrutiny, Carnegie was recognized as "the most conspicuous apostle of the doctrine that great private wealth is a more or less accidental result of what has been hitherto our faulty economic system," according to the *American Monthly Review of Reviews*, and was under a moral obligation to redistribute to best serve his fellow men.[12] In May 1901, a writer for the *Annals of the American Academy of Political and Social Science* noted, "It is most hopeful to find a man, rising from humble station, attaining to success which gives him power superior to that of kings, still announcing a doctrine full of patriotic devotion to the institutions that have been favorable to his rise, keenly sympathetic with his fellows and enthusiastic for the amelioration of conditions against which the less fortunate must struggle."[13] More powerful than kings—this Carnegie was well aware of. His wealth, of which everyone wanted a piece, continued to grant him access to the Executive Mansion in Washington and Parliament in London, as well as to open doors to academia. As far as he was concerned, he was indeed of national interest; and as a trustee of wealth, and by extension, civilization, he was prepared for the task. The world had never before witnessed such philanthropy as was about to be committed, and it was an opportune moment for Carnegie to demonstrate enlightenment.

His philanthropic philosophy had changed very little since he wrote "Gospel of Wealth" twelve years earlier, and he would defend it to the hilt. Through cajoling and scolding, he also prodded his fellow capitalists to live the gospel. "The thought comes to my mind—" he wrote the retail million-aire John Wanamaker, "is it not about time that you were beginning to prac-tice distribution? I saw your immense new structure going up in Philadelphia, and Mrs. Carnegie has been patronizing your establishment here, and I can-not but feel that you should begin giving instead of using the whole of your exceptional talents in grabbing for more dollars. There! That is a better sermon than you hear in any of your chapels, including your own Sunday School!"[14] For Mrs. Russell Sage, inheritor of millions, he wrote his "RULES FOR A PHILANTHROPIST," which reiterated points in his "Gospel" and provided such sound advice as "Don't begin any *new* departure without first testing fully upon a small scale." He signed it, "Your fellow sufferer, A.C."[15]

John D. Rockefeller, who had paid heed to Carnegie's work for some time, required no prodding. After receiving a handout of oatmeal, he wrote the retired steel titan:

> My Dear Mr. Carnegie:
>   I thank you for the oatmeal of your own manufacture, which you were kind enough to send me. It is very good and I hope you enjoy the eating of it as much as I do. Be sure to eat it very slowly and masticate well.
>   You grind oatmeal: I grind apples, and have ordered a bottle of my sweet cider sent you from Pocantico.
>   Keep right on with your grand work of giving away money, regardless of the criticisms of cranks and fools. You have already given away more money than any man living.
>   The good Lord bless you and give you wisdom for your great responsi-bilities.
>
>   Very sincerely yours,
>   John D. Rockefeller[16]

Rockefeller's philanthropy chieftain, Frederick Gates, was not so compli-mentary. "Mr. Carnegie's intimate friends tell me that it is no secret between them and him that he does these things for the sake of having his name written in stone all over the country," he wrote his boss concerning the library giving. "Have you observed that he always gives buildings while somebody else furnishes the money to keep them in repair?"[17] Gates was raising the old debate: altruism versus personal glorification. But he was missing Carnegie's point in forcing communities to take an interest; it gave them ownership of their respective libraries. As for Carnegie's propensity to publicize his doings, he himself had written years earlier, "To *do* things *is* not one-half the battle, Carlyle is all wrong about this. To be able to tell the world what you have done, that is the greatest accomplishment!"[18] Publicity, he hoped, would beget good deeds by others.

Transferring his energy from business to philanthropy, Carnegie was now determined to *improve mankind,* a term he would use in a number of the philanthropic deeds he wrote. The power Carnegie's money wielded frightened the general public, communities, and institutions, however, and one of the foremost objections to his philanthropy, regardless of its manifestation, was that he would use it to intrude on society and impose his own set of moral codes—a form of social control. Individuals and communities also found his almsgiving demeaning and patronizing and resented it, and, to a lesser degree, rejected his money as tainted because it was the result of draconian economics. Each major benefaction would arouse feverish deliberation and criticism that he would have to contend with in turn, some more virulent than others. As to Carnegie's motives, an ongoing great debate was conducted: does he give money to alleviate his conscience and to make up for industrial crimes; to satisfy an insatiable desire for attention, notoriety, and immortality; because he is in fact a socialist in disguise; or perhaps, just perhaps, for altruistic reasons? Sure he had a desk drawer labeled Gratitude and Sweet Words, but regardless of how he conducted his philanthropy, he was always going to be labeled a notorious egotist because he so adamantly voiced his opinion and acted on his convictions. Certainly, philanthropy was an opportunity for the capitalists to cleanse their image, but these men also truly desired to create models for moral leadership. They considered themselves the high priests of civil religion, and Carnegie wanted to be a leading player in civilization's progress at the dawn of the twentieth century. And unlike Morgan and Rockefeller, his philanthropy would give him an opportunity to reconcile internal conflicts between his radical heritage and capitalistic present that had made him a man of contradictions. But what did the gods have in store for him? Was it too late? Was there enough time left, or would he die disgraced?

Library giving remained Carnegie's preferred means of advancing civilization, at least initially. It was his centerpiece. It was holy, a monument to his father and Colonel Anderson and his own proverbial success. It was also subject to the harshest scrutiny.

Just days after his retirement, Carnegie was reading the *Scottish American* newspaper (which he noted in the introspective memorandum to himself), when a quote struck him—"the gods send thread for a web begun." The web begun was his library work. He resolved to use his multimillion-dollar thread to continue the web, to create a network of intellectual centers that would raise collective intelligence. On March 16, Carnegie announced a $5.2 million gift to New York City to build sixty-five branch libraries, on the now standard condition that the city provide the sites and the money to maintain the facilities. "I give you the seed," Carnegie said in his press release. "Cultivate it as you will."[19] *Harper's Weekly* considered the benefaction "an example not only of princely but of most intelligent generosity" that would add to the educational powers of the public schools; R. R. Bowker, the renowned editor of the *Library Journal*, praised it as a supreme gift; and the *New York Daily Tribune*, once his sternest critic, was equally effusive in praise.[20] It was expected the necessary legislation would be enacted so the gift could be accepted posthaste.

Through 1898, Carnegie had provided for just 9 libraries. Over the next two years, he added 38 to the list.[21] Now the pace leaped to such a jarring speed the newspapers couldn't keep track; the *Tribune* noted just over 50 libraries for 1901 in the paper's index, while, in fact, he gave 131. In addition to New York, other notable donations included $1 million for St. Louis, $500,000 for Glasgow—in gratitude, Glasgow University conferred on Carnegie the degree of LL.D.—and $100,000 for San Juan, Puerto Rico. Although there was an impression that Carnegie forced his libraries on communities, it wasn't true; thousands of requests came from mayors, councils, committees, women's clubs, and clergymen in remote villages.

He had now moved from a retail phase of library giving to wholesale, but the need for control remained paramount as Carnegie, now dubbed the "Patron Saint of Libraries," wanted his library benefactions to run as efficiently as his mills had. To ensure that control, once a request was received, Carnegie's secretaries Bertram and Franks opened a dossier on the town. Bertram would send out a basic questionnaire requesting information on the town's size, its current library facilities, site availability, and whether any collection had been raised for a new building.[22] More questions were added over time as Bertram and Franks became ever-more vigilant. They also reviewed the architect's building plans to ensure there were no unnecessary extravagances and waste, which reflected Carnegie's tastes; when the boss happened to see the proposed drawing of the Denver library, he wrote, "I am sorry to have my money wasted in this way—This is no practical library plan. Too many pillars."[23] Eventually Bertram had a pamphlet of architectural guidelines made. After receiving approval, the town council had to sign a pledge committing to provide the site and maintenance, and then money was sent in small amounts as work progressed.

Carnegie had little to do with the day-to-day administration, implicitly trusting Bertram and Franks, who would remain guardians of his ideals and wealth long after his death. The fact that they remained loyal said much about how well Carnegie treated them personally, as opposed to how he

Carnegie, who was much kinder to his personal help than his partners, dictates a letter to his secretary James Bertram. (Courtesy of the Carnegie Library of Pittsburgh)

manipulated Frick and other business partners. Bertram would come into Carnegie's study and say, "Here are forty or fifty more libraries, Mr. Carnegie. They need your O.K."

"Have you examined them all, my boy?"

"Yes."

Carnegie, who was made an honorary member of the American Library Association, might peruse a few of the applications, then nod his approval. "All right, go ahead with them."[24]

Some towns were refused for being too indebted already or for fumbling management of the library request, or for having what were deemed as adequate facilities, or because Carnegie knew a local capitalist who should be forced to give the building. Also, he did not give to state libraries, state historical society libraries, and proprietary or subscription libraries because they had access to alternative funding.

Detractors of his library giving naturally came to the fore with a reprise of the standard criticism that Carnegie was such a fervent building giver because he was Ramses II incarnate—he wanted to immortalize himself by demanding his name be carved above each threshold. "He has bought fame and paid cash for it," his anti-imperialist ally Twain noted, "he has deliberately projected and planned out his fame for himself; he has arranged that his name shall be famous in the mouths of men for centuries to come. He has planned shrewdly, safely, securely, and will have his desire."[25] It was an easy criticism to make, but contrary to these loud and belligerent claims, Carnegie's name being used was not a prerequisite to winning funds. While vain, he remained tasteful and practical. When the town of Lincoln, Illinois, proposed naming their library the Lincoln-Carnegie Memorial Library, Carnegie objected, declaring he "would consider it a desecration to have any name linked with that of Lincoln." He also demurred when he gave a considerable sum to the Franklin Institute of Boston and it was proposed to rename the school the Franklin-Carnegie Institute.[26] And as he explained to Charles Eliot, president of Harvard, "I find it difficult to avoid having gifts for new things called after the donors. Carnegie Hall New York was called by me *The Music Hall* a la Boston. Foreign artists refused to appear in 'A Music Hall' — London idea. The Board changed it in my absence in Europe without consulting me. . . . The way of the Philanthropist is hard but I don't do anything for popularity and just please my sel' — do what I think is useful. I never reply to attacks. Altho I confess I was surprised that you should have for a moment imagined there was a man living who could dream of coupling his name with Franklin *or with any founder.*"[27] Carnegie held heroes in such high esteem that he never wanted or expected his name attached to theirs. Not one of the eventual 115 libraries in Indiana used his name, and only 27 percent of the libraries he provided for chose to do so.

Another blanket censure of his library program was that he was putting the proverbial cart before the horse. A taste for reading was a precious possession, Carnegie had said again and again, so why didn't he provide the books?[28] The books contained the knowledge, not the bricks, after all, and the quality of reading material at his libraries appeared to suffer. "Go to the nearest Carnegie Library and examine its catalog of books," H. L. Mencken wrote years later. "The chances are five to one that you will find the place full of literary bilge and as bare of good books as a Boston bookshop."[29] Carnegie was steadfast in his refusal to give money for books; it was up to the locals to select what would best serve their community. When he did make exceptions — he gave $100 to Conneautville, Pennsylvania, $1,000 to Manassas, Virginia, and $6,000 to Erie, Pennsylvania, as well as about twenty-four other communities, for books — he came under fire for being a socialist.[30] If giving free books, why not free clothes and furniture? And then there were the socialists who claimed his libraries were a devious means of distracting the worker from his daily suffering. Meanwhile, the allegedly distracted laborers, who were to be uplifted by the libraries, had no time or energy for books. In 1901, most steelworkers were still working twelve-hour days, seven-day weeks. It was a clear case of damned if you do and damned if you don't.

It has been assumed that there was a broad-based movement against accepting his donations due to it being tainted money, but this is a false impression. Of the some 3,000 communities that applied and were offered libraries, only 225 ended up choosing not to sign the pledge when it was put to a vote; and of those, 98 already had library facilities. For the remainder, the majority of the reasons had nothing to do with Carnegie personally. The most frequent explanation was the community simply could not commit to the 10 percent maintenance clause because either it didn't have the legal authority to raise the necessary taxes, or it simply couldn't afford the added economic burden. Also, in some towns the paving of streets, the installation of sewers, and the building of new schools were the priorities, and there were instances when a single council member shot down the gift because of a pet project taking precedence. In yet other towns, people wanted more money than Carnegie was willing to give, or politically messy site controversies erupted that ended any hope for a gift. Across the southern states there was antagonism toward all northern industrialists, so communities there were less likely to accept his gifts. Ultimately, about 6 percent of those who rejected Carnegie money did so because it was tainted.[31] It was a very small minority, but the most shrill.

When a Detroit contingent requested a library in 1902 and Carnegie offered $750,000, reaction was swift and cut to the bone. "We ought to be able to take care of ourselves, I should think," said the city's treasurer. "Who told Mr. Carnegie that we were worthy objects of charity, I wonder? . . . It doesn't seem to me as though it would be a proper thing for this town to accept a big chunk of money as a gift from a man who has made his money the way Carnegie did." The city was a labor stronghold, reflected vividly in the opposition's opinions. "Carnegie ought to have distributed his money among his employees while he was making it," said C. H. Johnson, Detroit resident and secretary of the Street Railway Employees. "No man can accumulate such wealth honorably. It may be legally honest, but it's not morally honest."[32] When put to a vote, the offer was soundly rejected. Five years later, the people passed an issuance of bonds to fund a library.

The same reaction occurred in most labor and union strongholds; it was just a question of whether the labor contingent was large enough to vote down the offer. Labor leader Eugene V. Debs said, "We want libraries, and we will have them in glorious abundance when capitalism is abolished and working men are no longer robbed by the philanthropic pirates of the Carnegie class. Then the library will be as it should be, a noble temple dedicated to culture and symbolizing the virtues of the people."[33] Samuel Gompers thought Carnegie's wealth could be put to more important uses but wrote a comrade in Toronto, "After all is said and done, he might put his money to a much worse act. Yes, accept his library, organize the workers, secure better conditions and particularly, reduction in hours of labor and then workers will have some chance and leisure in which to read books."[34] Labor leaders still carried the Homestead torch, echoing the 1892 St. Louis Dispatch editorial: "Ten thousand 'Carnegie Public Libraries' would not compensate the country for the direct and indirect evils resulting from the Homestead lockout."

A handful of towns in England and Canada refused libraries because the money was considered tainted, but for a different reason: Carnegie spoke insultingly of Queen Victoria and the monarchy.[35]

Any criticism rolled off Carnegie because he knew millions of people derived pleasure from the libraries. In his lifetime, Carnegie and his foundations would establish 2,811 libraries at a cost of over $60 million. He could proudly say that the sun never set on his libraries. But not until the 1930s would scholars recognize that Carnegie had aided in the democratization of culture with his libraries.[36] They were truly seeds.

The Patron Saint of Libraries also achieved the dubious distinction as a church organ donor, a seemingly quixotic choice for the agnostic. As a young man attending the Swedenborg society meetings in Allegheny City, he had found only the music exhilarating and was fond of quoting Confucius: "Music sacred tongue of God, I hear thee calling and I come." When asked why he donated only organs to churches, he replied, "To lessen the pain of the sermons."[37] On another occasion he elaborated: "You can't always trust what the pulpit says, but you can always depend upon what the organ says."[38] Organs were a means for the agnostic to hedge his bet, too, just in case God was up there, watching Carnegie with a wry smile.

Contrary to all appearances, Carnegie was not completely antagonistic toward religion. He understood the need for a system of beliefs, wanted to believe there was a great Creator, and desired to reconcile religion and science, but he despised the oppressive creeds handed down by the various sects, and their branding of those who didn't share their particular creed as heathens. So churches, as declared in his gospel, were not a top priority. In fact, Carnegie never intended organ giving to become such a popular component of his philanthropy, a position he divulged in explaining to Elizabeth Haldane, a Scottish author wanting to found a charity school in Edinburgh, why he would not aid her cause: "Sorry, I cannot extend my field to cover the cause you have at heart. It would be a case of Organs over again. I gave one Organ to a church in Allegheny City, my home, and it has resulted in giving or contributing to over four thousand Church Organs, and the correspondence really takes the greater part of one Secretary's time. We have seven thousand Church Organs, arranged in order awaiting attention in this one department."[39] It was the uncontroversial nature of giving a beautiful organ that made the donations popular with the public and spurred thousands of requests.

Organ requests became so overwhelming that Bertram and Franks had to resort to the same process used for libraries: the request came in and a questionnaire went out. The U.S. church organ tally eventually reached 4,092, at a cost of $3,604,718.75. Pennsylvania received the most at 1,351, next was Ohio at 440, and then New York at 290. Nevada received 1. Another 3,597, at a cost of $2,643,593, were given to other countries, although 3,124 of those went to England and Scotland. The grand total: 7,689 organs costing $6,248,311.75.[40] A good many clergymen's voices were drowned out.

Nicely bronzed from their Mediterranean respite in the spring of 1901, the Carnegies made their customary visit to London for hobnobbing and shopping before proceeding to Skibo. Morgan was also in town, so talk of U.S.

Steel could not be avoided. If Carnegie still had the feelings of a bereft father, he didn't show it when both Morgan and he attended a dinner hosted by the London Chamber of Commerce for the New York Chamber of Commerce at Grocer's Hall. Carnegie appeared to be the happiest man there, while, the newspapers noted, Morgan with his deformed nose hid behind a Mr. Morton when the photographer's camera flashed.[41] Besides being the world's richest man and in the spotlight, Carnegie had another good reason to be happy—he was in the midst of planning a great benefaction for Scotland.

The Scottish universities at Aberdeen, Edinburgh, Glasgow, and St. Andrews had been neglected for years, while the Scottish aristocracy sent their boys to Oxford or Cambridge. The *Fortnightly Review* had published a piece titled "The Scottish University Crisis" in December 1900, pointing out that the Scottish universities were second-rate educational institutions and estimating that it would take an endowment of $7.5 million to reorganize and modernize the schools.[42] Thomas Shaw, a native of Dunfermline and a member of Parliament, was actively trying to revitalize the schools. As part of his campaign, he proposed some money be used to help students pay their tuition, thus attracting a larger and hopefully brighter body. In stepped Carnegie.

He approached Shaw shortly after arriving in Britain and offered $5 million in U.S. Steel bonds, the income to subsidize tuition. Based on the desired student enrollment, it was quickly determined that amount wouldn't be sufficient, so Carnegie offered an additional $5 million. It appeared he was breaking from his creed of self-help. British critics certainly thought so, charging he would "pauperize" youth who should earn their education, and they resented his intrusion. *Blackwood's Magazine* was ferocious: "Maybe Mr. Carnegie has never heard the fable of Midas. If for a moment he can overcome his loathing of the past, we would urge him to read it. . . . Push and screw; buy cheap and sell dear. . . . To get money you must strangle joy and murder peace. . . . Presently the American ideal of life will be our own. . . . In old days, a rich man enjoyed his wealth—and if he did the community 'no good' at least he did not insult it with 'patronage.'"[43] "Loathing of the past" referred to Carnegie's derision of a classical education. More than ten years earlier, in the *New York Daily Tribune*, he had written an article titled "How to Win Fortune," in which he concluded, based on the overwhelming number of businessmen dominating industry who started poor and had no university degree, that "college education as it exists seems almost fatal to success in that domain."[44] He had seen no use in studying the classics and dead languages; instead, he supported polytechnic and scientific schools, which were turning out men who made a real impact on manufacturing. Since then Carnegie, under the influence of men like John Morley, had modified his views. He had realized both technical and classical education played a role, but *Blackwood's* cut him no slack. Other critics warned of Carnegie invading their country in an attempt to change their way of life, thus corrupting their educational system. Still others argued the money would be better spent refurbishing facilities, buying equipment, and building labs. Carnegie was caught off guard by the outcry, but if the likes of *Blackwood's* thought it was going to bully him into shelving the idea, the editors were very wrong.

Supporters of tuition relief rallied around Carnegie, charging the English critics with desiring to suppress Scottish youth. Before proceeding, Carnegie wisely elected to consult with Lord Balfour of Burleigh, secretary of Scotland, the earl of Elgin, and Prime Minister Arthur James Balfour. Willing to hear all sides, Carnegie was hardly the autocratic monster his enemies made him out to be, but he was tenacious in his determination to help his homeland. Over a series of meetings, the group decided a balance between tuition aid and funds to enhance scientific research would be the most beneficial and would quiet the critics. Just before leaving London for Skibo, he received a crucial letter of encouragement from the prime minister, who congratulated him for his "splendid generosity, which is, so far as my knowledge goes, on quite an unexampled scale." As for providing students with tuition relief, Balfour still reserved judgment. "But as regards that part of it by which the adequate equipment of our scientific teaching would be permanently secured, I must express myself at once. . . . One discovery which adds to our command over the forces of nature may do more for mankind than the most excellent teaching of what is already known, absolutely necessary to national welfare as this latter is. And yet for sheer want of money our provision both in the department of teaching and that of research is deplorably deficient. It gives me intense gratification to think that, so far as Scotland is concerned, this wretched state of things is now, through your liberality, to be brought to an end."[45] Balfour's emphasis on the crucial importance of scientific discovery influenced Carnegie now and in later benefactions. As he subsequently told Morley, "I get many letters telling me how important is the remission of fees, but I don't place that feature as of first importance. *Research* is the soul."[46]

After the deliberations, he judiciously created the Carnegie Trust for the Universities of Scotland and endowed it with $10 million in U.S. Steel bonds, with revenue from $5 million going toward tuition aid for qualified youth who might otherwise not have a chance to attend a university, and revenue from the second $5 million going toward "improving and extending the opportunities for scientific study and research."[47] History, literature, and modern languages were also provided for. Based in Edinburgh, the elite board of trustees included Prime Minister Balfour, ex–prime minister Rosebery, future prime minister Sir Henry Campbell-Bannerman, the earl of Elgin, and Morley, among others. These names alone were testimony to the power Carnegie and his money wielded in Britain.

To assuage any fears that he was trampling on British mores, Carnegie included in the deed a clause that allowed the trustees, by a two-thirds vote, to modify the regulations governing the trust if new conditions demanded it. As difficult as it was for him, he gave them a free hand. At one of the first meetings, the earl of Elgin actually protested the clause, arguing that as a trustee he wanted to be told what to do, which prompted Carnegie to turn to Balfour and say, "Mr. Balfour, I have not known a man in any country who could legislate wisely for the next generation—and I have seen people that did not make a very great success in legislating for their own."

"That is true," Balfour said with a smile. As for the clause, he said, "It is the wisest provision I have ever seen included on a trust deed."[48]

There was little ammunition left for the critics, especially considering that the preexisting combined endowments of the four universities—Aberdeen, Edinburgh, Glasgow, and St. Andrews—generated just $350,000 annually, while Carnegie's gift would generate $500,000. Beginning in 1901, Carnegie met with the heads of the Scottish universities annually at Skibo, and the first week of September became known as "Principals' Week." By 1910, a St. Andrews official could claim, "At the present time, the University has a larger number of students and is doing a greater variety of work in all departments of study than at any period in its history."[49]

At Skibo, the renovation was still under way. The main hall and new wings were completed but now required decorating and furnishing. Other ambitious projects were in various stages of completion: a man-made lake, Loch Ospisdale, which would be stocked with brown trout; two ponds, Lake Louise and Margaret's Loch, for water lilies and other plants; a dam at the mouth of the Evelix River to create a loch with a salmon ladder; a nine-hole golf course, which would be expanded to eighteen, nestled between Loch Evelix and Dornoch Firth; and the marble, indoor swimming pool, twenty-four meters long and nine meters wide, heated and filled with salt water pumped from the sea. The county of Sutherland prospered as both the unskilled and skilled found plenty of work, with even "walkers" hired to walk the estate's roads looking for bumps and ruts to repair.

There was still one thing missing, however—a waterfall. Carnegie solved the problem by convincing the duke of Sutherland to sell him a large tract of land to the north and west, nearly doubling the estate's property, which included a section of the River Shin and a fine waterfall. The river also offered excellent salmon fishing. Without the intensity of business competition to expend his energy, he punished the fish mercilessly, his passion famous among friends. Charles Flint enjoyed telling the story of when he took Carnegie fishing: "I was interested to see how $300,000,000 would fish. He went at it as though he were pulling in another million."[50]

Carnegie also attacked golf with greater vigor, playing frequently at the challenging Dornoch course, where he became vice president of the club. He later invited J. H. Taylor, five-time British Open champion, to visit Skibo and instruct Louise and him. In notes to Dod and friends, he crowed, "I beat Lucy today badly at golf—really broke my record & now feel I can do something creditable. . . . I am beating my friends at golf, so all goes well. I played eighteen holes today with Taylor. Beat him! Beat Murray Butler Saturday. Beat Franks the day before. I am playing better! P.S. They gave me a stroke a hole, but that's a detail."[51] A *stroke a hole.* Anyone was free game in his insa-

Skibo Castle, which Carnegie purchased in 1898, was said to be cursed. (Courtesy of the Carnegie Library of Pittsburgh)

tiable need to compete, and whether playing golf or backgammon, if Carnegie lost he was miserable for hours afterward.

Every day that first summer of retirement he read a little Shakespeare or Burns, endeavored to peruse a dozen or more daily newspapers—at least that's what he told the press—and reviewed his own essays as he prepared an anthology, *The Empire of Business*, to be published the next year by Doubleday, Page. It would include seventeen essays dating back to 1885, covering commerce, industry, and business success. Carnegie also kept himself well acquainted with business conditions on both sides of the Atlantic, digesting everything of significance, especially any news related to U.S. Steel, the company paying the interest on his $200 million plus in bonds.

As the bereft father, Carnegie harbored ill-founded ill-feeling toward U.S. Steel and Morgan, and, to assuage his pain, he made disparaging remarks about the company in the press, contributing to the billion-dollar steel trust's bad public relations image. In the same manner he had belittled Frick, he told Skibo guests: "Pierpont is not an ironmaster, he knows nothing about the business of making and selling steel. I managed my trade with him so that I was paid for my properties in bonds, not stocks! He will make a fizzle of the business and default in payment of the interest. I will then foreclose and get my properties back, and Pierpont and his friends will lose all their paper profits. Pierpont feels that he can do anything because he has always got the best of the Jews in Wall Street. It takes a Yankee to beat a Jew, and it takes a Scot to beat a Yankee!"[52]

In retirement, Carnegie pursued golf as avidly as he had business. Losing put him in a foul humor for hours. (Courtesy of the Carnegie Library of Pittsburgh)

Carnegie must have watched with a mocking smile as Morgan contended with his first labor agitation that summer with not even six months having passed since the formation of U.S. Steel. Striking was sporadic, but in the end, the Amalgamated was no match for the greatest industrial Goliath ever created. Ten fewer mills were union after the summer strikes, and conditions remained deplorable for the slingshot-wielding steelworkers.

A greater threat to Morgan and big business emerged in the wake of President McKinley's assassination, carried out on September 6, 1901—the president would die on September 14—while he was visiting the Pan-American Exposition in Buffalo, a festival to celebrate progress. The assassin was an anarchist, Leon Czolgosz, who had been inspired by one of Emma Goldman's speeches. To think, if Goldman had been linked to her boyfriend Alexander Berkman and the Frick murder attempt, the McKinley assassination might never have happened, as she would have been in jail. Now the cowboy Roosevelt was president of the United States; as a reformer, he was a menace to Morgan and, by association, U.S. Steel and the company's largest bondholder, Carnegie. Such was the work of the gods.

"President McKinley gone," Carnegie lamented to his cousin Dod. "Isn't it dreadful. I was quite depressed by the shock & not very confident of Roosevelt's wisdom but power may sober him."[53] To Morley, he reiterated his concern about the would-be imperialist Rough Rider: "Anxious about Roosevelt, an unknown quantity, capable of infinite mischief. . . ."[54] In a memorandum to himself and for posterity's sake, Carnegie wrote: "President Roosevelt. If he would only act as he tells one that he feels. Plenty good advice given & apparently taken & then some wild erratic outburst on stump. Prest. Eliot Harvard sums it all up when he said recently, 'I knew Teddy when he was a boy. I know him now when he is still a boy, and I'll never know him anything else but a boy.' But one can't help loving him. He has high & pure ideals."[55] In time, Roosevelt would come to have the same respect and distrust for Carnegie.

Wall Street was rattled by this new, unpredictable force who as governor of New York had forced reforms on Tammany Hall and municipal corruption. Roosevelt, with an ego to rival Carnegie, Morgan, and Rockefeller's, was not going to pander to the industrialists or to Wall Street. In fact, he had both Morgan and Rockefeller in his gun sights and, walking quietly while wielding his big stick, launched a trust-busting campaign. His first move was to instruct Attorney General Philander Knox (who had been highly recommended by Carnegie and Morgan) to dissolve one of Morgan's railroad consolidations, Northern Securities, a holding company controlling three railroads, for restraint of trade. When in February 1902 the charges were filed, Morgan was first surprised, then livid. Although the stock market plunged, the public approved—the people despised the Morgan monopolies. The case ultimately went to the Supreme Court in 1904 and Knox won. The attorney general had made a good show of it, but he was careful ultimately to protect the Morgan interests—in particular, U.S. Steel.

Wisely, Carnegie did not take an aggressive posture with Roosevelt; instead, he pursued the canny course of ingratiating himself with the new president. Interestingly, the month before the charges were levied against Northern Securities, Carnegie had delivered a speech to railroad men in New York titled "Railroads Past and Present." It was harmless enough, mostly a retrospective of his career with the Pennsylvania and the importance of railroads, but vigilant observers, and perhaps cynics, could not easily dismiss the coincidence. No doubt, Carnegie was feeding Roosevelt information, especially considering several years later he wrote Senator Moses Clapp of Minnesota: "A few great railroad organizations control the situation, combining they divide the business between them—agree not to build in certain territory, fix rates, &c. That govt. must control them & prevent unlimited sway to public or private injury seems obvious. . . . The President is right upon this question sure."[56] For decades Carnegie had harbored a grudge against the railroads, and still did. Even in retirement he could be extremely spiteful. He would also soon be advising the president, welcomed or not, on a host of issues, political and economic.

When Carnegie returned to the United States in the fall, he still found retirement hard to accept. "I felt myself entirely out of place," he recalled, "but was much cheered by seeing several of 'the boys' on the pier to welcome me—the same dear friends, but so different. I had lost my partners, but not my friends. This was something; it was much. Still a vacancy was left."[57] With that sense of vacancy came the heightened awareness of his mortality, a sense of urgency, the need to push inordinately. The expanding void had to be filled at an ever-greater pace; therefore, Carnegie threw himself violently into his philanthropy. The Carnegie Institute in Pittsburgh continued to nourish him; at a November 12 afternoon meeting of trustees, he announced his intention to increase the endowment of the technical school from $1 million to $3 million. Later in the month, at the 145th annual St. Andrew's Society dinner at Delmonico's, attended by five hundred, he donated $100,000 to aid the aged and decrepit Scottish poor in the city. As the society's president, he said a toast for President Roosevelt and King Edward. A piper played Scottish airs, there was a small orchestra, haggis was the prize dish, and on the dais with Carnegie was Mayor-elect Seth Low and Mark Twain, who arrived late and received a hearty cheer. And Carnegie was deep into planning his next great venture, a U.S.-based foundation modeled on the Scottish universities trust.

But then the Dunfermline branch of the family suffered a terrible loss with the death of eighty-seven-year-old Uncle Lauder. The teacher who seemed as though he would live forever was gone. It shocked Carnegie, rendered him childlike, and left him gasping for breath:

> Sunday night
> December 22, 1901
>
> Dear Dod:
>   I am stunned and somehow protected from severe shocks, except every now and then one comes that seems almost to stop the heart.
>   What this loss is to you and to me no one knows but ourselves; they cannot know. I don't believe there ever was so sweet, so fond an attachment on earth, as between us three men—the Teacher and his pupils.
>   But I can't write about it; I must quit.
>   It is so saddening. What on earth will Scotland be to me now? He was Scotland.
>   Well, I must bite my lips and say nothing. This life, so delightful to us when it touches the precious relationship, is, apart from these sweet touches of affection, a fearful mockery; but good night. Do write a few lines and tell me how you are. This blow doesn't draw us closer—nothing could do that; but it does send the thoughts more to you.
>
> Ever yours,
> Naig

Uncle Lauder, like his mother, Margaret, had been a driving force, a guiding force he still needed. "I feel so lonely," he wrote Morley. "The intense interest he took in all my doings gave me satisfaction. 'How this will please Uncle Lauder!' was always present in my mind as events came."[58]

Except for his mother, Carnegie had never had such definitive emotional attachment to any human being. There was no quoting from Burns or Shakespeare to express his emotions now.

Within days of Uncle Lauder's death, Carnegie was again fully immersed in his philanthropy; it served to heal this wound as well as old ones.

For over a year his friend Andrew White, the ambassador to Germany and a former Cornell president, recalling that George Washington had wanted a national university and using the lure of heroic immortality, had been pushing the idea of one on Carnegie. Carnegie replied: "You suggested a National University at Washington—Washington's desire, several have; but while this does, as you say, ensure immortality to the Founder, it has hitherto seemed to me not needed, and this puts immortality under foot. . . . Don't care two cents about future 'glory.' I must be satisfied that I am doing good, wise, beneficial work in my day."[59] He pointed out that Johns Hopkins could very well serve as an embryo for a national university, and he had no desire to duplicate others' efforts; redundancy had been anathema at his mills and remained so. The promises of immortality did nothing for Carnegie—that was already secure—but there was an appeal to linking himself indirectly to George Washington, of committing a great act in his spirit. After talking over the subject with Daniel Gilman, president of Johns Hopkins, he decided it would be best to give the United States a gift similar to what he'd given Scotland, in the form of a Washington-based national trust supporting all American universities. The focus would be on science alone—no tuition aid or other peripheral projects that would just drain funds and scatter his efforts.

Carnegie, like fellow New York philanthropist Peter Cooper, dreamed of science conquering misery, and he recalled the words of Prime Minister Balfour: "One discovery which adds to our command over the forces of nature may do more for mankind than the most excellent teaching of what is already known." The glory of discovery, of pushing mankind one great leap forward, was far more intoxicating to Carnegie than large-scale tenement reform, or filtration plants, or urban high schools. As the plan evolved, Carnegie consulted a number of renowned educators, just as he had in creating the Scottish trust. Daniel Gilman recalled: "Mr. Carnegie raised many hard questions: How is it that knowledge is increased? How can rare intellects be discovered in the undeveloped stages? Where is the exceptional man to be found? Would a new institution be regarded as an injury to Johns Hopkins, or to Harvard, Yale, Columbia, or any other university? What should the term 'knowledge' comprise? Who should be the managers of the institution? How broad and how restricted should be the terms of the gift?"[60] Carnegie was clearly as thorough in how he should give away his money as he was when making it; there'd be no slapdash decisions.

He was so enthused that on Thanksgiving Day he took the time to express his intentions to create a foundation that would benefit all American universities in a letter to Roosevelt. To bolster the idea, he presumed what George Washington would desire: "For some time, I have been considering the propriety of fulfilling one of Washington's strongest wishes, the founding of a university at Washington, but the conclusion reached was that, if with us today, he would decide that under present conditions greater good would result from cooperation with, and strengthening of, existing universities throughout the country, than by adding to their number. . . . If established and managed as I believe it can be, our country will possess a potent instrument for discovery and invention and the pursuit of knowledge, for it aims at the cooperation of all our higher educational institutions, thus ensuring unity and effort hitherto lacking, from which I think we are not too sanguine in predicting a surprising harvest."[61]

Realizing this was an opportunity to revolutionize science and education while he was in power, Roosevelt invited Carnegie to the White House for lunch on December 1 and again on December 12 to discuss his plans. Carnegie divulged that the Carnegie Institution of Washington, as it was now being called, was to receive an unheralded endowment of $10 million (another $22 million would follow in later years). The money was significant, but to give the institution national prominence, Carnegie wanted Roosevelt—the man he deemed capable of "infinite mischief"—to serve as a trustee, along with several other Washington politicians. "I will serve with the greatest pleasure . . . ," Roosevelt wrote Carnegie on New Year's Eve. "It seems to me to be precisely the institution most needed to help and crown our educational system by providing for and stimulating original research."[62] Including Roosevelt was a shrewd move on Carnegie's part; not only was it a feather in his cap, it was a means of keeping tabs on the Rough Rider.

The trustees numbered twenty-seven, including Roosevelt, Grover Cleveland, William N. Frew, Abram Hewitt, John Hay, Elihu Root, and Andrew White—such a collection of men was yet more clear evidence of the power Carnegie commanded. At the first meeting, held at the State Department, the trustees elected seventy-year-old Daniel Gilman to serve as the first president, which he did until 1904. In the Founder's Deed of Trust, Carnegie charged his trustees to "in the broadest and most liberal manner encourage investigation, research, and discovery—show the application of knowledge to the improvement of mankind . . . To promote original research . . . To discover the exceptional in every department of study whenever and wherever found, inside or outside of schools, and enable him to make the work for which he seems specially designed his life work." As with the Scottish trust, the trustees were given absolute power, a difficult concession on Carnegie's part but necessary to give the organization legitimacy. After Carnegie outlined his goals at the meeting, he declared, "Gentlemen, your work begins. Your aims are high; you seek to extend known forces, and to discover and utilize new forces for the benefit of man."[63]

What was particularly unique was that the institution had no tangible goals such as those demanded in business or in Carnegie's library giving and

Relief Fund. Its purpose was far more abstract, its precise benefits unknown. It was a testament to Carnegie's expansive mind that he was now able to disconnect himself from the narrow purpose of profit making. But then again, just as he had in the steel business, he knew an investment needed to be made today for profits tomorrow. "You are one of the very few who realizes that the world's activities of tomorrow will found their very existence upon the research of today," complimented Professor Theodore W. Richards of Harvard. The chancellor of Vanderbilt University, J. H. Kirkland, also lavished praise on the institution, comparing its spirit with Harvard, Yale, and Columbia; but Kirkland worried that such large endowments would discourage the small givers, who were equally important in supporting institutions at large. He predicted individual benefactors would play an increasingly important role in the educational system—a thought that worried the critics. A suspicious public wanted its say and feared the money of the Carnegies, Rockefellers, and Stanfords would muffle its voice.

At the annual meeting in November 1902, the institution's trustees confirmed the need to promote original research and support projects that attempted to fill knowledge gaps. They would not enter into anything being done well by other groups or that could be done better by others.[64] Over the first six years, the institution established departments to support work in experimental evolution, marine biology, historical research, economics and sociology, terrestrial magnetism, astronomy, geophysics, botany, and nutrition. Eventually, research labs and stations would be established around the world.

One of Carnegie's dreams was for the research to discover cures to disease, not just for humans, but for plant and wildlife that would ultimately benefit mankind. He didn't leave all the work to his trusts; he also gave $50,000 to Madame Curie and $120,000 to Robert Koch for his studies in bacteriology. Koch, a German, was awarded the 1905 Nobel Prize for physiology or medicine for discovering the bacillus that causes tuberculosis, a tremendous step toward controlling and defeating the disease. This was the kind of result Carnegie fantasized about and made him impervious to criticism. Did not saving millions of future lives justify the trampling under of thousands of past ones, his laborers?

CHAPTER 30

Human Frailty

C arnegie's first twelve months of retirement were marked by triumph as he gave away some $30 million to libraries and educational foundations, but the philanthropy didn't bring internal peace. His personal life remained filled with conflict and disappointment as he contended with the shortcomings of friends, family, and himself. In his relationships with those close to him, he would continue to reveal polarized characteristics, from callous cruelty to sentimental empathy; it was the same maddening, dichotomous Carnegie who had yet to discover a place in life that brought him contentment.

Human frailty surrounded the world's greatest philanthropist, Carnegie's protégé Schwab included. The sale of Carnegie Steel made instant millionaires out of dozens of vested partners, and they indiscreetly bathed in the riches, prompting one of them to observe that "the sudden flood of gold dazed and demoralized some of the younger partners, who, masters now of riches they have never dreamed of, began to kick up their heels like pasture colts. Some of them never recovered."[1] In addition to a mansion-building spree and conspicuous consumption, there were Caligula-like parties. The newspaper reporters gawked and reported it all. It was distasteful to Carnegie. "These young men were models as long as they knew they had to be — besides they had my example & they were poor," he wrote Oswald Villard, who had run an editorial in the *New York Evening Post* on Pittsburgh's nouveaux riches. "Altho making large sums, these went to their credit paying for their interests. Now they see stock gamblers prominent in the Company & behind it. They become demoralized. . . . It is too sad for me to see such ruination morally. You will see I cannot speak of it publicly."[2]

In private, Carnegie would lament: "Have you seen Charlie's house? Mine is a cottage by comparison." On a block-long piece of property at Seventy-second Street and Riverside Drive, Schwab was building a mansion modeled after a French Loire Valley chateau. It was four stories with a 116-foot lookout tower, a 60-foot swimming pool, a bowling alley, a gymnasium, six elevators serving ninety bedrooms, and a power plant consuming ten tons of coal every day. It was to reflect his million-dollar salary. But his chateau was not the worst of his extravagances or his crimes.

The very month Carnegie officially incorporated the Carnegie Institution of Washington—January—Schwab was in hedonistic Monte Carlo celebrating his fortieth birthday without his wife. On a lucky roll at roulette, a frenzied crowd pursued him from one table to the next, and the *New York Sun* ran the headline: SCHWAB BREAKS THE BANK. Considering U.S. Steel already suffered from bad press, a gambling president made for great fodder, and the newspapers did their best to embarrass him. No one was more outraged than Carnegie, who felt as though a son had stabbed him. He cabled Schwab immediately, informing him that the public was shocked and he would probably have to resign. "Serves you right," he concluded unsympathetically, and followed it with a punishing letter that amounted to an excommunication. Schwab was literally heartbroken by the cruel denunciations.[3]

Carnegie also wrote Morgan a letter fraught with sadness, anger, and unforgiving condemnation: "I feel in regard to the enclosed as if a son had disgraced the family. . . . He is unfit to be the head of the United States Steel Co.—brilliant as his talents are. Of course he would never have so fallen when with us. . . . I have had nothing wound me so deeply for many a long day, if ever."[4] Morgan did not heed the call for Schwab's resignation; as far as he was concerned, Schwab's only crime was that he had indulged himself while in the public's eye, instead of behind closed doors.

Now all the gossipers scurried out from the woodwork, and Carnegie heard stories of Schwab's gambling episodes with Bet-a-Million Gates and the rich poker games in Waldorf Astoria suite rooms and at Canfield's casino. Imperiously righteous and exceedingly spiteful, Carnegie smacked Schwab with yet another barbed letter laced with accusation based on hearsay that echoed the Leishman episode years earlier. An emotionally drained Schwab replied he was deeply hurt that "you would be willing to listen to and believe the stories someone has seen fit to tell you. . . . I am no gambler. . . . But be what I may, there is no condition of affairs that would make me even listen to a tale of such a character concerning you. I'd defend you or any of my friends until I knew the truth." Schwab regretted the loss of Carnegie's "confidence and friendship" but concluded the letter by saying, "Do not send for me for I should not come."[5] He had had enough of the preaching.

Once back in New York, Schwab sought Morgan's forgiveness, and as Schwab recalled, "he simply said, 'Forget it, my boy, forget it.' He was, of course, the direct opposite of Carnegie in many ways. Carnegie was little and spare and at times narrow. Morgan was big and human, with human failings and human virtues."[6] When Carnegie summoned Schwab, he refused to visit with his old and spare mentor: "I have not as yet been able to muster up sufficient courage to come to see you. Your very severe letters to me and especially your letter to Mr. Morgan has depressed me more than anything that has ever occurred."[7] For the president of U.S. Steel to be afraid to visit Carnegie said all that was necessary about the force of the latter's character and the contents of the letters. Carnegie, despite growing more expansive in his views as he delved into philanthropy, did remain narrow in many ways, as Schwab contended. He was still too reactionary, too impulsive.

As a result of the scandal, Schwab started suffering bouts of insomnia and nervous irritability. He lost weight, complained of numbness in his extremities, and occasionally fainted. His anxiety was at a dangerous level. Smilin' Charlie resigned as president of U.S. Steel on August 4, 1903. U.S. Steel's common stock price was also spiraling downward. From $55 in 1901, it slumped to $47 in 1902; after a financial panic in 1903, it would eventually crash below $10 the next year. "I see U.S. stocks way down," Carnegie gloated to Dod. "Guess our Bonds are better than both together—I thought they would prove so."[8] When the stock crashed, his tune changed.

Carnegie feared the company wouldn't have the cash to pay the interest on his bonds, and, if so, what would happen to his noble benefactions endowed with those U.S. Steel bonds? He anxiously wrote Elbert H. Gary, chairman of U.S. Steel's executive committee: "More and more I think the managers will see the wisdom of accumulating an enormous reserve fund by holding fast to a large portion of the earnings in prosperous years, so that regular, though moderate, dividends can be maintained."[9] He couldn't help but give advice.

Following Schwab's fall from grace, in the summer of 1902, another trusted aide-de-camp failed Carnegie. Two years earlier, he had hired Hew Morrison to purchase a library of books for Skibo, the canon of western literature, and specifically told him "that I do not wish rare or curious books or elaborate bindings. It is to be a working library, only of the gems of literature."[10] When he discovered Morrison had found the gems but stripped them of their covers, he was livid: "I never said one word to you about changing the bindings of these gems, never. Now I learn that you have spent more money on bindings than the precious gems cost. This is, to my mind, not only a waste of money, which is wrong in itself, but an insult to the great Teachers from whom I draw my intellectual & emotional life—my spiritual existence."[11] For his entire adult life, Carnegie had used literary gems to help define his emotions and himself, and now Morrison, unwittingly, had made a mockery of that. Still, Carnegie loved to browse his library, the collective books giving his soul substance—although he never touched most of the volumes, the spines never cracked.

Other than the library debacle, Skibo was in stunning shape and ready for hordes of visitors. "Fishing, yachting, golfing," Carnegie wrote Morley. "Skibo never so delightful; all so quiet. A home at last. . . . The average American wouldn't like our life at Skibo. There aren't enough of 'other people' to go around—no casinos, nor dancing, and all that. But we love it. . . . I am off to the moors, all alone. Mist on the hills. But I'm a Celt, not a prosaic En-glishman like—well, like a very good fellow I know."[12] When tramping through the moors, Carnegie was like a boy; he never hesitated to lay in the heather and, looking up at the sky, croon o'er an auld Scotch sonnet. At such moments, he was unspoiled by wealth.

Yet the fleeting peace he discovered at Skibo also forced introspection; he would confront his lost youth, regretting that he had missed out on such care-free days as a boy. This was evident when a visitor, T. P. O'Connor, remarked how he envied Carnegie's wealth, and the laird replied, "I would give you all my millions if you would give me your youth." A moment of silence passed, and then Carnegie added a comment that O'Connor never forgot. In a hushed and bitter voice, he said, "If I could make Faust's bargain I would gladly sell anything to have half my life over again."[13]

Carnegie was haunted by the specter of death. When his friend Herbert Spencer lay on his death bed in Brighton, in the fall of 1903, Carnegie sought answers from his master on the most profound of questions, "You come to me every day in thought and the everlasting 'Why?' intrudes."[14] *Why must we die?*

"The why? and the Why? and the Why?" Spencer replied, "are questions which press ever more and more as the years go by; and time passed wholly in bed, save when on occasion, being rather better, my nurse helps me stag-ger to the sofa, gives abundant opportunity for them."[15] The torturous intro-spection rattled Carnegie, particularly Spencer's inability to answer *Why?* With Spencer's health rapidly declining, Carnegie's only solution to answer-ing the big question was to buy a memorial to immortalize his master. On December 8, 1903, Spencer died.

Age didn't appear to be having any ill effects on Carnegie, however. Now in his late sixties, he surprised visitors with his perpetual youth, his bronze face accentuated by white hair, his walk jaunty, and the line of his mouth and chin retaining its hardness.

June and early July were traditionally quiet months at Skibo as Louise re-quired time to settle in, unpack the trunks, and help Margaret adjust. Then came the storm of personalities. Although it overwhelmed his wife, Carnegie was generous with his invitations and enjoyed a large group of mixed com-pany—Dunfermline natives and American capitalists, American Republicans and British liberals—all together at once. There were old friends like Robert Pitcairn, who stayed for a week in July, and John D. Rockefeller Jr. and his wife, Abby, who visited in August. And then there were the "Old Shoes"—that is, those who were as comfortable as an old shoe, like Morley, the Yates-Thompsons, and Andrew White—who never required an invitation. The next summer they were even honored by an unexpected visit from King Edward VII; Buckingham Palace was being refurbished, and he wanted to review the modern amenities installed at Skibo.

While Carnegie was a social creature, his favorite companion at Skibo was Laddie the collie. There were few people he could trust because everyone wanted his money. (Courtesy of the Carnegie Library of Pittsburgh)

At Skibo, two of Carnegie's favorite companions were a pair of collies the family owned and kept at the castle. In photographs taken by Louise—on the stone porch, walking the moors, or picnicking in the heather—the dogs appeared at Carnegie's side more than his guests. Always sanguine about the human race, always needing to be surrounded by adoring people, always gravitating toward one hero or another, Carnegie ultimately knew who his best friend was.

So the parade continued. The bagpipes sounded at 8 A.M. to rouse the guests—a small manifestation of Carnegie's autocracy in the Highlands. Breakfast was porridge, kippers, and scrambled eggs while the organist played Beethoven, Bach, and Wagner—Carnegie's morning devotions. Early each morning Louise would review the plans for the day with the butler: what activities the guests would pursue, what vehicles might be needed, any special meals, who was coming and who was going. Each guest, on his or her first visit, was given a bone spoon embossed with the word *Skibo* in silver letters, and those visitors of note were given the privilege of planting a tree under which was placed a tablet inscribed with the variety of tree, the name of the planter, and the date. Daily activities had not changed much since the days of Cluny, except now there was yachting. With the North Sea accessible, yachting became a favorite of the guests who might sail for a picturesque coastal spot for a picnic or dock at a village and hand out candy to all the children who scurried over to the magnificent boat. On one occasion, when the engines died while they were skirting the coast, Carnegie and his party feared they would be dashed against the rocks. The yachting party—Sir Henry Fowler, Sir Walter and Lady Foster, Reverend Robert L. Ritchie, the pastor of a local parish, and James Bertram, among others—ran up signals of distress, using towels and broomsticks, and a trawler came to their rescue. During the return to port, waves started kicking up and Carnegie's party sought shelter in an empty hold, but they discovered a woman and two ragged children there and chose not to venture in; the yachting party either feared disease or were arrogant. Instead, they covered themselves with one of the trawler's spare sails. After spending the night in the fishing village of Cromarty, they reached Skibo the following afternoon.[16]

For dinner, it remained a tradition for the bagpiper to lead the guests to the table. The estate provided most of its own meat and produce, the heated greenhouses producing the usual vegetables, as well as peaches, apricots, figs, and grapes. Evenings involved a game of billiards, backgammon, or the card game Pit, and conversation might include a debate over which author's work they would bring with them if condemned to live on a desert island. Dante and Shakespeare were invariably at the top. Carnegie considered Dante too gloomy, while Morley thought two-thirds of Shakespeare was padded. Ever loyal, Carnegie consistently chose Spencer, which always elicited a groan—the philosopher was too dry. Regardless of who was visiting, every day the Carnegies would go to Louise's boudoir, where she would play the piano while they sung hymns. It was sacred time, a quiet moment in the day Louise desperately needed.

The Skibo visitors, so many requiring delicate handling, her husband's autocratic demands, and the frantic pace of their lives while trying to raise a young daughter took its toll on Louise, and she suffered from nervous exhaustion. Instead of looking forward to Skibo with pleasure, she began to do so with apprehension. "She has no long Holiday term as you lucky Scotch Professors and I have," Carnegie admitted to St. Andrews principal James Donaldson. "Skibo I call one interrupted playtime. Not quite so for the 'Boss of the show' however—woman's work is never done."[17] Even when on vacation, Louise felt as though the daily demands ran her ragged. "Mr. Carnegie is busy and happy but it is anything restful for me," she wrote to a friend while vacationing in Hot Springs, Arkansas. "Everyone laughs when we say we are here for my benefit, on account of my high color, but what with callers for Mr. C's registered letters, Doctor's instructions in regard to the care he needs, etc., it is hopeless for me to try and rest. Home is a perfect haven of rest in comparison."[18]

Contrary to being upset by her weakness—or weariness, really—Carnegie was understanding and tackled the issue with his usual gusto. On the piece of adjacent property he had purchased from the duke of Sutherland, secluded in the moors, was a stone cottage known as Auchinduich, where they could escape the hordes, the servants, and the chaotic schedule. No visitors were permitted. The cottage required serious refurbishing, but he made certain it was ready that summer of 1904, explaining to Morley: "It is an experiment we are to try. I think a wise one." At first feeling forced into the solitary confine-ment, Carnegie quickly appreciated what it meant to his wife and him. "We must manage somehow that you do not have so much energy in your doings," he told Louise prior to one summer's flitting. "A slow, quiet-going life is needed. I wish we could all go to Auchinduich direct and play at homekeep-ing."[19] It was a rare show of sympathy.

This annual period of relative isolation also afforded him the opportunity to bond with his daughter, Baba, who seldom interacted with her father for any extended length of time. His adoration for her was all too obvious in let-ters to family and friends. To Dod, who now lived in nearby Ospisdale, he wrote: "So sorry I shall miss you . . . Baba fine—in third class now and read-ing a little. She repeated a verse she had learned at school, which I praised highly. Then she said, 'Yes, and that isn't Shakespeare either, Papa. Glad some people could do better than he could.' Mean, wasn't it, to attack my God among men?" He bragged to Morley: "Baba keeps on showing her American precocity. Tells her mother and me names of flowers we don't know. Her latest remark: 'Don't step on the nemophila.' Gardener says he told her the name a few days ago. Madam has been told several times but forgotten it." In another letter to Morley, he proudly announced that eight-year-old Margaret "made golf score of 54 to-day. Her mother beaten badly."[20] And to Richard Watson Gilder, editor of *Nineteenth Century* magazine, "Madam and I very well and Margaret very sprightly. We think she is pro-gressing well. Eats well, sleeps well and keeps us on the go. Her chief work is making up parties who never had a motor ride and taking them as her guests. Already the young socialist crops out. Why should some be rich and others poor? Why do we invite rich people and give them everything when they have plenty at home—and the poor haven't? Questions easier to ask than to answer. Her babble for a day would enrich even the Century columns."[21]

Come August, the Carnegies' hectic schedule resumed. That month in 1902, Carnegie and Morley spent a day cruising on Moray Firth. When they re-turned, Louise ran to greet them, shaking a newspaper with a story announc-ing that King Edward had instituted an Order of Merit and Morley was one of the first twelve members. Of such recognition the two men differed greatly in their attitudes. Morley preferred to avoid pomp and circumstance, while Carnegie, of course, invited it. When the provost of Montrose wanted to give Freedoms to both men together, Morley refused even though his friend pres-sured him, explaining how "double pleased" he would be.[22] As his philanthropy now exploded exponentially, the libraries and Freedoms were being exchanged so rapidly that the London *Times* couldn't keep track. Morley wrote: "How dog-sick you must be of all these meetings, addresses and Hallelujah business. I shouldn't wonder at your longing for Skibo, and what Mr. Smith calls 'the quiet stream of self-forgetfulness'—blessed waters for us all."[23] Knowing his friend's disdain for pomp, Carnegie poked fun at him by purposefully apprising him of every award. When he received the Freedom at Glasgow, he wrote Morley: "I thought you would like the close of my Glasgow speech, but you should have heard the vast audience cheer the sentiment, Civilized Warfare! . . . I never spoke with more abandon. It was great." And he crowed to Dod: "So sorry I shall miss you—but 'engagements' call—I go to Salisbury for 'Freedom' in the morning and next morning North'd—Think I can get over to Dulloch over Wednesday night—six freedoms in six days last week, rather exhausting."[24] Carnegie claimed he never bored of receiving Freedoms because each ceremony was a little different than the last, each town was unique with unique problems, and he enjoyed counseling the various mayors and provosts on their problems. He eventually received fifty-seven Freedoms, a record Winston Churchill was unable to surpass. After accepting his fifty-second, he wrote a friend, bragging that he had fifty-two to Gladstone's seventeen—so maybe, after all, there was a wee bit of ego involved in collecting the Freedoms.

In the fall of 1902, he opened libraries and received Freedoms at Perth, Falkirk, Greenock, and Stirling, making two speeches at each town. The Carnegies also visited the Gladstone family at Hawarden and attended the dedication of St. Deniol's Library, a memorial to William Gladstone. The last stop of the whirlwind tour was the University of St. Andrews. Founded in 1411, it was the oldest institution for learning in Scotland, presided over by Catholic bishops and archbishops until the Reformation and now affiliated with the Presbyterian Church. Carnegie and Louise were to attend the ceremonial introduction of the new Lord Rector, an honorable chair held for three years. It was the right of the students to elect the Lord Rector, and traditionally it was a statesman, an aristocrat, or a man of letters, never a capitalist. *Carnegie was the first.* The students were well aware that he had made the largest donation toward an endowment for educational purposes by an individual when he gave $10 million to establish the Carnegie Trust for the Universities of Scotland, and many of them benefited from the tuition aid. But considering university students were a notoriously independent lot, this was a sign of heartfelt acceptance. When the train pulled in, a fine carriage awaited Louise and him; and when they arrived on campus, the students rushed to greet him. The introduction of the new Lord Rector took place in Volunteer Hall, which was decorated in a blazing mass of red, purple, and gold. After hymns and prayers, Andrew Carnegie, LL.D., was installed in the honorary position. As St. Andrew's principal Sir James Donaldson was reading the rector's oath in Latin, there were jeers and one student yelled, "Oh! Jamie, why don't ye tell Andra what ye're saying?" At the conclusion, when Carnegie uttered "Juro"—"I swear"—there were peals of laughter.[25] They were all well aware of Carnegie's mocking of dead languages, and he laughed with them. The most important event, the rectorial address, followed, and was the only potential source for real scandal.

When Carnegie had submitted a twenty-five-page draft of his speech, then titled "A Confession of Religious Faith," for Donaldson to review, the principal had been startled by what he read. It was a soul-baring essay on a most controversial subject, the replacing of traditional Christian religious creed with a new belief system reflecting Darwin and Spencer. In this confession, Carnegie reflected on his father's rejection of the Presbyterian Kirk and his own rejection of Swedenborg and Channing. He embraced science as a means for explaining the universe, and he concluded by calling on the young men to obey "the judge within" and to concentrate on their duty in this life, not thinking of the next.[26] It was too much for Donaldson, who kindly rejected the heresy.

As a substitute, Carnegie drafted a second speech, "The Industrial Ascendency of the World," on America's uncontested march to industrial supremacy and what Europe must do to respond. He did not discard everything from his first draft, as he opened by imploring the young men to listen to their conscience and quoted one of his favorite Burns lines: "Thine own reproach alone do fear." With little segue, he then endeavored to review the great economic changes the world was experiencing; to the delight of his audience, he determined that "material progress is Britain's child." The nation's destiny lay with America, however, and he briefly promulgated his desire for reunion. As for continental Europe, he contested, it would survive only if the Continent became a political and economic federation based on the American model. He finished with a rousing declaration: Britain was the modern-day Greece, even more than Greece was to its world.[27] The students approved and would elect him to a second term. Another man who appreciated Carnegie's speech was Kaiser Wilhelm II, who read it in the newspapers. The notion of a unified Europe was appealing.

Carnegie returned to Skibo triumphant. "Home again. Great excursion, big crowds, all passed off well," he notified Morley. But to Dod, he gravely admitted he was not the morally superior man others considered him: "Of course St. Andrews was the apex, and there from the beginning to end triumphant. I may turn out quite spoiled—I am not the man they take me for, as none knows better than you except myself. So that keeps me half ashamed of it all and I am humbled."[28] Carnegie had allowed his mask, carved of ego and vanity, to fall, and he revealed himself ever so briefly. The mask was just as quickly replaced, necessary to disguise the self-doubts from not only others, but himself.

Before returning to the United States, the Carnegies toured Switzerland in early November. While there, they ate contaminated food and all three fell sick. Louise and Margaret recovered quickly, but the elder Carnegie did not, so they returned to London to consult a top doctor, who assured them it was nothing more than a bad case of food poisoning. Still, they postponed sailing for New York, and a week later found him confined to a London hotel bed for his sixty-seventh birthday. Louise had to assure the press corps that he was recovering and expected to sail for America in a fortnight. When it came time to return to New York, Carnegie, dreading the grim reaper would harvest him before he sowed all of his seeds, insisted on being accompanied across the Atlantic by a physician. Upon disembarking on December 10, the newspaper reporters crowding the pier noticed he leaned heavily on Louise's arm and that she forcefully permitted them but a few questions. From the dock, the family was driven directly to a newly constructed home on Ninety-first Street, where the badgering reporters again awaited their arrival, peppering Carnegie with questions about his health, his philanthropy, and the landmark New York residence.

To purchase the property, he had used a clever ruse: he hired a broker to quietly buy options on all the plots on the Fifth Avenue block between Ninetieth and Ninety-first Streets and insisted that the expiration date for each be set for the same day. On that day, Carnegie emerged from the shadows and bought them all, catching the various owners by surprise. If they had known he was behind it, prices would have soared. The property, located on a slight rise, prompting Carnegie to dub it "the Highlands," was just across from the great expanse of Central Park, where Louise and he had first ridden together twenty years earlier. As for the Fifty-first Street home, they kept it so his sister-in-law, Lucy, would have a New York headquarters when in town.

The Scottish-Georgian mansion cost $1.5 million to build, not much more than the option money won from Frick, Phipps, and Moore in 1900. So, while on the British side of the Atlantic he was joking that Skibo was a gift from Frick, he also did so on the New York side about his new Fifth Avenue mansion; when Carnegie had a good joke running, he couldn't let go. On reading about the block-long mansion and its extravagant amenities in the newspapers, Dod admonished Carnegie, who replied, "I don't like building any more than you do & am sorry the house grew to a mansion while my thots were on selling out. But I do believe it is far healthier up here & would not return to 51st St. for anything."[29] It was another weak excuse from a celebrated hypocrite.

Schwab's chateau, incidentally, didn't quite reduce this home to a cottage, considering it had sixty-four rooms on six levels, including two gymnasiums—one for Carnegie and one for Margaret—leaded glass windows, an entry canopy by Tiffany, an Aeolian organ with three-story-high pipes in a great oak-paneled hall, private and public living rooms, and servants quarters. It was also the first private residence to have an Otis passenger elevator (Schwab's home wouldn't open until 1904). There were extensive gardens with beds of pansies, daffodils, crocuses, hyacinths, and roses, as well as lilacs, wisteria, dogwood, and rhododendron, and a lead-and-glass greenhouse to nourish the more exotic. A wrought-iron fence around the perimeter protected the property from prying reporters, intruders, and vandalism.

Carnegie's library at his Ninety-first Street mansion served as a war room for his philanthropy and his crusade for world peace. (Courtesy of the Carnegie Library of Pittsburgh)

The iron fence was a prudent decision considering the overzealous authors, the destitute, the cranks, and the crazies who staked out his residence and stalked him for years. The first case to seriously aggravate Carnegie occurred in December 1904, and Roosevelt actually dispatched Secret Service agents to protect him until it was resolved. It began when Carnegie received a unique Christmas present that year: news of an illegitimate daughter. In early December, he learned that a Mrs. Chadwick of Cleveland had convinced her husband and a Cleveland bank officer, a Mr. Reynolds, that she was Carnegie's illegitimate daughter and had access to his wealth. She pedaled notes, one as high as $500,000, claiming they were as good as gold, backed by A. C. himself. Not until Reynolds traveled to New York did he discover the notes were worthless. In the ensuing lawsuits, Carnegie was forced to testify against the insane Mrs. Chadwick, who was locked up.[30]

In spite of the loonies, every day Carnegie would endeavor to walk in Central Park, his favorite course a two-mile loop around the reservoir he often did twice. Savvy reporters would ambush him, but rather than shoo them away, he would take them by the elbow and bring them along on his jaunt, telling one story or another, but never quite giving them the information they wanted. Other times, Carnegie would go into the park and find a strategic bench for people watching. He relished the days he was anonymous and indulged a stranger or two in a story. Most of his time was spent in his war room for benevolence, the modest study off his library at the west end of the house. To inspire himself, the walls were not graced with fine art—although there was a painting of Captain Bill Jones in his bedroom, where he slept on the same brass bed he had as a boy in Allegheny City. Instead, the walls were adorned with mementos and engraved maxims: "The Kingdom of Heaven is within you"; "The Gods send thread for a web begun"; "All is well since all grows better"; and "Thine own reproach alone do fear." The maxims reinforced Carnegie's belief that he was both destiny's child and in control of his own fate; and yet, as he always had, he continued an internal battle with these two forces, predestination and free will. The fact that he didn't sleep with his wife wasn't necessarily unusual; sleeping in his old bed was, as even now he still felt compelled to remind himself of his childhood bout with poverty. By keeping himself tied to the past, he drove himself mercilessly forward.

The first formal dinner to christen the home was for the Carnegie Veterans' Association, a group of about thirty men who'd been partners in Carnegie's company, from Phipps to Schwab to Gayley, and the other juniors. The dinners were held annually, usually in November, and gave the sentimental Carnegie a chance to reminisce with his boys and reconnect with the past. The first was held on December 18, 1902, for which Louise and Margaret elected to leave the house for the evening. When they returned around 10 P.M., they were stuck in the vestibule for about ten minutes on the cold night before the butler finally heard them over the raucous dinner. The spying reporters noted it all for the next day's editions.[31]

At the Highlands residence, Carnegie entertained a gaggle of powerful politicians—the prime minister of Canada, Elihu Root, Theodore Roosevelt, and Woodrow Wilson—as well as celebrity scientists and activists, including Madame Curie and Helen Keller. Of all these, he preferred the company of authors and poets and started hosting an annual Literary Dinner. Richard Watson Gilder helped organize the affairs and recruited John Burroughs, William Dean Howells, and Henry James, among dozens of others. Carnegie and Gilder, who first met at the Author's Club, were initially drawn together by mutual regard for Matthew Arnold and then by shared tastes in literature. As an editor, Gilder was characterized as prissy; Walt Whitman never appeared in his pages, and he considered Twain to be coarse. Gilder wanted to elevate American tastes. Such lofty ideals suited Carnegie, and soon he was playing golf and dining regularly with him.

With straight, serious hair parted flatly in the middle and a full but bland mustache encroaching over his upper lip, Gilder's most prominent feature was his large round eyes, oversized porous disks absorbing all that was around him. Although aware of the egoist Carnegie's faults, he genuinely admired the industrialist for his appreciation of classic literature, which was why he agreed to help with the literary dinners. "A.C. is truly a 'great' man"; he wrote a friend, "that is, a man of enormous faculty and a great imagination. I don't remember any friend who has such a range of poetical quotation, unless it is Stedman. (Not so much *range* as numerous quotations from Shakespeare, Burns, Byron, etc.) His views are truly large and prophetic. And, unless I am mistaken, he has a genuine ethical character. He is not perfect, but he is most interesting and remarkable; a true democrat; his benevolent actions having a root in principle and character."[32]

Carnegie held the inaugural literary dinner in March 1903, to honor Sidney Lee, the renowned Shakespeare scholar visiting from Britain. Handsomely engraved invitations were mailed out to men Carnegie came to call the "Knights of the Cloth." This playful name was given because each guest would pencil his autograph on a cloth placed at his seat, and then Louise would have them embroidered. The guests were often a quixotic bunch typified by John Burroughs, who as a renowned naturalist and author was the antithesis of Carnegie. He was attracted to Carnegie's wealth, but he also never forgot Carnegie's kindness to Walt Whitman. Carnegie had bought many copies of *Leaves of Grass* and made sure Whitman's appearances for readings and talks were sold out.

A guest of honor in 1904 was none other than John Morley, who last visited the United States in 1868. Carnegie had invited Morley to accompany him and the family home to New York after their sojourn at Skibo in time to observe the 1904 presidential election and to deliver the Founder's Day Address at his Pittsburgh institute, as well as tour about and hobnob with important people. In making preparations, Carnegie forwarded a draft of the Founder's Day program to Morley, who couldn't help but mock his friend when he read the proceedings were to open with prayers and blessings: "By the way, I'm both perplexed and scandalized at the discovery that proceedings at Pittsburgh on your Day seem to begin with Invectives of the unseen & unknowable power. I don't mind this sort of thing in places of ancient endowment. It disappoints me to find theological appeals started fresh in your new foundation. I would have *no theology*."[33]

That October, Morley accompanied the Carnegies on the *Celtic*, which arrived to a pack of waiting reporters who accosted Carnegie on the economy and the Russo-Japanese War, which had erupted back in February. On the latter topic, he said he was very sorry for the underdog, Japan, and predicted Russia would win—a complete misreading of the situation, for the Russian fleet would be annihilated in the Battle of Tsushima Strait. Carnegie was expecting to give Morley a grand tour of New York; that is, until the host came down with a severe case of gout and was ordered to bed for a month. It was terribly disappointing, a cruel hoax it seemed, and he began to wonder if his days in New York were limited considering he had been sick most of last winter while there. Gilder took over the chore as tour director. After experiencing the chaos of New York's seamy melting pot, Morley took the train to Niagara Falls to witness the raw beauty "human hands could not control, destroy, or otherwise blemish." From there it was to Pittsburgh, where he delivered the library's Founder's Day address, "Some Thoughts on Progress." "Pittsburgh was an unalloyed pleasure and gratification and interest," Morley wrote his bedridden friend. "It gave me a completely new vision of your work in the world. Of course, I have always known it in a general way; but 1) to see Homestead, its magnitude, order, system and discipline; 2) the Museum, Institute &c. &c.; 3) to hear the position you hold in so great a community, brought all home to me in a way that was at once striking, half-unexpected, and wholly delightful."[34] Carnegie's tainted image had certainly been cleansed in the twelve years since Homestead; as B. C. Forbes noted toward the end of the benefactor's life, "It is as a giver, not as a maker, of millions that Carnegie will live in history."[35]

Once back in New York, Morley was the honored guest of the Knights of the Cloth literary dinner on November 22, hosted by Gilder at the Carnegie residence, while poor Carnegie suffered in his bedroom. The hospitality overwhelmed Morley; as he reflected on his visit, he was a bit kinder than Matthew Arnold, who, in the prior decade, condemned the Philistines. "Materialistic, practical, and matter-of-fact as the world of America may be judged," Morley observed, "or may perhaps rightly judge itself, everybody recognises that commingled with all that is a strange elasticity, a pliancy, an intellectual subtlety, a ready excitability of response to high ideals, that older worlds do not surpass, even if they can be said to have equaled it." Since Arnold's visit, the philanthropy of men like Carnegie, Morgan, and Rockefeller was bringing culture to America and a higher awareness of the fine arts and music.

"House quiet since our swell visitor left us," a melancholy Carnegie wrote to Morley the first week of December. "I am over my gout, but careful these stormy days. . . . Am busy on Watt. . . . It has been a source of great pleasure to me while cooped up." He was writing a biography of James Watt, the Scottish inventor who lived a century ago and pioneered work on steam engines. The book would be published by Doubleday, Page in 1905, and while it didn't become part of the literary canon, it did help Carnegie better understand the roots of the Industrial Revolution that destroyed his father and he himself rode to prominence. He comprehended that it was an unstoppable force that his father had no choice but to submit to.

There was one guest at the literary dinners who was never charmed by Carnegie and was openly contemptuous of his host: Hamlin Garland, a reputable author who ten years earlier had written the scathing piece on Homestead. He complained how pathetic it was that "money could command genius and genius would obey"; at one dinner, he whispered to Burroughs that without his millions Carnegie "would not interest any of us." He was particularly disgusted by the ostentation, from the Scotch pipers leading the guests to the dining room to the butler handing Carnegie note cards to read from. In a bitter mood, Garland observed that Carnegie was in "a false position . . . it was clearly evident that he would have been helpless without the actual text of his commendation." Regardless of how Garland viewed him in light of Homestead, Carnegie knew his Shakespeare, appreciated scholarship, and was never at a loss for words, with or without a text. Garland's other cause for complaint was that each of them had to pay a witty tribute to the guest of honor, and he sarcastically noted his words were his price for a sumptuous meal. While attending one literary dinner, he refused to speak, and to Burroughs he said, "I shall accept no more of these invitations."

"You may not have another," replied Burroughs. He was quite right.[36]

Despite harsh comments by Hamlin Garland, the literary community continued to embrace Carnegie for his genuine interest in literature and his library work. At Mark Twain's seventieth birthday party, held at Delmonico's in November 1905, Carnegie and Louise were two of only half a dozen nonliterary types out of two hundred guests that included the eminent John Burroughs, Willa Cather, Richard Watson Gilder, William Dean Howells, and Emily Post. After a cocktail reception, dinner was served in the Red Room, decorated with potted palms and huge gilt mirrors and air enlivened with the music of the Metropolitan Opera's forty-piece orchestra. The meal included fillet of kingfish, saddle of lamb, terrapin, quail, and redhead duck, washed down with champagne. Claret was served to soften five hours of toasts and speechmaking. Mixing the absurd with humor, Twain amused the audience in advising on how to reach seventy: "I stopped frolicking with mince pie after midnight. . . . I have made it a rule never to smoke more than one cigar at a time. . . . As for drinking I have no rule about that. When the others drink, I like to help. . . . I have never taken any exercise, except for sleeping and resting."[37] At the end of the evening, the group had its photo taken and each guest received a cheap plaster cast of Mark Twain that reportedly did not compliment the author.[38]

As Twain's health deteriorated, Carnegie visited him often in New York. Like much of America, except Gilder perhaps, he appreciated Twain's coarse humor, but he also said that there was more to the "amusing cuss, Mark Twain"—there were his political and social convictions, such as his anti-imperialism work—to be greatly respected. On Twain's death in 1910, Carnegie wrote a moving tribute for the *North American Review*: "Mark Twain gone!—such is the refrain that comes to my lips at intervals. The gaiety of nations eclipsed, the most original genius of our age and one of the sweetest, noblest men that ever lived. Fortunate was I that we met so many years ago upon the ocean and became friends. . . . No man I ever knew could throw such pathos into a single sentence."[39]

Carnegie's relationship with Gilder also strengthened as both men slid into old age. When Carnegie embarked on a tour through Ohio and Canada in April and May of 1906 to collect a basketful of honorary doctorates for his library and educational work, Gilder accompanied him and subsequently provided insight into why he had befriended the capitalist. At the first stop, Kenyon College in Ohio, Carnegie delivered a speech honoring hometown hero Edwin Stanton, Lincoln's war secretary, which included stories that fascinated Gilder. "A.C.'s address was remarkably brilliant and vital this morning, on Stanton whom he knew"; he wrote a friend, "after which we had a reception at the Bishop's and then lunch with the ladies, and speeches. A.C. again was brilliant." Gilder found his friend "dramatic, willful, generous, whimsical, at times almost cruel in pressing his own conviction upon others, and then again tender, affectionate, emotional, always imaginative." Once in Canada, he again reflected on Carnegie:

> A.C. is truly a "great" man, i.e., a man of enormous faculty and a great imagination. I don't remember any friend who has such a range of poetical quotation, unless it is Stedman. (Not so much range as numerous quotations from Shakespeare, Burns, Byron, etc.) His views are truly large and prophetic. And, unless I am mistaken, he has a genuine ethical character. He is not perfect, but he is most interesting and remarkable; a true democrat; his benevolent actions having a root in principle and character. . . . He has greatly grown since I first knew him. As he himself said, his life is now so much more worth while than if he had kept on making money. "I wouldn't have known you and Butler!" "I have changed my views"—I should think so! I remember how he attacked any one who said a good word for higher education, and now he has done more for it from the point of view of moneyed contributions, than any other man who ever lived. He is inconsistent in many ways, but with a passion for lofty views; the brotherhood of man, peace among nations, religious purity. . . .

The affection was mutual, and when Gilder died in November 1909, Carnegie mourned his passing in a letter to Roosevelt: "Gilder's death gives me a keen pang indeed. He went often with me to the golf links at St. Andrews and no one can take his place. One of the whitest souls that ever lived."[40]

Before Gilder and Twain passed on, they joined Carnegie in a venture the newspapers ridiculed as a monstrous, barbarous absurdity. It was an assault on spelling. Melvil Dewey, the New York State librarian who developed the Dewey decimal system, wrote a letter to Carnegie in which he promoted the idea of simplifying the spelling of English words, to make the language more phonetic like Italian or Spanish. Dewey argued that with the simplification, English could then take its place as the world language.[41] How could the race imperialist Carnegie resist? What the usually sentient benefactor failed to notice was that Dewey's letter was dated April 1, 1903—April Fools' Day. Was it coincidence or not?

A group of distinguished Americans—men of letters, politicians, businessmen—organized the Simplified Spelling Board, its mission to "gradually substitute for our present caotic spelling, which is neither consistent nor etimologic, a simpler and more regular spelling." Carnegie, Dewey, Henry Holt, Andrew White, Gilder, scholars at Columbia, Yale, and Oxford, and even Teddy Roosevelt, among others, signed a pledge to adopt the simplified versions of twelve common words, including *altho, catalog, tho, thoro, thru,* and *thruout.* The board created a list of some three hundred words to be reformed, and advocated the dropping of "u" in such words as *labour* and the "e" at the end of a word if it didn't indicate a long vowel, as in *love,* the omission of other useless or silent letters, and using "f" to phonetically render the "gh" and "ph," among other phonetic butchery.

Roosevelt adopted the core changes in all White House correspondence, a major boost to the movement's legitimacy that prompted Carnegie to write him, "The reform of our language may seem a small task compared to the establishment of arbitration instead of war, and so it is, yet the former is no mean accomplishment. If we can ever get our language as fonetic as the Italian and Spanish, as Pioneer you will have rendered no small service to the race. . . . I have just received from the editor of the Worcester (Mass.) Telegram his issue of August 27th, the first paper publisht with the improved spelings—the world moves."[42] Carnegie, who endowed the group with $170,000 and pledged $25,000 a year, went too far in his reforms, according to Twain, who said, "Torquemada had never committed any crime comparable to 'St. Andrew's' treatment of the English language." Twain then admitted that he regretted the scheme "won't make any hedway. I am sory as a dog. For I do lov revolutions and violens." [43] The cynics also ridiculed the "moovment" with glee, an editorial in the *New York Times* noting sarcastically, "The Bored of Speling start with their own names: Androo Karnege . . ." Cartoonists also satirized Roosevelt, one depicting him with pistol in hand taking aim at the dictionary.

Convinced the simplified language would indeed be adopted as the world language—a critical step toward better communication between nations and world peace—Carnegie refused to drop the idea. "The editors who are disposed to ridicule the effort themselves use words, and especially spellings, which their predecessors of a century ago would have denounced as degrading to literature," he said in a rebuttal to the critics. "The editors of the next century will, in turn, marvel at the uncouth spelling of our present scribes." He pointed out that in Queen Anne's reign *spite* was spelled "spighte" and in Queen Elizabeth's time *fish* was spelled "fysshe." Reformed spelling would prove a passing fad for most everyone except Carnegie, who, at times, had unshakable convictions and didn't know when to quit.[44]

Even as Carnegie pushed forward into what he believed to be the more enlightened literary and academic realms, he could not escape his robber baron past. Hamlin Garland's appearance at the literary dinners was merely a vague, ghostly reminder of the Homestead violence compared to a more striking token of remembrance that appeared in 1903. It was a book written by James Bridge, Carnegie's former literary assistant, which was called *The Inside History of the Carnegie Steel Company.* As the title suggests, it was assumed to be a juicy tell-all from an insider with access. In fact, two other insiders were behind the book, Frick and Phipps, who passed along valuable information to Bridge. Not only did Frick and Phipps have an agenda, which was to portray themselves in a better light now that Carnegie had captured all the glory, but Bridge, due to a dispute with Carnegie two years earlier, was seeking revenge.

When Bridge had helped Carnegie with the monumental *Triumphant Democracy* in 1886, Carnegie duly noted in the preface, "I acknowledge with great pleasure the almost indispensable aid received in the preparation of this work from my clever secretary, Mr. Bridge." According to Bridge, Carnegie later gave him the copyright to *Triumphant Democracy* as a reward, which permitted him to issue revisions over the years and reap the profits. But when he was working on a revision in 1901, Carnegie attempted to thwart the project; Bridge, intent on knocking Carnegie down a notch, then decided to write his insider's story.[45] He presented a plethora of useful facts, but there was plenty of bias, too, as he gave more credit to Phipps and Frick and disparaged Carnegie; specifically, in the opening chapters of the story, Bridge claimed Carnegie used underhanded tactics to push out Thomas Miller and to sink his claws into the Kloman business. Although Bridge's prejudices were obvious to many, the book succeeded in creating a media stir and in ripping open old wounds.

When Miller learned the book would be issued that June, he warned Carnegie: "Look out for a scorching in which your humble Scot I fear will take a small part. He expects to sell an edition de luxe of 1000 copies at $25 each. Now don't you go and buy it up for the libraries—I am sure you will enjoy the spice of it all even if you are hard hit by the author—You know Hamlet says 'treat every man as he deserves, and who shall 'scape whipping?'"[46] Too distraught to appreciate Miller's humor and fearing for his legacy, Carnegie couldn't fathom that he was being charged with stealing the very business that had made him the greatest philanthropist the world had ever witnessed, and he immediately asked his friend to publicly refute portions of the story and verify facts. Miller agreed and wrote a letter to the editor of the *Pittsburgh Leader,* clarifying how Carnegie gained control of the Kloman firm. He explained how he had asked Andy to buy him out and stated, "Andy took no advantage of me. He never did; all was strictly straightforward negotiations." Miller then added one criticism: "The only fault I found, and in the business world it is rarely deemed a fault, was that to Andy, Napoleon that he was in business, blunder was worse than crime. He could forgive the one; he could never excuse the other, and we parted as business associates on this line."[47]

The other extremely sensitive point in the book was Homestead. In an attempt to portray Frick more positively, Bridge mercilessly denigrated Carnegie's behavior, so much so that Carnegie called on the weasel Phipps for help. In January 1904, Phipps submitted to an interview with the *New York Herald* in an attempt to clear his old partner. To the question of whether Carnegie acted in a cowardly manner by not returning to the United States during the strike, Phipps confirmed Carnegie's assertion that he had offered to take the first ship home. "I have never known of any one interested in the business to make any complaint about Mr. Carnegie's absence at that time," Phipps concluded, "but all the partners rejoiced that they were permitted to manage the affair in their own way."[48]

Not long after the appearance of Bridge's book, John Milholland, White-law Reid's canvassing manager from the 1892 election who had approached Frick about resolving the Homestead strike, wrote Carnegie explaining he had been asked to write a short piece on Homestead from his perspective, and he was letting him know as a courtesy. There would be nothing discred-itable or slanderous, he assured.

Bertram responded for Carnegie, relaying that his boss had no objection. He then added, "Perhaps you do not know that Mr. Carnegie had received a cable from the Committee of the men, as follows, 'Kind master, tell us what you wish us to do; will do anything for you.'" At first, Milholland was con-fused by the mention of this mysterious cable, but Bertram was referring to the period when union leader Hugh O'Donnell had approached Reid about contacting Carnegie to negotiate an end to the strike. In his mind, Carnegie had twisted the story, fabricating the cable; when Milholland realized this was an attempt at revisionism he was incredulous. "No, I did not know," he replied sharply, "when I cabled you O'Donnell's terms for the settlement for the Homestead Strike, that you had already received a cable from the Com-mittee of the men, whom he represented, begging you to make known your wishes to them. I never imagined such a thing at the time; I am unable to do so now. . . . If you look up your private cable book, I think you will find that you had no such message from the men up to the time I opened correspon-dence with you by O'Donnell's consent and on behalf of the National Com-mittee." There was no such message in the cable book, of course. In his reply, Carnegie lamely quibbled with Milholland over when he first heard from Reid. He did not mention the mysterious cable again.[49]

The Bridge book stirred to life more skeletons in the closet. Captain Jones's son-in-law, D. D. Gage, concluded his family was owed millions more than the paltry sum of $35,000 that was paid them for the patents in the days immediately after the Captain's death, and he wrote Carnegie for restitution. When there was no response to his first letter, he wrote a second demanding the injustice be corrected. Carnegie either refused to accept any responsibil-ity in the matter or couldn't bear to dredge up more memories, so he asked Dod to deal with Gage. Dod did so in a perfunctory manner, claiming Jones was lucky to have gotten even $35,000—a stark contradiction to what Dod had told Schwab, who recalled, "Jones was not very much impressed with his mixer. He seemed to think it was just part of the day's work. But 'Dod'

Lauder, who used to sit in my office and tell me he was 'lending dignity' to my administration, was the man most enthusiastic. He knew its full import and although it was costly—well, it meant revolution in the business."[50]

Carnegie was still haunted by the Frick suit, too, as were his old friends. When Miller visited him at Lucy's Dungeness estate in early 1903, he mentioned that Callie Wilson, the widow of Original Six member John Wilson and once the holder of Frick Coke Company stock, was anxious about Carnegie's being angry with her for not publicly denouncing Frick during the conflict. She was well aware of his demands for absolute loyalty, but Carnegie insisted he was not upset. Miller wrote her immediately: "Yesterday we had a chat when out sailing about your good self which other matters bro't up—He expressed surprise that you think that he felt aggrieved that you did not join him in the Frick matter—He said—'Tell Callie, if you see her, that I have nothing but the warmest feelings for her and for her family, and there is nothing I would not do for her'—So, you see, Andy is all O.K. in his friendship for you."[51]

If there was any question about Carnegie's sentimentality over boyhood friends and alliances, it was put to rest by a chance encounter on the HMS *Baltic* during his 1905 Atlantic crossing. The grandson of Edwin Bennett, whose brother James had met the Carnegie family when they arrived in Pittsburgh almost sixty years earlier, was on board. He was surprised by how approachable the multimillionaire was and immediately wrote his grandfather:

> He [Carnegie] said that several weeks ago his sister [sister-in-law Lucy] had come across a box of old letters which she sent him to go over—among them he found a letter from James Bennett to him telling him what a grand, good woman his mother was and how they had appreciated her services in their trouble—it appears that Mrs. Carnegie went to help out at the home of James Bennett when Mrs. B was sick. . . . Mr. Carnegie is an unusually small man. . . . Has blue eyes and whether it was the subject or not I found him a most unassuming conversationalist—wears a yellow flannel shirt and has a huge rough overcoat with a hood—he is quite spry in his movements and has a good grip—for when he parted he shook hands and said how glad he was that I had given him the chance of talking about his early days.

Still aboard the *Baltic*, Carnegie took the time to write to Edwin Bennett, age eighty-seven, living in Baltimore, and an astonished Bennett replied, "I have your letter of April 30th written in mid ocean. I could scarce realize I was reading a letter from the beloved and renowned millionaire whose unparalleled donations have astonished the world. . . . I well remember your parents and the two boys when they arrived in Pittsburgh, PA. about 60 years ago."[52]

While Carnegie cherished such memories evoked by the chance meeting with the Bennett boy, he, like Shakespeare's Macbeth, still lived with the ghosts of the past. Carnegie would continue to attempt to slay those ghosts with an increasing mania for philanthropy and by breaking from his gospel in pursuing a self-imposed mission to achieve world peace that would bring him into increasing conflict with the Roosevelt administration.

CHAPTER 31

The Peace Mission Begins

If Carnegie could effect cooperative relations between labor and capital with his benefactions, if he could effect greater equality between classes, if he could effect peace between nations, he could achieve internal peace. It was that simple and that difficult. While Carnegie would continue to support libraries and education, among other endeavors, over the coming years he would begin to focus his philanthropy on achieving peace on a grand scale. He would become more embroiled in politics than ever before as he sought to realize the old dream of a reunion with Britain and to prevent increasingly belligerent European colonial powers from declaring war on each other. His peace mission would take time to evolve and straddle the presidencies of Roosevelt, Taft, and Wilson.

A fortuitous opportunity toward achieving that inner peace was realized in 1902. It first presented itself when Colonel Thomas Hunt, owner of the Pittencrieff estate, expressed interest in selling the property to the hometown hero in 1900. The least he would accept, however, was a rich $350,000, twice what Carnegie's solicitor John Ross thought the property worth.[1] At the time of Hunt's initial offer, Carnegie was immersed in his battle with Morgan and had just committed money to build new baths and a gymnasium for Dunfermline. The price tag wasn't justifiable, but the mere possibility of owning the historic property stirred up vivid memories, for a generation ago James Hunt had banned the Morrison family from Pittencrieff due to a dispute with Uncle Thomas, who was always pushing for more public access to the estate. Over fifty years later, James Hunt's son wanted to sell, and it was a chance to settle an old score. Carnegie bided his time, but now in late 1902 he instructed Ross to approach Hunt. They also enlisted the help of Lord Shaw of Dunfermline, whose somewhat clandestine job was to bump into Hunt's solicitor and, in the course of conversation, suggest Hunt sell to Carnegie at a reasonable price. Even treasures were not to be purchased too dear.

On Christmas Eve, Hunt agreed to sell for $225,000, a far better price than he first demanded, and Carnegie trumpeted to Morley, "My new title beats all. I am Laird of Pittencrieff—that's the glen & Palace ruins at Dunfermline, the most sacred spot to me on Earth. Would rather be Pittencrieff than King Edward by a long shot. I laugh at the importance of it. It really tickles me. But Oh-those who have passed should be here to enjoy it. What it would have meant to my Grandfather, Father, Uncles. Ah, Uncle Lauder more than any." To cousin Dod he sent a simple cable that said it all: "*Pittencrieff* is ours."[2]

For Carnegie, it was a small, personal effort toward the death of privilege. Not only could all Morrisons now romp across the historic property, but no longer would the townspeople be limited to visiting it once a year because he intended to present it to the town. Yet it couldn't be a stand-alone bequest; Carnegie desired a grander benefaction. With the recent thrust of his philanthropy having been toward higher education and science, he decided to return to an old path, a path that had led to the Pittsburgh library, museum, and art gallery, the theme of community education and pleasure side by side. He wanted to uplift the laboring masses. Throughout the spring and summer of 1903, Carnegie and a commission he organized worked on what would be called the Carnegie Dunfermline Trust. Ross, who would receive the Freedom of Dunfermline in 1905, was his point man and eventual lifetime trustee. When it came to selecting the trustees, Carnegie wanted a true cross section of society to serve on the board so desires and needs from all walks were voiced. His vision included laborers, artists, lawyers, and even a Catholic priest, but as for the latter Ross protested vehemently—it would be scandalous in the Calvinist stronghold. "All right, Boss," Carnegie agreed. "Exit Holy Father, but I like to keep in with one who can really grant absolution. It may be handy someday."[3] The trustees numbered fifteen, and in the first week of August 1903, the laird summoned them to Skibo, the first of annual meetings held there.

Carnegie's first order of business was to transfer $2.5 million in bonds for the endowment, "all to be used in attempts to bring into the monotonous lives of the toiling masses of Dunfermline more sweetness and light; to give to them—especially the young—some charm, some happiness, some elevating conditions of life which residence elsewhere would have denied; that the child of my native town, looking back in after years, however far from home it may have roamed, will feel that simply by virtue of being such, life has been made happier and better. If this be the fruit of your labors, you will have succeeded; if not, you will have failed."[4] To bring "sweetness and light," he exhorted the trustees to experiment freely with various social programs, to discard projects just as freely, to be willing to make mistakes, and to keep in touch with the masses and constantly aim to improve their tastes.[5] It was a flash of liberal laissez-faire. The trust also took over management of Carnegie's gymnasium and public baths, as well as Pittencrieff. The Hunt's old estate house was converted into a museum for displaying the processes of area industries; the property's gardens were used for teaching horticulture; playgrounds, a theater, and a pavilion were built. Some sixteen hundred people might attend a Saturday evening concert, and almost daily in the summer, pipe or brass bands or a symphony orchestra took the stage.

The trust provided more than just entertainment to break the monotony Carnegie presumed to exist (and probably did in the Auld Grey Toun). At the time, there were no laws enforcing the medical examination of schoolchildren, so the trust championed and performed the duty through its school clinic. It also established a College of Hygiene and Physical Training, as well as a department of civics to raise the tone of citizenship and teach young people heroic qualities; a craft school for woodcarving, metalwork, metal enameling, and jewelry; and Louise opened a Women's Institute to teach embroidery, cookery, and such things. The trust had a tremendous impact on a modest town like Dunfermline, and programs like medical examination for children truly lifted civilization up a notch.

The year Carnegie agreed to purchase Pittencrieff, the world appeared to be engulfed in violence and wars. So far, Carnegie had avoided any major benefactions in the name of peace, such an amorphous goal being beyond the parameters of his gospel. Even when in 1899 his good friend Andrew White had passed along the noble suggestion of providing for a temple of peace to house a court of arbitration and an international law library at The Hague, Carnegie demurred. For all his idealistic faith in arbitration, Carnegie was simply unsure of the value of such a temple, and he also questioned why he should take on the burden because it appeared to be government's responsibility.

Now Carnegie began to reconsider his position as he absorbed the current military activity around the world. Granted, America's bloody campaign against Filipino nationalists had just ended at a trifling cost of 4,200 American dead and 2,800 wounded, with about 20,000 rebels killed with another estimated 200,000 dead from disease and famine and other side effects of the war. But then the United States had immediately become embroiled in a revolution in Panama, where the nationals were fighting occupying forces from Columbia. The Boer War had also ended. But then the British started slaughtering Somalis armed with spears.[6] Disgusted by his native country's behavior, Carnegie publicly denounced Britain at a dinner hosted by Collier's Weekly at the Metropolitan Club in honor of war correspondents. "The killing of men by men under the name of war," he pronounced, "is the foulest blot upon humanity to-day. . . . We have made little progress in the path of genuine civilization, as long as we can find no better substitute for the settling of international disputes than the brutal murder of one another."[7] The ongoing hostilities involving the United States and Britain were significant catalysts in changing how Carnegie viewed the relationship between philanthropy and peace between nations.

Meanwhile, White and his friend Frederick Hols, who had served as secretary for the American delegation to the 1899 Hague Conference, continued to drop hints to Carnegie about building a peace temple for an international court of arbitration and library. (Czar Nicholas, concerned about the escalating military buildup in Europe, had called for the Hague Conference to discuss disarmament and peaceful means for settling conflict. The only act of substance was to move forward on creating the Permanent Court of Arbitration at The Hague.) In early 1902, it was Hols who applied the pressure to build the temple for the court; and again, although Carnegie considered himself the man for the task, he hesitated. Foremost, he feared the tribunal would not garner the respect it deserved if he stepped forward with the money. Also, the time was still not opportune, as he wrote Hols: "Please let the idea rest for the present. Let us get our English speaking race at peace first. This forcing ourselves upon unwilling peoples & shooting resisters down is so incongruous with the Hague Peace idea that neither Britain nor America seems in place— doing right (Hague) with one hand and (Filipinoes & Boers) wrong with the other. I am not going to think of it at present."

By the summer of 1902, Carnegie had reconsidered his position and invited White to Skibo to discuss a temple of peace. They golfed, fished, walked the moors, and debated every topic except the very one behind White's visit as Carnegie toyed with him by letting the dramatic tension build. As guest, White knew better than to initiate the discussion. On his last full day there, his host suggested yet another fishing expedition, which didn't bode well for White in winning any commitment from Carnegie because he made it abundantly clear: "I never talk while I fish." White recalled ruefully that he didn't catch a fish all day. "Then, that very evening—the last of our stay—as the men, after smoking, entered the drawing room to join the ladies, Mr. Carnegie, with whom I happened to be walking at the time, somewhat ahead of the others, suddenly turned to me and said: 'Now, as to that Peace Palace which you have been writing me about—I'll build it.'"[8] It was the same game Carnegie had played with Sir Swire concerning the Keighley library, a game he found humorous at the expense of others.

Slightly contrary to White's recollections, the actual sequence of events was that initially Carnegie agreed to ante up $250,000 for a library of international law for The Hague, and then offered to provide the funding for a modest peace temple on the condition that the Dutch government request it. This last caveat served two purposes: it satisfied Carnegie's ego, and it made the temple more acceptable to other governments and the public because it had been *requested*.[9] It still took an interminable amount of time—as most diplomacy does—for the temple to be realized. Not until October did he write the deed for a $1.5 million gift, in which he stated his belief that the Permanent Court of Arbitration was the most important step yet toward abolishing war; and not until the spring of 1903 did he establish the endowed trust.[10] It took another two years to agree on a site; in 1907 the cornerstone would be laid; and in 1913 the temple would be dedicated. In the interim, there would be a number of battles over it.

"The gift which fairly takes my breath away is your provision for the Temple of Peace," a long-denied White exulted in April 1903. "That will result undoubtedly in saving hundreds of thousands of lives. It is an immense thing, to have made such a provision."[11] The gift was a fraction of what would be another fantastic year of beneficence, with the London *Times* estimating that Carnegie gave $21 million in 1903 versus Rockefeller's $10 million.[12] For all the attention being lavished on the philanthropy and the Permanent Court of Arbitration at The Hague, Europe continued to slide pell-mell toward war. As the political situation became more dire, Carnegie would increase his efforts, desperate to be mankind's savior.

At the very time Carnegie was handing over the funds for his temple of peace, the United States and Britain became entangled in another dispute over Venezuela, a sequel to the 1895 conflict. The current conflict erupted when Britain, along with Germany and Italy, imposed a naval blockade on Venezuela because the country was not paying its debts, which outraged the other South American countries, especially when the United States didn't invoke the Monroe Doctrine. "I dread the Venezuelan trouble," Carnegie wrote William T. Stead. "A spark and there's no telling the end. Occupation of territory on this continent by European powers, even temporary, may result in war."

Carnegie's fears were confirmed when, ignoring Roosevelt's call for arbitration, on December 9, 1902, British and German boats sailed into La Guaira, seized all Venezuelan warships, and bombarded Puerto Cabello. In hopes of easing the heightened tensions between the United States and Britain, Carnegie cabled Morley to warn him that Prime Minister Balfour was playing with fire, and he suggested the cable be passed along to Balfour. According to Morley, the cable did indeed give the British cabinet the right cue. Sir Henry Campbell-Bannerman, who would succeed Balfour as prime minister, concurred: "I saw the strongly worded message you sent to John Morley regarding this ridiculous but most dangerous Venezuelan folly of our Government, and I cannot but believe that your warning had its effect on the Cabinet, to whose members it was shown." Even Prime Minister Balfour expressed his obligations to Carnegie for the telegram, and promised there would be no invasion of Venezuela as Britain fully respected the Monroe Doctrine. Carnegie shuttled down to Washington and shared the letters with Roosevelt and Secretary of State Hay, and the conflict was resolved shortly.[13] While Roosevelt and Hay resented his meddling, on occasion Carnegie did play a pivotal, yet unappreciated, role as messenger on the political stage.

After his successful involvement in the latest Venezuela conflict, reinforced greatly by the letters from Campbell-Bannerman and Balfour, Carnegie started considering himself one of the few who could accomplish anything at all toward peace. He assumed a Christ-like complex in promoting the brotherhood of man as his talk of an English-speaking race reunion and promotion of arbitration eventually evolved into an all-out campaign to save the world from war. The first years of the twentieth century should have heralded a golden age, Carnegie knew, considering the scientific work of the institution in Washington; the appearance of motorcars, making man ever more mobile; and the work of the Wright brothers. To think, in 1903, man would fly with the birds. But what of Icarus? Had we become too greedy for knowledge and material gain? Was humankind's insatiable appetite leading to war after war?

In early 1904, Carnegie continued his campaign for peace, although, inspired by a tragic event, it took a slightly different course than expected. It was a bitterly cold Monday morning, January 25, 1904, when at 8:15 a massive explosion rocked the coal-mining town of Harwick, twelve miles north of Pittsburgh. A small amount of gas had ignited in a shaft and the entire mine exploded in a chain reaction, killing most of the employees. Rescue parties began to arrive from the surrounding area. Selwyn M. Taylor, a Pittsburgh mining engineer, and a small crew descended the main shaft and found a seventeen-year-old at the bottom, badly burned but alive. Hoping others were alive, Taylor advanced into the mine, only to become asphyxiated by gas. He was survived by a wife and a stepson. The next day a coal miner, Daniel A. Lyle, also working with a search party, ventured farther than others dared into the mine, and he, too, was overcome by gas and died, leaving behind a wife and five children. They were but 2 among 181 who were killed in what was one of the worst mining disasters of the twentieth century.

"I can't get the women and children of the disaster out of my mind," Carnegie, who was often taunted by the clarity of images emblazoned on his conscious, wrote to a friend, and he matched the $40,000 in public donations for relief efforts, as well as commissioned two gold medals to commemorate Selwyn M. Taylor and Daniel A. Lyle for their surviving families. The two men's deaths made him realize that heroism didn't require an act of war, and if he could just demonstrate to the country, to the world even, how heroic one could be in times of peace, perhaps young men wouldn't be so likely to join the blood thirst as soon as there was a chance to prove their manhood in war: "Not seldom are we thrilled by deeds of heroism where men or women are injured or lose their lives in attempting to preserve or rescue their fellows; such the heroes of civilization. The heroes of barbarism maimed or killed theirs."

Thus, the Harwick mine disaster inspired him to found the Carnegie Hero Fund Commission to reward acts of heroism with a medal and money. He wasted no time. The deed was completed and signed on March 12; he gave $5 million in U.S. Steel bonds; and he appointed a twenty-one-member commission to administer the fund. Sometimes it was the commission that read of a heroic act in the papers, other times it was brought to their attention by those directly affected; either way, an application for the reward had to be on their desk within three years of the incident. The commission then investigated thoroughly before a medal and a monetary reward were forthcoming. On one side of the medal was a profile of Carnegie (who was smart enough not to demand his name on libraries, but used it and his image liberally with his trusts and foundations), on the other the name of the hero and his courageous act. There was also a quote from the Bible, John 15:13: "Greater love hath no man than this, that a man lay down his life for his friends." As for the money, it varied depending on the need and was paid either monthly as a pension or in one lump sum.

Carnegie was extremely proud of what he considered to be a unique project—his pet—and promoted it with passion. As he told a friend, it was folly to waste time upon worrying about God and Heaven, for we "have only duties in this life, let us attend to these—as the only action approaching worship. By the way I send you Hero Fund, my pet child—Here's worship of Humanity in its highest form—Heroism."[14] In touting it to John Ross, he also gave a glimpse of a painful childhood memory: "It is the fund that may be considered my pet. I used to hate that word, becaus the children at school cald me 'Martin's pet,' but now I like it."[15]

Cynics criticized the Hero Fund immediately, claiming it would spawn would-be, misguided heroes seeking reward and result in more tragedy. "I do not expect to stimulate or create heroism by this fund," Carnegie responded vigorously, "knowing well that heroic action is impulsive; but I do believe that, if the hero is injured in his bold attempt to serve or save his fellows, he and those dependent upon him should not suffer pecuniarily." Rewards were most often given for rescues from drowning or burning buildings or from automobile and industrial accidents. Eventually, the cynics were drowned out; and by December 1907, Carnegie could write Morley triumphantly: "Our Hero pension has triumphed, its last annual report swept the Country. . . . I don't believe there's a nobler fund in the world."[16] It was so noble in his estimation that he gave $10,540,000 to create eleven hero foundations, in the United States, Great Britain, France, Germany, Denmark, Norway, Sweden, Netherlands, Belgium, Italy, and Switzerland.

While Carnegie considered it an original inspiration, when Peter Cooper had founded Cooper Union he wanted $500 appropriated each year to be awarded to a woman who exhibited great heroism or sacrifice for humanity.[17] Carnegie may or may not have been aware of this—it was on a much smaller scale than what he had in mind, in any case—but just that March he had given an address at a memorial honoring Peter Cooper, saying of his predecessor in philanthropy: "He pointed the way that all millionaires should follow."[18] As he had in business, Carnegie remained adept at borrowing ideas and expanding on them until they reached heroic proportions.

In his mania for peace, Carnegie even allowed a family scandal to play out in the press, which provided him the opportunity to prove his goodwill toward all. Initially unknown to the public and decisively suppressed by Lucy Carnegie, her daughter Nancy was married to the family's coachman, James Hever, a widower and father of two. They had eloped in 1904, causing the estrangement of Lucy and Nancy, and in April 1905, the newspapers got hold of the story. Now that the marriage was public, Carnegie gave them $20,000 as a wedding gift in a show of support and defended Nancy in the newspapers: "Mr. Hever is not rich, but he is a sober, moral well doing man, and the family would rather have such a husband for Nancy than a worthless duke." Carnegie was adept at twisting almost any situation to serve his agenda; in this case, he used a family elopement to swipe at the privileged class. Unable to stomach family infighting, he set about playing arbitrator; but Lucy, as he knew she would be, was stubborn. She had grander designs in mind for her children, and eventually her branch of the Carnegie family would marry into the Rockefellers.

Not until October did he negotiate—in public—peace between Lucy and Nancy. As part of the settlement, he presented his niece and her husband, who now had a baby in addition to his two children, with a hundred-acre estate on Long Island.[19] Always quick to intertwine his life with the nation's, Carnegie noted with particular satisfaction that while he was settling the family conflict, Roosevelt mediated the peace treaty between Japan and Russia, which was signed on September 5.

While Carnegie slowly became more vested in peace work, he didn't abandon his gospel. In 1905, he returned to his central theme of planting seeds for higher education. As of 1904, his total benefactions were just over $100 million, and Carnegie still had more than $200 million to dispense with—it was time to accelerate the munificence, it was time for a grand gesture.[20] It would result in a benefaction the ever-sarcastic and caustic Mark Twain actually thought Carnegie deserved a halo for, one that would provide the Scotsman with another chance to assuage any guilt he felt in forsaking his radical ancestors. It would also create the greatest public furor since his retirement.

The canny president of MIT, Henry Pritchett, had planted the idea while visiting Skibo in 1904, when, in discussing the American educational system, he pointed out that one of its major faults was the poor salaries and absence of pensions. Now Carnegie wasn't going to augment salaries, but because he had already created the Relief Fund, a pension plan for teachers at universities, colleges, and technical schools was an idea to which he could become easily attached. It was a natural extension of his work, especially considering he had already supplied buildings, facilities, equipment, grants for research, and tuition aid through other endowments. In April 1905, he created the Carnegie Foundation for the Advancement of Teaching, appointed Pritchett president, and signed on a host of brilliant and devoted trustees, including Nicholas Murray Butler, president of Columbia; Woodrow Wilson; banker Frank Vanderlip; Robert Franks; and his nephew, T. Morris Carnegie, among others. He endowed the pension fund with $10 million of his 5 percent bonds and he added $5 million the next year as the foundation extended the pensions to widows of college professors. (Schwab, busy rehabilitating himself as president of Bethlehem Steel, was in Carnegie's library when the deed was signed and recalled that immediately afterward his mentor, still an avid penny-pincher, looked up, realized unnecessary lights were on, and turned them off.)

In the deed letter, Carnegie included a most interesting but not entirely unexpected clause: no aid was to be given to sectarian institutions. There would be nothing for schools under control of a sect that decreed its trustees, officers, faculty, or students must be members of a particular church.[21] This clause was untouchable; and Pritchett, for one, agreed wholeheartedly with it. To ensure its enforcement, a questionnaire was designed to weed out those sectarian colleges and universities, as well as those that were financially unstable or academically too weak. Initially, it was sent to 627 institutions; of the 421 replies, only 52 were accepted. An immediate cry of dissent erupted from the hallowed halls of academia. Those presidents who desired inclusion but whose schools were rejected protested, as did Carnegie's detractors who disdained the intrusion of a capitalist into their sacred realm. It was a replay of the Scottish universities trust. Representing the opposition were statements by a renowned historian at the University of Pennsylvania, Dr. John Bach McMaster, who declared he didn't want to be patronized or pauperized by Carnegie.

When William Jennings Bryan, an alumnus and a trustee of Illinois College, learned his school had been accepted, he fought participation; and when the school's president took the pensions, he resigned. "Our college cannot serve God and Mammon," Bryan wrote in his resignation letter. "It cannot be a college for the people and at the same time commend itself to the commercial highwaymen who are now subsidizing the colleges to prevent the teaching of economical truth. It grieves me to have my alma mater converted into an ally of plutocracy, but having done what I could to prevent it, I have no other resource than to withdraw from its management."[22] Bryan's position was expected—he and Carnegie had had a nasty falling out years earlier—and "Our college cannot serve God and Mammon" became the popular cry among critics.

College and university presidents and provosts generally differed with the likes of Bryan. They believed the foundation would rightfully reward faithful teachers who had been unable to save for retirement and stimulate scholarly work since teachers wouldn't be distracted by the specter of future destitution. Nicholas Murray Butler considered it Carnegie's most important benefaction yet because not just the teachers benefited.[23] Some of the rejected schools raised their admission and academic standards to qualify in the mad scramble for pension money, thus benefiting students and the educational system as a whole. The Carnegie Foundation also took an unexpected turn, morphing into a form of bribe for a college or university to change its charter by eliminating any sectarian connections or requirements. Once Carnegie perceived this unintended effect, he played it the hilt to create a secularization revolution. As he explained to one university president, in his travels around the world he had discovered that denominationalism resulted in destructive competition as one sect condemned the other.[24] He refused to compromise for even the president of the United States.

With Northwestern being one of the rejected schools, President Abram Harris turned to Theodore Roosevelt, who then pleaded the university's case. The stubborn Scotsman refused to bend, and in reply to Roosevelt he praised the foundation for "doing great work, rooting out denominational control in colleges. . . . Like yourself, we are depending less and less upon the doctrine of grace and more upon the doctrine of works, not what a man believes but what he does, which was the great doctrine laid down."[25] Although Carnegie was rapidly approaching his own mortality, he took no solace in the prospects of an afterlife; rather, he was more convinced than ever that doing good deeds during life on earth was all that mattered. He was also wholly embracing his radical heritage by condemning the church in his continuing search for internal peace. Defending the foundation would soon be unnecessary because it was widely embraced. A century later it was still providing pensions and other benefits under the name of Teachers Insurance and Annuity Association.

Carnegie's creation and management of trusts and foundations continued to impress John D. Rockefeller. On encountering a Pittsburgh institute trustee during a transatlantic crossing aboard the *Amerika*, the oil baron drilled him with questions about the thinking and the mechanics behind various philanthropic endeavors, which the trustee then relayed to Carnegie:

> He placed his hand on my shoulder and, elevating his forefinger, said in a most impressive way: "I want you to tell Mr. Carnegie—for I cannot tell Mr. Carnegie anything myself—never to make a verbal promise. I have had much embarrassment by men telling me that I had promised them so and so when I had never meant to make any promise at all."
>
> Mr. Rockefeller was particularly solicitous in inquiring how you felt when men misunderstood you or when newspapers enlarged upon incorrect motives, and I told him that you relied upon your work to vindicate you without giving heed to anybody's rash judgment.
>
> "I wish" he said, "that Mr. Carnegie and I could call others into this splendid field of work. It is the happiest life a man can lead."[26]

Carnegie was a pioneer in foundations, to be followed by Rockefeller and Henry Ford, among others, and his pension work is still lauded a century later.

Carnegie and Rockefeller both shared a detestation for the aristocracy and a love for the underdog. A meritocracy was their preference, and this attitude spilled over into their support for smaller educational institutions and, in

Carnegie, walking next to Woodrow Wilson, was honored at Princeton University for giving the school a lake in 1906. Wilson, then president of the university, would have preferred cash. (Courtesy of the Carnegie Library of Pittsburgh)

particular, schools for minorities. For Carnegie, there was no giving to already well-endowed institutions. Even when his friend Andrew White, who was back at his post as Cornell's president, had requested monetary support, Carnegie shamed him for begging and refused to give. Naturally, White, who didn't consider it begging, took offense: "Doubtless you are 'bored to extinction' with requests and suggestions, and my letter may have been a sort of 'last straw.'"[27]

Woodrow Wilson, who was president of well-endowed Princeton University, made his bid, too. Hoping to impress the capitalist, he neatly listed Princeton's needs, from endowing a new graduate school to hiring fifty tutors—or "reference librarians," as he called them—to push the undergraduates. At Wilson's invitation "to see Princeton from the inside," Carnegie toured the campus and determined the school needed a lake for rowing.[28] It wasn't on Wilson's list, but the titan insisted. At the lake's dedication in December 1906, the students cheered while Wilson ruefully commented, "We asked for bread and you gave us cake."[29] At least the lake was more than White received.

In his dedication speech, Carnegie said he hoped the lake would promote water sports while discouraging football, which to him was another manifestation of raw blood thirst and war. The man who once manufactured projectiles couldn't stomach boys and men groveling in the dirt like animals.[30] Sport, according to Carnegie, should be educative and virtuous according to Victorian sensibilities, not a commercialized bloody affair in Roman coliseum-like arenas.

As with Cornell and Princeton, Carnegie now also considered the Pittsburgh area to be well endowed. When the Pittsburgh College for Women fell on hard times and would cease to exist if the trustees couldn't raise $150,000, they approached Carnegie for help, but he refused, explaining, "I think that I have already done enough for Pittsburgh from an educational standpoint. Pittsburghers now have an opportunity of showing whether or not they are able to help themselves."[31] But there was another motive behind his decision. The Carnegie Technical Schools (later Carnegie Mellon University) had finally opened, including the Margaret Morrison College for Women, and competition with a school named after his mother wouldn't be tolerated.

When Stanford president David Starr Jordan solicited funds, Carnegie demurred, explaining, "The colleges I have been helping for two years, already about two hundred in number, do not average more than $200,000 to $250,000 in endowments and after deep consideration, I decided it was better to help smaller colleges than larger ones."[32] He eventually gave almost $20 million to those modest U.S. colleges and universities.[33] One of his pet schools was Tuskegee Institute in Tuskegee, Alabama, the black vocational school founded by Booker T. Washington, whom he greatly respected because Washington espoused helping one's self.

Carnegie's interest in blacks and attempts to uplift them was genuine. In the spring of 1906, he traveled to Tuskegee for the school's silver jubilee. At the ceremony, he delivered a closing address that while lavishly praising the school's accomplishments, demonstrated his omnipresent race consciousness: "The colored race having done this here and in several other similar colleges and schools in widely scattered parts of the South, proves that the whole race is capable of being eventually elevated through education to a high state of general civilization."[34] Afterward, Washington was proud to say that Carnegie not only bought shoes from Tuskegee's shoemaking department, but wore them. Of slightly more importance, he gave $620,000, including a library, to the school, making him the largest single contributor.[35]

Once made aware that blacks in the South would be barred from entering his libraries due to segregation, Carnegie further demonstrated his concern for them by offering libraries specifically for them in Chattanooga, Tennessee, and other southern cities. And when Carnegie was given the honor to speak before the Edinburgh Philosophical Institution in 1907, he delivered an address titled "The Negro in America." Three years later, he was still helping black schools even though there was little public interest and little recognition compared to giving a large benefaction to a Harvard or a Columbia. He donated $200,000 to the Lincoln Institution and $400,000 to Berea College, and gave annually to Hampton and Tuskegee.[36] And he supported Booker T. Washington, whom he considered a "self-sacrificing hero" and a "rare privilege" to know.[37] When Washington scheduled a tour of Britain, Carnegie touted his accomplishments to a friend there, unabashedly calling him "the most remarkable man living today, taking into account his birth as a slave and his position now as the acknowledged leader of his people. . . . I should think he would be a drawing card. He has recently made a triumphal tour thru the Southwestern States, being received by white and black—no hall big enough to hold his audiences."[38]

Supporting education for blacks made Carnegie feel ever-more enlightened, more tolerant of all races, and more convinced that his mission in life was to be an apostle of goodwill among men. Therefore, the Carnegie Foundation for the Advancement of Teaching was his last great benefaction to education. It was time to take a more prominent stage where he could play savior as the arms race in Europe continued unabated.

While always quick to condemn war and promote arbitration, it was his October 17, 1905, rectorial address at St. Andrews that marked his ascension as a recognized leader of the peace movement. That was the day Carnegie was credited with the first public call for nations to form a League of Peace. (The concept was, however, on many statesmen's minds, including that of British prime minister Sir Henry Campbell-Bannerman, who had used the phrase "League of Peace" earlier in the year.) To make his case against war, Carnegie, a preacher completely absorbed in his fevered sermon, quoted Rousseau, Homer, Euripides, Thucydides, Andocides, Isocrates, Sallust, Virgil, Seneca, Plutarch, and Luther, among many other authors, philosophers, and theologians, including his friend Morley. The quotes were pithy and hard-hitting, such as this one from Rousseau: "War is the foulest fiend ever vomited forth from the mouth of Hell." And he charged the students "to adopt [George] Washington's words as your own, 'My first wish is to see this plague of mankind, war, banished from the earth.'"[39] The speech was filled with such vivid imagery and notable phrases that Baron d'Estournelles de Constant, head of the Society for International Conciliation, ordered several hundred thousand copies of the speech printed in thirteen languages to distribute throughout the world.[40]

Carnegie's speech was a reaction to the fact that Europe had recently come to the brink of war when Germany challenged France's domination of Morocco, with the kaiser publicly supporting Morocco's independence. Fearing Germany's growing military power, Britain and France entered into a treaty, the Entente Cordiale, which recognized each other's sovereignty and committed them to defend each other against any German aggression. The longtime antagonists were finally allies. Three years later, Russia would join the two in the Triple Entente and Germany would be completely isolated. The same month of his St. Andrews speech, Carnegie's essay "Anglo-French-American Understanding" was published in the *North American Review*. He lavishly complimented England, France, and the United States, but he appeared to work hard, almost too hard, to foster good feelings among the three nations.

His unrelenting public invectives on peace annoyed Roosevelt, an assumed ally in the work for peace. "I have tried hard to like Carnegie," Roosevelt wrote Whitelaw Reid shortly after the St. Andrews address, "but it is pretty difficult. There is no type of man for whom I feel a more contemptuous abhorrence than for one who makes a God of mere money-making and at the same time is always yelling out that kind of utterly stupid condemnation of war which in almost every case springs from a combination of defective physical courage, of unmanly shrinking from pain and effort, and of hopelessly twisted ideals. All the suffering from Spanish war comes far short of the suffering, preventable and non-preventable, among the operators of the Carnegie steel works, and among the small investors, during the time that Carnegie was making his fortune." Roosevelt had no respect for businessmen like Carnegie who ventured outside of their realm and believed he was unfit to speak on matters of war and peace.[41] However, Roosevelt found Carnegie and his British connections useful tools to further his agenda, so he kept up the politically astute charade of playing friend. It was, in part, the case of the young and vital forty-seven-year-old president thinking he could take advantage of the doddering seventy-year-old do-good philanthropist.

The idealistic world Carnegie inhabited sorely tested Roosevelt's patience, too, as was the case when Secretary of State Hay negotiated arbitration treaties with ten countries, all modeled on the British-French Entente Cordiale. The Star-Spangled Scotchman was exuberantly active in encouraging the negotiations and relaying information to and from his British contacts; this was the first step toward the reunion he had been dreaming of. Meanwhile, a wary Roosevelt ensured each participating country's national sovereignty and honor was not compromised. Even so, during the ratification process, the Senate, fearing any constrictions and breaking sharply with Roosevelt, amended the treaties to the point where they were essentially useless, characterized as "empty shells." Roosevelt was furious and refused to sign them. Carnegie fervently urged him to sign them anyway: "Such is the opinion of all of us who have labored for these treaties from Ex-Sec'y Foster down—No one in half a million will ever note the amendments. . . . We shall have the substance and this is what you are after."[42]

Humiliated by the Senate, a spiteful Roosevelt didn't see it that way: "I do not agree with you about the treaties. I am not willing to go into a farce."[43] Carnegie was deeply disappointed and frustrated; at times it appeared civilization would take one step forward, only to take two backward. It was also not the last time the two egoists butted heads over national policy.

Having endorsed disarmament since the first Hague Conference, Carnegie was overjoyed when, on the heels of the failed arbitration treaties, an apparently enlightened Roosevelt promised to him that "from now on I do not wish to increase our navy beyond its present size."[44] This conciliatory decree reopened the communication valve, and that summer of 1906 a gush of correspondence poured forth from Scotland. On July 26, Carnegie informed the president that he had passed along the note on not expanding the navy to Morley who, in turn, showed it to the prime minister. It was well received, and the British cabinet actually hinted at a willingness to reduce its military forces. A week later, the president, resting at the family's summer home at Oyster Bay, New York, replied, "Your letter is most interesting. Do you know, I sometimes wish that we did not have the ironclad custom which forbids a President ever to go abroad? If I could meet the Kaiser and the responsible authorities of France and England, I think I could be of help in this Hague Conference business; which is now utterly impossible, and as facts are, unadvisable." He also dredged up regrets over the prior year's failed arbitration treaties and criticized the peace activists: "I have always felt that our special peace champions in the United States were guilty of criminal folly in their failure to give me effective support in my contest with the Senate over the arbitration treaties." The peacemakers had wanted too much, were too radical, Roosevelt believed, and a reactionary Senate had found their position so repulsive that it reduced the treaties to nothing more than pieces of paper. It was an indirect shot at Carnegie.

Still, considering himself more useful than he was, Carnegie continued to funnel information on British political positions to Roosevelt. "Sir Edward Grey, Foreign Minister, has read what Secretary Root sent me and is full of sympathy with you," he wrote from Skibo in late August. "Mr. and Mrs. Morley have been with us for two weeks. Mr. and Mrs. Bryce [the Irish Secretary] are now here. Never was there a British Cabinet so keenly favorable to peace and so anxious for cooperation with America, and especially with you; you have won their confidence." He went on to suggest to Roosevelt that he should make a statement in support of arbitration, which would then, hopefully, act as an embryo for a League of Peace. Using the very argument White had once used with him to convince him to part with money for a national university, Carnegie said, "The man who passes into history as the chief agent in banishing or even lessening war, the great evil of his day, is to stand for all time among the foremost benefactors." Being immortalized as a peacemaker was not what Roosevelt desired, however, but he did promise to talk to his newly appointed secretary of state Elihu Root, about Carnegie's proposal for a statement favoring arbitration.[45]

Ultimately, Roosevelt was Frick incarnate, a man willing to challenge Carnegie's authority and unwilling to share power; but unlike Frick, Roosevelt disguised his feelings. Fortunately, for both Carnegie and Roosevelt, they weren't legally bound to each other, as Carnegie had been to Frick, and the philanthropist could pursue his own peace agenda along different courses than pandering to Washington—especially when, he believed, it was Washington that should have been courting him. Empowered by a sense of destiny, he shook off Roosevelt's failure to ratify the arbitration treaties or then to publicly support arbitration and persevered. A statement of global proportions was in the making in the summer of 1906 as plans for the temple of peace at The Hague moved forward. There was one problem, however. The modest temple Carnegie envisioned had spun out of control.

The first warning sign flashed when he heard rumors the temple's cost might run into the millions, well over the $1.5 million he'd given. "It seems clear to me that they must make a fresh start," he anxiously wrote the U.S. minister to the Netherlands, Dr. David Jayne Hill, who had the unpleasant task of playing go-between. "I fear they found that such a structure as that proposed might run into several millions, and not a dollar more will I ever give. A million and a half, with accrued interest equal to 10 % more, is ample for a simple Temple of Peace and an International Law Library for the use of the court. To me the building proposed is no temple of peace, but shouts all over of the pomp, pride and vain circumstance of inglorious war."[46] When he received news the library alone would consume one-third of his $1.5 million donation, Carnegie's sensibilities were offended and he protested more vigorously: "A large, showy building would I feel be incongruous. A moderate structure only is needed. The Court, the principal chamber, should be small, so that the members can sit close together, in touch with each other mentally and almost physically, proximity being always conducive to friendly conference and harmony. It dampens excited oratorical discussion."[47] Carnegie was demanding the same functional simplicity he did for his libraries; after all, these buildings were extensions of himself—you are what you build—and he envisioned himself as nobly pragmatic and prudent.

Then came news the temple was to be called the Library and Court of Arbitration, a pathetic name according to Carnegie, who, just two days after his last protestation, injected his feelings into a more strongly worded letter. "This is to me shocking. I am positively wounded. The day that a permanent tribunal was established to settle international disputes humanity took a great step forward, and when a Temple of Peace is erected it will in my opinion be the holiest structure in the world. To speak of 'The Library and Court of Arbitration' is as if a bereaved husband were to ask plans for a sacred shrine to 'my nephew and my dear wife.'"[48] Now having reviewed the architect's drawings, his fears were confirmed. He was severely disappointed that a French architect had been selected over an American—he was not fond of the Frenchy look; it was too ornate and frilly—and that the French architect had indeed debased the high ideal of the temple by turning it into an ostentatious palace.

To Carnegie, the temple now palace appeared to be a Flemish guildhall, with a brick facade, steeply pitched roof, and towers—useless towers. It was more warlike than peaceful. Haunted by the Frenchy palace and unable to sleep, he dispatched his director at the Carnegie Institute of Pittsburgh, Samuel Harden Church, who, according to Carnegie, was all-knowing of things aesthetic, to The Hague to review the plans and recommend revisions. The director of the temple, Jonkheer van Karnebeek, quickly learned it was futile to resist Carnegie. In mid-July, he acquiesced to the revisions proposed by Church, who updated his anxious boss: "The only unpleasant thing he is yet tenacious of is *red brick*. How a Peace Palace could be beautiful in red brick I fail to see. He thinks the climate of Holland will not stand stone or marble. But you can get him out of this heresy."[49]

At this point, the floundering Dutchman van Karnebeek reluctantly ascended Mount Olympus to pay homage to the roaring Zeus—that is, he went to Skibo to see Carnegie. The Scotsman demanded the same granite used for Skibo be cut for the temple, but as it turned out the quarry had little left to yield. He then insisted van Karnebeek import the stone used in building the city of Aberdeen, but it was too expensive. Red brick it would be. With an exasperated sigh, Carnegie wrote Richard Watson Gilder: "If you knew what efforts were made to obtain the very 'temple' idea your artistic sense instinctively suggested you would be surprised. It's a long story. I'll tell you when we meet. Of course I must bow my head and say 'all right.' That is the part of the giver always."[50] Perhaps not always. Whereas Carnegie had given the reins to the trustees of his various endowments, along with the power to modify their respective missions, he was still very controlling under certain circumstances, especially when dealing with men and nations he considered inferior.

The other instrument Carnegie controlled for pushing his peace agenda outside the purview of Washington and Roosevelt was the New York Peace Society, which he became president of in 1907. The membership included powerful editors and clergymen who influenced public opinion, a potent weapon. He wasted no time and used his influence to attract big names—Harvard president Eliot, Earl Grey, d'Estournelles, and Root, among others—to the society's annual three-day conference. "I am drawn more to this cause than to any—Just as when young I became a rabid anti-slavery zealot," he admitted to Eliot, "so in regard to war, far more heinous than owning and selling men is killing men by men."[51] There could be no doubt that world peace was now Carnegie's mission.

The group wielded enough influence that after Carnegie's speech at the conference made the papers, Roosevelt actually attempted to persuade Carnegie to modify his views. "Have just read your splendid letter to the Peace Congress. Only one point that seems to me weak. 'Righteousness' vs. Peace. Disputants are both seeking 'righteousness,' both feel themselves struggling for what is just. Who is to decide? No one. According to you, they must go to War to decide not what is 'Right' but who is Strong. Pray reflect."[52] Righteousness justified war, according to Roosevelt, whereas Carnegie, who was once "not a man of peace at any cost," now flatly denied there existed any reason for man to kill man. Such a radical position, Roosevelt rightly perceived, would undercut Carnegie's chance for success.

New York Peace Society board meetings were held at his Ninety-first Street home, and through these gatherings Carnegie befriended Hamilton

Holt, editor of the *Independent*. Holt shared Carnegie's views on peace, race union, and even spelling reform, and, reasoning "the views of a multimillionaire being always good 'newspaper stuff,'" he soon consulted Carnegie on all public issues. Following Gilder's death, they became golfing partners at St. Andrews, the most pleasurable time to be with Carnegie. "We always went to St. Andrews by motor," Holt recalled, "Mr. Carnegie being bundled up by Mrs. Carnegie and numerous butlers till the only part of him visible was his nose under his goggles and drawn-down cap and over his muffler and turned-up collar."[53] Carnegie could putt, the editor observed, but couldn't drive; and if he had a bad lie in the fairway, he didn't hesitate to tee up the ball. Other than that indiscretion, Carnegie played strictly by the rules and, of course, counted his opponent's strokes. After a round, he and Holt would retire to his small cottage, where Carnegie would take off his shoes, wrap himself in a blanket, and nap until the two servants and a St. Bernard dog presiding over the cottage served lunch.

At one such lunch, Holt asked Carnegie if he ever lost faith in human nature when so many people, even good friends, tried to wheedle money out of him. "No," Carnegie replied, "that doesn't trouble me at all, for I don't see people unless they are properly introduced and I don't become intimate with those I don't like. And besides, as long as I have money and others have ideas, I am more than obliged to those that are good enough to bring me their proposals. They benefit me more than they do themselves."

On the way back to New York, they had a flat tire. Carnegie motioned to Holt to walk a short distance away; he didn't want the chauffeur to become flustered by the two men watching over his shoulder as he changed the tire. If only Roosevelt had only been so lucky.

CHAPTER 32

The Metamorphosis
of Andrew Carnegie

R oosevelt's bellicose attitude toward capitalists and big business continued to rattle Wall Street in early 1907 as he proclaimed his intention to regulate all large trusts and opened a preliminary investigation of Standard Oil for an antitrust suit. Compounding the investment community's anxiety, England's and Germany's cash-starved governments, which had witnessed their capital depleted during the Boer War, raised their interest rates to attract investors, causing money to drain from the United States and credit to tighten. All of this made for stormy seas: by March 1907, the public's confidence had reached ebb tide, and the stock market was a floundering ship. As distasteful as it was to him, Roosevelt was forced to seek advice from Pierpont Morgan, who visited him in Washington on March 12, and Carnegie, who wrote him the day Morgan was there. In support of Roosevelt, Carnegie called for strict federal regulations to govern Wall Street and encouraged the president: "We cannot trust this to the Gamblers, for such they are."[1]

It was too late. Two days later the stock market crashed, the Dow Jones losing 25 percent of its value. While men like Woodrow Wilson, then president of Princeton, blamed Roosevelt and his policies, Carnegie attempted to bolster his confidence by supporting his position that the government must take a stronger hand in regulating private enterprise. "Nothing radical needed, but this is imperative," Carnegie concluded. He promulgated this message in letters to the editor and interviews in an attempt to force change.[2]

Contrary to what Carnegie told Roosevelt, radical medicine was needed. In October, yet another banking panic would hit New York. It was precipitated by the rapacious Wall Street speculators F. Augustus Heinze and Charles W. Morse, who attempted to corner the copper market and failed. The alarm sounded. There was a run by depositors on the trust companies that had financed their ill-advised venture, causing those banks to fail; stocks tumbled to a new low; interest on short-term loans shot to 125 percent; and the ex-president of the devastated Knickerbocker Trust killed himself. It took Morgan and a syndicate of powerful men—as well as many lost meals and smoked cigars—to bail out the banks. Even John D. Rockefeller came out of hiding to tell the Associated Press he would ante up half of his fortune to thwart the panic; he eventually provided $10 million to improve liquidity. Even with Morgan skillfully playing the role of central banker, a severe economic downturn couldn't be avoided.

While economic value and lives were being destroyed, one man found Carnegie's utterances on regulation sanctimonious and highly amusing. He was the former secretary of the Frick Coke Company, M. M. Bosworth. "Through your great wealth and your philanthropy, libraries, etc.," he screeched in condemnation, "you have become a public character of prominence and international interest. Some of your public utterances and writings are read with interest. To some of your old employees they are both interesting and highly amusing. Recently you publicly referred to persons who buy and sell stocks in Wall Street as stock gamblers. . . . Why don't you tell the public that through the great volume of your business, you were able to take railroads by the throat and to compel them to secretly violate state and Federal laws . . . ? Why are you apparently afraid to acknowledge that you were the 'chiefest rebater' of the Pennsylvania RR Co. as charged in last June's Pearson's Magazine by James Creelman."[3] If Carnegie responded, he left no record.

On the political front, Roosevelt also sought Carnegie's aid. The titan had made it well known that Kaiser Wilhelm II, Germany's emperor, had made several overtures to him to be his guest in Germany, but each time Carnegie had taken pleasure in denying him. Ever since Carnegie's St. Andrews' rectorial address in 1903, which the kaiser had read with great interest—especially the bit about a unified Europe—he was interested in meeting the philanthropist. Now, with all the sword rattling in Europe, Roosevelt and Secretary of State Root encouraged Carnegie to meet with the kaiser, who had recently extended another invitation. A second Hague Conference was scheduled to assemble on June 15, 1907, at which disarmament, arbitration, and other means of obtaining peace were to be discussed. Roosevelt was hoping Carnegie might be able to discern where Germany stood on these topics, as the kaiser was fighting the agenda.

"The Kaiser is the difficulty," Morley complained to Carnegie. "He is moving heaven and earth against the whole thing, and makes no secret of it that if the topic of disarmament is raised, his men will walk out."[4] While Morley condemned the kaiser, Roosevelt's position on disarmament was no different. "We must always remember," the president wrote Carnegie on the importance of arming the military, "that it would be a fatal thing for the great free peoples to reduce themselves to impotence and leave the despotisms and barbarisms armed."[5] With such powerful leaders unwilling to yield, Carnegie was certain that it was his duty to intervene. Thus he accepted the kaiser's invitation to visit with him in Germany. Charlemagne Tower, the U.S. ambassador to Germany, arranged for the two to meet in Kiel during a popular regatta in June.

Carnegie had not been completely ignoring the emperor, and his correspondence could be as heavy and blunt as a sledgehammer. In a January 1907 letter, he included a lengthy, suggestive soliloquy in which he imagined himself the emperor. In the spirit of a Shakespearean tragedy, in which a king, racked with self-doubts, takes the stage alone and questions his purpose, it opened: "God has seen fit to place me in command of the greatest military power ever known. For what end? Surely for the good and not for evil; surely for peace and not war. To prove the servile follower of a Caesar, Frederick, or Napoleon, who prevailed by brute force? Never! That day is past." The *self-exhortations* for peace continued throughout: "Thank God, my hands, *as yet*, are guiltless of human blood. What part, then, can I play worthy of my power and position? It must be—shall be—in the direction of Peace on earth. . . . I am the only man who can bring Peace among men. Can it be that God has destined me so to work his glory, and so to benefit the world? . . . I have it! Eureka! An International Police! A League of Peace! Propose to the Hague Conference that this be formed . . . Yes! This is my work! Thank God. Now I see my path and am happy." Carnegie was obviously attempting to manipulate the kaiser psychologically, but his own consciousness, his own voice, was too strong; it was his destiny of which he spoke as much as that of the kaiser's or Roosevelt's.

At the end of the soliloquy, Carnegie returned to himself and concluded, "If that kindred soul, our President, had 'The Emperor's' role to play, I should have been at his side long ago urging it. His part in some measure is yet to play, and he means to play it well—*and for Peace too*—but there is only one on earth to whom has been given the power to resolve and execute—the Emperor of Germany." While Carnegie massaged the emperor's ego, he was, in fact, at Roosevelt's side exhorting him to take up the mantle of peace, too. "An international police should really be the aim of the next Hague Conference," Carnegie wrote the president the month after his creative monologue to the kaiser. "If the German Emperor would rise to his destiny and stand with you favoring this, instead of pegging away, trifling over petty questions!—chasing rainbows in the form of a colonial empire which he cannot get, and which would do Germany no good if he did."[6] For Carnegie, an international police force, backed by a League of Nations, was a most viable option to arbitration. He hoped the martial, the imperialist, the expansionist leaders of the world—namely, Roosevelt and Kaiser Wilhelm II—would find the active enforcement of peace more enticing than passive arbitration.

Carnegie had high hopes for tangible accomplishments when he sat down with the kaiser. Before embarking on his adventure, he penned a short piece titled "The Next Step—a League of Nations" for the May 25 edition of *Outlook* magazine, to further promote such an international association and the German emperor's participation, in particular. He acknowledged that he was not presenting a novel idea, but asked that nations in conflict simply ask themselves, "Is war imperative?" and "Is there no honorable escape?" He devoutly believed an international police force, however difficult to organize, would abolish "at one stroke the killing of men by men in battle like wild beasts." What he feared most was the politicians and diplomats becoming bogged down in petty details: "Not seldom the easiest way to secure agreement in a great problem is to treat it boldly as a whole, go to the root, and settle it upon permanent foundations. I believe the world peace problem to be a case in point. Petty details often arouse more hostility in meetings of men than the sweep of large principles."

Carnegie also dashed off a last note to Morley, full of hope and inspiration: "I told our Ambr. I'd go only if H.M. [the kaiser] *really wished the interview after my speech putting the Peace of Nations on him.* He really is responsible. No other man has the power to draw a League of Nations competent to keep the peace for an agreed upon period just as an experiment. . . . Fortunately, he's very devout—very. He sent me his address to his son upon his Consecration & it wouldn't discredit a Holy Father of the Catholic Church. Well, never was a holy Father more convinced of his Mission than I am of mine. I *know* I offer H.I.M. the plan that makes him the greatest agent known so far in human history. The Peace Maker."[7] Unfortunately, the Catholic Church had been responsible for more than a few wars over the centuries, so being a devout Catholic promised nothing in terms of peace. And Morley was highly skeptical that Carnegie, whose tone was becoming ever more righteous, would accomplish anything positive: "How interesting it will be. That you can inflame him with your own Crusader's Zeal, I am not sure. But the effort is *noble.*"[8]

Once they arrived in the seaport of Kiel, Ambassador Tower accompanied the Carnegies to the emperor's yacht, which had been made available to them. Carnegie and Louise were introduced to various admirals and dignitaries, and were deep in conversation when the emperor unexpectedly approached from behind. Tower tapped Carnegie on the shoulder. "Mr. Carnegie, the Emperor."

Carnegie raised both hands in delight and exclaimed with a hint of condescension, "Your Majesty, I have traveled two nights to accept your generous invitation, and never did so before to meet a crowned head."

"Oh! yes, yes, I have read your books. You do not like kings."

"No, Your Majesty, I do not like kings, but I do like a man behind a king when I find him."

That evening Carnegie sat opposite the emperor at a dinner attended by sixty guests. It was difficult for Carnegie to indulge in any meaningful discourse, but when he mentioned that Roosevelt wished he could leave the country to visit with His Majesty, it elicited a positive response from the kaiser, who thought it would be quite enjoyable. "Well, Your Majesty, when you two do get together, I think I shall have to be with you. You and he, I fear, might get into mischief." Carnegie then told Wilhelm he would like to see Roosevelt and him hitched together in the cause of peace.

"Oh, I see!" the kaiser said. "You wish to drive us together. Well, I agree if you make Roosevelt the first horse, I shall follow."

"No, Your Majesty, I know horse-flesh better than to attempt to drive such gay colts tandem. You never get proper purchase on the first horse. I must yoke you both in the shafts, neck and neck, so I can hold you in."[9]

On departing Kiel, Carnegie wanted to believe the emperor was anxious for peace, that he cherished the fact he had reigned for twenty-four years without shedding a drop of German blood. After all, the forty-eight-year-old Wilhelm II had been very polished, dressed in a military parade uniform and sporting a trim mustache curled gently at the ends, and he was the grandson of the late Queen Victoria—why would he desire war with Britain? "I had three interviews with the German Emperor and dined with him twice—a wonderful man, so bright, humorous, and *with a sweet smile*," he wrote St. Andrews principal James Donaldson. "I think he can be trusted and declares himself for peace."[10] To Richard Watson Gilder, he effused: "Our visit to the Emperor was a decided success. He's a rare man, as free and informal as the President; chuck full of fun. Very engaging smile—very; can't help liking him."[11] Charm could easily sway Carnegie, and the emperor could be exceedingly charming.

Carnegie was not completely fooled. While telling everyone his détente had been a success (because it had to be), he had recognized the kaiser's warlike traits. He wrote a lengthy letter to the German chancellor Prince von Bülow, pleading that Germany should adopt every means possible "to show the people of Britain, as distinguished from the official classes, Naval and Military, that Germany is anxiously desirous of bringing about, as occasion may serve, a reign of peace among nations, and that she has no warlike policy at heart." Carnegie also wrote Germany's ambassador to Washington, Speck von Sternburg: "Knowing you enjoy his [the emperor's] confidence I write freely to you. Let me say, therefore, that, as you know, I feel that His Majesty has the greatest mission ever entrusted to man. Something tells me he will sooner or later fulfill his destiny and become the world's peacemaker."[12] Applying pressure from all points, he hoped one of these men would talk some sense into the emperor. The need to do so became far more imperative with the failure of the second Hague Conference to yield any tangible results beyond such mild declarations as agreeing not to drop projectiles from balloons in times of war. Even the establishment of the court of arbitration at The Hague was thrown into doubt.

British and American diplomats blamed the Germans for blocking any progress, criticism the Germans resented and that only served to increase tensions. Carnegie had accepted that disarmament was a futile cause, but arbitration was a must. How could the court of arbitration be in doubt when he was building a temple of peace? Arbitration, an international police force, a league of peace—all these grand visions seemed to be fading fast.

Secretary of State Elihu Root did attempt to salvage the conference by suggesting all participants negotiate separate treaties with one another since a general arbitration and armament treaty was out of the question. This was a cause Carnegie would take up with gusto, but not until Roosevelt was out of the picture.

Roosevelt was too militaristic for Carnegie's tastes, a characteristic that was confirmed in November 1907 when the president reneged on his promise to not increase naval forces to meet what he perceived to be rising German and Japanese threats. When word reached Carnegie, he cabled immediately. "You stand before the world today committed to the policy of only maintaining efficiently the present number of ships in the navy, the only ruler of a great nation who has ever reacht this height . . . ," he praised, hoping to change the president's mind. "Pause and reflect how the world will regard and bemoan your sudden change into the ruler reversing his policy and asking the most unexpected increase. Why? Why? Verily, the question needs your most serious attention."[13]

A short-tempered Roosevelt's response was impenitent: "I shall recommend an increase in the navy. I shall urge it strongly as I know how. I believe that every far sighted and patriotic man ought to stand by me. . . . You say the question needs my serious attention. It has had it, and, as I say, I cannot imagine how anyone . . . can fail to back me up."[14]

Carnegie, however, did fail to back him up. Hoping a face-to-face meeting might convince the president to change course, Carnegie went to Washington during Thanksgiving week, but Roosevelt was adamant. A second meeting on December 9 also proved fruitless. Eventually, the hardened president was forced to rebuke Carnegie over his view that Japan was not a reason to increase the U.S. Navy's size. "My dear sir," Roosevelt wrote in exasperation, "it would be the very highest unwisdom for us to act on the belief that you so lightly express that 'Japan is really a negligible quantity.'"[15]

When Roosevelt announced he would not run for reelection that December, Carnegie greeted it with mixed feelings: "Sorry for my country that you are not to be at the helm for some years more during which I am confident you would have secured for the Republic the reforms essential for her welfare. You have done the preparatory work which only needs continued attention to give us a prouder position than hitherto occupied in some departments."[16] Carnegie had appreciated the progressive's reform measures; but, as he hinted in the letter, Roosevelt's work was merely preparatory, a subtle jab that he had accomplished little in the way of definitive reforms—at least according to Carnegie's agenda. But with Roosevelt's announced departure from politics and detrimental economic conditions plaguing the great Republic, Carnegie actually evolved into a progressive reformer.

Anarchy now ruled New York. After the financial panic in October 1907, an economic downturn choked the city. The "industrial paralysis and prostration," contended the Commercial and Financial Chronicle, was "the very worst ever experienced in the country's history."[17] The breadlines were longer than ever. The socialists were marching in the streets. Failed assassin Alexander Berkman was out of prison and a favored speaker at labor protests. And Morgan, the man who imposed order on the financial markets, was accused of orchestrating the chaos for his own benefit. (For the record, Morgan's American firms lost $21 million in 1907.)

Carnegie's old partners suffered, too. He received a pathetic letter from Jane Fleming Lovejoy, the wife of one his favorite partners who had nobly resigned during the Frick conflict rather than pick sides. Her husband had made ill-advised investments out West and was now faced with bankruptcy, she explained, surely to be followed by unpleasant press, as such circumstances did for all old Carnegie associates. She pleaded with Carnegie to buy their property for $550,000 (he already held the mortgage of $125,000) for the sake of her own children.[18] His response is unknown. But for certain, economically and politically, it was a dark winter.

The failure of both The Hague Peace Conference and the U.S. banking system forced Carnegie to look inward; in April, he actually went to church for the first time in years.[19] He considered how he reflected the failures and how they reflected him. A round of self-analysis would lead to the self-admission that the United States—for all its high and mighty ideals—was fallible and to a momentous change in Carnegie that was not evolutionary, but revolutionary. He removed his rose-colored glasses. He transformed from a Republican who worshipped free enterprise blindly to a critical Roosevelt progressive.

The metamorphosis took place in his Ninety-first Street study, where a haunting epigram hung above him: "All is well since all grows better." The change manifested itself in a series of essays he wrote. Writing had always been a means of purging his anxieties and restless energies, and over the next months he expressed his evolving emotions in a surge of political and economic essays. First, he penned "The Worst Banking System in the World," published in the February 29 issue of Outlook, in which he admitted the U.S. banking system was the most inferior in Western civilization. Once a devout laissez-faire capitalist, he was now not averse to the government guaranteeing individual's deposits and creating a central bank. To promote his ideas, his contribution to the great banking debate from which would arise the Federal Reserve System, he had 70,500 reprints made of the essay and mailed them to every member of Congress, bank and manufacturer chiefs, and sundry men of importance. His friend Nicholas Butler, president of Columbia University, called it "a masterpiece."[20]

The second sign of his self-imposed revolution appeared in the March 1908 issue of Century Illustrated Monthly, which published Carnegie's "My Experience with Railway Rates and Rebates." He did indeed review his experience, and he complimented President Roosevelt for tackling the evil of preferential rates, but he failed to recall the rebates he had won from the Pennsylvania Railroad. The closest he came to outright self-condemnation was in writing: "The dead past is to bury its past. It is rapidly doing so." Yes, he wanted it buried forever, entombed and forgotten. Yet the past was linked to Carnegie; he could not escape it. He had made millions due to rebates that now flowed into libraries, foundations, and trusts.

The transformation from conservative Republican to a Roosevelt progressive continued with his most startling essay yet. In a second essay for *Century Illustrated Monthly*, "My Experience with, and Views upon, the Tariff," he advocated the termination of the tariff for most imports, including steel. Carnegie acknowledged that having once been classified as a "robber tariff baron," he would be accused of being a convert due to retirement from business, but he honestly believed it was time for change. The article was so inflammatory, especially since it was an election year, that the *Century's* editor, Robert Underwood Johnson, who told Roosevelt it contained "campaign dynamite," shared it with Roosevelt's heir apparent, Secretary of War William Howard Taft, to ascertain if its publication should be postponed until after the election. Taft thought Carnegie's essay would prove very useful in revising the tariff, but he worried "that some of his positions would be misunderstood or would be perverted in the campaign."[21] So the publication was postponed until December. True to the expectations, the reaction was indeed explosive. His moral rectitude smacked of rank hypocrisy and his pious remarks drew critical fire, especially from U.S. Steel officials.

Carnegie's antitariff position immediately attracted the attention of Congress, which assembled a Tariff Commission in December and requested his testimony. Knowing better, he declined in an act of civil disobedience—only to be served a subpoena by Sereno Payne, chairman of the House Ways and Means Committee. Carnegie protested: "I have been seven years out of the Steel business and have no detailed figures to give you, and I cannot be induced to enter into a Tariff controversy. All that I have to say upon the Tariff has been published in the Century Magazine and I beg to enclose a copy of the article."[22] To no avail. "Off for Washington tomorrow to answer Tariff Comm," he wrote Dod on December 19. "They will get short responses. We are approaching great crisis in 'Combination' Monopoly vs. Competition."[23] To the contrary, Carnegie's responses were anything but short, and Payne would come to regret the day he ordered the subpoena.

These congressmen were toys to Carnegie, foils for his leading role, and the witness stand another stage. It was Chairman Payne who sweated while Carnegie entertained the audience with his wit. When Payne was finally able to ask about the tariff on steel, Carnegie unloaded a bomb. He explained that U.S. Steel could make a profit selling steel so cheap the tariff was moot; then, pointing at Payne, he brazenly mocked: "Does that enter into your brain? Can you arrive at any other conclusion than that the steel industry can stand on its own legs? . . . The time for free trade has come so far as steel is concerned. The total abolition of the tariff will leave the steel companies in a better position as far as this country is concerned, than a continuance of the present coddling system."[24]

Elbert H. Gary, chairman of U.S. Steel's executive committee, was outraged when reports reached him about Carnegie's call for the end of the steel
tariff and wrote him a strongly worded letter of protest, charging him with
diabolical hypocrisy. Having retired from a business in which he made millions because of the tariff, what right did he have to proclaim its obsoles-
cence, thus possibly denying current and future generations of steelmakers
from enjoying the same protection? An unapologetic Carnegie replied, "I am
done now with the subject, having done my duty when subpoenaed. I told
the truth—the whole truth as I know it."[25] It was no wonder Carnegie had
had so many enemies in the steel industry.

Agricultural leaders who had always despised the tariff because they believed it only served to fatten the wallets of their industrial brethren saluted
Carnegie as a "powerful new champion of reform."[26] The champion of
reform didn't stop at the tariff in attacking the great industrial concerns.

In March 1908, Roosevelt invited Carnegie to take an active part in the
upcoming Conference on the Conservation of Natural Resources. He agreed,
and at the May conference he delivered a paper titled "The Conservation of
Ores and Related Minerals." It amounted to a condemnation of how he had
conducted business for twenty-five years. Using an arsenal of facts, he vividly
illustrated how the country's ore, coal, and other natural resources had been
and were being wastefully exploited and consumed. "The same spirit of reck-
lessness that leads to waste in mining and in the consumption of coal leads to
unnecessary risk of human life," he continued. "During the year 1907 in the
United States the killed and wounded in coal mining operations exceeded
9,000." In his contrite evaluation, he concluded that conservation of human
and natural resources was the only course, predicting that "the most useful
minerals will shortly become scarce and may soon reach prohibitive cost unless steps to lessen waste are taken in the interest of the future."[27] Never had
Carnegie demonstrated such concern for Frick Coke laborers or his own in
steel; as a ravenous industrialist, he had ravaged iron ore, coal, and lime.
Now, however, like a reborn Christian full of righteous piety, he spewed forth
his new gospel—and the likes of Morgan and Frick cringed.

The transformation was complete when he wrote a glowing introduction
to *The Roosevelt Policy*, a two-volume collection of the president's letters,
speeches, and papers. The fact that if Carnegie was still in business, his pro-
fuse tribute to Roosevelt would be considered an enormous conflict of interest—along the lines of a Southern plantation owner applauding Lincoln—
was not lost on reviewers. "At first sight it seems a little odd that this book,"
wrote the reviewer for the *Times Literary Supplement*, "which attacks the
undue concentration of wealth, and has many severe things to say about
'swollen fortunes' should be sent into the world with an introductory bene-
diction from one of the two richest men in America. But Mr. Andrew Carnegie, as we all know, has always been 'on the side of angels' and the reformers,
and this is not the first time he has come forward as a Roosevelt man."[28] As
for Roosevelt, even though he made disparaging remarks about Carnegie's

peace initiatives, he undoubtedly welcomed the introduction because it guaranteed sales to thousands of libraries.

Could the 1907 panic and the failed Hague Conference alone have inspired such a marked turn in Carnegie's thinking? No. His philanthropic endeavors were having a major impact on him, too. He was literally a new man, a result of his foundations, trusts, and institutions, which acted as a rewired and refurnished nervous system feeding him with impulses never felt before. Since 1901, the Relief Fund's annual reports unequivocally showed that hundreds were being killed each year at Carnegie Steel operations. Since 1904, one of the top reasons the Hero Fund Commission presented rewards was for acts of rescue from industrial accidents. And the Carnegie Institution of Washington was pioneering research to cure disease and aid the suffering. All of this made him more cognizant of torment and anguish. In addition, *The Shame of the Cities* by Lincoln Steffens, *The Jungle* by Upton Sinclair, and exposés on the harsh underside of American industry by Jack London and Ida Tarbell all contributed to a rising national consciousness regarding the plight of labor. That new sense of responsibility toward the working class affected Carnegie, who had always been a creature of his environment. He respected and befriended Samuel Gompers, chief of the American Federation of Labor and who supported labor's "Bill of Grievances" sent to Roosevelt. He had joined and hosted dinners for the National Civic Federation, which brought together prominent capitalists and labor leaders. John Mitchell, once a child laborer in the mines and now president of the United Mine Workers, was at many of the National Civic Federation meetings and had Carnegie's ear. It was difficult to ignore Mitchell, who eloquently spoke out against child labor as he struggled "to reconcile the humanity and flaunted intelligence of this era with the wholesale employment of children in industry. Childhood should be a period of growth and education."[29] The words struck Carnegie to the core, especially when he cast his eye on his Baba.

All of this, along with the media's recent and brutal attacks on Rockefeller and Morgan, forced Carnegie to realize "the day of the multi-millionaire is over, the people won't have it," as he wrote industrialist Sir Charles Macmara.[30] And in explaining his position on the tariff to Seth Low, a former mayor of New York, he said, "You will have to agree that time brings changes, and it is fully time that the Tariff was changed to meet present conditions. As far as protection is concerned, great reductions can be made without injuring our manufacturers in any degree."[31] Roosevelt calling it quits also had affected Carnegie, for the president, a worthy ally and foe, had inspired him like no president before. Carnegie yearned to extend the Progressive Era; he desperately desired a better world for Margaret, his Baba, now eleven years of age, the age of thousands of girls in the textile factories and boys in the mines.

In the twilight of his life, the startling essays and proclamations acted as a confession, an act of self-absolution as he reacted to the times and his self-realization.

CHAPTER 33

Covert Deal with Taft

F ailure at The Hague, the economic chaos, and the troubling ruminations as the progressive reformer emerged from his chrysalis caused Carnegie to lose his bearing in his philanthropic ventures. As he walked the two-mile loop around the Central Park reservoir in the bitterly cold month of January 1908, he mulled over what new direction he should take, how to continue to best spend the surplus wealth with which he had been entrusted.

To reorient himself, he sent a questionnaire to about a dozen top American authors, educators, scientists, and statesmen that contained but one question for them: How could he spend $5 or $10 million to best uplift society? He offered a prize for the most insightful, useful answer. Grover Cleveland, who had resumed his law practice in Princeton, New Jersey, and become a trustee of Princeton University, jumped at the chance to offer advice after having been on the receiving end of it for years. The former president replied with alacrity, "If in asking the question propounded in your note, you had followed the formula so often used and had written, 'If *you* were in my place what would you do' in the circumstances mentioned, I would not compete for the prize offered for the 'best answer.'" Cleveland must have smiled as he wrote the line; how many times had he received a Carnegie letter with the clause, "If I were in your place . . . "

"Perhaps you will remember that once," Cleveland continued, "while enjoying your delightful hospitality, I confessed to mental but unexpressed criticism touching the direction of your benevolences; and it may be that you will recall that I thereupon put myself under bonds never to allow myself to again harbor the thought that anyone could impose upon your own generous and correct impulses related to the distribution of your noble gifts." But since Carnegie had asked, he added unhesitatingly that a liberal sum for the Graduate School of Princeton would be most welcome. The program was just a few years old and required equipment, facilities, and an endowment.[1] The suggestion hardly benefited the general public, and Carnegie never did award the prize.

Not until his return to Skibo did Carnegie reinvigorate himself and decide to continue to pursue his own course of action in the name of peace. This mission would involve not only straightforward benefactions for additional temples of peace and the usual propaganda, but covert dealings with Taft, who would be elected president in November, allowing both men to further their respective agendas. The one man they both had to be wary of was Roosevelt, who was still very much in the public eye.

At the prompting of Elihu Root, Carnegie's first action was to offer $100,000 to build a Central Court of Justice to be erected in Cartago, Costa Rica. Root had been involved with the Central American Peace Conference, which had been held in Washington the prior December and attended by Costa Rica, Guatemala, Honduras, Nicaragua, and Salvador, as well as invited guests from Mexico and the United States. Nine treaties were signed, and the countries agreed to build a court to settle any disputes—thus the need for funding. "One more step in the right direction—the peace of our hemisphere," Carnegie congratulated Root in June. He would also give $850,000 in total gifts toward a building for the Pan American Union, the Washington-based organization dedicated to promoting better communication and peace in the Americas.[2] Again, Root, who was honorary chairman of the Pan American Union (subsequently renamed the Organization of American States), was instrumental in tapping the philanthropist. These two buildings, dedicated in 1910, and the one in The Hague became Carnegie's triumvirate of temples of peace, of which he was exceptionally proud—all accomplished without the endorsement of Roosevelt.

That summer of 1908, with Carnegie closing in on age seventy-three, the prolific entertaining continued unabated at Skibo. When Woodrow Wilson visited in August, he reported to his wife, Ellen: "They have a perfect stream of visitors at Skibo: I should think that a season of it would utterly wear poor Mrs. Carnegie out. The Castle is like a luxurious hotel. Some twenty or thirty persons sit down to every meal. Guests are received, for the most part (if— say—of less than cabinet rank) by the servants; shown to their room; and received by the host and hostess when all assembled for the next meal."[3]

Across the Atlantic, the Republican Convention offered a flash of excitement when Roosevelt was greeted with a forty-nine-minute ovation. Carnegie and much of America thought Roosevelt might consider running for reelection after such a show of support, but Taft was nominated. At three hundred pounds, the obese, roly-poly Taft, who had twists on the end of a full mustache, was almost comic looking, and cynics chuckled over his last name being an acronym for "Take advice from Teddy." The 1908 presidential election was hardly inspiring, with the Democrats nominating William Jennings Bryan, yet again, to run against Taft. A future Democratic congressman from Manhattan who refused to vote, Herbert C. Pell, observed, "I couldn't see much difference in the candidates. One had a big head and no brains, and the other had a big belly and no guts."[4] Taft won with 52 percent of the votes to Bryan's 43, the latter losing a chunk of votes to labor leader Eugene Debs, who garnered 3 percent. While cynics like Pell derided Taft, Carnegie, who gave $20,000 to the Republican Campaign Fund, harbored hope that the nation's rotund, triple-chinned leader did have the guts to move forward on arbitration treaties as suggested by Root after The Hague Conference. "Mr. Taft is going to secure what Roosevelt rendered securable. He'll prove a good binder of the sheaves," he predicted to Morley.[5]

Since The Hague, Secretary of State Root had succeeded in negotiating twenty-five bilateral arbitration treaties with most nations in the Americas and Europe. To ensure these agreements would be acceptable to the fastidious Senate, he wisely included a clause that provided for the Senate's involvement in giving advice and consent of arbitration. The treaties, however, left much to be desired for the peacemakers. As in the agreement with Austria ratified by the Senate in January 1909, the treaties were restricted to arbitrating matters that didn't affect a nation's vital interests, independence, and honor, nor involve the interests of third parties. In February, for example, the United States and Britain arbitrated a Newfoundland waters fishing dispute at The Hague, a relatively harmless issue. While limited in scope, the treaties were a small step in the right direction. Now Carnegie desired Taft to improve on them, but there was one potential complication: Philander Knox was Taft's secretary of state, not Root. As secretary of state, Knox's statesmanship, shaped in the age of the robber baron by robber barons, was oafish and heavy-handed. And although Carnegie had first supported his ascent to national office, Knox had harbored a grudge against him ever since the Frick conflict and was planning to fight any meddling by him.

Oblivious to the fact he had an enemy in the jovial Taft administration, Carnegie was eager to pursue elusive unconditional arbitration treaties. (With Roosevelt on his way to Africa for a yearlong safari, a potential roadblock was removed.) It was time to begin wooing Taft. After a March visit to the White House, Carnegie sent the president a barrel of fine Scotch. The other key player in the quest for peace remained the kaiser. But actually winning Wilhelm's cooperation was futile, according to Root, who bluntly told Carnegie: "The fact is, and no well informed person can doubt it, that Germany under present Government, is the great disturber of peace in the world. At every turn, the obstacle to the establishment of arbitration agreements, to the prevention of war, to disarmament, to the limitation of armament, to all attempts to lessen the suspicion and alarm of nations toward each other, is Germany, who stands, and has persistently stood since I have been familiar with foreign affairs, against that kind of progress."[6]

Regardless, Carnegie was spurred on by supporters. "America is in advance in many things over Europe—but in the peace-movement the advance is a stupendous one. And most of it is due to *you*," Baroness Berthe von Suttner wrote him in May.[7] And Samuel Gompers, vice president of the Peace Congress meeting held in Chicago, noted, "The United States has had no more earnest worker for world-peace than Andrew Carnegie who gave time and money to the cause."[8]

Enduringly faithful to the hope the kaiser could be turned, it dawned on Carnegie that only one man had a chance of influencing him: Colonel Theodore Roosevelt, the man who before leaving for Africa, at a breakfast in his honor, was found "roaring as only a human volcano can roar!—leading the laugh and singing and shouting, like a boy out of school, pounding the table with both noisy fists when they sang:—'There'll be a hot time, in the Jungle, To-night.'"[9] After the safari concluded in the spring of 1910, he was to travel through the capitals of Europe, visiting cities and dignitaries he had been barred from seeing as a country-locked president. The German emperor was not on the itinerary, but Carnegie calculated this would be an opportune time for Roosevelt to meet with him and discuss European hostilities and the armament buildup. Ideally, if Roosevelt could win some expression of desire from the kaiser to end the tensions, it might very well lead to permanent peace. Now Carnegie just had to convince Roosevelt, recently considered a roadblock, to meet the emperor and then come to London for a debriefing with top diplomats. It was a daunting challenge, and Carnegie enlisted a sympathetic Root to assist.

Roosevelt's safari was purportedly a scientific expedition to collect specimens, from bugs to lion skins, for the National Museum, but it more closely resembled a military expedition designed to aid his lust for big-game hunting. Although well financed, after just five weeks he started to worry over his rapidly dwindling funds. From Nairobi, on June 1, he humbly wrote Carnegie that he needed another $30,000 to complete his scientific expedition. In the four-page letter, he admitted the cost was much greater than he had foreseen, with having to buy four tons of salt to preserve the skins and hiring so many porters for carrying supplies, including fifty-seven of Roosevelt's favorite books, like *Paradise Lost*. In his defense, Roosevelt also claimed he had already collected over a thousand specimens to ship to the National Museum. (The expedition as a whole would collect 4,900 mammals, 4,000 birds, 500 fish, and 2,000 reptiles.)[10] Once again, Roosevelt played the hypocrite; even though he bad-mouthed Carnegie's ostentatious lifestyle behind his back, he was willing to take the multimillionaire's money to fulfill his own pleasures.

Carnegie, who had just arrived at Skibo after touring the Continent and having had an audience with King Victor Emmanuel of Italy, was in a buoyant mood when he received Roosevelt's request and only too happy to oblige. The unexpected communiqué gave him the very opening he needed to coerce the former president into sitting down with the kaiser. "Rest easy. I will arrange," he cabled. Roosevelt's call for help opened a flood of correspondence from Carnegie in which he cajoled and complimented and otherwise buttered up his anointed instrument of peace. Roosevelt eventually cracked and agreed to a summit with the kaiser. "I've told the President the Big game he should hunt is the Emperor, Germany, France, Russia, & especially You big fellows in London," Carnegie informed Morley in late June 1909.[11] Incredibly eager to be in the fray, in another note, he lamented, "I wish I were Prime Minister. . . . I'd settle matters finally, *Peace* or War for Peace."[12]

Into autumn, Carnegie kept the fire lit under Roosevelt, playing to his ego as he was so good at doing: "If any man can get the Emperor in accord for peace, you are that man. He will go far to act in unison with you, of this I am certain. You are sympathetic souls."[13]

Roosevelt responded to the heavy-handed encouragement with a touch of sarcasm: "When I see the Kaiser, I will go over the matter at length with him, telling him I wish to repeat our whole conversation to you; then I will tell it all to you when I am in London. . . . I only fear, my dear Mr. Carnegie, that you do not realize how unimportant a man I now am, and how little weight I shall have in the matter."[14] Undaunted, Carnegie's persuasive magic was in peak form in November when he convinced Roosevelt to add Sweden to his itinerary and accept the Nobel Peace Prize he had been awarded in 1906 for settling the Russo-Japanese conflict; it was another opportunity to make a statement in the name of peace.[15]

Carnegie also busied himself with logistical matters. He was frequently in contact with Ambassador Hill, now serving in Berlin, and Ambassador Reid in London, not to mention Morley, who set aside his gloomy skepticism to aid in organizing a London conference expected to follow Roosevelt's triumphant détente. Top British politicians were to attend and debrief the former president. "Do take care of yourself," Carnegie wrote his old friend enthusiastically, "for believe me you are going to be in position to do great work in May when Roosevelt is with us there or I am mistaken. . . . It is time for statesmen (not politicians) to understand each other & act in Unison re War."[16]

The most crucial element in the preparations for the summit with the kaiser was not the handling of Roosevelt's travel schedule, but the words he would speak, the position he would take. It could not be that of the gung ho expansionist. As early as December, more than five months before the tête-a-tête, Carnegie, along with Root, started feeding Roosevelt advice on how he should conduct himself: not as a dictator of policy, but as a leader conferring with other leaders on equal terms. "The only question," Carnegie wrote, "is whether the idea of promoting World Peace stirs you. If it does, you will not fail, but even failure in such a cause would be noble."[17]

From Nairobi, an uncharacteristically submissive Roosevelt responded, "I entirely agree with the views you and Root hold. Now, can't you get Root to put in writing, in a letter to you of which you could send a copy to me, these views? It would offer the way of all others for my introduction of the matter with the Kaiser. Root's gift of phrasing things is unequalled."[18]

Although Roosevelt specifically asked for a letter from Root, Carnegie couldn't restrain himself from providing his own opinion. Ever presumptuous, he never did learn the art of subtlety as indicated by his opening line: "In reply to yours, here is what I should say to His Imperial Majesty, were I in your place." He advised Roosevelt to open his impending conversation with the kaiser by complimenting him for talking and acting peace, "for your hands are giltless of shedding human blood during your long reign." Then he should suggest to the kaiser that he be the one to officially propose a League of Peace, and to say to him, "Your Majesty, I have felt it to be my duty to lay this matter before you in the hope that you would recognize the holy mission of bringing Peace to the world rest upon you. No service ever man has rendered to man since the world began equals this." By laying the peace mission squarely on the kaiser and by saying he was the only man capable of succeeding, Carnegie hoped it would shame him into accepting the mission. "Let me assure you, dear Mr. Roosevelt," he concluded, "that the Emperor can be trusted. I believe in him. He is a true man and means what he says, although probably inclined to rank physical before moral force."[19] (If only Carnegie were as suspicious as he had been in dealing with the Pennsylvania Railroad and Illinois Steel.)

A full month later, Root's letter followed. He again cautioned Roosevelt to not appear to be lecturing Europe on its duties; and, echoing Carnegie's sentiments, he suggested telling the emperor that a great opportunity had been presented. If he ignored it, he would be just another forgotten figure of history; whereas if he seized it, he would render a service toward peace and would win everlasting renown.[20]

All the pieces appeared to be falling into place, concluding with a debriefing with Britain's leaders at the chosen site of Wrest Park in London. Yet Roosevelt's overly responsive desire to please was suspect. While in colonial Africa, had the onetime assistant secretary of the navy, Rough Rider, expansionist, and imperialist finally recognized the dire political situation in Europe, with each country seeking more foreign treasures to plunder and threatening world war in the process? Or was he simply not in the mood to spar with Carnegie? Confident there were no hitches, in February 1910 Carnegie left for a vacation in the Southwest, but the next month he received a disturbing letter from Roosevelt. No longer was he playing the submissive good guy, and he had serious reservations about meeting the kaiser.

After confirming he would travel to Germany to meet Wilhelm at his convenience, Roosevelt added, "Now, however for some reservations. First, and least important, personal. I want to go home! I am homesick for my own land and my own people! Of course it is Mrs. Roosevelt I most want to see; but I want to see my two youngest boys; I want to see my own house, my own books and trees, the sunset over the sound from the window in the north room, the people with whom I have worked, who think my thoughts and speak my speech. So far from Mrs. Roosevelt's wishing to see more of Europe, she has written me that even if I can't get home in June she'll have to—and I am not going to be separated from her again."

More potent, Roosevelt declared he would not align himself with the peace-at-any-price men, such as Carnegie's friend William Stead (and Carnegie for that matter), whose ideas on unconditional arbitration Roosevelt considered to be "rarely better than silly; and the only reason that the men themselves are not exceedingly mischievous is that they are well-nigh impotent for either good or evil." While he agreed with the basic concept of a League of Peace, he also harbored serious reservations about pursuing any diplomacy not supported by the United States. "I cannot work for a policy which I think our country might repudiate; I cannot work for anything that does not represent some real progress; and it is useless to expect to accomplish everything at once," he explained. "But I will do all in my power, all that is feasible, to help in the effort to secure some substantial advance towards the goal."[21] Roosevelt feared he would lack credibility if he pushed a peace platform not endorsed by the Taft administration.

If he wanted public support from home, Carnegie determined, he would get it. It could hardly be coincidence that Taft, to whose election Carnegie gave $20,000, stood before the Peace and Arbitration Society at the Hotel Astor in New York on March 22 and made an unexpected and unequivocal speech in favor of arbitration to settle all matters of dispute, including those of national honor. The speech was a major coup for Carnegie, who, while on vacation at the Grand Canyon, gushed in a letter to Taft: "Your repeated earnest utterances in favor of International Peace entitle you to rank with Washington, whose first wish was to 'banish war, the plague of mankind, from the earth.' . . . If you only prove true to your great promise and propose to Germany and Great Britain at first (other invitations to follow) that they confer confidentially with our country, basing this suggestion upon their repeated declarations that their earnest desire is International Peace, I believe you will succeed . . . and when peace is established, as it finally must be, you would be as clearly the father of Peace on Earth as Washington is father of his country or Lincoln its preserver."[22] Relieved that Roosevelt now had Taft's public blessing, Carnegie wrote Hill in Berlin, "What a pair T.R. and H.M. to hobnob—well they will love each other like vera brithers and I have faith in both."[23] On the eve of Roosevelt's summit with the kaiser, however, a wisp of poison slipped into the air.

With just three weeks to go, in a speech at the Sorbonne in Paris, Roosevelt, now touring Europe, suggestively advocated righteous wars, two words that made Carnegie cringe. After all the preparation and nervous anticipation, was Roosevelt about to stab him? "I notice in your speech at the Sorbonne," Carnegie wrote anxiously, "you speak of 'righteous wars.' I am sure that upon serious reflection you will no longer be satisfied to send disputes between nations to war for adjustment, the crime of war being inherent. . . .

It has no regard for 'righteous.' Every citizen in a civilized community is under the reign of law compelled to submit his wrongs to the law for redress. . . . Ponder over this. You have a conscience."[24]

The scolding attempt to influence Roosevelt's scruples failed. A week before the summit with Kaiser Wilhelm II, in his Nobel Peace Prize acceptance speech at Christiana (Oslo), Norway, he supported the creation of a League of Peace, believing it would be a masterstroke, but then declared man must fight when faced with infamy rather than submit to it. "No nation deserves to exist if it permits to lose the stern and virile virtues!" he declared in direct opposition to Taft's New York speech.[25] If Carnegie only knew what Roosevelt had told Reid—"There is no type of man for whom I feel a more contemptuous abhorrence than for one who makes a God of mere money-making and at the same time is always yelling out that kind of utterly stupid condemnation of war . . . "—he wouldn't have been so shocked by Roosevelt's blunt proclamations.

But Roosevelt had good reason to take a strong and guarded position. It was partly in response to the belligerent rhetoric filling the German newspapers to rile the public up against the United States and Roosevelt. The German nationalists were incensed that Roosevelt might attempt to dictate their responsibilities concerning disarmament and peace. The propaganda was unanticipated by a naive Carnegie and worse than expected by the seasoned Roosevelt, who now believed he would accomplish little with the kaiser.[26]

Contrary to Roosevelt's skepticism, the meeting of two men with the potential to shake the world started very cordially. All precedents were broken when the kaiser invited him (the first civilian to do so) to review field maneuvers of the German army. But their subsequent meetings proved unproductive, and Roosevelt later reflected that "there were many points in international morality where he and I were completely asunder. But at least we agreed in a cordial dislike of shams and of pretense, and therefore in a cordial dislike of the kind of washy movement for international peace with which Carnegie's name has become so closely associated."[27]

A sign of things to come, King Edward VII died suddenly of heart failure on the eve of Roosevelt's historic visit, throwing Britain into a state of mourning. "The sad news of the passing of the King saddened us all," Carnegie wrote Whitelaw Reid. "Mr. Roosevelt's visit will naturally be greatly changed by the event."[28] Still, Carnegie hoped some political breakthrough might be salvaged if the kaiser and Roosevelt traveled together to the funeral.[29] Any optimism for measurable accomplishments was crushed as the London debriefing of Roosevelt was canceled, and a despondent Carnegie, still at Skibo, passed along the news to Reid in London: "The King's death has changed all and as there is to be no meeting at least for some time there is not need for my running up to London. . . . We will keep out of London hubbub and rest quietly here."[30]

Roosevelt, for his part, made the best of his time in England, anyway. "My last twenty-four hours on England have really been the pleasantest of all, as I spent them with Edward Grey in the valley of the Itchen and the New Forest, listening to bird songs," he informed Carnegie. Then, after having denigrated Carnegie in the presence of the kaiser, he had the impudence to add, "Well, I wish I could have seen a little more of you. . . . When you reach New York, come out in an auto and take lunch with us in Oyster Bay."[31] A presidential election was only two years away, and Roosevelt had to keep his options open.

It appeared, for the moment, Carnegie had but one last hope in securing peace: Taft, who had spoken so bravely for unconditional arbitration.

Nicholas Murray Butler, who was president of the American branch of the Association for International Conciliation, and Hamilton Holt, editor of the *Independent*, deserved the credit for inspiring Carnegie to make his boldest strike yet for peace. But Carnegie took all the acclaim for himself.

During discussions at a 1908 New York Peace Society dinner in honor of Elihu Root, Butler and Holt decided to propose to Carnegie the creation of a well-endowed foundation loosely modeled on the Carnegie Institution that worked for the cause of peace. They went so far as to draft a charter, but the concept proved too nebulous for Carnegie. His attitude began to change when, in the summer of 1910, Congress authorized Taft to create a Peace Commission charged with studying the prospects of organizing an international naval force to police the seas. It was a glimmer of hope for Carnegie in what had been a disastrous year to date. From Skibo, he immediately cabled Taft suggesting Butler, Charles W. Eliot, and Seth Low, among others, as candidates for the commission. Apparently Taft wasn't put off by the intrusion because he considered Carnegie a candidate, too, but then he thought the better of it. "There is a suggestion of Carnegie," he told Knox, "but Mr. Roosevelt and I both agreed, in discussing it, that he might be a hard man to be responsible for because he talked so much."[32] In mulling over this latest development along with Taft's position on arbitration, which was now endorsed by Britain's foreign secretary, Sir Edward Grey, Carnegie decided the time was ripe for a magnanimous gesture toward peace.

On October 28, Taft, who hoped his peace policy would be his jewel, his legacy that distinguished him from Roosevelt, hosted the Carnegies at the White House for an overnight stay, giving the two men a chance to talk privately about the explosive military buildup in Europe and arbitration treaties.[33] Over the course of the evening, Carnegie introduced the Peace Institution concept, and the two men agreed to help each other: Taft would vigorously pursue a series of unprecedented arbitration treaties, and Carnegie would create the organization to support him, a propaganda machine promoting peace. As a sign of good faith, Carnegie wanted Taft to announce publicly his resolve to win ratification of the treaties in his upcoming message to Congress, but wary of showing his hand before Carnegie's organization was up and running, Taft confided to a White House aide: "The trouble with old Carnegie is, he might secure what he wants in my message and then not give the money. I think I will go a little slow until old Andrew becomes more specific."[34]

Taft's suspicions were unfounded as Carnegie now adopted the 1908 Butler-Holt idea of a peace institution as his own. "Private. I have a new idea," he wrote Morley on November 4, "or rather I have decided once for all my course upon action upon a new idea but will take some time before announced—President approves heartily so does Root."[35] Now entered Root, veteran arbitrator and respected man of peace, who became indispensable in helping Carnegie create the specific organization Taft wanted, from focusing its mission to crafting the language in the deed. Sensing time was of the essence, less than two weeks after his meeting with Taft and after frantic shuttling between New York and Washington by Root, on November 11 Carnegie sent a working draft of the deed for the Carnegie Endowment for International Peace to Knox, who, along with Taft, approved it.[36] As a seventy-fifth birthday present to himself and for dramatic effect, Carnegie decided to publicly announce the creation of the endowment on November 25. "Tomorrow you will be 75 years young!" Butler congratulated him. "What a grand 75 years they have been! Lincoln was a raw-boned young man when you were born & Napoleon had not long been dead. Think of the change! Today Napoleon is unthinkable. Peaceful industry and enlightenment are putting an end to war. Just think how much you have helped it all on, & are helping it on. Thank God for your health & strength & broad vision."[37]

With his end of the bargain well under way, Carnegie wrote Taft a gentle reminder to keep his promise, warning him that to assure his legacy "among the masses" he must take "a grandly bold forward step. Nothing Commonplace will do." He continued, "Excuse me for presuming to tender counsel, you can justly charge it to an intense desire to see you occupy the Commanding position you have deserved and which entitles you not only to another term—that goes without saying—but to foremost place in history which will be yours if you stand firm in advocacy of the views you have been the first Ruler to declare."[38] How could Taft question his presumption to tender counsel when he had just set aside a $10 million endowment to back the president's policy? Carnegie was simply too tenacious and too rich to ignore. The deal, however, was an act of calculated desperation by both men. Carnegie desired to rescue Western civilization from the clutches of war, while Taft desired to secure his legacy in history.

On December 14, the world's first institution dedicated to peace research and abolishing war was officially established in Washington. Taft was appointed honorary president and Root was appointed president, a post he would hold until 1925. Twenty-eight trustees in total were named, including: Charles W. Eliot, president emeritus of Harvard; Joseph Choate, former ambassador to Great Britain; former secretary of state John W. Foster; Henry S. Pritchett, president of the Carnegie Foundation for the Advancement of Teaching and former president of the Massachusetts Institute of Technology; Andrew D.

The cartoonists had great fun with Carnegie when he endowed the
Carnegie Endowment for International Peace with $10 million—no one
could comprehend how the money would be spent. (Courtesy of the
Carnegie Library of Pittsburgh)

White, former ambassador to Germany; Robert S. Woodward, president of
the Carnegie Institution; and Luke E. Wright, former ambassador to Japan
and secretary of war. "I thought of asking you to be a trustee but this seemed
too small for you and besides I feared you might dislike to refuse," Carnegie
wrote Roosevelt, "so I kept you free. If you ever wished to join very easy to
arrange."[39] In the final draft of the letter, he deleted the last line—Roosevelt,
he had finally admitted to himself, was not a man of peace. A trusteeship was
offered to Knox, who declined, an indication that he wanted to keep his distance from Carnegie.

In the deed (still using reformed spelling), Carnegie wrote, "I hav transferred to you as Trustees of the Carnegie Peace Fund, Ten Million Dollars of
Five Percent First Mortgage Bonds, the revenue of which is to be adminis-
tered by you to hasten the abolition of war, the foulest blot upon our civilization. Altho we no longer eat our fellow men, nor torture prisoners, nor sack
cities killing their inhabitants, we still kill each other in war like barbarians."
Once war was banished, he stated further, the trustees were then to "consider
what is the next degrading evil of evils whose banishment—or what new elevating element or elements if introduced or fathered, or both combined—

would most advance the progress, elevation, and happiness of man, and so on from century to century without end."[40]

The *Independent* called it Carnegie's greatest gift. Baron d'Estournelles de Constant thanked him on behalf of "the children of all the world."[41] Morley cheered: "This last noble stroke of wisdom and beneficence is the crowning achievement, and is universally recognized for what it is—a real ascent in the double spheres of ideal and practical. . . . Today, my dear Carnegie, you have truly made us, who are your friends, proud of you, including especially one who has been your friend longest of them all, to wit, John Morley."[42] And Taft did indeed hold up his end of the bargain. Three days after the endowment was made legal, on a Saturday evening, he stood before the attendees of the first annual conference of the Society for the Judicial Settlement of International Disputes in the New Willard Hotel in Washington and intimated the United States would establish a treaty with another major power. Shortly thereafter he authorized Knox to negotiate arbitration treaties on broader terms than ever before, with Britain and France the first targets. Carnegie offered hearty congratulations and some advice, of course: the key to success was for Knox "to prepare the ground" by consulting with the Foreign Relations Committee in the Senate, rather than making unilateral decisions.[43] But would Knox heed what was sound advice from a man he had come to detest?

Certainly, the Endowment for International Peace had its work cut out; the European armament buildup appeared unstoppable. First, however, the men had to settle a conflict amongst themselves: some of the trustees were disturbed by the intrusion of private interests and money on Washington. Yes, there had always been campaign contributions and reciprocal favors, some not so legal, but never on this scale. The pact between Carnegie and Taft was an extremely dangerous precedent. Also, they feared that if it became known Carnegie was essentially funding Taft's peace agenda, it would destroy Taft's work. And a weak Taft would make for a weak Endowment for International Peace if they worked hand in hand. The trustees wanted to freely pursue their own course toward peace, without constriction that might hinder success, and Butler pushed for the organization to relocate in New York, where greater autonomy could be had. It remained in Washington; however, insiders took note when Taft's name did not appear in the first annual report as the trustees moved to distance themselves somewhat from the administration.

For all the publicity and compliments Carnegie garnered from around the world, the public was curious—and rightly so—as to how such a prodigious endowment would be spent on such a cause. The usual cynics came forth, typified in a rancorous letter received by Trustee Jacob G. Schmidlapp, in which the author attacked Carnegie's benefaction and raised the old robber baron tariff issue:

> Your brother peacemaker Carnegie reminds me of a verse that I learned at an early period of my life: "There was an old woman who lived in a shoe. She had so many children, she didn't know what to do." Carnegie seems to

know no better what to do with his money than this old lady knew what to do with her children. . . . He gives you ten millions of dollars to promote peace, every penny of which was the Dead Sea fruit of a war tariff which he has himself admitted was unnecessary and therefore oppressive, and he selects forty of the most conspicuous men of his acquaintance in the country, pretty nearly everyone of whom is a stand pat protectionist, and a red-handed partisan of war upon every commercial nation, including our own, to spend millions for peace, without the suggestion of a single step they were to take to accomplish it.[44]

So how would the income from a $10 million endowment be expended in the name of peace?

The mission was "To promote a thorough and scientific investigation and study of the causes of war and of the practical methods to prevent and avoid it." Other stated purposes included aiding the development of international law, diffusing information, cultivating friendly feelings among nations, and promoting peaceable methods to settle international disputes.[45] But how would these goals manifest themselves specifically? Butler attempted to answer some of these questions in an essay he penned for Holt's *Independent*. Part of the process for preventing war involved infusing a new attitude in governments and people, he said. The principle of nationalism had to have superimposed on it a new political structure of internationalism, which involved shaping the evolution of the highest institutions in the judicial, legislative, and executive branches from viewing war as an accepted means for settling international disputes to embracing judicial methods for settling them. "To accomplish these ends elaborate and prolonged studies, highly scientific in character, must be made and their results published to the world."[46]

To begin such a noble crusade, the endowment secured the cooperation of some two hundred eminent international economists, historians, lawyers, and scholars to aid in the research and promotion of peace. In July 1912, for example, the trustees appointed a commission to study and dissect the economic, social, and political causes and effects of the Second Balkan War. It was hoped that by publishing the outrages committed during the war and clearly illustrating how it could have been avoided, future bloodshed would be averted. Published reports and the endowment's activities were disseminated on every continent. The endowment paid for exchange lecturers to travel to various countries to promote mutual understanding and peace. Money was donated to peace societies and kindred institutions. Spending the money was not a problem, as it turned out; finding useful causes yielding concrete results remained the difficult part.

There was one prize Carnegie still yearned to capture: an arbitration treaty with Great Britain that would be akin to a race reunion, his dream since the early 1890s. By February 1911, Taft and Knox were moving forward on such a treaty, but an impatient Carnegie pushed for information on the progress, chiding one of Taft's representatives that he wanted more than the mere updates he could read in the newspapers.[47] Although a treaty was far from signed, there was a backlash from nationalist forces in the Roosevelt camp, who feared the treaty might evolve into a dreaded mutual defense pact. To alleviate any such concerns, Carnegie took to the newspapers, telling the United Press he was in almost daily communication with Taft, and he went so far as to write a model for the treaty with Great Britain, which he then forwarded to the president. He had crossed the line. By assuming the role of the secretary of state, he did more than step on toes; he greatly offended Taft, who instructed Knox to muzzle the endower of peace. "I confess," Carnegie admitted to Knox, concerning the treaty work, "I thought it was like most extremely great things, quite easy, the right key to open the door having been found and exhibited by the President, a real open sesame; but after seeing you I may realize that much has yet to be done. So be it! I can be patient."[48]

His patience didn't last long. Within months, he again intruded on Knox's territory, when a popular revolt against the Manchu dynasty swept through parts of China and Carnegie recognized the name of one of the leaders based in Shanghai. It was Wu Ting Fang, an acquaintance from years ago. He cabled Fang: "Our hearts go out to you. Success attend you." Two days later, Fang replied: "Grateful good Wishes. We are fighting for liberty and good government. Kindly ask your government to recognize us." There was no need to ask the government! Carnegie immediately cabled: "Our country certain among first to welcome heartily sister Republic."[49] Only afterward did he forward the cables to Taft's office. Carnegie had wrongly come to believe that the deal with Taft entitled him to speak for the country, and his presumptuous enthusiasm threatened the broad arbitration treaties as much as Knox's heavy-handedness or Roosevelt's opposition.

In spite of his meddling, on May 19, 1911, an overjoyed Carnegie was finally able to congratulate Knox when it appeared arbitration treaties with Britain and France were to be a reality. "What a hit. Must strengthen you in the Senate . . . I imagine you, pen in hand, signing the greatest document in its influence upon the world ever signed. Your piloting superb. I am rejoicing that I live in these days."[50] The very next day, however, Roosevelt fired a vicious volley in his personal crusade against the arbitration treaties when an article he authored appeared in *Outlook*, attacking Taft's foreign policy.[51]

When Roosevelt's *Outlook* article made headlines, Carnegie immediately questioned him as to why now, at this pivotal point, was he so vehemently against arbitration? In a condescending and patronizing note, the former president replied, "You know that one reason why I hesitated long before writing that article was just because I hated to do anything that might seem distasteful to you. I finally came to the conclusion that it would be a weakness on my part not to write it. . . . If it had not been for the very unfortunate statement that we would arbitrate questions of honor, I do not think any trouble would have come about the treaty at all."[52] Despite the Roosevelt factor, Taft remained optimistic. "I am sorry that Theodore thought it necessary to come in advance of a definite knowledge of what we are planning to do," he wrote Carnegie, but he didn't believe Theodore's invectives wouldn't "interfere with the consummation of what you and I both desire."[53]

The days dragged into another month as the sensitive diplomats word-smithed the documents into acceptable terms for their respective countries. Carnegie's impatience was evident as the dickering continued; on June 24, Britain's ambassador in Washington, James Bryce, perceptively cautioned tolerance.[54] Four days later, Bryce assured Carnegie the end was in sight: "There is really very little between us & as the President is genuinely wishful to put the thing through now, this session we hope this may be achieved. The political situation in the Senate is so odd, & unprecedented, that one fears to prophesy, but I don't see why they should refuse the Treaty; it doesn't infringe what they think is their prerogative. In all our discussions over the wording of the Treaty, Knox has been very fair and reasonable; he is genuinely wishful that the thing should be done & done well."[55] Carnegie still had his suspicions about Knox, whom he had previously advised to ingratiate himself with the Senate to secure passage of the treaties.

At this critical juncture, there was an unexpected and magnificent display of support: the pope issued an autographed brief supporting Taft's peace work. "It will be the duty of each priest to read this in public," Taft's secretary wrote Carnegie. "I understand that the brief praises the President for his part in this stroke of statesmanship, and commends you for the interest you have taken in the cause, and the substantial aid you have rendered it."[56] The operative words were most certainly "substantial aid"—money and propaganda.

On June 29, as the final drafts of the treaties with Britain and France were completed, Carnegie cabled his friend: "Shake friend Morley, Shake. I am the happiest mortal alive. Couldn't call snakes snake this morning if naming created things."[57] The joyful but cryptic message flew right past Morley, who was baffled by it. Carnegie clarified: "Sorry my telegram not understood—thot you knew the celebrated American who being elected declared he felt so happy that he couldn't libel snakes by calling them by their real name. I had just heard that the Race—our race had agreed to banish war—the greatest step upward ever taken by any race since history began. . . . Other nations will soon follow."[58] The glorious race reunion was at hand in the form of a treaty. All the effort in the name of peace, all the money, the $10 million pact with Taft was now justifiable.

On the eve of the family's traditional July sojourn in the Highland lodge (now at newly constructed quarters called Aultnagar), a rejuvenated Carnegie again wrote Morley: "Skibo never so beautiful. I mourn our departure in many respects, but I am going to begin my memoirs [for the third time or so] up on the moors, opening with my retirement from business eleven years ago. I have a new life to describe, acquisition & distribution of surplus wealth, & as I have had to organize & gather sound men above the sordid love of gain & adhere myself to my vow never to make another dollar, it is an interesting development. At least it should be—I dout if any business man so far as I have known then could perform the task I'm going to try."[59]

There appeared to be little concern of a Senate defeat when, on August 3, Taft signed the arbitration treaties with Britain and France. The *Los Angeles Times* considered the treaties the most praiseworthy presidential action since the Emancipation Proclamation, and the *New York Times* proclaimed them Taft's crowning achievement. Only Roosevelt, mulling over the prospect of running for president, remained a thorn in Taft's side: all personal communication between the two men had broken off. The Rough Rider continued his high-decibel attack against the "tomfool" treaties and "mollycoddles" who feared using force to protect the country.

Roosevelt was the lesser of Taft's worries. Just as Carnegie feared, Knox had not consulted the Senate adequately—at least not adequately enough to soothe their egos—and the senators were now busy ripping apart the treaties. Knox, showing his lack of diplomacy, turned the ratification process into such a political disaster that he appeared to be sabotaging them. At the end of August, an unhappy Root informed Carnegie, "The trouble could have been averted easily if some of the Senate had been consulted before the treaty was signed."[60] While this was not a revelation to Carnegie, he was caught off guard by the strong opposition. "The disappointment is too great to cause annoyance, or wrath," he wrote Ambassador Bryce. "It falls like a heavy dull load of disaster which we must slowly surmount. It is a serious struggle to get two thirds majority from a body that changes so slowly. I hope some compromise can be reached. Taft's reelection, however, seems so certain by an overwhelming majority that he may win without changing form of treaty, but it seems more probable to me that some change can be arranged without sacrificing much."[61] While Carnegie and Taft were willing to compromise, Knox was so adamantly opposed to the idea that his loyalty to Taft was thrown into question.

Carnegie could take little comfort in the fact that in October Root and he were nominated separately for the Nobel Peace Prize. Root would win.

On his return to New York that October, Carnegie took to the soapbox in support of the treaties. He shuttled back and forth between his home and Washington, where he either cajoled Senate members, consulted with the president, or urged his Endowment for International Peace trustees to use all their resources in support of Taft. The endowment trustees were having a crisis of conscious, however, over their role as a propaganda machine. After a morning meeting with Carnegie on October 26, the trustees reconsidered their position in a battle that had mired the country in constitutional, legal, and political arguments. Did they want to be caught in the cross fire between Taft, Roosevelt, and the Senate? No. They wanted to step back and carry on their peace mission without being tainted by political malarkey. "After careful consideration of the opinion advanced at the morning session and of the attitude of Mr. Carnegie . . . ," the endowment's secretary wrote in the minutes, "the committee agreed that the work of propaganda begun at the instance of Mr. Carnegie should cease."[62] The entry was later deleted, but Carnegie was now aware of the disenchantment.

Always willing to go it alone, he continued his campaign, speaking on behalf of the treaties before an audience at Carnegie Hall, the address marked by disturbances attributed to the "ignorant Irish Americans."[63] Carnegie still held his belief that publicity of one's work was as important as the work. "Well do I remember my apprehension when you advocated keeping all you did quiet," he would write Morley the next year. "*No show*. No advocacy. Only go on & do the work in a quiet way, when I knew that advertizing was essential for success, i.e. to spreading abroad what could be done. . . . Of course its disagreeable work & puts me forward as a vain trumpeter but one who isn't willing to play this part *for the good* to be done, isn't much of a man."[64] His high-profile involvement in the peace movement was becoming an impediment, however; Knox resented his intrusion, as did the Senate, which could vote against the treaties simply to spite him. As Knox had warned him earlier in the year, "exaggerated public discussion" might hinder the process. As Root later observed, "The thing which has made me feel very certain about the importance of keeping out of political matters is that what we do carries a certain prejudice; this is the Carnegie Endowment; Mr. Carnegie is still living, and active and prominent. The people of the country are exceedingly sensitive as to the employment of the money of rich men toward influencing public opinion. I think that is the great trouble." [65]

Roosevelt complicated matters further by declaring his intention to run for president—"My hat is in the ring! The fight is on and I am stripped to the buff"—which served to fracture Taft's Republican support in the Senate.[66] Now Taft's reelection, which Carnegie had predicted, was far from guaranteed.

Feeling betrayed and wounded, Carnegie wrote Roosevelt a long, rambling letter in an attempt to induce him to reconsider. He considered the Taft-Roosevelt relationship to be "idyllic," and begged him to meet with the president "face to face and just let your hearts speak. It is not too late. You are both big enough to discard mean petty trifles and renew your idyllic relations before history records you as false or worse." Carnegie closed the letter by reminding Roosevelt that Taft's wife was ill, perhaps mortally so, suggesting the Rough Rider should not add to such a terrible burden and withdraw from the race.[67] Guilt, a weapon Carnegie used repeatedly, had no effect.

Roosevelt's reply was impenitent: "You oblige me to speak frankly by what you say about Mr. Taft—I would not say this for publication. I have never been so bitterly disappointed in any man. I care not one whit as to his attitude toward me. But I care immensely as to his attitude toward the people. He has completely reversed the position he held when he was my lieutenant."[68] Unwilling to provoke further animosity, Carnegie replied, "No more of this. It will work out somehow. The republic is invulnerable."[69] He was not so strong in faith when he wrote Morley two days later: "I am mourning over the pitiable disagreement between Roosevelt & Taft. . . . Roosevelt wrong in not agreeing second term for President who has done so well—Roosevelt & Niagara. Quite true. Both uncontrollable."[70]

It was now apparent the treaties with Britain and France, as they were, would not be ratified by the Senate, at least not until after the election. For Carnegie, the unconditional arbitration treaties were like dividends to Phipps in days past—just as they appeared on the horizon, they were gone again. Even though Henry Cabot Lodge, chairman of the Foreign Relations Committee and the Senate's opposition leader, hinted at compromise, Taft, like Roosevelt before him, felt humiliated by the Senate and wasn't going to cave. Instead, he decided to incorporate the treaties directly into his reelection platform. "The people of the country have manifested a very general and unusual degree of interest in these treaties and I believe that the preponderance of public sentiment is overwhelmingly in their favor. . . ," he explained to Carnegie.[71] The fight wasn't over yet, and Carnegie would donate a whopping $100,000 to Taft's reelection campaign.[72]

CHAPTER 34

The Last Great Benefaction

C arnegie's obsession with peace was evident in that since his 1905 creation of the Foundation for the Advancement of Teaching, there had
been no major new philanthropic endeavors outside the realm of peace.
Libraries did remain his pet, and he continued to fund them at a torrid pace;
yet, in 1910, he still had about $180 million to disburse. Time was not on his
side, and so, under the growing fear of dying rich, he realized radical action
was called for to purge both his Hoboken, New Jersey, vault and any final
doubts lingering in his conscience.

One creation that had still been consuming a relatively large percentage
of Carnegie's interest, energy, and money was his Pittsburgh institute. In April
1907, Carnegie was in Pittsburgh celebrating the historic opening of the institute's magnificent Art Gallery and Natural Museum of History, six years in
the making. Railroad carloads of celebrities were brought from Europe, as
were heads of state from around the world, for the three-day celebration held
over April 11, 12, and 13. The night before the dedication, as Carnegie and
Louise prepared to retire, the benefactor became overwhelmed by what had
been accomplished in Pittsburgh, by the sudden grandeur of the Carnegie
Institute, which now measured among the elite museums of the world. In a
tremulous voice, he said to his wife, "It is like the mansion raised in the night
by the genii, who obeyed Aladdin."

"Yes, and you did not even have to rub the lamp."

Speaking at the dedication, his words reflected the amazement expressed
to Louise the night before. "I have been in a dream ever since I arrived here,"
he told the enraptured audience, "and I am still in a dream. As I look upon
this building, I can hardly realize what has been done in my absence by the
men who have made it. I have tried to make myself realize that I have anything to do with it, and have failed to do so."[1] Many a time Carnegie
attempted to comprehend just exactly how he'd come to have such enormous

wealth, but he could not—it was like attempting to grasp the unfathomable size of the universe. A correspondent for *Cosmopolitan* concurred: "All the people, in a general way, know about Mr. Carnegie; but how few really grasp the fairy-tale in all its fulness! It extinguishes the glory of Croesus and makes the story of Aladdin seem cheap."[2]

Almost quadruple the size it once was, the institute was now an imposing three-story building of gray sandstone in the American Renaissance style. The entrance to the gallery and museum was graced with bronze statues of Bach, Galileo, Michelangelo, and Shakespeare, and the interior was lavishly decorated, including a generous use of variegated marble—six thousand tons imported from Europe. The top floors of the art galleries and museum opened to a glass roof and a brooding Hall of Architecture, capped by a pyramidal roof, bridged the new building and the old.

As visitors entered the Hall of Architecture, they felt as though they had stepped back into the ancient and the medieval worlds as they encountered a re-creation of the tomb of King Mausolus of Halicarnassus and the entire facade of a twelfth-century Romanesque church, among other casts of architectural monuments. Carnegie had commissioned an army of agents to seek out the best models in architecture and sculpture to be cast in plaster for the museum, and the agents had spent five years traipsing about Europe to secure the casts. Also home to such casts, the museum's Hall of Sculpture was built to the scale of the Parthenon, with white columns of Pentelic marble and a duplicate of the Parthenon frieze. As for the art galleries, Carnegie didn't want old masters; he wanted new masters who would then become old, his logic being that the masses of the people would better appreciate contemporary work they could relate to.[3] And the institute's Natural Museum of History could finally display the *Diplodocus carnegii*, discovered in 1898, in the bone-chilling Hall of Dinosaurs. As could have been expected, the satirists had a field day comparing the capitalist to the dinosaur: both had huge appetites, and the robber baron was now on the verge of extinction in the Roosevelt era. The museum would soon have one of the most important collections of South American fishes, among other superlative collections, and plundered treasures that would garner a world-renowned reputation.

Carnegie capped off the festivities by giving another $5 million toward the endowment, bringing the total to $6 million. It was estimated he had now given some $25 million to the institute in money and material in his zeal as a trustee of civilization.[4]

On the library front, requests dwindled in 1907–1908 as towns couldn't make the financial commitment due to the economic downturn. For those keeping score, *Collier's* magazine provided a tally. As of December 31, 1908, the magazine noted, Carnegie had given $51,596,903 to libraries in these countries:

United States	959 buildings
England and Wales	329
Scotland	105
Canada	86
Ireland	42
New Zealand	14
British West Indies	5
South Africa	3
Australia and Tasmania	2
Seychelles Islands	1
Fiji Islands	1

Libraries had been built in 47 states and the District of Columbia, with Illinois leading the way at 81, followed by Iowa and Ohio with 78 and 71, respectively. Pennsylvania had 39 and New York, 47. In an interview for the *Collier's* article, Carnegie confirmed his joy in giving to libraries: "The letters received from parents thanking me for libraries established and telling of the change these have made upon their children are numerous. It is not only what a library does in a community; that is only one-half of its sphere. What it prevents is equally important. If young men do not spend their evenings in the library, where will they be spending them? If the young do not acquire a taste for reading, what will they otherwise acquire?"[5] By now, Carnegie recognized that it was the youth who would benefit, not the workingmen in the mills he originally intended to aid.

For his unheralded munificence, King Edward had wanted to honor Carnegie and offered a title in 1908, but he respectfully demurred. He preferred a letter of appreciation for his study wall, which the King accommodated. "You have no doubt seen the action of the king," Carnegie, who still reveled in receiving commendations, wrote his Dunfermline solicitor Ross. "The question was whether there was any way in which His Majesty could honor me which I would appreciate. My, what a chance I lost! I might have been a duke! Then you would have treated me with respect, and to get over your bossing me was something of a temptation."[6]

Contrary to any lack of respect Ross may have displayed on occasion, Carnegie, with a face as craggy as the rough Highlands and thinning white hair, was, in the general public's opinion, a national treasure, not a ruthless robber baron. No longer did his name evoke images of smoky Homestead with trigger-happy Pinkertons and bloodthirsty steelworkers. Now he was a wizened benefactor and sage, and the newspapers on both sides of the Atlantic continued to seek his opinion on all the issues of the day.

The papers also continued to keep a scorecard of his philanthropy versus that of Rockefeller. On December 21, 1910, the *New York American* estimated Carnegie's total lifetime giving at $179,300,000 versus Rockefeller's $134,271,000. Moreover, Rockefeller still demurred to Carnegie as the king of benefaction, and even sought his advice on setting up a trust company to administer his estate.[7] Far more discreet than his Scottish peer, the oil baron appeared detached from his philanthropy, which prompted Carnegie's friend Charles Eliot to observe, "Mr. Rockefeller's method of giving away money impersonally on the basis of investigation by others was careful and conscientious; but it must have cut him off almost completely from the real happiness which good deeds brought to the doer."[8]

In spite of the king's letter of commendation and beating Rockefeller in the benefaction race, Carnegie was forced to admit that his money giving had bogged down and that the eternally infernal headaches that arose with each new benefaction were beginning to depress him. During a speech in Edinburgh, he had paused and, breaking from his prepared text, he said, "Millionaires who laugh are rare, very rare, indeed."[9] No longer was philanthropy as enjoyable as golf. He found himself with about $180 million still in the bank, and he despaired over leaving Louise with the responsibility of dispensing with his surplus wealth if he were to die. Despondent, he turned to one of the few men who had proved trustworthy: Elihu Root.

An earnest and worried-looking man, Root's mouth appeared carved into a frown, but his short bangs and trim mustache balanced his seriousness with a touch of boyishness. Overall, he did not leave a domineering impression. What made him unique was his direct frankness with any man and his skill in tempering the impulsiveness of such men as Carnegie and Roosevelt. Once, when debating policy with Root, an irritated Roosevelt said, "Oh, go to the devil, Root!" Unflustered, the secretary raised his glass in mock salute to the president and responded blithely, "I come, Sir, I come."[10] Unlike Roosevelt, Root harbored no duplicitous feelings toward Carnegie. Like the philanthropist, he was a devout disciple of peace and would win the 1912 Nobel Peace Prize. He also agreed with Carnegie's "Gospel of Wealth," becoming an invaluable adviser to the benefactor—but never asking for money for his own pet causes like Roosevelt, Wilson, and White, among so many others.

Carnegie's first step was to draft a revision of his will, adding a provision for a great philanthropic trust to be created on his death to take the onus off Louise, which he then gave to Root for review. After examining it, he pointed out what had happened to Samuel J. Tilden, a case Carnegie knew well. Tilden's trust had been challenged in court and tied up for years. To avoid any legal entanglements, Root suggested he create such a trust now to administer the bulk of his remaining wealth and therefore take the burden off Carnegie himself, who, along with his secretaries, shouldered overwhelming responsibilities. At first he was reluctant, but as Root told him, "You have had the best run for your money I have ever known."[11] It was time to cross the finish line. On June 9, 1911, the New York State legislature passed an act to establish the Carnegie Corporation, the trust Root envisioned. He endowed it with $25 million to start, then added $75 million in January 1912, and another $25 million the next October to bring the total to $125 million. Carnegie served as the first president, Root as vice president, Robert Franks as vice president and treasurer, and Bertram as secretary. These men plus five others—including Carnegie's newly hired personal secretary, John A. Poynton—comprised the board of trustees.

At the first meeting, held at his Ninety-first Street home on November 11, Carnegie delivered the charge "to promote the advancement and diffusion of knowledge and understanding among the people of the United States by aiding technical schools, institutions of higher lerning, libraries, scientific research, hero funds, useful publications, and by such other agencies and means as shall from time to time be found appropriate therefore." The trustees were given "full authority to change policy or clauses hitherto aided, from time to time, when this, in their opinion becomes necessary or desirable. They shall best conform to my wishes by using their own judgment." It was the first endowment that gave the trustees a completely free hand to distribute the money as they thought best—in perpetuity—and he concluded his gift letter by stating, "My chief happiness as I write these lines lies in the thot that even after I pass away the welth that came to me to administer as a sacred trust for the good of my fellow men is to continue to benefit humanity for generation untold."[12] This idea of being made immortal by the trust appealed to him.

While the corporation did not target a specific cause, it would predominantly support his existing projects and initiatives, with the corporation's largest contributions being to the Carnegie Foundation for the Advancement of Teaching ($15,250,000), the building of libraries ($14,174,148.91), and the Carnegie Institute at Pittsburgh ($6,500,979.67). Eventually it would give away almost $50 million prior to Carnegie's death.

Certainly, in any moments spared from his peace campaign, Carnegie remained active in promoting his foundations' work, both to the benefit and to the chagrin of his trustees. Work by the Carnegie Institution of Washington always intrigued him. Entranced with astronomy, in January 1911, Carnegie visited the Mount Wilson observatory in the mountains of southern California, a site funded by the institution, to gaze on his godless heavens. The observatory enjoyed the most advanced facilities yet, including a telescope tube with a sixty-inch aperture, the largest at the time. Carnegie enjoyed telling friends that the telescope revealed sixty thousand new suns, while cynics remarked that was akin to finding sixty thousand new gallons of water in Lake Michigan. When he learned that for $500,000 the observatory could obtain an even more powerful telescope one hundred inches in diameter, he decided to give another $10 million in bonds (yielding $500,000 annually) to the institution's endowment, shooting tremors through the scientific community, but with the money came the demand for the new telescope. "I hope the work at Mount Wilson will be vigorously pushed because I am so anxious to hear the expected results from it," he wrote his "independent" trustees. "I should like to be satisfied, before I depart, that we are going to repay to the old land some part of the debt we owe them by revealing more clearly than ever to them the new heavens."[13] How gloriously righteous if the telescope could prove the Heaven guarded by St. Peter was pure myth.

Another major undertaking by the institution was the launching of the *Carnegie*, a uniquely designed brigantine with auxiliary power that would ultimately sail nearly four hundred thousand miles, charting the oceans. The hull was made of wood, and all the metalwork was of nonmagnetic bronze or copper to eliminate any interference with the magnetic compasses used. Without a doubt, the chart work saved untold lives, and the innovative boat fired Carnegie's competitive spirit as he sought to secure his place, and the Republic's place, in scientific history.

"The declared object of the Carnegie Institution was to attain preeminence if possible in investigations, discovery, etc., for the Republic," he wrote his newly elected president of the institution, Robert Woodward. "I quite agree with you that the money given in Britain, as far as I know, is not well managed. Too many doctrinaires and too little managing ability. My impression is that rather than assist projects already started, if the Carnegie Institution does anything in foreign lands it should be in some new field, where success will be credited to the Republic. Rivalry between nations is beneficent when it is rivalry for good ends."[14]

At the time the institution was making great strides, Carnegie's Foundation for the Advancement of Teaching provided another unforeseen benefit. One of the staff members, Abraham Flexner, was charged with evaluating medical schools to determine if they were worthy of pension money. What he discovered disturbed him. A zealot, he visited some 155 schools personally and concluded that their quality was scandalously poor; many were merely degree factories run for profit. One school's physiology lab consisted of nothing but a pulse-taking device; another school had not one scrap of scientific apparatus; and of the 155 medical schools, only 23 required more than a high school diploma for matriculation. Flexner issued a scathing report evaluating facilities and teaching staff; if he believed the institution was purely a money-making scam, he said so. That prompted one of the schools to sue the foundation for "injuring its business." The 1910 "Flexner Report" had a definite, positive impact on improving the quality of medical education; so much so that John D. Rockefeller's vigilant minister of philanthropy, Frederick Gates, recruited Flexner to help manage Rockefeller's medical benefactions.

Not all of Carnegie's endeavors were a success. The spelling-reform movement died a quiet death, much to the pleasure of Whitelaw Reid, who called it a "fictitious movement." A retort from Carnegie was quick in coming: "Amused at your calling improved spelling movement 'a fictitious movement' . . . move up, move on before old age comes—don't be an old fogey—*if you can* help it."[15] But by 1911, what movement there had been was faltering badly, and the trustees of his foundations, once ordered to use the reformed words, were rebelling. "You will see from this report that in deference to my eminent colleagues of the Executive Committee and the Board of Trustees I have taken what we would call a step backwards in reference to spelling," Carnegie Institution of Washington president Woodward informed him. "My experiment with the two proceeding reports met with a degree of disfavor which was unanticipated. . . . I have concluded that the relatively small question of the spelling of the English language should not be allowed to jeopardize the larger interests of the Institution."[16] Less than four years later, Carnegie, who continued to use the revised spellings, cut off funding for the Simplified Spelling Board. Spiteful and quick to place the blame elsewhere, he wrote Henry Holt: "A more useless body of men never came into association, judging from the effects they produced. . . . I think I hav been patient long enuf. . . . I have a much better use for the Twenty-five thousand dollars a year."[17]

Another flash of Carnegie's that failed at this time was model housing for the poor. It was a revelation that came thirty years too late. In 1911, he finally recognized that libraries did not bring indoor plumbing, sewage systems, and better living conditions to the submerged tenth, the destitute. Like Horace Greeley had sixty years earlier, he realized certain segments of society simply could not help themselves. Newly inspired, Carnegie was now actually willing to break from his dictum of only helping those who help themselves. He wrote Ross in Dunfermline, "I know of no way of diffusing sweetness and lite more easily and practically than by improving housing conditions among the poor."[18] But he had picked the wrong country in which to build model houses: class-conscious Britain would not tolerate *un*-natural uplifting of the lower classes. "Where is this experiment to stop?" Ross responded shrilly. Ross feared antagonizing powerful landowners, even though he agreed that "the improvement of houses for the poorer classes is one of the most urgent social needs."[19] To overcome the annoying objections that always seemed to plague politicians and the narrow-minded, Carnegie suggested fixing up existing houses as long as landlords pledged not to raise the rent.[20] The trustees, who distrusted any program smelling of social revolution, essentially ignored the suggestion. It was their prerogative.

As time passed, Ross and other trustees of Carnegie's foundations sought greater autonomy and became more resentful of his meddling. Slowly and sadly, Carnegie was being locked out of what he had created.

Another conflict arose with Ross when, in January 1913, the Dunfermline Trust approved an extension for *the* library, Carnegie's *first* library building, a structure he held sacred. Under the impression the extension was to be for scholars and researchers alone, Carnegie, already miffed *his* library was to be tampered with, argued that it was a pitiable use of funds because it would serve such a narrowly defined group. Ross, incensed that Carnegie was once again attempting to impose his views on what was supposed to be an *inde-*

pendent board of trustees, censured the benefactor for his intrusion. An injured Carnegie, who would never mellow with age, responded:

> You surely regret the words you have riten me but I forgive you. . . . Has it come to this, that I cannot be permitted to forcibly express my feelings? I have had and am having as much experience as you with Libraries for the Masses which is what I consider most important. Libraries for antiquarians are within reach of Dunfermline as I point out—not for working man as you have it. My Friend, beware of the weaknesses of old age—which as I begin to learn from experience sometimes betray us into regretful words or action against those we love and honor most. I have laid aside your letter, sad, indeed, feeling that I have not deserved at your hands such a blow—not angry, no, no—but oh so sorry.[21]

Both could be crotchety old men and the conflict passed quickly by, for less than a month later Carnegie, who had stormy relationships with so many, was sharing intimate feelings with Ross. After revising his will and setting up trusts for Louise and Margaret, the next month he admitted to Ross, "The final dispensation of one's wealth preparing for the final exit is I found a heavy task—all sad—deep regrets that one isn't allowed to live here in this *heaven on earth forever,* which it is to me. None other satisfactory . . . You have no idea the strain I have been under."[22] But Carnegie had no intention of going quietly into the night.

Carnegie also came into conflict with the Carnegie Corporation trustees. As an afterthought, in 1912, he decided to found a Carnegie Corporation–like foundation in Britain called the Carnegie United Kingdom Trust, to be headquartered in Dunfermline under Ross's eye. There was just one problem: he had run out of money. Well, there was still $25 million in the bank, but it had been set aside for the family and sundry bequests he desired to make on his demise. The best course, he decided, was simply to take $10 million from the Carnegie Corporation, so he submitted his request to Henry Pritchett, who was now heading the organization. It wasn't that easy, Pritchett explained, for only the trustees could make such a decision, and their decision would be limited to the deed of the endowment. In fact, the deed limited the scope of the corporation's activities to aiding the people of the United States, so the answer was no. Unwilling to accept no, Carnegie went to Root for support, but Root concurred with Pritchett.

Determined to found the United Kingdom Trust, the next year he appropriated $10 million of his U.S. Steel bonds, and in the deed he charged that the income was to be used "for the improvement of the well-being of the masses of the people of Great Britain and Ireland, by such means as are embraced within the meaning of the word 'charitable,' according to Scotch or English law, and which the Trustees may from time to time select as best fitted from age to age for securing these purposes, remembering that new needs are constantly arising as the masses advance."[23] As with the Carnegie

Corporation, the trustees were given a free hand, but the trust's initial work focused on Carnegie's existing programs: the building of libraries, especially in rural areas, and the shoring up of existing libraries. Other priorities included donating public baths and organs and sponsoring musical competitions. By 1917, social welfare and health projects were being funded, projects desperately needed by citizens on both sides of the Atlantic for decades, only to have been ignored by robber barons focused on haute culture.

Carnegie was forced to realize that his days as an influential adviser in politics and charity were coming to a close and he didn't relish entering his twilight; as he told Ross, "deep regrets that one isn't allowed to live here in this *heaven on earth forever.*" Carnegie's life had always been a tight cycle of emotional ups and downs—extremely fluctuant waves if charted on graph paper. Now was a depressed period, particularly so in the wake of creating the Carnegie Corporation and with the arbitration treaties floundering in the Senate. To make matter worse, the House of Representatives was investigating U.S. Steel, and Taft's attorney general charged the company with violating the Sherman Antitrust Act. Carnegie, retired for a dozen years, was named a codefendant. It was unthinkable.

CHAPTER 35

House of Cards

B ack in May 1911, the House of Representatives had appointed a committee, chaired by Augustus Stanley of Kentucky, to investigate the history of U.S. Steel and alleged violations of the Sherman Antitrust Act. As evidence of monopolistic behavior mounted, Taft came under pressure to act, and on October 27 Carnegie picked up the morning newspaper to discover the attorney general had filed suit against U.S. Steel, as well as against other officers and him. His lawyer, D. A. Reed, had warned Carnegie the prior week about the impending charges, but considered them unwarranted.[1] Reed then arranged a deal in which the government agreed to drop the rather senseless charges against Carnegie in exchange for his testimony as a witness, a worrisome development for Elbert H. Gary and Pierpont Morgan, considering the Scotsman had long ago proved himself a verbal loose cannon. Subsequently, Carnegie was subpoenaed to appear before the Stanley Committee in mid-January.

Louise and he spent New Year's Eve at their cottage on St. Andrew's golf course in Yonkers, and they decided to make the traditional rounds on New Year's Day. They visited with the Rockefellers, who were six miles away in Pocantico Hills, near North Tarrytown, where Rockefeller owned a weekend escape on three thousand acres overlooking the Hudson River that included a twelve-hole golf course he had plowed in winter so he could play. (Rockafellow was, after all, Carnegie's kind of man.) A tall and spare Rockefeller, smiling as he greeted them, had just finished riding and was wearing a paper jacket for warding off the cold wind. He promptly presented the Carnegies a paper jacket each and two large photographs of himself. Indulging in the friendship that day, Carnegie was gloating nine days later when, recounting his ore deal before the Stanley Committee, he proceeded to say, "Don't you know, it does my heart good to think I got ahead of John D. Rockefeller on a bargain."

It was the tenth day of January, a Wednesday, when Carnegie climbed the steps of the Capitol as sprightly as he could to testify before the committee.

Dressed for a funeral, in a dark suit, he appeared rather jovial as he once again mounted the stage in the grandest of theaters. Here he could play both the coy operator and the lovable, doddering old man. He attempted to open with a soliloquy on the history of steel, only Chairman Stanley insisted on interrupting with anticipatory questions that resulted in the dialogue disintegrating into a marginal comedy with Carnegie's personal counsel opening the routine:

MR. REED: I think you are just a step ahead of Mr. Carnegie's story, Mr. Chairman, if you will permit me to suggest it.

THE CHAIRMAN: Very well. Do not let me anticipate.

MR. CARNEGIE: Yes. If you would let me go right along, I would prefer to continue my story first, and then you can ask me questions.

THE CHAIRMAN: Very well. I will not interrupt you.

MR. CARNEGIE: Where was I?

He was reminded and the story continued; but of course, a moment later the chairman again interrupted with a question and Carnegie again forgot where he was in his story.[2] The stenographer read back Carnegie's last sentence — that is, before the previous exchange. In this polite clash of egos, the substance of the story mattered little (everyone already knew the story); it was victory in the verbal fencing that took the day.

After two days of Carnegie on the stand, one exasperated congressman declared, "We have been sitting here for two days and we have learned nothing." A quiet chuckle shook Carnegie's frame. That was precisely what he intended; after all, as he told the investigators again and again, his memory was too faulty to commit to details when under oath. The newspapers noted that Carnegie, while entertaining, didn't seem to get "anywhere in particular" and was simply "enjoying his own reminisces."[3] Carnegie not only suppressed information, but he lied. When told the Sherman Antitrust Act was passed in 1890, he appeared surprised, according to one newspaper correspondent, and claimed he didn't hear of it until much later. However, in 1890 he was very much involved in the trust debate and had even written essays on the topic. He also insisted he never studied the Carnegie Company's books and was not apprised of any of the details in running the business, which was a bold-faced lie considering how meticulously oppressive he was in monitoring all facets of the operations. Revisionist history aside, even his severest critics had to appreciate how deftly he fenced with the Stanley Committee. A mutual friend of Stanley and Carnegie wrote the latter: "I long ago told Stanley he would catch a tartar when he caught you; and I guess by this time he too thinks so."[4]

As for the government's case against U.S. Steel, in 1920 the Supreme Court would find in favor of the company.

Old wounds were once again ripped open by the hearings and the lawsuit. Based on revelations provided during the testimony, Bridge decided to revise his book—*The Inside History of the Carnegie Steel Company*—and in April asked for Carnegie's cooperation. Even though Bridge admitted to being mis-led on certain issues, Carnegie wanted no part.[5] Behind his jocular thrusts and parries with the Stanley Committee, there was a pained soul still haunted by the past. Like a mortally wounded sinner desperately seeking redemption, Carnegie wrote Alexander Peacock (as he had Lovejoy) in desperate hopes of finding that missing telegram in which Amalgamated leader Hugh O'Donnell begged the kind master to instruct them as to what to do during the Home-stead strike. "It seems to me that ritely managed," he wrote within days of hearing from Bridge, "those who had part in signing that cablegram would be glad to pass into history as having shown friendly relations between the chief owner and themselves. It mite be presented to them in this lite, I am sure. Explain fully that what I wish is to leav a record of the past and is not to be publisht at present." If the cable could not be found and if those who signed would not testify, Carnegie suggested to Peacock that perhaps he should tes-tify to the existence of the cable.[6]

As Carnegie contemplated the cable that offered an exorcism, redemp-tion, and emancipation from the past, on April 15, the invincible luxury pas-senger ship *Titanic* sank. Many notable American and British passengers were among the 1,513 who drowned out of the 2,224 on board. Four days later he cabled Dod, "Glad you are home again—*take it easy*. Cant get the Titanic out of mind."[7] The O'Donnell cable, incidentally, never surfaced—because it didn't exist.

At the family's isolated Highland retreat in the rugged countryside that summer of 1912, Carnegie ruminated over the trials of the past as he worked on his autobiography. While contemplating death and all too cognizant that his own years were numbered, he thought of Louise, of living without her if she were to die:

> I cannot imagine myself going through these twenty years without her. Nor can I endure the thought of living after her. In the course of nature I have not that to meet; but then the thought of what will be cast upon her, a woman left alone with so much requiring attention and needing a man to decide, gives me intense pain and I sometimes wish I had this to endure for her. But then she will have our blessed daughter in her life and perhaps that will keep her patient. Besides, Margaret needs her more than she does her father.
>
> Why, oh why, are we compelled to leave the heaven we have found on earth and go we know not where![8]

Facing death without a god was a frightening specter for Carnegie, but to fully shoulder the responsibilities of life on earth without a god as crutch was noble.

Carnegie's mood darkened further when it became clear there was an irreparable breach between Roosevelt and Taft that would not be resolved in time for the Republican National Convention. If Taft was not nominated and then elected, all the treaty work would be for naught. With Roosevelt calling

Taft a "fathead" with "brains less than a guinea pig" and Taft calling him "a demagogue" and "a man who can't tell the truth," the Republican Party did indeed rupture into two factions. Come November, Democrat Woodrow Wilson won the election. "The election has not surprised many—Roosevelt's power for mischief is unlimited," Carnegie wrote Morley. He then added with his eternal optimism, "Have written Wilson, of course, a nice letter. You knew he is on the board University Professor's Trust, & has been at Skibo with his wife. *He is for Peace* & will I think manage better than Taft who really failed in Treaty thru poor management."[9]

It was now time for Carnegie the political chameleon to charm Wilson, a process that was initiated with a not so subtle mix of congratulations and personal agenda pushing: "Having done my best to elect President Taft to the second term I now find myself impelled to congratulate you upon your election to the heist office upon the earth—the elected ruler of the majority of the English speaking race. My second choice. . . . What the fates have in store for you is unknown. Perhaps you are destined to succeed in banishing war between the most enlitened nations where President Taft failed. . . . I am sincerely your admirer and cannot help it."[10]

Wilson's answer was cautious but gave Carnegie hope: "I note with the greatest interest what you say about the effort to get a definite foundation of treaty of the international peace for which we are all striving, and I need not tell you again what my own sympathies and feelings are in the matter. I shall always be on that side."[11]

To acknowledge Carnegie's generous financial support during the campaign, Taft invited him to the White House for dinner on December 12. He accepted, but in the weeks between the invitation and the dinner, Carnegie's disenchantment with Taft over the failed arbitration treaty with Britain became highly bitter, and he vented his frustration on Bryce, who resigned as British ambassador a week after the election: "I hoped your crowning glory was to be The Treaty, which was lost by poor management, nothing else. It will come some day."[12]

"As you say," Bryce replied, "the Treaty was lost for want of promptitude & management. But we mustn't say that except to each other. It grieved me surely as it grieved you. How often do great enterprises fail for the want of a little tact or a little energy at the right moment."[13]

Further put out when William Barnes, chairman of the Republican State Committee, requested $10,000 to help pay debts incurred during the election, Carnegie dictated a curt response to his personal secretary, Poynton, "Mr. Carnegie . . . asks me to say that he has not recovered from the effects of the campaign and must have a rest for a time before considering anything of the nature you suggest."[14] Then came the December 12 dinner, during which conversation was strained. There was nothing Taft could salvage from his presidency, and the blustering president, questioning what he could have done differently, spent the evening lamenting the failed ratification of the treaty. As Carnegie studied the obese man, the more incensed he became with his, as well as Knox's, inept statesmanship. It had been physically and figuratively heavy-handed.

Three days later, Carnegie could no longer contain his emotions, and he exploded at Taft: "Why did you fail? The answer given by Republicans and Democrats alike was you failed to remember that the Constitution gives the Senate the right not only to consider and approve or reject, but also to advise. . . . When I learnt in Scotland the treaty had been sent to the Senate duly signed I concluded you had submitted it to the Senate Committee and cabled you my joy. I lived for days in a happier world. . . . Believe me, failure to consult the Senate Committee was the *fatal* mistake; keeping leading Senators ignorant of your presuming to make a treaty which they read for the first time to their surprise in the morning papers." The perfectly gratuitous retrospection was salt to the wounds and, across the top of the letter an offended Taft carved the letters, "Refer to Sec. Knox. Isn't it pleasant to be told how it could have been done. WHT."

After Knox read the letter, in a response to Taft the fuming secretary of state unleashed an irate tirade that been pent up over the years:

> As an exhibition of ignorance, mendacity and impudence, this communication of Mr. Carnegie's is quite up to his well known and well deserved international reputation for these mental and moral failings. It should be appropriately tagged and filed and given no further attention. His statement that we did not consult leading Senators about the peace treaties is untrue. . . . His characterization of your making a treaty without consulting the Senators as presumption upon your part is an exhibition of pitiable ignorance and a piece of colossal impudence. . . .
>
>   When Carnegie's epitaph is honestly written, its author may well use the monkish rhyme:
>   "Mel in ore, verba lactis
>   Fel in corde, fraus in factis."[15]

Carnegie's relationships with Taft and Knox were discarded in the trash, just like those with Harrison and Bryan. They no longer served a function.

Carnegie would quickly discover where Wilson stood on arbitration and peace as the first year of his administration witnessed violence on several continents: bloodshed engulfed Mexico as revolution swept the country; Turkey was warring with Italy over Libya; the Balkan countries battled the Ottoman Empire, which occupied Macedonia and had been encouraged to expand into the region by the kaiser; and Bulgaria would attack its former Balkan allies in June 1913, the month Carnegie would be in Berlin to honor the German emperor's peaceful reign and just two months before Carnegie was to finally attend the dedication of the Palace of Peace, as it was now called, in The Hague.

Endowment for International Peace trustee Nicholas Murray Butler, hoping to promote future peace, had proposed the kaiser be awarded a memorial signed by top officials of leading American societies and corporations to celebrate the twenty-fifth anniversary of the kaiser's reign, a reign without the blot of war—this despite the kaiser's ongoing massive military build-up. Carnegie, still foolishly dreaming the kaiser would prove the champion of peace, heartily endorsed the project and left New York in May with eager anticipation. First on the itinerary was Berlin, followed by Paris, and then to Skibo, before going to The Hague.

Carnegie arrived in Berlin on June 13 to convey felicitations to the kaiser. At the palace, he delivered the address of congratulations to the "Imperial Majesty as the foremost apostle of peace in our time," and then he approached with an ornate casket containing the memorial address. As he did, the emperor, with outstretched arms, said emphatically, "Remember, Carnegie! Twenty-five years of peace! If I am Emperor for another twenty-five years not a shot will be fired in Europe!" But the soothing promise belied the belligerent talk of a European war.

Perhaps a sign from the goddess of fortune, the Balkan Wars ended with the August 10 signing of the Treaty of Bucharest. The sunshine was glorious on August 28, when notables from around the world gathered in The Hague for the Palace of Peace dedication. It was "certainly unlike anything else in the world," wrote a journalist attending the opening ceremonies. In a show of unity, countries from around the world contributed gifts to furnish the palace's interior: a Gobelin tapestry from France, gates and railings from Germany, marble from Italy, a candelabra and vases from Austria-Hungary, and silk cartoons from Japan, among so many others. The director of the palace, Jonkheer Van Karnebeek, and the Dutch minister of foreign affairs made the keynote speeches before the queen of the Netherlands and the four hundred others in attendance, while Carnegie kept a low profile.

The next day, at the unveiling of a bust of King Edward VII and Sir William Randall Cremer in the Great Court, Carnegie delivered his address promoting peace among the Teutonic nations—Britain, Germany, and the United States—and repeating the call for a League of Peace.[16] After the emotionally exhausting day, Louise wrote in her diary, "Thus the great day has passed, perhaps the greatest in Andrew's life, when he has been permitted to see inaugurated the permanent building which he has given wherein the great ideal for peace may be wrought—until Peace and good will may be realized upon the earth."[17] Coincidentally and not so ironically, after the peace ceremonies the Carnegies traveled to Brussels, Belgium, a neutral country soon to be ravaged by war.

While Carnegie was in Europe, Wilson, who cut a far more impressive figure than Taft, quickly established his presidency, prompting Carnegie to characterize him as bold and earnest to Morley. "Naturally I think it's the Scotch in him, the do or die."[18] The honeymoon didn't last long, however; none ever did with Carnegie. When a revolutionary bloodbath swept through Mexico, the president was no longer spared from Carnegie's advice. In a military coup, General Victoriano Huerta had overthrown the country's president, Francisco Madero, who had angered the peasants for not fulfilling promised reforms and angered the landowners for promising anything. Wilson, refusing to recognize Huerta, attempted to force the dictator to hold free elections. On November 3, Carnegie jumped into the fray with his trademark "if I were you." "If I were you I'd let Mexico manage her own destiny," he advised Wilson, "limiting my charge to taking care of our citizens here."[19] When Wilson's rhetoric became more belligerent toward Huerta, two weeks later, Carnegie cabled, "Beware! Beware Invasion."[20] Like many before him, Wilson must have paused to contemplate the maze of contradiction threaded through Carnegie's personality. On the one hand, the philanthropist was an avid preacher of "triumphant democracy," but when it came to aiding the Mexican people's fight for the right to vote he jumped off the pedestal. Perhaps he feared the resurgence of imperialistic designs.

The jingoists did indeed come forth when, in April 1914, a crew of American sailors in Tampico, Mexico, were arrested by Mexican soldiers. Although they were held only briefly and the government issued an apology, the U.S. commanding admiral in the Caribbean fleet demanded the Mexican navy honor the American flag with a twenty-one-gun salute. The Mexicans refused, insisting the Americans honor the Mexican flag first. Then came news that German merchants were to land with a cargo of weapons at the port of Vera Cruz. The newspapers clamored for war just as they had in 1898, and, patience tested, Wilson ordered the American fleet to capture and hold the city. Exasperated by the turn of events, Carnegie chided the president as though he were a schoolboy, using one of his favorite lines, "What fools these mortals be," that illustrated his general contempt for the human race: "Such a war as seems pending will in after years be held akin to the fabled war of the two kings to decide which end of the egg should first be broken. 'How or when should the salute be fired' is a trifle unworthy of consideration. 'What fools these mortals be.' I am very sorry for you. Just on the eve of your unequaled triumph, the gods threaten you with defeat; but I still hope for a miraculous triumph. War is defeat, no true victory is possible here."[21] He was relieved when Argentina, Brazil, and Chile offered to mediate and Wilson accepted. "If mediation fails," Carnegie reminded the president, "you can still blot out the past by prompt withdrawal, and inform your countrymen that your desire to save poor Mexico . . . from a reign of misrule had been found wholly impracticable."[22]

By midsummer, the fickle Carnegie was extolling Wilson's virtues to Morley: "Rejoicing this morning that our noble President is likely to escape from his Mexican blunder."[23] Mexican leader Huerta did resign, but Pancho Villa would lead a revolt against the next regime. Carnegie also rejoiced when it became clear that Wilson and Bryan were intent on pursuing the treaties Taft and Knox had laid the groundwork for. Bryan spearheaded the negotiations, but in his zealousness to win "conciliation treaties" with any nation of marginal import that would be acceptable to the Senate, the terms of the treaties lacked real substance, not unlike the empty shells Roosevelt refused to sign a decade earlier. Real détente with Britain, France, and Germany remained elusive as Bryan signed pacts with lesser nations. "Secretary Bryan's completed arbitration treaties with Switzerland, Denmark, and Uruguay take a great load off our minds," wrote a columnist for the *Memphis Commercial-Appeal* sarcastically. "The thought of war with them was terrible."[24] Any progress in the direction toward peace, however useless, was acceptable to Carnegie, and after Bryan concluded negotiations with Denmark, he congratulated the secretary of state: "I wish you speedy success, and more treaties of the same character."[25]

Communication between Carnegie and the Wilson administration was relatively minimal when compared to Carnegie's exhortations and protestations during the Roosevelt and Taft years. It was as though the great titan of industry and philanthropy had finally purged himself: the bulk of his surplus wealth now rested with the trustees of the Carnegie Corporation and the Palace of Peace had opened. Yet violence around the world continued unabated. What more could be done? He had attacked cancerous war on a number of fronts: through education; through monuments to peace; through his hero funds; through diplomacy; through playing to egos, fears, and moral conscience. Other than war itself, there was one avenue to peace left unexplored: through the church.

In 1914, Carnegie engineered one last major endowment when he convinced the Carnegie Corporation trustees to give $2 million to create the Church Peace Union, an organization comprised of members of various religious bodies. Although millions had died in sundry holy wars, he prayed that in this age of enlightenment religious men would respond strongly to an appeal for peace. The stated mission: "To promote peace, through the rallying of men of all religions to supplant war by justice and international brotherhood." The goals and means were very similar to those of the Endowment for International Peace, the mission to be achieved through diplomacy, improving communication between nations and peoples, and educating the masses. Carnegie proudly trumpeted his latest effort to Morley: "Would you believe that I have the cordial, delighted acceptance of Cardinal Gibbons of Washington (R.C. of course) Bishop Greer, Episcopal Head, and two dozen heads of various sects, *not one* refused. I am so pleased at union of the separate Sects, Jews included, two Rabbies, Universalists, Baptists, etc. etc., esteeming that in itself a step forward toward the coming brotherhood of man. Have called all to meet here 5th February to organize—Episcopalians here not being unfairly pampered by the nation, cooperate freely with other sects."[26]

For the agnostic Carnegie to appeal to religious men to join his fight for peace demonstrated just how desperate he was. At the urging of Carnegie, the trustees of the Church Peace Union organized a conference of the churches of Europe and Asia and scheduled it for the first three days in August 1914 in Constance, Germany. They would be caught in the maelstrom.

As he had for the last thirty years, Carnegie made plans for his Scotland sojourn. "Due Plymouth 31st—Coburg Hotel for four days," he informed Morley the first week of May, "then Freedoms of Coventry & Lincoln enroute to Skibo, join Madam & c on northward at York for Skibo. Return London for Liberal Club address 16th & Burt banquet—& Aberdeen University Society these two following 17 & 18th, then am free."[27] Morley was scheduled to visit the Highlands in August, as was Lucy and her son Andrew and his wife. It was shaping up to be a typical summer on June 6, 1914, when the Carnegie family arrived at Skibo. Carnegie was seventy-eight years of age, Louise was fifty-seven, and Margaret was now a young lady of seventeen. Her parents had been married for twenty-seven years and were still very much in love. The same could be said for Archduke Francis Ferdinand, heir apparent to the Austro-Hungarian Empire, and his wife, Sophie.

Celebrating fourteen years of marriage on June 28, the royal couple was to spend the day touring Sarajevo, the capital of Bosnia, and hobnobbing with the city's dignitaries. As their open motorcar, in a procession of four, passed through unguarded streets, seven nationalist Serbs belonging to a terrorist group called the Black Hand, and filled with murderous intent, spread out to strategic points and waited for their quarry. The motorcade passed the first conspirators at the Cumuria Bridge, where, without warning, a home-made bomb was flung through the air. Seeing the motion, the archduke lifted his arm and deflected the bomb, which, on hitting the street, exploded. The cars now sped through the streets, but then the archduke's driver made a wrong turn and screeched to a halt to reverse course. Before he could accelerate, from just five feet away, another assassin stepped forward and fired two bullets from his pistol. One hit Ferdinand in the neck, the other Sophie in the abdomen. Both were fatally wounded. "Es ist nichts. Es ist nichts," the archduke responded, when asked if he was suffering.[28] His last words—"*It is nothing*"—couldn't have been more wrong.

The murder of the archduke and his wife was a tragedy, the work of senseless terrorists, nothing more, and life at Skibo continued as usual. The only violence that concerned Carnegie was in Ireland, where the Protestant Irish of Ulster were threatening a civil war if Britain allowed a Free State of Ireland to annex the region. Still active in politics, Morley condemned the threats of violence, and Carnegie applauded him on his position on July 16: "You made a clear strong speech the other day. The situation seems incredible—to think of a Civil War in Britain. Surely impossible."[29] At the end of the letter, he added, "We are off to our retreat in a few minutes where we spend two or three weeks, and then return to greet coming friends, among them yourself and Lady." The family was to spend the remainder of July and the first week of August at their Aultnagar hideaway.

Through the hot weeks of July, while the Carnegies enjoyed the cool solitude of Aultnagar, an inquisition was held in Sarajevo to determine who was behind the assassinations. At the time, it was determined the conspiracy apparently started and ended with the Black Hand, and a Viennese bureaucrat in Sarajevo agreed with the findings. Even so, the Austrian foreign minister, Count Leopold von Berchtold, strongly favored punishing Serbia by invading Belgrade, the capital. Other officials, realizing a mobilization of their troops would likely provoke Serbia's powerful ally Russia, attempted to rein in Berchtold. But when Emperor Francis Joseph received assurances from Kaiser Wilhelm II that Germany would support Austria-Hungary, Berchtold issued the command.

Deceit, miscommunication, missed chances, and fumbled diplomacy—in short, a series of small decisions and events—created a massive, unstoppable domino effect. On July 25, Russia initiated a partial mobilization of her troops as expected; on July 28, Austria declared war on Serbia; on July 30, Czar Nicholas II agreed to a full mobilization; on July 31, France mobilized; and on August 1, the kaiser called for full mobilization when the czar refused to call his off. The unwritten law was mobilization means war; as Russia's interior minister N. A. Maklakov said on signing the mobilization orders, "With us the war cannot be popular deep down among the masses, to whom revolutionary ideas mean more than a victory over Germany. But one cannot escape one's fate."[30]

The day the kaiser called for mobilization, the attendees of the Church Peace Union conference assembled at the Insel Hotel in Constance, Germany, on the shore of shimmering Lake Constance. At Aultnagar, Carnegie remained unaware of the sudden and grave developments on the Continent.

The British attempted to remain noncommittal; that is, until the kaiser stated his intent to invade Belgium and from there to strike at France. Now there was no choice but to intervene if neutral Belgium was violated. When word spread that Britain was about to declare war on Germany, a Carnegie family friend, Reverend Robert L. Ritchie, minister of a local parish, drove immediately to Aultnagar to inform Carnegie. The greatest champion of peace was incredulous. "It can't be true. Are you sure it's true?" he burst out. Then he paced, deep in thought for a few moments, before again bursting out, "Can't America do something to stop it?" Louise, fearing he might die from the shock, attempted to console him, but he collapsed into a chair and became very distracted, unable to focus on anything about him. "All my air-castles have fallen about me like a house of cards," he muttered.[31]

CHAPTER 36

The War to End All Wars

The Church Peace Union conference called it quits on Sunday, August 2nd, and accepted an invitation from the German government to take the last train out of the country bound for France, where the delegates could then board a steamer for London. It was horrifying to Carnegie as he visualized these peaceful men being swept before the armies, their lives threatened. Having rushed back to Skibo, he immediately cabled Allen Baker, the leader of the British delegation in Constance: "We shall be with you all today in spirit, and full in the faith that our cause is righteous and therefore must prevail amid many deplorable catastrophes such as the present outburst. We know that man is created with an instinct for development, and that from the first he has developed to higher and higher standards and that there is no limit to his future ascent."[1] The optimism rang hollow, however.

In the first week of August, 6 million soldiers were on the move, and the lines were distinctly drawn between two armed camps: the Central Powers of Germany, Austria-Hungary, Turkey, and Bulgaria; and the Allied Powers of Britain, France, Italy, Poland, and Russia, among others. Only the Netherlands, Switzerland, and Spain remained neutral. Belgium cast aside any hope for neutrality when Germany invaded it on August 4, the country's landscape offering the only level path to France and thus permitting a rapid deployment of troops. Belgium's King Albert had no intention of submitting, however, and in the battle for the strategic city of Liège, he ordered his general to "hold to the end." It took the Germans ten days to take Liège, a critical delay as France and Britain, having declared war on Germany as of midnight, August 4, mustered their forces. "The war news is terrible and shocking," Robert Franks cabled Carnegie's personal secretary, John Poynton. "I do feel so sorry for Mr. C. after having peace so close to his grasp."[2] Once Britain entered the fray, Carnegie was engulfed with despair. Gutted of hope. A dried locust carcass. He suffered attacks of perplexity and dejection. He had to find a way to sustain himself or die.

Morley was also shaken and despondent. Refusing to support the war on any terms, he resigned from the cabinet the day Britain resolved to declare war, and from his Wimbledon home, he informed Carnegie and noted: "But what a black panorama!! To nobody will it seem blacker than to you. Hell in full blast."[3] Morley's skepticism had darkened to the point of giving up hope for mankind. He abhorred the Machiavellian spirit among nations, the survival of the fittest mentality that drove countries to war, each warlike nation always wanting to answer the ultimate question, "Can I kill thee, or canst thou kill me?" Man was too violence prone, never to be more than a base animal.

Two days after the hostilities commenced in earnest, Carnegie was relieved to hear from Frederick Lynch, an American member of the Church Peace Union delegation who had arrived safely in London. In his letter, he conveyed harrowing scenes from their escape out of Germany:

> We saw all the men being taken from work and corralled at every railroad station. We saw one young man go crazy at being torn from his wife and children. We saw four foreigners shot deliberately down because they would not take arms for Germany. We saw lines of women weeping and wailing. Worst of all, we saw great crowds of young men in mad orgies of drink and war fever, howling, with wild eyes for the blood of Russians and French and Englishmen. I saw a Russian family pulled out of a train by the German soldiers and the mother so frightened that her milk stopped and the poor little baby got nothing to eat for two days. We took them along in our party and on the steamer Lady Barlow, one of our group, found a mother with a baby who offered to give the little Russian baby a drink from her breasts. The poor little thing snatched at the breast with a cry that was pathetic. . . .
>
> It was the unanimous feeling of everyone present that we must devote our lives to it [peace] as never before. Many felt that the very fact that the world was now witnessing the collapse of the military system as the preserver of peace, the utter incapacity of the present international political order to secure justice for any nation, would reach in our favor. Never again can anyone say that armaments make for peace. . . .
>
> I hope you have not lost courage. You must have felt heartsick and dejected as have we all. But I believe this catastrophe will witness the beginning of the end of trust in might and brute force. That trust has failed at last.[4]

The arrival of Lucy Carnegie on August 8 and Morley two days later brought momentary relief to an overwhelmed Carnegie. The failure of peace was his personal failure, he believed, and with it came a crushing burden. But now, if he could just talk with the vital Lucy and the logical Morley, perhaps their words alone would make the world right. Other guests who arrived that August to pay homage to the man of peace and comfort him, included the former British ambassador to the United States, Lord Bryce, the Yates-

Thompsons, Sir Swire Smith, and John Ross, among others. While Morley was totally against Britain's participation in the war, Carnegie, through conversations with his guests, realized Britain had no choice but to act. So much so that when he received an invitation from a group of British pacifists to join in denouncing Britain's participation, Carnegie declined, and proceeded to publish his answer in the August 8 London *Times*: "Protest today useless. German Emperor refused Britain's friendly invitation to peaceful conference of the Powers, signed by no less able and peaceful a statesman than Sir Edward Grey." He referred to the German emperor, once his anointed champion of peace, as the "War Lord of Europe."[5]

But he was also not convinced the kaiser was completely at fault, and rightly so. The day after German forces engaged the British at Mons, on August 22, a battle that would cost the British 4,244 casualties, a second letter from Carnegie was published in the London *Times:* "The German Emperor has not yet been proved guilty. I believe he has been more sinned against than sinning. Rulers are not seldom overruled and, at best, are unable to supervise wisely all the varying conditions of international quarrels. History alone will record the truth. Meanwhile the Emperor, who alone of all ruling potentates has preserved his country's peace for twenty-six years, is at least entitled to the benefit of the doubt."[6] This went against the popular view. Now, having opened himself to severe criticism, he was accused of being pro-German, of embracing the kaiser; yet anyone who knew his loyalty to Scotland realized such charges were ridiculous. In his own way, however fanciful and illusionary, Carnegie was attempting to open a dialogue with the German emperor, hoping that his own sign of forgiveness might convince the emperor to recall his armies.

The fairyland castle of Skibo was not protected from the realities of war. The estate's young male tenants were called into the armed forces, and the British government commandeered horses and even cut down beautiful trees for lumber because wood had become a scarce commodity. At times, Carnegie found himself weeping uncontrollably. To bolster the laird's fragile psyche, John Ross and John Morley kept up a steady stream of correspondence. "Thanks for your notes," Carnegie wrote Ross. "We are in perilous times. Our horses, traps &c commandeered—our territorials, ditto. All the household servants included steadily at work, sewing & knitting for the Army. It is all too sad to contemplate but we can indulge the hope that out of this eruption there is to spring the resolve to form an organization among the nations to prevent war hereafter. In this I hope our race will tell."[7]

During the third week of August, the French were retreating across the entire front, building barricades, and digging entrenchments for the defense of Paris. On the eastern front, the Russians were about to overrun Prussia, so on August 25, the German command pulled two corps from France and shipped them to Prussia, saving Paris. Three days later Morley wrote: "The only days of peace and refreshment in this Trough of Despair, for me at least, have been my fortnight at Skibo. The company was both genial and understanding. The young people were most delightful. The weather was ideal. The host and hostess were almost kinder, more considerate, and more sympathetic than usual. . . . We are seeing evil war at its worst—worst in carnage, worst in its depravation of all moral sense, worst as a murderous gamble. . . . Words are in vain or worse than vain." How strange it was to enjoy delightful Skibo, to desperately hang on to a semblance of normalcy, while men were being slaughtered in the beautiful European countryside.

As Carnegie read Morley's declaration—"Words are in vain"—he sensed an absolute truth. As he further reflected on the madness and read over the last passages he had written for his autobiography, recounting his 1913 visit with the kaiser, the celebration of his twenty-fifth year of peace, he realized words were indeed vain:

> As I read this to-day, what a change! The world convulsed by war as never before! Men slaying each other like wild beasts! I dare not relinquish all hope. In recent days I see another ruler coming forward upon the world stage, who may prove himself the immortal one. The man who vindicated his country's honor in the Panama Canal toll dispute is now President. He has the indomitable will of genius, and true hope which we are told,
>
> "Kings it makes gods, and meaner creatures kings."
>
> Nothing is impossible to genius! Watch President Wilson! He has Scotch blood in his veins.[8]

Carnegie never wrote another word in his autobiography. He set it aside, unfinished.

The mid-September farewells at Skibo were difficult, physically painful to face, especially when acknowledging the young men who were not there, and the hugs and tears were prolonged. At Liverpool, where the Carnegies were to take the steamer *Mauretania*, Morley came to see them off. Again, the scene was emotionally grim. As Morley stood on the dock, waving, both men wondered when they would see each other next and under what circumstances. Morley's figure blended into the crowd of well-wishers as the ship pulled away.

The expanse of the Atlantic Ocean was medicinal for Carnegie. The air was clean; he could breathe again. His mind cleared, and he considered his next move. President Wilson and Kaiser Wilhelm II were the only two men with enough power to end the atrocities. In his cabin, Carnegie composed a letter to Wilson on how best to stop the conflagration that threatened to become Armageddon. As soon as he arrived at Ninety-first Street, he wrote a second letter. His plan was simple and direct: Wilson must step forward and offer to arbitrate while the warring nations honored a cease-fire. He naively expected Wilson to act as Roosevelt had during the Russo-Japanese conflict and, by sheer force of character, settle the conflict. The political situation was a bit more complicated now, however, and Roosevelt had succeeded only after Japan's navy had crushed the Russian fleet. Still, Wilson appreciated the advice from Carnegie, who did have a tremendous breadth of experience to draw upon. "I have your letter written from the Mauretania and also the little note which followed it after you reached this country. I am warmly obliged to you for lodging in my mind a suggestion which may later bear fruit."[9]

Carnegie's other present concern was America's position vis-à-vis the war. So far it was neutral, and he wanted it to remain so. At least thousands of American boys could be saved from unnecessary deaths. Wilson and Bryan shared this view. The administration was even willing to continue to pursue a "conciliatory treaty" with Germany despite its aggression. If the kaiser were to sign such a treaty, they calculated, it might be viewed as an act of good faith that he did indeed desire peace, a pivotal first step in opening negotiations to end the war. Invigorated with renewed purpose, Carnegie, considering the pursuit of the treaty a heroic gesture, volunteered to serve as an intermediary between the State Department and the kaiser, an offer Wilson accepted. In the first week of October, Bryan forwarded to Carnegie a selection of "conciliation treaties" signed with other European nations for the kaiser to evaluate and for the two countries to use as models. "I most sincerely hope your words will have weight with him," Bryan wrote.[10] Carnegie then drafted a letter to the kaiser in support of the treaty. After Bryan reviewed and edited it, he sent it to Germany via diplomatic courier.

> May it please Your Majesty:
>
> Of your earnest desire for World Peace I am convinced. This you probably know, since I have not failed repeatedly to proclaim it here. . . . In my opinion, nothing would please or affect our people so much as your participation in the proposed treaty, thus giving additional proof of your devotion to International Peace. . . .
>
> I had opportunity yesterday morning of consulting at Hamilton College your friend and admirer, Charlemagne Tower, who introduced Mrs. Carnegie and myself to your Majesty at Kiel, and found him enthusiastic upon the proposed treaty of giving statesmen a year to cool, which would generally ensure peace upon some terms. . . .
>
> Meanwhile I find accord among statesmen of both parties here. All support our President in maintaining strict neutrality between the two unfortunate warring nations. Silence for the present; but also I find remarkable unanimity in the belief that this unparalleled war is at last to result in a stern resolve among the best of the nations that men shall no longer be permitted to slay each other, as they are now doing. War must be abolished by a union of the civilized nations, possessing the will and power to maintain peace.[11]

The temperamental kaiser did not dismiss the overture out of hand. He had no quarrel with the United States, after all, and keeping the industrial power neutral was to his advantage, so he signed a conciliation treaty with the United States. Now the Senate had to ratify it, not an easy nor a necessarily desirable task, especially with Rough Rider Teddy Roosevelt clamoring for war and flogging President Wilson for not condemning Germany's invasion of Belgium. The general sentiment of the public disagreed with Roosevelt, however; the majority supported neutrality and read about the war with detached interest, not jingoistic outrage.

Such disinterest was obviously not the case in Britain, where war engulfed the people. Morley kept his old friend advised: "The war fever is raging here in heavy strength. It is not yet realised that we at any rate might well have kept out of it; that its results can bring us no solid gain; and that the cost in carnage, waste, and demoralization of the public mind, will be monstrous."[12] Carnegie replied that it was useless to consider what might have been and instead to change what will be. He for one was still willing to "try his hand" for the cause of peace.

"You say you are 'trying your hand' at a presentation of the case for abolishing war," Morley, in a dark, but pragmatic mood, replied. "I fear the time has not yet come. People will not listen." He then chided Carnegie, who had admitted he was severely depressed. "It cuts me to the heart that you of all men—the bravest and most confident of men—should write that 'happiness is all over for the nonce.' Today is black—yes, black at best. But you have a right—and a duty—to find several hours of happiness *per diem* in thinking that you have fought your best and hardest for your fellow creatures."[13] The mask had fallen from Carnegie. Behind his optimism that the kaiser could be influenced was the face of despair, belonging to a man who could not muster a flicker of joy in any aspect of his daily life. His protracted peace mission had been burned to ashes, his other missions no longer needed him, and now, left with just himself, just his mind and body to give his character substance, he found nothing to like.

Over the holidays, John Ross offered subdued greetings and expressed hope that the Carnegie family was planning to return to Skibo in the spring. Hopelessly downtrodden, Carnegie replied that they would not, explaining that his own depressed presence would serve only to further sadden the tenants, who had enough burdens. "On the contrary," Ross wrote, in a spirited attempt to enliven the old laird. "I feel sure that the very fact that you abstain from coming here will increase the sadness. . . . Your presence will tend to encourage and comfort them [the tenants] far more than any letters you could write. . . . You are so much committed to the 'Peace Crusade,' and you have been so often the exponent of the belief that amidst all the contradictions in this world, the world grows better, that if you now make a public announcement that your sadness has altered your life, it would be accepted as a confession that your faith has been shattered. This will never do." Ross, Morley, and all of Carnegie's friends needed him to "remain the same happy, optimistic person as ever you were."[14] For Carnegie to lose his eternal optimism was for life itself to end.

But the idea of crossing the Atlantic, with German U-boats disrupting the shipping lanes, was not particularly attractive. "Consider what it means to go upon a small steamer across the Atlantic," Carnegie described to Ross, "lites all out, shut in every evening—all dark until the sun rises—crawling along on the look-out for bergs—such our experience home." He also believed he had "a part to play" in the United States, where he was "in constant touch with our President and Secretary of State," advising them on the British position.[15]

The next month, February, Germany announced that the waters around the British Isles were a war zone and that unrestricted submarine warfare would terrorize every ship approaching Britain, regardless of purpose.

The month Germany initiated a blockade of the British Isles, Carnegie was forced to testify before another U.S.-government grade-A commission—only it had nothing to do with war. President Wilson had created the United States Commission on Industrial Relations, chaired by Frank P. Walsh and charged with studying the relationships between capital and labor, the conditions of the working class, and related topics, which gave it wide discretion in its investigation. Carnegie was summoned to testify because the commission had elected to explore whether philanthropic foundations were a menace to individual rights, democracy, and the American way of life. There was a fear of large sums of money being concentrated in the hands of a few trustees who may or may not act responsibly, and of the impact if the directorates of these trusts were interlocked. These concerns mirrored those addressed by the 1912 Pujo hearings, a congressional witch-hunt led by Arsène Pujo, a representative from Louisiana.

In 1912, there had been a belief among congressmen, as well as the American public, that a handful of men, using interlocked directorates that spanned American industry and commerce, controlled the movement of money, the markets, and the entire economy. At the center of the conspiracy was Pierpont Morgan, age seventy-five, who testified before the committee on December 18 and 19. Morgan's evident sincerity and frankness in testifying, according to the New York Times, created a favorable impression, and the hearings never did uncover a sinister conspiracy—it was indeed a witch-hunt.[16] However, the harsh allegations weighed heavily on Morgan, and his health began to fail. Two weeks later, he, his daughter, Louisa, and several friends departed for Egypt. While touring the Nile, he fell ill and the party hastily retreated to Rome. Morgan died there on March 31, mercifully in his sleep.

Now, with Carnegie's health fragile, if he were to undergo a similar grilling, his life could be put in jeopardy. Meanwhile, the beleaguered titan, protecting the American way, had just protested to President Wilson a bill passed by Congress that would require literacy tests for immigrants. It would be unfair to those who "have no opportunity for education in their native land," he argued. "I would not exclude illiterates. The parents may not become intensely literary Americans, but the children will. They cannot help it; such is the Republican atmosphere."[17] Carnegie may have had his quirks, but in 1915 he was hardly the most imminent threat to the American way of life, and it was difficult not to sympathize with him as he prepared to take the stand.

On February 5, he appeared in the meeting hall of the Metropolitan Life Building in New York, where Walsh was conducting the hearings. He was greeted by hoots and hollers from a mostly hostile crowd, including a contingent of vocal IWW union members. The seventy-nine-year-old Carnegie, dressed in black frock coat, black bow tie, and white stiff-bosomed dress shirt, refused to be ruffled; after climbing up on the dais, he bowed to the commission and gave everyone a winning smile. As he had with the Stanley Commission, he addressed his answers to the audience and played to them. Now came the inquisition on philanthropy and the creating of foundations and trusts.

"Do you not believe, Mr. Carnegie . . ."

"Now, Mr. Chairman," he interrupted. "You say, 'do you not believe?' That implies that *you* believe and you want me to agree. I don't like that. Please be kind enough to say 'do you believe?'"

Laughter rolled through the audience, and once the noise settled, a somewhat perturbed Walsh said, "We had no trouble in keeping order until you came, Mr. Carnegie."

"I'm glad of that." And extending his arms toward the crowd, he added, "What an audience! See how many ladies there are here! That's one of the greatest triumphs of my life." Laughter and applause erupted, and the socialists were charmed.[18] Ultimately, there was little information gained by the commission, but the strain of this last public appearance did affect Carnegie as feared.

He suffered a severe attack of grippe in late February and was confined to bed for two weeks. His mental outlook and physical health weren't helped when the newspaper headlines shrieked of a poison gas attack at the French village of Langemarck. On the morning of April 22, following a German mortar barrage, two greenish yellow clouds appeared over the French lines, merged, and then, like a low fog, swept over five miles of the front. It was like mist over meadows on a frosty night, said one transfixed observer; except that more than fifteen thousand men suffered a painful death or invalidism, choking, falling to the ground, and writhing in pain. The lucky ones urinated on handkerchiefs or shirts and wrapped them around their faces and then ran. Hideous, ignoble gas warfare was now an integral part of battle.[19]

Another blow to Carnegie came on May 7, when a German submarine torpedoed the *Lusitania*, a Cunard luxury liner. It sank in twenty minutes, taking with her 1,198 lives, 128 of them American; most of the victims were women and children. Any chance of the Senate ratifying a treaty with Germany sank, too. The public was now incensed. Wilson fired off a series of protests, demanding an indemnity for the loss of American life and demanding the end of unrestricted submarine warfare.

Even though it was detrimental to his health, every day Carnegie pored over the newspapers and journals, reading the fiery rhetoric and the gory descriptions. The horror of war continued to grind him down, and influenza set in. His longtime doctor, Jasper Garmany, advised a trip to Bar Harbor, Maine. Carnegie heeded his advice and spent the summer of 1915 fishing, yachting, and golfing. He regained his physical strength, but not his vitality. The clarity of his piercing blue eyes had yellowed. He relinquished all duties at the Carnegie Corporation and suspended writing letters to Morley, a Sunday tradition that was now given to Louise. For companionship, he bought a collie and named it Laddie, just like his favorite dog at Skibo. When the dog died suddenly, Louise immediately arranged to have the true Laddie at Skibo shipped to Bar Harbor.

Friends feared for his health. In mid-May, Morley wrote Louise:

> I had heard one day last week that something was amiss with him, and have been wondering how I should approach you. Nothing has caught my eye about it in our newspapers.
>
> It is indeed distressing. I cannot bear to think of that pulse of such extraordinary vitality and force going down by a single beat. You are evidently doing all that tenderness and good sense could lead you to. That I know full well, you may be very sure.
>
> It is no surprise to me that the strain of the war should be counted among the causes of his illness. I don't believe there is a man in America, or here, to whom this black cloud of misery and horror that has swept over mankind could bring more mortification of heart and soul than to him. . . . [20]

Morley would continue to scan the papers for news of his old friend, but Carnegie's name was rapidly fading from the public eye.

Toward the end of July, the household mood at Bar Harbor brightened. "I am delighted to tell you that Mr. Carnegie is very much stronger and spends most of his time on the yacht, the strong sea air proving the very elixir of life for him," Louise wrote a family friend, and in mid-August she reported to Robert Franks: "I have still further good news of Mr. Carnegie. He wrote Lord Morley a most delightful letter last week which we were able to send!!"[21] In September, she heard from Charlie Schwab, whose feelings for Carnegie remained strong despite past differences: "Every thought of yourself and Mr. Carnegie is always one of deepest affection. What a man and what a friend he has always been!! A father indeed!"[22] He offered to help them in any way, no matter how trivial.

Once the Maine coastal weather cooled, the family returned to the Highlands at Ninety-first Street, where they enjoyed the early autumn glory of the gardens for the first time.

"This morning I had a waking dream—that I was at Skibo and should once more find myself, on going downstairs, at that joyful and hospitable breakfast table, with the cordial cheerful talk all around, followed by the feeding of the dog, the bustle of the cars, the walks in the glorious garden, the day on the yacht, the kind return home in the late afternoon, the brisk discussions over letter and newspapers. Then how painful to awake to the realities—the cheerless skies, the trees stripped of leaves, the black pall of war outspread, poor Skibo deserted, and you two, battling with home anxieties across the Atlantic out of sight and reach." These were the words of Morley in a letter to Louise, dated October 31, but they very well could have been Carnegie's. "Peace does not seem very near," Morley added. "If it were not unmanly, I could wish that I had slipped off my mortal coil, before these myriad horrors had come upon the earth. There can be no compensation."[23] Always skeptical and pessimistic, Morley now preferred his own death over witnessing the destruction of life, a reaction to the latest war development. The prior month, the French had attempted to break the German army in the Champagne. Over a 15-mile front, they concentrated 35 divisions, about 500,000 men, and 900 heavy artillery guns and 1,600 light. After a furious 3-day bombardment that carved out interlocked craters, the ground assault was launched. It cost the French 145,000 men and no strategic advantage was won. As for the Britain, by the end of the year, she would witness 400,000 of her soldiers cut down.[24]

Although significantly stronger in November, Carnegie did not submit to the annual birthday interview with reporters, a ritual for years. Instead, on his eightieth birthday he asked Louise to issue a statement:

> Say to the reporters who usually call on my birthday that all goes well with me. Dr. Garmany marvels at the splendid return to health which a summer on the Maine coast has wrought.
>
> The world grows better and we are soon to see blessed peace restored and a world court established when, in the words of Burns:
>
> > "Man to man the world o'er
> > Shall brothers be for a' that."[25]

There was a birthday dinner that night, his close friends and colleagues invited. It was subdued; Carnegie was too weak to come downstairs until the last dinner course was served, and then he was propped up in his chair with pillows. Rather than engaging in lively conversation, he contented himself with listening to the Hampton Negro Quartet, hired for the evening to sing plantation melodies.

The winter of 1915–1916 was spent on a houseboat, the *Everglades*, in Miami, Florida. "We now begin to feel more at home and I can truly say I like it," Louise wrote Margaret, who was now a senior at an all-girls private school, where she was separated from her father by distance and ideas. Disillusioned by the war, Margaret recognized little purpose to her father's philanthropy and had little tolerance for his idealistic proclamations on peace. The Florida life her mother described was equally hollow. "While we were at breakfast this morning the *Everglades* moved near the shore and anchored off the Club House," Louise continued her letter. "This meant that we could go ashore easily, without a long launch trip—so after Daddy had his nap, he was willing to take an excursion! I let everybody go ashore and see the town and the Captain took just Daddy and me in the launch up the Miami river. . . . We went up the river under several bridges to a fruit farm where they are experimenting on new kinds of fruit. The Captain went ashore and brought us out a delicious kind of drink made from the juices of grapefruit, oranges, pineapples, lemons, and kumquats—it was very delicious and I let Daddy have a little which pleased him greatly."[26]

Louise's mollycoddling of her husband could not shield him from the barbaric war. Morley wouldn't allow it. Bogged down in reflective melancholy, Morley wrote the Carnegies a morbid New Year's Eve greeting that reached them on the houseboat. "My best of friends. Here's the last day of the year—the worst of years! . . . The carnage is hideous. . . . The Britain that you and I have known all these long years is pretty rapidly disappearing. Well, we must face our fates as we best can. . . . I often think of that parting night in the Liverpool hotel."[27] Nor could Louise shield her husband from the January 1916 death of Lucy Coleman Carnegie, the monarch of Dungeness. "The whole family revolved around her," Louise wrote Robert Franks, "and life can never be quite the same to any of us. Mr. Carnegie bore the news better than I expected. I tried to break it very gently, and his quiet acceptance of it was very pathetic. He does not say much, but he is not brooding over it." It was indeed a pathetic sight, the steel tycoon slumped in a lounge chair, every need catered to, babied by his wife, he silent and marking time, waiting for his turn.

The tone of tributes from friends suggested he was already dead, as was the case when Earl Grey wrote a mutual friend, Oscar Strauss, who then forwarded the letter to Louise, hoping it might cheer up her husband. "I hear from Doctor Ross," Grey wrote, "the head of the Carnegie Trust at Dunfermline, that this war has broke our friend Carnegie's health and his heart; and you tell me that the effort he made in giving testimony before the Federal Commission broke him down. When you see him tell him that many of us look to him as the great pioneer who has blazed the way to future peace because if his policy of collective responsibility on the part of signatory nations to the Hague convention had been adopted, the United States would have been obliged to come into this war at the very beginning and the knowledge that she would come in would have kept Germany quiet."[28] Grey might very well have been reading a statement at Carnegie's memorial service.

Morley, who wished he could be whisked across the Atlantic aboard a "rapid aircraft, now devoted to more diabolical purposes," continued his stream of letters through the winter. "I never get one of the publications of your Peace Endowment," he wrote in March while the bloody Battle of Verdun raged, "without a warm feeling for the founder of the Endowment, and of the comfort it must be to him to have had such a happy inspiration, in spite of the unspeakable discouragement of the hour. Europe is devastated by Plague and the Black Death, but that is no reason why Pasteurs and Listers should not persevere in search of healings."[29] The Carnegie Endowment for International Peace was active in fighting the war, as well as funding the reconstruction of devastated villages in France, Belgium, Serbia, and Russia. The Carnegie Corporation gave $2.5 million to the Red Cross, the YMCA, and the Knights of Columbus, among other organizations, for relief efforts. The Carnegie family wasn't completely paralyzed, either. Louise gave $100,000 to the Netherlands Red Cross Society, as well as money to Edith Wharton, who was raising funds for the Children of Flanders Rescue Committee.[30]

The cruelest month, April, found the Carnegies back in New York, and then in Noroton, Connecticut, on the Long Island Sound, for the summer. Carnegie had hoped for a cool breeze off the sound to duplicate the salt air of Dornoch Firth, but, to the contrary, it was hot and muggy. It was made all the more hellish when on July 1, the Allies launched the Battle of the Somme, hoping it would be "an open sesame to final victory." The British and French soldiers went over the top, intent on cutting the German army in two and marching into Berlin. Instead, by the end of the first day, sixty thousand British corpses lay rotting in the field. At such a cost, Carnegie calculated, ground surely must have been won and the Germans pushed to the brink of suing for peace. Dreaming of peace negotiations at The Hague, Carnegie wrote Morley in August to plan a triumphant return to Skibo the next spring. Morley replied, "You speak of The Hague, and I hope it may come in good time, but whether there is any Hague or not, Skibo will do just as well for you and me to have our own private congress in the spring."[31] Another English friend, Frederic Harrison, tempered Carnegie's hopes of a return: "There is, I fear, no prospect of your visiting Britain whilst the horrors continue; and I am some years your senior—when this letter reaches you, I shall have completed my 85 years on earth—so there is little chance of my being here should you come across the Atlantic when this war is ended. It must end one day from sheer exhaustion if nothing else. So, whilst I have strength to write I send you a few words to express my grateful sense of our friendship in happier days and my profound sense of admiration for the long and universal efforts you have made in the Old & the New Worlds to avert the cataclysm that is a menace to human civilization."[32] The letter was of little consolation. Neither was the putting green Louise had installed at Ninety-first Street; it was a cruel reminder of the courses at Skibo and Dornoch and their rugged beauty.

The first presidential election in decades in which Carnegie was not heavily involved, financially or otherwise, came and went in November; Wilson won reelection with the slogan, "He Kept Us Out of the War." Another birthday came and went. Margaret's coming-out party was held on December 8, a bittersweet celebration for Carnegie as he gazed on her innocent beauty, regretting that she must blossom in a world gone mad. "Baba had at least a hundred bouquets and baskets of flowers"; Louise wrote in her diary, "a wonderful tribute to our little girl. She looked very sweet in her white tulle dress with a few threads of silver and her string of pearls her Daddy and I gave her—so very simple and sweet. We had dinner of twenty-six covers and people began to come at 8:30. About 800 people here. Baba had nine girls receiving with her; all so lovely. Party was over at 2 A.M., a very great success. Daddy very happy greeting guests."[33]

With the Allied and Central Powers hopelessly entrenched in a war of attrition, on January 22, 1917, President Woodrow Wilson called for a peace without victory. Even Carnegie realized this was not possible, so, in a burst of ferocious energy, he dictated an urgent letter to Wilson in which he promoted what he detested most—war.

> Dear Mr. President:
>
> Sometime ago I wrote you "Germany is beyond reason." She has ever since become more and more so until today she shows herself completely insane. No wonder the Cabinet in today's paper shows restlessness. Were I in your place there would soon be an end to this. There is only one straight way of settlement. You should proclaim war against her, however reluctantly, and then settlement would soon come. . . . Let me predict you will have the greatest of all careers before you; hope it will be soon clearly defined. Be of good cheer.
>
> > Yours devotedly,
> > Andrew Carnegie[34]

At the time, the Germans were withdrawing to regroup and to reinforce positions after the Somme offensive. As they retreated, they systematically razed and poisoned the landscape. Thousands of homes were destroyed, orchards and forests torched, water wells and reservoirs poisoned, and bridges, railways, and roads demolished. By April 5, the Germans were positioned along the Hindenburg Line, a foreboding tier of concrete-revetted fortifications.

With the kaiser reinstituting unrestricted submarine warfare on February 1, and the interception of the Zimmermann communication, in which Germany's foreign secretary proposed an alliance with Mexico to fight the United States—Texas, New Mexico, and Arizona to be given Mexico upon victory—Carnegie didn't have to wait long for America's entry. In April, the president asked Congress to declare war; on April 6, it obliged him. Just after delivering his war message on April 2 and receiving a tremendous ovation, the president had turned to his secretary and said, "Think of what it is they were applauding. My message of today was a message of death for our young men. How strange it seems to applaud that."[35] Carnegie was among them. "You have triumphed at last," he cabled Wilson. "God bless you. You will give the world peace and rank the greatest hero of all."[36]

In May, Congress passed a Selective Service Bill, requiring every able-bodied man between the ages of the twenty-one and thirty-one to serve, and the next month 9.5 million registered to fight. Among them were Harry

Whitfield, husband and father and Louise's younger brother, who was commissioned a lieutenant; and Robert Morrison, their faithful valet, who enlisted in the marines.

The convulsion of America entering the war racked Carnegie, and he suffered another attack of the grippe and influenza. Nurses attended to him daily from that point on. When allowed in the Highlands' gardens, he was wrapped in blankets and rested in a steamer chair, the collie at his feet. At least there would be no muggy Noroton this summer; Louise had purchased a glorious nine-hundred-acre estate, the former home of railroad baron Anson Phelps Stokes christened Shadowbrook, in the Berkshire Mountains of Massachusetts. Only one private residence in America was larger than this fifty-four-room native gray stone mansion—the Vanderbilts' Biltmore estate in Asheville, North Carolina.

Located in the village of Lenox, a summer community during the Gilded Age, Shadowbrook immediately attracted Louise because the home had a music room with a beautiful organ where Carnegie could listen to music for hours. There was also a lookout tower so the laird could gaze out over the entrancing green hills and blue lakes, including the adjacent Lake Mahkeenac, where he would often fish and boat. Always accompanied by his personal secretary Poynton on outings, Carnegie was fond of playfully asking him, "How much did you say I had given away, Poynton?"

"$324,657,399," was the reply.

"Good Heaven! Where did I ever get all that money?" an energized Carnegie would say in jest.

Louise was revitalized, too, writing a friend:

> I am charmed with my first glimpse of it which I had in the setting sun last evening. It is a grand mixture of Aultnagar and the Cottage; the fine trees at the back suggest this; all on the scale of Skibo. The Patersons' house and furnishings are so Scotch I feel I have crossed the ocean and am in Scotland itself on a fine estate.
>
> I am now considering the *human* element. There are pros and cons, but life is a mixture and we must take it as we find it. Our life here would be an Americanized Skibo, with a fair amount of social life but not as hectic as Bar Harbor. One can be independent here; but more when we meet.[37]

There was no need for such a huge estate—Carnegie's social life was limited to lunches and teas with a few friends—but the feeling of having been transported to Scotland was crucial to sustaining Carnegie. He was desperate to live to see peace restored.

Events unfolding in Europe were on a revolutionary scale, but none portended the end of hostilities. To the contrary, in fact. Riots struck Petrograd, Russia,

Unable to return to Skibo in 1917 due to the war, Andrew and Louise Carnegie summered in the Berkshire Mountains of western Massachusetts. There, Louise had purchased the second-largest private home in the United States. (Courtesy of the Carnegie Library of Pittsburgh)

in March 1917, the result of severe food shortages. Russian soldiers refused to suppress the uprisings, further undermining the government. Czar Nicholas was forced to abdicate and was exiled to western Siberia, later to be executed along with his entire family. At first, the provisional government pledged to continue the war, but with the subsequent Bolshevik Revolution in November, which put Lenin and Trotsky in power, all alliances were nullified. In March 1918, an armistice with Germany was signed. The capitulation was a potential disaster for western Europe, for it permitted the kaiser to transfer all his troops to that arena.

Carnegie and Morley, seemingly oblivious to the events, preferred to take a tour of the past that winter, the catalyst being the publication of Morley's memoirs. In New York, Carnegie devoured every word and rediscovered fleeting contentment:

> Your wonderful book of recollections has given me rare and unalloyed pleasure. You have dealt with matters of state as no others could in my opinion, especially those of India and Ireland, and everyone here is extolling the

book. I have read every word and it is as if I were again talking these things all over with you face to face on the terrace at Skibo. Your references to me are all too flattering, but I am not altogether displeased, though you know my modest nature.

I feel confident that with America's help, the great war cannot last much longer, and Madam and I are thinking and talking of the time when we will return to Skibo and have you with us once more.[38]

He had good cause to anticipate the war's conclusion: Wilson had made his seminal Fourteen Points speech, a statement on war aims and a proposal for peace, while troops under John "Black Jack" Pershing prepared to flood the western European theater in the nick of time.

Reinforced German troops pushed forward in the spring after Russia's withdrawal, but there was a marked change in the soldiers: new recruits were mostly very green youngsters or men over forty. Due to war, starvation, and disease, the German population was depleted. On the Allied side, by contrast, the Yankee doughboys filling out the ranks were filled with eager anticipation and revitalized the front. By the end of July, a counteroffensive was under way; and by September, all of Germany's gains from the spring were erased. In mid-September, the Allied forces launched the Saint-Mihiel offensive, and on November 4, the British broke through the German lines. "Now that the world war seems practically at an end I cannot refrain from sending you my heartfelt congratulations upon the great share you have had in bringing about its successful conclusion," Carnegie wrote Wilson on November 10. "The Palace of Peace at the Hague would, I think, be the fitting place for dispassionate discussion regarding the destiny of the conquered nations, and I hope your influence may be exerted in that direction."[39]

That same day, the kaiser boarded a train bound for the Netherlands, where he would die in exile. On the 11th day of the 11th month at 11:00 A.M. the war was officially declared over. "I know your heart must rejoice at the dawn of peace after these terrible years of struggle," Wilson replied to Carnegie two days after the signing, "for I know how long and earnestly you have worked for and desired such conditions as I pray God it may now be possible for us to establish. The meeting place of the Peace Conference has not yet been selected, but even if it is not held at The Hague, I am sure you will be present in spirit."[40]

While Carnegie and the world celebrated, Morley remained his gloomy self. He would come to believe the ensuing peace process was a mockery, declaring that "to the end of time" it would "always be a case of 'Thy head or my head.'"[41] Indeed, the humiliating Versailles Treaty forced on Germany would ensure his prophecy. In a birthday greeting to Carnegie, Morley was surprisingly upbeat, reflecting on the old days once again and pondering, "I sometimes dream that you may cross the Atlantic this summer. Shall I? 'I hae ma doots.' Do you reproach me? You were always the bolder and more valiant of the two."[42]

With the war concluded, Carnegie pressed his personal physician, Dr. Garmany, for permission to go. Without it, Louise would never agree. "If you go," the doctor would say, "you may not come back."

"What difference does it make if I don't?"[43]

The Great War was the war to end all wars. The Republic had saved Europe. Peace reigned. Order was restored. And Margaret fell in love with Roswell Miller Jr., who had driven ambulances in Europe during the war, before enlisting as an ensign in the U.S. Navy. Carnegie was friends with Roswell Sr., the highly respected former chairman of the Chicago, Milwaukee & St. Paul Railroad, so when the ensign asked for his Baba's hand in marriage, he didn't hesitate to answer. "He wept," Louise wrote in her diary, "but was dear and gave it."[44]

On April 22, the thirty-second anniversary of Andrew and Louise's marriage, Margaret and Roswell were married at the Highlands home. "Margaret made a very lovely bride," Louise faithfully noted in her diary. "Decorations of spring flowers were fine. Andrew so well and alert. He and I gave Baba away and later we walked down the aisle together." But between her private schools and his travels, Carnegie was giving away a daughter he never really knew nor she him; Louise even admitted to Margaret that circumstances prevented her "from ever really knowing your dear Daddy." She didn't serve a function in his life other than that of a daughter to be raised by her mother. Unlike Rockefeller and Morgan, who included their sons in their business dealings and desired a dynasty, Carnegie pursued a solitary agenda as he had his entire life.

Certainly, Carnegie had been a doting father when home, and he had never hesitated to sing her praises and was particularly pleased when Margaret asked hard questions about God. "She is developing fast—puzzles her mother about certain things in Holy Writ now & then that gives Madam some anxiety," he divulged to Morley. "She does her best & I say, all right, Lou—I'll not give you away. Do the best you can—but remember she'll find out the truth before long for herself & Lou agrees, Yes, she won't rest until she is satisfied."[45] On another occasion, he wrote that "she grows troublesome on Bible Stories, *very*, her Mother stalled & sometimes appalled at her temerity—but she has past the Fairytale period."[46] She had grown up to be much like her father, independent and stubborn, which led to clashes with him. Peace at home was as elusive as peace on the international stage.

Now a freethinking twenty-two-year-old adult, Margaret was more skeptical of her father's benefactions in the name of peace than ever before. What purpose did they serve? What had been gained? Over two decades, Carnegie had expended an estimated $25 million toward peace, and yet there were an estimated 13 million military deaths in World War I alone. By now, she was also well versed in the robber baron heritage he embodied and found it impossible to reconcile his business legacy with that of the benevolent philanthropist. As she later directed her father's official biographer, "Tell his life like it was. I'm sick of the Santa Claus stuff."[47] There was too much hypocrisy for her; she wanted nothing to do with his philanthropic work, along with its pomp and circumstance, which rang so hollow to her.

When John Barrett, president of the Pan American Union, representing the twenty-one Central and South American countries, expressed his hope Margaret would accept an award and speak on her father's behalf at a celebration scheduled for that May in Washington, she demurred. Even though she was going to be in town, it was her honeymoon, she complained. Disappointed, Louise wrote her daughter a stern reprimand: "Mrs. Miller told me yesterday that John Barrett was on your track. I know how you will feel about this, but know although you will be firm, you will be polite to him, for he means well; he is a great friend of Daddy's in carrying out his work for conciliation in Central and South America; besides now that you are married you are no longer irresponsible children, but owe something to the dignity of both your families and I know you will not fail us."

Margaret relented and agreed to attend the ceremony. Elated, Louise wrote: "It makes me so happy to know that you are gaining a true appreciation of Daddy and his wonderful work in the world; and to have him still with us, so that you can come back to him with this new attitude in your heart, makes me very happy. . . . If you could have seen the heavenly smile that broke over his face as I rushed up to him after breakfast and told him about your letter it would have made you very happy. I am going to show him his gold medal from the twenty-one Republics. You see how much pleasure you are giving Daddy by being happy and appreciative yourself."[48]

More so than ever, Carnegie, forever desperate to conquer an illusionary world, could proclaim, "All is well since all grows better."

The Carnegie Legacy

A ndrew Carnegie died on August 11, 1919, at his Shadowbrook estate, the cause of death given as bronchial pneumonia. Louise was at his side and later that day wrote in her diary, "I was called at 6 A.M., and remained with my darling husband, giving him oxygen until he gradually fell asleep, at 7.14. I am left alone."[1]

Hundreds of telegrams and letters of consolation from family, friends, and heads of state arrived at Shadowbrook.[2] "I cannot realize that my most steadfast of all friends has gone," John Morley wrote Louise, "nor do I realize that this letter will find you lonely in your home. Though he was far from me in place and sight, in thought he was close and constant. How little when we last said goodbye at the Liverpool Station, could we suppose that we were to meet no more, and that the humane hopes we had lived in, and lived by, were on the very eve of ruin. Our ideas and aims were just the same, but the fire and glow of his spirit was his own, and my debt to him from the year when Arnold made us acquainted, was more than I can find words for. His interest in me and my doings was for all this long span of time active, eager, indulgent, long-sighted, high pitched. My days of survival cannot be very far prolonged, but they will be much the more dull now that the beacon across the Atlantic has gone out." Carnegie's death, although expected, also dealt a blow to his cousin Dod, who, growing feeble, found consolation in that "I am tottering on the same brink."[3]

Louise invited Charlie Schwab to ride with the family for the funeral services at Shadowbrook. Despite the Monte Carlo gambling episode, Carnegie had always regarded Schwab as a favored son, and almost twenty years later Louise and Schwab were still in contact. After his wife died in 1939, Schwab wrote Louise movingly, "We had fifty-six long years together, and they were happy years, I can assure you. It means a complete change in my life, which at my age is not easily arranged, and I will live on the happy memories of my associates of the years gone by, and none of these was more delightful or happy and with such genuine affection, than my association with

Mr. Carnegie and yourself."[4] While Carnegie could be so cruel, he had a magnetic charm that left men like Schwab enraptured two decades after his death. Henry Clay Frick, who would die that December of 1919, was one of the few who resisted his allure.

Following the services, the Carnegie family, bound for Sleepy Hollow Cemetery, took a special train to nearby Tarrytown, New York. Carnegie had debated between there and the Pittencrieff Glen as his final resting place, but settled on Sleepy Hollow, home to many of New York's elite families, as well as renowned author Washington Irving. A Celtic cross, the granite cut from a Skibo quarry, was placed above his grave and carved into its base these words: "Andrew Carnegie Born Dunfermline Scotland 25 November 1835 Died Lenox Massachusetts 11 August 1919." It was simple and unostentatious, the image Carnegie had always wanted for himself.

On his death, there was great speculation as to Carnegie's net worth. Newspapers estimated his fortune at $500 million to $600 million, but he had given away most of it. For once, he had done what he said he would. Measured in today's dollars, Carnegie would have been worth over $100 billion at the height of his wealth, bested only by Rockefeller, who would have been worth over $200 billion. Software baron Bill Gates would then be third with a paltry $50 billion, depending on Microsoft's stock price.[5] However, as of June 1, 1918, Carnegie had given a total of $350,695,653.40 to philanthropic causes, and there was but $25 million left in the Hoboken bank vault.[6] Rockefeller, who died in 1937, eventually gave away almost $500 million, but he also passed along over $500 million to his children—a disgrace according to Carnegie's principles.

In his will, there were no provisions for Louise or Margaret; their financial security had already been arranged. All real estate was bequeathed to Louise. She returned to Skibo in 1920, where she kept Carnegie's spirit alive until 1939, when world war again plagued mankind. She would die in 1946. Of the $25 million, Carnegie gave $20 million to the Carnegie Corporation and set $4 million aside for an expanded private pension list, to include $10,000 a year to former President Taft, $5,000 each to Mrs. Grover Cleveland and Mrs. Theodore Roosevelt, and $10,000 to John Morley. He provided gifts for the gamekeepers, foresters, crofters, and others on the Skibo estate; the Carnegie family butler, George Irvine, the housekeeper, Mrs. Nicoll, nurse, Nannie Lockerbie, and the eldest servant, Maggie Anderson, each received a legacy, too. Mrs. Nicoll had been with the family since the Carnegies' marriage thirty-two years earlier, and that relationship says a good deal about the real Carnegie, the hardworking boy from Dunfermline. He was tolerable and likable in the congenial setting of home life, but often a tyrant otherwise. The final $1 million was divided among educational institutions, including a $200,000 gift each to Pittsburgh University, Stevens Institute, and the St. Andrew's Society.

Andrew Carnegie's name remains prominent today, forever gracing the pages of national periodicals and haunting libraries across America. His major trusts and foundations—the Carnegie Trust for the Universities of Scotland, the Carnegie Dunfermline Trust, the Carnegie Institute, the Carnegie Endowment for International Peace, the Carnegie Hero Fund Commission, the Carnegie Institution of Washington, and the Carnegie Corporation—continue his work. The Carnegie Corporation, with a capital fund of about $2 billion, remains a force in philanthropy and still supports libraries with a passion, giving $15 million in 1999 alone to urban libraries used heavily by immigrant populations.[7] The Dunfermline cottage Carnegie was born in is now a museum dedicated to his life; the Fifth Avenue mansion is a world-class art museum, the Cooper-Hewitt National Design Museum; and Skibo Castle is a private club, playing host to international jet-setting members.

As B. C. Forbes predicted in 1917, Carnegie is remembered "as a giver, not as a maker," and the titan remains a model for philanthropy. Peter Drucker, one of the great students of business, credits Carnegie with establishing the template for charitable foundations.[8] When the media evaluates benevolence, it is measured against Carnegie. Before his death, David Packard, cofounder of Hewlett-Packard, gave away $5 billion, almost his entire estate, and in 1997 was anointed "today's Carnegie."[9] And the journal *American Libraries* asks, "Is Bill Gates the New Andrew Carnegie?"[10] The philanthropic legacy has whitewashed the incisive statement made by the correspondent for the London *Times* at the time of the titan's death: "Carnegie's naturally kind and generous disposition and the memories and traditions of his Dunfermline proletariat days came into conflict with his consuming ambition. The business side always won."[11] Today, the Homestead strike has become shrouded in legend and the robber baron is part of American lore, along with Johnny Appleseed and Daniel Boone. It did take time for Carnegie's image to take on a sort of benign legendary status.

In the mid-twentieth century, a feature in *American Heritage* titled "Epitaph for the Steel Master" didn't gloss over Carnegie's hypocritical behavior and fallibility, but the author did allow for an excuse, believing that Carnegie was "struggling to retain his convictions in an age, and in the face of a career, which subjected them to impossible temptations." He then concluded, "In the failures of Andrew Carnegie we see many of the failures of America itself."[12] The steel master was merely part of a collective experience and therefore a collective guilt, unavoidable and expected. Today, when Carnegie's business legacy is evoked, he is remembered with sweeping classifications, such as a business builder who embraced change, an executive trainer

At a ceremony honoring his benefactions, Carnegie, who had a mask for every occasion, was at his animated best. This trip to Braddock in 1914 was his last to the Pittsburgh area. (Courtesy of the Carnegie Library of Pittsburgh)

who was a master motivator, and a fanatic cost accountant who demanded perfect efficiencies. In excusing some of his unsavory tactics, we say, What is morally repugnant to us now was not back then. Yes, he was a typical employer to a degree. As a businessman, however, Carnegie was the most driven and competitive, the most obsessive and compulsive, the most independent and daring. He was so convinced of his own rightness—on business, politics, and philanthropy—that he couldn't conceive of being wrong. He was intoxicated by his own holiness.

And yet, at times he harbored doubts. Even in 1914, about to turn seventy-nine years old, he allowed his mask of conviction to slip when he spoke at the twenty-fifth anniversary of the Braddock Carnegie Library: "I don't know how every one thinks about the way I spend money but I'm willing to put this library and institution against any other form of benevolence. It's the best kind of philanthropy I can think of·and I'm willing to stand on that record. This is a grand old world and its always growing better. And all's well since it is growing better and when I go for a trial for the things done on earth, I think I'll get a verdict of 'Not Guilty' through my efforts to make the earth a little better than I found it."[13] He thought he would be judged not guilty; but clearly, being guilty was on his mind.

Why the guilt complex at such a late stage in Carnegie's life? Because he suspected he had exacted too high of a price from his laborers, and the visit to Braddock reminded him of it. Living and working conditions for laborers in the steel industry had yet to improve. In fact, the year Carnegie died there was a great steel strike. With the shortage of labor during the war, union leaders had hoped to organize the steel industry, and eighty-nine-year-old Mary "Mother" Jones declared, "We are to see whether Pennsylvania belongs to Kaiser Gary or Uncle Sam."[14] The campaign for better conditions began in 1918 and culminated on September 22, 1919, when 275,000 steelworkers in Illinois, Ohio, and Pennsylvania went on strike. After three months, the workers were forced to return without any concessions in hand and old Mother Jones was locked up in jail. Not until almost twenty years later, when the Steel Workers Organizing Committee, the embryo of the United Steelworkers of America, was formed, did conditions begin to improve. During World War II, the high demand for steel finally aided the union's cause.

Today, the Edgar Thomson steel mill is the sole survivor of the Carnegie mills along the Monongahela River; the others have been razed. Its hometown of Braddock remains bleak, however; many shops on the main street are boarded up, and the town is empty of spirit. The stark contrast between the desolate streets of Braddock and the vitality discovered in Carnegie's libraries best symbolize the great contradictions within Carnegie himself.

Notes

Manuscript Collections

ACLOC—Papers of Andrew Carnegie, 1803–1935, Library of Congress, Washington, D.C.

ACNYPL—Carnegie Autograph Collection, 1867–1945, New York Public Library, New York, N.Y.

ACWPHS—Carnegie Steel Company, Records, 1853–1912, Historical Society of Western Pennsylvania, Pittsburgh, Pa.

Preface

1. S. J. Kleinberg, *The Shadow of the Mills: Working-Class Families in Pittsburgh, 1870–1907* (Pittsburgh: University of Pittsburgh Press, 1989), pp. 74, 86.
2. Ibid., p. 29.
3. In 1870, the composition of the male iron and steel workforce was 50 percent native-born white, 20 percent British, 21 percent Irish, 8 percent German, and 1 percent other. U.S. Census Bureau, *Ninth Census, 1870,* vol. 1, p. 795.
4. Kleinberg, p. 19.

Chapter 1: Flesh and Blood

1. James B. Mackie, *Andrew Carnegie: His Dunfermline Ties and Benefactions* (Dunfermline, Scot.: Dunfermline Journal Printing Works, 1916), p. 4. Genealogical information is from Mackie and the Carnegie Birthplace Museum, Dunfermline, Scotland.
2. Andrew Carnegie, *The Autobiography of Andrew Carnegie* (Boston: Northeastern University Press, 1986), p. 3.
3. Mackie, p. 4.
4. Burton J. Hendrick, *The Life of Andrew Carnegie,* vol. 1 (Garden City, N.Y.: Doubleday, Doran, 1932), pp. 4–5. Hendrick was selected by Louise Carnegie to be her husband's official biographer.
5. Hendrick, *Carnegie,* vol. 1, p. 3; Mackie, p. 7; Carnegie, *Autobiography,* p. 2.
6. Mackie, p. 7.
7. Joseph Frazier Wall, *Andrew Carnegie* (New York: Oxford University Press, 1970), p. 33.
8. Ebenezer Henderson, *Annals of Dunfermline* (Glasgow: n.p., 1879), p. 107. Henderson was the town's historian.
9. Norman Murray, *The Scottish Hand Loom Weavers, 1790–1850: A Social History* (Edinburgh: John Donald Publishers, 1978), p. 13.
10. Wall, *Carnegie,* p. 21; Carnegie, *Autobiography,* p. 6. Dunfermline historians dispute whether the Morrisons moved from Edinburgh. There is also no proof that Thomas Morrison Sr. squandered the family's business. Some historians think he may have lost the business during a severe economic downturn during the early Napoleonic Wars.

11. Thomas Morrison, "Rights of Land," unpublished manuscript, Carnegie Papers, Carnegie Museum, Dunfermline, Scot.

12. Wall, *Carnegie*, p. 22.

13. The first issue appeared in January 1833 and sold for two pence a copy.

14. Alexander Wilson, *The Chartist Movement in Scotland* (Manchester, Engl.: University Press, 1970), pp. 1–4.

15. Ibid., p. 13.

16. R. H. Campbell, *Scotland Since 1707: The Rise of an Industrial Society* (New York: Barnes & Noble, 1965), pp. 167–168.

17. Ibid., p. 184.

18. Eric Simpson, *The Auld Grey Toun: Dunfermline in the Time of Andrew Carnegie* (Dunfermline, Scot.: Carnegie Dunfermline Trust, 1987), p.17.

19. Ibid., p. 46.

20. William Shakespeare, *Macbeth*, I, iii, l. 50, in David Bevington, ed., *The Complete Works of Shakespeare*, 3rd ed. (Glenview, Ill.: Scott, Foresman, 1980).

21. Carnegie, *Autobiography*, p. 7.

22. Ibid., p. 22.

23. David Robinson, ed., *William Ellery Channing: Selected Writings* (New York: Paulist Press, 1985), p. 23.

24. Hendrick, *Carnegie*, vol. 1, p. 15.

25. Carnegie, *Autobiography*, p. 22.

26. Wall, *Carnegie*, p. 38.

27. Henderson, p. 640.

28. Ibid., p. 642; Simpson, p. 24.

29. For a detailed account of the movement, see Richard Brown, *Chartism* (Cambridge, U.K.: Cambridge University Press, 1998).

30. Notes of James Shearer, ACLOC, vol. 244; *Dunfermline Journal*, February 26, 1841.

31. Simpson, p. 28.

32. Mackie, pp. 15–16.

33. *Edinburgh Monthly Democrat*, July 7, 1838.

34. Carnegie, *Autobiography*, p. 15.

35. Notes of James Shearer, ACLOC, vol. 244.

36. Carnegie, *Autobiography*, p. 14.

37. Simpson, p. 13.

38. Mackie, p. 36.

39. Carnegie, *Autobiography*, pp. 13–14.

40. Hendrick, *Carnegie*, vol. 1, p. 28.

41. Mackie, pp. 38–40.

42. Wall, *Carnegie*, p. 44.

Chapter 2: Odyssey to America

1. Annie Aitken to Sisters and Friends, October 7, 1840, ACLOC, vol. 1.

2. Local Chartist organizations in Scotland numbered 78 in 1838, 169 in 1839, and 127 in 1840, illustrating the falloff in activism. See Wilson, p. 269.

3. Simpson, p. 29.

4. Hendrick, *Carnegie*, vol. 1, pp. 34–35; Carnegie, *Autobiography*, pp. 8–9.

5. Hendrick, *Carnegie*, vol. 1, p. 37.

6. Carnegie, *Autobiography*, p. 21.

7. Ibid., p. 11.

8. Hendrick, *Carnegie*, vol. 1, p. 23; Carnegie, *Autobiography*, pp. 9–10.

9. Simpson, pp. 52–53; Henderson, pp. 654–655.

10. Henderson, p. 652.

11. *Dunfermline Journal*, July 4, 1846.

12. Annie Aitken to Margaret Carnegie, May 30, 1844. ACLOC, vol. 1.

13. Carnegie, *Autobiography*, p. 12.

14. Ibid., p. 12.

15. Hendrick, *Carnegie*, vol. 1, p. 37.

16. Thomas Morrison's letter was published in *Cobbett's Political Register*, December 21, 1833.

17. Carnegie, *Autobiography*, p. 6.

18. *Dunfermline Journal*, July 2, 1847.

19. Hendrick, *Carnegie*, vol. 1, p. 36.

20. Murray, p. 23.

21. Carnegie, *Autobiography*, p. 24.

22. Samuel Gompers, *Seventy Years of Life and Labor: An Autobiography* (New York: E. P. Dutton, 1957), pp. 18–19.

23. Wall, *Carnegie*, p. 73.

24. Richard Woodman, *The History of the Ship* (London: Conway Maritime Press, 1997), p. 138.

25. *New York Daily Tribune*, May 11, 1902. There is a picture of the ship and a brief history.

26. William Doak, "A Scotch-Irish Emigrant Writes Home," *Pittsburgh History* (Winter 1994–1995). His letter provides an excellent accounting of what a typical voyage was like.

27. Carnegie, *Autobiography*, p. 27.

28. Edwin G. Burrows and Mike Wallace, *Gotham: A History of New York City to 1898* (New York: Oxford University Press, 1999), p. 456.

29. Ann Novotny, *Strangers at the Door* (Riverside, Conn.: Chatham Press, 1971), p. 43.

30. Page Smith, *The Nation Comes of Age* (New York: McGraw-Hill, 1981), p. 738.

31. Carnegie, *Autobiography*, p. 27.

32. Ibid., p. 27.

33. *New York Herald*, July 6, 1848.

34. Carol Sheriff, *The Artificial River: The Erie Canal and the Paradox of Progress* (New York: Hill & Wang, 1996), pp. 139, 141.

35. Carnegie, *Autobiography*, pp. 28–29.

36. Smith, *The Nation Comes of Age*, p. 767. The observation was made in 1847.

37. Stefan Lorant, *Pittsburgh* (Lenox, Mass.: Author's Edition, 1980), p. 79.

38. David W. Lonich, "Metropolitanism and the Genesis of Municipal Anxiety in Allegheny County," *Pittsburgh History* 76, no. 2, p. 80.

39. Jacqueline Sardi and Paul Roberts, introduction to William Doak, "A Scotch-Irish Writes Home," *Pittsburgh History* (Winter 1994–1995), p. 172; Peter Chalmers, *Historical and Statistical Account of the Town and Parish of Dunfermline*, vol. 2 (Edinburgh: n.p., 1859).

40. Lorant, p. 103.

41. Carnegie, *Autobiography*, p. 29.

Chapter 3: $1.20 a Week

1. Carnegie, *Autobiography*, p. 29.

2. Carnegie, *Autobiography*, p. 31.

3. Ibid., p. 33; Andrew Carnegie, "How I Served My Apprenticeship," *Youth's Companion*, April 23, 1896.

4. Carnegie, *Autobiography*, p. 33.

5. Carnegie, "How I Served My Apprenticeship."

6. Carnegie, *Autobiography*, p. 34.

7. John K. Winkler, *Incredible Carnegie* (New York: Vanguard Press, 1931), p. 51.

8. Thomas N. Miller to Andrew Carnegie [hereafter abbreviated as AC], quoted in Hendrick, *Carnegie*, vol. 1, p. 53.

9. Hendrick, *Carnegie*, vol. 1, p. 56.

10. Carnegie, *Autobiography*, p. 37.

11. James D. Reid, *The Telegraph in America* (New York: Derby Brothers, 1879), pp. 160, 161.

12. Hendrick, *Carnegie*, vol. 1, p. 56.

13. Carnegie, *Autobiography*, p. 35.

14. Ibid., pp. 37–38; Henry Wysham Lanier, "The Many-Sided Andrew Carnegie: A Citizen of the Republic," *World's Work* 1 (April 1901), p. 620.

15. Carnegie, "How I Served My Apprenticeship."

16. David H. Wollman and Donald R. Inman, *Portraits in Steel* (Kent, Ohio: Kent State University Press, 1990), p. 29.

17. Reid, p. 177.

18. Carnegie, *Autobiography*, p. 47.

19. "Carnegie on the Verge of Seventy," *Current Literature* 42 (May 1907), pp. 501–502.

20. Carnegie, *Autobiography*, p. 42.

21. T. B. A. David to AC, May 20, 1903, ACLOC, vol. 96.

22. Carnegie, *Autobiography*, p. 53.

23. Ibid., p. 54.

24. T. B. A. David to AC, May 20, 1903, ACLOC, vol. 96.

25. Andrew Carnegie, "The Road to Business Success," speech delivered before Curry Commercial College, June 23, 1885.

26. Carnegie, *Autobiography*, p. 56. Carnegie states that it was 1852 in his autobiography, but a June 22, 1851, letter to Dod shows that it was 1851.

27. AC to George Lauder Jr., June 22, 1851, ACLOC, vol. 1.

28. Frances C. Cooper to Burton J. Hendrick, July 5, 1927, ACLOC, vol. 239.

29. Wall states that Aunt Annie moved with the Hogans; however, in his March 14, 1853, letter to Uncle Lauder, Carnegie writes that his mother was helping Aunt Annie at her store, so she couldn't have moved then.

30. AC to George Lauder Sr., May 30, 1852, ACLOC, vol. 1.

31. Carnegie, *Autobiography*, p. 60.

Chapter 4: The Scotch Devil

1. T. B. A. David to AC, May 20, 1903, ACLOC, vol. 96.

2. See AC to George Lauder Sr., March 14, 1853, ACLOC, vol. 1. Carnegie states that "we all thought that the situation held out better prospects for the future. . . ." It was not his decision alone.

3. Carnegie, *Autobiography*, p. 61.

4. T. K. Collins and P. G. Collins, *Guide to the Pennsylvania Railroad* (Philadelphia: n.p., 1855). Parts of the depot were still under construction when Carnegie joined the company.

5. Carnegie, *Autobiography*, pp. 62–63.

6. AC to George Lauder Sr., March 14, 1853, ACLOC, vol. 1.

7. Carnegie speech at Grangemouth, Scotland, September 1887, quoted in Hendrick, *Carnegie*, vol. 1, p. 67.

8. *Pittsburgh Dispatch* letters to the editor quoted in Hendrick, *Carnegie*, vol. 1, pp. 68–70.

9. AC to George Lauder Sr., March 14, 1853, ACLOC, vol. 1.

10. AC to George Lauder Jr., June 1, 1853, ACWPHS, ser. 1, subser. 2.

11. George Bancroft, *History of the United States* (Boston: C. C. Little and J. Brown, 1838), pp. 1–3.

12. AC to George Lauder Jr., March 14, 1853, ACLOC, vol. 1; AC to George Lauder Jr., August 18, 1853, ACLOC, vol. 1.

13. *New York Daily Tribune*, May 9, 1853.

14. AC to George Lauder Jr., August 18, 1853, ACLOC, vol. 1.

15. AC to George Lauder Jr., February 8, 1854, ACWPHS, ser. 1, subser. 2.

16. AC to George Lauder Jr., February 24, 1855, ACWPHS, ser. 1, subser. 2.

17. AC to George Lauder Jr., November 12, 1855, quoted in Wall, *Carnegie*, p. 100.

18. AC to George Lauder Jr., May 1857, ACWPHS, ser. 1, subser. 2.

19. Jeter A. Isely, *Horace Greeley and the Republican Party, 1853–1861: A Study of the New York Tribune* (Princeton, N.J.: Princeton University Press, 1947), p. 81.

20. Lorant, p. 121.

21. Carnegie, *Autobiography*, p. 64.

22. Ibid., p. 65.

23. Ibid., pp. 67–69.

24. Ibid., p. 67.

25. See William Carnegie's application for citizenship, ACLOC, vol. 1.

26. Carnegie, *Autobiography*, p. 74.

Chapter 5: Tree of Knowledge

1. See stock transfer, April 17, 1856, and IOU to Scott, May 17, 1856, ACLOC, vol. 1.

2. See promissory note, November 14, 1856, ACLOC, vol. 1.

3. Mortgage dated March 27, 1858, ACLOC, vol. 1. The house was mortgaged to Richard Boyce of Columbiana County, Ohio.

4. Carnegie, *Autobiography*, p. 76.

5. James A. Ward, *J. Edgar Thomson: Master of the Pennsylvania* (Westport, Conn.: Greenwood Press, 1980), pp. 110–115. Ward's research is extensive, including PRR Board Minutes and Thomson's letters, among other material.

6. Ibid., pp. 118–121.

7. Carnegie states in his autobiography that the year was 1856, and Wall does not dispute that date; however, evidence points strongly to January 1, 1858, when the organizational changes took effect. The Pennsylvania Railroad's 1857 annual report, published on January 30, 1858, states that Scott had just been made general superintendent.

8. Carnegie, *Autobiography*, p. 80.

9. Hendrick, *Carnegie*, vol. 1, p. 98.

10. Carnegie, *Autobiography*, pp. 81–82.

11. Ibid., pp. 85–86.

12. Thomas N. Miller to AC, April 10, 1903, ACLOC, vol. 95.

13. Thomas Miller to AC, April 10, 1903, ACLOC, vol. 95.

14. Carnegie, *Autobiography*, p. 86.

15. Thomas Miller to AC, April 10, 1903, ACLOC, vol. 95.

16. AC to Mrs. Grant (Rebecca Stewart), January 9, 1868, ACWPHS, Union Iron Mills Letterbook, 1866–1869.

17. John H. White Jr., *The American Railroad Passenger Car* (Baltimore: Johns Hopkins University Press, 1978), pp. 213–214.

18. T. T. Woodruff to AC, June 12, 1886, ACLOC, vol. 9.

19. Carnegie, *Autobiography*, p. 83.

20. See income statement for 1863, ACLOC, vol. 3.

21. Hendrick, *Carnegie*, vol. 1, pp. 95–96.

22. Carnegie, *Autobiography*, p. 87.

23. Ibid., p. 87.

24. Ibid., pp. 89–90.

25. Lorant, pp. 126–127, 129.

26. Collins and Collins, p. 33.

27. Hendrick, *Carnegie*, vol. 1, p. 101.

28. Carnegie, *Autobiography*, pp. 91–92.

29. George M. Alexander to Thomas N. Miller, May 12, 1903, ACLOC, vol. 96.

30. Carnegie, *Autobiography*, p. 89.

31. George M. Alexander to Thomas N. Miller, May 12, 1903, ACLOC, vol. 96.

32. Hendrick, *Carnegie*, vol. 1, p. 104.

33. *New York Tribune*, April 13, 1861.

34. *New York Tribune*, April 15, 1861.

Chapter 6: Blood Money and Black Gold

1. Edwin Bennett to AC, May 16, 1905, Bennett Family Papers, ACWPHS, MFF2190.
2. AC to W. R. Plum, November 25, 1879, ACSHC, ser. 1, subser. 3.
3. David Homer Bates, "Lincoln in the Telegraph Office," *Century Magazine*, 74 (May 1907), p. 124.
4. Ibid., p. 128.
5. Carnegie, *Autobiography*, p. 96.
6. James M. McPherson, *Battle Cry of Freedom* (New York: Ballantine, 1988), p. 347.
7. AC to W. H. Holmes, July 26, 1861, ACLOC, vol. 1.
8. Carnegie, *Autobiography*, p. 97.
9. Ibid., pp. 98–99.
10. Leland D. Baldwin, *Pittsburgh: The Story of a City* (Pittsburgh: University of Pittsburgh Press, 1937), p. 317; Lorant, p. 137.
11. AC to Enoch Lewis, October 5, 1861, ACLOC, vol. 1.
12. Ibid.
13. AC to Enoch Lewis, October 4, 7, 10, and 18, 1861, ACLOC, vols. 1, 2, 3.
14. Ward, p. 128.
15. Andrew Carnegie, *An American Four-in-Hand in Britain* (New York: Charles Scribner's Sons, 1883), p. 112.
16. Lorant, p. 119.
17. Ibid., p. 25; Paul H. Giddens, *The Birth of the Oil Industry* (New York: Macmillan, 1938), p. 82.
18. Ibid., p. 133.
19. Carnegie, *Autobiography*, p.132.
20. Giddens, p. 82; see also Andrew Carnegie's statement of earnings for 1863, ACLOC, vol. 3.
21. Carnegie, *Autobiography*, p. 125.
22. Articles of Agreement, February 1, 1862, and May 21, 1863, ACWPHS, Keystone Bridge Files.
23. Ward, p. 127.
24. AC to George Lauder Jr., May 26, 1862, ACLOC, vol. 3.
25. Carnegie, *Autobiography*, p. 106.
26. Ibid., p. 106.
27. Ibid., p. 107.
28. AC to Dod, June 21, 1863, ACLOC, vol. 3.

Chapter 7: An Iron Coup

1. T. B. A. David to AC, May 20, 1903, ACLOC, vol. 96.
2. See Memorandum of Agreement for coal mining patent, February 1, 1865; Articles of Association for Neptune Coal, October 1, 1864; George Boulton to AC, March 27, 1865; Ferree Property Agreement, n.d., among other documents in ACWPHS, Early Investments File.
3. Baldwin, p. 222.
4. James Howard Bridge, *The Inside History of the Carnegie Steel Company* (Pittsburgh: University of Pittsburgh Press, 1991), p. 3.
5. Thomas N. Miller to AC, quoted in ibid., p. 10.
6. Bridge, p. 11.
7. See receipt for the $850, dated June 19, 1864, and the Certificate of Non-Liability, dated July 19, 1864, ACWPHS, Miscellaneous Papers File.
8. Carnegie, *Autobiography*, p. 135.
9. Wall, *Carnegie*, p. 224.
10. See resignation letter, March 28, 1865, ACLOC, vol. 3.
11. Bridge, p. 21.
12. Hendrick, *Carnegie*, vol. 1, pp. 136–137.

13. Hendrick and Wall don't raise this possibility, but it is the only explanation.

14. Niccolo Machiavelli, *The Prince and the Discourses* (New York: Modern Library, 1950), p. 372.

15. AC to Thomas N. Milller, September 4, 1867, quoted in Bridge, p. 23.

16. Hendrick, *Carnegie*, vol. 1, p. 141; Carnegie, *Autobiography*, p. 129.

17. AC to Thomas N. Miller, June 3, 1867, ACWPHS, Union Iron Mills Letterbook, 1866–1869.

18. Bridge, p. 30; AC to Thomas N. Miller, September 4, 1867, quoted in Bridge, p. 29.

19. Thomas N. Miller to AC, April 2, 1903, ACLOC, vol. 95.

20. AC to William J. Holland, December 22, 1911, quoted in Hendrick, *Carnegie*, vol. 1, p. 142.

Chapter 8: Many Hands, Many Cookie Jars

1. Carnegie, *Autobiography*, p. 137.

2. Herbert N. Casson, *The Romance of Steel* (New York: A. S. Barnes & Company, 1907), p. 86; AC to Margaret and Tom Carnegie, Travel Letters, 1865–1866, quoted in Wall, *Carnegie*, p. 230. The travel letters are still privately held by Carnegie descendants and were unavailable at the time.

3. John Franks Letterbook, Dresden, November 19, 1865, ACLOC, vol. 3; John Franks Letterbook, Frankfurt am Main, October 18, 1865, ACLOC, vol. 3.

4. AC to Margaret and Tom Carnegie, Amsterdam, November 5, 1865, Travel Letters, 1865–1866, quoted in Wall, *Carnegie*, p. 231; AC to Margaret and Tom Carnegie, Amsterdam, November 5, 1865, Travel Letters, 1865–1866, quoted in Wall, *Carnegie*, p. 233.

5. Carnegie, *Autobiography*, p. 137.

6. AC to Margaret and Tom Carnegie, Mannheim, October 16, 1865, Travel Letters, 1865–1866, quoted in Wall, *Carnegie*, p. 232.

7. John Franks Letterbook, Frankfurt am Main, October 18, 1865, ACLOC, vol. 3; John Franks Letterbook, quoted in Hendrick, *Carnegie*, vol. 1, p. 139.

8. Excerpts from AC's letters to Tom Carnegie, summer and fall of 1865, Travel Letters, 1865–1866, quoted in Wall, *Carnegie*, p. 236.

9. AC to Margaret and Tom Carnegie, Adlesburg, Austria, December 3, 1865, Travel Letters, 1865–1866, quoted in Wall, *Carnegie*, pp. 236–237.

10. AC to Margaret and Tom Carnegie, London, July 26, 1865, Travel Letters, 1865–1866, quoted in Wall, *Carnegie*, p. 234.

11. AC to Margaret Carnegie, Dunfermline, September 2, 1865, Travel Letters, 1865–1866, quoted in Wall, *Carnegie*, p. 232.

12. AC to Tom Carnegie, n.d. (autumn of 1865), Travel Letters, 1865–1866, quoted in Wall, *Carnegie*, p. 234.

13. AC to Margaret and Tom Carnegie, Mannheim, October 16, 1865, Travel Letters, 1865–1866, quoted in Wall, *Carnegie*, p. 235.

14. J. Edgar Thomson to AC, March 12, 1867; J. Edgar Thomson to AC, March 12 and 15, 1867, ACWPHS, Dodd Patent Files.

15. AC to Messrs. Cass & McCullough, September 1, 1866, and AC to A. Stone, September 1, 1866, ACWPHS, Union Iron Mills Letterbook, 1866–1869.

16. AC to Henry Blackwell, November 4, 1867, ACWPHS, Union Iron Mills Letterbook, 1866–1869.

17. AC to Thomas A. Scott, March 8, 1869, ACWPHS, Union Iron Mills Letterbook, 1866–1869.

18. See agreements between AC and the Pacific and Atlantic Telegraph Company, September 13, 1867, ACWPHS, Telegraph File.

19. Ibid.

20. G. H. Thurston to AC, November 6, 1867, ACWPHS, Telegraph File.

21. AC to George H. Thurston, November 9, 1867, ACWPHS, Telegraph File.

22. AC to Thomas A. Scott, January 19, 1869, ACWPHS, Union Iron Mills Letterbook, 1866–1869.

23. AC to W. D. Judson, November 4, 1867, ACWPHS, Union Iron Mills Letterbook, 1866–1869.

24. Ward, p. 185.

25. Reid, p. 520.

26. David McCargo to AC, January 17, 1872, ACWPHS, Telegraph File.

27. Wall, *Carnegie*, 218.

28. Henry Spackman to AC, May 23, 1873, ACWPHS, Telegraph File.

29. AC to William Orton, June 3, 1873, ACWPHS, Telegraph File.

30. Henry Spackman to AC, June 9, 1873, ACWPHS, Telegraph File.

31. W. G. Johnston to AC, May 24, 1873, ACWPHS, Telegraph File.

32. W. G. Johnston to AC, June 3, 1873, ACWPHS, Telegraph File.

33. AC to J. W. Weir, September 4, 1873, ACWPHS, Telegraph File.

34. AC to George Roberts, May 26, 1874, ACWPHS, Letterbook, 1873–1874.

35. Liston E. Leyendecker, *Palace Car Prince: A Biography of George Mortimer Pullman* (Niwot: University Press of Colorado, 1992), p. 77.

36. Carnegie, *Autobiography*, p. 154.

37. See ibid., pp. 154–155, and Leyendecker, pp. 100–102.

38. AC to George M. Pullman, May 29, 1867, ACWPHS, Central Transportation File.

39. AC to Charles W. Angell, May 21, 1868, ACWPHS, Union Iron Mills Letterbook, 1866–1869.

40. AC to George M. Pullman, February 22, 1869, ACWPHS, Central Transportation File.

41. AC to George M. Pullman, March 1869, ACWPHS, Central Transportation File.

42. Ward, p. 184.

43. Leyendecker, pp. 146–147.

44. Ward, p. 184; Leyendecker, p. 102.

Chapter 9: Bridges to Glory

1. Carnegie, *Autobiography*, p. 144.

2. Statement of Business Holdings, ACNYPL.

3. Hendrick, *Carnegie*, vol. 1, pp. 146–147. The original is in possession of the Carnegie family descendents.

4. Wall, *Carnegie*, p. 225.

5. Ron Chernow, *Titan: The Life of John D. Rockefeller Sr.* (New York: Vintage Books, 1998), p. 114.

6. Jean Strouse, *Morgan: American Financier* (New York: Random House, 1999), p. 127.

7. Carnegie, *Autobiography*, pp. 144–145.

8. Sidney B. Whipple, "Notes on Mr. Schwab's Life," unpublished manuscript, Hagley Library, Wilmington, Del., p. 93.

9. Carnegie, *Autobiography*, p. 146; Jerry E. Patterson, *The City of New York* (New York: Harry Abrams, 1978), p. 136.

10. See notice dated May 16, 1865, ACWPHS, early investment file; Ward, p. 177.

11. AC to J. H. Linville, January 20, 1868, ACWPHS, Union Iron Mills Letterbook, 1866–1869.

12. AC to President & Directors of the Keystone Bridge Co., January 25, 1868, ACWPHS, Union Iron Mills Letterbook, 1866–1869.

13. Carnegie, *Autobiography*, pp. 148–149.

14. G. F. McCandless to Tom Carnegie, November 7, 1870, ACWPHS, Letterbook, November 1, 1870–March 14, 1871.

15. Joseph Gies, *Bridges and Men* (Garden City, N.Y.: Doubleday, 1963), p. 156.

16. Ibid., p. 161.

17. See AC to Amos Cutting, March 7, 1870, ACWPHS, Letterbook, 1869–1870; AC to J. Edgar Thomson, March 1, 1870, ACWPHS, Letterbook, 1869–1870; AC to Thomas A. Scott, March 7, 1870, ACWPHS, Letterbook, 1869–1870.

18. Strouse, p. 138.

19. Carnegie, *Autobiography*, pp. 150–151.

20. W. H. Holmes to AC, February 21, 1871, ACWPHS, Davenport File.

21. J. P. Morgan to AC, July 23, 1872, ACWPHS, Davenport File.

22. Sulzbach Brothers to AC, November 18, 1872, ACWPHS, Davenport File.

23. Sulzbach Brothers to AC, May 9, 1873, ACWPHS, Davenport File.

24. AC to Edward J. Allen, December 14, 1871, ACWPHS, Letterbook, March 16, 1871–March 8, 1872.

25. Sulzbach Brothers to AC, May 9, 1873, ACWPHS, Davenport File.

26. Charles Edgar Ames, *Pioneering the Union Pacific* (New York: Appleton-Century-Crofts, 1969), p. 406.

27. Ibid., pp. 407–409; Carnegie, *Autobiography*, p. 160; C. S. Bushnell to President and Treasurer Union Pacific Railroad, January 26, 1871, and C. S. Bushnell to AC, March 20, 1871, ACWPHS, Union Pacific File.

28. Ames, p. 23.

29. Ibid., p. 407.

30. Leyendecker, p. 104.

31. AC to Messrs. Boyd, Falls, and Vincent, March 20, 1871, AC to Messrs. Norton, Bliss & Co., March 22, 1871, ACWPHS, Union Pacific File; G. F. McCandless to George M. Pullman, May 8, 1871, ACWPHS, Union Pacific File.

32. Carnegie, *Autobiography*, p. 159.

33. AC to E. J. Thomson, March 20, 1872, ACWPHS, Union Pacific File; AC to C. S. Bushnell, September 26, 1872, ACWPHS, Letterbook, 1872–1873; E. H. Rollins to AC, September 27, 1872, ACWPHS, Union Pacific File.

34. Ames, pp. 436, 454.

35. Carnegie, *Autobiography*, p. 160.

36. AC to R. D. Barclay, November 3, 1871, ACWPHS, Union Pacific File.

37. See Miller letter to AC, quoted in Hendrick, *Carnegie*, vol. 1, p. 179.

38. AC to John Ross, Esq., March 28, 1873, Union Iron Mills Letterbook, 1866–1869; AC to Thomas M. Carnegie, January 3, 1870, ACWPHS, Letterbook, 1869–1870.

Chapter 10: Epiphany of Legend

1. Hendrick, *Carnegie*, vol. 1, p. 225.

2. David Wiltshire, *The Social and Political Thought of Herbert Spencer* (Oxford, U.K.: Oxford University Press, 1978), pp. 197, 199; Jonathan H. Turner, *Herbert Spencer* (London: Sage Publications, 1985), p. 38.

3. Hendrick, *Carnegie*, vol. 1, p. 223.

4. Ibid., p. 221.

5. S. M. Shoemaker to AC, December 2, 1871, ACWPHS, Box 5, Folder 2.

6. Frances C. Cooper to Burton Hendrick, July 5, 1927, ACLOC, vol. 239.

7. Hendrick, *Carnegie*, vol. 1, pp. 227–228.

8. Carnegie, *Autobiography*, p. 170.

9. John A. Fitch, *The Steel Workers* (Pittsburgh: University of Pittsburgh Press, 1989), p. 3.

10. Henry Bessemer, *An Autobiography* (London: Offices of Engineering, 1905), pp. 153–154.

11. Bridge, pp. 72–75.

12. Burton J. Hendrick interview with William L. Abbott, August 1929, ACLOC, vol. 239.

13. AC to Edgar Thomson, October 30, 1872, ACWPHS, Edgar Thomson Operating File.

14. See Co-Partnership agreements, ACLOC, vol. 4.

15. Peter Temin, *Iron and Steel in Nineteenth-Century America* (Cambridge, Mass.: Massachussetts Institute of Technology, 1964), p.166.

16. See AC to Hon. W. D. Bishop, January 22, 1877, ACWPHS, ser. III, subser. 4.

17. J. Edgar Thomson to AC, November 14, 1872, ACWPHS, Edgar Thomson Operating File.

18. Thomas J. Misa, *A Nation of Steel* (Baltimore: Johns Hopkins University Press, 1995), p. 17.

19. Strouse, p.150.

20. Lewis Sanders to AC, September 6, 1873, ACWPHS, Miscellaneous Files.

21. Carnegie, *Autobiography*, p. 182.

22. *New York Times*, September 19, 1873.

23. *New York Times*, September 21, 1873.

24. Carnegie, *Autobiography*, p. 167.

25. AC to G. F. McCandless, July 30, 1873, ACWPHS, Superior Iron File.

26. J. E. Thomson to AC, October 3, 1873, ACNYPL.

27. Carnegie, *Autobiography*, p. 167.

28. Thomas N. Miller to AC, April 10, 1903, ACLOC, vol. 95.

29. See Burrows and Wallace, pp. 1020–1032, for a detailed description of New York City during the depression.

30. Carnegie, *Autobiography*, p. 187.

31. See G. F. McCandless to AC, April 8, 1879, ACWPHS, Davenport and St. Paul File.

32. George French to AC, February 24, 1876, ACWPHS, Davenport and St. Paul File.

33. George French to G. F. McCandless, March 22, 1879, ACWPHS, Davenport and St. Paul File.

34. George Dallas to AC, February 12, 1884, ACWPHS, Davenport and St. Paul File.

35. See Limited Partnership papers dated October 12, 1874, ACWPHS, Edgar Thomson Operating File.

36. William P. Shinn to AC, January 24, 1874, ACWPHS, Edgar Thomson Operating File.

37. Wall, *Carnegie*, pp. 318–319.

38. *United States Steel Corporation: Hearings Before the Committee on Investigation of the United States Steel Corporation: House of Representatives* (Washington, D.C.: U.S. Government Printing Office, 1911–1912), p. 1738.

39. D. J. Morrell to AC, November 14, 1872, ACWPHS, Edgar Thomson Operating File.

40. D. J. Morrell to AC, December 3, 1872, ACWPHS, Edgar Thomson Operating File.

41. Captain Jones Manuscript, n.d., ACLOC, vol. 243.

42. William Thomas Hogan, *Economic History of the Iron and Steel Industry in the United States*, vol. 1 (Lexington, Mass.: Heath, 1971), pp. 34–35.

43. Captain Jones Manuscript, n.d., ACLOC, vol. 243.

44. Kleinberg, p. 291.

45. For a detailed account, see Kevin Kenny, *Making Sense of the Molly Maguires* (Oxford, U.K.: Oxford University Press, 1998).

46. Hogan, p. 117; Burrows and Wallace, p. 1022.

Chapter 11: Template for Domination

1. Joseph G. Butler, *Recollections of Men and Events* (New York: G. P. Putnam's Sons, 1927), p. 151.

2. William R. Jones to E. V. McCandless, February 25, 1875, quoted in Bridge, pp. 81–82. This letter was to be shared with David McCandless and William Coleman.

3. AC to William P. Shinn, June 11, 1875, ACWPHS, Letterbook, 1874–1875.

4. AC to Samuel Reeves, December 29, 1870, ACWPHS, Iron Beam Agreements File.

5. D. J. Morrell to William P. Shinn, June 10, 1875, ACWPHS, Edgar Thomson Operating File; L. S. Durfee, July 14, 1875, ACWPHS, Pneumatic Steel Association File.

6. AC to William P. Shinn, December 9, 1875, ACWPHS, Letterbook, 1875–1876.

7. AC to William P. Shinn, November 20, 1875, quoted in Temin, p. 175.

8. AC to William P. Shinn, November 29, 1875, ACWPHS, Letterbook, 1875–1876.

9. AC to William P. Shinn, December 9, 1875, ACWPHS, Letterbook, 1875–1876.

10. AC to William P. Shinn, January 15, 1876, ACWPHS, Letterbook, 1875–1876.

11. William P. Shinn to AC, December 13, 1875, ACWPHS, Edgar Thomson Operating File.

12. AC to William P. Shinn, December 14, 1875, ACWPHS, Letterbook, 1875–1876.

13. William P. Shinn to AC, November 26, 1875, ACWPHS, Edgar Thomson Operating File.

14. AC to William P. Shinn, November 30, 1875, quoted in Hendrick, *Carnegie*, vol. 1, p. 217.

15. AC to William P. Shinn, April 10, 1876, ACLOC, vol. 4.

16. See agreement between AC and William Coleman, May 1, 1876, ACWPHS, Edgar Thomson Operating File.

17. Hogan, p. 117.

18. Carnegie, *Autobiography*, pp. 129–130.

19. Ibid., p. 169.

20. AC to Tom Carnegie, April 19, 1869, ACWPHS, Union Iron Mills Letterbook, March 2–June 28, 1869.

21. AC to Henry Phipps Jr., March 8, 1870, ACWPHS, Letterbook, 1869–1870.

22. AC to Henry Phipps Jr., August 9, 1871, ACWPHS, ser. I, subser. 2.

23. Hendrick interview with William Abbott, August 1829, ACLOC, vol. 239.

24. Henry Phipps Jr. to AC, November 27, 1875, ACWPHS, W. R. Jones File.

25. AC to Andrew Kloman, November 6, 1874, ACWPHS, Lucy Furnace Company File.

26. AC to Andrew Kloman, March 17, 1875, ACWPHS, Lucy Furnace Company File.

27. William P. Shinn to AC, October 21, 1876, ACWPHS, Edgar Thomson Operating File.

28. AC to Carnegie Bros. & Co., April 2, 1878, ACWPHS, Lucy Furnace Company File; Hendrick, *The Life of Andrew Carnegie*, vol. 2 (Garden City, N.Y.: Doubleday, Doran, 1932), pp. 35–36; David Brody, *Steelworkers in America: The Non-Union Era* (Cambridge, Mass.: Harvard University Press, 1960), p. 2.

29. AC to Baily, Lang and Co., May 8, 1876, ACWPHS, Edgar Thomson Rail Order File.

30. AC to William P. Shinn, May 12, 1876, ACWPHS, Edgar Thomson Rail Order File.

31. AC to William P. Shinn, February 1, 1876, and AC to William P. Shinn, May 10, 1876, ACWPHS, Edgar Thomson Rail Order File.

32. See Hendrick, *Carnegie*, vol. 1, pp. 209–210.

33. Ibid., vol. 1, pp. 298–299.

34. AC to William P. Shinn, April 10, 1876, ACLOC, vol. 4.

35. AC to William P. Shinn, August 26, 1876, ACLOC, vol. 4.

36. John Scott to AC, January 16, 1877, ACWPHS, Edgar Thomson Operating File.

37. AC to William P. Shinn, April 3, 1877, ACWPHS, Letterbook, 1877.

38. William P. Shinn to AC, April 4, 1877, ACWPHS, Edgar Thomson Operating File.

39. AC to James Swank, May 8, 1876, ACWPHS, Letterbook, 1876.

40. AC to H. M. Curry, April 3, 1877, ACWPHS, Letterbook, 1877.

41. William P. Shinn to AC, April 27, 1877, quoted in Bridge, p. 119.

42. AC to William P. Shinn, May 1, 1877, ACLOC, vol. 4.

43. William P. Shinn to AC, November 15, 1877, ACWPHS, Edgar Thomson Operating File.

44. William R. Jones to AC, April 14, 1876, ACWPHS, W. R. Jones File.

45. William R. Jones to AC, February 22, 1877, ACWPHS, W. R. Jones File.

46. William R. Jones to AC, May 6, 1878, ACWPHS, W. R. Jones File.

47. Tom Gage, "'Hands-on, All-over': Captain Bill Jones," *Pittsburgh History* 80 (Winter 1997–1998).

48. William R. Jones to AC, March 24, 1878, ACWPHS, W. R. Jones File.

49. William R. Jones to AC, May 24, 1878, ACWPHS, W. R. Jones File.

50. Hendrick, *Carnegie*, vol. 1, pp. 212–213.

51. AC to E. Y. Townsend, April 19, 1877, ACWPHS, Letterbook, 1877.

52. AC to William P. Shinn, April 30, 1877, ACWPHS, Letterbook, 1877.

53. AC to Carnegie Bros. & Co., December 8, 1877, ACWPHS, Letterbook, 1877.

54. AC to John Fritz, December 8, 1877, ACWPHS, Letterbook, 1877.

Chapter 12: Rekindling the Flame

1. AC to William P. Shinn, October 1878, ACLOC, vol. 4.

2. Hendrick, *Carnegie*, vol. 1, p. 216.

3. Andrew Carnegie, *Round the World* (New York: Charles Scribner's Sons, 1884), p. 38.

4. Ibid., p. 47.

5. Ibid., p. 76.

6. Ibid., p. 114.

7. Ibid., p. 198.

8. Ibid., p. 203.

9. Ibid., p. 251.

10. Ibid., pp. 249, 256.

11. William P. Shinn to AC, December 1, 1878, ACWPHS, Edgar Thomson Operating File.

12. AC to William P. Shinn, February 22, 1879, ACLOC, vol. 4.

13. Carnegie, *Round the World*, p. 273.

14. Ibid., p. 324.

15. AC to William P. Shinn, quoted in Bridge, p. 100.

16. Carnegie, *Autobiography*, p. 198.

17. Carnegie, *Round the World*, pp. 359–360.

18. Carnegie, *Autobiography*, p. 199.

19. Ibid., p. 327.

20. Wiltshire, p. 197.

21. Carnegie, *An American Four-in-Hand in Britain*, p. 182.

22. Burton J. Hendrick and Daniel Henderson, *Louise Whitfield Carnegie* (New York: Hastings House, 1950), p. 54.

23. Louise Whitfield, diary entry, February 7, 1881, quoted in Hendrick and Henderson, p. 57. The diaries and intimate letters remain in the possession of the Carnegie family and at the time of my research were not available; therefore, it is necessary to rely on excerpts quoted in the Louise Whitfield Carnegie biography.

24. Louise Whitfield, diary entry, February 10, 1881, quoted in Hendrick and Henderson, p. 57.

25. Louise Whitfield, diary entries, quoted in Hendrick and Henderson, pp. 58–59.

26. Hendrick and Henderson, p. 59.

27. Louise Whitfield, diary entry, April 16, 1881, quoted in Hendrick and Henderson, p. 59.

28. Hendrick and Henderson, p. 59.

29. Carnegie, *Autobiography*, p. 168; quoted in Hendrick, *Carnegie*, vol. 1, p. 210.

30. Thomas A. Morrison to AC, January 20, 1880, ACWPHS, Box 11, Folder 2.

31. *Liverpool Daily Albion*, August 5, 1882, ACLOC, vol. 263.

32. *New York Herald*, July 6, 1884, ACLOC, vol. 263.

33. Carnegie, *An American Four-in-Hand in Britain*, p. 34.

34. Ibid., p. 81.

35. Lillian Gilchrist-Thompson, *Sidney Gilchrist-Thomas* (London: Faber & Faber, 1940), p. 169.

36. Carnegie, *An American Four-in-Hand in Britain*, p. 195.

37. Hendrick and Henderson, pp. 60–61.

38. Carnegie, *An American Four-in-Hand in Britain*, p. 133.

39. Ibid., pp. 140, 150.

40. Anonymous, "Through Great Britain on a Drag," *Lippincott's Monthly* (September 1882).

41. Quoted in Hendrick, *Carnegie*, vol. 1, p. 236.

42. Carnegie, *Autobiography*, p. 203.

43. Carnegie, *An American Four-in-Hand in Britain*, pp. 336–337.

Chapter 13: War against the Steel Aristocracy

1. See Archive MFF 457 and document dated July 30, 1879, WPHS.

2. AC to William P. Shinn, April 4, 1879, ACLOC, vol. 4.

3. AC to John Scott, April 7, 1879, ACWPHS, Shinn Suit File.

4. See testimony given by AC, January 7–15, 1880, and testimony given by Daniel Garrison and O. L. Garrison of the Vulcan Iron Company, ACWPHS, William Shinn Suit File.

5. Bridge, p. 128.

6. Ibid., p. 124.

7. AC to William P. Shinn, September 14, 1879, ACWPHS, Letterbook, 1878–1879.

8. Bridge, p. 126. The stories associated with William P. Shinn's ouster are based on the testimony of Carnegie, William P. Shinn, and John Scott.

9. Ibid., pp. 125–130.

10. Machiavelli, p. 86.

11. William R. Jones to AC, November 5, 1880, ACWPHS, Jones Correspondence File.

12. AC to William R. Jones, November 8, 1880, ACWPHS, Letterbook, 1880–1881.

13. Robert Hessen, *Steel Titan: The Life of Charles M. Schwab* (New York: Oxford University Press, 1975), p. 20.

14. See documents, ACWPHS, Folder 6, Box 50.

15. Gage, pp. 165, 166.

16. Carnegie, *Autobiography*, p. 196.

17. William R. Jones to AC, October 29, 1880, ACWPHS, Jones Correspondence File.

18. William R. Jones to AC, December 19, 1880, ACWPHS, Jones Correspondence File.

19. Frances C. Cooper to Hendrick, July 5, 1927, ACLOC, vol. 239.

20. Burton J. Hendrick interview with William L. Abbott, August 1929, ACLOC, vol. 239.

21. Whipple, p. 85.

22. Kleinberg, p. 7.

23. AC to Julian Kennedy, March 14, 1884, ACWPHS, Letterbook, 1884.

24. AC to E. A. Macrum, March 14, 1884, ACWPHS, Letterbook, 1884.

25. William R. Jones to AC, March 22, 1881, ACWPHS, Jones Correspondence File.

26. William R. Jones speech to the British Iron and Steel Institute, May 1881, quoted in Bridge, pp. 109–110.

27. Hessen, pp. 15–16.

28. William R. Jones to AC, December 5, 1879, ACWPHS, Jones Correspondence File.

29. William R. Jones to AC, April 2, 1880, ACWPHS, Jones Correspondence File.

30. Allan Nevins, *Abram S. Hewitt* (New York: Harper & Brothers, 1935), p. 243.

31. George Lauder Jr. to AC, February 19, 1872, ACWPHS, Union Mills Folder.

32. Herbert N. Casson, *The Romance of Steel* (New York: A. S. Barnes, 1907), p. 147.

33. Carnegie, *Autobiography*, p. 211.

34. See Henry Phipps Jr. to AC, quoted in Kenneth Warren, *Triumphant Capitalism* (Pittsburgh: University of Pittsburgh Press, 1996), p. 29.

35. Samuel A. Schreiner Jr., *Henry Clay Frick* (New York: St. Martin's Press, 1995), pp. 34–35.

36. Warren, p. 18.

37. *National Labor Tribune*, July 2, 1881.

38. Warren, p. 32; Wall, *Carnegie*, p. 485.

39. Henry Phipps to AC, January 4, 1882, quoted in Warren, p. 31.

40. See H. C. Frick Memorandum dated March 10, 1885, ACWPHS, Frick Papers. On March 10, 1885, Carnegie Brothers and Company, Limited, paid $15,000 for three hundred shares of unissued stock in the H. C. Frick Coke Company, at par. The shares were then allotted to Andrew Carnegie, Tom Carnegie, Harry Phipps, D. A. Stewart, John Vandevort, George Lauder, John Walker, William R. Jones, John D. Thompson, Henry M. Curry, W. H. Singer, H. W. Borntraeger, W. L. Abbott, S. E. Moore, John Walker (guardian), Amelia Walker, and Caroline Wilson. Another $30,000 was issued for present stockholders to buy. If not bought by March 20, it was to be offered in the market at a price no less than par. Captain Jones owned one hundred shares worth $5,000.

41. See memorandum dated August 17, 1885, ACWPHS, Frick Papers.

42. Henry C. Frick to AC, August 13, 1883, quoted in Warren, p. 34.

43. Henry C. Frick to AC, November 18 and 19, 1883, quoted in Warren, p. 36.

44. George Lauder Jr. to AC, November 14, 1883, quoted in Warren, p. 36.

45. See memorandum dated December 1, 1884, ACWPHS, Frick Papers.

46. AC to E. Y. Townsend, April 20, 1882, ACWPHS, Edgar Thomson Operating File.

47. E. Y. Townsend to AC, April 21, 1882, ACWPHS, Edgar Thomson Operating File.

48. AC to E. Y. Townsend, April 22, 1882, ACWPHS, Edgar Thomson Operating File.

49. A. L. Griffin to AC, November 23, 1883, ACWPHS, Edgar Thomson Operating File.

50. See documents dated April 1, 1881, ACLOC, vol. 5.

51. Bridge, p. 134.

52. Ibid., p. 135.

53. William R. Jones to AC, December 21, 1880, ACWPHS, Jones Correspondence File.

54. Bridge, p. 152.

55. William R. Jones to AC, February 20, 1882, ACWPHS, Jones Correspondence File.

56. See Hendrick, *Carnegie*, vol. 1, pp. 302–303.

57. John N. Ingham, *Making Iron and Steel* (Columbus: Ohio State University Press, 1991), p. 66.

Chapter 14: An Attack on Britain

1. Carnegie, *An American Four-in-Hand in Britain*, p.17.

2. Quoted in Hendrick, *Carnegie*, vol. 1, pp. 263–264.

3. AC to Samuel Storey, October 18, 1884, ACLOC, vol. 8.

4. Interview in *Philadelphia Bulletin*, August 27, 1884, ACLOC, vol. 265.

5. AC to Colonel Thomas Higginson, December 10, 1884, ACWPHS, General Correspondence.

6. AC to Samuel Storey, January 3, 1883, quoted in Hendrick, *Carnegie*, vol. 1, pp. 267–268.

7. Frances Wentworth Cutler Knickerbocker, *Free Minds: John Morley and His Friends* (Cambridge, Mass.: Harvard University Press, 1943), pp. 59, 268.

8. Carnegie, *Autobiography*, pp. 310–311.

9. Hendrick, *Carnegie*, vol. 1, pp. 239–240; Herbert Spencer, *An Autobiography*, vol. 1 (New York: D. Appleton, 1904), pp. 423–424.

10. Ibid., p. 240.

11. Herbert Spencer, *An Autobiography*, vol. 2 (New York: D. Appleton, 1904), p. 468.

12. John Morley, *Recollections: Book IV* (New York: Macmillan, 1917), pp. 110–112.

13. Carnegie, *Autobiography*, p. 286.

14. Matthew Arnold to AC, September 15, 1883, ACNYPL.

15. Matthew Arnold to Frances Arnold, n.d. (October 1883), quoted in Clinton Machann and Forrest D. Burt, eds., *Selected Letters of Matthew Arnold* (Ann Arbor: University of Michigan Press), pp. 262–263.

16. Hendrick, *Carnegie*, vol. 1, pp. 244–245.

17. Ibid., p. 242.

18. AC to Miss Louise Whitfield, n.d. (1883), ACWPHS, General Correspondence.

19. Hendrick and Henderson, p. 44.

20. Burton J. Hendrick interview, quoted in Wall, *Carnegie*, p. 404.

21. Burton J. Hendrick interview with William L. Abbott, August 1929, ACLOC, vol. 239.

22. Ibid.

23. Maria C. Hogan to Gardner McCandless, December 5, 1879, ACWPHS, General Correspondence; S. E. Moore to AC, December 8, 1888, ACWPHS, Letterbook, 1888–1892.

24. AC to Mrs. Jas. R. Wilson, November 22, 1883, ACWPHS, Carnegie Company Papers.

25. See H. C. Frick Memorandum dated March 10, 1885, ACWPHS, Frick Papers.

26. Hendrick and Henderson, p. 62.

27. Louise Whitfield to AC, July 23, 1883, quoted in Hendrick and Henderson, pp. 62–63.

28. Louise Whitfield, diary entries, quoted in Hendrick and Henderson, pp. 64–65.

Chapter 15: Bleeding Hearts and Bleeding Newspapers

1. Hendrick and Henderson, p. 66.

2. Ibid., p. 66.

3. AC to Louise Whitfield, n.d. (1884–1885), ACWPHS, General Correspondence.

4. Hendrick and Henderson, p. 66.

5. Ibid., p. 66.

6. See newspaper clipping dated May 7, 1884, ACLOC, vol. 264.

7. Herbert Spencer to AC, May 26, 1884, ACNYPL.

8. AC to Louise Whitfield, June 11, 1884, quoted in Hendrick and Henderson, p. 67.

9. Carnegie, *Autobiography*, p. 287.

10. Wall, *Carnegie*, p. 436.

11. *New York Daily Tribune*, July 4, 1884.

12. Louise Whitfield to AC, n.d., quoted in Hendrick and Henderson, p. 56.

13. AC to Louise Whitfield, July 19, 1884, quoted in Hendrick and Henderson, pp. 67–68.

14. Joseph Frazier Wall believed Carnegie never made such a commitment, but Carnegie's official biographer claimed he did. A letter dated July 22, 1886, from Carnegie to Louise, quoted in Hendrick and Henderson, p. 76, strongly suggests that he did make such a promise.

15. Carnegie, *Autobiography*, p. 329.

16. James G. Blaine to AC, August 20, 1884, ACNYPL.

17. James G. Blaine to AC, November 22, 1884, ACNYPL.

18. James G. Blaine to AC, August 28, 1886, ACNYPL.

19. Hendrick and Henderson, p. 69.

20. Ibid.

21. Ibid., p. 74.

22. AC to John Morley, October 8, 1884, quoted in Hendrick, *Carnegie*, vol. 1, p. 249.

23. See Trial Balance document dated April 30, 1887, ACWPHS, Box 20, Folder 4.

24. Wall, *Carnegie*, p. 415.

25. AC to Louise Whitfield, July 23, 1885, quoted in Hendrick and Henderson, p. 75.

26. Wall, *Carnegie*, p. 415.

27. AC to Samuel Storey, January 14, 1883, quoted in Hendrick, *Carnegie*, vol. 1, p. 268.

28. AC to Samuel Storey, February 28, 1884, quoted in Hendrick, *Carnegie*, vol. 1, pp. 268–269.

29. AC to Samuel Storey, April 22, 1884, ACWPHS, Letterbook, 1884.

30. AC to Samuel Storey, November 5, 1884, ACWPHS, Letterbook, 1884–1885.

31. Carnegie, *Autobiography*, p. 316.

32. AC to William Gladstone, April 27, 1885, ACLOC, vol. 8.

33. AC to William Gladstone, July 14, 1885, ACLOC, vol. 8.

34. AC to William Gladstone, January 25, 1886, ACLOC, vol. 8.

35. Wall, *Carnegie*, p. 441; Hendrick, *Carnegie*, vol. 1, p. 270.

36. Hendrick, *Carnegie*, vol. 1, p. 270.

37. Andrew Carnegie, *Triumphant Democracy* (New York: Charles Scribner's Sons, 1886), p. 1.

38. Ibid., p. 125.

39. Hendrick, *Carnegie*, vol. 1, p. 274.

40. Ibid., pp. 275–276.

41. Herbert Spencer to AC, May 18, 1886, quoted in Hendrick, *Carnegie*, vol. 1, pp. 277–278.

42. Letters of Matthew Arnold, vol. II, p. 396, quoted in Hendrick, *Carnegie*, vol. 1, p. 277.

43. Charles A. Cole to AC, August 3, 1886, ACLOC, vol. 10.

44. "Triumphant Democracy," *Dial*, April 1, 1894.

45. John Morley to AC, May 17, 1886, quoted in Hendrick, *Carnegie*, vol. 1, pp. 278–279.

46. Carnegie, *Triumphant Democracy*, p. 7.

47. Ibid., p. 135.

48. Ibid., p. 319.

49. Ibid., pp. 297–298.

50. T. T. Woodruff to AC, June 12, 1886, ACLOC, vol. 9.

51. Ibid.

52. AC to T. T. Woodruff, June 15, 1886, ACLOC, vol. 9.

53. See income for 1863, ACLOC, vol. 3.

54. Carnegie, *Autobiography*, pp. 75–76.

Chapter 16: Patronizing the Peasants

1. David A. Stewart to AC, April 1, 1882, ACWPHS, Edgar Thomson Operating File.
2. Whipple, p. 32.
3. William R. Jones to AC, November 2, 1883, ACWPHS, Jones Correspondence File.
4. *Pittsburgh Dispatch*, December 13, 1883.
5. *Pittsburgh Dispatch*, December 16, 1883.
6. Thomas N. Miller to AC, December 16, 1883, ACWPHS, Edgar Thomson Operating File.
7. AC to A. L. Griffin, April 21, 1884, ACWPHS, Letterbook, 1884.
8. Warren, p. 95.
9. Carnegie interview, quoted in Fitch, p. 113.
10. Warren, p. 95.
11. AC to Louise Whitfield, n.d. (fall of 1885), quoted in Hendrick and Henderson, p. 79.
12. Strouse, p. 225.
13. AC to W. C. Whitney, October 11, 1884, ACWPHS, Letterbook, 1884–1885.
14. AC to Frank Thomson, January 23, 1884, ACWPHS, Letterbook, 1884–1885.
15. AC to George Roberts, January 10, 1885, ACWPHS, Letterbook, 1884–1885.
16. Bridge, p. 102.
17. Strouse, p. 244.
18. *National Labor Tribune*, January 23, 1886; also see Warren, pp. 44, 64–65, for background on strike.
19. Burrows and Wallace, pp. 1095–1096; Joanne Reitano, *The Tariff Question in the Gilded Age* (University Park: Pennsylvania State University Press, 1994), p. 76.
20. Andrew Carnegie, "An Employer's View of the Labor Question," *Forum* (April 1886).
21. *Pittsburgh Dispatch*, March 23, 1886; Sharon A. Brown, *Historic Resource Study: Cambria Iron Company* (Washington, D.C.: U.S. Department of the Interior, 1989), p. 178.
22. Figures cited in Bridge, p. 102.
23. Brody, p. 35.
24. AC to W. R. Thompson, April 1887, ACWPHS, Letterbook, 1887–1888.
25. William R. Jones to AC, July 17, 1880, ACWPHS, Jones Correspondence File.
26. Kleinberg, p. 31.
27. *National Labor Tribune*, June 14, 1879.
28. Brody, p. 44; Kleinberg, p. 26.
29. Bridge, p.102.
30. Nevins, *Abram S. Hewitt*, p. 425.
31. Page Smith, *The Rise of Industrial America* (New York: McGraw-Hill, 1984), p. 137.
32. Bridge, p. 199.
33. Tom Carnegie to Henry C. Frick, n.d., ACWPHS, Frick Papers.
34. AC to Henry C. Frick, February 25, 1886, quoted in Warren, pp. 41–42.
35. Hendrick, *Carnegie*, vol. 1, p. 295.
36. Jay Morse to Henry C. Frick, June 1, 1887, quoted in Warren, pp. 52–53.
37. J. N. Schoonmaker to Henry C. Frick, May 4, 1887, quoted in Warren, pp. 46–47.
38. Henry C. Frick to Henry Phipps Jr. and John Walker, June 7, quoted in George Harvey, *Henry Clay Frick: The Man* (Privately printed, 1936), pp. 85–86.
39. See Warren, pp. 44–49, and Bridge, p. 191, for the story of the strike.
40. Hendrick, *Carnegie*, vol. 1, p. 295.
41. Gage, p. 165.
42. Ibid., p. 157.
43. Fitch, p. 115.
44. Quoted in Hendrick, *Carnegie*, vol. 1, p. 374.
45. Ibid., p. 374.
46. See detailed analysis in Fitch, pp. 116–118; *National Labor Tribune*, April 7, 1888; Bridge, p. 102.
47. *National Labor Tribune*, April 14, 1888.
48. *National Labor Tribune*, April 28, 1888.

49. Fitch, pp. 116–118.

50. *National Labor Tribune*, April 28, 1888; Fitch, p. 115. Fitch cites the Knights of Labor District Assembly No. 3 Quarterly Meeting held in April 1888.

51. Brown, *Historic Resource Study*, p. 92.

52. G. Brooks, "Typical American Employer," *Blackwood's* (October 1892), p. 561.

53. Ingham, p. 134.

Chapter 17: The Pale Horse and the Gray Dress

1. Matthew Arnold to AC, July 7, 1886, ACNYPL.

2. Matthew Arnold to his sister, July 26, 1886, quoted in Hendrick, *Carnegie*, vol. 1, p. 248.

3. AC to Louise Whitfield, July 22, 1886, quoted in Hendrick and Henderson, pp. 76–77.

4. AC to Louise Whitfield, September 23, 1886, quoted in Wall, *Carnegie*, p. 416.

5. AC to Louise Whitfield, n.d., quoted in Hendrick and Henderson, p. 79.

6. See statement of Carnegie Brothers and Company, April 1, 1881, ACLOC, vol. 5; and Carnegie, Phipps and Company, Articles of Association, January 1, 1886, ACLOC, vol. 8.

7. Burton J. Hendrick interview with John Walker, n.d., ACLOC, vol. 239.

8. Charles T. O. Mackie to AC, October 29, 1886, ACWPHS, Letterbook, 1885–1887.

9. Hendrick, *Carnegie*, vol. 1, p. 254.

10. Louise Whitfield, diary entry, n.d., quoted in Hendrick and Henderson, p. 80.

11. Aunt Aitken to Rachel Pattison, 1887, ACNYPL.

12. Carnegie, *Autobiography*, p. 204.

13. Hendrick and Henderson, p. 53.

14. AC to Louise Whitfield, November 24, 1886, quoted in Wall, *Carnegie*, p. 419.

15. AC to Louise Whitfield, n.d., quoted in Hendrick and Henderson, p. 80.

16. AC to Louise Whitfield, n.d., quoted in Hendrick and Henderson, p. 81.

17. AC to Louise Whitfield, December 2, 1886, quoted in Hendrick and Henderson, p. 81.

18. Frederic S. Dennis to Mr. Moore, January 22, 1887, ACWPHS, General Correspondence, ser. 1, subser. 1–2.

19. See Iron Clad Agreement, ACLOC, vol. 10.

20. AC to C. P. Huntington, April 2, 1887, ACWPHS, Letterbook, 1887–1888.

21. Walt Whitman to R.W.G., April 20, 1887, ACNYPL.

22. AC to Charles Eaton, April 16, 1887, quoted in Wall, *Carnegie*, p. 420.

23. Marriage settlement, April 22, 1887, quoted in Hendrick and Henderson, pp. 86–87.

24. See Trial Balance, April 30, 1887, ACWPHS, Box 20, Folder 4.

25. Louise Carnegie to Mrs. Whitfield, n.d., quoted in Hendrick and Henderson, p. 90.

26. Jno. G. MacConnell to Samuel Storey, May 25, 1887, ACLOC, vol. 10.

27. AC to Lord Rosebery, May 24, 1887, ACLOC, vol. 10.

28. Louise Carnegie to Mrs. Whitfield, June 10, 1887, quoted in Hendrick and Henderson, p. 94.

29. Louise Carnegie to Mrs. Whitfield, July 10, 1887, quoted in Hendrick and Henderson, p. 99.

30. William Roscoe Thayer, *The Life and Letters of John Hay*, vol. 2 (Boston: Houghton Mifflin, 1915), p. 74.

31. Mrs. James G. Blaine to Emmons Blaine, quoted in Hendrick, *Carnegie*, vol. 1, p. 317.

32. Louise Carnegie to Mrs. Whitfield, July 17, 1887, quoted in Hendrick and Henderson, pp. 101–102.

33. Hendrick and Henderson, pp. 118–119.

34. Ibid., pp. 117–118.

35. Ibid., p. 119.

36. AC to William L. Abbott, July 25, 1888, ACLOC, vol. 10.

37. Hendrick and Henderson, pp. 128–129.

38. Herbert Spencer to AC, August 10, 1888, ACNYPL.

39. Hendrick and Henderson, p. 127.

40. See AC to William L. Abbott, July 4, 1888, ACLOC, vol. 10, quoted in Hendrick and Henderson, pp. 123–124.

41. Quoted in Hendrick, *Carnegie*, vol. 1, p. 324.

Chapter 18: Gospel of Conscience

1. See James A. Kehl, *Boss Rule in the Gilded Age: Matt Quay of Pennsylvania* (Pittsburgh: University of Pittsburgh Press, 1981), p. xv.

2. See Allan Nevins, *Grover Cleveland: A Study in Courage* (New York: Dodd, Mead, 1934), pp. 423, 436–437, and Harry J. Sievers, *Benjamin Harrison: Hoosier Statesman* (New York: University Publishers, 1959), pp. 415–421, for a litany of bribery and fraud schemes.

3. Nevins, *Grover Cleveland*, p. 420.

4. Benjamin Harrison to AC, November 22, 1888, ACNYPL.

5. Richard Welch Jr., *The Presidencies of Grover Cleveland* (Lawrence: University Press of Kansas, 1988), p. 17.

6. See Carnegie's personal financial statements dated January 1, 1890, listing total assets as $15,317,514.81, ACLOC, vol. 10.

7. Alan Schom, *Napoleon Bonaparte* (New York: HarperCollins, 1997), p. 11.

8. Machiavelli, p. 23.

9. Nevins, *Abram S. Hewitt*, p. 505.

10. See Edward C. Mack, *Peter Cooper: Citizen of New York* (New York: Duell, Sloan & Pearce, 1949), pp. 243–252, for more on Cooper Union and Cooper's philosophy on philanthropy.

11. Andrew Carnegie, "The Gospel of Wealth," reprinted in Edward C. Kirkland, ed., *The Gospel of Wealth and Other Timely Essays* (Cambridge, Mass.: Harvard University Press, 1962), pp. 14–29.

12. AC to Joseph G. Schmidlapp, December 30, 1890, quoted in Hendrick, *Carnegie*, vol. 1, pp. 338–339.

13. George Lauder Sr. to AC, April 5, 1891, ACLOC, vol. 12.

14. Kleinberg, pp. 297–298.

15. Louise Carnegie to William Gladstone, June 19, 1889, quoted in Hendrick, *Carnegie*, vol. 1, p. 339.

16. Quoted in Hendrick, *Carnegie*, vol. 1, pp. 343–344.

17. *New York Daily Tribune*, November 30, 1890.

18. "Irresponsible Wealth," *Nineteenth Century* (December 1890).

19. Andrew Carnegie, "The Advantages of Poverty," *Nineteenth Century* (March 1891).

20. Quoted in Wall, *Carnegie*, pp. 810–811.

21. Ingham, p. 177.

22. Strouse, p. 216.

23. Chernow, p. 237.

24. Ibid., p. 320.

25. Ibid., p. 312.

26. Ibid., p. 237.

27. Ibid., p. 237.

28. Ibid., pp. 240–241.

29. Ibid., p. 306.

30. Strouse, pp. 216, 235–236.

31. Ibid., p. 236, 272.

32. Ibid., p. 275.

33. AC to William Gladstone, June 13, 1890, quoted in Hendrick, *Carnegie*, vol. 1, pp. 355–356.

34. Hendrick, *Carnegie*, vol. 2, p. 253; see also newspaper clippings, ACLOC, vol. 263.

35. *New York Tribune*, February 7, 1890.

36. AC to Louise Carnegie, January 1890, quoted in Hendrick and Henderson, pp. 138–139.

37. William B. Shaw, "The Carnegie Libraries," *Review of Reviews* (October 1895).

38. *New York Tribune*, February 21, 1890.

39. Kleinberg, p. 299.

Chapter 19: Rewards from the Harrison Presidency

1. AC to the president's secretary, September 21, 1891, ACNYPL.

2. Carnegie, *Autobiography*, p. 341; AC to President Harrison, January 25, 1892, ACNYPL.

3. Harry J. Sievers, *Benjamin Harrison: Hoosier President* (Indianapolis: Bobbs-Merrill, 1968), p. 193.

4. Hogan, p. 347.

5. Andrew Carnegie, "Do Americans Hate England?" *North American Review* (June 1890); Andrew Carnegie, "Summing Up the Tarriff Discussion," *North American Review* (July 1890); Andrew Carnegie, "The McKinley Bill," *Nineteenth Century* (June 1890).

6. Nevins, *Abram S. Hewitt*, p. 423.

7. Andrew Carnegie, "ABC of Money," *North American Review* (June 1891).

8. Andrew Carnegie, "The Bugaboo of Trusts," *North American Review* (February 1889).

9. Andrew Carnegie, "Pennsylvania's Industrial and Railroad Policy," reprinted in Burton J. Hendrick, ed., *Miscellaneous Writings of Andrew Carnegie*, vol. 1 (Garden City, N.Y: Doubleday, Doran, 1933), pp. 265–305; *Philadelphia Times*, April 8, 1889.

10. Misa, p. 111.

11. W. H. Emory to AC, June 30, 1890, ACLOC, vol. 11.

12. AC to Mr. Tracey, n.d., ACLOC, vol. 11.

13. AC to Mr. Tracey, July 5, 1890, ACLOC, vol. 11.

14. AC to Philander Knox, March 22, 1890. All letters pertaining to the City Poor Farm purchase are quoted from Paul Krause, *The Battle for Homestead, 1880–1892: Politics, Culture, and Steel* (Pittsburgh: University of Pittsburgh Press, 1992), pp. 387–389.

15. AC to Philander Knox, March 22, 1890.

16. AC to Philander Knox, March 25, 1890.

17. Krause, p. 275. See also pp. 273–281 for a detailed explanation of the entire transaction.

18. Philander Knox to Henry C. Frick, August 1, 1890.

19. Krause, p. 279.

20. AC to Henry C. Frick, August 3, 1890, quoted in Warren, p. 147.

Chapter 20: Prelude to Homestead

1. Warren, p. 54.

2. Henry C. Frick to AC, February 4, 1899, quoted in Warren, p. 54.

3. Henry C. Frick to AC, August 9, 1889, quoted in Warren, p. 54.

4. AC to Henry C. Frick, September 3, 1889, quoted in Warren, p. 55.

5. Henry C. Frick to AC, January 2, 1890, quoted in Warren, p. 61; Henry C. Frick to Jay Morse, April 24, 1890, quoted in Warren, p. 61.

6. Henry C. Frick to AC, July 14, 1891, quoted in Warren, p. 62.

7. AC to William L. Abbott, September 7, 1889, ACLOC, vol. 10.

8. AC to William L. Abbott, August 13, 1888, ACLOC, vol. 10.

9. AC to William L. Abbott, March 20, 1889, ACLOC, vol. 10.

10. Quoted in Krause, pp. 231–232.

11. Bridge, p. 199.

12. Gage, p. 157.

13. See David McCullough, *The Johnstown Flood* (New York: Simon & Schuster, 1968) for details.

14. AC to William L. Abbott, n.d. (early July 1889), ACLOC, vol. 10.

15. See Ingham, pp. 132–133, and Fitch, pp. 119–121, for good documentation of the 1889 Homestead strike; see also *National Labor Tribune*, June 15, July 13 and 15, 1889.

16. *National Labor Tribune*, September 17, 1889.

17. AC to Louise Carnegie, September 26, 1889, quoted in Hendrick and Henderson, p. 138.

18. Captain Jones Manuscript, n.d., ACLOC, vol. 243.

19. Quoted in Bridge, pp. 105–106.

20. See Gage, pp. 158–159, for the Jones family version.

21. AC to J. G. A. Leishman, August 1, 1895, ACLOC, vol. 35.

22. Henry Phipps to AC, November 1, 1889, quoted in Bridge, p. 294.

23. AC to William Gladstone, November 24, 1890, ACLOC, vol. 11.

24. Charles Schwab to Henry C. Frick, October 20, 1890, quoted in Warren, pp. 68–69.

25. See Dennis Diaries, ACLOC, vol. 10.

26. *New York Tribune*, May 14, 1890.

27. Burrows and Wallace, pp. 1074–1075; Elkhonon Yoffe, editor, and Lidya Yoffe, translator from Russian, *Tchaikovsky in America* (New York: Oxford University Press, 1986), p. 111.

28. Secretary of the New York Botanical Garden to AC, May 25, 1891, ACLOC, vol. 12.

29. Charles Schwab to Henry C. Frick, January 1, 1891, quoted in Warren, p. 71.

30. Henry C. Frick to Charles Schwab, January 1, quoted in Warren, p. 71.

31. Charles Schwab to Henry C. Frick, January 1, 1891, quoted in Warren, p. 72.

32. Henry C. Frick to AC, January 1, 1891, quoted in Warren, pp. 69–71.

33. Henry C. Frick to James Gayley, January 2, 1891, quoted in Warren, p. 72.

34. Henry C. Frick to AC, January 2, 1891, quoted in Warren, p. 69.

35. Henry C. Frick to AC, January 3 1891, quoted in Warren, p. 69.

Chapter 21: The Homestead Tragedy

1. Kimball to AC, January 27, 1892, ACLOC, vol. 14, and Estee to AC, March 15, 1892, ACLOC, vol. 14, as well as other letters in volume.

2. Board of Managers Meeting Minutes, June 28, 1892, ACLOC, vol. 16.

3. See Fitch, pp. 102–103; Brody, p. 53.

4. Hendrick, *Carnegie*, vol. 1, p. 383.

5. Brody, p. 50.

6. A. C. Buell to a Mr. Cramp, January 8, 1892, Papers of Secretary of the Navy Benjamin F. Tracy, Library of Congress.

7. Harvey, p. 163.

8. Bridge, p. 204.

9. Harvey, pp. 165–166.

10. Henry C. Frick to John A. Potter, May 30, 1892, quoted in Wall, *Carnegie*, p. 552; Henry C. Frick to AC, May 31, 1892, quoted in Warren, p. 80.

11. Warren, pp. 168–169.

12. AC to Henry C. Frick, June 10, 1892, quoted in Bridge, p. 205.

13. AC to Henry C. Frick, June 17, 1892, quoted in Bridge, p. 206.

14. See June 23, 1892, letter from William Farmer, owner of Coworth Park, ACLOC, vol. 17.

15. Henry C. Frick to AC, June 24, 1892, quoted in Warren, p. 84.

16. William C. Oates, "The Homestead Strike: A Congressional View," *North American Review* 155 (1892), pp. 355–375; Henry C. Frick to Robert A. Pinkerton, June 25, 1892, quoted in Harvey, pp. 114–115.

17. Bridge, p. 210.

18. Henry C. Frick to AC, July 4, 1892, quoted in Warren, p. 84.

19. A number of books have been written on the Homestead strike. For a detailed account of events, see Paul Krause, *The Battle for Homestead 1880–1892: Politics, Culture, and Steel* (Pittsburgh: University of Pittsburgh Press, 1992).

20. Harvey, pp. 129–131.

21. AC to Henry C. Frick, July 7, 1892, quoted in Hendrick, *Carnegie*, vol. 1, p. 402.

22. Krause, p. 42.

23. Leon Wolff, *Lockout* (New York: Harper & Row, 1965), p. 181.

24. G. Brooks, "Typical American Employer," *Blackwood's* (October 1892).

25. Bridge, pp. 233–234.

26. C. F. Black, "Lessons of Homestead," *Forum* (September 1892); Lorant, p. 214.

27. Henry C. Frick to AC, July 11, 1892, quoted in Warren, p. 85.

28. Henry C. Frick to AC, July 11, 1892, quoted in Warren, pp. 85–86.

29. W. W. Chamberlin, "Labor Troubles at Homestead," *Harper's Weekly* (July 23, 1892).

30. AC to George Lauder Jr., July 17, 1892, ACLOC, vol. 17.

31. Hugh O'Donnell to Whitelaw Reid, July 16, 1892, quoted in Hendrick, *Carnegie*, vol. 1, pp. 406–407; Wolff, pp. 203–204.

32. Quoted in Hendrick, *Carnegie*, vol. 1, p. 399.

33. Henry C. Frick to AC, July 23, 1892, quoted in Warren, p. 89.

34. John Milholland memo on visit, July 30, 1892, in Harrison MSS, vol. 145, Library of Congress, quoted in Warren, p. 400.

35. Quoted in Harvey, p. 149.

36. Ibid.

37. AC to Henry C. Frick, July 28, 1892, ACLOC, vol. 17.

38. AC to William T. Stead, August 6, 1892, ACLOC, vol. 17.

39. AC to Henry C. Frick, September 28, 1892, quoted in Warren, p. 91.

40. See Warren, p. 93.

41. Oates, "The Homestead Strike: A Congressional View," pp. 355–375.

42. *New York Tribune*, October 2, 1892.

43. *New York Tribune*, October 12, 1892.

44. See AC letter written on Grand Hotel de Sienne letterhead, November 27, 1892, ACLOC, vol. 17.

45. Henry C. Frick to AC, November 21, 1892, quoted in Warren, p. 92; AC to Henry C. Frick, November 27, 1892, quoted in Harvey, p. 172.

46. Harvey, p. 173.

47. Henry C. Frick to AC, September 8, 1892, quoted in Warren, p. 95.

48. Henry C. Frick to AC, November 28, 1892, quoted in Warren, p. 92.

49. *Pittsburgh Press*, December 9, 1892, quoted in Bridge, p. 252.

50. Hamlin Garland, "Homestead and Its Perilous Trades," *McClure's* (June 1894).

51. Fitch, p. 104.

52. William Cahn, *A Pictorial History of American Labor* (New York: Crown Publishers, 1972), p. 164.

53. Hermann Suter, "Recollections," unpublished manuscript, p. 34, WPHS, 1996.0325.

54. S. A. Ford to AC, October 24, 1891, ACLOC, vol. 13.

55. Wolff, 34.

56. Sievers, *Hoosier President*, p. 236.

57. Ibid., p. 249.

58. AC to Henry C. Frick, November 9, 1892, and undated from Venice, quoted in Harvey, p. 157.

59. See Scottish Home Rule Association invitation dated September 15, 1892, ACLOC, vol. 17; and Lord Rosebery to AC, October 10, 1892, ACLOC, vol. 13.

60. John Morley to AC, April 3, 1893, ACLOC, vol. 19.

61. George Lauder Sr. to AC, March 25, 1893, ACLOC, vol. 19.

62. Abram S. Hewitt to AC, May 9, 1893, ACLOC, vol. 20.

63. Editor of *Engineering* Magazine to AC, February 17, 1893, ACLOC, vol. 18.

64. Thomas Mellon to AC, January 30, 1893, ACLOC, vol. 18.

65. Philander Knox to AC, February 24, 1893, ACLOC, vol. 18.

66. Fourth Assistant P.M. General to AC, May 15, 1893, ACLOC, vol. 20; AC to John S. Robb, March 7, 1893, ACLOC, vol. 19; V. Robert Agostino, *A Track through Time: A Centennial History of Carnegie, PA* (Pittsburgh: Wolfson Publishing, 1994), p. 15.

67. William Gladstone to AC, September 19, 1892, quoted in M. R. D. Foot, ed., *The Gladstone Diaries, vol. 13* (Oxford, U.K.: Clarendon Press, 1968–1994).

68. AC to William Gladstone, September 24, 1892, ACLOC, vol. 17.

69. William Shakespeare, *King Lear,* act III, scene iv.

70. Ibid., act I, scene i.

71. Ibid., act III, scene ii.

72. AC to James Reid, March 20, 1893, ACLOC, vol. 19.

73. Carnegie was always receiving requests for money, but based on the plethora of chari-table letters to and from Carnegie in ACLOC vols. 18–23, in the spring and fall of 1893 he was definitely more active in giving money to family, friends, and even strangers.

74. Margaret Marshall Fuller to AC, January 19, 1893, ACLOC, vol. 18; Susie Robertson to AC, October 17, 1894, ACLOC, vol. 28; R. A. Slater to AC, December 16, 1893, ACLOC, vol. 23.

75. Mrs. Henderson to AC, February 13, 1893, ACLOC, vol. 18.

76. Sarah Kerr Heistand to AC, March 13, 1893, ACLOC, vol. 19.

77. William A. Clark to AC, February 3, 1893, ACLOC, vol. 18.

78. Elizabeth Curtiss to AC, November 23, 1893, ACLOC, vol. 23.

79. AC to Mrs. Alexander King, February 18, 1893, ACLOC, vol. 18.

80. William Carnegie to AC, May 8, 1893, ACLOC, vol. 20; Charlotte Carnegie to AC, December 16, 1894, ACLOC, vol. 29; Robert Franks to AC, November 21, 1893, ACLOC, vol. 23.

81. AC to Robert Pitcairn, December 30, 1893, ACLOC, vol. 24; Lorant, p. 196.

82. John Morley to AC, December 31, 1893, ACLOC, vol. 24.

83. J. G. A. Leishman to AC, May 4, 1893, ACLOC, vol. 20.

84. Krause, p. 348.

85. Peter Wild, "The Strange Story of 'Honest' John McLuckie," *Pittsburgh History* (Sum-mer 1997).

86. Carnegie, *Autobiography,* p. 228.

87. *New York Daily Tribune,* July 27, 1896.

88. Wild, "The Strange Story of 'Honest' John McLuckie."

89. J. A. Potter to AC, October 19, 1893, ACLOC, vol. 22.

90. Gage, "'Hands-on, All-over': Captain Bill Jones," *Pittsburgh History* (Winter 1997–1998), pp. 166–167.

Chapter 22: The Great Armor Scandal

1. AC to Grover Cleveland, April 22, 1893, ACLOC, vol. 20.

2. Cleveland to the United Press, April 23, 1893, quoted in Alan Nevins, ed., *Letters of Grover Cleveland: 1850–1908* (Boston: Houghton Mifflin, 1933), p. 324.

3. Hogan, p. 237.

4. *Pittsburgh Dispatch,* November 10, 1893, quoted in Warren, p. 126.

5. Brody, p. 5.

6. AC to Henry C. Frick, February 13, 1894, ACLOC, vol. 24.

7. John Gates's testimony before the Stanley Commission, May 27 and June 8, 1911.

8. Edison Electric Illuminating Co. of New York to AC, September 26, 1893, ACLOC, vol. 22.

9. Henry C. Frick to Charles Schwab, September 16, 1893, quoted in Warren, p. 154.

10. See Hessen, pp. 45–58, for more details on the armor scandal.

11. *Washington Post,* December 21, 1893, quoted in *New York Daily Tribune,* March 2, 1894.

12. AC to Grover Cleveland, December 20, 1893, ACLOC, vol. 23.

13. AC to Grover Cleveland, December 27, 1893, ACLOC, vol. 24.

14. Burrows and Wallace, p. 1187; and for more details, pp. 1185–1190.

15. *New York Daily Tribune,* January 5, 1894.

16. AC to Henry C. Frick, February 13, 1894, ACLOC, vol. 24.

17. *New York Daily Tribune,* March 2, 1894.

18. *New York Herald,* May 30, 1893, ACLOC, vol. 21.

19. AC to Mr. John Dalzell, December 6, 1893, ACLOC, vol. 23.

20. AC to Senator Arthur P. Gorman, January 2, 1894, ACLOC, vol. 24.

21. AC to Andrew White, April 28, 1894, ACLOC, vol. 24.
22. *New York Daily Tribune*, August 31, 1894.
23. Krause, p. 358.
24. AC to Mr. Ditch, July 3, 1895, ACLOC, vol. 32.
25. AC to Henry C. Frick, September 7, 1894, quoted in Warren, p. 157.
26. Henry C. Frick to AC, September 19, 1894, ACLOC, vol. 27.
27. Henry C. Frick to AC, December 18, 1894, ACLOC, vol. 29.
28. Henry C. Frick to C. A. Stone, October 30, 1894, quoted in Warren, p. 214.
29. Henry C. Frick to Millard Hunsiker, November 8, 1894, quoted in Warren, p. 214.
30. Henry C. Frick to AC, December 18, 1894, quoted in Warren, p. 215.
31. AC to Henry C. Frick, December 18, 1894, ACLOC, vol. 29.
32. AC to Henry C. Frick, December 18, 1894 (second letter), ACLOC, vol. 29.
33. Henry C. Frick to AC, December 20, 1894, ACLOC, vol. 29.
34. Henry Phipps to AC, December 22, 1894, ACLOC, vol. 29.
35. AC to Henry C. Frick, December 23, 1894, ACLOC, vol. 29.
36. Henry C. Frick to AC, December 24, 1894, ACLOC, vol. 29.
37. AC to J. G. A. Leishman, December 24, 1894, ACLOC, vol. 29.
38. AC to Henry C. Frick, December 26, 1894, ACLOC, vol. 29.
39. Henry C. Frick to AC, January 1, 1895, ACLOC, vol. 30.
40. AC to Henry C. Frick, January 3, 1894, ACLOC, vol. 30.
41. AC to Board of Managers, November 26, 1899, quoted in Whipple, p. 61.
42. Warren, p. 218.
43. Henry C. Frick to AC, February 14, 1895, quoted in Warren, p. 220.
44. AC to Carnegie Steel, May 16, 1895, ACLOC, vol. 31.
45. Henry Phipps to AC, June 2, 1895, ACLOC, vol. 32.
46. George Lauder Jr. to AC, June 12, 1895, ACLOC, vol. 32.
47. AC to J. G. A. Leishman, August 5, 1895, ACLOC, vol. 32.
48. Warren, p. 97.
49. AC to J. G. A. Leishman, September 2, 1895, ACLOC, vol. 32.
50. AC to Robert P. Linderman, February 25, 1895, ACLOC, vol. 31.
51. AC to Francis Lovejoy, February 11, 1895, ACLOC, vol. 30.
52. AC to J. G. A. Leishman, December 23, 1895, ACLOC, vol. 35.
53. AC to Francis Lovejoy, December 9, 1895, quoted in Hendrick, *Carnegie*, vol. 2, p. 44.
54. AC to Henry C. Frick, December 30, 1896, ACLOC, vol. 40.
55. AC to Charles Scribner's Sons, December 30, 1896, ACLOC, vol. 40.
56. Hendrick, *Carnegie*, vol. 1, pp. 297–298.
57. Hendrick Notes, August 1929, ACLOC, vol. 239.
58. AC to Francis Lovejoy, January 20, 1896, ACLOC, vol. 36.
59. Quoted in Hendrick, *Carnegie*, vol. 2, p. 73.
60. Henry Phipps to AC, September 25, 1897, ACLOC, vol. 45.
61. AC to Henry C. Frick, October 9, 1897, ACLOC, vol. 45.
62. Board Meeting Minutes, Carnegie Steel, October 19, 1897, ACLOC, vol. 46.

Chapter 23: Seeking a Measure of Peace

1. B. C. Forbes, *Men Who Are Making America* (New York: B. C. Forbes Publishing, 1917), p. 36.
2. AC to William N. Frew, October 24, 1894, ACLOC, vol. 28.
3. AC to William N. Frew, December 2, 1895, ACLOC, vol. 34.
4. See AC to William N. Frew, March 12, 1895, ACLOC, vol. 31; AC to William N. Frew, September 19, 1895, and AC to Grover Cleveland, September 20, 1895, ACLOC, vol. 33.
5. AC to William N. Frew, November 1, 1895, ACLOC, vol. 33; AC to William N. Frew, November 4, 1895, ACLOC, vol. 34.
6. Simon Goodenough, *The Greatest Good Fortune* (Edinburgh: Macdonald Publishers, 1985), p. 48.

7. Krause, p. 331.
8. AC to Editor, *Outlook* (May 11, 1896), ACLOC, vol. 38.
9. Goodenough, p. 62.
10. William B. Shaw, "The Carnegie Libraries," *Review of Reviews* (October 1895).
11. Ibid.
12. *New York Daily Tribune*, November 11, 1895.
13. AC to Charles Schwab, January 23, 1896, ACLOC, vol. 36.
14. Charles Schwab to AC, May 21, 1896, ACLOC, vol. 38.
15. AC to W. W. Sage, February 3, 1896, ACLOC, vol. 36.
16. AC to Ann MacGregor, November 19, 1895, ACLOC, vol. 34.
17. AC to R. Anderson, November 19, 1895, ACLOC, vol. 34.
18. See AC to J. Lindley Smith, December 27, 1895, ACLOC, vol. 35, and AC to J. H. Linville, December 1, 1896, ACLOC, vol. 39.
19. AC to Ella J. Newton, November 26, 1895, ACLOC, vol. 34.
20. Nevins, *Hewitt*, pp. 579–580.
21. *New York Daily Tribune*, December 20, 1891.
22. AC to John Patterson, January 13, 1892, ACLOC, vol. 14.
23. Burrows and Wallace, p. 1116. For more details on ethnic neighborhoods during this period, see Burrows and Wallace, pp. 1111–1131, and Lloyd Morris, *Incredible New York* (New York: Random House, 1951), pp. 273–279.
24. Burrows and Wallace, p. 1122.
25. AC to John Morley, April 16, 1893, ACLOC, vol. 20.
26. AC to William T. Stead, July 22, 1893, ACLOC, vol. 21; Hendrick, *Carnegie*, vol. 1, p. 420.
27. AC to Lawrence T. Neal, October 19, 1893, quoted in *New York Daily Tribune*, October 20, 1893.
28. AC to William T. Stead, August 11, 1893, ACLOC, vol. 21.
29. See Herbert Spencer to AC, September 23, 1891, ACNYPL, in which Spencer wishes a Carnegie essay on race alliance was more widely distributed.
30. Reported in *New York Daily Tribune*, December 25, 1895; Andrew Carnegie, "The Venezuela Question," *North American Review* (February 1896).
31. AC to the duke of Devonshire, December 26, 1895, ACLOC, vol. 35.
32. AC to John Morley, January 27, 1896, ACLOC, vol. 36.
33. AC to William N. Frew, February 16, 1896, ACLOC, vol. 36.
34. AC to Carl Schurz, April 20, 1896, ACLOC, vol. 37.
35. AC to J. G. A. Leishman, April 21, 1896, ACLOC, vol. 37.
36. William Black to AC, February 6, 1896, ACLOC, vol. 36; William Black to Louise Carnegie, May 14, 1895, ACNYPL.
37. Robert L. Heilbroner, "Epitaph for the Steel Master," reprinted in Alex Groner and the Editors of American Heritage, *The American Heritage History of American Business and Industry* (New York: American Heritage, 1972).

Chapter 24: Illegal Rebates and a Fight with Rockefeller

1. AC to Henry C. Frick, December 9, 1896, ACLOC, vol. 40.
2. Warren, p. 196.
3. *New York Daily Tribune*, February 20, 1896.
4. James H. Creery to AC, October 25, 1895, quoted in Warren, p. 191.
5. AC to Henry C. Frick, February 7, 1896, ACLOC, vol. 36; Andrew Carnegie, "My Experience with Railway Rates and Rebates," *Century Illustrated Monthly* (March 1908), p. 725.
6. AC to J. G. A. Leishman, February 4, 1896, ACLOC, vol. 36.
7. AC to John Stewart, April 18, 1896, ACLOC, vol. 37.
8. AC to George Lauder Jr., April 16, 1896, ACLOC, vol. 37.
9. AC to Frank Thomson, May 5, 1896, ACLOC, vol. 37.

10. Hendrick, *Carnegie*, vol. 2, pp. 30–33; Carnegie, "My Experience with Railway Rates and Rebates," pp. 10–14; Warren, p. 175; also see agreement dated May 16, 1896, ACLOC, vol. 37.

11. AC to Henry C. Frick, March 30, 1898, quoted in Warren, p. 193.

12. See Strouse, pp. 339–358, for more details of the monetary crisis and Morgan's involvement.

13. AC to J. G. A. Leishman, August 21, 1896, ACLOC, vol. 32.

14. AC to President and the Board, August 6, 1896, ACLOC, vol. 38.

15. Warren, p. 162.

16. AC to Henry C. Frick, August 29, 1892, quoted in Warren, pp. 162–163.

17. Bridge, p. 259; AC to Henry C. Frick, September 4, 1894, quoted in Warren, p. 163.

18. AC to Henry M. Curry, December 9, 1895, ACLOC, vol. 35.

19. Letter in the Board of Managers Meeting Minutes, January 21, 1896, ACLOC, vol. 36.

20. AC to the Board of Managers, August 21, 1896, ACLOC, vol. 39.

21. AC to John D. Rockefeller, October 30, 1896, ACLOC, vol. 39.

22. Warren, p. 104.

23. *United States Steel Corporation. Hearings before the Committee on Investigation of United States Steel Corporation, House of Representatives* (Washington, D.C.: Government Printing Office, 1911–1912), p. 2392. (Hereafter to be cited as U.S. Steel Hearings.)

24. George T. Fleming, *History of Pittsburgh and Environs* (New York: American Historical Society, 1922), p. 172.

25. *Iron Age*, December 17, 1896, quoted in Warren, p. 104.

26. Henry Oliver to Henry C. Frick, July 27, 1897, ACLOC, vol. 43.

27. *New York Daily Tribune*, October 13, 1897.

28. AC to Henry C. Frick, October 9, 1897, quoted in Warren, pp. 165–166.

29. AC to Chairman, President, and Managers of Carnegie Steel, December 31, 1896, ACLOC, vol. 40.

30. Ibid.

31. AC to Henry C. Frick, February 15, 1897, ACLOC, vol. 41; AC to Henry C. Frick, February 7, 1897, quoted in Warren, p. 133.

32. John Gates to Henry C. Frick, September 24, 1897, quoted in Warren, p. 282.

33. Whipple, p. 53.

34. AC to Henry C. Frick, December 11, 1896, ACLOC, vol. 40.

35. AC to Henry C. Frick, September 20, 1897, quoted in Warren, pp. 135–136.

36. Warren, p. 137.

37. AC to Henry C. Frick, November 31, 1897, quoted in Warren, p. 138.

38. AC to J. G. A. Leishman, January 4, 1896, ACLOC, vol. 35.

39. J. G. A. Leishman to AC, January 11, 1896, ACLOC, vol. 35.

40. AC to J. G. A. Leishman, January 27, 1896, ACLOC, vol. 36.

41. AC to J. G. A. Leishman, January 28, 1896, ACLOC, vol. 36.

42. AC to Henry C. Frick, February 5, 1898, quoted in Warren, p. 138.

43. Mark Hanna to AC, October 17, 1896, ACLOC, vol. 39.

44. AC to Wayne McVeagh, October 26, 1896, ACLOC, vol. 39.

Chapter 25: A Point of Disruption and Transition

1. Henry C. Frick to AC, December 16, 1896, ACLOC, vol. 40.

2. AC to William McKinley, December 17, 1896, ACLOC, vol. 40.

3. *New York Daily Tribune*, March 31, 1897.

4. AC to Louise Carnegie, two letters, n.d., quoted in Hendrick and Henderson, pp. 144–145.

5. Louise Carnegie to Stella Whitfield, n.d., quoted in Hendrick and Henderson, p. 146.

6. Louise Carnegie to AC, n.d., quoted in Hendrick and Henderson, p. 147.

7. See Charles R. Flint, *Memories of an Active Life* (New York: G. P. Putnam's Sons, 1923), pp. 39, 40, for his visit to Cluny.

8. AC to Charles Schwab, September 14, 1897, ACLOC, vol. 44.

9. AC to Charles Schwab, October 1, 1897, ACLOC, vol. 45.

10. AC to Charles Schwab, October 6, 1897, ACLOC, vol. 46.

11. Nathan Miller, *Theodore Roosevelt: A Life* (New York: William Morrow, 1992), pp. 264–267.

12. Andrew Carnegie, "Americanism Versus Imperialism," *North American Review* (January 1899).

13. Henry C. Frick to AC, April 4, 1898, ACLOC, vol. 50.

14. AC to Charles Schwab, September 24, 1897, ACLOC, vol. 45.

15. See statement, ACLOC, vol. 50.

16. AC to Henry C. Frick, April 23, 1898, ACLOC, vol. 51.

17. Board Meeting Minutes, May 17, 1898, ACLOC, vol. 51.

18. Henry C. Frick to AC, March 19, 1898, ACLOC, vol. 50.

19. Henry C. Frick to AC, April 19, 1898, ACLOC, vol. 51.

20. AC to Henry C. Frick, April 23, 1898, ACLOC, vol. 51.

21. Louise Carnegie to Charles H. Eaton, n.d., quoted in Hendrick and Henderson, pp. 147–148.

22. Louise Carnegie to Hew Morrison, May 8, 1898, ACLOC, vol. 51.

23. Louise Carnegie to Charles H. Eaton, n.d., quoted in Hendrick and Henderson, p. 152.

24. Herbert Spencer to AC, August 22, 1898, ACNYPL.

25. AC to Dr. Adolf Gurlt, June 1, 1898, ACLOC, vol. 52.

26. AC to George Lauder Jr., June 9, 1898, ACLOC, vol. 52.

27. AC to General Nelson Miles, cablegram, n.d., ACLOC, vol. 53.

28. Nelson A. Miles, *Serving the Republic* (New York: Harper & Brothers, 1911), pp. 273–274.

29. G. J. A. O'Toole, *The Spanish War* (New York: W. W. Norton, 1984), p. 322.

30. Andrew Carnegie, "Distant Possessions—the Parting of the Ways," *North American Review* (August 1898).

31. John Hay to AC, August 22, 1898, quoted in Thayer, pp. 175–176.

Chapter 26: The Crusades

1. Charles Schwab to AC, March 7, 1898, ACLOC, vol. 49.

2. Strouse, p. 396.

3. Hogan, p. 258.

4. Henry C. Frick to AC, March 22, 1898, ACLOC, vol. 50.

5. AC to Henry C. Frick, April 5, 1898, ACLOC, vol. 50.

6. See agreement, n.d., ACLOC, vol. 40.

7. John A. Potter to Charles Schwab, June 23, 1898, quoted in Warren, p. 202.

8. Hogan, p. 266.

9. AC to Board of Managers, July 25, 1898, ACLOC, vol. 54.

10. AC to Board of Managers, August 23, 1898, ACLOC, vol. 54.

11. Board of Managers Meeting Minutes, October 18, 1898, ACLOC, vol. 55.

12. *New York Daily Tribune*, December 3, 1898.

13. Richard Sassaman, "Carnegie Had a Dinosaur Too," *American Heritage* (March 1988), pp. 72–73.

14. Henry Phipps to Henry C. Frick, November 23, 1898, quoted in Warren, p. 227.

15. George Lauder Jr. to Henry Phipps, November 28, 1898, quoted in Warren, p. 228.

16. Henry C. Frick to AC, December 10, 1898, ACLOC, vol. 58.

17. Reprinted in Andrew Carnegie, *Empire of Business* (New York: Doubleday, Page, 1902), pp. 303–307.

18. AC to George Lauder Jr., January 17, 1899, ACLOC, vol. 60.

19. AC to George Lauder Jr., n.d. (1898), ACLOC, vol. 59.

20. AC to Francis Lovejoy, December 30, 1898, and Board Meeting, January 3, 1899, ACLOC, vol. 60.

21. Board Meeting Minutes, March 4, 1899, ACLOC, vol. 63.

22. AC to Charles Schwab, December 22, 1898, ACLOC, vol. 58.

23. Board Meeting Minutes, January 31, 1899, ACLOC, vol. 61.

24. Board Meeting Minutes, February 7, 1899, ACLOC, vol. 62.

25. Board Meeting Minutes, February 14, 1899, ACLOC, vol. 62.

26. Board Meeting Minutes, February 21, 1899, ACLOC, vol. 62.

27. Henry Phipps to Henry C. Frick, April 17, 1899, quoted in Warren, p. 198.

28. *New York Tribune*, September 3, 1898.

29. *New York Tribune*, November 3, 1898.

30. AC to John Hay, November 24, 1898, ACLOC, vol. 57.

31. John Hay to Whitelaw Reid, November 29, 1898, quoted in Thayer, pp. 198–199.

32. AC to William McKinley, November 28, 1898, ACLOC, vol. 57.

33. *New York Daily Tribune*, March 4, 1898.

34. AC to John Hay, December 11, 1898, ACLOC, vol. 58.

35. Andrew Carnegie, "Americanism versus Imperialism," *North American Review* (March 1899); *New York Daily Tribune*, December 22, 1898.

36. William Jennings Bryan to AC, December 24, 1898, ACLOC, vol. 59.

37. Ibid.

38. William Jennings Bryan to AC, December 30, 1898, ACLOC, vol. 59.

39. *New York Journal*, January 30, 1899; AC to Andrew D. White, March 16, 1899, ACLOC, vol. 63.

40. Brody, p. 87.

41. Board Meeting Minutes, May 28, 1898, ACLOC, vol. 52.

42. See T. J. Shaffer to Samuel Gompers, March 19, 1900, quoted in Fitch, pp. 298–299.

43. Charles Schwab to AC, May 26, 1899, ACLOC, vol. 65.

44. Board Meeting Minutes, June 13, 1899, ACLOC, vol. 66.

45. Board Meeting Minutes, June 27, 1899, ACLOC, vol. 66.

46. AC to Charles Schwab, July 1, 1899, ACLOC, vol. 66.

47. Charles Schwab to AC, July 6, 1899, ACLOC, vol. 67.

48. U.S. Steel Hearings, p. 2372.

49. Printed for the first time in *Iron Age*, August 14, 1899.

50. Agreement dated April 24, 1899, ACLOC, vol. 64.

51. *New York Daily Tribune*, May 6 and 7, 1899.

52. U.S. Steel Hearings, p. 2373.

53. *New York Daily Tribune*, May 13 and 17, 1899.

54. Hendrick and Henderson, p. 151.

55. AC to Louise Carnegie, n.d., quoted in Hendrick and Henderson, p. 155.

56. Ibid.

57. From the Keighley Library Dedication speech by Sir Swire Smith, quoted in Hendrick, *Carnegie*, vol. 2, pp. 162–163.

58. Henry C. Frick and Henry Phipps to AC, May 20, 1899, ACLOC, vol. 51.

59. Board Meeting Minutes, May 22, 1899, ACLOC, vol. 51.

60. "The Carnegie Fortune," *American Monthly Review of Reviews* (June 1899).

61. Board Meeting Minutes, June 27, 1899, ACLOC, vol. 66.

62. Henry Phipps to Henry C. Frick, July 15, 1899, quoted in Warren, pp. 238–239.

63. Board Meeting Minutes, June 27, 1899, ACLOC, vol. 66.

64. Henry Phipps to Henry C. Frick, n.d. (late August), quoted in Warren, p. 239.

Chapter 27: UnCivil War

1. Board Meeting Minutes, September 11, 1899, quoted in Warren, p. 243.

2. AC letter read to Board Meeting, October 16, 1899, ACLOC, vol. 69.

3. O'Toole, p. 389.

4. Miller, p. 335.

5. *New York Daily Tribune*, February 3, 1900.

6. Board Meeting Minutes, November 20, 1899, ACLOC, vol. 70.

7. AC to Henry C. Frick, November 21, 1899, quoted in Warren, p. 249.

8. AC to George Lauder Jr., November 23, 1899, ACLOC, vol. 70.

9. George Lauder Jr. to AC, November 24, 1899, ACLOC, vol. 70.

10. AC to George Lauder Jr., November 25, 1899, ACLOC, vol. 70.

11. Burton J. Hendrick interview with John Walker, February 1928, ACLOC, vol. 239.

12. AC to Henry Phipps, n.d. (November 1899), ACLOC, vol. 70.

13. AC to Charles Schwab, November 26, 1899, Whipple, p. 60.

14. AC to Board of Managers, November 26, 1899, Whipple, pp. 60–62.

15. Charles Schwab to AC, November 27, 1899, ACLOC, vol. 70.

16. Charles Schwab to Henry C. Frick, September 26, 1899, ACLOC, quoted in Warren, pp. 244–245.

17. Herbert Spencer to AC, October 28, 1899, ACLOC, vol. 70.

18. Herbert Spencer to AC, January 29, 1900, ACLOC, vol. 72.

19. AC to Whitelaw Reid, December 1, 1899, ACLOC, vol. 70.

20. AC to John Hay, February 26, 1900, ACLOC, vol. 73.

21. *New York Daily Tribune*, June 1, 1899.

22. A. M. F. Campbell and J. C. Campbell, *Anti-Carnegie Scraps and Comments* (Pittsburgh: Privately printed, 1899), pp. 5–6.

23. AC to George Lauder Jr., n.d., ACLOC, vol. 70.

24. AC to Henry C. Frick, n.d., quoted in Harvey, p. 225.

25. AC to Henry C. Frick, n.d. (December 1899), quoted in Warren, p. 255.

26. AC to Henry C. Frick, December 19, 1899, ACLOC, vol. 70.

27. AC to Lauder, n.d., ACLOC, vol. 70.

28. Henry C. Frick to Thomas Lynch, December 26, 1899, quoted in Warren, p. 256.

29. Charles Schwab to AC, December 27, 1899, ACLOC, vol. 71.

30. AC to George Lauder Jr., December 27, 1899, ACLOC, vol. 71.

31. *New York Daily Tribune*, December 23, 1899.

32. AC to John Morley, December 17, 1899, ACLOC, vol. 70.

33. *New York Times*, January 1, 1900.

34. Harvey, p. 242.

35. Burton J. Hendrick interview with John Walker, February 16, 1928, ACLOC, vol. 239.

36. Ibid.

37. Warren, p. 261.

38. Henry C. Frick and Henry Phipps to AC, January 29, 1900, ACLOC, vol. 72.

39. AC to Caroline Wilson, March 2, 1900, ACWPHS, Frick Suit Folder.

40. A. B. Farquhar to AC, March 14, 1900, ACLOC, vol. 73.

41. George Westinghouse to AC, February 8, 1900, ACLOC, vol. 73.

42. *New York Daily Tribune*, February 15, 1900.

43. See "Joint and Several Answer of the Carnegie Steel Company Limited and Andrew Carnegie," dated March 1900, ACLOC, vol. 73.

44. Board Meeting Minutes, January 3, 1899, ACLOC, vol. 60.

45. Gibson D. Packer to AC, February 3, 1900, ACLOC, vol. 72.

46. Board Meeting Minutes, October 19, 1897, ACLOC, vol. 46.

47. W. H. Singer to AC, March 8, 1900, ACLOC, vol. 73.

48. Henry C. Frick to AC, June 10, 1898, ACLOC, vol. 52.

49. Henry Phipps to Henry C. Frick, January 17, 1900, quoted in Warren, p. 262.

50. *New York Daily Tribune*, February 15, 1900.

51. J. Moritzen, "The Great Steel Makers of Pittsburgh and the Frick-Carnegie Suit," *Review of Reviews* 21, p. 432.

52. *New York World*, February 13, 1900.

53. Net Earnings Statement for March 1900, and Board Meeting Minutes, April 23, 1900, ACLOC, vol. 74.

54. Harvey, p. 254.

55. Charter of Carnegie Company, March 22, 1900, ACLOC, vol. 73.

56. Harvey, p. 256.
57. James Laughlin to AC, March 26, 1900, ACLOC, vol. 74.
58. John Morley to AC, April 25, 1900, ACLOC, vol. 74.
59. F. W. Haskell to Henry C. Frick, February 12, 1900, quoted in Warren, 266.
60. Samuel A. Schreiner, *Henry Clay Frick* (New York: St. Martin's Press, 1995), p. 9.
61. AC to Charles Schwab, March 29, 1900, quoted in Whipple, p. 69.

Chapter 28: The World's Richest Man

1. AC to Charles Schwab, July 11, 1900, quoted in Board Meeting Minutes, July 31, 1900, ACLOC, vol. 76.
2. AC to George Lauder Jr., June 3, 1900, ACLOC, vol. 75.
3. AC to Charles Schwab, June 4, 1900, ACLOC, vol. 75.
4. Quoted in Hendrick, *Carnegie*, vol. 2, p. 119.
5. Warren, p. 271.
6. AC to Charles Schwab, June 20, 1900, ACLOC, vol. 75.
7. AC to Board, June 22, 1900, ACLOC, vol. 76.
8. AC to Charles Schwab, June 26, 1900, quoted in Board Meeting Minutes, July 9, 1900, ACLOC, vol. 76.
9. AC to Charles Schwab, July 7, 1900, quoted in Board Meeting Minutes, July 9, 1900, ACLOC, vol. 76.
10. AC to Charles Schwab, July 11, 1900, quoted in Board Meeting Minutes, July 31, 1900, ACLOC, vol. 76.
11. Carnegie Company, Board Meeting Minutes, July 16, 1900, ACLOC, vol. 76.
12. *New York Daily Tribune*, September 5, 1900.
13. Henry C. Frick to AC, August 1900, quoted in Harvey, p. 257.
14. Henry Phipps to Henry C. Frick, September 11, 1900, quoted in Warren, p. 276.
15. John Morley to AC, July 23, 1900, ACLOC, vol. 76.
16. Samuel Clemens to Margaret Carnegie, May 28, 1900, ACNYPL.
17. AC to Andrew D. White, June 23, 1900, ACLOC, vol. 76.
18. Strouse, p. 392.
19. Diana Preston, *The Boxer Rebellion* (New York: Walker, 1999), p. 285.
20. *New York Daily Tribune*, August 11, 1900.
21. Andrew D. White to AC, June 18, 1900, ACLOC, vol. 75.
22. AC to Andrew D. White, June 23, 1900, ACLOC, vol. 76.
23. William T. Stead to AC, September 21, 1900, ACLOC, vol. 78.
24. AC to William T. Stead, October 4, 1900, ACLOC, vol. 78.
25. Herbert Spencer to AC, September 24, 1900, ACLOC, vol. 78.
26. AC to Herbert Spencer, October 10, 1900, ACLOC, vol. 78; Herbert Spencer to AC, October 10, 1900, ACLOC, vol. 78.
27. *New York Tribune*, November 16, 1900.
28. Whipple, p. 86.
29. AC to George Lauder Jr., December 8, 1900, ACLOC, vol. 81.
30. Warren, pp. 277–278.
31. Hendrick, *Carnegie*, vol. 2, p. 123.
32. Warren, p. 275.
33. Flint, pp. 168–170.
34. AC to Charles Schwab, October 9, 1900, ACLOC, vol. 78.
35. Wayne McVeagh to AC, January 26, 1901, ACLOC, vol. 81.
36. Wayne McVeagh to AC, January 31, 1901, ACLOC, vol. 81.
37. AC to George Lauder Jr., January 24, 1901, ACLOC, vol. 81.
38. Hendrick, *Carnegie*, vol. 2, p. 128.
39. Willis L. King, "Recollections and Conclusions from a Long Business Life," *Western Pennsylvania Historical Magazine* 23, no. 4, pp. 228–229.

40. Carnegie, "My Experience with Railway Rates and Rebates," pp. 726–727. See Robert L. Frey, ed., *Railroads in the Nineteenth Century* (New York: Facts on File, 1988) for more details on Cassatt's management of the Pennsylvania Railroad.

41. Whipple, pp. 87–88. Versions on the Morgan-Schwab meeting vary. Also see Robert Irving Warshow, *Bet-a-Million Gates: The Story of a Plunger* (New York: Greenberg, 1932), pp. 50–51, and Hendrick, *Carnegie*, vol. 2, pp. 132–133.

42. Hendrick, *Carnegie*, vol. 2, p. 135; Whipple, p. 88.

43. Charles Schwab to AC, January 24, 1901, ACLOC, vol. 81.

44. Wall, *Carnegie*, p. 792.

45. Board of Carnegie Corporation to AC, February 4, 1901, ACLOC, vol. 81.

46. AC to John Morley, February 3, 1901, ACLOC, vol. 81.

47. John Morley to AC, February 16, 1901, ACLOC, vol. 81.

48. AC to George Lauder Jr., February 5, 1901, ACLOC, vol. 81.

49. Hendrick, *Carnegie*, vol. 2, pp. 139, 192.

50. John Brisbane Walker, "The World's Greatest Revolution," *Cosmopolitan* (April 1901).

51. *Wall Street Journal*, March 25, 1901.

52. AC to George Lauder Jr., March 6, 1901, ACLOC, vol. 82.

53. AC to Henry Phipps, n.d., and Phipps's response, n.d., quoted in Hendrick, *Carnegie*, vol. 2, pp. 140–143.

54. Herbert L. Satterlee, *J. Pierpont Morgan: An Intimate Portrait* (New York: Macmillan, 1939), p. 345.

55. Flint, p. 169.

56. King, "Recollections and Conclusions from a Long Business Life," pp. 228–229.

57. Memorandum in AC's handwriting, n.d., ACLOC, vol. 81.

Chapter 29: Tainted Seeds

1. AC to George Lauder Jr., March 12, 1901, ACLOC, vol. 82.

2. John Morley to AC, April 5, 1901, ACLOC, vol. 82.

3. AC to John Morley, April 9, 1901, ACLOC, vol. 82.

4. Carnegie, *Autobiography*, p. 247.

5. "Mr. Carnegie's Gift," *Harper's Weekly*, March 30, 1901.

6. *New York Daily Tribune*, January 25, 1903.

7. *New York Daily Tribune*, January 22, 1905; and Homestead Committee to AC, February 23, 1903, quoted in Carnegie, *Autobiography*, p. 247.

8. Carnegie, *Autobiography*, p. 248.

9. "Persons of Interest," *Harper's Bazaar* (April 1901), p. 1017.

10. Quoted in Hendrick, *Carnegie*, vol. 2, pp. 271, 356.

11. Wall, *Carnegie*, p. 831.

12. "The Progress of the World," *American Monthly Review of Reviews* (April 1901).

13. Frederick Cleveland, "Mr. Carnegie as Economist and Social Reformer," *Annals of the American Academy of Political and Social Science* (May 1901), pp. 78–79.

14. AC to John Wanamaker, November 11, 1904, quoted in Hendrick, *Carnegie*, vol. 2, p. 276.

15. AC to Mrs. Russell Sage, February 26, 1901, ACLOC, vol. 174.

16. John D. Rockefeller to AC, February 2, 1903, quoted in Hendrick, *Carnegie*, vol. 2, p. 277. Also see John D. Rockefeller to AC, January 29, 1896, ACLOC, vol. 36. Rockefeller greatly appreciated Carnegie's philanthropy.

17. Frederick Gates to John D. Rockefeller, April 24, 1905, quoted in Chernow, p. 314.

18. Carnegie, *An American Four-in-Hand in Britain*, p. 140.

19. *New York Daily Tribune*, March 17, 1901.

20. "Mr. Carnegie's Gift"; *New York Daily Tribune*, March 24, 1901.

21. George S. Bobinski, *Carnegie Libraries* (Chicago: American Library Association, 1969), p. 14.

22. Ibid., pp. 203–204.

23. Ibid., p. 57.

24. Hendrick, *Carnegie*, vol. 2, p. 207.

25. Bobinski, p. 105.

26. Hendrick, *Carnegie*, vol. 2, p. 201.

27. AC to Charles Eliot, December 31, 1904, ACLOC, vol. 110.

28. Goodenough, p. 177.

29. Bobinski, p. 108.

30. Ibid., pp. 82–83.

31. See Robert Sidney Martin, *Carnegie Denied* (Westport, Conn.: Greenwood Press, 1993). Martin studied 47 of the 225 communities that rejected or failed to follow through on the offer of Carnegie libraries. He concluded only 3 of these 47 opposed the libraries due to significant labor antipathy.

32. Bobinski, pp. 90–91.

33. Ibid., p. 103.

34. Ibid., p. 104.

35. *New York Daily Tribune*, April 26, 1904.

36. Bobinski, p. 185.

37. Hamilton Holt, "The Carnegie That I Knew," *Independent* (August 23, 1919).

38. Quoted in Hendrick, *Carnegie*, vol. 2, p. 261.

39. Wall, *Carnegie*, p. 830.

40. *A Manual of the Public Benefactions of Andrew Carnegie* (Washington, D.C.: The Carnegie Endowment for International Peace, 1919), pp. 320–321.

41. *New York Daily Tribune*, June 6, 1901.

42. Hendrick, *Carnegie*, vol. 2, p. 215.

43. Goodenough, p. 83.

44. Andrew Carnegie, "How to Win Fortune," *New York Tribune*, April 13, 1890.

45. Hendrick, *Carnegie*, vol. 2, pp. 218–219.

46. AC to John Morley, June 24, 1901, ACLOC, vol. 83.

47. *A Manual of the Public Benefactions of Andrew Carnegie*, p. 233.

48. Hendrick, *Carnegie*, vol. 2, p. 221.

49. Goodenough, pp. 80–81; Hendrick, *Carnegie*, vol. 2, p. 223.

50. Flint, pp. 167–168.

51. AC to George Lauder Jr., March 1, 1902, ACLOC, vol. 87; Hendrick, *Carnegie*, vol. 2, p. 267.

52. Satterlee, p. 348.

53. AC to George Lauder Jr., September 26, 1901, quoted in Wall, *Carnegie*, p. 926.

54. AC to John Morley, n.d. (probably September 1901), ACLOC, vol. 84.

55. Theodore Roosevelt to AC, June 13, 1902, ACLOC, vol. 89. Carnegie wrote the note on the back of the letter, which was an invitation for AC to join TR at Oyster Bay.

56. AC to Moses H. Clapp, March 29, 1906, quoted in Wall, *Carnegie*, p. 956.

57. Carnegie, *Autobiography*, p. 248.

58. Hendrick, *Carnegie*, vol. 2, p. 258.

59. AC to Andrew D. White, April 26, 1901, ACLOC, vol. 82.

60. Quoted in Hendrick, *Carnegie*, vol. 2, p. 230.

61. AC to Theodore Roosevelt, November 28, 1901, quoted in Hendrick, *Carnegie*, vol. 1, pp. 227–228.

62. Theodore Roosevelt to AC, December 31, 1901, ACLOC, vol. 86.

63. *A Manual of the Public Benefactions of Andrew Carnegie*, pp. 97–98; *New York Daily Tribune*, January 30, 1902.

64. *New York Daily Tribune*, November 26, 1902.

Chapter 30: Human Frailty

1. Frank C. Harper, *Pittsburgh: Forge of the Universe* (New York: Comet Press, 1957), p. 191.

2. AC to Oswald Villard, December 8, 1905, quoted in Wall, *Carnegie*, p. 799.

3. Charles Schwab to AC, January 26, 1902, ACLOC, vol. 90.

4. Hessen, pp. 134–135.

5. Charles Schwab to AC, January 28, 1902, ACLOC, vol. 90.

6. Whipple, pp. 90–91.

7. Hessen, p. 137.

8. AC to George Lauder Jr., July 1, 1902, ACLOC, vol. 89.

9. AC to Elbert H. Gary, March 14, 1904, ACLOC, vol. 104.

10. AC to Hew Morrison, December 18, 1900, ACLOC, vol. 80.

11. AC to Hew Morrison, March 11, 1902, ACLOC, vol. 88.

12. Hendrick, *Carnegie*, vol. 2, p. 154.

13. Ibid., p. 157.

14. AC to Herbert Spencer, September 14, 1903, quoted in David Duncan, *Life and Letters of Herbert Spencer* (London: Methuen, 1908), p. 472.

15. Herbert Spencer to AC, September 18, 1903, quoted in Duncan, p. 472.

16. Edith Hartley Fowler, *The Life of Henry Hartley Fowler* (London: Hutchinson, 1912), p. 634.

17. AC to James Donaldson, March 20, 1904, ACLOC, vol. 104.

18. Hendrick and Henderson, pp. 197–198.

19. AC to John Morley, June 29, 1904, ACLOC, vol. 105; Hendrick and Henderson, p. 174.

20. AC to George Lauder Jr., June 4, 1905, ACLOC, vol. 117; AC to John Morley, quoted in Hendrick, *Carnegie*, vol. 2, p. 170.

21. Hendrick, *Carnegie*, vol. 2, p. 170.

22. AC to John Morley, August 29, 1905, ACLOC, vol. 119; John Morley to AC, September 1, 1905, ACLOC, vol. 119.

23. John Morley to AC, April 19, 1902, ACLOC, vol. 88.

24. AC to John Morley, September 26, 1901, quoted in Hendrick, *Carnegie*, vol. 2, p. 165; AC to George Lauder Jr., June 4, 1905, ACLOC, vol. 117.

25. Hendrick, *Carnegie*, vol. 2, p. 211.

26. Reprinted in Burton J. Hendrick, ed., *Miscellaneous Writings of Andrew Carnegie*, vol. 2 (Garden City, N.Y.: Doubleday, Doran, 1933), pp. 291–319.

27. Reprinted in Hendrick, *Miscellaneous Writings of Andrew Carnegie*, vol. 1, pp. 78–125.

28. AC to John Morley, September 26, 1901; AC to George Lauder Jr., July 1, 1902; AC to John Morley, October 18, 1902; AC to George Lauder Jr., November 7, 1902, all quoted in Hendrick, *Carnegie*, vol. 2, pp. 164–165.

29. AC to George Lauder Jr., January 9, 1903, ACLOC, vol. 93.

30. *New York Daily Tribune*, November 29, December 5, December 12, and December 30, 1904.

31. *New York Daily Tribune*, December 19, 1902.

32. Rosamond Gilder, ed., *Letters of Richard Watson Gilder* (Boston: Houghton Mifflin, 1916), p. 374.

33. John Morley to AC, September 6, 1904, ACLOC, vol. 106.

34. John Morley to AC, November 6, 1904, ACLOC, vol. 108.

35. Forbes, p. 43.

36. Edward J. Renehan, *John Burroughs: An American Naturalist* (Post Mills, Vt.: Chelsea Green Publishing, 1992), pp. 229–231.

37. *New York Daily Tribune*, December 6, 1905.

38. Renehan, p. 258.

39. Hendrick, *Carnegie*, vol. 2, pp. 273–274.

40. See letters dated April 26, 28, and 30, 1906, reproduced in Gilder, pp. 373–375; AC to Theodore Roosevelt, November 24, 1909, ACLOC, vol. 171.

41. Melvil Dewey to AC, 1 April 1903, ACLOC, vol. 95.

42. Goodenough, p. 222; AC to Theodore Roosevelt, August 8, 1906, ACLOC, vol. 132.

43. Hendrick, *Carnegie*, vol. 2, p. 262; Goodenough, p. 223.

44. *New York Daily Tribune*, March 25, 1906; see also Goodenough, pp. 222–225.

45. James Bridge to AC, June 27, 1901, ACLOC, vol. 83; James Bridge to AC, July 23, 1901, ACLOC, vol. 83.

46. Thomas N. Miller to AC, May 21, 1903, ACLOC, vol. 96.

47. Thomas Miller to the *Pittsburgh Leader*, September 23, 1903.

48. Quoted in Carnegie, *Autobiography*, pp. 219–220.

49. John E. Milholland to AC, July 1, 1904, ACLOC, vol.106; P. Secretary to John E. Milholland, July 5, 1904, ACLOC, vol. 106; John E. Milholland to AC, July 12, 1904, ACLOC, vol. 106; AC to John E. Milholland, July 16, 1904, ACLOC, vol. 106.

50. D. D. Gage to AC, May 12, 1905, ACLOC, vol. 116; D. D. Gage to AC, August 30, 1905, ACLOC, vol. 119; George Lauder Jr. to D. D. Gage, August 31, 1905, ACLOC, vol. 119; AC to D. D. Gage, September 6, 1905, ACLOC, vol. 119; Whipple, p. 19.

51. Thomas Miller to Mrs. J. R. Wilson, March 11, 1903, ACWPHS, Frick Suit Folder.

52. Grandson to Edwin Bennett, April 28, 1905; AC to Edwin Bennett, April 30, 1905; and Edwin Bennett to AC, May 16, 1905, Bennett Family Papers, 1841–1962, Historical Society of Western Pennsylvania, MFF 2190.

Chapter 31: The Peace Mission Begins

1. John Ross to AC, September 8, 1900, and John Ross to AC, September 20, 1900, ACLOC, vol. 78.

2. AC to John Morley, January 18, 1903, ACLOC, vol. 93; and AC to George Lauder Jr., June 16, 1903, ACLOC, vol. 97.

3. AC to John Ross, n.d., ACLOC, vol. 98.

4. Quoted in Goodenough, p. 118.

5. *New York Daily Tribune*, August 7, 1903.

6. *New York Daily Tribune*, December 31, 1902, and April 26, 1903.

7. *New York Daily Tribune*, January 28, 1902.

8. Hendrick, *Carnegie*, vol. 2, pp. 163–164.

9. AC to Frederick Hols, April 4, 1902, and AC to Frederick Hols, August 7, 1902, quoted in Wall, *Carnegie*, pp. 904–905; AC to Andrew D. White, August 10, 1902, ACLOC, vol. 90.

10. *A Manual of the Public Benefactions of Andrew Carnegie*, p. 273.

11. Andrew D. White to AC, April 30, 1903, ACLOC, vol. 96.

12. Wall, *Carnegie*, pp. 880–881.

13. See letters quoted in Hendrick, *Carnegie*, vol. 2, pp. 179–183.

14. AC to Frederic Harrison, June 8, 1904, ACLOC, vol. 115.

15. AC to John Ross, March 16, 1911, ACLOC, vol. 189.

16. AC to John Morley, December 29, 1907, ACLOC, vol. 146.

17. Mack, p. 244.

18. *New York Daily Tribune*, March 9, 1904.

19. *New York Daily Tribune*, April 20 and October 24, 1905.

20. "Carnegie as a Socialist," *Independent* (January 12, 1905), p. 105.

21. *A Manual of the Public Benefactions of Andrew Carnegie*, p. 149.

22. Wall, *Carnegie*, p. 874.

23. *New York Daily Tribune*, April 29, 1905.

24. Henry Pritchett to AC, March 13, 1909, ACLOC, vol. 163; AC to Abram Harris, March 16, 1909, ACLOC, vol. 164.

25. Theodore Roosevelt to AC, February 2, 1909, ACLOC, vol. 162; AC to Theodore Roosevelt, February 3, 1909, ACLOC, vol. 162.

26. Carnegie Institute Trustee to AC, July 31, 1906, ACLOC, vol. 132.

27. Andrew D. White to AC, January 25, 1904, ACLOC, vol. 102.

28. Woodrow Wilson to AC, April 17, 1903, ACLOC, vol. 95.

29. Henry Wilkinson, *Woodrow Wilson: The Academic Years* (Cambridge, Mass.: Harvard University Press, 1967), p. 288.

30. *New York Daily Tribune*, December 6, 1906.

31. *New York Daily Tribune*, January 1, 1906.

32. AC to David Starr Jordan, n.d., ACLOC, vol. 136.

33. *A Manual of the Public Benefactions of Andrew Carnegie*, p. 318.

34. *New York Daily Tribune*, April 6, 1906.

35. Goodenough, p. 262.

36. AC to Charles W. Eliot, February 3, 1910, ACLOC, vol. 173.

37. Carnegie, *Autobiography*, pp. 265–266.

38. AC to William Archer, August 15, 1910, ACLOC, vol. 179.

39. Hamilton Holt, "The Carnegie That I Knew," *Independent* (August 23, 1919), p. 252.

40. Wall, *Carnegie*, p. 918.

41. Theodore Roosevelt to Whitelaw Reid, November 13, 1905, quoted in Wall, *Carnegie*, p. 1109.

42. Larry L. Fabian, *Andrew Carnegie's Peace Endowment: The Tycoon, the President, and Their Bargain of 1910* (Washington, D.C.: Carnegie Endowment for International Peace, 1985), p. 24; AC to Theodore Roosevelt, February 5, 1905, ACLOC, vol. 111.

43. Theodore Roosevelt to AC, February 6, 1905, ACLOC, vol. 111.

44. Theodore Roosevelt to AC, May 19, 1906, ACLOC, vol. 129.

45. AC to Theodore Roosevelt, July 27, 1906; Theodore Roosevelt to AC, August 6, 1906; AC to Theodore Roosevelt, August 27, 1906; and Theodore Roosevelt to AC, September 6, 1906, quoted in Hendrick, *Carnegie*, vol. 2, pp. 302–308.

46. AC to David J. Hill, June 10, 1906, ACLOC, vol. 130.

47. AC to David J. Hill, June 18, 1906, ACLOC, vol. 130.

48. AC to David J. Hill, June 20, 1906, ACLOC, vol. 131.

49. Samuel Harden Church to AC, July 18, 1906, ACLOC, vol. 131.

50. Unless otherwise noted, all peace palace letters are quoted in Hendrick, *Carnegie*, vol. 2, pp. 334–336.

51. AC to Charles W. Eliot, March 15, 1907, ACLOC, vol. 140.

52. Theodore Roosevelt to AC, April 10, 1907, ACLOC, vol. 141.

53. Holt, "The Carnegie That I Knew," p. 252.

Chapter 32: The Metamorphosis of Andrew Carnegie

1. AC to Theodore Roosevelt, March 12, 1907, ACLOC, vol. 140.

2. AC to Theodore Roosevelt, April 7, 1907, ACLOC, vol. 141.

3. M. M. Bosworth to AC, May 4, 1907, ACLOC, vol. 142.

4. John Morley to AC, September 30, 1906, ACLOC, vol. 133.

5. Theodore Roosevelt to AC, August 6, 1906, ACLOC, vol. 132.

6. AC to Wilhelm II, January 19, 1907, quoted in Hendrick, *Carnegie*, vol. 2, pp. 311–313; AC to Theodore Roosevelt, February 14, 1907, quoted in Hendrick, *Carnegie*, vol. 2, p. 310.

7. Andrew Carnegie, "The Next Step—a League of Nations," *Outlook* (May 25, 1907); AC to John Morley, n.d. (probably early June 1907), ACLOC, vol. 142.

8. John Morley to AC, June 14, 1907, ACLOC, vol. 142.

9. Carnegie, *Autobiography*, pp. 354–357.

10. AC to James Donaldson, July 3, 1907, ACLOC, vol. 143.

11. Hendrick, *Carnegie*, vol. 2, p. 315.

12. Ibid., pp. 317–319.

13. AC to Theodore Roosevelt, November 18, 1907, ACLOC, vol. 145.

14. Theodore Roosevelt to AC, November 19, 1907, ACLOC, vol. 145.

15. Theodore Roosevelt to AC, January 22, 1908, ACLOC, vol. 148.

16. AC to Theodore Roosevelt, December 15, 1907, ACLOC, vol. 146.

17. Strouse, pp. 593–594.

18. Jane Fleming Lovejoy to AC, September 14, 1908, ACLOC, vol. 156.

19. AC to George Lauder Jr., April 20, 1908, ACLOC, vol. 152.

20. Andrew Carnegie, "The Worst Banking System in the World," *Outlook* (February 29, 1908); Wall, *Carnegie*, p. 960.

21. Andrew Carnegie, "My Experience with Railway Rates and Rebates"; "My Experience with, and Views upon, the Tariff," *Century Illustrated Monthly* (December 1908); Wall, *Carnegie*, p. 960.

22. AC to Sereno Payne, December 17, 1908, ACLOC, vol. 159.

23. AC to George Lauder Jr., December 19, 1908, ACLOC, vol. 160.

24. Wall, *Carnegie*, pp. 964–965; AC statement before Tariff Revision Committee, December 21, 1908, ACLOC, vol. 160.

25. AC to Elbert H. Gary, December 23, 1908, ACLOC, vol. 160.

26. George P. Hampton to AC, January 1, 1908, ACLOC, vol. 147.

27. Theodore Roosevelt to AC, March 4, 1908, ACLOC, vol. 149; see also Carnegie, "The Conservation of Ores and Related Minerals," reprinted in *Miscellaneous Writings*, vol. 2.

28. *Times Literary Supplement*, July 16, 1908.

29. Cahn, p. 194.

30. Wall, *Carnegie*, p. 957.

31. AC to Seth Low, September 22, 1908, ACLOC, vol. 156.

Chapter 33: Covert Deal with Taft

1. *Letters of Grover Cleveland*, pp. 621–623.

2. AC to Elihu Root, June 9, 1908, ACLOC, vol. 154.

3. Eleanor Wilson McAdoo, ed., *The Priceless Gift: The Love Letters of Woodrow Wilson and Ellen Axson Wilson* (New York: McGraw-Hill, 1962), p. 251.

4. Strouse, p. 601.

5. AC to John Morley, February 24, 1909, ACLOC, vol. 163.

6. Elihu Root to AC, April 3, 1909, ACLOC, vol. 165.

7. Baroness Berthe von Suttner to AC, May 22, 1909, ACLOC, vol. 166.

8. Gompers, p. 328.

9. Gilder, p. 483.

10. Theodore Roosevelt to AC, June 1, 1909, ACLOC, vol. 166; Bartle Bull, *Safari: A Chronicle of Adventure* (New York: Viking, 1988), pp. 169, 173, 175; H. W. Brands, *T.R.: The Last Romantic* (New York: Basic Books, 1997), p. 657.

11. AC to John Morley, June 20, 1909, ACLOC, vol. 167.

12. AC to John Morley, n.d., ACLOC, vol. 167.

13. AC to Theodore Roosevelt, October 6, 1909, ACLOC, vol. 170.

14. Theodore Roosevelt to AC, October 16, 1909, ACLOC, vol. 170.

15. Theodore Roosevelt to AC, November 22, 1909, ACLOC, vol. 171.

16. AC to John Morley, October 22, 1909, ACLOC, vol. 170.

17. AC to Theodore Roosevelt, December 24, 1909, ACLOC, vol. 172.

18. Theodore Roosevelt to AC, December 14, 1909, quoted in Hendrick, *Carnegie*, vol. 2, p. 326

19. AC to Theodore Roosevelt, January 3, 1910, ACLOC, vol. 173.

20. Elihu Root to AC, February 11, 1910, ACLOC, vol. 174.

21. Theodore Roosevelt to AC, February 18, 1910, ACLOC, vol. 174.

22. AC to William H. Taft, March 26, 1910, ACLOC, vol. 175.

23. AC to David J. Hill, March 25, 1910, ACLOC, vol. 175.

24. AC to Theodore Roosevelt, April 27, 1910, ACLOC, vol. 176.

25. Brands, p. 662.

26. Theodore Roosevelt to AC, April 22, 1910, ACLOC, vol. 176.

27. Theodore Roosevelt, *Theodore Roosevelt: An Autobiography* (New York: Da Capo Press, 1985), p. 314.

28. AC to Whitelaw Reid, May 10, 1910, ACLOC, vol. 176.

29. AC to David J. Hill, May 11, 1910, ACLOC, vol. 176.

30. AC to Whitelaw Reid, May 14, 1910, ACLOC, vol. 176.

31. Theodore Roosevelt to AC, June 14, 1910, ACLOC, vol. 177.

32. AC to William H. Taft, July 22, 1910, ACLOC, vol. 178; William H. Taft to Philander Knox, July 7, 1910, quoted in Wall, *Carnegie*, p. 981.

33. Fabian, p. 39.

34. Ibid., p. 4.

35. AC to John Morley, November 4, 1910, quoted in Fabian, p. 3.

36. Fabian, p. 42.
37. Nicholas Murray Butler to AC, November 24, 1910, ACLOC, vol. 182.
38. AC to William H. Taft, December 10, 1910, quoted in Fabian, p. 42.
39. Fabian, p. 20.
40. "Carnegie's Greatest Gift," *Independent* (December 15, 1910).
41. Baron d'Estournelles de Constant to AC, December 15, 1910, ACLOC, vol. 184.
42. John Morley to AC, December 15, 1910, ACLOC, vol. 184.
43. Fabian, p. 45.
44. John Bigelow to J. G. Schmidlapp, December 22, 1910, ACLOC, vol. 185.
45. *A Manual of the Public Benefactions of Andrew Carnegie*, p. 165.
46. Nicholas Murray Butler, "The Carnegie Endowment for International Peace," *Independent* (November 27, 1913).
47. Fabian, p. 47.
48. Ibid., pp. 48–49.
49. Wall, *Carnegie*, pp. 912–913.
50. AC to Philander Knox, May 19, 1911, quoted in ibid., p. 983.
51. Fabian, p. 51.
52. Theodore Roosevelt to AC, May 23, 1911, ACLOC, vol. 193.
53. William H. Taft to AC, May 20, 1911, ACLOC, vol. 193.
54. James Bryce to AC, June 24, 1911, ACLOC, vol. 194.
55. James Bryce to AC, June 30, 1911, ACLOC, vol. 194.
56. Charles D. Hilles to AC, June 28, 1911, ACLOC, vol. 195.
57. AC to John Morley, June 29, 1911, ACLOC, vol. 195.
58. AC to John Morley, July 2, 1911, ACLOC, vol. 195.
59. AC to John Morley, July 16, 1911, ACLOC, vol. 196.
60. Elihu Root to AC, August 29, 1911, ACLOC, vol. 197.
61. AC to James Bryce, September 2, 1911, quoted in Wall, *Carnegie*, p. 988.
62. Fabian, p. 54.
63. Francis B. Loomis to AC, December 13, 1911, ACLOC, vol. 201.
64. AC to John Morley, July 11, 1912, ACLOC, vol. 207.
65. Philander Knox to AC, March 27, 1911, quoted in Wall, *Carnegie*, p. 983; Fabian, p. 56.
66. Miller, p. 522.
67. AC to Theodore Roosevelt, March 1, 1912, ACLOC, vol. 204.
68. Theodore Roosevelt to AC, March 5, 1912, quoted in Wall, *Carnegie*, pp. 992–993.
69. AC to Theodore Roosevelt, March 10, 1912, ACLOC, vol. 204.
70. AC to John Morley, May 12, 1912, ACLOC, vol. 206.
71. William H. Taft to AC, March 28, 1912, ACLOC, vol. 204.
72. Charles D. Hilles to AC, November 1, 1912, ACLOC, vol. 210. Carnegie's note at bottom: "I gave . . . in all 100,000$. Glad I was the largest contributor for Taft."

Chapter 34: The Last Great Benefaction

1. "Carnegie on the Verge of Seventy," *Current Literature* (May 1907).
2. Charles S. Gleed, "Andrew Carnegie," *Cosmopolitan* 33 (July 1902).
3. "Pittsburgh and Carnegie," *Independent* (April 11, 1907), p. 865.
4. Goodenough, p. 48; "Pittsburgh and Carnegie," p. 864.
5. "Fifty Million Dollars," *Collier's* (June 5, 1909).
6. AC to John Ross, December 23, 1908, quoted in Hendrick, *Carnegie*, vol. 2, p. 175.
7. John D. Rockefeller Jr. to AC, May 8, 1909, ACLOC, vol. 166; John D. Rockefeller Jr. to AC, June 23, 1909, ACLOC, vol. 167.
8. Chernow, p. 474.
9. Joseph Frazier Wall, *Skibo* (New York: Oxford University Press, 1984), p. 87.
10. Fabian, p. 8.
11. Goodenough, p. 153.

12. A *Manual of the Public Benefactions of Andrew Carnegie*, pp. 206–207; Goodenough, pp. 153–154.

13. Hendrick, *Carnegie*, vol. 2, p. 240.

14. AC to Robert S. Woodward, September 28, 1909, ACLOC, vol. 170.

15. AC to Whitelaw Reid, October 11, 1909, ACLOC, vol. 170.

16. Robert S. Woodward to AC, November 18, 1911, ACLOC, vol. 200.

17. AC to Henry Holt, February 25, 1915, ACLOC, vol. 238.

18. AC to John Ross, February 25, 1911, ACLOC, vol. 188.

19. John Ross to AC, March 9, 1911, ACLOC, vol. 189.

20. AC to John Ross, March 22, 1911, ACLOC, vol. 189.

21. AC to John Ross, January 14, 1913, ACLOC, vol. 212.

22. AC to John Ross, February 11, 1913, ACLOC, vol. 213.

23. A *Manual of the Public Benefactions of Andrew Carnegie*, p. 222.

Chapter 35: House of Cards

1. D. A. Reed to AC, October 22, 1911, ACLOC, vol. 244.

2. U.S. Steel Hearings, pp. 2351–2352.

3. "Confessions of Carnegie," *Literary Digest* 44, pp. 107–108.

4. Henry Watterson to AC, January 16, 1912, ACLOC, vol. 203.

5. John A. Poynton to James Bridge, April 22, 1912, ACLOC, vol. 205.

6. AC to Alexander Peacock, April 20, 1912, ACLOC, vol. 206.

7. AC to George Lauder Jr., April 19, 1912, ACLOC, vol. 205.

8. Carnegie, *Autobiography*, p. 210.

9. AC to John Morley, November 7, 1912, ACLOC, vol. 210.

10. AC to Woodrow Wilson, November 6, 1912, ACLOC, vol. 210.

11. Woodrow Wilson to AC, November 19, 1912, ACLOC, vol. 210.

12. AC to James Bryce, November 12, 1912, quoted in Wall, *Carnegie*, p. 994.

13. James Bryce to AC, November 13, 1912, ACLOC, vol. 210.

14. AC to William Barnes, December 6, 1912, ACLOC, vol. 211.

15. AC to William H. Taft, December 15, 1912, and Philander Knox to William H. Taft, March 3, 1913, quoted in Wall, *Carnegie*, pp. 995–996.

16. Carnegie, *Autobiography*, p. 272; London *Times*, August 30, 1913.

17. Hendrick and Henderson, p. 181.

18. AC to John Morley, October 11, 1913, ACLOC, vol. 218.

19. AC to Woodrow Wilson, November 3, 1913, ACLOC, vol. 218.

20. AC to Woodrow Wilson, November 17, 1913, ACLOC, vol. 218.

21. AC to Woodrow Wilson, April 21, 1914, ACLOC, vol. 223.

22. AC to Woodrow Wilson, May 11, 1914, ACLOC, vol. 223.

23. AC to John Morley, July 17, 1914, ACLOC, vol. 225.

24. Wall, *Carnegie*, p. 1001.

25. AC to William Jennings Bryan, February 9, 1914, ACLOC, vol. 221.

26. AC to John Morley, January 25, 1914, ACLOC, vol. 220.

27. AC to John Morley, May 3, 1914, ACLOC, vol. 223.

28. S. L. A. Marshall, *World War I* (Boston: Houghton Mifflin, 1964), pp. 8, 12.

29. AC to John Morley, July 16, 1914, ACLOC, vol. 225.

30. Marshall, p. 39.

31. Hendrick, *Carnegie*, vol. 2, p. 345.

Chapter 36: The War to End All Wars

1. AC to J. Allen Baker, August 2, 1914, ACLOC, vol. 225.

2. Robert Franks to John A. Poynton, August 3, 1914, ACLOC, vol. 225.

3. John Morley to AC, August 4, 1914, ACLOC, vol. 225.

4. Frederick Lynch to AC, August 6, 1914, ACLOC, vol. 225.

5. Hendrick, *Carnegie*, vol. 2, p. 347.

6. Ibid., p. 348.

7. AC to John Ross, August 17, 1914, ACLOC, vol. 225.

8. John Morley to AC, August 28, 1914, ACLOC, vol. 225; Carnegie, *Autobiography*, pp. 359–360.

9. Woodrow Wilson to AC, September 29, 1914, ACLOC, vol. 225.

10. William Jennings Bryan to AC, October 7, 1914, ACLOC, vol. 226.

11. AC to Kaiser Wilhelm II, October 16, 1914, ACLOC, vol. 226.

12. John Morley to AC, November 6, 1914, ACLOC, vol. 226.

13. John Morley to AC, November 30, 1914, ACLOC, vol. 227.

14. John Ross to AC, January 5, 1915, ACLOC, vol. 228.

15. AC to John Ross, January 18, 1915, ACLOC, vol. 228.

16. Strouse, pp. 13–14.

17. AC to Woodrow Wilson, January 23, 1915, ACLOC, vol. 228.

18. Hendrick, *Carnegie*, vol. 2, pp. 360–362; Winkler, pp. 298–300.

19. Marshall, pp. 167–168.

20. John Morley to Louise Carnegie, May 19, 1915, quoted in Hendrick, *Carnegie*, vol. 2, pp. 363–364.

21. Louise Carnegie to Theodore Marburg, July 29, 1915, ACLOC, vol. 231; Louise Carnegie to Robert Franks, August 10, 1915, ACLOC, vol. 278.

22. Charles Schwab to Louise Carnegie, September 15, 1915, ACNYPL.

23. John Morley to Louise Carnegie, October 31, 1915, quoted in Hendrick, *Carnegie*, vol. 2, pp. 364–365.

24. Marshall, pp. 227–228, 242.

25. Winkler, pp. 300–301.

26. Louise Carnegie to Margaret Carnegie, January 14, 1916, quoted in Hendrick, *Carnegie*, vol. 2, pp. 201–202.

27. John Morley to AC, December 31, 1915, ACLOC, vol. 232.

28. Earl Grey to Oscar S. Strauss, February 24, 1916, ACNYPL.

29. John Morley to AC, February 16 and March 6, 1916, quoted in Hendrick, *Carnegie*, vol. 2, pp. 367–369.

30. Edith Wharton to Louise Carnegie, n.d. (1916), ACNYPL.

31. John Morley to AC, September 15, 1916, quoted in Hendrick, *Carnegie*, vol. 2, pp. 370–371.

32. Frederic Harrison to AC, October 9, 1916, ACLOC, vol. 233.

33. Hendrick and Henderson, pp. 208–209.

34. AC to Woodrow Wilson, February 14, 1917, ACLOC, vol. 234.

35. Marshall, p. 281.

36. AC to Woodrow Wilson, April 7, 1917, ACLOC, vol. 235.

37. Hendrick, *Carnegie*, vol. 2, p. 383; Hendrick and Henderson, p. 209.

38. AC to John Morley, January 21, 1918, ACLOC, vol. 236.

39. AC to Woodrow Wilson, November 10, 1918, ACLOC, vol. 237.

40. Woodrow Wilson to AC, November 13, 1918, ACLOC, vol. 237.

41. Warren Staebler, *The Liberal Mind of John Morley* (Princeton, N.J.: Princeton University Press for University of Cincinnati), p. 200.

42. John Morley to AC, November 21, 1918, ACLOC, vol. 238.

43. Hendrick, *Carnegie*, vol. 2, p. 381.

44. Hendrick and Henderson, p. 211.

45. AC to John Morley, n.d. (March 1909), ACLOC, vol. 164.

46. AC to John Morley, April 25, 1909, ACLOC, vol. 166.

47. Burton J. Hendrick, interview with Margaret Carnegie, quoted in "The Richest Man in the World: Andrew Carnegie," produced, written, and directed by Austin Hoyt for *The American Experience*, WGBH, Boston, 1997.

48. Hendrick and Henderson, pp. 214–215.

The Carnegie Legacy

1. Hendrick and Henderson, p. 216.

2. See Queen Mary to Louise Carnegie, n.d., ACNYPL, and others in ACLOC, vol. 239.

3. John Morley to Louise Carnegie, n.d. (August 1919), ACLOC, vol. 239; Hendrick, *Carnegie*, vol. 2, p. 382.

4. Charles Schwab to Louise Carnegie, January 23, 1939, ACNYPL.

5. Floyd Norris, "Outlook 2000: A Century of Business," *New York Times*, December 20, 1999.

6. *Iron Age*, August 14, 1919; London *Times*, August 29, 1919.

7. Beverly Goldberg, "Carnegie Corporation Gives $15 Million to Libraries," *American Libraries* (August 1999).

8. Peter F. Drucker, "Good Works and Good Business," *Across the Board* (October 1984).

9. "The Disinheritors," *Forbes* (May 19, 1997).

10. Patricia Martin, "Is Bill Gates the New Andrew Carnegie?" *American Libraries* (September 1997).

11. London *Times*, August 12, 1919.

12. Heilbroner, p. 259.

13. Bobinski, p. 185.

14. Cahn, p. 236.

Selected Bibliography

Agostino, V. Robert. *A Track through Time: A Centennial History of Carnegie, PA.* Pittsburgh: Wolfson Publishing, 1994.

Ames, Charles Edgar. *Pioneering the Union Pacific.* New York: Appleton-Century-Crofts, 1969.

Baldwin, Leland D. *Pittsburgh: The Story of a City.* Pittsburgh: University of Pittsburgh Press, 1937.

Bessemer, Henry. *An Autobiography.* London: Offices of Engineering, 1905.

Bevington, David, ed. *The Complete Works of Shakespeare.* 3rd ed. Glenview, Ill.: Scott, Foresman, 1980.

Bobinski, George S. *Carnegie Libraries.* Chicago: American Library Association, 1969.

Brands, H. W. *T. R.: The Last Romantic.* New York: Basic Books, 1997.

Bridge, James Howard. *The Inside History of the Carnegie Steel Company.* Pittsburgh: University of Pittsburgh Press, 1991.

Brody, David. *Steelworkers in America: The Nonunion Era.* Cambridge, Mass.: Harvard University Press, 1960.

Brown, Richard. *Chartism.* Cambridge, U.K.: Cambridge University Press, 1998.

Brown, Sharon A. *Historic Resource Study: Cambria Iron Company.* Washington, D.C.: U.S. Department of the Interior, 1989.

Bull, Bartle. *Safari: A Chronicle of Adventure.* New York: Viking, 1988.

Burrows, Edwin G., and Mike Wallace. *Gotham: A History of New York City to 1898.* New York: Oxford University Press, 1999.

Butler, Joseph G. *Recollections of Men and Events.* New York: G. P. Putnam's Sons, 1927.

Cahn, William. *A Pictorial History of American Labor.* New York: Crown Publishers, 1972.

Campbell, R. H. *Scotland Since 1707: The Rise of an Industrial Society.* New York: Barnes & Noble, 1965.

Carnegie, Andrew. *An American Four-in-Hand in Britain.* New York: Charles Scribner's Sons, 1883.

————. *The Autobiography of Andrew Carnegie.* Boston: Northeastern University Press, 1986.

————. *Round the World.* New York: Charles Scribner's Sons, 1884.

————. *Triumphant Democracy.* New York: Charles Scribner's Sons, 1886.

Casson, Herbert N. *The Romance of Steel.* New York: A. S. Barnes, 1907.

Chernow, Ron. *Titan: The Life of John D. Rockefeller, Sr.* New York: Vintage Books, 1998.

Collins, T. K., and P. G. Collins. *Guide to the Pennsylvania Railroad.* Philadelphia: n.p., 1855.

Duncan, David. *Life and Letters of Herbert Spencer.* London: Methuen, 1908.

Fabian, Larry L. *Andrew Carnegie's Peace Endowment: The Tycoon, the President, and Their Bargain of 1910.* Washington, D.C.: Carnegie Endowment for International Peace, 1985.

Fitch, John A. *The Steel Workers.* Pittsburgh: University of Pittsburgh Press, 1989.

Fleming, George T. *History of Pittsburgh and Environs.* New York: American Historical Society, 1922.

Flint, Charles R. *Memories of an Active Life.* New York: G. P. Putnam's Sons, 1923.

Foot, M. R. D., ed. *The Gladstone Diaries.* 14 Vols. Oxford, U.K.: Clarendon Press, 1968–1994.

Forbes, B. C. *Men Who Are Making America.* New York: B. C. Forbes Publishing, 1917.

Fowler, Edith Herietta. *The Life of Henry Hartley Fowler.* London: Hutchinson, 1912.

Frey, Robert L., ed. *Railroads in the Nineteenth Century.* New York: Facts on File, 1988.

Giddens, Paul H. *The Birth of the Oil Industry.* New York: Macmillan, 1938.

Gies, Joseph. *Bridges and Men.* Garden City, N.Y.: Doubleday, 1963.

Gilder, Rosamond, ed. *Letters of Richard Watson Gilder.* Boston: Houghton Mifflin, 1916.

Gompers, Samuel. *Seventy Years of Life and Labor: An Autobiography.* New York: E. P. Dutton, 1925.

Goodenough, Simon. *The Greatest Good Fortune.* Edinburgh: Macdonald Publishers, 1985.

Harper, Frank C. *Pittsburgh: Forge of the Universe.* New York: Comet Press, 1957.

Harvey, George. *Henry Clay Frick: The Man.* N.p.: Privately printed, 1936.

Heilbroner, Robert L. "Epitaph for the Steel Master." Reprinted in Alex Groner and the Editors of American Heritage. *The American Heritage History of American Business and Industry.* New York: American Heritage, 1972.

Henderson, Ebenezer. *Annals of Dunfermline.* Glasgow: n.p., 1879.

Hendrick, Burton J. *The Life of Andrew Carnegie.* 2 vols. Garden City, N.Y.: Doubleday, Doran, 1932.

————, ed. *Miscellaneous Writings of Andrew Carnegie.* 2 vols. Garden City, N.Y.: Doubleday, Doran, 1933.

Hendrick, Burton J., and Daniel Henderson. *Louise Whitfield Carnegie.* New York: Hastings House, 1950.

Hessen, Robert. *Steel Titan: The Life of Charles M. Schwab.* New York: Oxford University Press, 1975.

Hogan, William Thomas. *Economic History of the Iron and Steel Industry in the United States.* 5 vols. Lexington, Mass.: Heath, 1971.

Ingham, John N. *Making Iron and Steel.* Columbus: Ohio State University Press, 1991.

Isely, Jeter A. *Horace Greeley and the Republican Party, 1853–1861: A Study of the New York Tribune.* Princeton, N.J.: Princeton University Press, 1947.

Kehl, James A. *Boss Rule in the Gilded Age: Matt Quay of Pennsylvania.* Pittsburgh: University of Pittsburgh Press, 1981.

Kenny, Kevin. *Making Sense of the Molly Maguires.* Oxford, U.K.: Oxford University Press, 1998.

Kirkland, Edward C., ed. *The Gospel of Wealth and Other Timely Essays.* Cambridge, Mass.: Harvard University Press, 1962.

Kleinberg, S. J. *The Shadow of the Mills: Working-Class Families in Pittsburgh, 1870–1907.* Pittsburgh: University of Pittsburgh Press, 1989.

Knickerbocker, Frances Wentworth Cutler. *Free Minds: John Morley and His Friends.* Cambridge, Mass.: Harvard University Press, 1943.

Krause, Paul. *The Battle for Homestead, 1880–1892: Politics, Culture, and Steel.* Pittsburgh: University of Pittsburgh Press, 1992.

Leyendecker, Liston E. *Palace Car Prince: A Biography of George Mortimer Pullman.* Niwot: University Press of Colorado, 1992.

Lorant, Stefan. *Pittsburgh.* Lenox, Mass.: Author's Edition, 1980.

Machiavelli, Niccolo. *The Prince and the Discourses.* New York: Modern Library, 1950.

Mack, Edward C. *Peter Cooper: Citizen of New York.* New York: Duell, Sloan & Pearce, 1949.

Mackie, James B. *Andrew Carnegie: His Dunfermline Ties and Benefactions.* Dunfermline, Scot.: Dunfermline Journal Printing Works, 1916.

A Manual of the Public Benefactions of Andrew Carnegie. Washington, D.C.: Carnegie Endowment for International Peace, 1919.

Marshall, S. L. A. *World War I.* Boston: Houghton Mifflin, 1964.

Martin, Robert Sidney. *Carnegie Denied.* Westport, Conn.: Greenwood Press, 1993.

McAdoo, Eleanor Wilson, ed. *The Priceless Gift: The Love Letters of Woodrow Wilson and Ellen Axson Wilson.* New York: McGraw-Hill, 1962.

McCullough, David. *The Johnstown Flood.* New York: Simon & Schuster, 1968.

McPherson, James M. *Battle Cry of Freedom.* New York: Ballantine, 1988.

Miles, Nelson A. *Serving the Republic.* New York: Harper & Brothers, 1911.

Miller, Nathan. *Theodore Roosevelt: A Life.* New York: William Morrow, 1992.

Misa, Thomas J. *A Nation of Steel.* Baltimore: Johns Hopkins University Press, 1995.

Morley, John. *Recollections.* 2 vols. New York: Macmillan, 1917.

Morris, Lloyd. *Incredible New York.* New York: Random House, 1951.

Murray, Norman. *The Scottish Hand Loom Weavers, 1790–1850: A Social History.* Edinburgh: John Donald Publishers, 1978.

Nevins, Allan. *Abram S. Hewitt.* New York: Harper & Brothers, 1935.

———. *Grover Cleveland: A Study in Courage.* New York: Dodd, Mead, 1934.

———, ed. *Letters of Grover Cleveland: 1850–1908.* Boston: Houghton Mifflin, 1933.

Novotny, Ann. *Strangers at the Door.* Riverside, Conn.: Chatham Press, 1971.

O'Toole, G. J. A. *The Spanish War.* New York: W. W. Norton, 1984.

Preston, Diana. *The Boxer Rebellion.* New York: Walker, 1999.

Reid, James D. *The Telegraph in America.* New York: Derby Brothers, 1879.

Reitano, Joanne. *The Tariff Question in the Gilded Age.* University Park: Pennsylvania State University Press, 1994.

Renehan, Edward J. *John Burroughs: An American Naturalist.* Post Mills, Vt.: Chelsea Green Publishing, 1992.

Robinson, David, ed. *William Ellery Channing: Selected Writings.* New York: Paulist Press, 1985.

Roosevelt, Theodore. *Theodore Roosevelt: An Autobiography.* New York: Da Capo Press, 1985.

Satterlee, Herbert L. *J. Pierpont Morgan: An Intimate Portrait.* New York: Macmillan, 1939.

Schom, Alan. *Napoleon Bonaparte.* New York: HarperCollins, 1997.

Schreiner, Samuel A., Jr. *Henry Clay Frick.* New York: St. Martin's Press, 1995.

Sheriff, Carol. *The Artificial River: The Erie Canal and the Paradox of Progress.* New York: Hill & Wang, 1996.

Sievers, Harry J. *Benjamin Harrison: Hoosier President.* Indianapolis: Bobbs-Merrill, 1968.

———. *Benjamin Harrison: Hoosier Statesman.* New York: University Publishers, 1959.

Simpson, Eric. *The Auld Grey Toun: Dunfermline in the Time of Andrew Carnegie.* Dunfermline, Scot.: Carnegie Dunfermline Trust, 1987.

Smith, Page. *The Nation Comes of Age.* New York: McGraw-Hill, 1981.

———. *The Rise of Industrial America.* New York: McGraw-Hill, 1984.

Spencer, Herbert. *An Autobiography.* 2 vols. New York: D. Appleton, 1904.

Staebler, Warren. *The Liberal Mind of John Morley.* Princeton, N.J.: Princeton University Press for University of Cincinnati, 1943.

Strouse, Jean. *Morgan: American Financier.* New York: Random House, 1999.

Temin, Peter. *Iron and Steel in Nineteenth-Century America.* Cambridge, Mass.: Massachussetts Institute of Technology Press, 1964.

Thayer, William Roscoe. *The Life and Letters of John Hay.* 2 vols. Boston: Houghton Mifflin, 1915.

United States Steel Corporation. *Hearings before the Committee on Investigation of United States Steel Corporation. House of Representatives.* Washington, D.C.: Government Printing Office, 1911–1912.

Wall, Joseph Frazier. *Andrew Carnegie.* New York: Oxford University Press, 1970.

———. *Skibo.* New York: Oxford University Press, 1984.

Ward, James A. *J. Edgar Thomson: Master of the Pennsylvania.* Westport, Conn.: Greenwood Press, 1980.

Warren, Kenneth. *Triumphant Capitalism.* Pittsburgh: University of Pittsburgh Press, 1996.

Warshow, Robert Irving. *Bet-a-Million Gates: The Story of a Plunger.* New York: Greenberg, 1932.

Welch, Richard, Jr. *The Presidencies of Grover Cleveland.* Lawrence: University Press of Kansas, 1988.

Whipple, Sidney B. "Notes on Mr. Schwab's Life." Unpublished manuscript. Hagley Library, Wilmington, Del.

White, John H., Jr. *The American Railroad Passenger Car.* Baltimore: Johns Hopkins University Press, 1978.

Wilkinson, Henry. *Woodrow Wilson: The Academic Years.* Cambridge, Mass.: Harvard University Press, 1967.

Wilson, Alexander. *The Chartist Movement in Scotland.* Manchester, Engl.: University Press, 1970.

Wiltshire, David. *The Social and Political Thought of Herbert Spencer.* Oxford, U.K.: Oxford University Press, 1978.

Winkler, John K. *Incredible Carnegie.* New York: Vanguard Press, 1931.

Wolff, Leon. *Lockout.* New York: Harper & Row, 1965.

Wollman, David H., and Donald R. Inman. *Portraits in Steel.* Kent, Ohio: Kent State University Press, 1990.

Woodman, Richard. *The History of the Ship.* London: Conway Maritime Press, 1997.

Acknowledgments

Foremost, I am exceedingly grateful to Hana Lane, my editor, and Ed Knapp-man, my agent, for setting such a great project right in my lap; it has been a thrilling experience. Throughout the research and writing, I was assisted by a number of people to whom I'm indebted. I wish to thank Sarah Rubenstein, Leslie Plaisted, Susannah Maurer, Joe and Sophie Mas, and Ruth Mills for giving me a jumpstart; Bill Krass for D.C. support; and the knowledgeable staffs at the Andrew Carnegie Birthplace Museum at Dunfermline, the Historical Society of Western Pennsylvania, the New York Public Library, the Carnegie Library of Pittsburgh, and the Library of Congress. A special thanks to Margaret Thomson and Ken Miller, who shared their insights into their legendary ancestor; Angus, Skibo's resident historian; the staff at Skibo, for their carte blanche hospitality and for tolerating a full-moon, midnight swim in the pool; Carol, for the Skibo séance; Jim and Joan Mitchell, for arranging the Skibo adventure; and to Dr. B., for medicinal aid. To my family—Diana, Pierson, Alex, Julia, Mom, and Dad—bless you for your patience and support.

Index